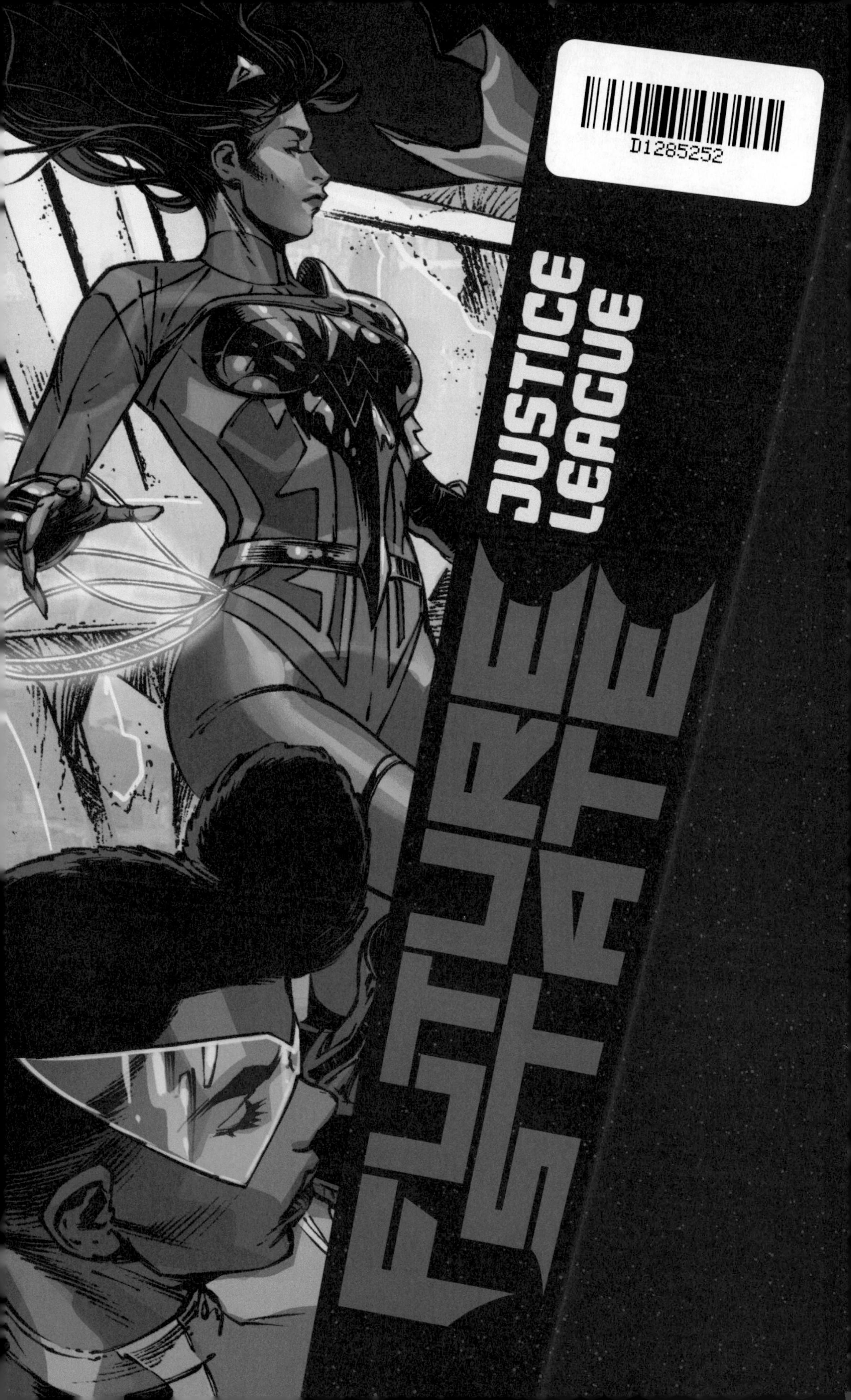
JUSTICE LEAGUE
FUTURE STATE

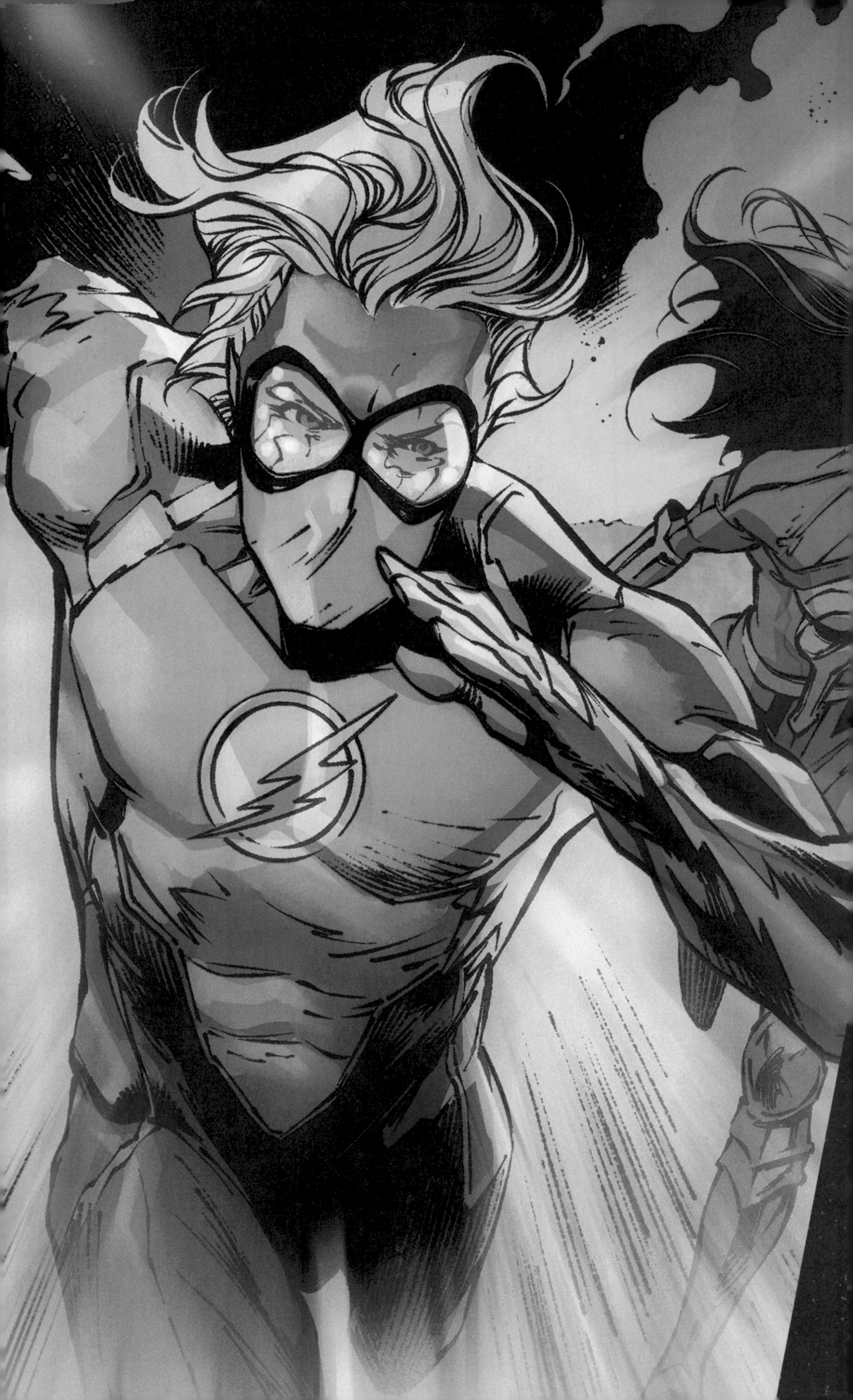

WRITERS
ERNIE ALTBACKER
RYAN CADY
JOSIE CAMPBELL
WILL CONRAD
BRANDON THOMAS
GEOFFREY THORNE
RAM V
ROBERT VENDITTI
BRANDON VIETTI
JOSHUA WILLIAMSON

ARTISTS
SAMI BASRI
DALE EAGLESHAM
DANIEL HENRIQUES
CLAYTON HENRY
BRANDON PETERSON
TOM RANEY
ROBSON ROCHA
DANIEL SAMPERE
DEXTER SOY
MARCIO TAKARA
ANDIE TONG

COLORISTS
MIKE ATIYEH
ROMULO FAJARDO JR.
HI-FI
ADRIANO LUCAS
MARCELO MAIOLO
WIL QUINTANA
ALEX SINCLAIR

LETTERERS
ANDWORLD DESIGN
CLAYTON COWLES
ROB LEIGH
TOM NAPOLITANO
DAVE SHARPE
STEVE WANDS

COLLECTION COVER ARTIST
DAN MORA

SUPERMAN CREATED BY
JERRY SIEGEL AND JOE SHUSTER.
BY SPECIAL ARRANGEMENT
WITH THE JERRY SIEGEL FAMILY.

JUSTICE LEAGUE

FUTURE STATE

ANDREA SHEA
Editor – Original Series & Collected Edition
ALEX R. CARR, MIKE COTTON
Editors– Original Series
MARQUIS DRAPER
Assistant Editor – Original Series
STEVE COOK
Design Director – Books
& Publication Design
CHRISTY SAWYER
Publication Production

MARIE JAVINS
Editor-in-Chief, DC Comics

DANIEL CHERRY III
Senior VP – General Manager
JIM LEE
Publisher & Chief Creative Officer
JOEN CHOE
VP – Global Brand & Creative Services
DON FALLETTI
VP – Manufacturing Operations & Workflow Management
LAWRENCE GANEM
VP – Talent Services
ALISON GILL
Senior VP – Manufacturing & Operations
NICK J. NAPOLITANO
VP – Manufacturing Administration & Design
NANCY SPEARS
VP – Revenue

FUTURE STATE: JUSTICE LEAGUE

DC Comics, 2900 West Alameda Ave., Burbank, CA 91505
Printed by LSC Communications, Owensville, MO, USA. 6/22/21. First Printing.
ISBN: 978-1-77951-065-5

Library of Congress Cataloging-in-Publication Data is available.

PEFC Certified
This product is from sustainably managed forests and controlled sources
PEFC/29-31-337
www.pefc.org

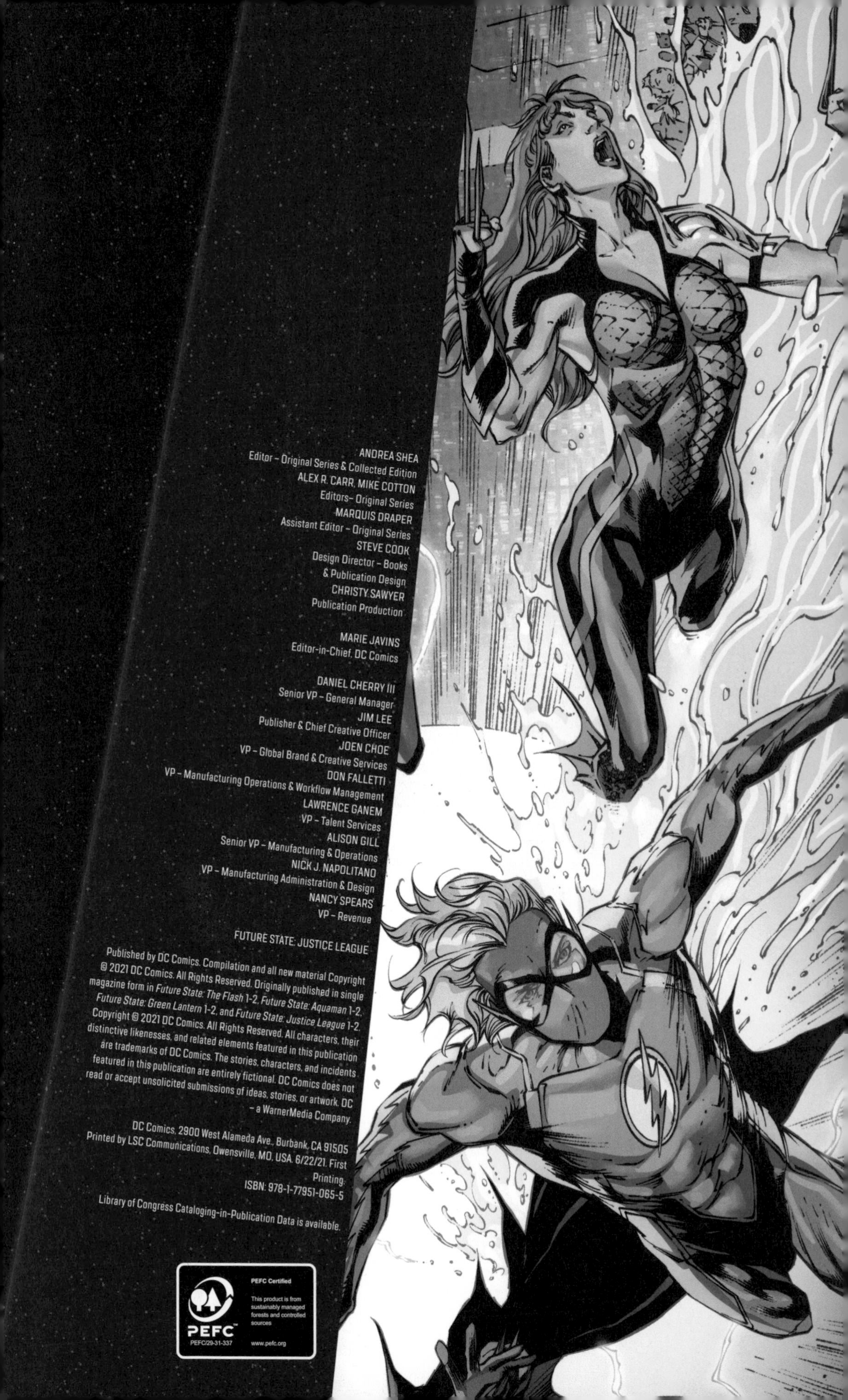

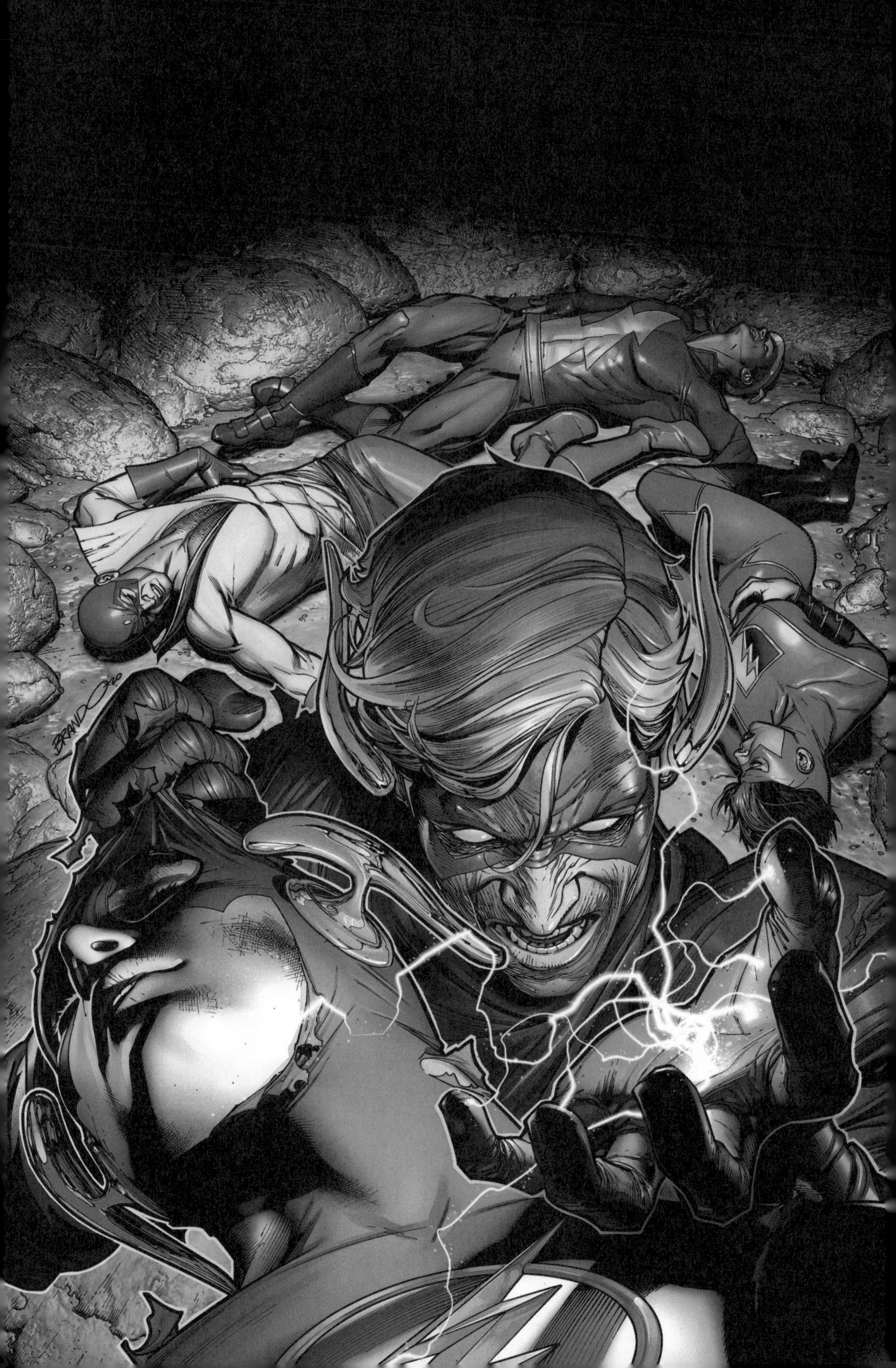

Future State: The Flash #1
cover art by **BRANDON PETERSON**

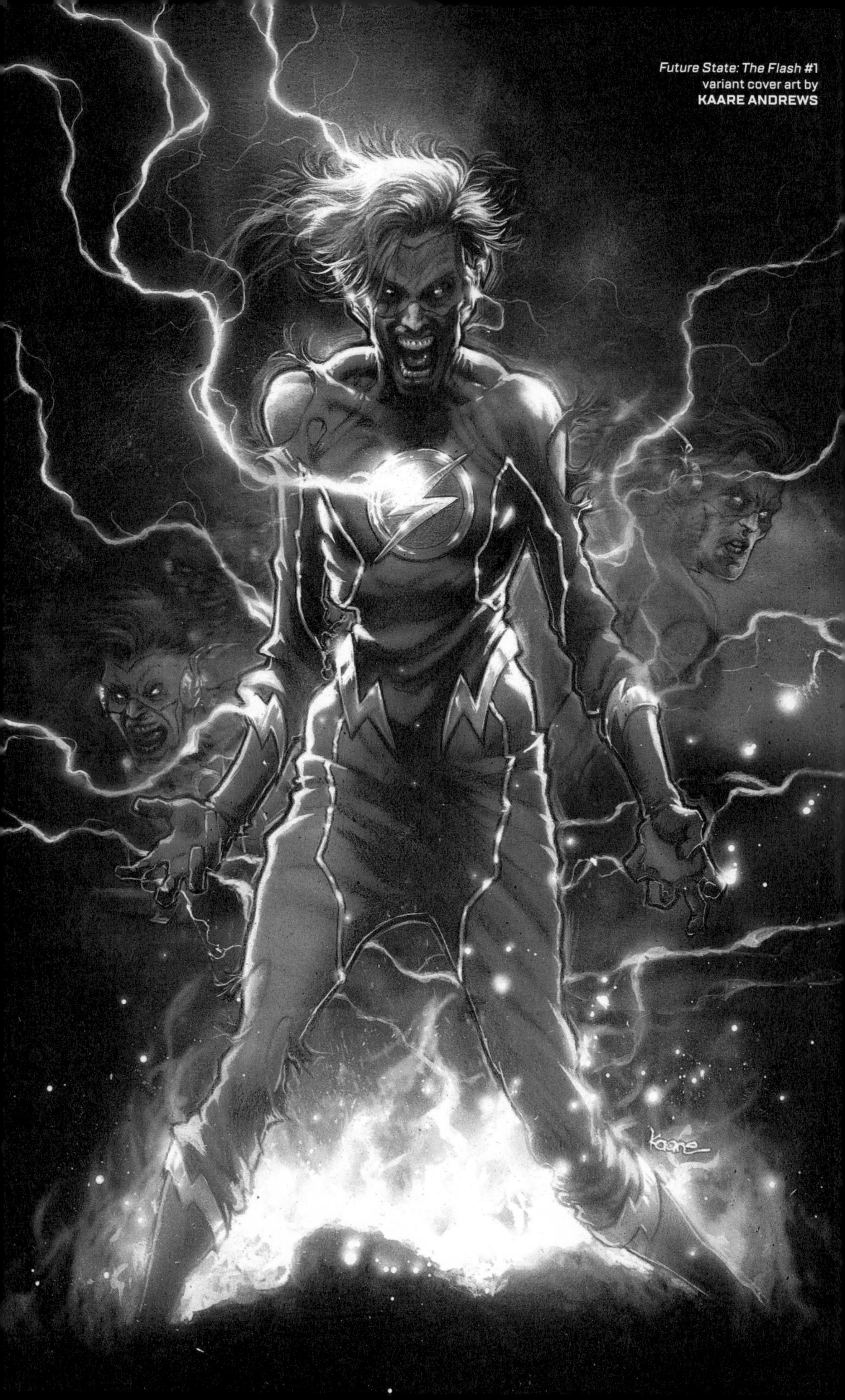
kaare

Future State: The Flash #1
variant cover art by
KAARE ANDREWS

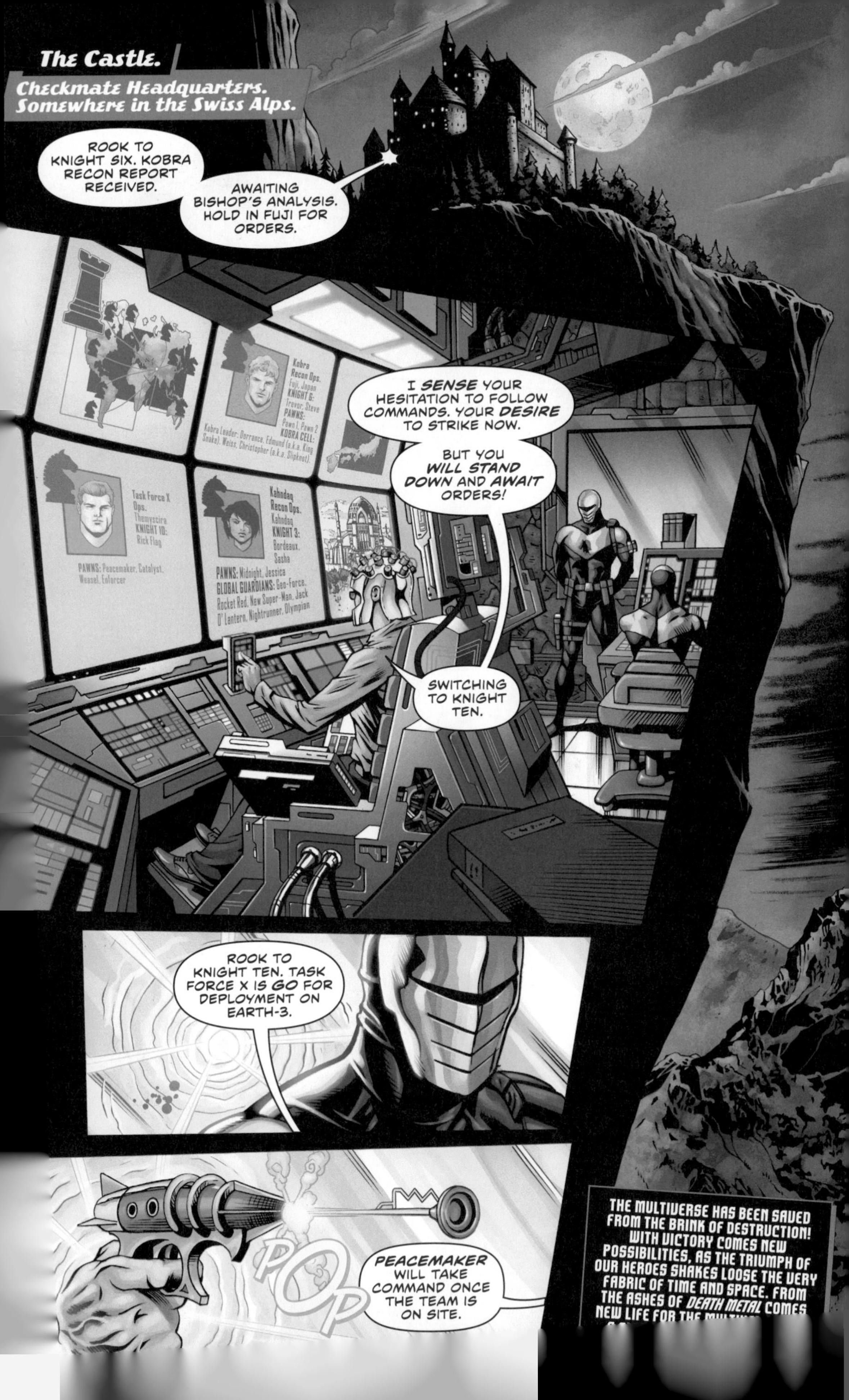
The Castle.
Checkmate Headquarters. Somewhere in the Swiss Alps.
ROOK TO KNIGHT SIX. KOBRA RECON REPORT RECEIVED.
AWAITING BISHOP'S ANALYSIS. HOLD IN FUJI FOR ORDERS.
Kobra Recon Ops. Fuji, Japan KNIGHT 6: Trevor, Steve PAWNS: Pawn 1, Pawn 2 KOBRA CELL: Kobra Leader: Dorrance, Edmund (a.k.a. King Snake). Weiss, Christopher (a.k.a. Slipknot).
Task Force X Ops. Themyscira KNIGHT 10: Rick Flag
PAWNS: Peacemaker, Catalyst, Weasel, Enforcer
Kahndaq Recon Ops. Kahndaq KNIGHT 3: Bordeaux, Sasha
PAWNS: Midnight, Jessica GLOBAL GUARDIANS: Geo-Force, Rocket Red, New Super-Man, Jack O' Lantern, Nightrunner, Olympian
I SENSE YOUR HESITATION TO FOLLOW COMMANDS. YOUR DESIRE TO STRIKE NOW.
BUT YOU WILL STAND DOWN AND AWAIT ORDERS!
SWITCHING TO KNIGHT TEN.
ROOK TO KNIGHT TEN. TASK FORCE X IS GO FOR DEPLOYMENT ON EARTH-3.
POP
PEACEMAKER WILL TAKE COMMAND ONCE THE TEAM IS ON SITE.
THE MULTIVERSE HAS BEEN SAVED FROM THE BRINK OF DESTRUCTION! WITH VICTORY COMES NEW POSSIBILITIES, AS THE TRIUMPH OF OUR HEROES SHAKES LOOSE THE VERY FABRIC OF TIME AND SPACE. FROM THE ASHES OF DEATH METAL COMES NEW LIFE FOR THE

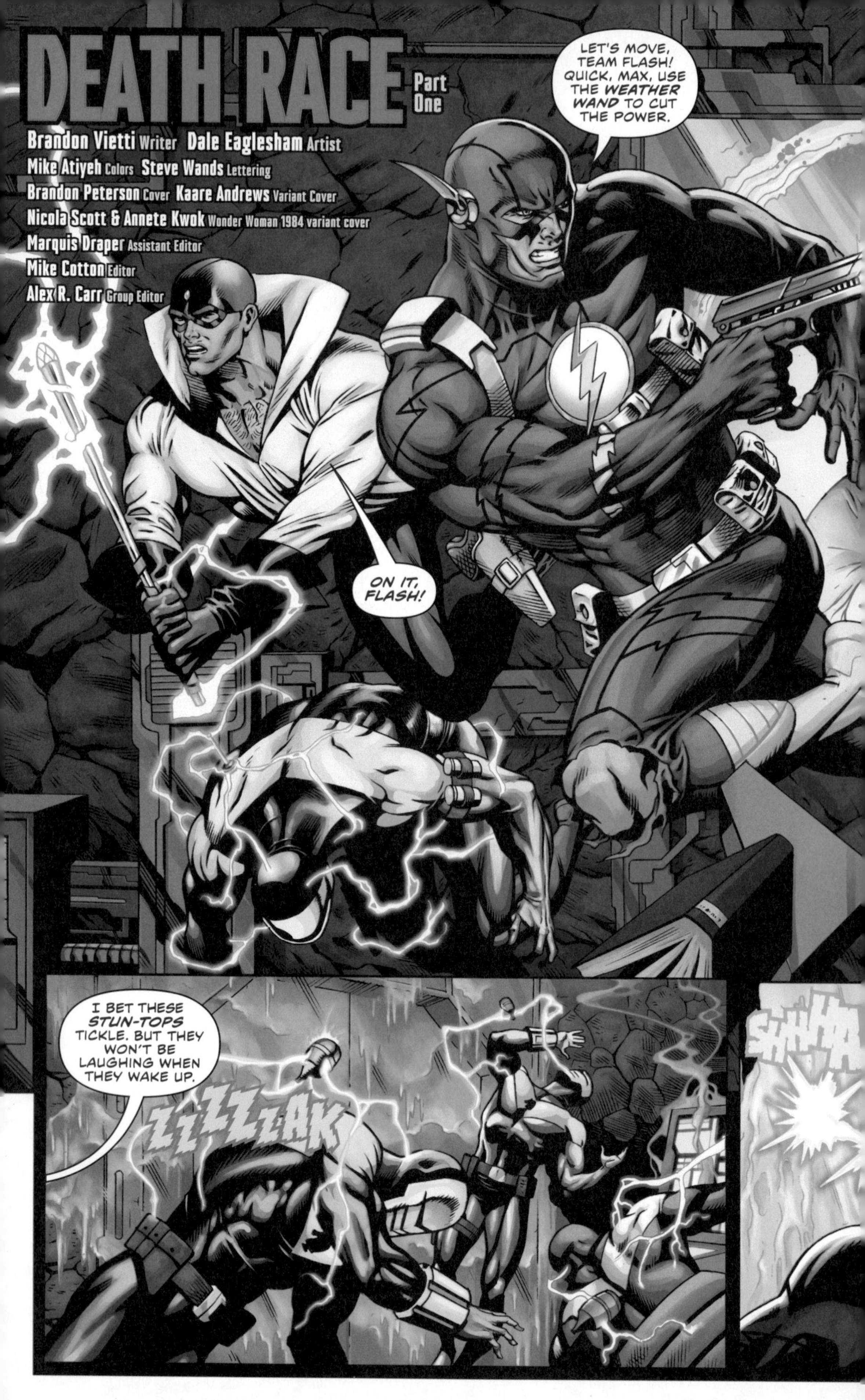
DEATH RACE Part One
Brandon Vietti Writer Dale Eaglesham Artist
Mike Atiyeh Colors Steve Wands Lettering
Brandon Peterson Cover Kaare Andrews Variant Cover
Nicola Scott & Annete Kwok Wonder Woman 1984 variant cover
Marquis Draper Assistant Editor
Mike Cotton Editor
Alex R. Carr Group Editor
LET'S MOVE, TEAM FLASH! QUICK, MAX, USE THE WEATHER WAND TO CUT THE POWER.
ON IT, FLASH!
I BET THESE STUN-TOPS TICKLE. BUT THEY WON'T BE LAUGHING WHEN THEY WAKE UP.
ZZZZZAK

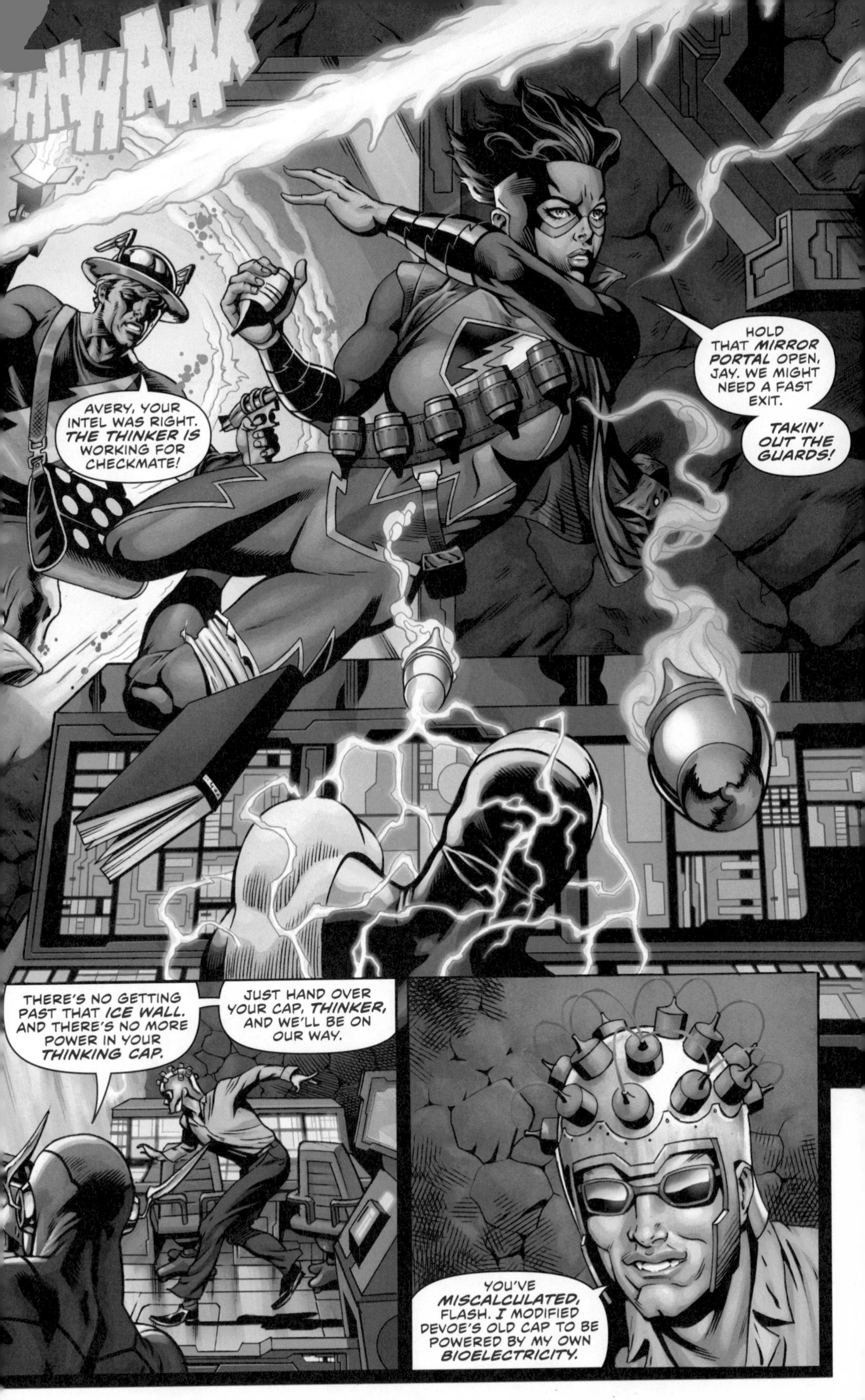
HHWAAK
AVERY, YOUR INTEL WAS RIGHT. THE THINKER IS WORKING FOR CHECKMATE!
HOLD THAT MIRROR PORTAL OPEN, JAY. WE MIGHT NEED A FAST EXIT.
TAKIN' OUT THE GUARDS!
THERE'S NO GETTING PAST THAT ICE WALL. AND THERE'S NO MORE POWER IN YOUR THINKING CAP.
JUST HAND OVER YOUR CAP, THINKER, AND WE'LL BE ON OUR WAY.
YOU'VE MISCALCULATED, FLASH. I MODIFIED DEVOE'S OLD CAP TO BE POWERED BY MY OWN BIOELECTRICITY.

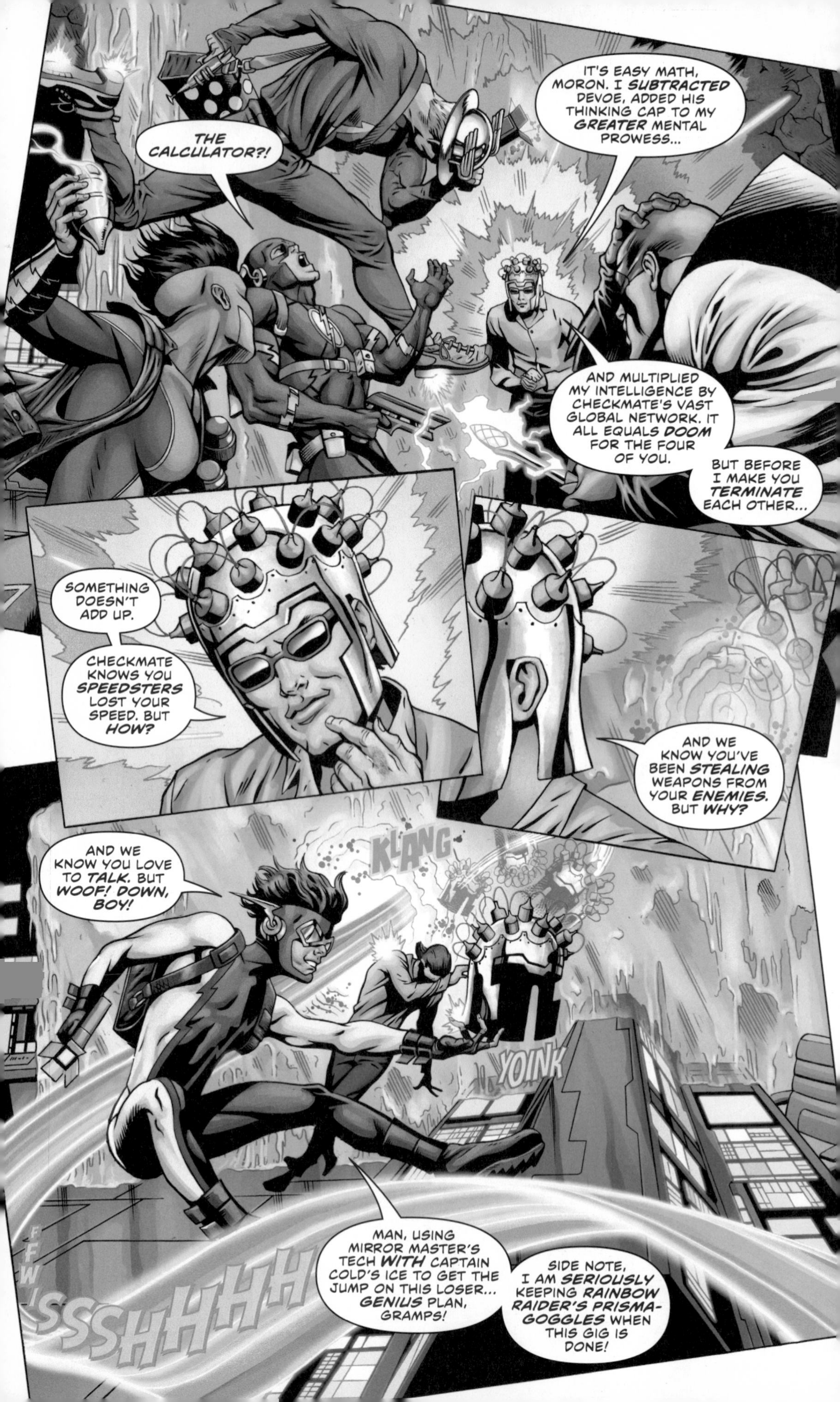
THE CALCULATOR?!
IT'S EASY MATH, MORON. I SUBTRACTED DEVOE, ADDED HIS THINKING CAP TO MY GREATER MENTAL PROWESS...
AND MULTIPLIED MY INTELLIGENCE BY CHECKMATE'S VAST GLOBAL NETWORK. IT ALL EQUALS DOOM FOR THE FOUR OF YOU.
BUT BEFORE I MAKE YOU TERMINATE EACH OTHER...
SOMETHING DOESN'T ADD UP.
CHECKMATE KNOWS YOU SPEEDSTERS LOST YOUR SPEED. BUT HOW?
AND WE KNOW YOU'VE BEEN STEALING WEAPONS FROM YOUR ENEMIES. BUT WHY?
AND WE KNOW YOU LOVE TO TALK. BUT WOOF! DOWN, BOY!
KLANG
YOINK
FFWISSSHHHHH
MAN, USING MIRROR MASTER'S TECH WITH CAPTAIN COLD'S ICE TO GET THE JUMP ON THIS LOSER... GENIUS PLAN, GRAMPS!
SIDE NOTE, I AM SERIOUSLY KEEPING RAINBOW RAIDER'S PRISMA-GOGGLES WHEN THIS GIG IS DONE!

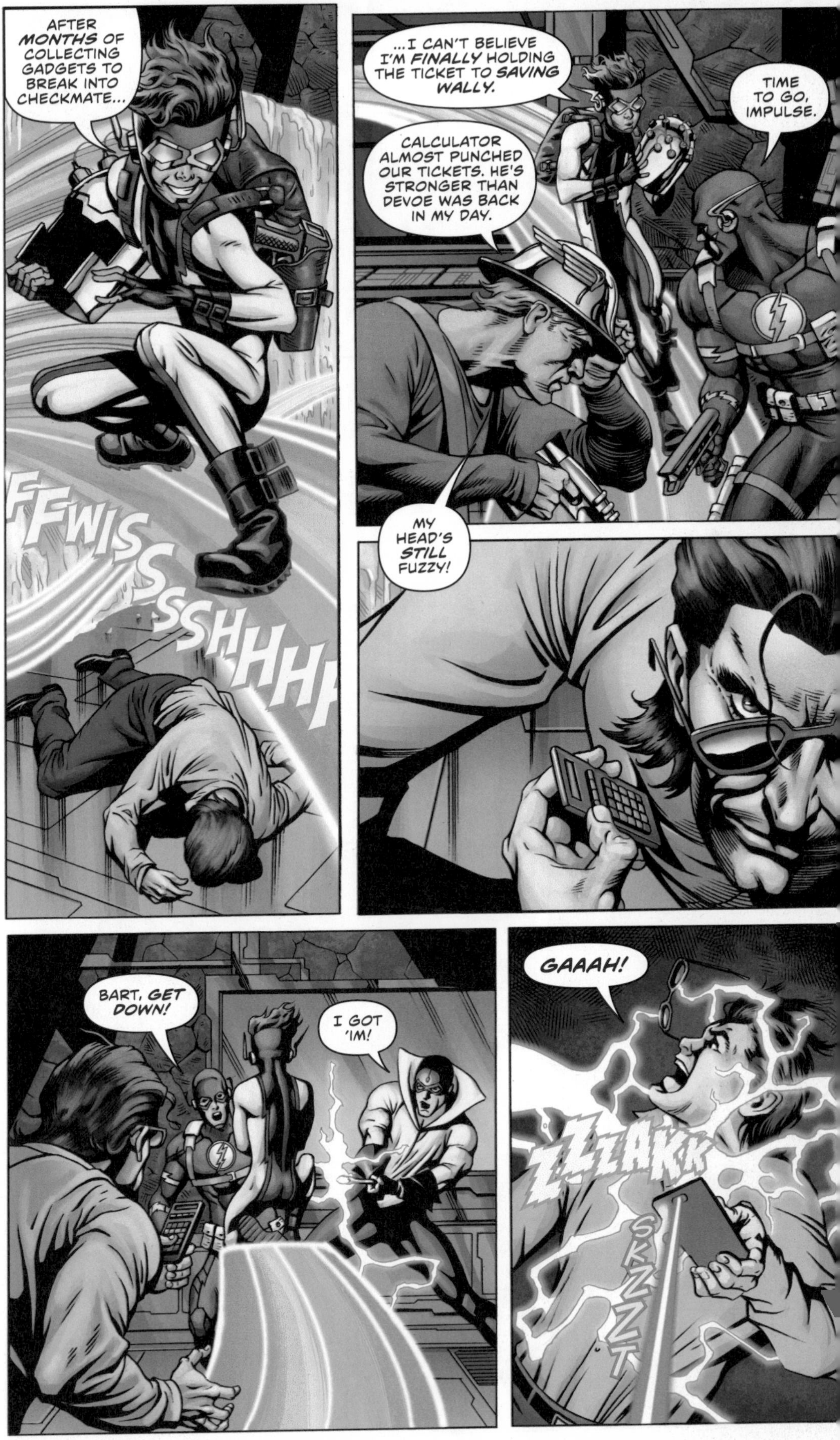
AFTER MONTHS OF COLLECTING GADGETS TO BREAK INTO CHECKMATE...
FFWISSSSHHHH
...I CAN'T BELIEVE I'M FINALLY HOLDING THE TICKET TO SAVING WALLY.
TIME TO GO, IMPULSE.
CALCULATOR ALMOST PUNCHED OUR TICKETS. HE'S STRONGER THAN DEVOE WAS BACK IN MY DAY.
MY HEAD'S STILL FUZZY!
BART, GET DOWN!
I GOT 'IM!
GAAAH!
ZZZAKK
SKZZZT

UHK--

SKRAAASHHHH

NOOO!

I--I WASN'T *FAST* ENOUGH.

"THAT MOMENT... STILL A SHARP, *BURNING* MEMORY.

"MY TEAM. *MY* FAILURE.

"I CAN'T REMEMBER WHAT HAPPENED AFTER BART FELL.

"CAN'T *LET* MYSELF REMEMBER.

"HAVE TO FOCUS ON WHAT BART'S SACRIFICE WAS FOR.

"HAVE TO FOCUS ON THIS DAMNED THINKING CAP."

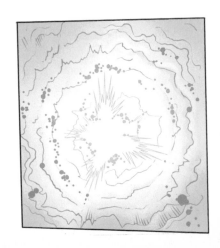

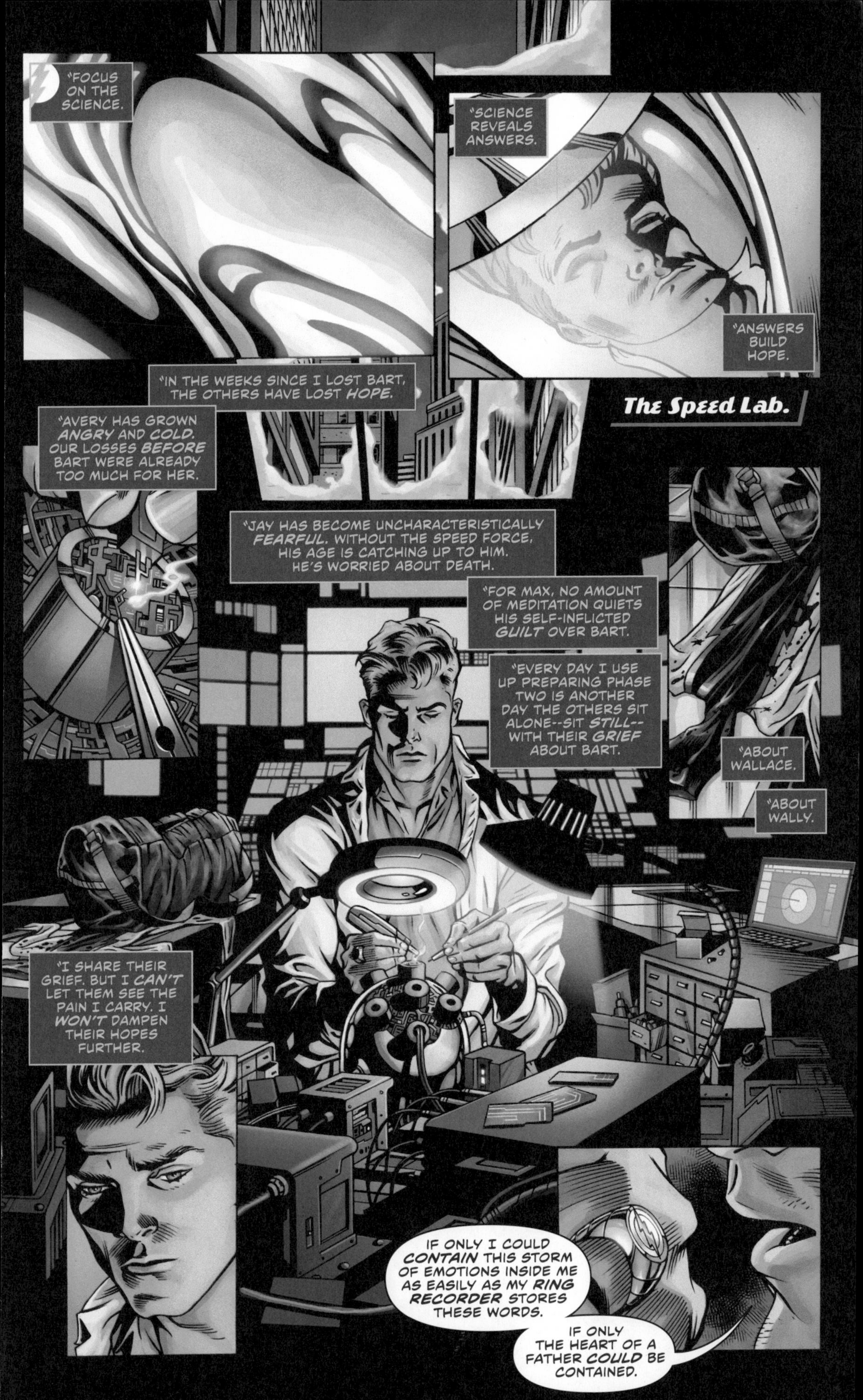
"FOCUS ON THE SCIENCE.
"SCIENCE REVEALS ANSWERS.
"ANSWERS BUILD HOPE.
"IN THE WEEKS SINCE I LOST BART, THE OTHERS HAVE LOST HOPE.
The Speed Lab.
"AVERY HAS GROWN ANGRY AND COLD. OUR LOSSES BEFORE BART WERE ALREADY TOO MUCH FOR HER.
"JAY HAS BECOME UNCHARACTERISTICALLY FEARFUL. WITHOUT THE SPEED FORCE, HIS AGE IS CATCHING UP TO HIM. HE'S WORRIED ABOUT DEATH.
"FOR MAX, NO AMOUNT OF MEDITATION QUIETS HIS SELF-INFLICTED GUILT OVER BART.
"EVERY DAY I USE UP PREPARING PHASE TWO IS ANOTHER DAY THE OTHERS SIT ALONE--SIT STILL--WITH THEIR GRIEF ABOUT BART.
"ABOUT WALLACE.
"ABOUT WALLY.
"I SHARE THEIR GRIEF. BUT I CAN'T LET THEM SEE THE PAIN I CARRY. I WON'T DAMPEN THEIR HOPES FURTHER.
IF ONLY I COULD CONTAIN THIS STORM OF EMOTIONS INSIDE ME AS EASILY AS MY RING RECORDER STORES THESE WORDS.
IF ONLY THE HEART OF A FATHER COULD BE CONTAINED.

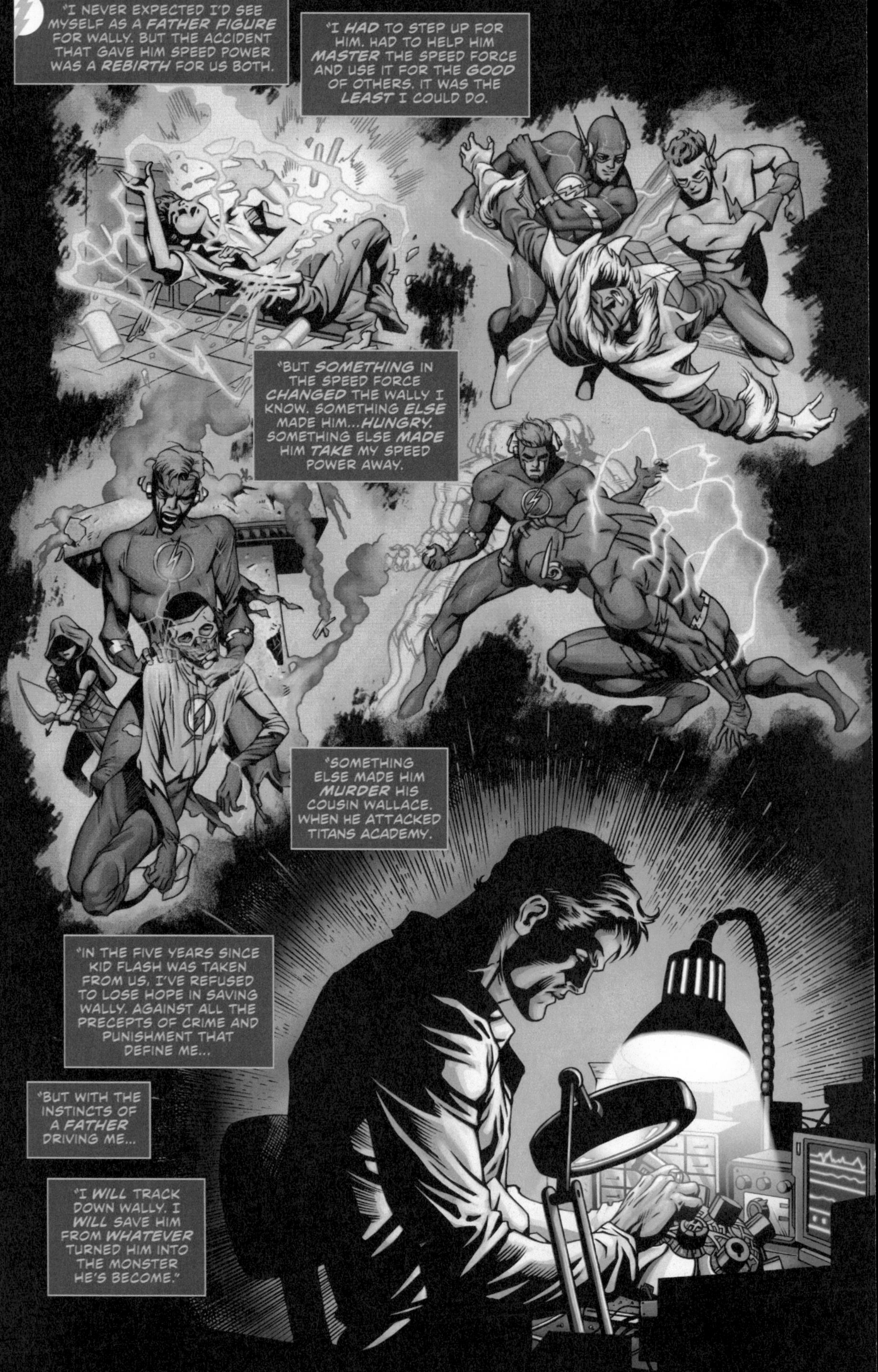
"I NEVER EXPECTED I'D SEE MYSELF AS A FATHER FIGURE FOR WALLY. BUT THE ACCIDENT THAT GAVE HIM SPEED POWER WAS A REBIRTH FOR US BOTH.
"I HAD TO STEP UP FOR HIM. HAD TO HELP HIM MASTER THE SPEED FORCE AND USE IT FOR THE GOOD OF OTHERS. IT WAS THE LEAST I COULD DO.
"BUT SOMETHING IN THE SPEED FORCE CHANGED THE WALLY I KNOW. SOMETHING ELSE MADE HIM...HUNGRY. SOMETHING ELSE MADE HIM TAKE MY SPEED POWER AWAY.
"SOMETHING ELSE MADE HIM MURDER HIS COUSIN WALLACE. WHEN HE ATTACKED TITANS ACADEMY.
"IN THE FIVE YEARS SINCE KID FLASH WAS TAKEN FROM US, I'VE REFUSED TO LOSE HOPE IN SAVING WALLY. AGAINST ALL THE PRECEPTS OF CRIME AND PUNISHMENT THAT DEFINE ME...
"BUT WITH THE INSTINCTS OF A FATHER DRIVING ME...
"I WILL TRACK DOWN WALLY. I WILL SAVE HIM FROM WHATEVER TURNED HIM INTO THE MONSTER HE'S BECOME."

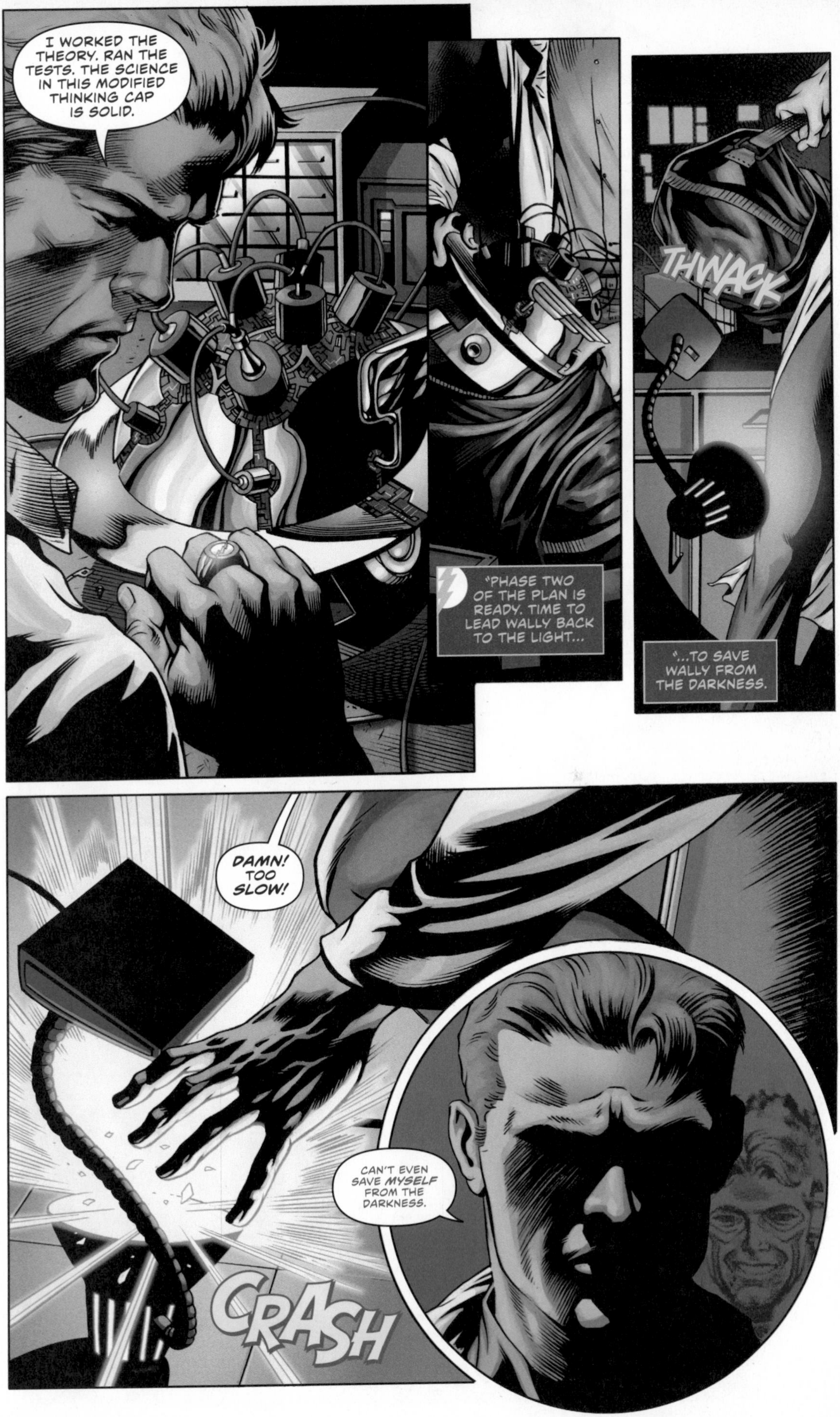
I WORKED THE THEORY. RAN THE TESTS. THE SCIENCE IN THIS MODIFIED THINKING CAP IS SOLID.
"PHASE TWO OF THE PLAN IS READY. TIME TO LEAD WALLY BACK TO THE LIGHT...
THWACK
"...TO SAVE WALLY FROM THE DARKNESS.
DAMN! TOO SLOW!
CRASH
CAN'T EVEN SAVE MYSELF FROM THE DARKNESS.

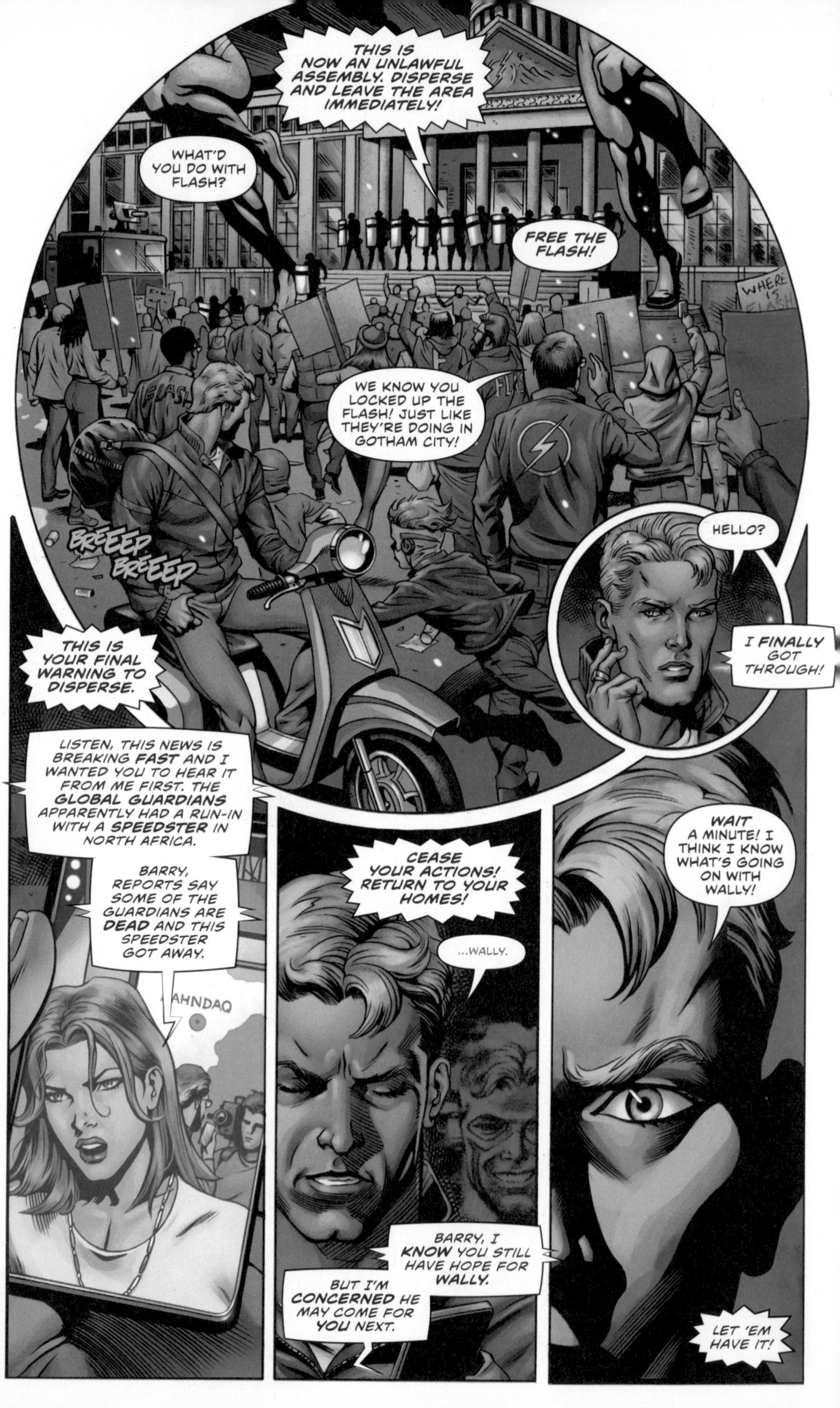

THIS IS NOW AN UNLAWFUL ASSEMBLY. DISPERSE AND LEAVE THE AREA IMMEDIATELY!
WHAT'D YOU DO WITH FLASH?
FREE THE FLASH!
WHERE IS FLASH
WE KNOW YOU LOCKED UP THE FLASH! JUST LIKE THEY'RE DOING IN GOTHAM CITY!
BREEEP BREEEP
HELLO?
I FINALLY GOT THROUGH!
THIS IS YOUR FINAL WARNING TO DISPERSE.
LISTEN, THIS NEWS IS BREAKING FAST AND I WANTED YOU TO HEAR IT FROM ME FIRST. THE GLOBAL GUARDIANS APPARENTLY HAD A RUN-IN WITH A SPEEDSTER IN NORTH AFRICA.
BARRY, REPORTS SAY SOME OF THE GUARDIANS ARE DEAD AND THIS SPEEDSTER GOT AWAY.
AHNDAQ
CEASE YOUR ACTIONS! RETURN TO YOUR HOMES!
...WALLY.
BARRY, I KNOW YOU STILL HAVE HOPE FOR WALLY.
BUT I'M CONCERNED HE MAY COME FOR YOU NEXT.
WAIT A MINUTE! I THINK I KNOW WHAT'S GOING ON WITH WALLY!
LET 'EM HAVE IT!

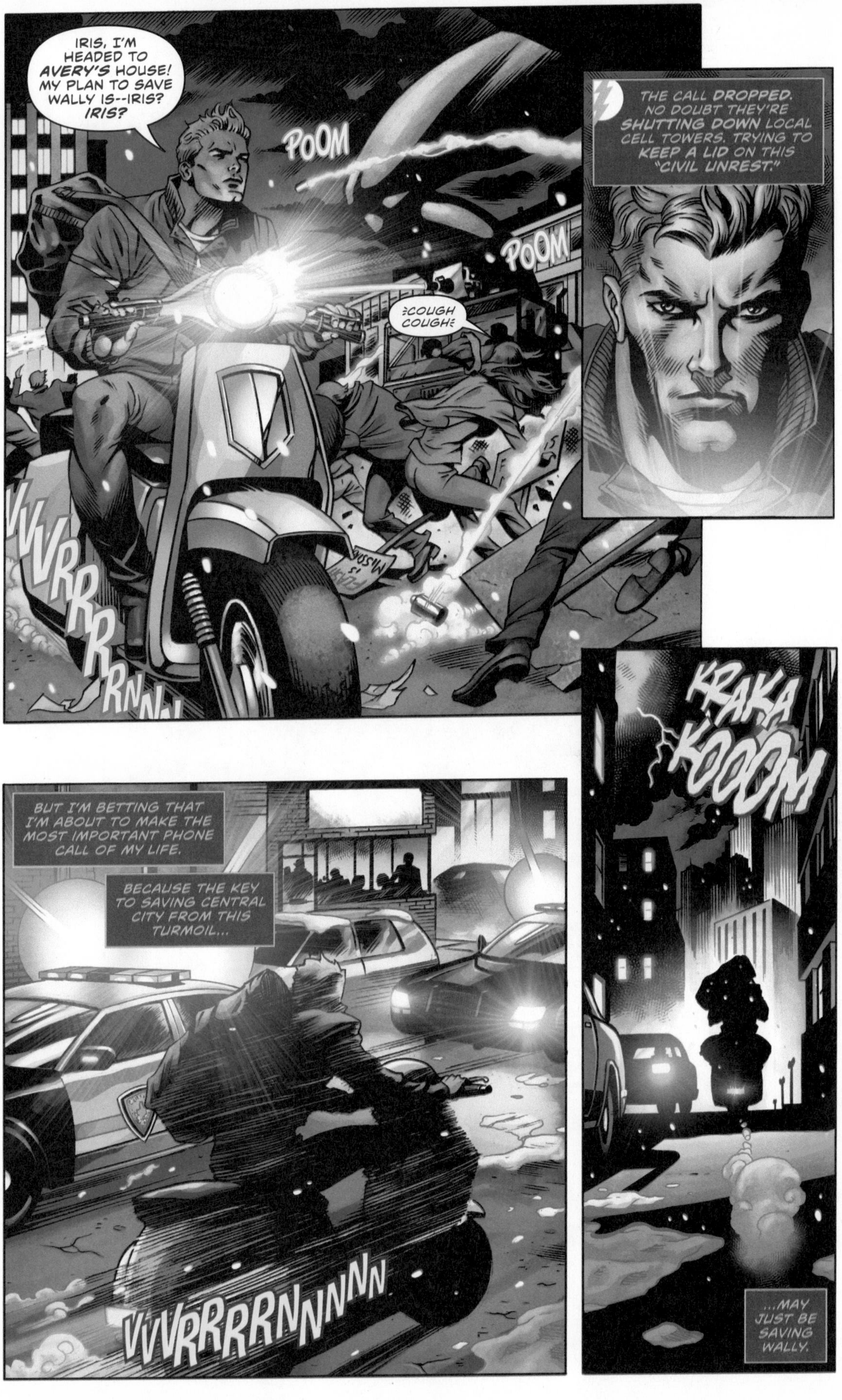
IRIS, I'M HEADED TO AVERY'S HOUSE! MY PLAN TO SAVE WALLY IS--IRIS? IRIS?
POOM
POOM
COUGH COUGH
VVVRRRRRNNNN
THE CALL DROPPED. NO DOUBT THEY'RE SHUTTING DOWN LOCAL CELL TOWERS. TRYING TO KEEP A LID ON THIS "CIVIL UNREST."
BUT I'M BETTING THAT I'M ABOUT TO MAKE THE MOST IMPORTANT PHONE CALL OF MY LIFE.
BECAUSE THE KEY TO SAVING CENTRAL CITY FROM THIS TURMOIL...
VVVRRRRRNNNNN
KRAKA KOOOM
...MAY JUST BE SAVING WALLY.

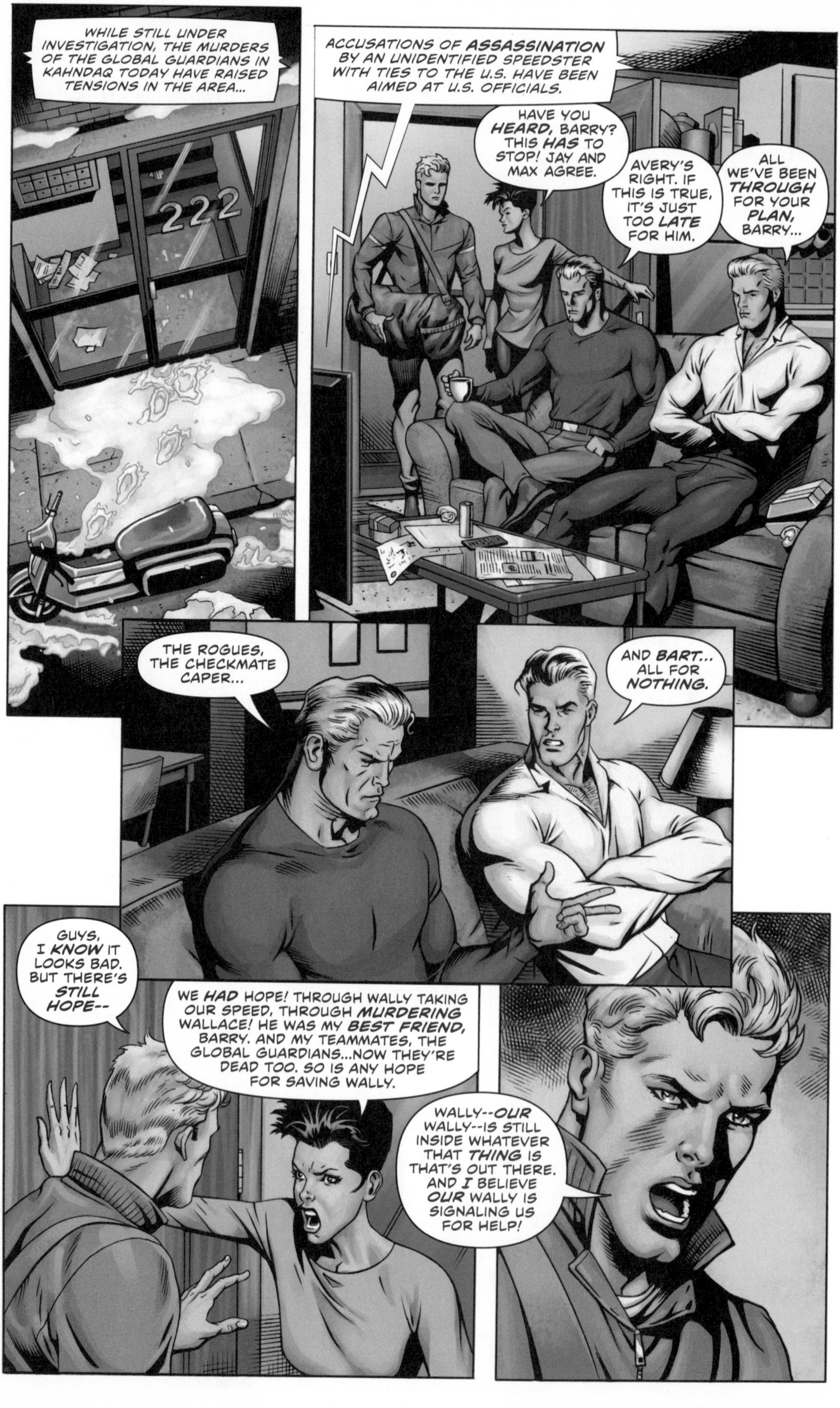
WHILE STILL UNDER INVESTIGATION, THE MURDERS OF THE GLOBAL GUARDIANS IN KAHNDAQ TODAY HAVE RAISED TENSIONS IN THE AREA...
222
ACCUSATIONS OF ASSASSINATION BY AN UNIDENTIFIED SPEEDSTER WITH TIES TO THE U.S. HAVE BEEN AIMED AT U.S. OFFICIALS.
HAVE YOU HEARD, BARRY? THIS HAS TO STOP! JAY AND MAX AGREE.
AVERY'S RIGHT. IF THIS IS TRUE, IT'S JUST TOO LATE FOR HIM.
ALL WE'VE BEEN THROUGH FOR YOUR PLAN, BARRY...
THE ROGUES, THE CHECKMATE CAPER...
AND BART... ALL FOR NOTHING.
GUYS, I KNOW IT LOOKS BAD. BUT THERE'S STILL HOPE--
WE HAD HOPE! THROUGH WALLY TAKING OUR SPEED, THROUGH MURDERING WALLACE! HE WAS MY BEST FRIEND, BARRY. AND MY TEAMMATES, THE GLOBAL GUARDIANS...NOW THEY'RE DEAD TOO. SO IS ANY HOPE FOR SAVING WALLY.
WALLY--OUR WALLY--IS STILL INSIDE WHATEVER THAT THING IS THAT'S OUT THERE. AND I BELIEVE OUR WALLY IS SIGNALING US FOR HELP!

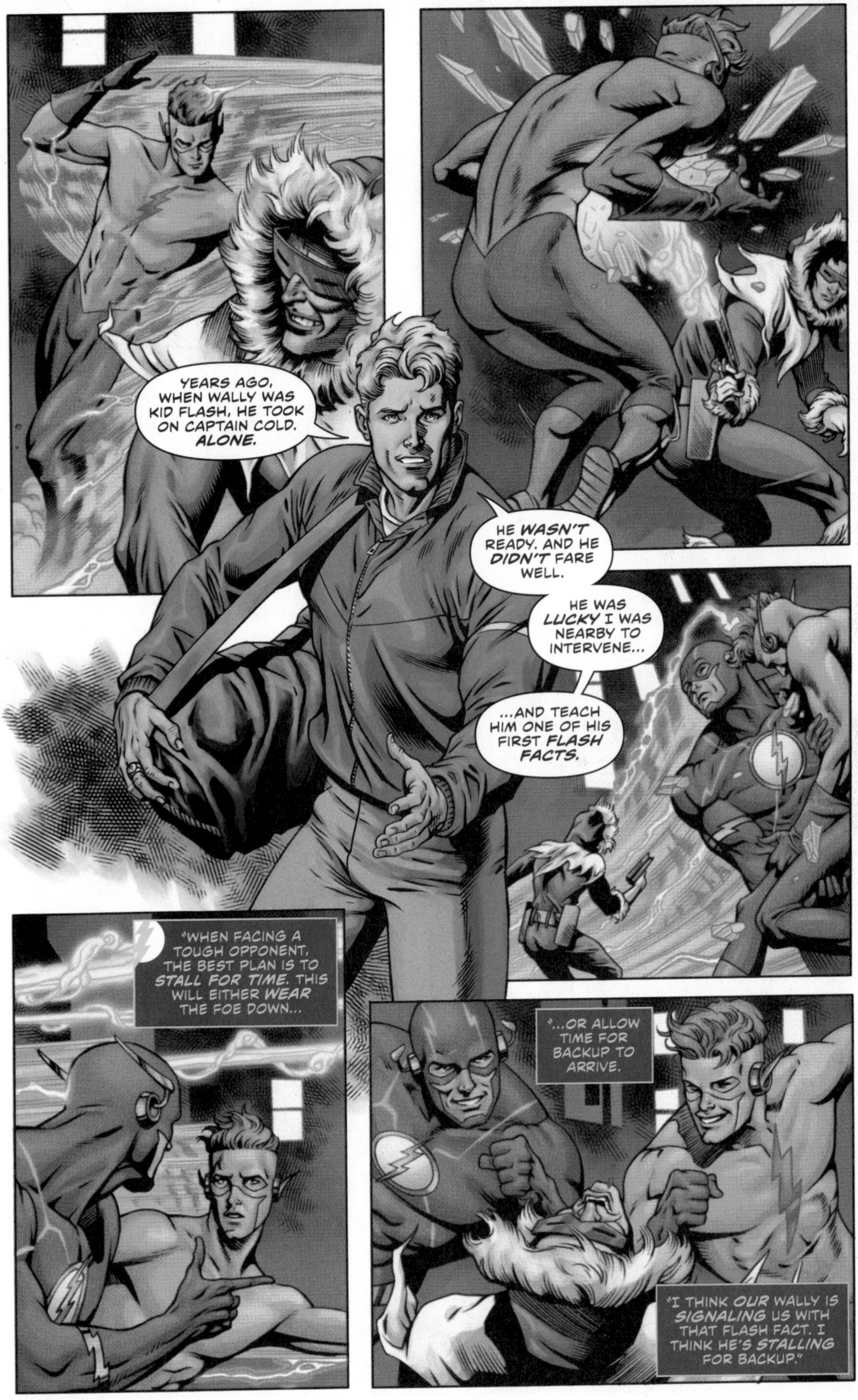
YEARS AGO, WHEN WALLY WAS KID FLASH, HE TOOK ON CAPTAIN COLD. ALONE.
HE WASN'T READY. AND HE DIDN'T FARE WELL.
HE WAS LUCKY I WAS NEARBY TO INTERVENE...
...AND TEACH HIM ONE OF HIS FIRST FLASH FACTS.
"WHEN FACING A TOUGH OPPONENT, THE BEST PLAN IS TO STALL FOR TIME. THIS WILL EITHER WEAR THE FOE DOWN...
"...OR ALLOW TIME FOR BACKUP TO ARRIVE.
"I THINK OUR WALLY IS SIGNALING US WITH THAT FLASH FACT. I THINK HE'S STALLING FOR BACKUP."

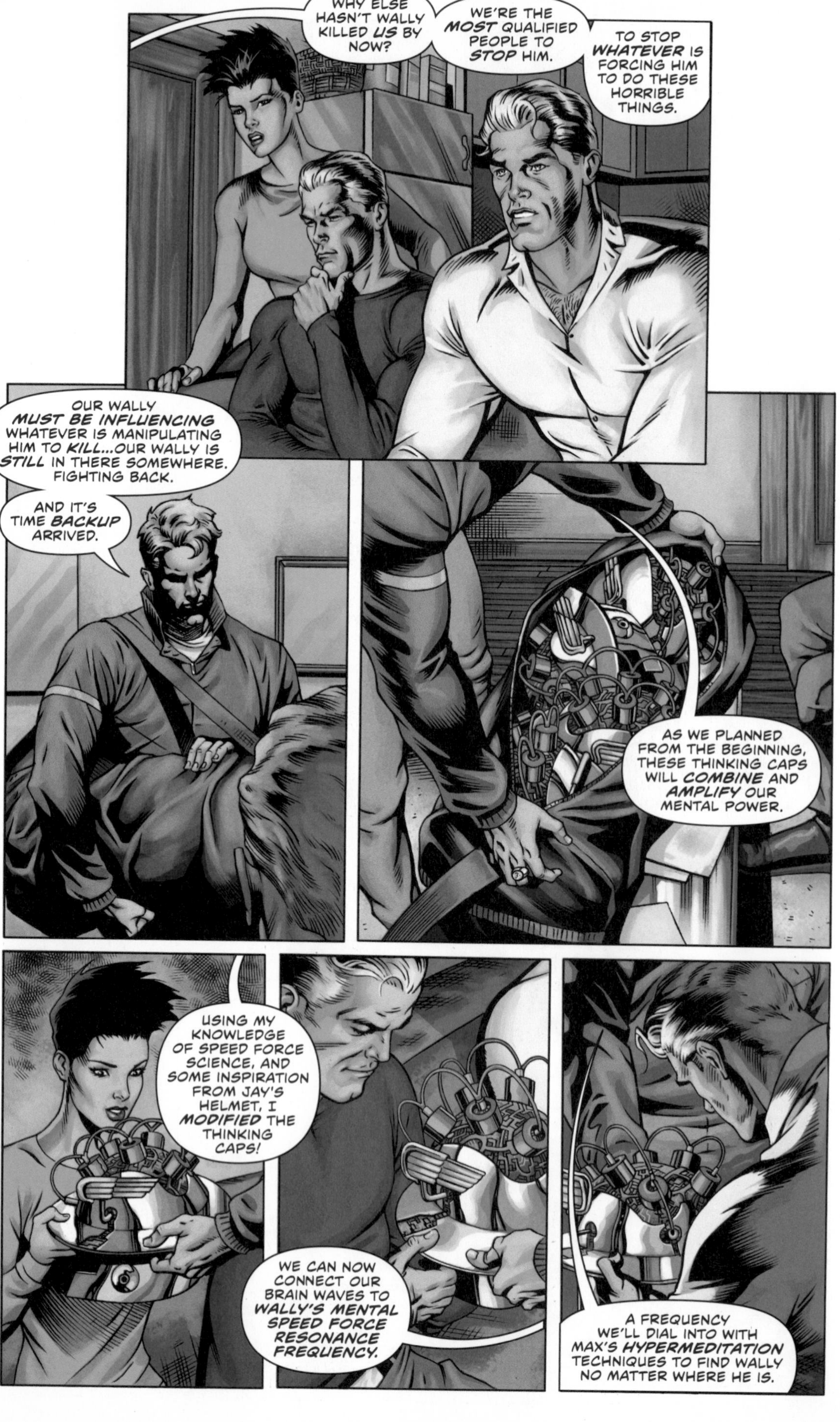
WHY ELSE HASN'T WALLY KILLED US BY NOW?
WE'RE THE MOST QUALIFIED PEOPLE TO STOP HIM.
TO STOP WHATEVER IS FORCING HIM TO DO THESE HORRIBLE THINGS.
OUR WALLY MUST BE INFLUENCING WHATEVER IS MANIPULATING HIM TO KILL...OUR WALLY IS STILL IN THERE SOMEWHERE. FIGHTING BACK.
AND IT'S TIME BACKUP ARRIVED.
AS WE PLANNED FROM THE BEGINNING, THESE THINKING CAPS WILL COMBINE AND AMPLIFY OUR MENTAL POWER.
USING MY KNOWLEDGE OF SPEED FORCE SCIENCE, AND SOME INSPIRATION FROM JAY'S HELMET, I MODIFIED THE THINKING CAPS!
WE CAN NOW CONNECT OUR BRAIN WAVES TO WALLY'S MENTAL SPEED FORCE RESONANCE FREQUENCY.
A FREQUENCY WE'LL DIAL INTO WITH MAX'S HYPERMEDITATION TECHNIQUES TO FIND WALLY NO MATTER WHERE HE IS.

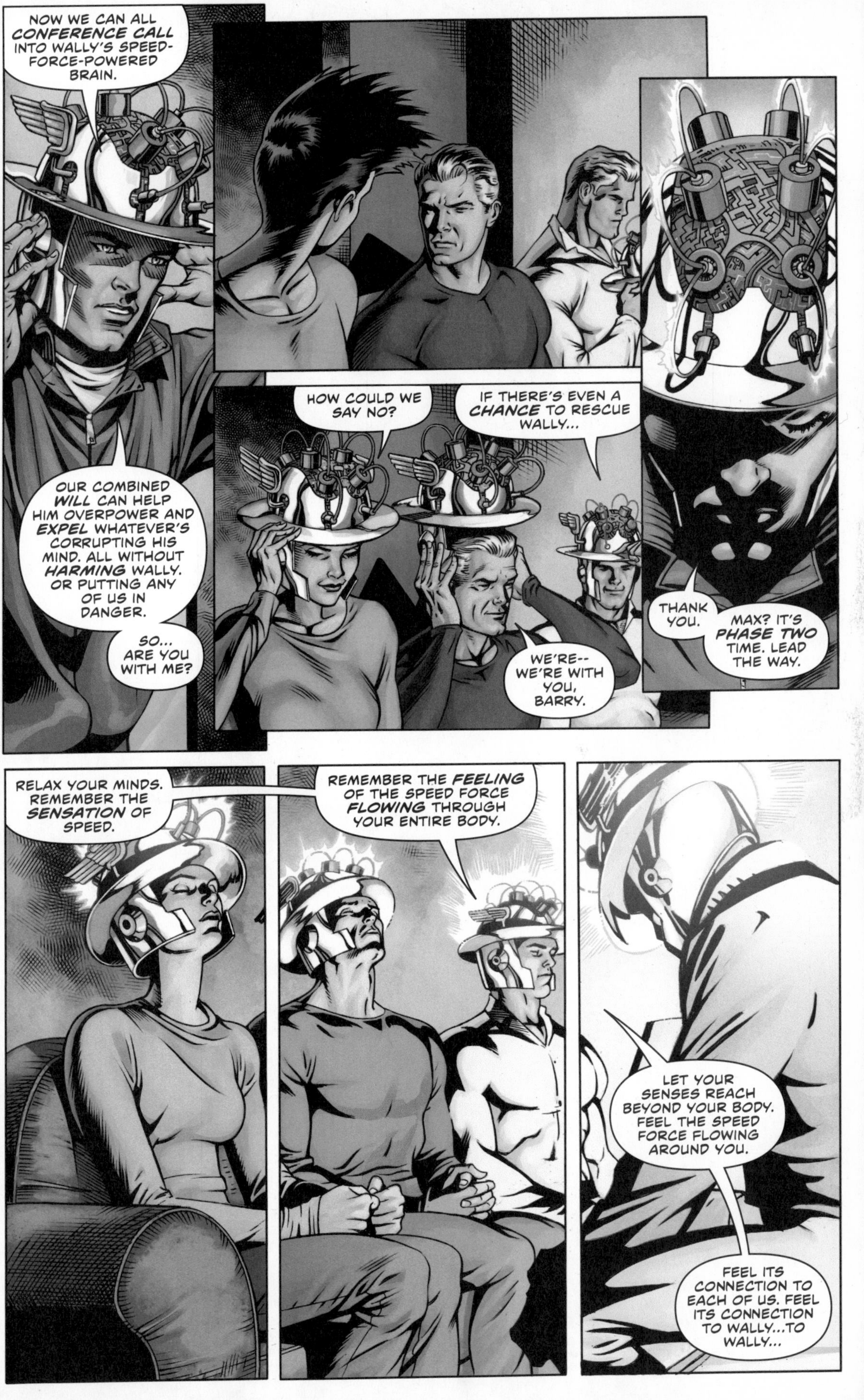
NOW WE CAN ALL CONFERENCE CALL INTO WALLY'S SPEED-FORCE-POWERED BRAIN.
OUR COMBINED WILL CAN HELP HIM OVERPOWER AND EXPEL WHATEVER'S CORRUPTING HIS MIND. ALL WITHOUT HARMING WALLY. OR PUTTING ANY OF US IN DANGER.
SO... ARE YOU WITH ME?
HOW COULD WE SAY NO?
IF THERE'S EVEN A CHANCE TO RESCUE WALLY...
WE'RE-- WE'RE WITH YOU, BARRY.
THANK YOU.
MAX? IT'S PHASE TWO TIME. LEAD THE WAY.
RELAX YOUR MINDS. REMEMBER THE SENSATION OF SPEED.
REMEMBER THE FEELING OF THE SPEED FORCE FLOWING THROUGH YOUR ENTIRE BODY.
LET YOUR SENSES REACH BEYOND YOUR BODY. FEEL THE SPEED FORCE FLOWING AROUND YOU.
FEEL ITS CONNECTION TO EACH OF US. FEEL ITS CONNECTION TO WALLY...TO WALLY...

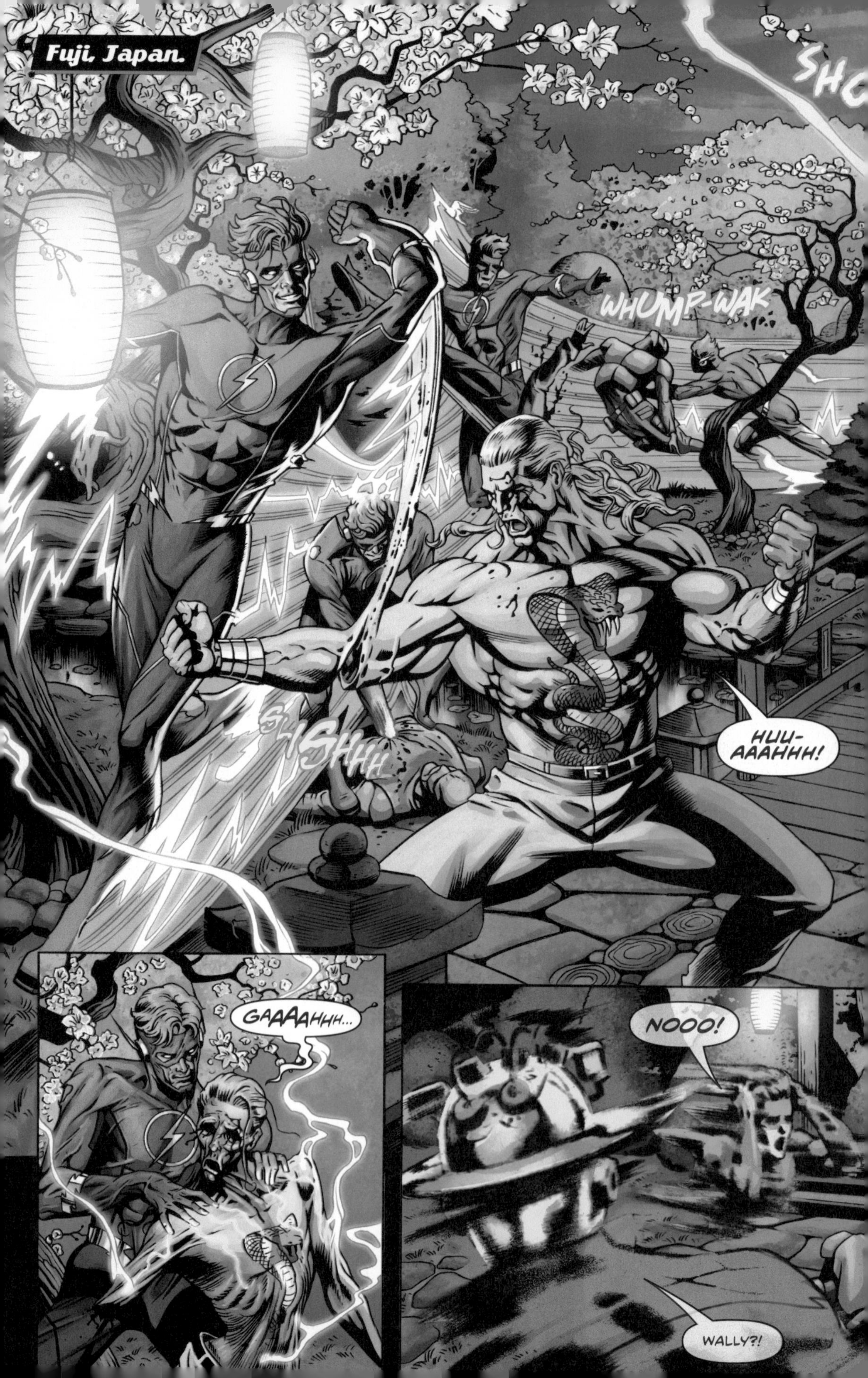

Fuji, Japan.
SHO
WHUMP-WAK
SHSHHH
HUU-AAAHHH!
GAAAAHHH...
NOOO!
WALLY?!

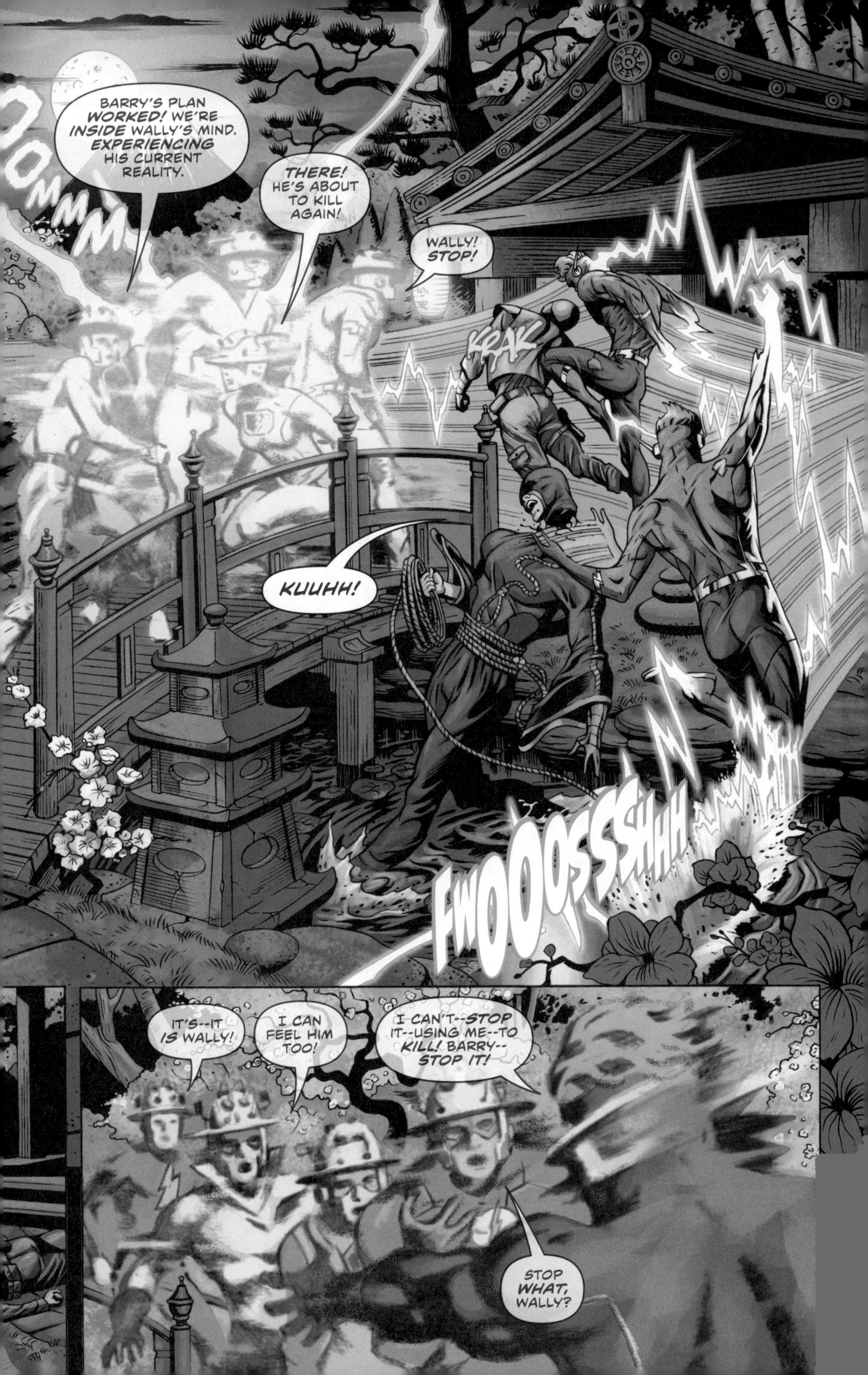

BARRY'S PLAN WORKED! WE'RE INSIDE WALLY'S MIND. EXPERIENCING HIS CURRENT REALITY.
THERE! HE'S ABOUT TO KILL AGAIN!
WALLY! STOP!
KRAK
KUUHH!
FWOOOSSSHHH
IT'S--IT IS WALLY!
I CAN FEEL HIM TOO!
I CAN'T--STOP IT--USING ME--TO KILL! BARRY--STOP IT!
STOP WHAT, WALLY?

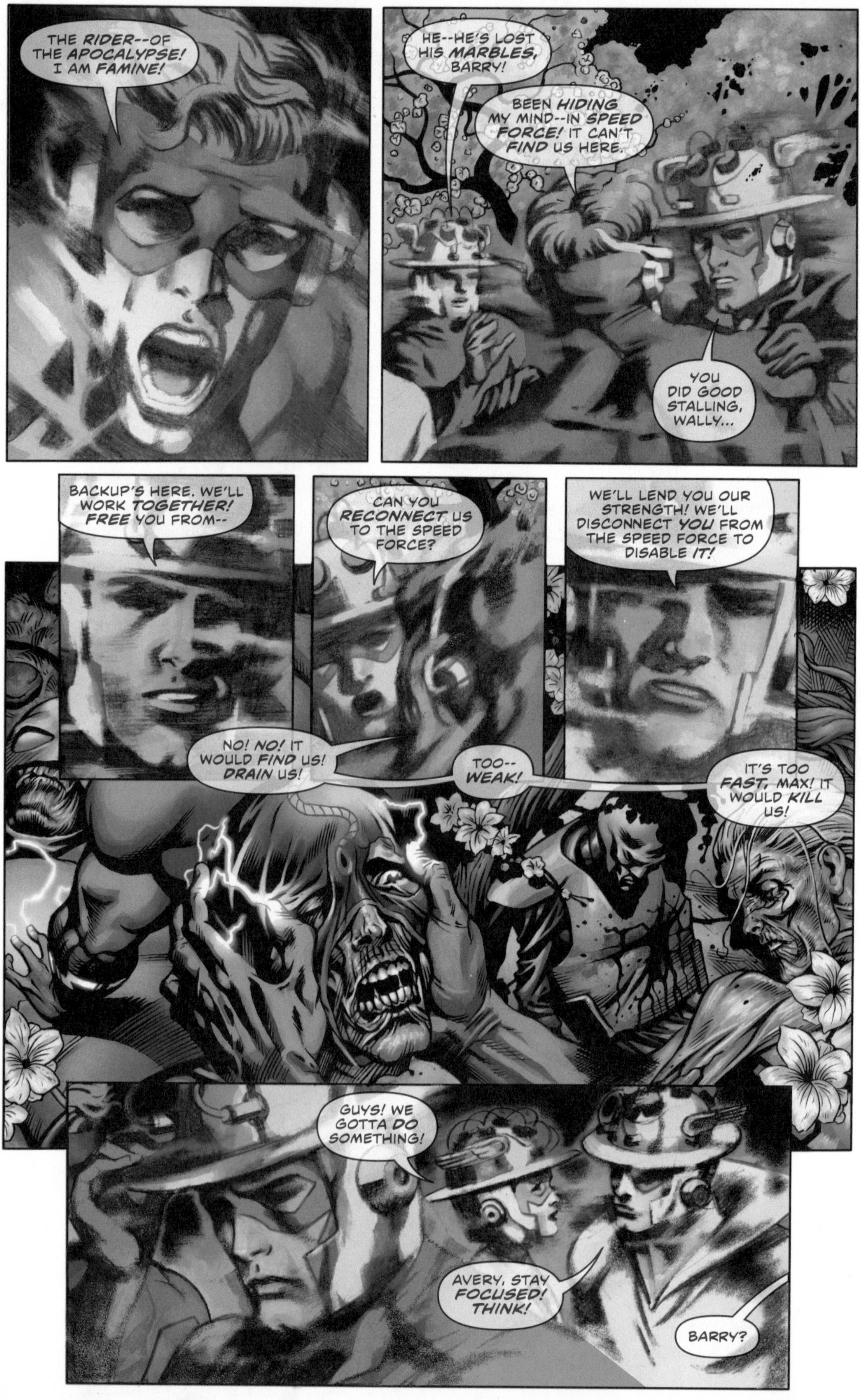
THE RIDER--OF THE APOCALYPSE! I AM FAMINE!
HE--HE'S LOST HIS MARBLES, BARRY!
BEEN HIDING MY MIND--IN SPEED FORCE! IT CAN'T FIND US HERE.
YOU DID GOOD STALLING, WALLY...
BACKUP'S HERE. WE'LL WORK TOGETHER! FREE YOU FROM--
CAN YOU RECONNECT US TO THE SPEED FORCE?
WE'LL LEND YOU OUR STRENGTH! WE'LL DISCONNECT YOU FROM THE SPEED FORCE TO DISABLE IT!
NO! NO! IT WOULD FIND US! DRAIN US!
TOO-- WEAK!
IT'S TOO FAST, MAX! IT WOULD KILL US!
GUYS! WE GOTTA DO SOMETHING!
AVERY, STAY FOCUSED! THINK!
BARRY?

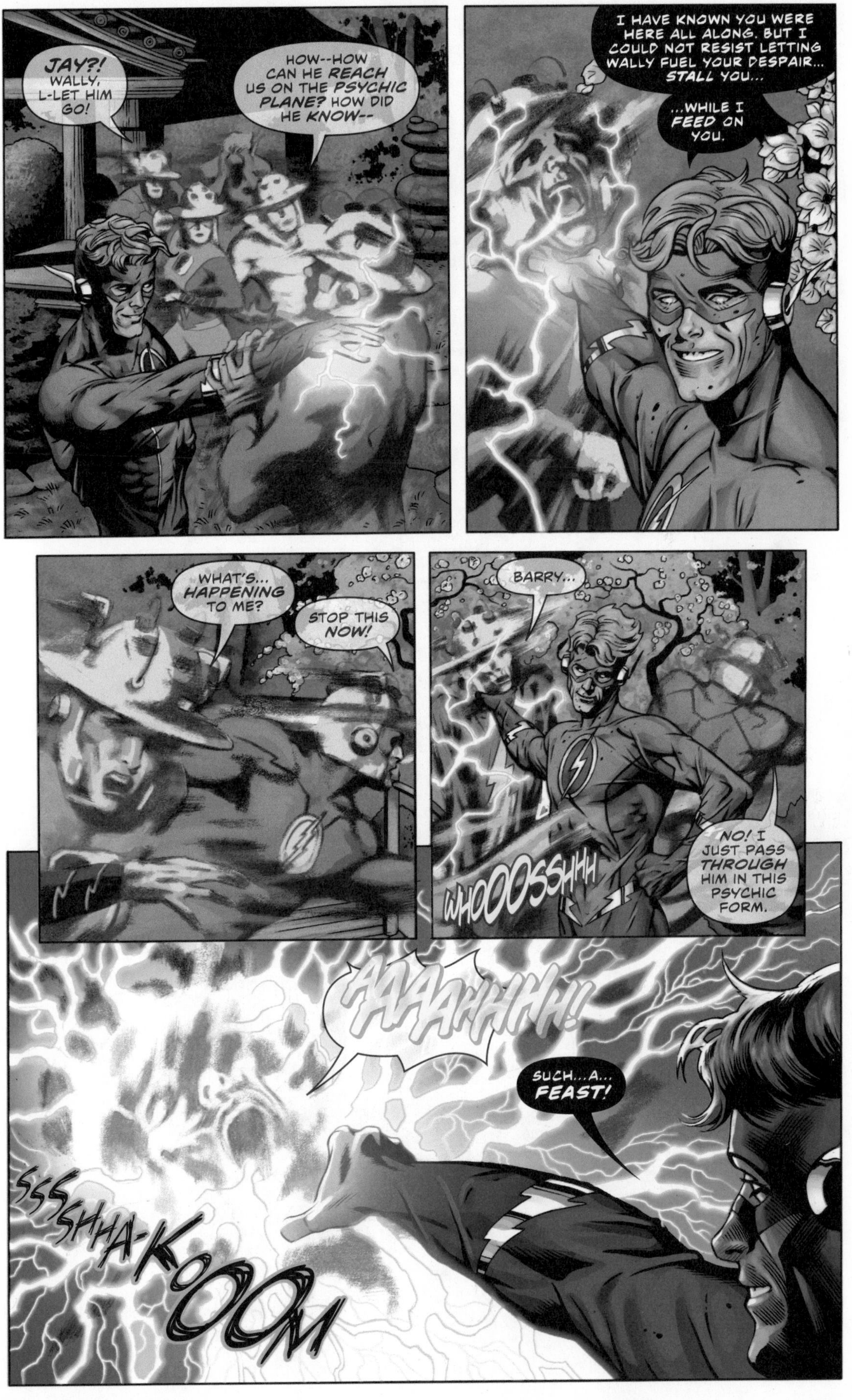
JAY?! WALLY, L-LET HIM GO!
HOW--HOW CAN HE REACH US ON THE PSYCHIC PLANE? HOW DID HE KNOW--
I HAVE KNOWN YOU WERE HERE ALL ALONG. BUT I COULD NOT RESIST LETTING WALLY FUEL YOUR DESPAIR... STALL YOU...
...WHILE I FEED ON YOU.
WHAT'S... HAPPENING TO ME?
STOP THIS NOW!
BARRY...
WHOOOSSHHH
NO! I JUST PASS THROUGH HIM IN THIS PSYCHIC FORM.
AAAAHHHH!
SUCH...A... FEAST!
SSSSHHA-KOOOM

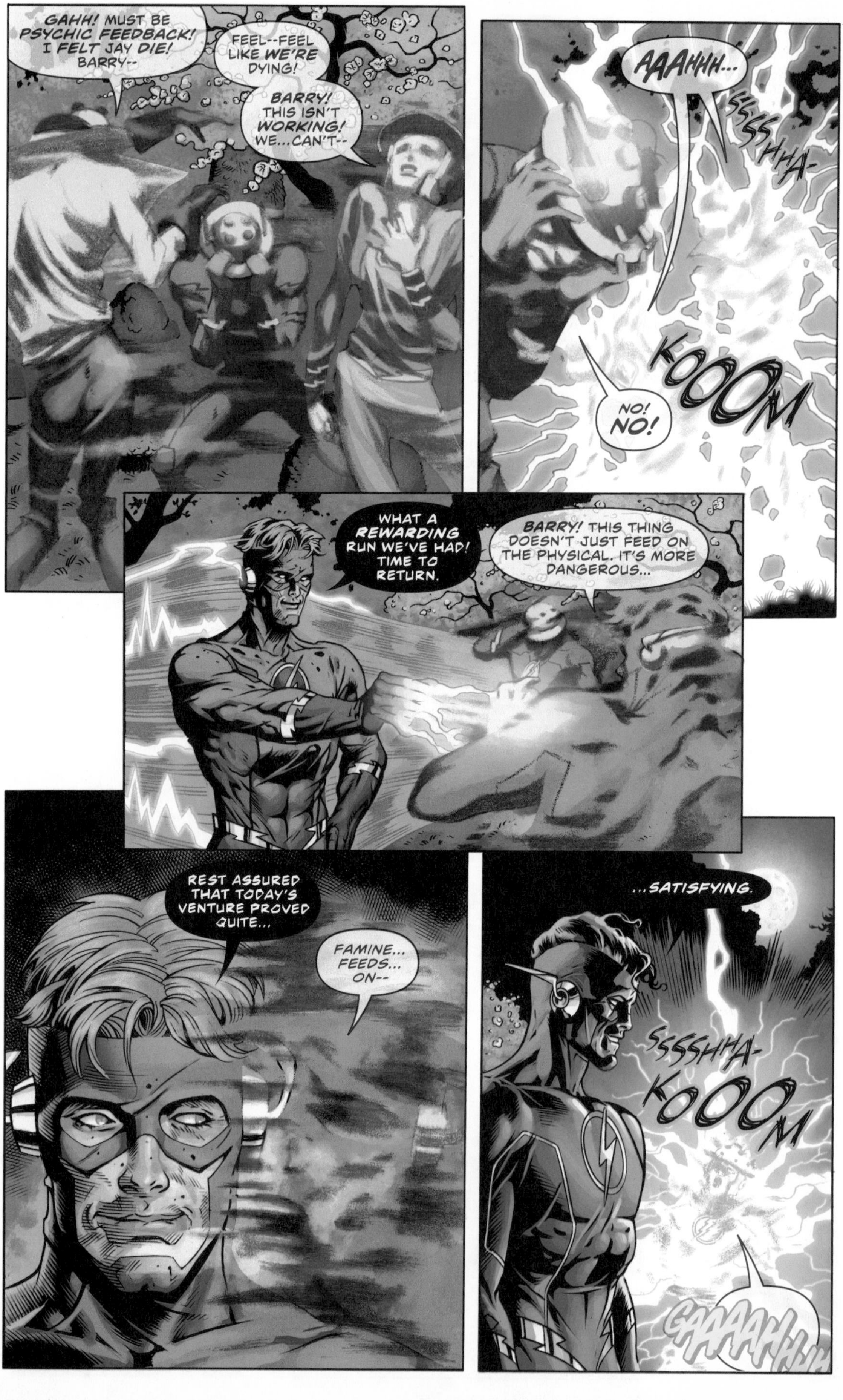
GAHH! MUST BE PSYCHIC FEEDBACK! I FELT JAY DIE! BARRY--
FEEL--FEEL LIKE WE'RE DYING!
BARRY! THIS ISN'T WORKING! WE...CAN'T--
AAAHHH...
SSSSHHA-
KOOOM
NO! NO!
WHAT A REWARDING RUN WE'VE HAD! TIME TO RETURN.
BARRY! THIS THING DOESN'T JUST FEED ON THE PHYSICAL. IT'S MORE DANGEROUS...
REST ASSURED THAT TODAY'S VENTURE PROVED QUITE...
FAMINE... FEEDS... ON--
...SATISFYING.
SSSSHHA-
KOOOM
GAAAAHHHH

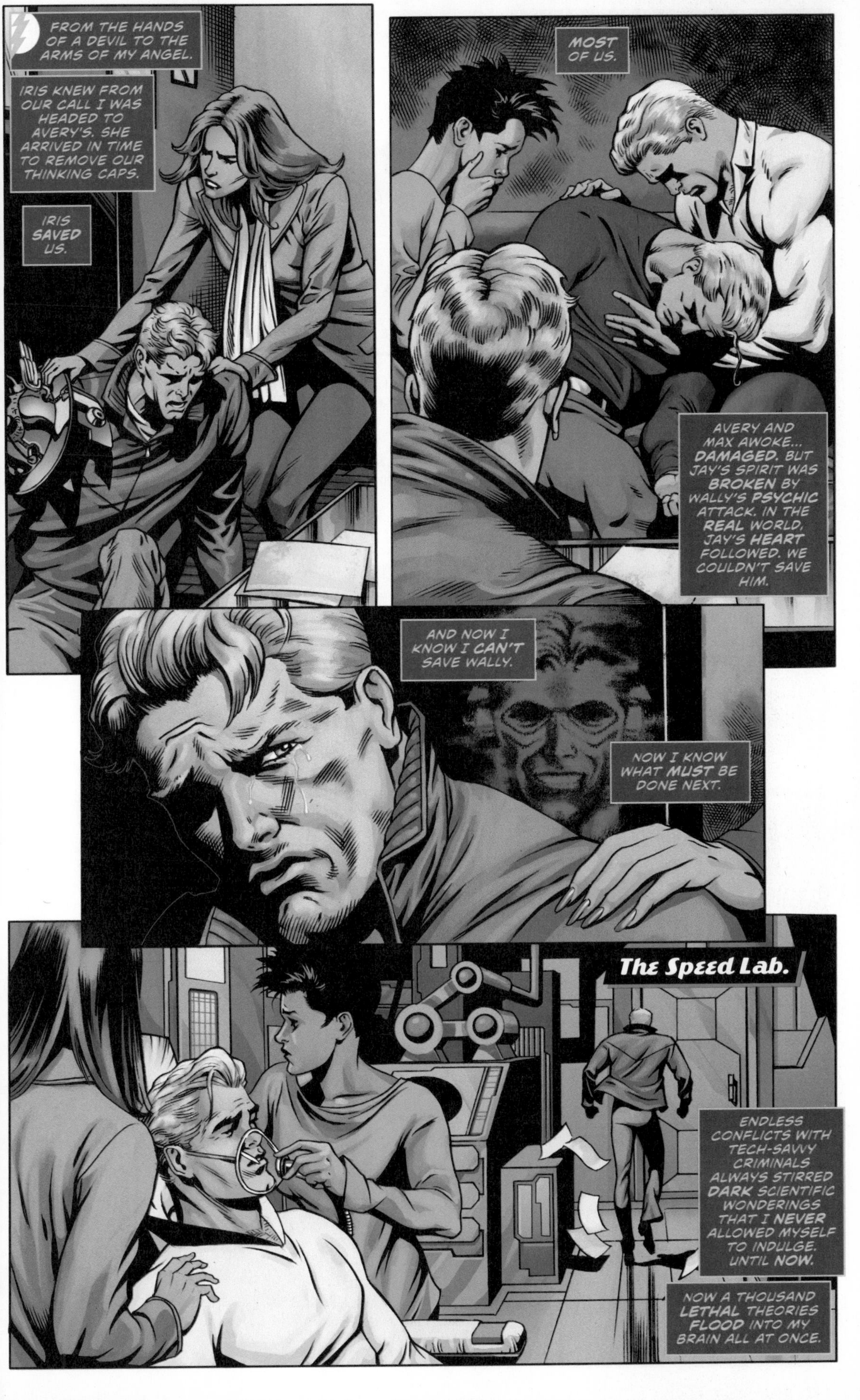

FROM THE HANDS OF A DEVIL TO THE ARMS OF MY ANGEL.
IRIS KNEW FROM OUR CALL I WAS HEADED TO AVERY'S. SHE ARRIVED IN TIME TO REMOVE OUR THINKING CAPS.
IRIS SAVED US.
MOST OF US.
AVERY AND MAX AWOKE... DAMAGED. BUT JAY'S SPIRIT WAS BROKEN BY WALLY'S PSYCHIC ATTACK. IN THE REAL WORLD, JAY'S HEART FOLLOWED. WE COULDN'T SAVE HIM.
AND NOW I KNOW I CAN'T SAVE WALLY.
NOW I KNOW WHAT MUST BE DONE NEXT.
The Speed Lab.
ENDLESS CONFLICTS WITH TECH-SAVVY CRIMINALS ALWAYS STIRRED DARK SCIENTIFIC WONDERINGS THAT I NEVER ALLOWED MYSELF TO INDULGE. UNTIL NOW.
NOW A THOUSAND LETHAL THEORIES FLOOD INTO MY BRAIN ALL AT ONCE.

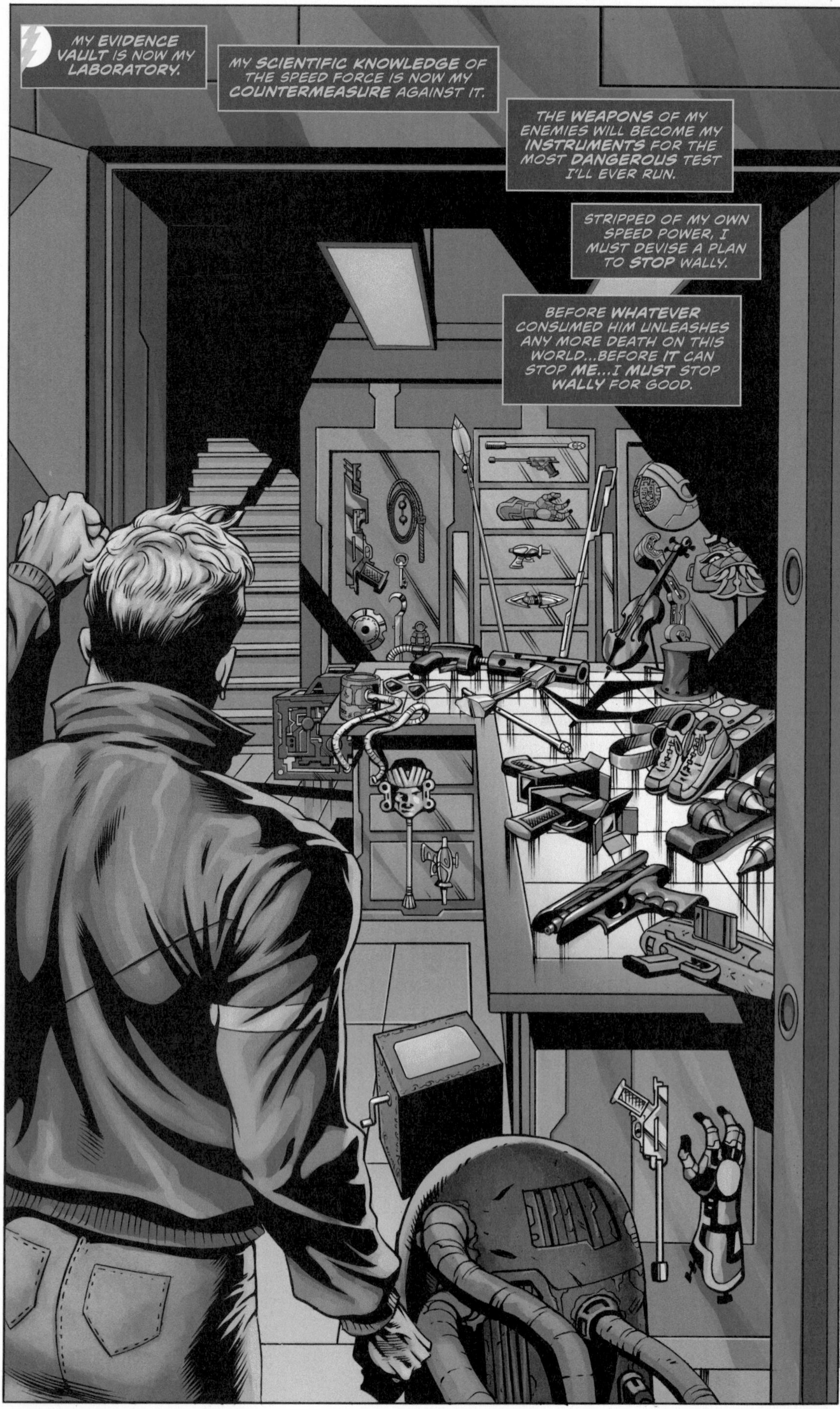
MY EVIDENCE VAULT IS NOW MY LABORATORY.
MY SCIENTIFIC KNOWLEDGE OF THE SPEED FORCE IS NOW MY COUNTERMEASURE AGAINST IT.
THE WEAPONS OF MY ENEMIES WILL BECOME MY INSTRUMENTS FOR THE MOST DANGEROUS TEST I'LL EVER RUN.
STRIPPED OF MY OWN SPEED POWER, I MUST DEVISE A PLAN TO STOP WALLY.
BEFORE WHATEVER CONSUMED HIM UNLEASHES ANY MORE DEATH ON THIS WORLD...BEFORE IT CAN STOP ME...I MUST STOP WALLY FOR GOOD.

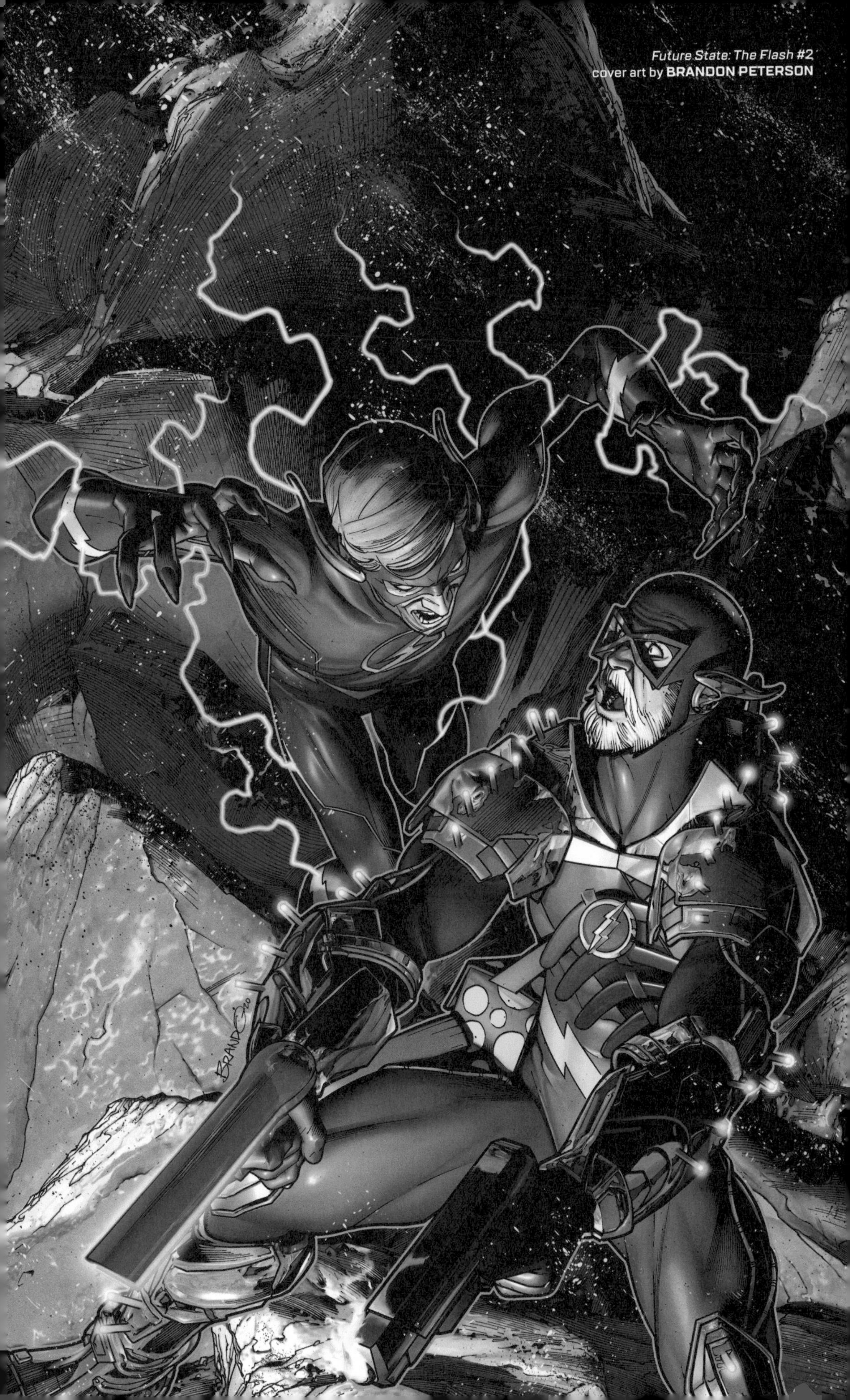

Future State: The Flash #2
cover art by **BRANDON PETERSON**

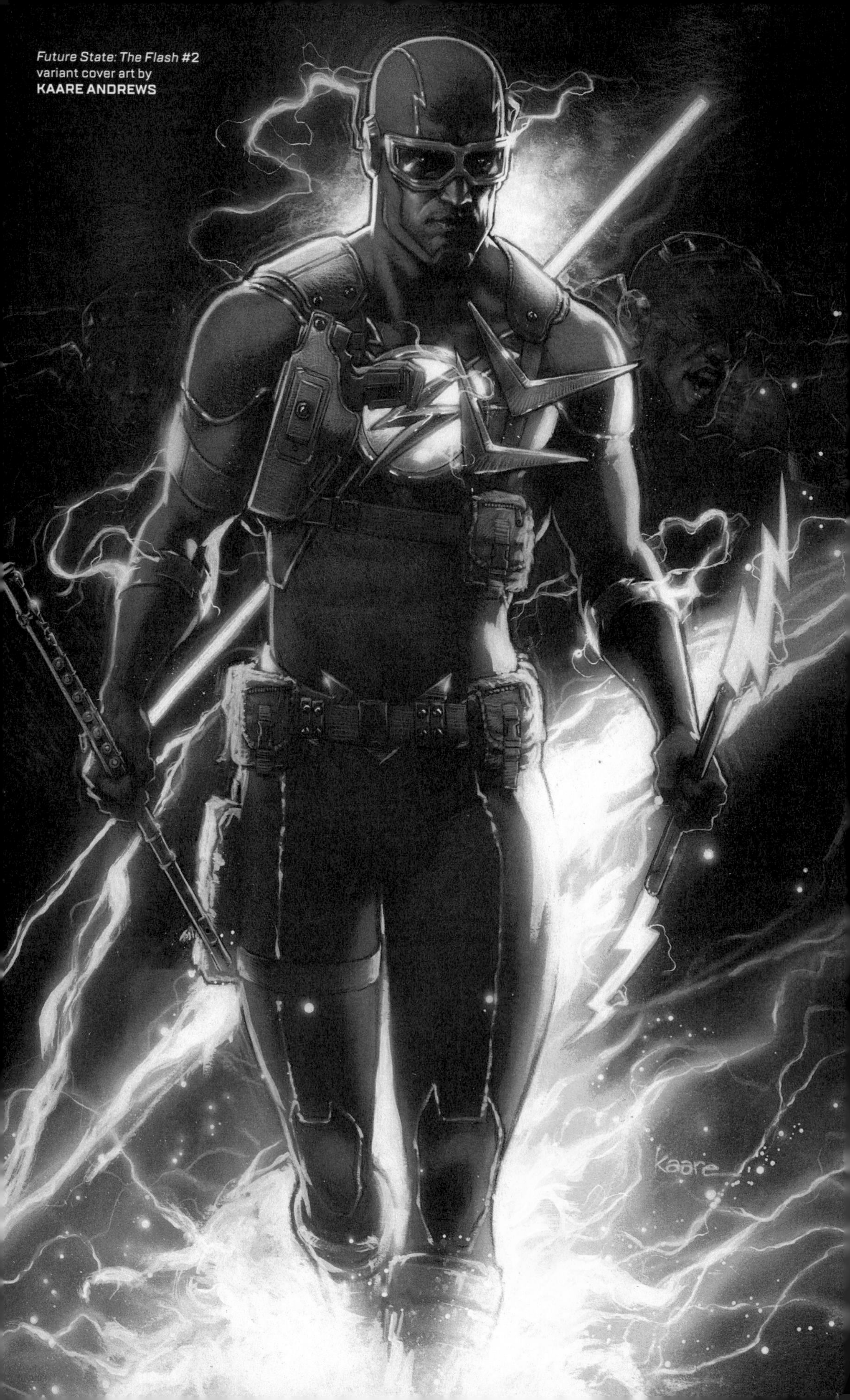
kaare

Future State: The Flash #2
variant cover art by
KAARE ANDREWS

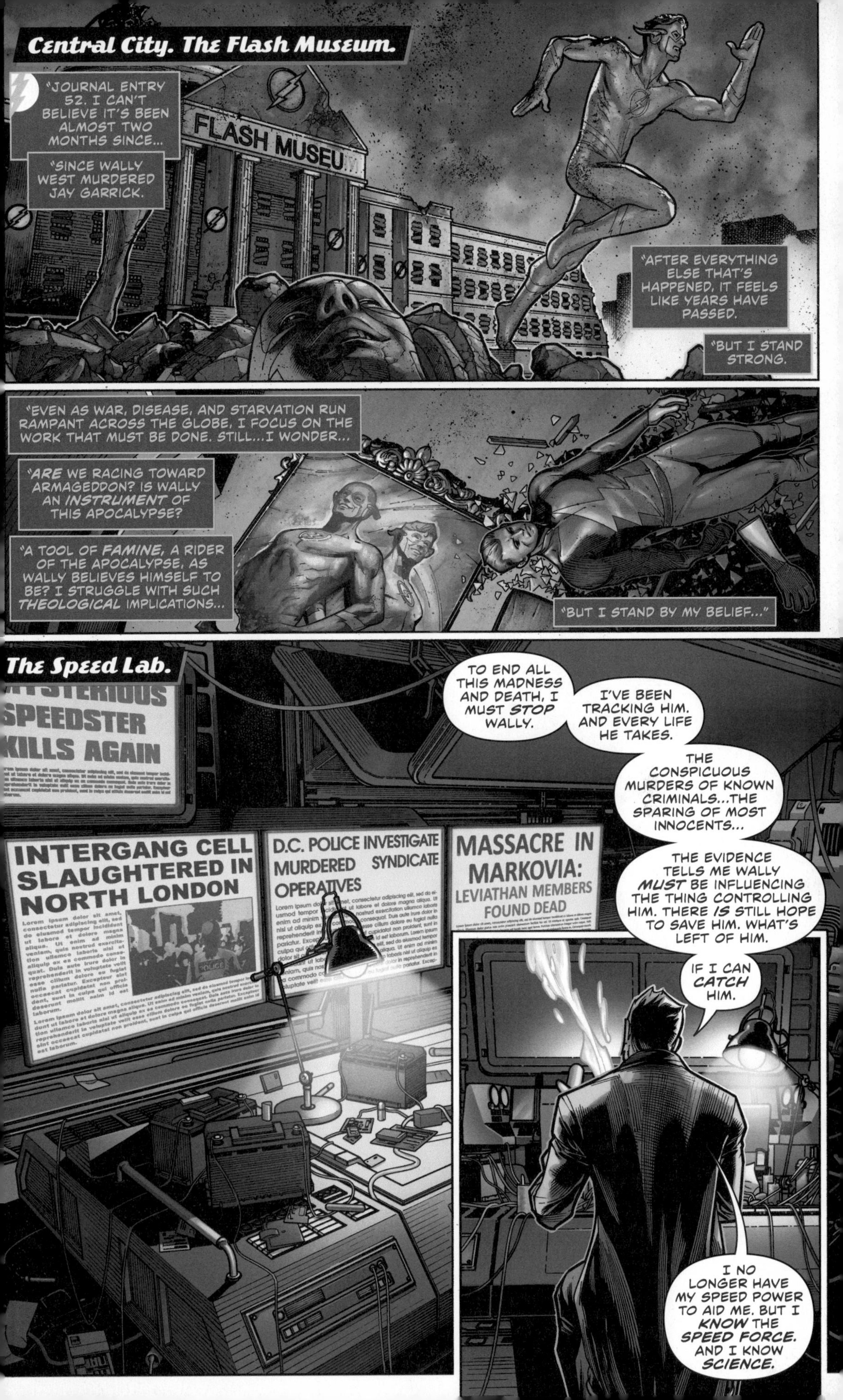
Central City. The Flash Museum.
"JOURNAL ENTRY 52. I CAN'T BELIEVE IT'S BEEN ALMOST TWO MONTHS SINCE...
"SINCE WALLY WEST MURDERED JAY GARRICK.
FLASH MUSEU
"AFTER EVERYTHING ELSE THAT'S HAPPENED, IT FEELS LIKE YEARS HAVE PASSED.
"BUT I STAND STRONG.
"EVEN AS WAR, DISEASE, AND STARVATION RUN RAMPANT ACROSS THE GLOBE, I FOCUS ON THE WORK THAT MUST BE DONE. STILL...I WONDER...
"ARE WE RACING TOWARD ARMAGEDDON? IS WALLY AN INSTRUMENT OF THIS APOCALYPSE?
"A TOOL OF FAMINE, A RIDER OF THE APOCALYPSE, AS WALLY BELIEVES HIMSELF TO BE? I STRUGGLE WITH SUCH THEOLOGICAL IMPLICATIONS...
"BUT I STAND BY MY BELIEF..."
The Speed Lab.
SPEEDSTER KILLS AGAIN
INTERGANG CELL SLAUGHTERED IN NORTH LONDON
D.C. POLICE INVESTIGATE MURDERED SYNDICATE OPERATIVES
MASSACRE IN MARKOVIA: LEVIATHAN MEMBERS FOUND DEAD
TO END ALL THIS MADNESS AND DEATH, I MUST STOP WALLY.
I'VE BEEN TRACKING HIM. AND EVERY LIFE HE TAKES.
THE CONSPICUOUS MURDERS OF KNOWN CRIMINALS...THE SPARING OF MOST INNOCENTS...
THE EVIDENCE TELLS ME WALLY MUST BE INFLUENCING THE THING CONTROLLING HIM. THERE IS STILL HOPE TO SAVE HIM. WHAT'S LEFT OF HIM.
IF I CAN CATCH HIM.
I NO LONGER HAVE MY SPEED POWER TO AID ME. BUT I KNOW THE SPEED FORCE. AND I KNOW SCIENCE.

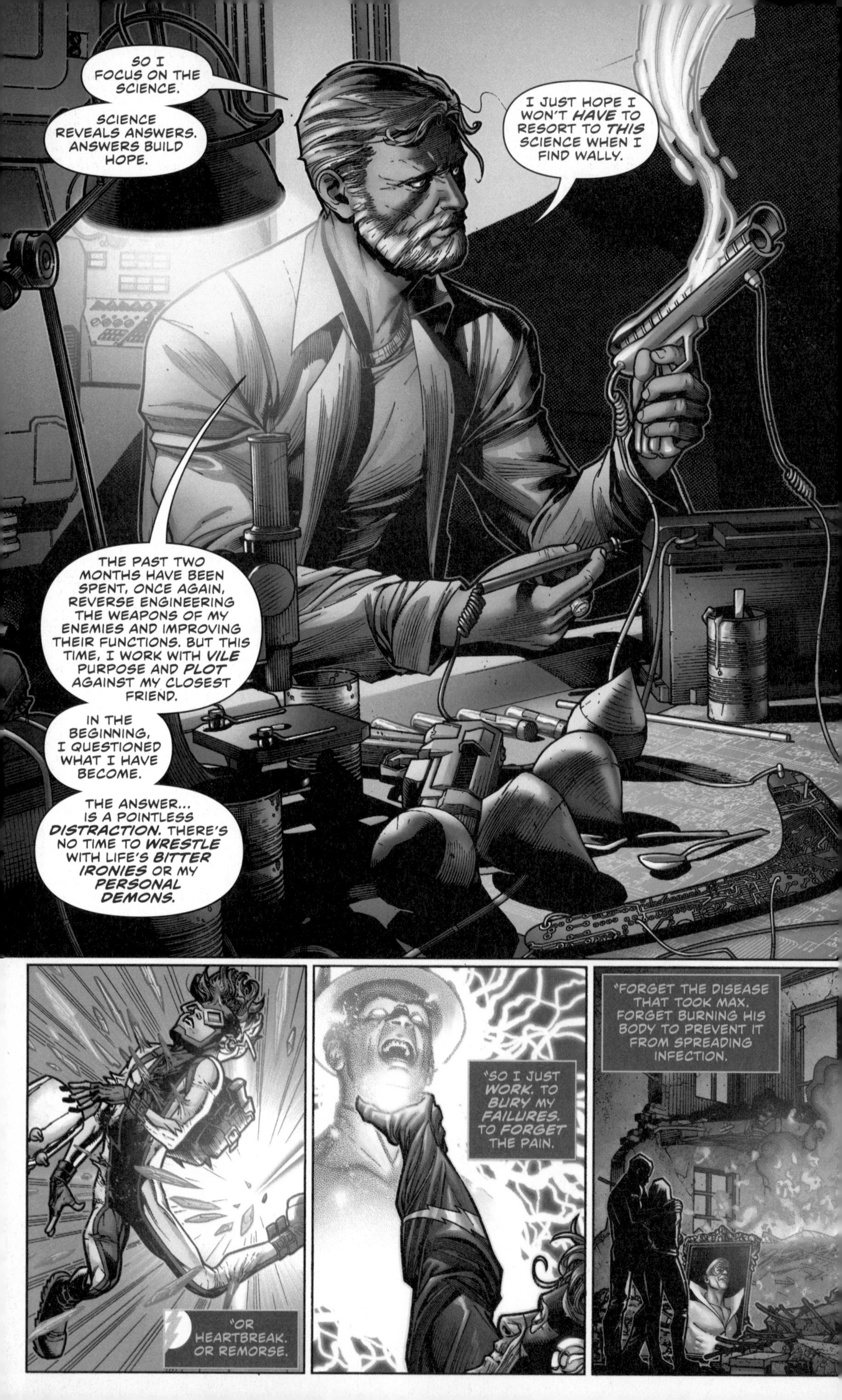
SO I FOCUS ON THE SCIENCE.
SCIENCE REVEALS ANSWERS. ANSWERS BUILD HOPE.
I JUST HOPE I WON'T HAVE TO RESORT TO THIS SCIENCE WHEN I FIND WALLY.
THE PAST TWO MONTHS HAVE BEEN SPENT, ONCE AGAIN, REVERSE ENGINEERING THE WEAPONS OF MY ENEMIES AND IMPROVING THEIR FUNCTIONS. BUT THIS TIME, I WORK WITH VILE PURPOSE AND PLOT AGAINST MY CLOSEST FRIEND.
IN THE BEGINNING, I QUESTIONED WHAT I HAVE BECOME.
THE ANSWER... IS A POINTLESS DISTRACTION. THERE'S NO TIME TO WRESTLE WITH LIFE'S BITTER IRONIES OR MY PERSONAL DEMONS.
"OR HEARTBREAK. OR REMORSE.
"SO I JUST WORK. TO BURY MY FAILURES. TO FORGET THE PAIN.
"FORGET THE DISEASE THAT TOOK MAX. FORGET BURNING HIS BODY TO PREVENT IT FROM SPREADING INFECTION.

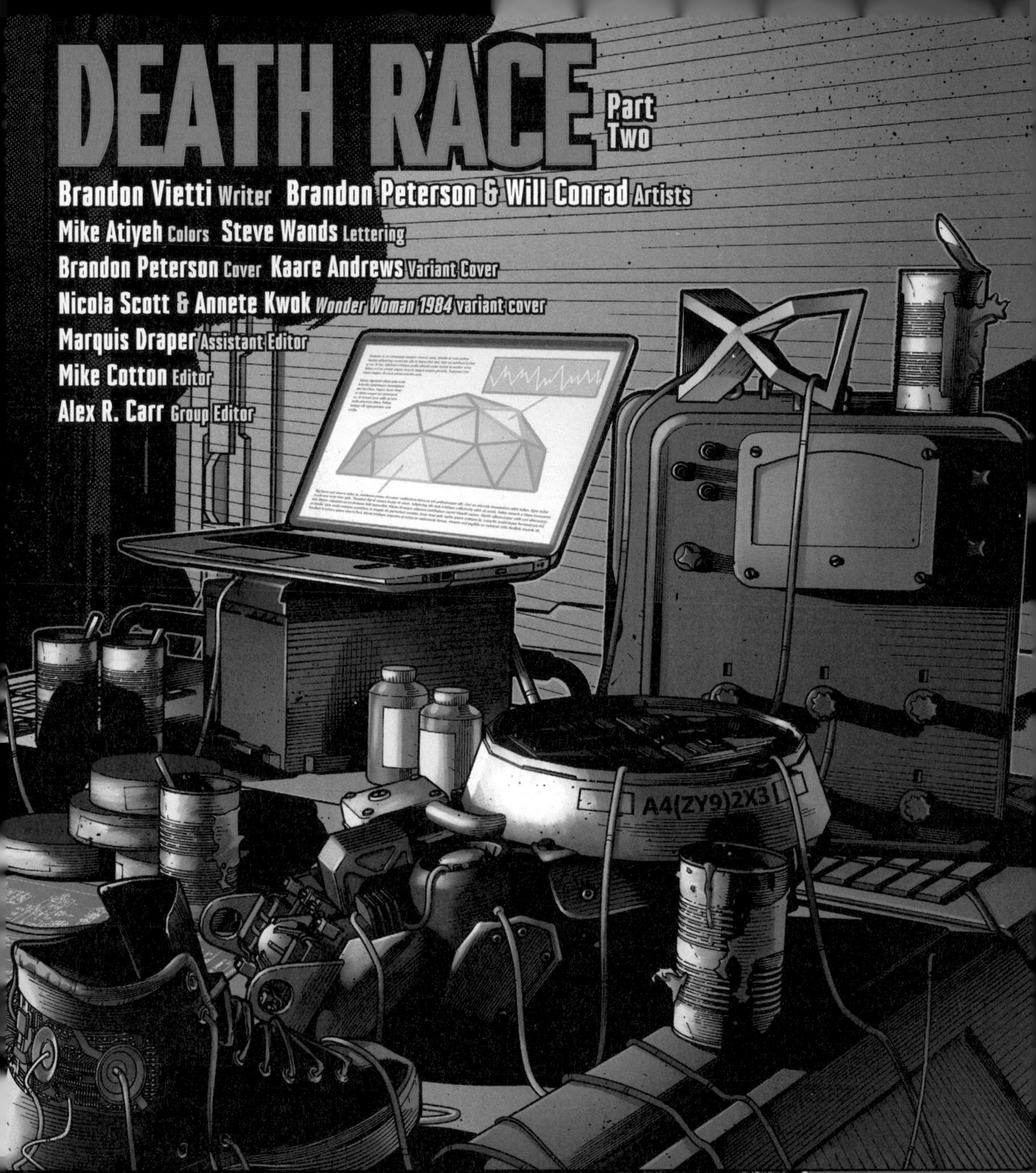
DEATH RACE Part Two
Brandon Vietti Writer Brandon Peterson & Will Conrad Artists
Mike Atiyeh Colors Steve Wands Lettering
Brandon Peterson Cover Kaare Andrews Variant Cover
Nicola Scott & Annete Kwok Wonder Woman 1984 variant cover
Marquis Draper Assistant Editor
Mike Cotton Editor
Alex R. Carr Group Editor
A4(ZY9)2X3

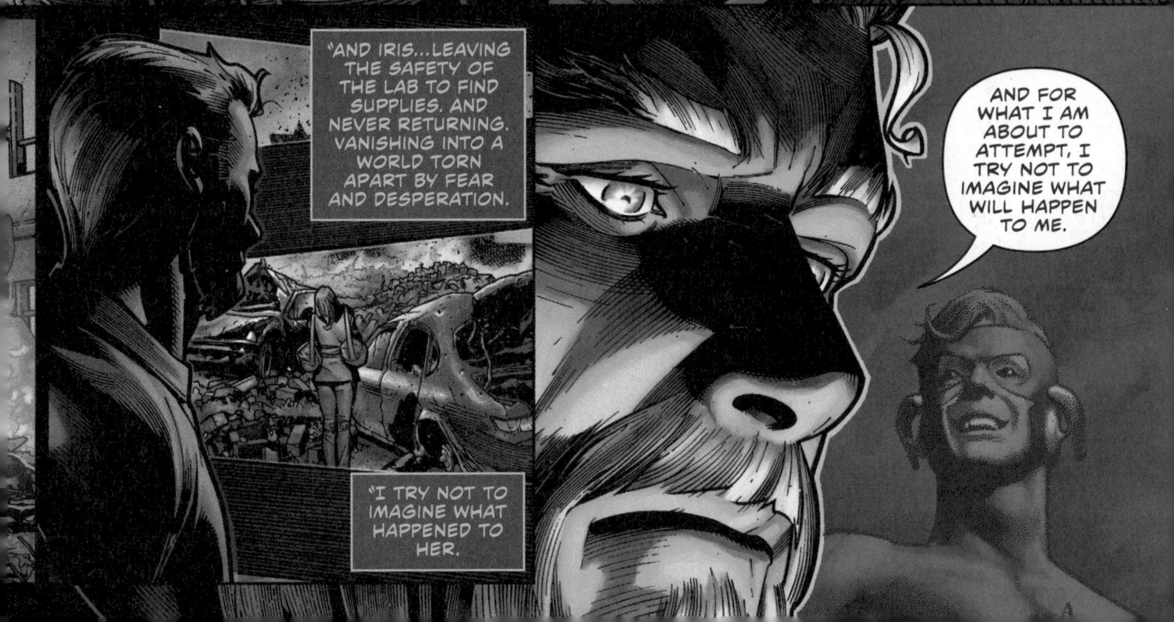
"AND IRIS...LEAVING THE SAFETY OF THE LAB TO FIND SUPPLIES. AND NEVER RETURNING. VANISHING INTO A WORLD TORN APART BY FEAR AND DESPERATION.
"I TRY NOT TO IMAGINE WHAT HAPPENED TO HER.
AND FOR WHAT I AM ABOUT TO ATTEMPT, I TRY NOT TO IMAGINE WHAT WILL HAPPEN TO ME.

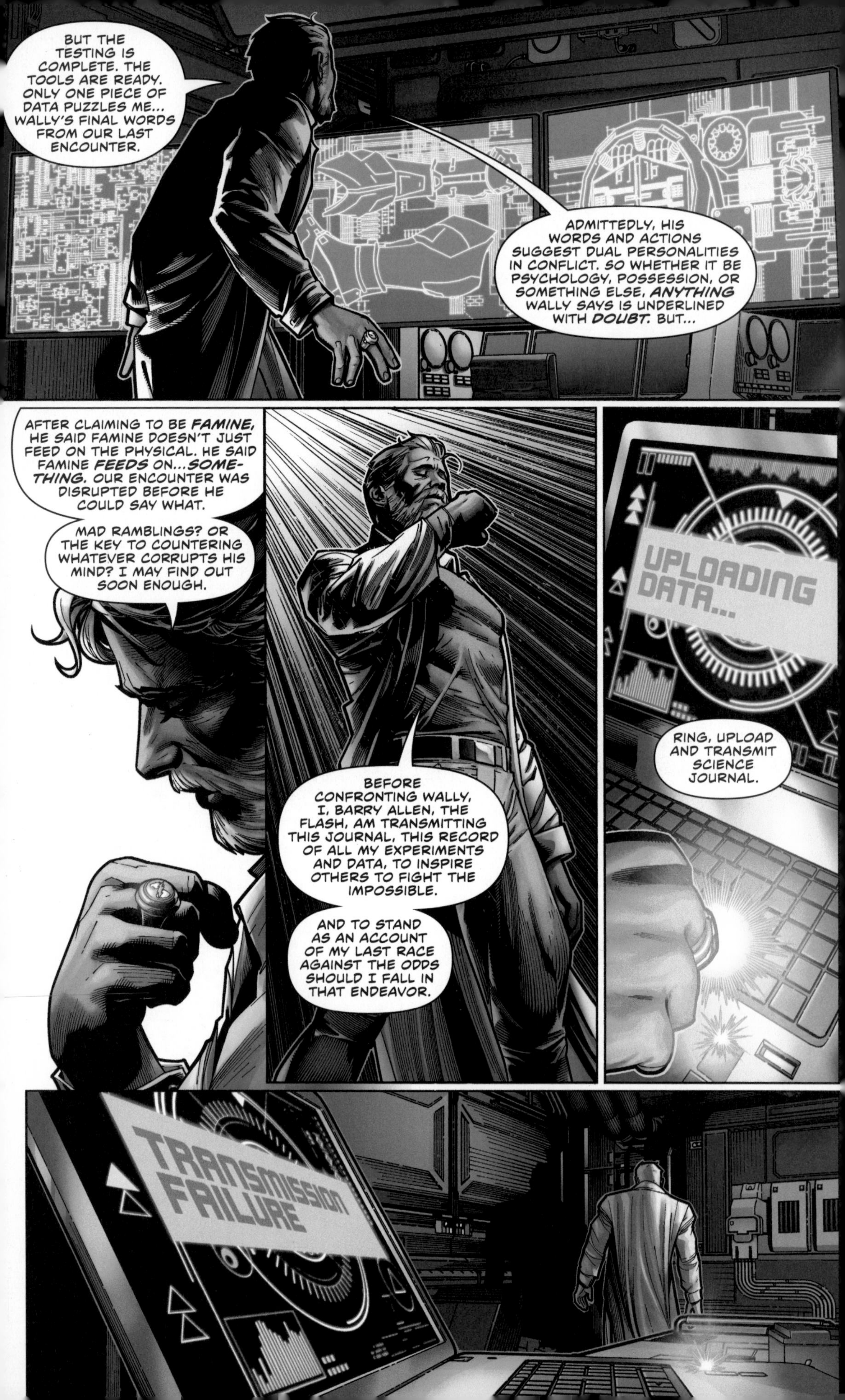
BUT THE TESTING IS COMPLETE. THE TOOLS ARE READY. ONLY ONE PIECE OF DATA PUZZLES ME... WALLY'S FINAL WORDS FROM OUR LAST ENCOUNTER.
ADMITTEDLY, HIS WORDS AND ACTIONS SUGGEST DUAL PERSONALITIES IN CONFLICT. SO WHETHER IT BE PSYCHOLOGY, POSSESSION, OR SOMETHING ELSE, ANYTHING WALLY SAYS IS UNDERLINED WITH DOUBT. BUT...
AFTER CLAIMING TO BE FAMINE, HE SAID FAMINE DOESN'T JUST FEED ON THE PHYSICAL. HE SAID FAMINE FEEDS ON...SOME-THING. OUR ENCOUNTER WAS DISRUPTED BEFORE HE COULD SAY WHAT.
MAD RAMBLINGS? OR THE KEY TO COUNTERING WHATEVER CORRUPTS HIS MIND? I MAY FIND OUT SOON ENOUGH.
BEFORE CONFRONTING WALLY, I, BARRY ALLEN, THE FLASH, AM TRANSMITTING THIS JOURNAL, THIS RECORD OF ALL MY EXPERIMENTS AND DATA, TO INSPIRE OTHERS TO FIGHT THE IMPOSSIBLE.
AND TO STAND AS AN ACCOUNT OF MY LAST RACE AGAINST THE ODDS SHOULD I FALL IN THAT ENDEAVOR.
UPLOADING DATA...
RING, UPLOAD AND TRANSMIT SCIENCE JOURNAL.
TRANSMISSION FAILURE

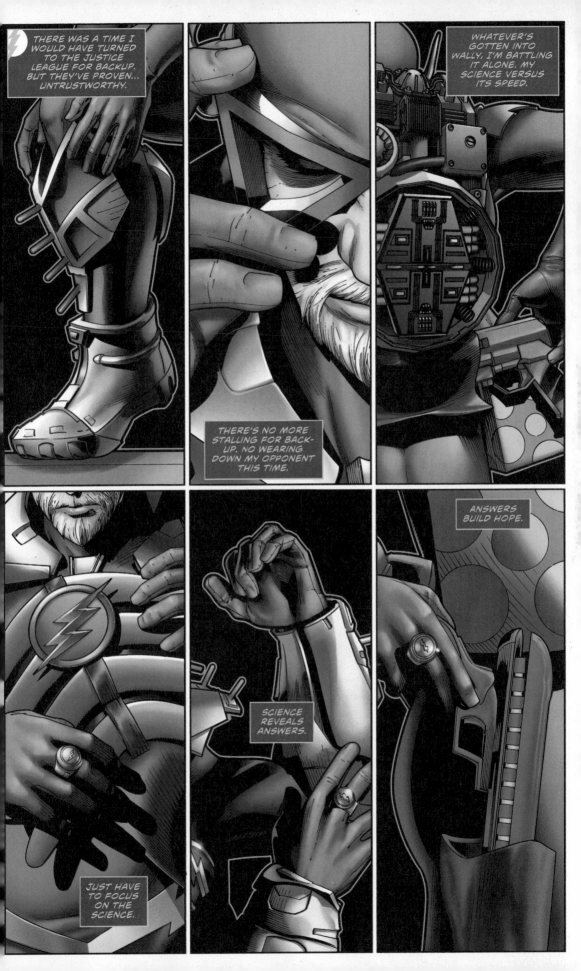

THERE WAS A TIME I WOULD HAVE TURNED TO THE JUSTICE LEAGUE FOR BACKUP. BUT THEY'VE PROVEN... UNTRUSTWORTHY.

THERE'S NO MORE STALLING FOR BACK-UP. NO WEARING DOWN MY OPPONENT THIS TIME.

WHATEVER'S GOTTEN INTO WALLY, I'M BATTLING IT ALONE. MY SCIENCE VERSUS ITS SPEED.

ANSWERS BUILD HOPE.

SCIENCE REVEALS ANSWERS.

JUST HAVE TO FOCUS ON THE SCIENCE.

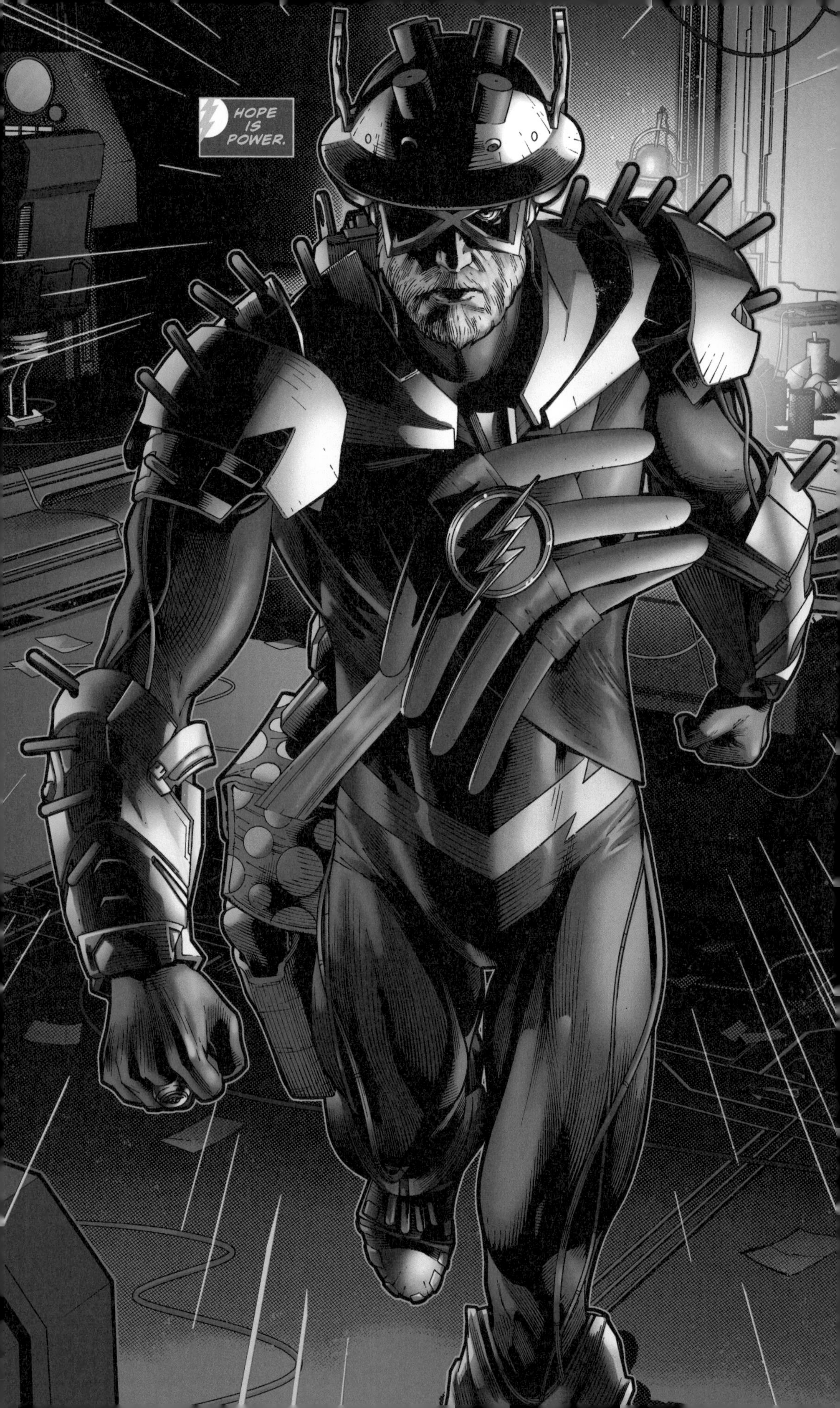
HOPE IS POWER.

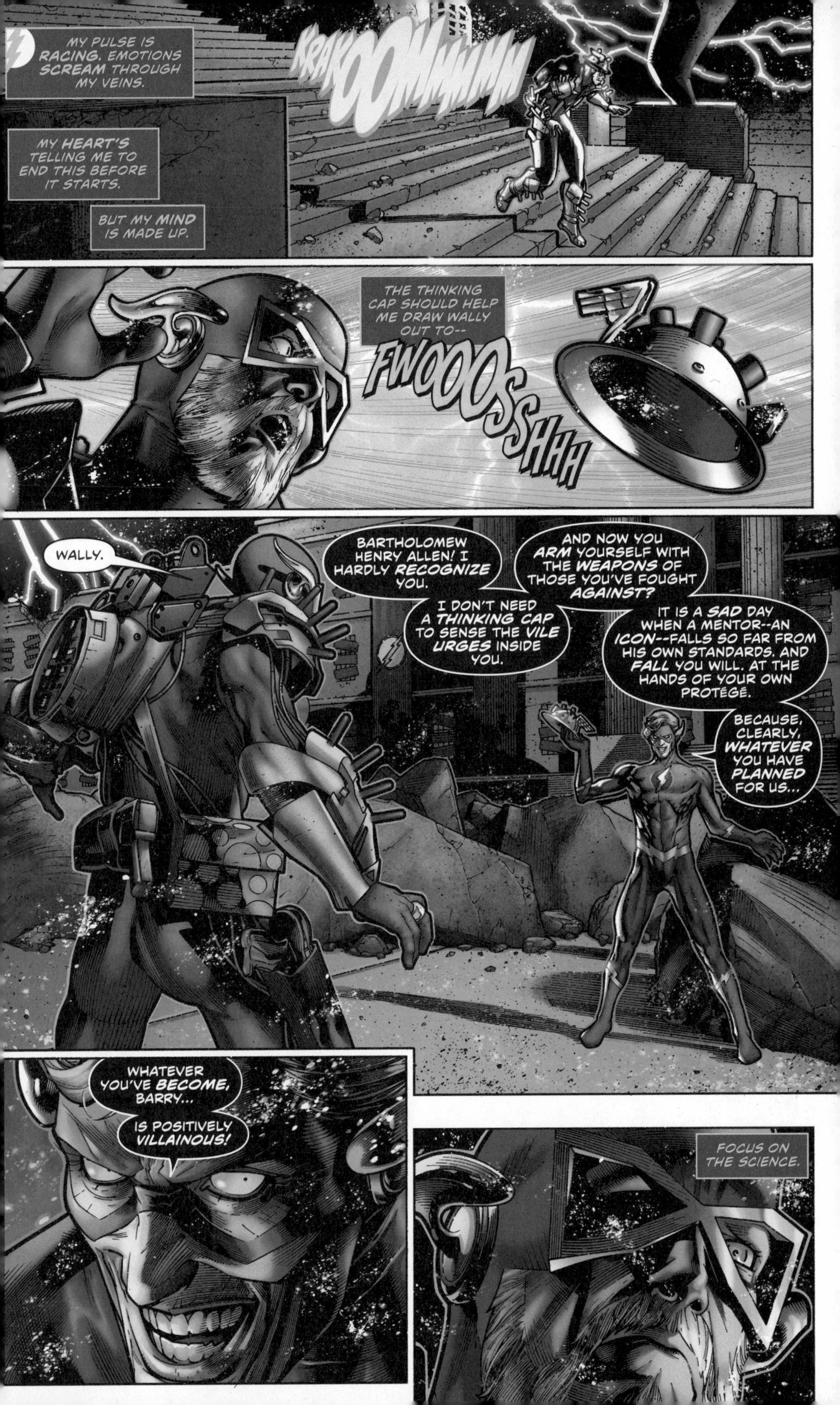
MY PULSE IS RACING. EMOTIONS SCREAM THROUGH MY VEINS.
KRAKOOMMMMM
MY HEART'S TELLING ME TO END THIS BEFORE IT STARTS.
BUT MY MIND IS MADE UP.
THE THINKING CAP SHOULD HELP ME DRAW WALLY OUT TO--
FWOOOSSHHH
WALLY.
BARTHOLOMEW HENRY ALLEN! I HARDLY RECOGNIZE YOU.
I DON'T NEED A THINKING CAP TO SENSE THE VILE URGES INSIDE YOU.
AND NOW YOU ARM YOURSELF WITH THE WEAPONS OF THOSE YOU'VE FOUGHT AGAINST?
IT IS A SAD DAY WHEN A MENTOR--AN ICON--FALLS SO FAR FROM HIS OWN STANDARDS. AND FALL YOU WILL. AT THE HANDS OF YOUR OWN PROTÉGÉ.
BECAUSE, CLEARLY, WHATEVER YOU HAVE PLANNED FOR US...
WHATEVER YOU'VE BECOME, BARRY...
IS POSITIVELY VILLAINOUS!
FOCUS ON THE SCIENCE.

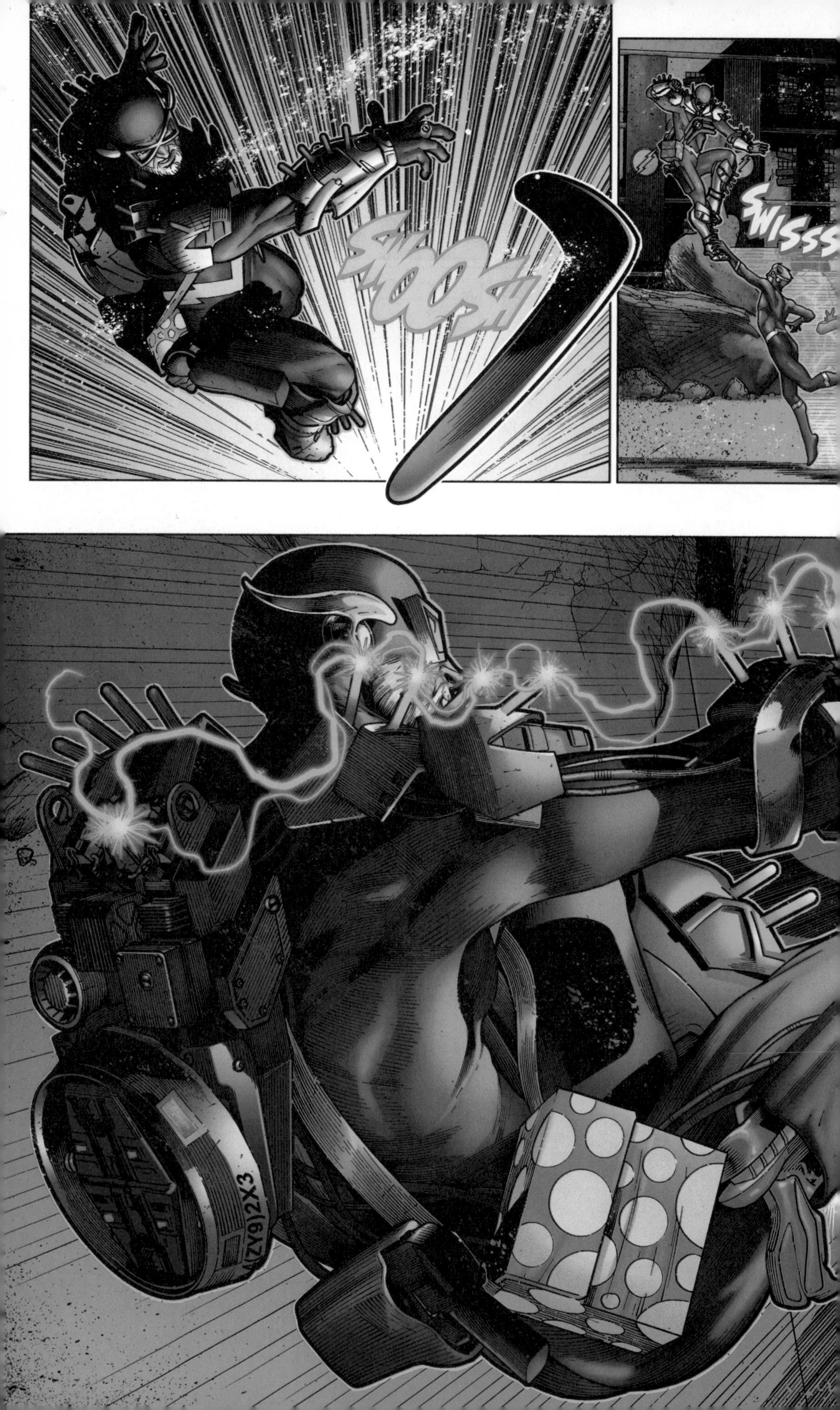
SWOOSH
SWISSS

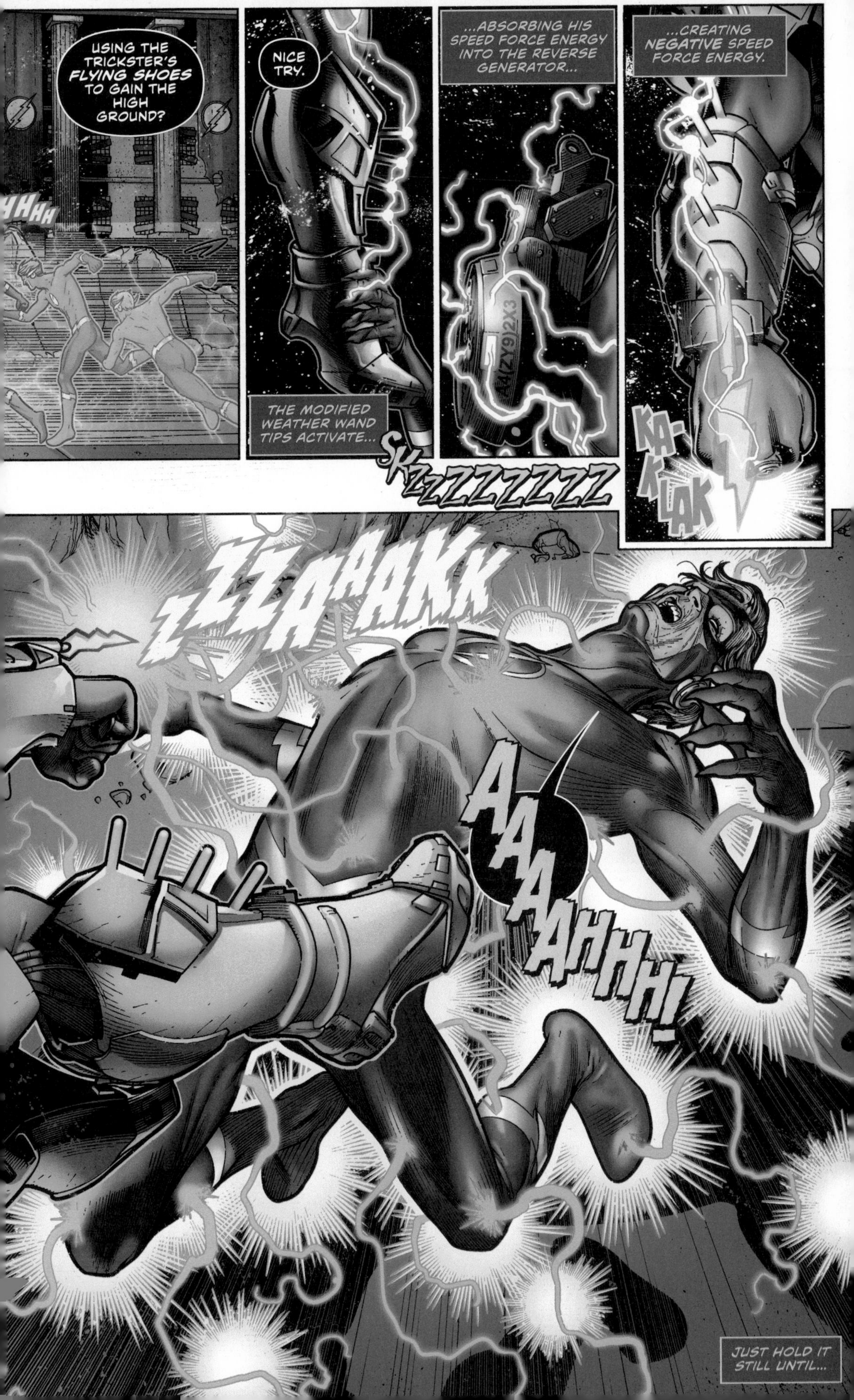

USING THE TRICKSTER'S FLYING SHOES TO GAIN THE HIGH GROUND?
NICE TRY.
THE MODIFIED WEATHER WAND TIPS ACTIVATE...
SKZZZZZZZZ
...ABSORBING HIS SPEED FORCE ENERGY INTO THE REVERSE GENERATOR...
A4(ZY9)2X3
...CREATING NEGATIVE SPEED FORCE ENERGY.
KA-KLAK
ZZZAAAKK
AAAAAHHH!
JUST HOLD IT STILL UNTIL...

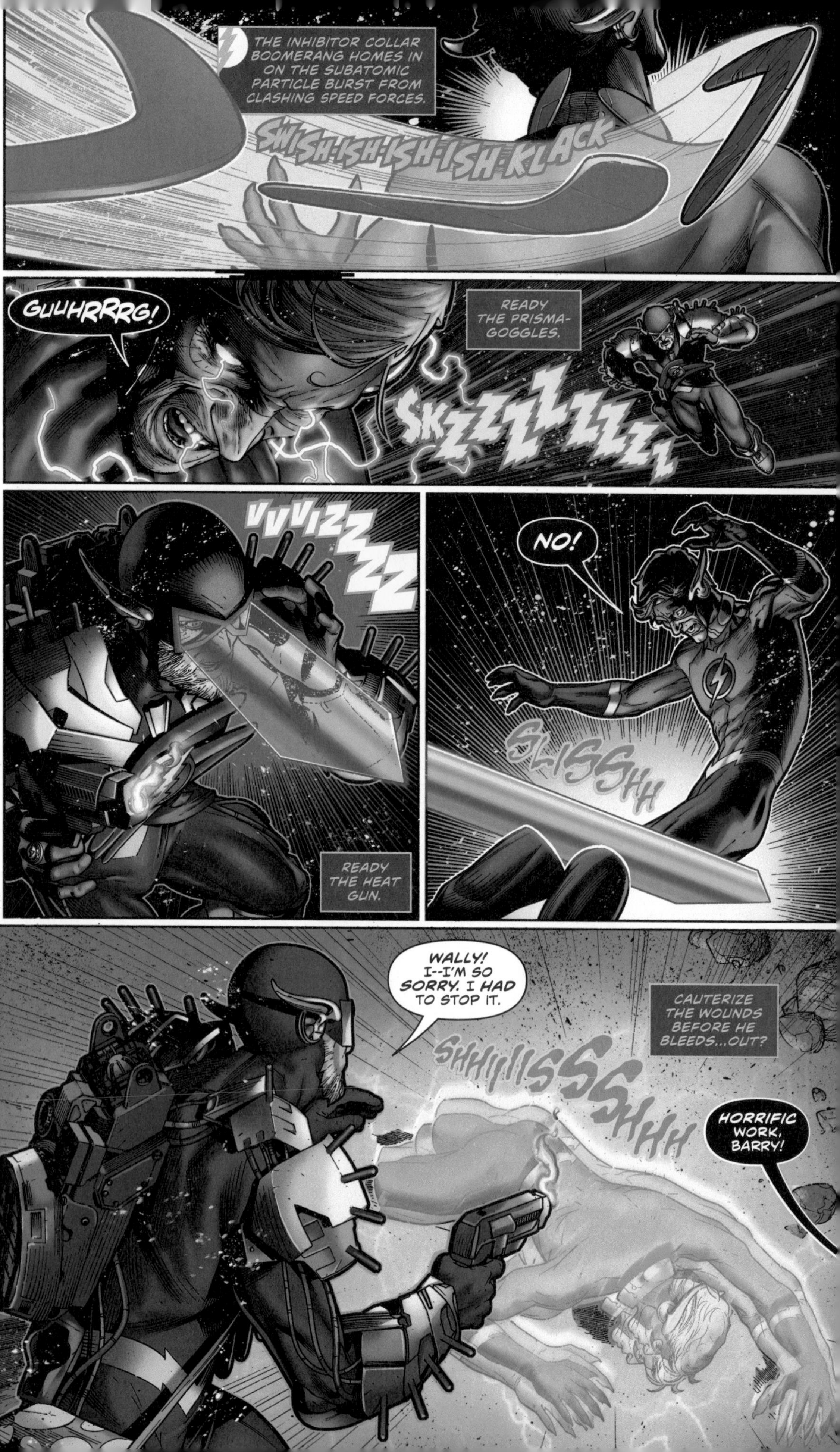
THE INHIBITOR COLLAR BOOMERANG HOMES IN ON THE SUBATOMIC PARTICLE BURST FROM CLASHING SPEED FORCES.
SWISH-ISH-ISH-ISH-KLACK
GUUHRRRG!
READY THE PRISMA-GOGGLES.
SKZZZZZZZZZZZ
VVVIZZZZZ
READY THE HEAT GUN.
NO!
SLISSHH
WALLY! I--I'M SO SORRY. I HAD TO STOP IT.
CAUTERIZE THE WOUNDS BEFORE HE BLEEDS...OUT?
SHHIIISSSSHHH
HORRIFIC WORK, BARRY!

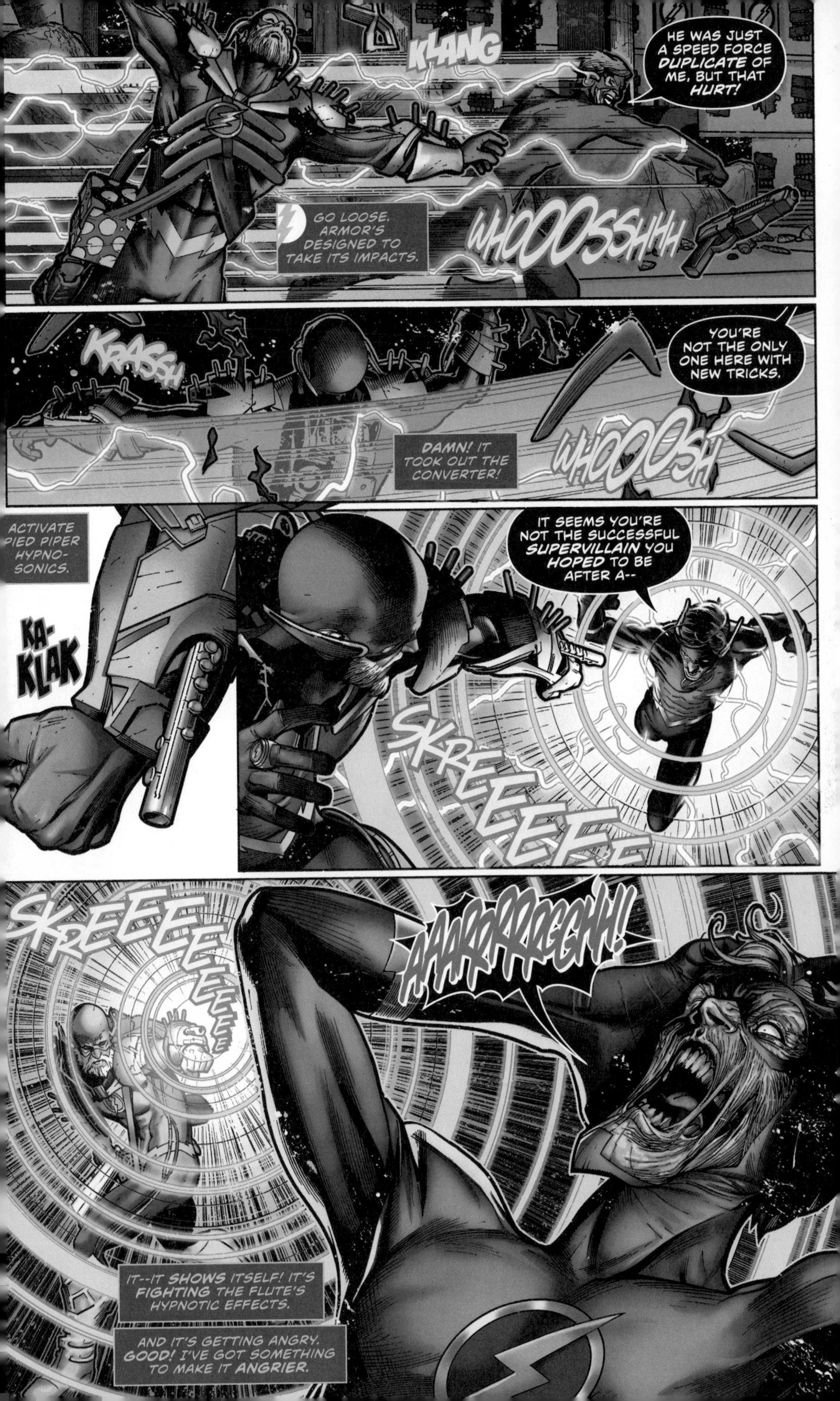
KLANG
HE WAS JUST A SPEED FORCE DUPLICATE OF ME, BUT THAT HURT!
GO LOOSE. ARMOR'S DESIGNED TO TAKE ITS IMPACTS.
WHOOOOSSHHH
KRASSH
YOU'RE NOT THE ONLY ONE HERE WITH NEW TRICKS.
DAMN! IT TOOK OUT THE CONVERTER!
WHOOOOSH
ACTIVATE PIED PIPER HYPNO-SONICS.
KA-KLAK
IT SEEMS YOU'RE NOT THE SUCCESSFUL SUPERVILLAIN YOU HOPED TO BE AFTER A--
SKREEEEEE
SKREEEEEEEEEE
AAARRRRGGHH!
IT--IT SHOWS ITSELF! IT'S FIGHTING THE FLUTE'S HYPNOTIC EFFECTS.
AND IT'S GETTING ANGRY. GOOD! I'VE GOT SOMETHING TO MAKE IT ANGRIER.

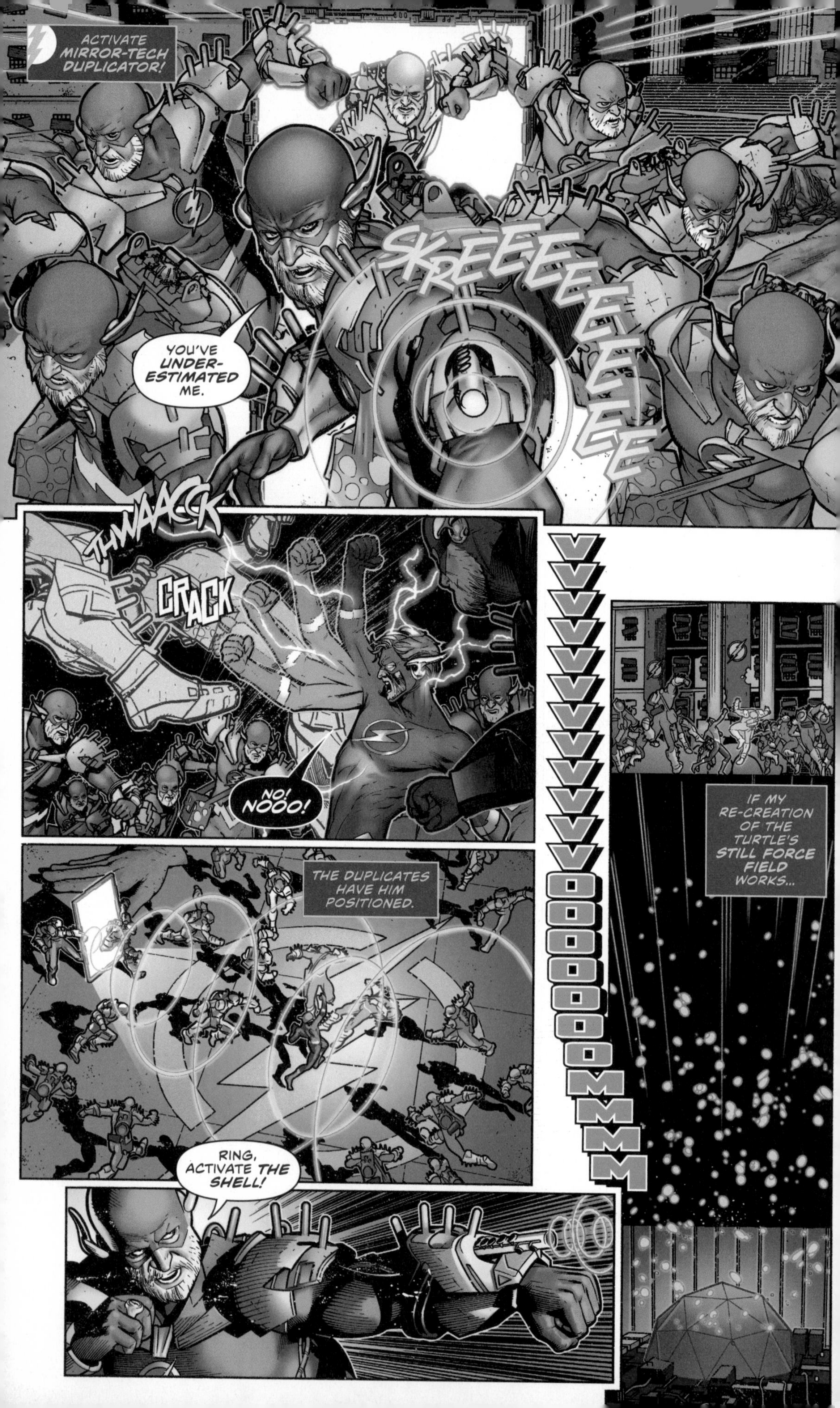

ACTIVATE MIRROR-TECH DUPLICATOR!
SKREEEEEEEEEEE
YOU'VE UNDER-ESTIMATED ME.
THWAACK
CRACK
NO! NOOO!
VVVVVVVVVVVVVVOOOOOOOOOMMMM
THE DUPLICATES HAVE HIM POSITIONED.
IF MY RE-CREATION OF THE TURTLE'S STILL FORCE FIELD WORKS...
RING, ACTIVATE THE SHELL!

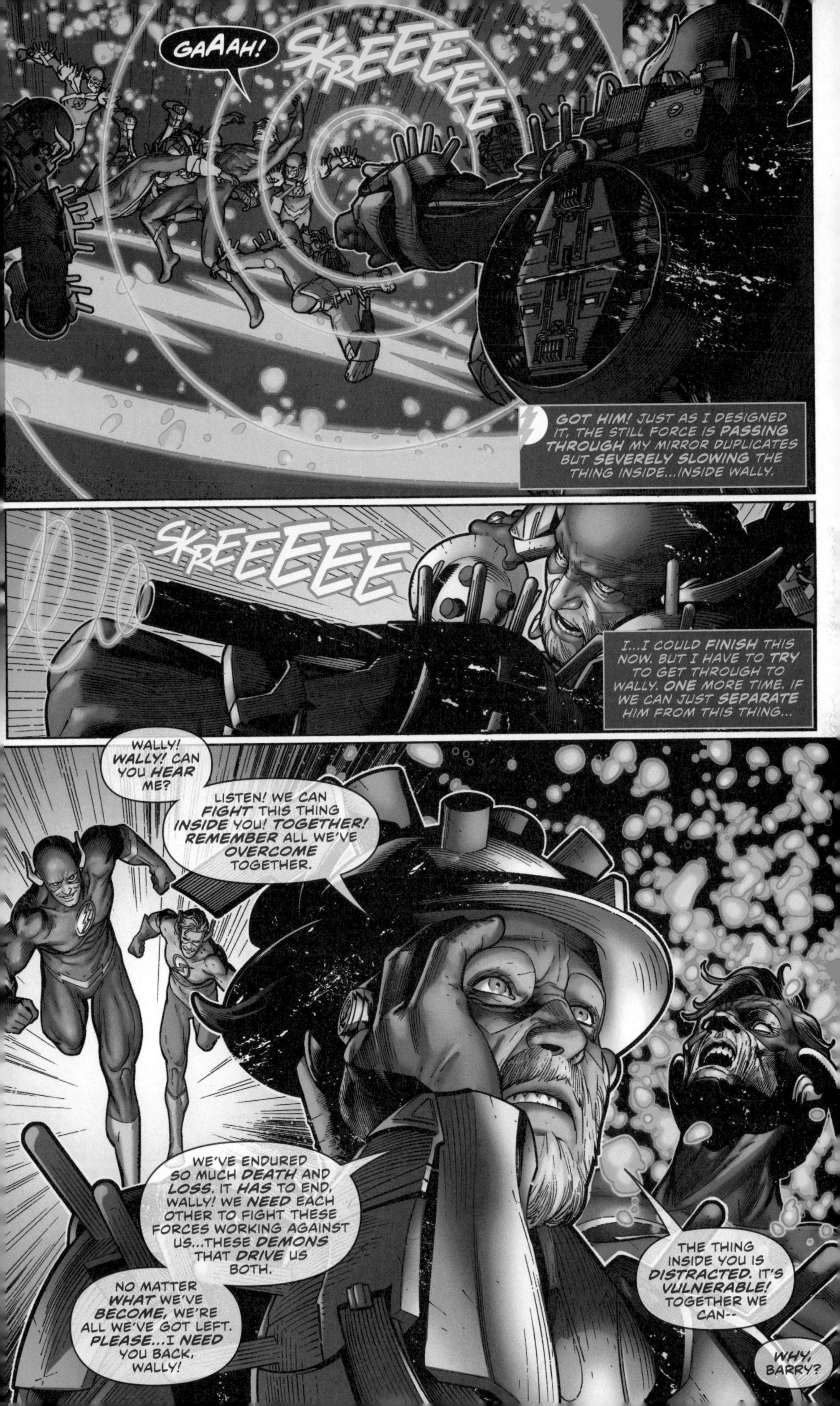

GAAAH!
SKREEEEEE
GOT HIM! JUST AS I DESIGNED IT, THE STILL FORCE IS PASSING THROUGH MY MIRROR DUPLICATES BUT SEVERELY SLOWING THE THING INSIDE...INSIDE WALLY.
SKREEEEEE
I...I COULD FINISH THIS NOW. BUT I HAVE TO TRY TO GET THROUGH TO WALLY. ONE MORE TIME. IF WE CAN JUST SEPARATE HIM FROM THIS THING...
WALLY! WALLY! CAN YOU HEAR ME?
LISTEN! WE CAN FIGHT THIS THING INSIDE YOU! TOGETHER! REMEMBER ALL WE'VE OVERCOME TOGETHER.
WE'VE ENDURED SO MUCH DEATH AND LOSS. IT HAS TO END, WALLY! WE NEED EACH OTHER TO FIGHT THESE FORCES WORKING AGAINST US...THESE DEMONS THAT DRIVE US BOTH.
NO MATTER WHAT WE'VE BECOME, WE'RE ALL WE'VE GOT LEFT. PLEASE...I NEED YOU BACK, WALLY!
THE THING INSIDE YOU IS DISTRACTED. IT'S VULNERABLE! TOGETHER WE CAN--
WHY, BARRY?

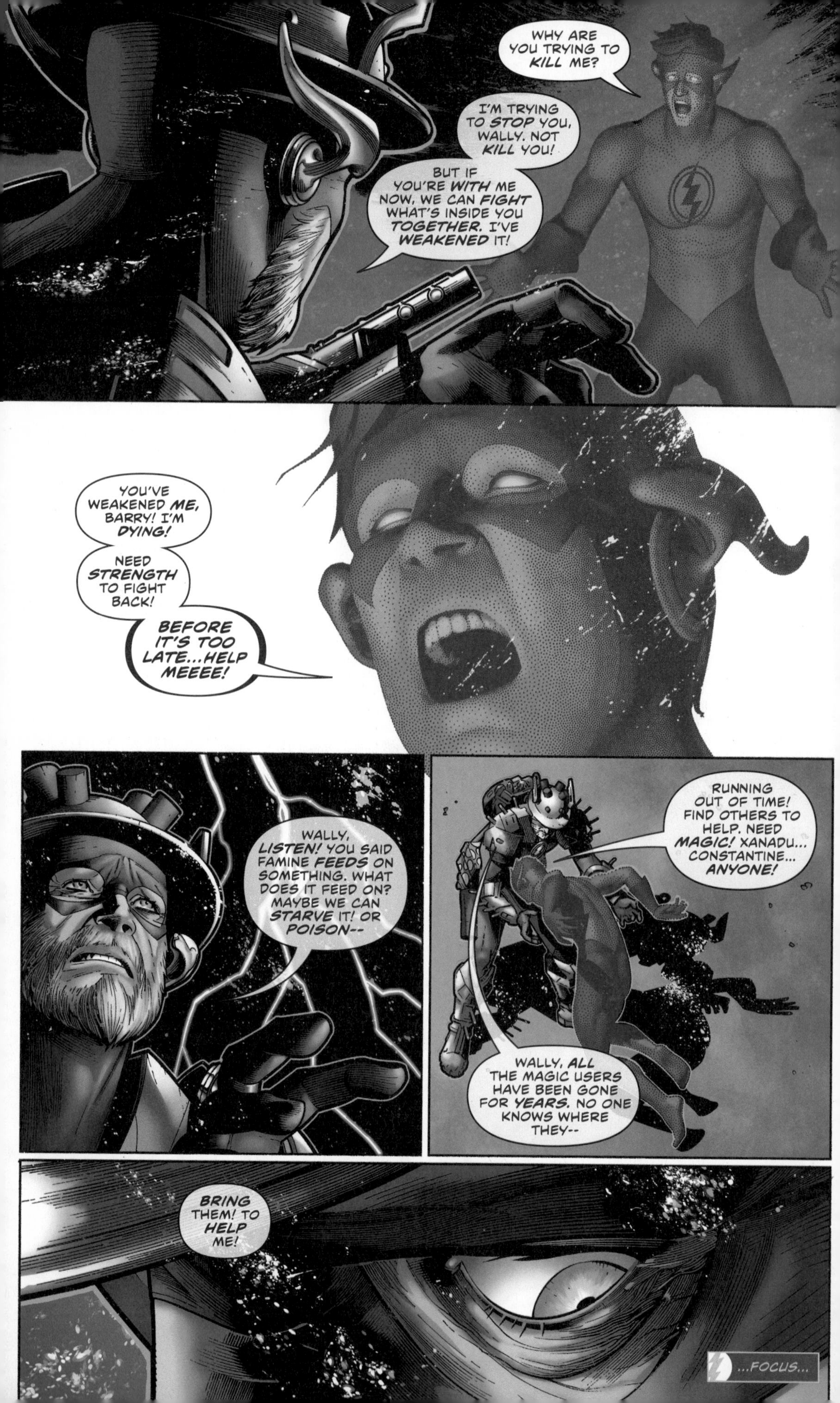
WHY ARE YOU TRYING TO KILL ME?
I'M TRYING TO STOP YOU, WALLY. NOT KILL YOU!
BUT IF YOU'RE WITH ME NOW, WE CAN FIGHT WHAT'S INSIDE YOU TOGETHER. I'VE WEAKENED IT!
YOU'VE WEAKENED ME, BARRY! I'M DYING!
NEED STRENGTH TO FIGHT BACK!
BEFORE IT'S TOO LATE...HELP MEEEE!
WALLY, LISTEN! YOU SAID FAMINE FEEDS ON SOMETHING. WHAT DOES IT FEED ON? MAYBE WE CAN STARVE IT! OR POISON--
RUNNING OUT OF TIME! FIND OTHERS TO HELP. NEED MAGIC! XANADU... CONSTANTINE... ANYONE!
WALLY, ALL THE MAGIC USERS HAVE BEEN GONE FOR YEARS. NO ONE KNOWS WHERE THEY--
BRING THEM! TO HELP ME!
...FOCUS...

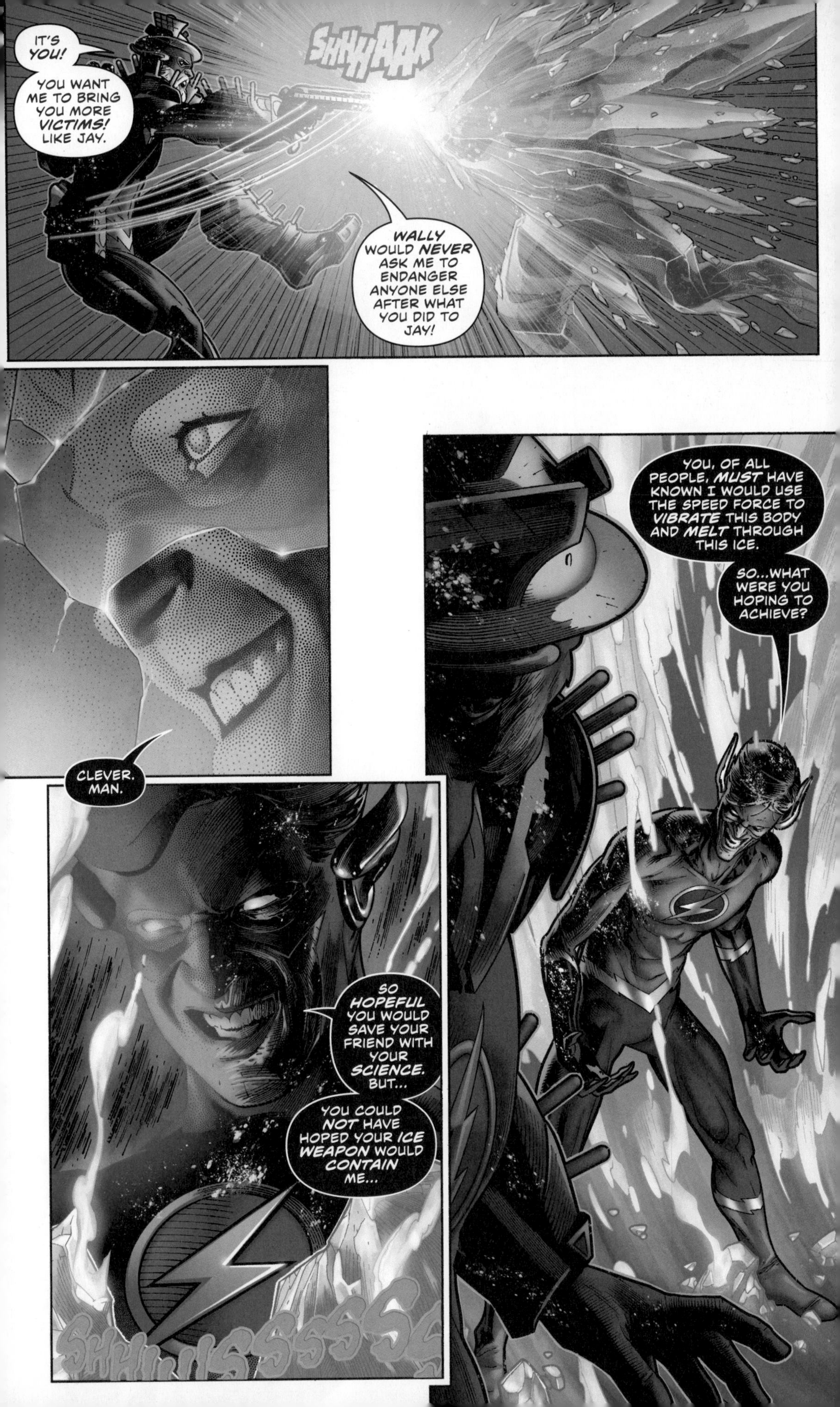
SHHHAAK
IT'S YOU!
YOU WANT ME TO BRING YOU MORE VICTIMS! LIKE JAY.
WALLY WOULD NEVER ASK ME TO ENDANGER ANYONE ELSE AFTER WHAT YOU DID TO JAY!
CLEVER. MAN.
YOU, OF ALL PEOPLE, MUST HAVE KNOWN I WOULD USE THE SPEED FORCE TO VIBRATE THIS BODY AND MELT THROUGH THIS ICE.
SO...WHAT WERE YOU HOPING TO ACHIEVE?
SO HOPEFUL YOU WOULD SAVE YOUR FRIEND WITH YOUR SCIENCE. BUT...
YOU COULD NOT HAVE HOPED YOUR ICE WEAPON WOULD CONTAIN ME...
SHHHISSSSSS

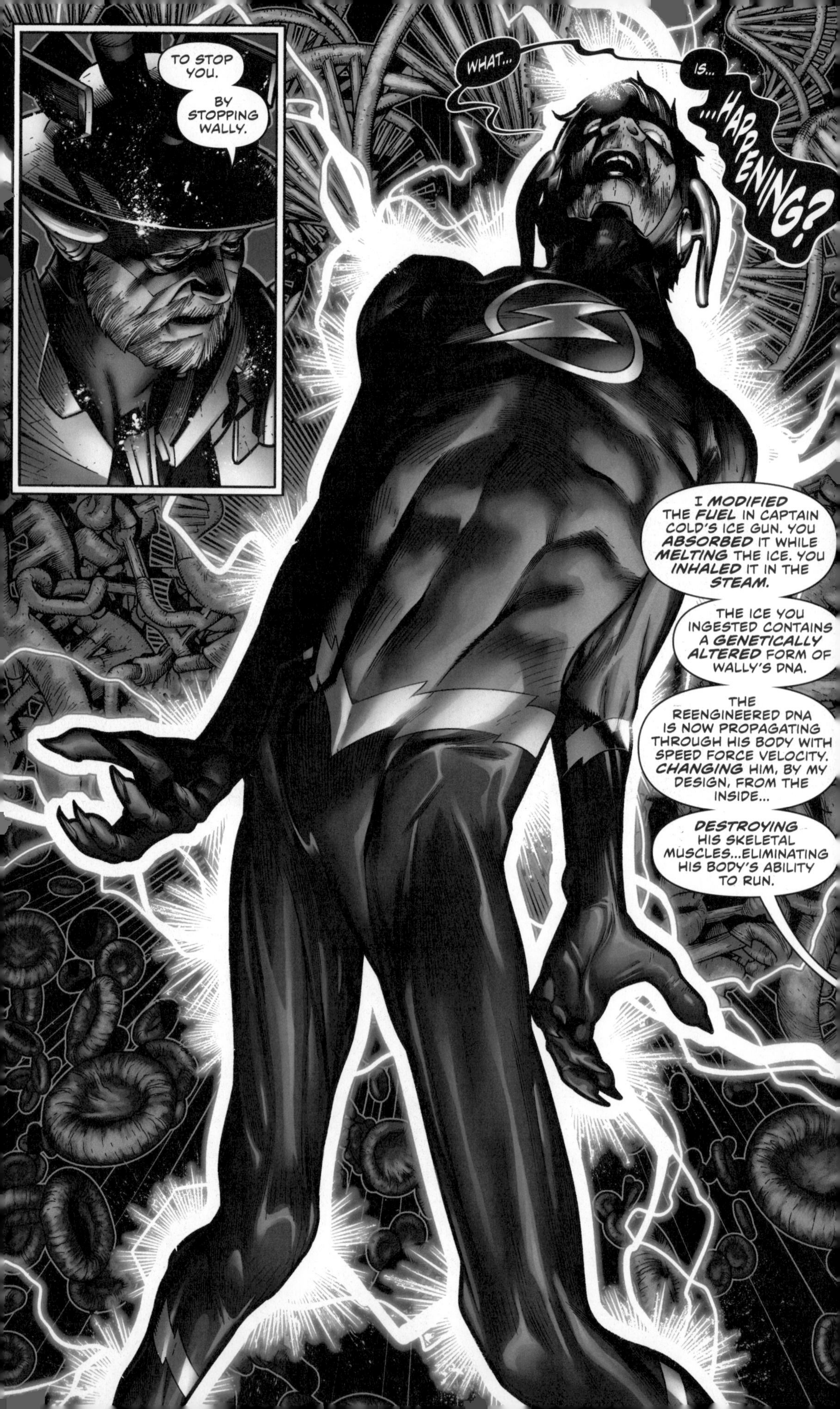
TO STOP YOU.
BY STOPPING WALLY.
WHAT...
IS...
...HAPPENING?
I MODIFIED THE FUEL IN CAPTAIN COLD'S ICE GUN. YOU ABSORBED IT WHILE MELTING THE ICE. YOU INHALED IT IN THE STEAM.
THE ICE YOU INGESTED CONTAINS A GENETICALLY ALTERED FORM OF WALLY'S DNA.
THE REENGINEERED DNA IS NOW PROPAGATING THROUGH HIS BODY WITH SPEED FORCE VELOCITY. CHANGING HIM, BY MY DESIGN, FROM THE INSIDE...
DESTROYING HIS SKELETAL MUSCLES...ELIMINATING HIS BODY'S ABILITY TO RUN.

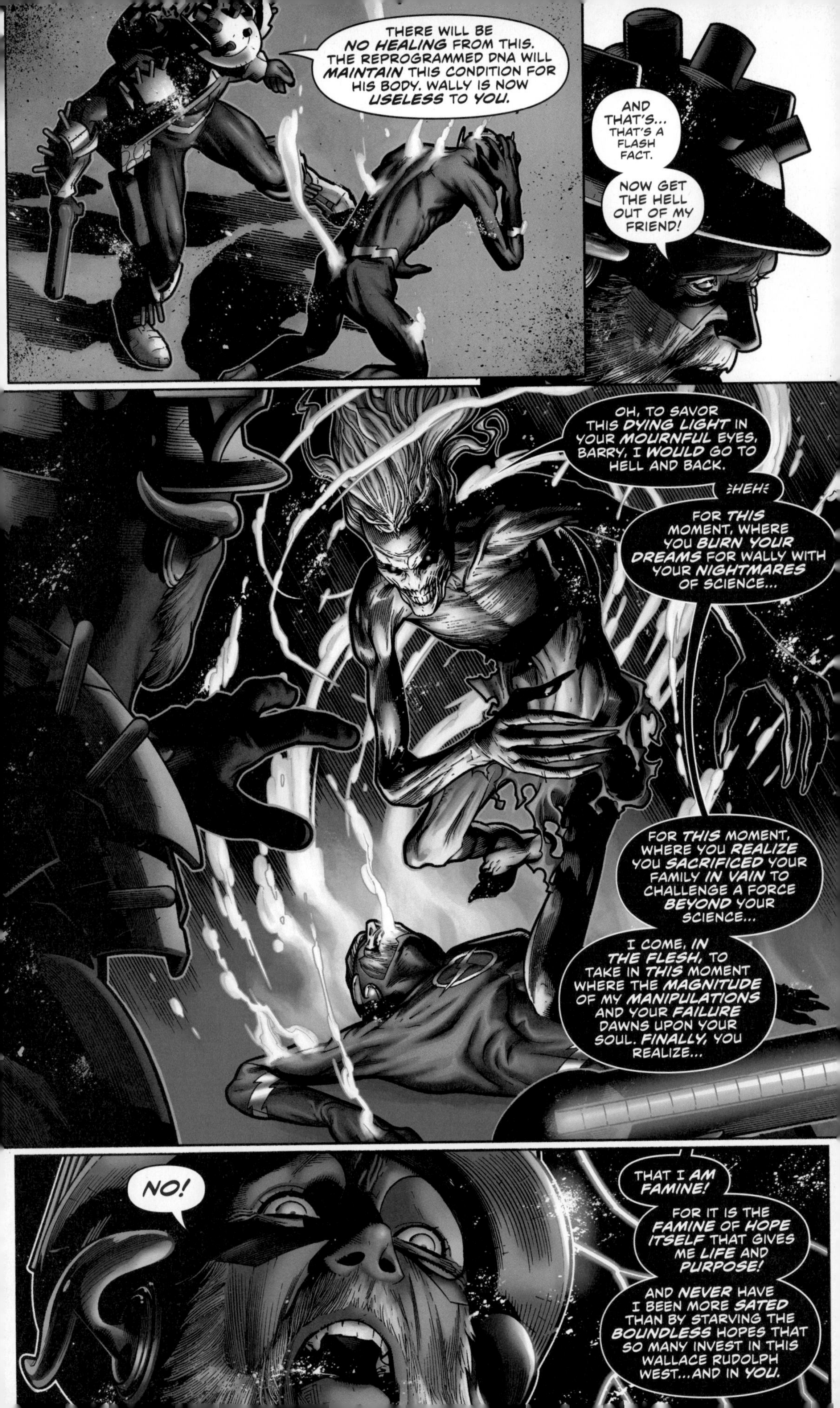

THERE WILL BE NO HEALING FROM THIS. THE REPROGRAMMED DNA WILL MAINTAIN THIS CONDITION FOR HIS BODY. WALLY IS NOW USELESS TO YOU.
AND THAT'S... THAT'S A FLASH FACT.
NOW GET THE HELL OUT OF MY FRIEND!
OH, TO SAVOR THIS DYING LIGHT IN YOUR MOURNFUL EYES, BARRY, I WOULD GO TO HELL AND BACK.
HEH
FOR THIS MOMENT, WHERE YOU BURN YOUR DREAMS FOR WALLY WITH YOUR NIGHTMARES OF SCIENCE...
FOR THIS MOMENT, WHERE YOU REALIZE YOU SACRIFICED YOUR FAMILY IN VAIN TO CHALLENGE A FORCE BEYOND YOUR SCIENCE...
I COME, IN THE FLESH, TO TAKE IN THIS MOMENT WHERE THE MAGNITUDE OF MY MANIPULATIONS AND YOUR FAILURE DAWNS UPON YOUR SOUL. FINALLY, YOU REALIZE...
NO!
THAT I AM FAMINE!
FOR IT IS THE FAMINE OF HOPE ITSELF THAT GIVES ME LIFE AND PURPOSE!
AND NEVER HAVE I BEEN MORE SATED THAN BY STARVING THE BOUNDLESS HOPES THAT SO MANY INVEST IN THIS WALLACE RUDOLPH WEST...AND IN YOU.

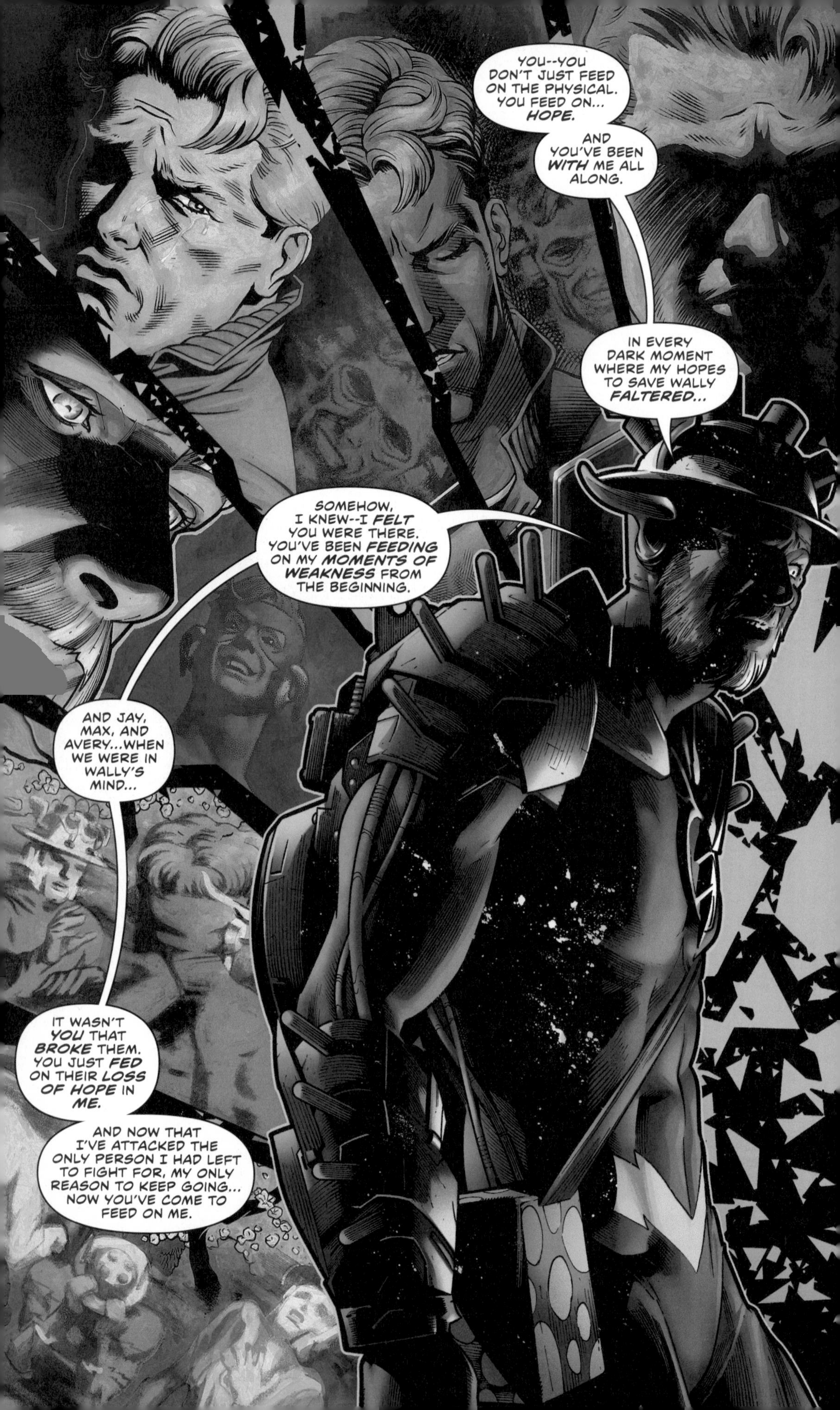
YOU--YOU DON'T JUST FEED ON THE PHYSICAL. YOU FEED ON... HOPE.
AND YOU'VE BEEN WITH ME ALL ALONG.
IN EVERY DARK MOMENT WHERE MY HOPES TO SAVE WALLY FALTERED...
SOMEHOW, I KNEW--I FELT YOU WERE THERE. YOU'VE BEEN FEEDING ON MY MOMENTS OF WEAKNESS FROM THE BEGINNING.
AND JAY, MAX, AND AVERY...WHEN WE WERE IN WALLY'S MIND...
IT WASN'T YOU THAT BROKE THEM. YOU JUST FED ON THEIR LOSS OF HOPE IN ME.
AND NOW THAT I'VE ATTACKED THE ONLY PERSON I HAD LEFT TO FIGHT FOR, MY ONLY REASON TO KEEP GOING... NOW YOU'VE COME TO FEED ON ME.

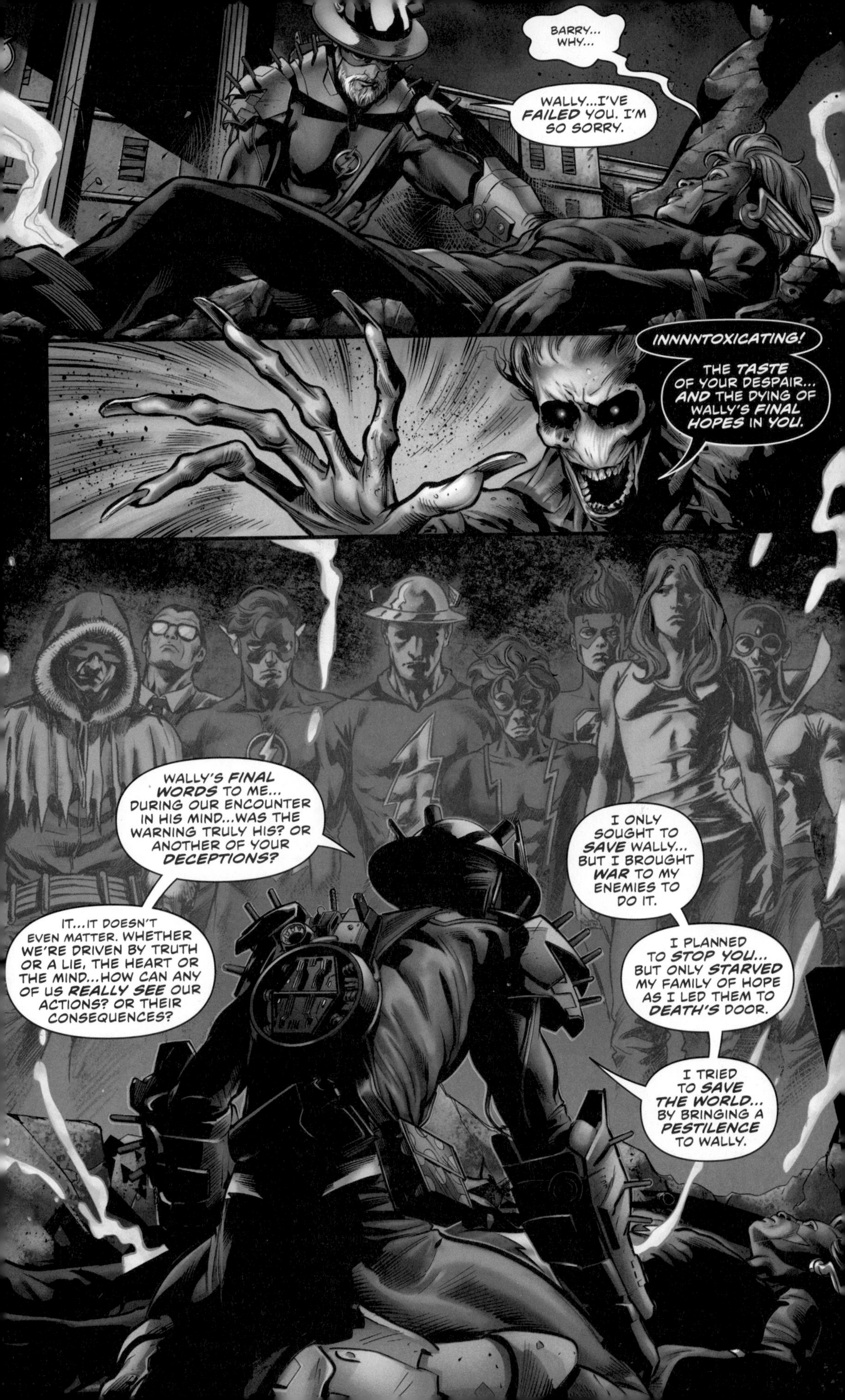
BARRY... WHY...
WALLY...I'VE FAILED YOU. I'M SO SORRY.
INNNNTOXICATING!
THE TASTE OF YOUR DESPAIR... AND THE DYING OF WALLY'S FINAL HOPES IN YOU.
WALLY'S FINAL WORDS TO ME... DURING OUR ENCOUNTER IN HIS MIND...WAS THE WARNING TRULY HIS? OR ANOTHER OF YOUR DECEPTIONS?
IT...IT DOESN'T EVEN MATTER. WHETHER WE'RE DRIVEN BY TRUTH OR A LIE, THE HEART OR THE MIND...HOW CAN ANY OF US REALLY SEE OUR ACTIONS? OR THEIR CONSEQUENCES?
I ONLY SOUGHT TO SAVE WALLY... BUT I BROUGHT WAR TO MY ENEMIES TO DO IT.
I PLANNED TO STOP YOU... BUT ONLY STARVED MY FAMILY OF HOPE AS I LED THEM TO DEATH'S DOOR.
I TRIED TO SAVE THE WORLD... BY BRINGING A PESTILENCE TO WALLY.

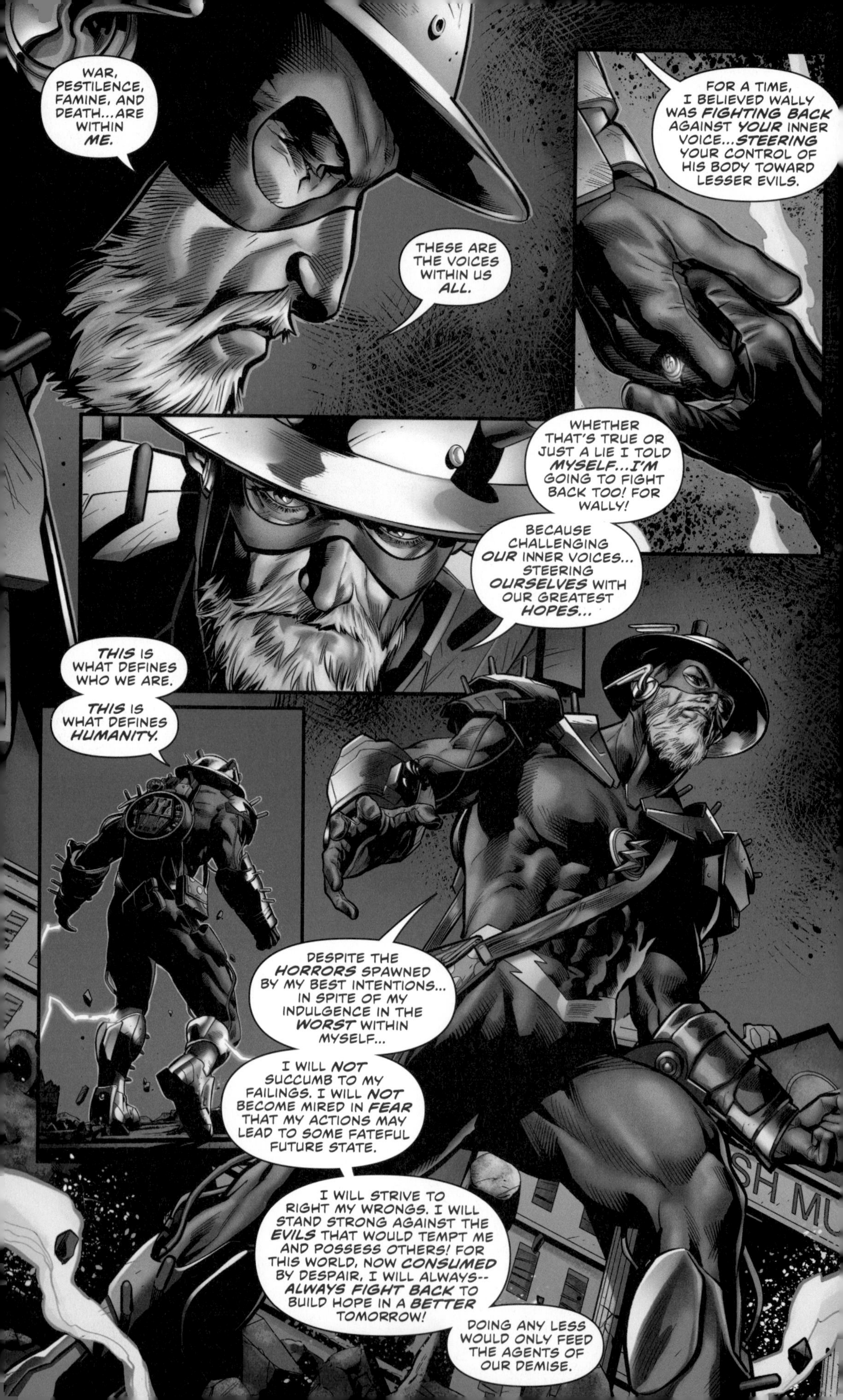
WAR, PESTILENCE, FAMINE, AND DEATH...ARE WITHIN ME.
THESE ARE THE VOICES WITHIN US ALL.
FOR A TIME, I BELIEVED WALLY WAS FIGHTING BACK AGAINST YOUR INNER VOICE...STEERING YOUR CONTROL OF HIS BODY TOWARD LESSER EVILS.
WHETHER THAT'S TRUE OR JUST A LIE I TOLD MYSELF...I'M GOING TO FIGHT BACK TOO! FOR WALLY!
BECAUSE CHALLENGING OUR INNER VOICES... STEERING OURSELVES WITH OUR GREATEST HOPES...
THIS IS WHAT DEFINES WHO WE ARE.
THIS IS WHAT DEFINES HUMANITY.
DESPITE THE HORRORS SPAWNED BY MY BEST INTENTIONS... IN SPITE OF MY INDULGENCE IN THE WORST WITHIN MYSELF...
I WILL NOT SUCCUMB TO MY FAILINGS. I WILL NOT BECOME MIRED IN FEAR THAT MY ACTIONS MAY LEAD TO SOME FATEFUL FUTURE STATE.
I WILL STRIVE TO RIGHT MY WRONGS. I WILL STAND STRONG AGAINST THE EVILS THAT WOULD TEMPT ME AND POSSESS OTHERS! FOR THIS WORLD, NOW CONSUMED BY DESPAIR, I WILL ALWAYS-- ALWAYS FIGHT BACK TO BUILD HOPE IN A BETTER TOMORROW!
DOING ANY LESS WOULD ONLY FEED THE AGENTS OF OUR DEMISE.

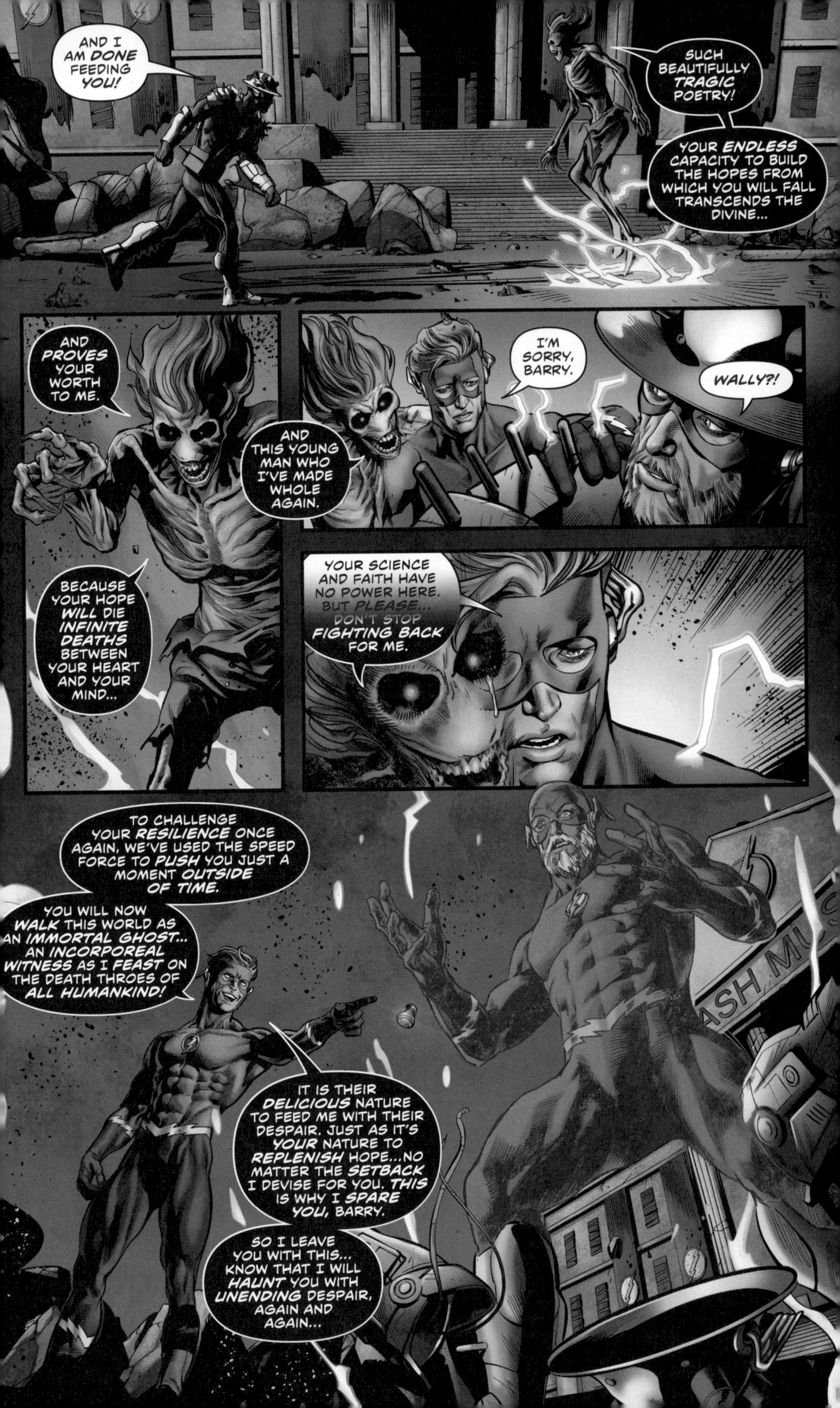

AND I AM DONE FEEDING YOU!
SUCH BEAUTIFULLY TRAGIC POETRY!
YOUR ENDLESS CAPACITY TO BUILD THE HOPES FROM WHICH YOU WILL FALL TRANSCENDS THE DIVINE...
AND PROVES YOUR WORTH TO ME.
AND THIS YOUNG MAN WHO I'VE MADE WHOLE AGAIN.
I'M SORRY, BARRY.
WALLY?!
BECAUSE YOUR HOPE WILL DIE INFINITE DEATHS BETWEEN YOUR HEART AND YOUR MIND...
YOUR SCIENCE AND FAITH HAVE NO POWER HERE. BUT PLEASE... DON'T STOP FIGHTING BACK FOR ME.
TO CHALLENGE YOUR RESILIENCE ONCE AGAIN, WE'VE USED THE SPEED FORCE TO PUSH YOU JUST A MOMENT OUTSIDE OF TIME.
YOU WILL NOW WALK THIS WORLD AS AN IMMORTAL GHOST... AN INCORPOREAL WITNESS AS I FEAST ON THE DEATH THROES OF ALL HUMANKIND!
IT IS THEIR DELICIOUS NATURE TO FEED ME WITH THEIR DESPAIR. JUST AS IT'S YOUR NATURE TO REPLENISH HOPE...NO MATTER THE SETBACK I DEVISE FOR YOU. THIS IS WHY I SPARE YOU, BARRY.
SO I LEAVE YOU WITH THIS... KNOW THAT I WILL HAUNT YOU WITH UNENDING DESPAIR, AGAIN AND AGAIN...

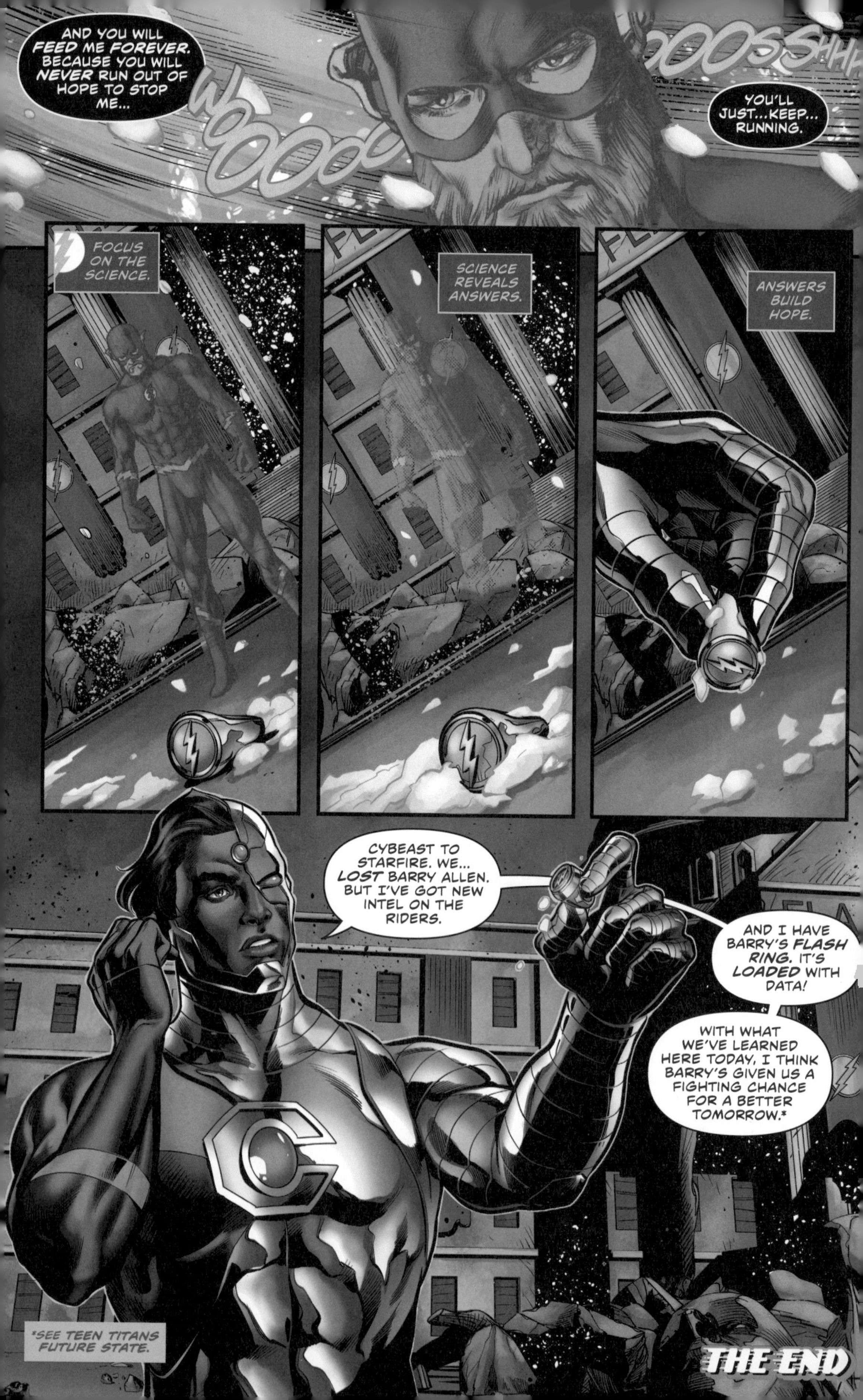

AND YOU WILL FEED ME FOREVER. BECAUSE YOU WILL NEVER RUN OUT OF HOPE TO STOP ME...
WHOOOOOOSSHHH
YOU'LL JUST...KEEP... RUNNING.
FOCUS ON THE SCIENCE.
SCIENCE REVEALS ANSWERS.
ANSWERS BUILD HOPE.
CYBEAST TO STARFIRE. WE... LOST BARRY ALLEN. BUT I'VE GOT NEW INTEL ON THE RIDERS.
AND I HAVE BARRY'S FLASH RING. IT'S LOADED WITH DATA!
WITH WHAT WE'VE LEARNED HERE TODAY, I THINK BARRY'S GIVEN US A FIGHTING CHANCE FOR A BETTER TOMORROW.*
*SEE TEEN TITANS FUTURE STATE.
THE END

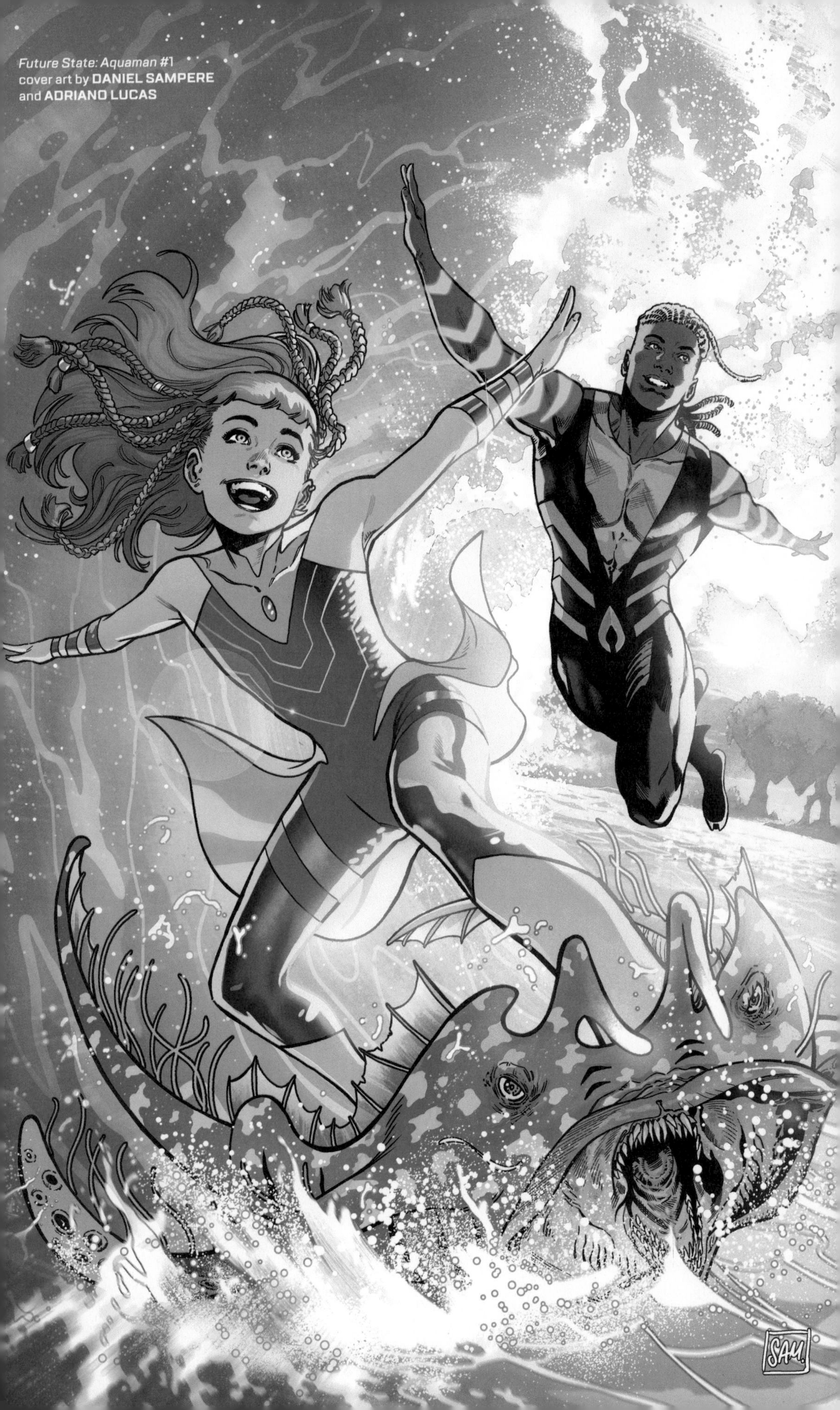

Future State: Aquaman #1
cover art by **DANIEL SAMPERE**
and **ADRIANO LUCAS**

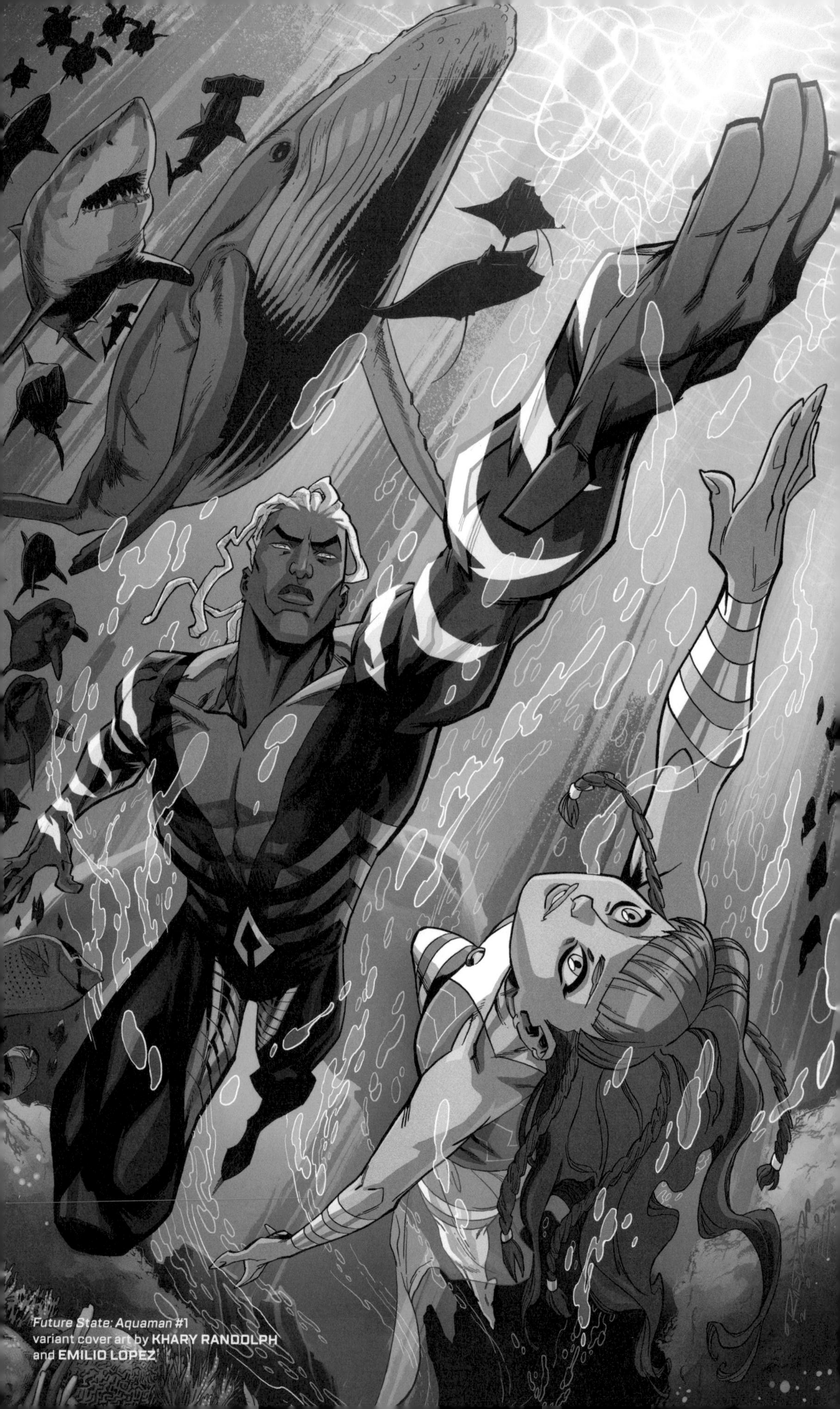

Future State: Aquaman #1
variant cover art by **KHARY RANDOLPH**
and **EMILIO LOPEZ**

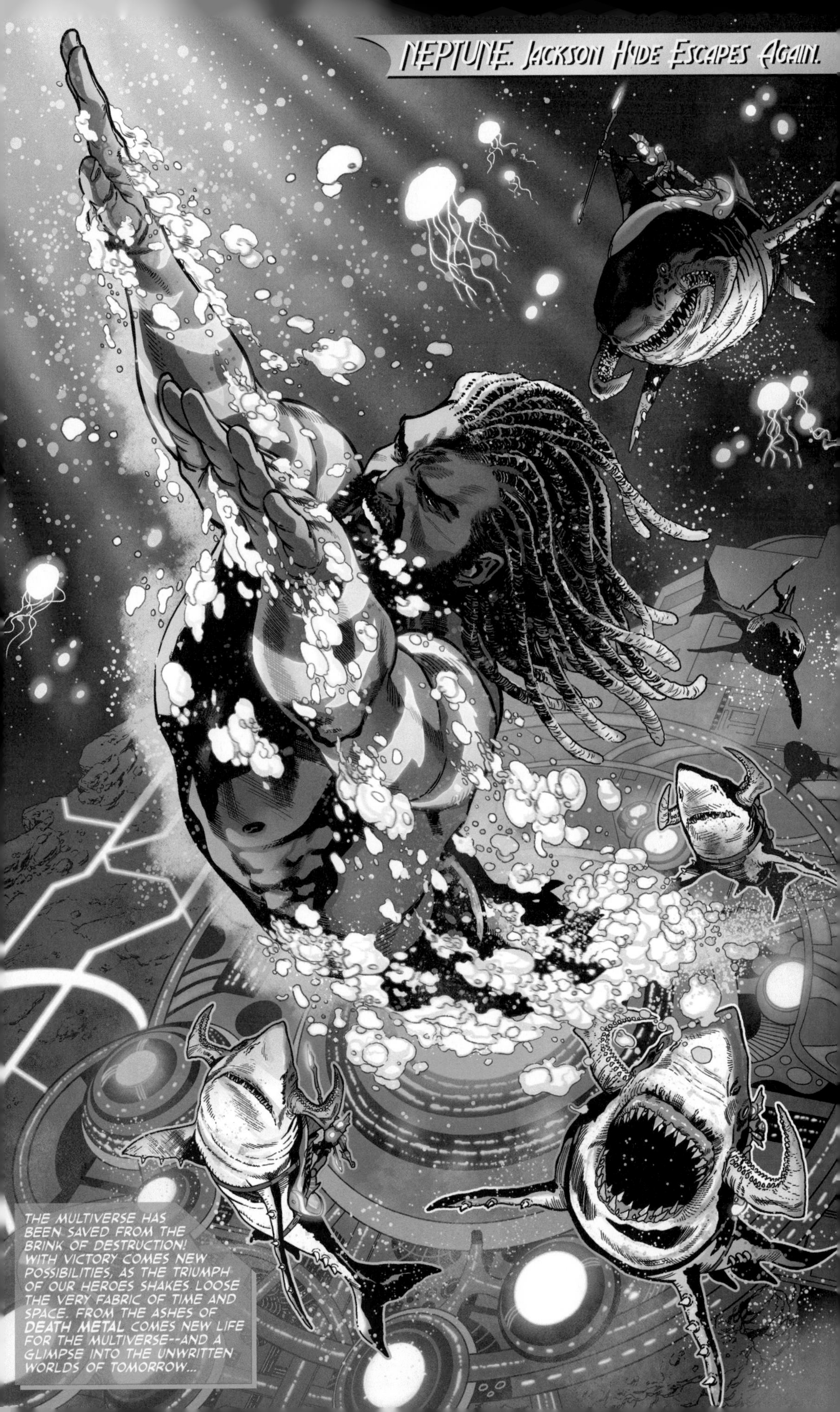
NEPTUNE. Jackson Hyde Escapes Again.
THE MULTIVERSE HAS BEEN SAVED FROM THE BRINK OF DESTRUCTION! WITH VICTORY COMES NEW POSSIBILITIES, AS THE TRIUMPH OF OUR HEROES SHAKES LOOSE THE VERY FABRIC OF TIME AND SPACE. FROM THE ASHES OF DEATH METAL COMES NEW LIFE FOR THE MULTIVERSE--AND A GLIMPSE INTO THE UNWRITTEN WORLDS OF TOMORROW...

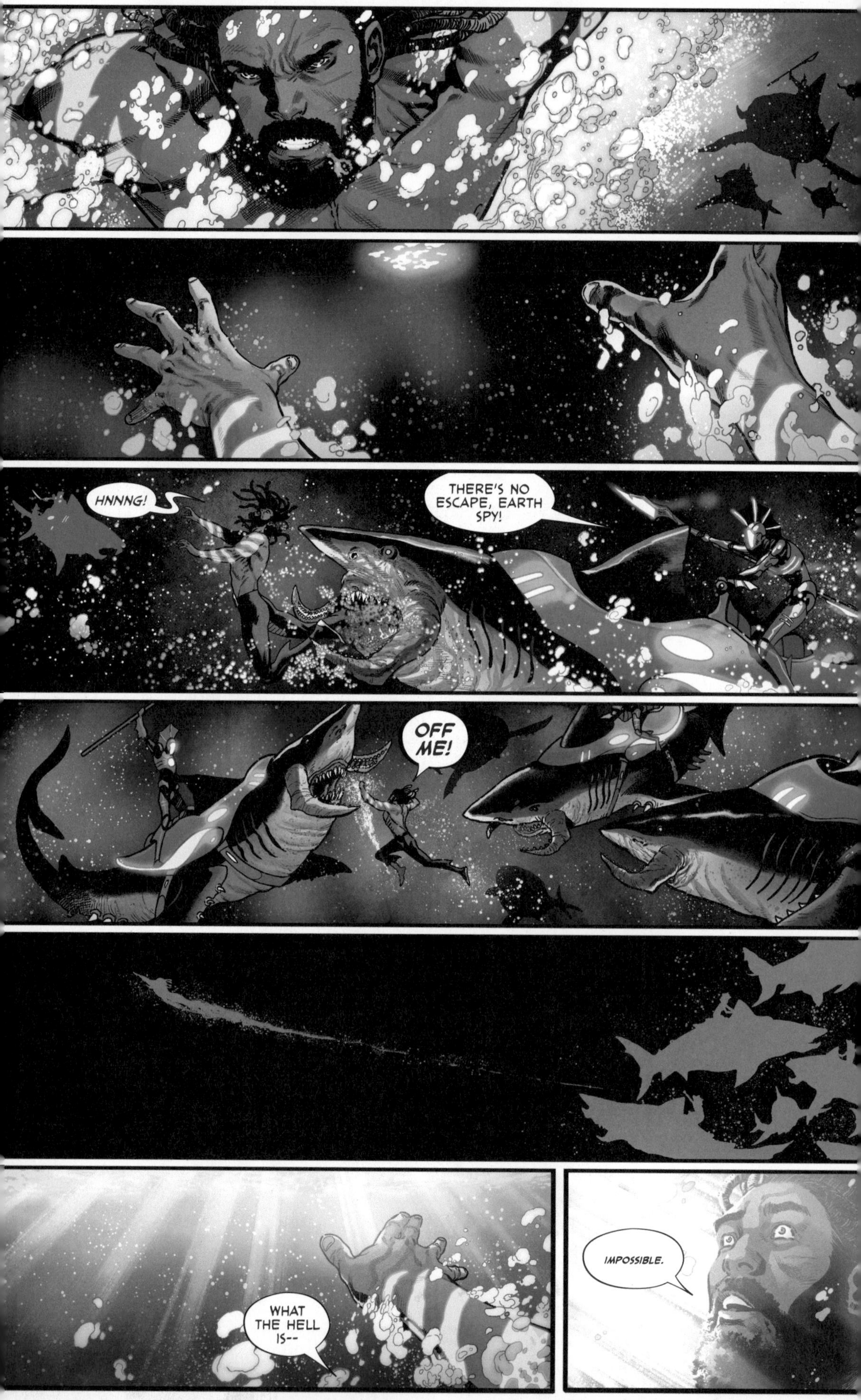
HNNNG!
THERE'S NO ESCAPE, EARTH SPY!
OFF ME!
WHAT THE HELL IS--
IMPOSSIBLE.

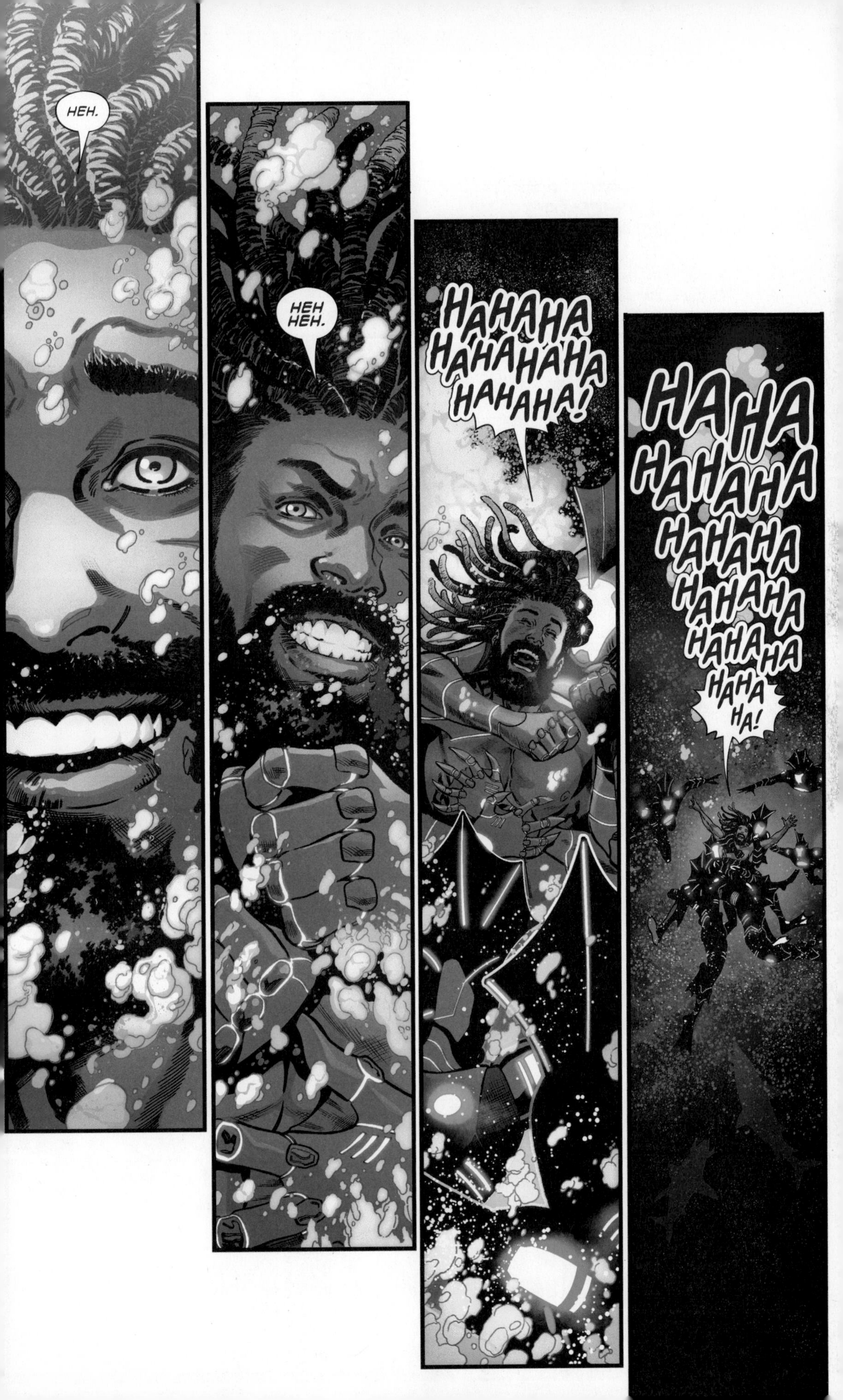
HEH.
HEH HEH.
HAHAHA HAHAHAHA HAHAHA!
HAHA HAHAHA HAHAHA HAHAHA HAHAHA HAHAHAHA HAHA HA!

FUTURE STATE: AQUAMAN

THE CONFLUENCE

PART ONE

BRANDON THOMAS WRITER DANIEL SAMPERE ARTIST
ADRIANO LUCAS COLORIST CLAYTON COWLES LETTERER
SAMPERE & LUCAS COVER ARTISTS
KHARY RANDOLPH & EMILIO LOPEZ VARIANT COVER ARTISTS
ANDREA SHEA EDITOR CHRIS CONROY SENIOR EDITOR
AQUAMAN CREATED BY PAUL NORRIS

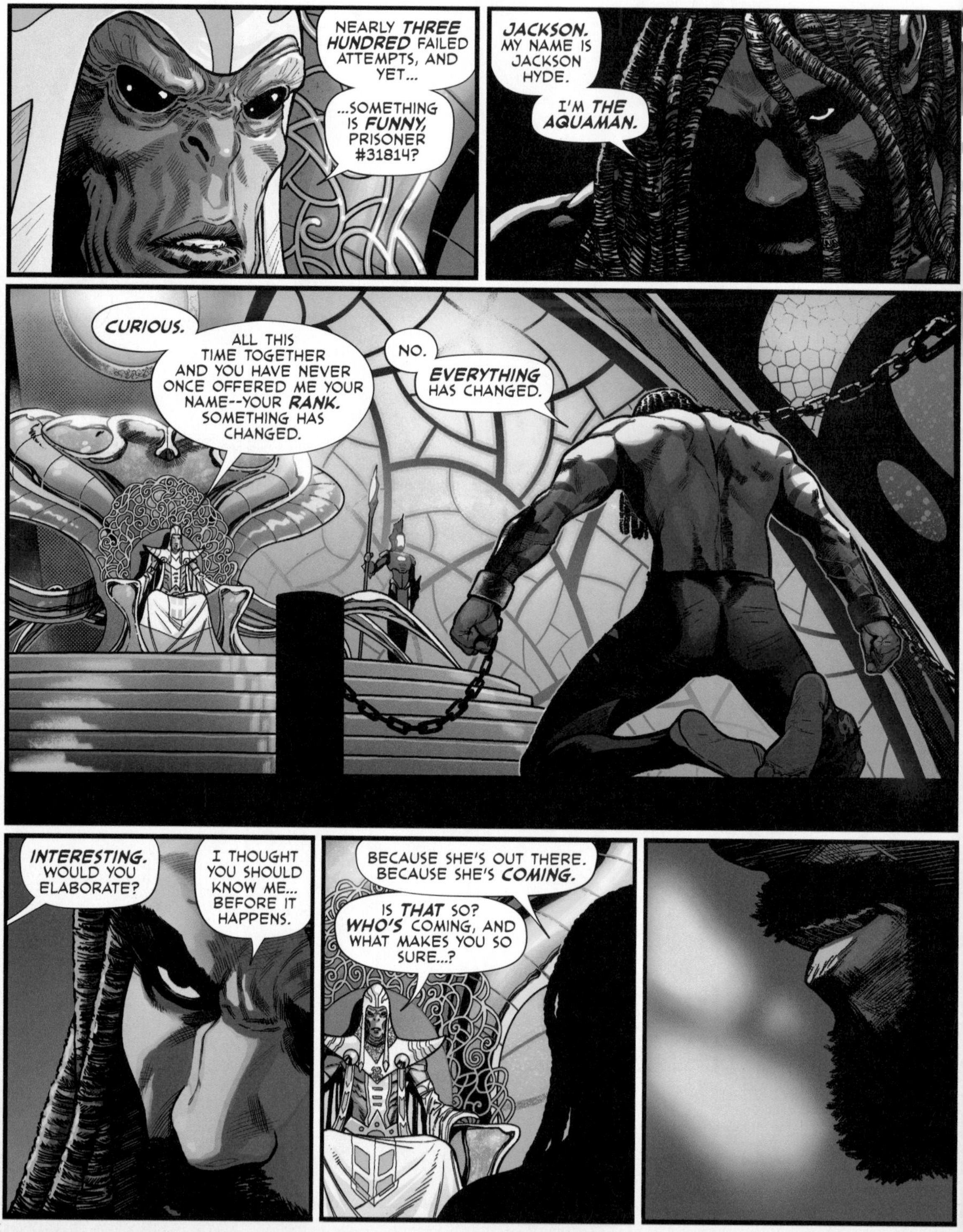

NEARLY THREE HUNDRED FAILED ATTEMPTS, AND YET...
...SOMETHING IS FUNNY, PRISONER #31814?
JACKSON. MY NAME IS JACKSON HYDE.
I'M THE AQUAMAN.
CURIOUS.
ALL THIS TIME TOGETHER AND YOU HAVE NEVER ONCE OFFERED ME YOUR NAME--YOUR RANK. SOMETHING HAS CHANGED.
NO.
EVERYTHING HAS CHANGED.
INTERESTING. WOULD YOU ELABORATE?
I THOUGHT YOU SHOULD KNOW ME... BEFORE IT HAPPENS.
BECAUSE SHE'S OUT THERE. BECAUSE SHE'S COMING.
IS THAT SO? WHO'S COMING, AND WHAT MAKES YOU SO SURE...?

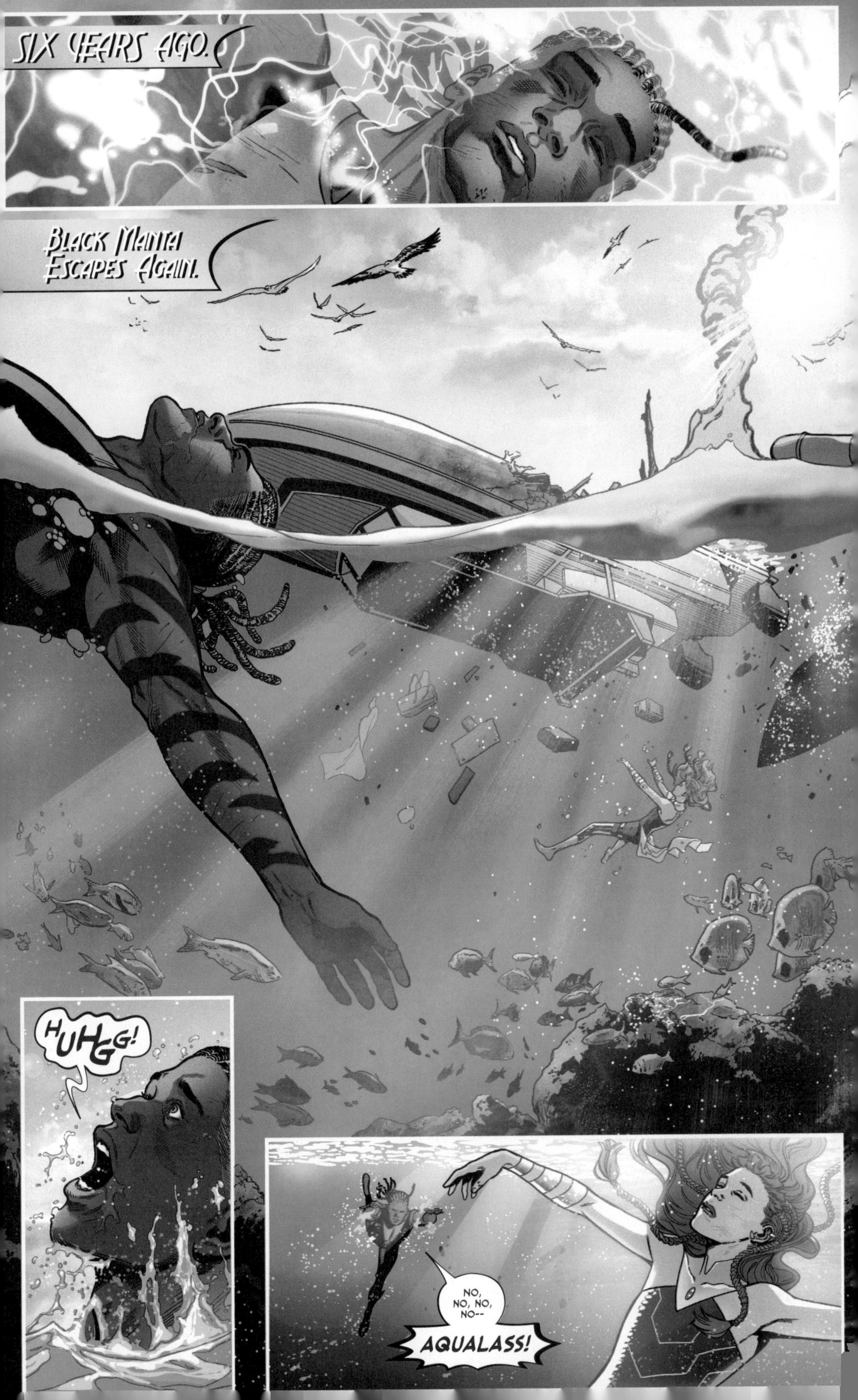
SIX YEARS AGO.
BLACK MANTA ESCAPES AGAIN.
HUHGG!
NO, NO, NO, NO--
AQUALASS!

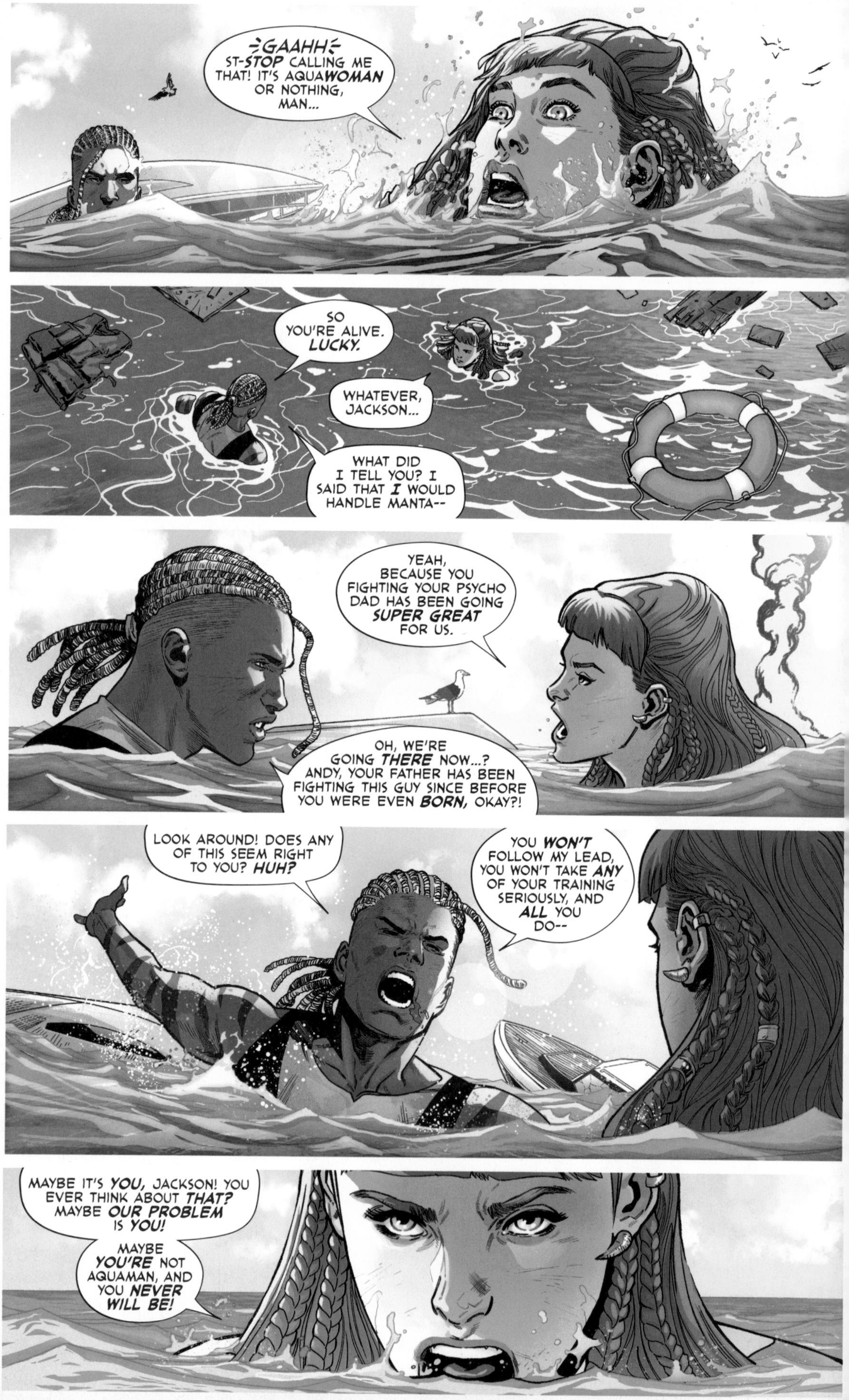
GAAHH
ST-STOP CALLING ME THAT! IT'S AQUAWOMAN OR NOTHING, MAN...
SO YOU'RE ALIVE. LUCKY.
WHATEVER, JACKSON...
WHAT DID I TELL YOU? I SAID THAT I WOULD HANDLE MANTA--
YEAH, BECAUSE YOU FIGHTING YOUR PSYCHO DAD HAS BEEN GOING SUPER GREAT FOR US.
OH, WE'RE GOING THERE NOW...? ANDY, YOUR FATHER HAS BEEN FIGHTING THIS GUY SINCE BEFORE YOU WERE EVEN BORN, OKAY?!
LOOK AROUND! DOES ANY OF THIS SEEM RIGHT TO YOU? HUH?
YOU WON'T FOLLOW MY LEAD, YOU WON'T TAKE ANY OF YOUR TRAINING SERIOUSLY, AND ALL YOU DO--
MAYBE IT'S YOU, JACKSON! YOU EVER THINK ABOUT THAT? MAYBE OUR PROBLEM IS YOU!
MAYBE YOU'RE NOT AQUAMAN, AND YOU NEVER WILL BE!

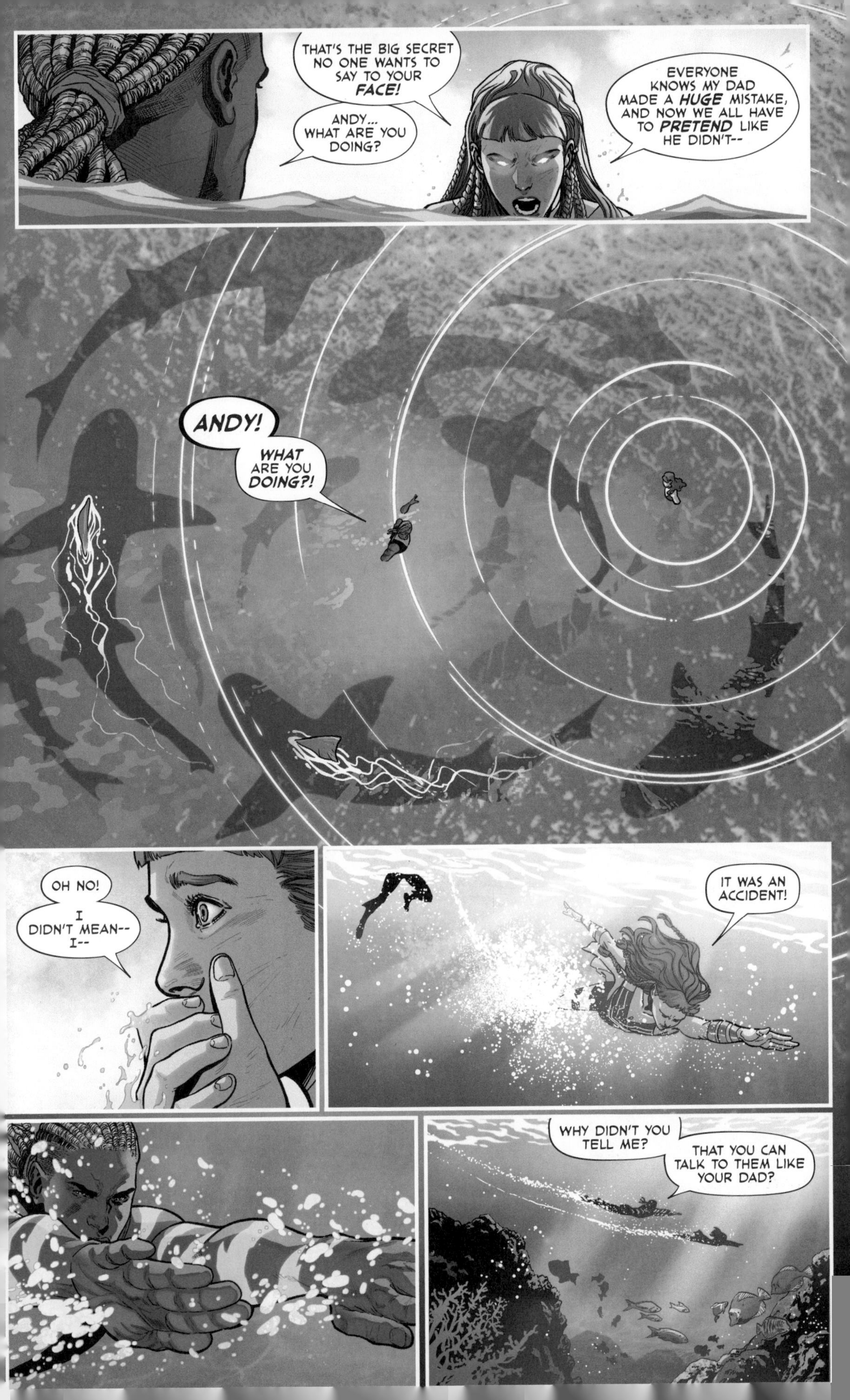
THAT'S THE BIG SECRET NO ONE WANTS TO SAY TO YOUR FACE!
ANDY... WHAT ARE YOU DOING?
EVERYONE KNOWS MY DAD MADE A HUGE MISTAKE, AND NOW WE ALL HAVE TO PRETEND LIKE HE DIDN'T--
ANDY!
WHAT ARE YOU DOING?!
OH NO!
I DIDN'T MEAN-- I--
IT WAS AN ACCIDENT!
WHY DIDN'T YOU TELL ME?
THAT YOU CAN TALK TO THEM LIKE YOUR DAD?

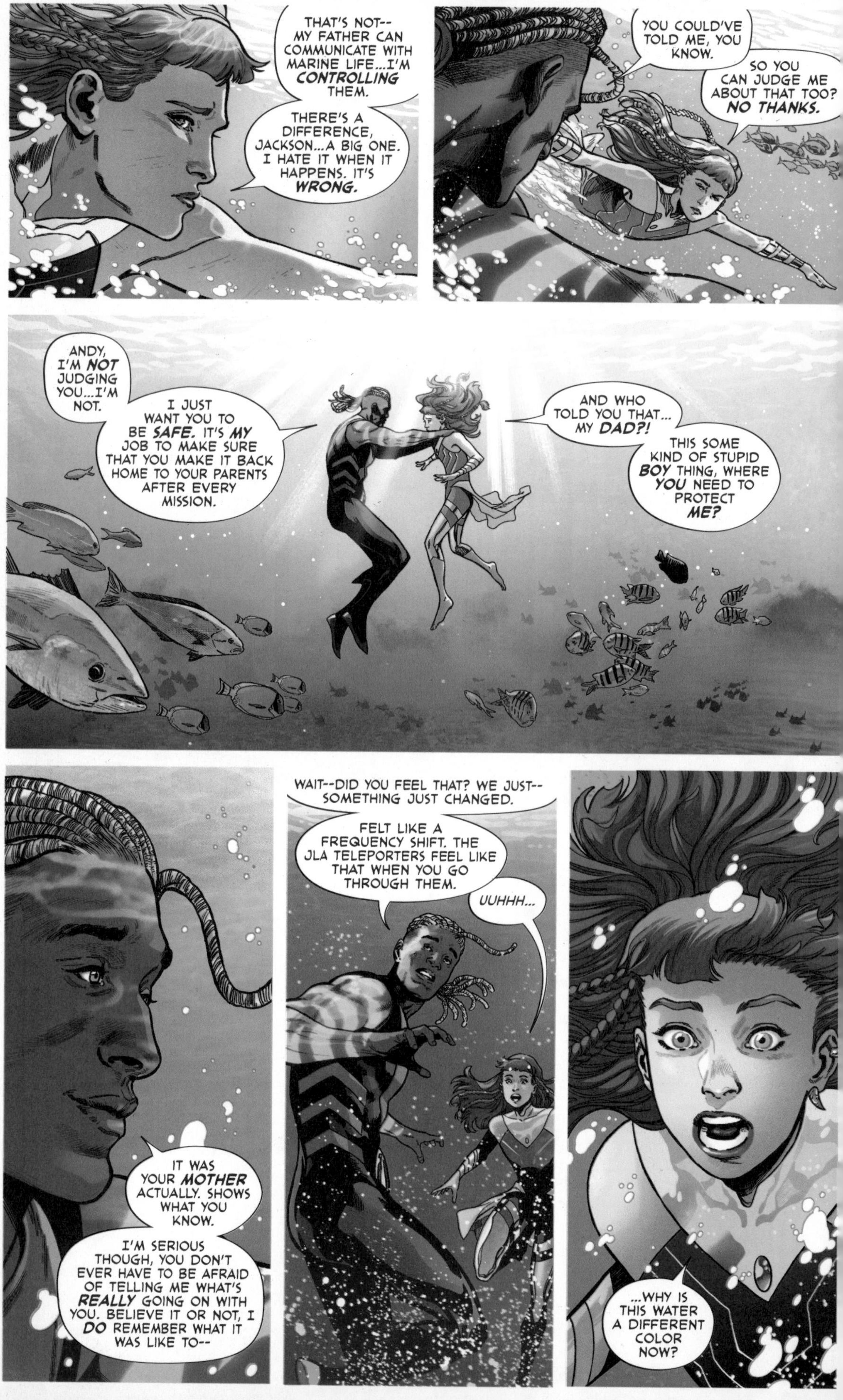
THAT'S NOT-- MY FATHER CAN COMMUNICATE WITH MARINE LIFE...I'M CONTROLLING THEM.
THERE'S A DIFFERENCE, JACKSON...A BIG ONE. I HATE IT WHEN IT HAPPENS. IT'S WRONG.
YOU COULD'VE TOLD ME, YOU KNOW.
SO YOU CAN JUDGE ME ABOUT THAT TOO? NO THANKS.
ANDY, I'M NOT JUDGING YOU...I'M NOT.
I JUST WANT YOU TO BE SAFE. IT'S MY JOB TO MAKE SURE THAT YOU MAKE IT BACK HOME TO YOUR PARENTS AFTER EVERY MISSION.
AND WHO TOLD YOU THAT... MY DAD?!
THIS SOME KIND OF STUPID BOY THING, WHERE YOU NEED TO PROTECT ME?
IT WAS YOUR MOTHER ACTUALLY. SHOWS WHAT YOU KNOW.
I'M SERIOUS THOUGH, YOU DON'T EVER HAVE TO BE AFRAID OF TELLING ME WHAT'S REALLY GOING ON WITH YOU. BELIEVE IT OR NOT, I DO REMEMBER WHAT IT WAS LIKE TO--
WAIT--DID YOU FEEL THAT? WE JUST-- SOMETHING JUST CHANGED.
FELT LIKE A FREQUENCY SHIFT. THE JLA TELEPORTERS FEEL LIKE THAT WHEN YOU GO THROUGH THEM.
UUHHH...
...WHY IS THIS WATER A DIFFERENT COLOR NOW?

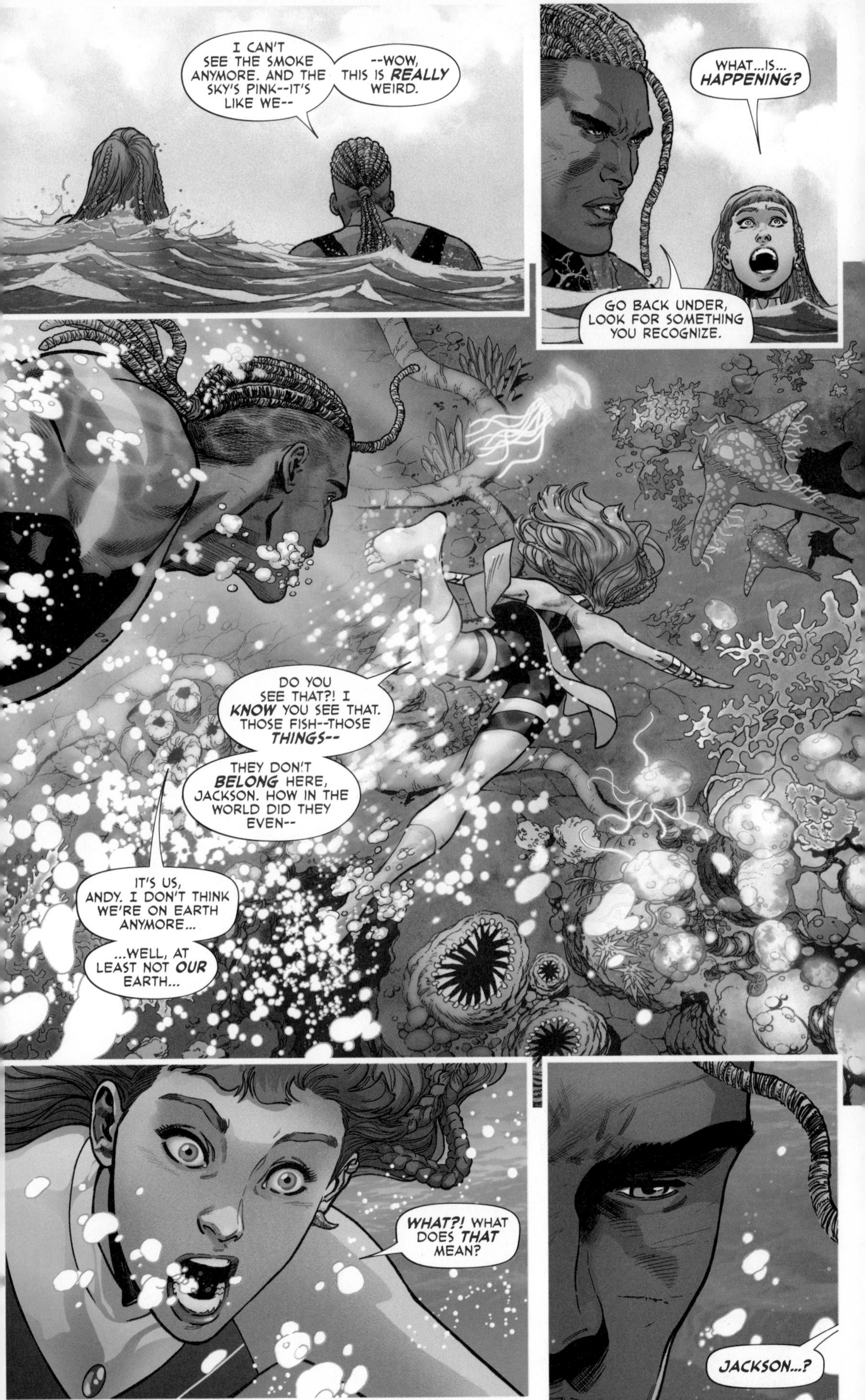

I CAN'T SEE THE SMOKE ANYMORE. AND THE SKY'S PINK--IT'S LIKE WE--
--WOW, THIS IS REALLY WEIRD.
WHAT...IS... HAPPENING?
GO BACK UNDER, LOOK FOR SOMETHING YOU RECOGNIZE.
DO YOU SEE THAT?! I KNOW YOU SEE THAT. THOSE FISH--THOSE THINGS--
THEY DON'T BELONG HERE, JACKSON. HOW IN THE WORLD DID THEY EVEN--
IT'S US, ANDY. I DON'T THINK WE'RE ON EARTH ANYMORE...
...WELL, AT LEAST NOT OUR EARTH...
WHAT?! WHAT DOES THAT MEAN?
JACKSON...?

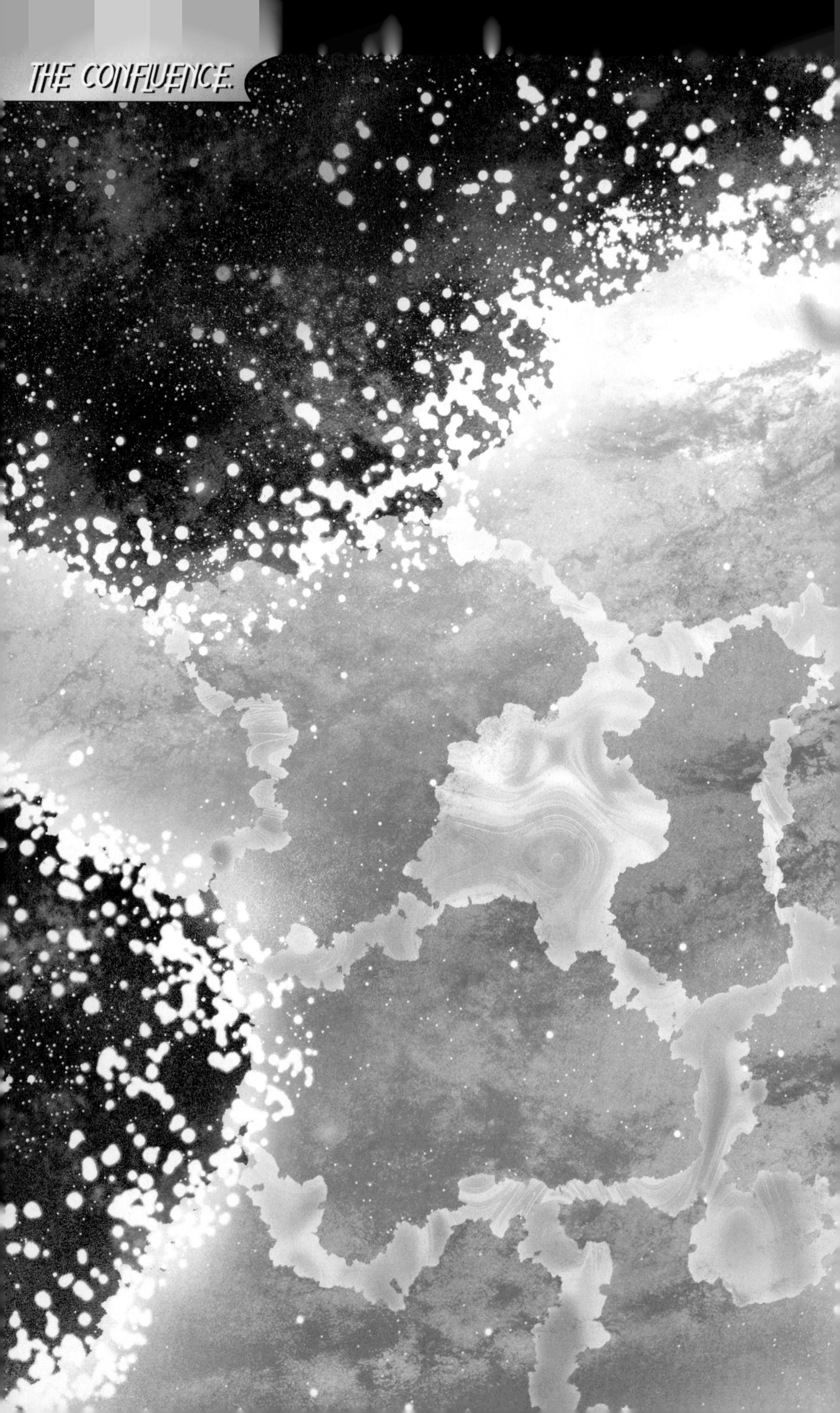
THE CONFLUENCE.

JACKSON, WHERE ARE WE...?

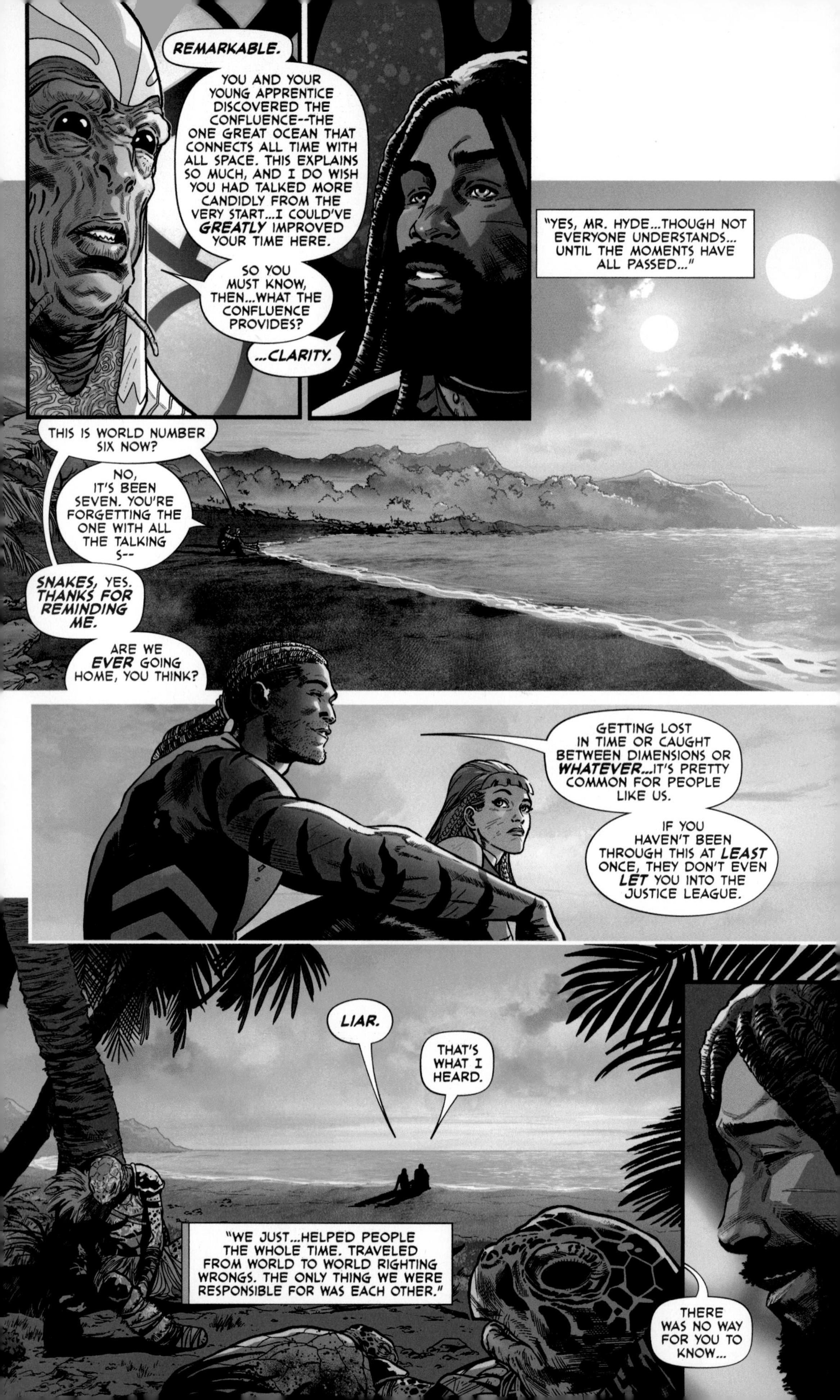

REMARKABLE.
YOU AND YOUR YOUNG APPRENTICE DISCOVERED THE CONFLUENCE--THE ONE GREAT OCEAN THAT CONNECTS ALL TIME WITH ALL SPACE. THIS EXPLAINS SO MUCH, AND I DO WISH YOU HAD TALKED MORE CANDIDLY FROM THE VERY START...I COULD'VE GREATLY IMPROVED YOUR TIME HERE.
SO YOU MUST KNOW, THEN...WHAT THE CONFLUENCE PROVIDES?
...CLARITY.
"YES, MR. HYDE...THOUGH NOT EVERYONE UNDERSTANDS... UNTIL THE MOMENTS HAVE ALL PASSED..."
THIS IS WORLD NUMBER SIX NOW?
NO, IT'S BEEN SEVEN. YOU'RE FORGETTING THE ONE WITH ALL THE TALKING S--
SNAKES, YES. THANKS FOR REMINDING ME.
ARE WE EVER GOING HOME, YOU THINK?
GETTING LOST IN TIME OR CAUGHT BETWEEN DIMENSIONS OR WHATEVER...IT'S PRETTY COMMON FOR PEOPLE LIKE US.
IF YOU HAVEN'T BEEN THROUGH THIS AT LEAST ONCE, THEY DON'T EVEN LET YOU INTO THE JUSTICE LEAGUE.
LIAR.
THAT'S WHAT I HEARD.
"WE JUST...HELPED PEOPLE THE WHOLE TIME. TRAVELED FROM WORLD TO WORLD RIGHTING WRONGS. THE ONLY THING WE WERE RESPONSIBLE FOR WAS EACH OTHER."
THERE WAS NO WAY FOR YOU TO KNOW...

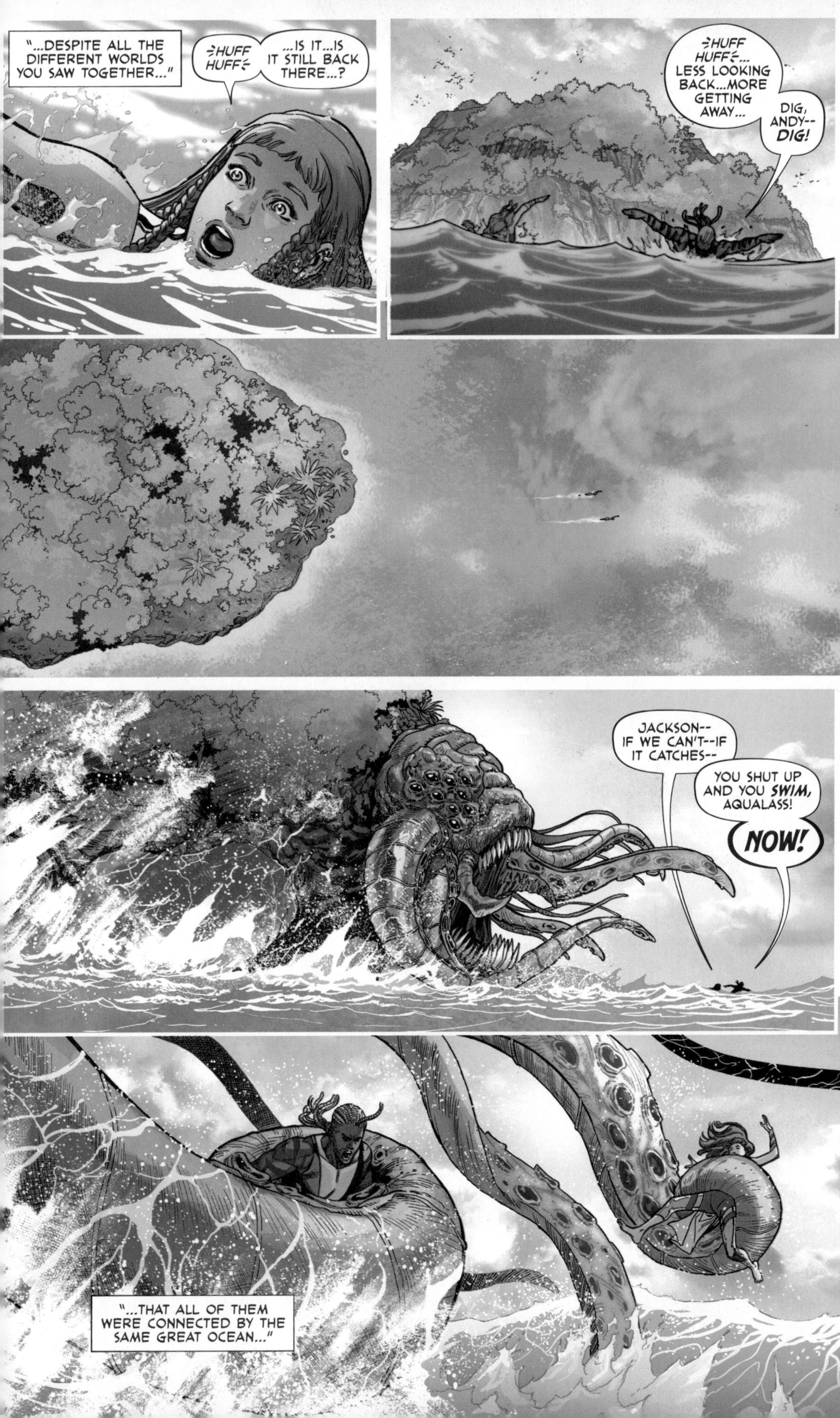
"...DESPITE ALL THE DIFFERENT WORLDS YOU SAW TOGETHER..."
HUFF HUFF
...IS IT...IS IT STILL BACK THERE...?
HUFF HUFF... LESS LOOKING BACK...MORE GETTING AWAY...
DIG, ANDY-- DIG!
JACKSON-- IF WE CAN'T--IF IT CATCHES--
YOU SHUT UP AND YOU SWIM, AQUALASS!
NOW!
"...THAT ALL OF THEM WERE CONNECTED BY THE SAME GREAT OCEAN..."

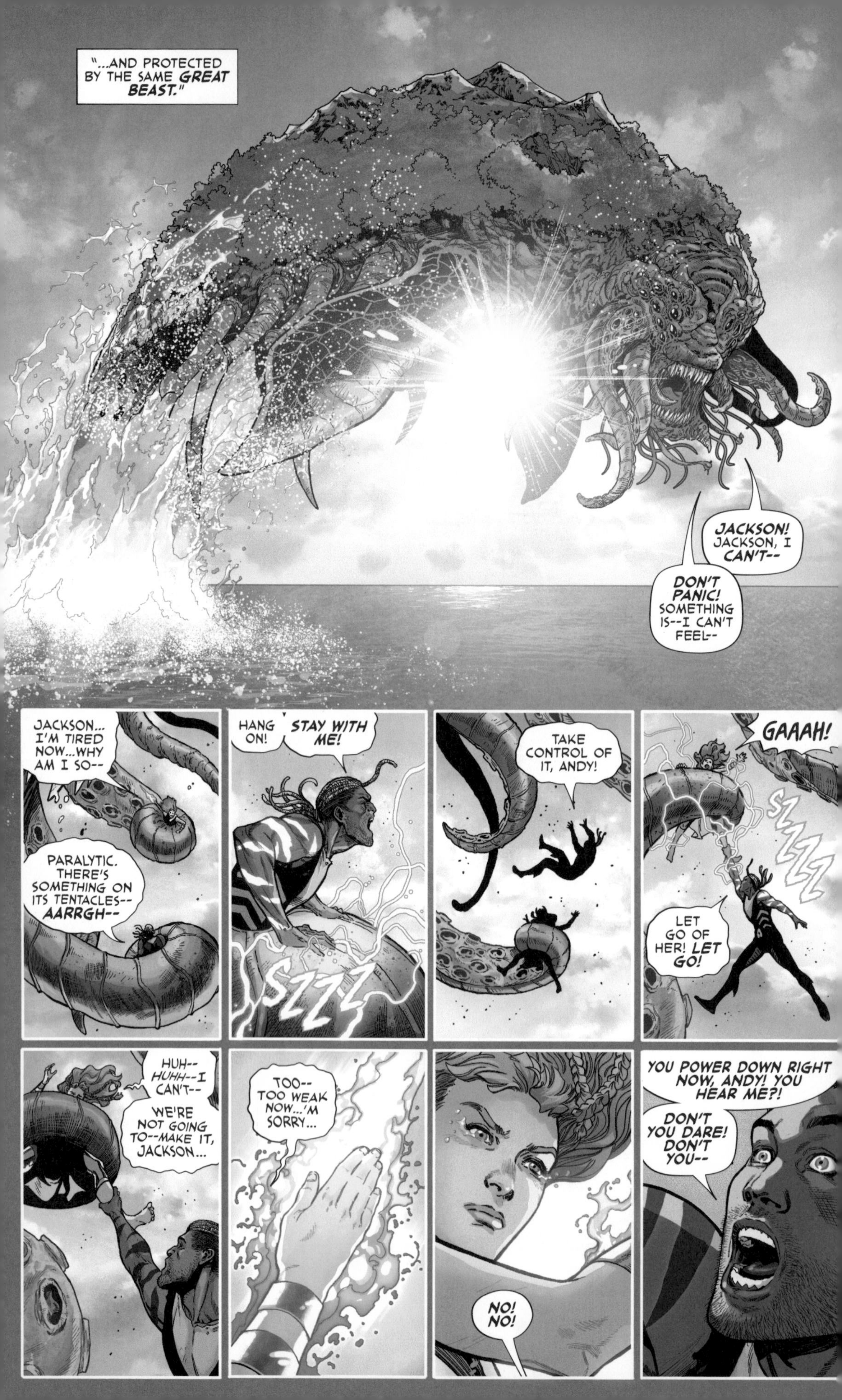
"...AND PROTECTED BY THE SAME GREAT BEAST."
JACKSON! JACKSON, I CAN'T--
DON'T PANIC! SOMETHING IS--I CAN'T FEEL--
JACKSON... I'M TIRED NOW...WHY AM I SO--
PARALYTIC. THERE'S SOMETHING ON ITS TENTACLES-- AARRGH--
HANG ON!
STAY WITH ME!
SZZZ
TAKE CONTROL OF IT, ANDY!
GAAAH!
SZZZ
LET GO OF HER! LET GO!
HUH-- HUHH--I CAN'T--
WE'RE NOT GOING TO--MAKE IT, JACKSON...
TOO-- TOO WEAK NOW...'M SORRY...
NO! NO!
YOU POWER DOWN RIGHT NOW, ANDY! YOU HEAR ME?!
DON'T YOU DARE! DON'T YOU--

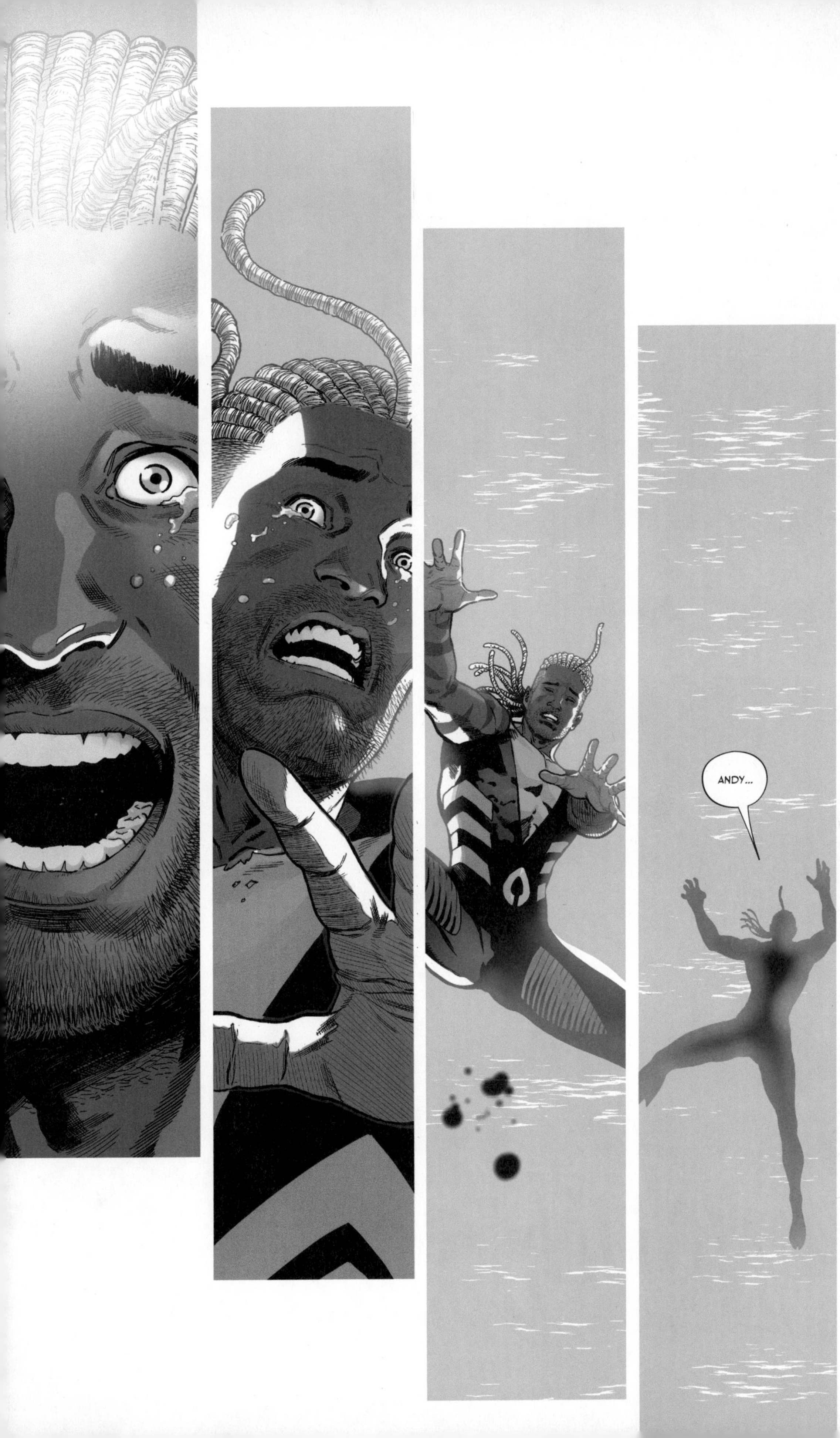
ANDY...

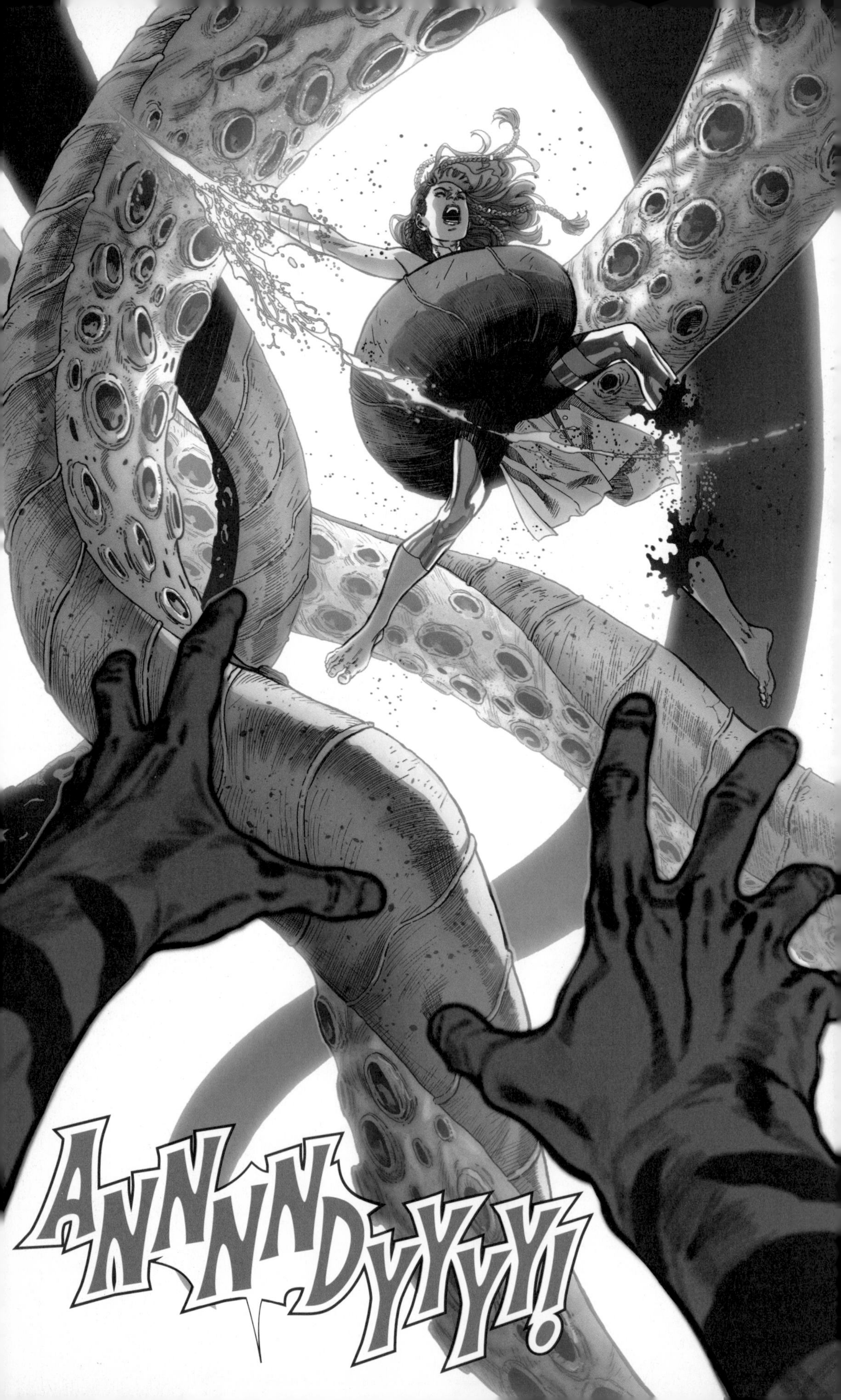
ANNNNDYYYY!

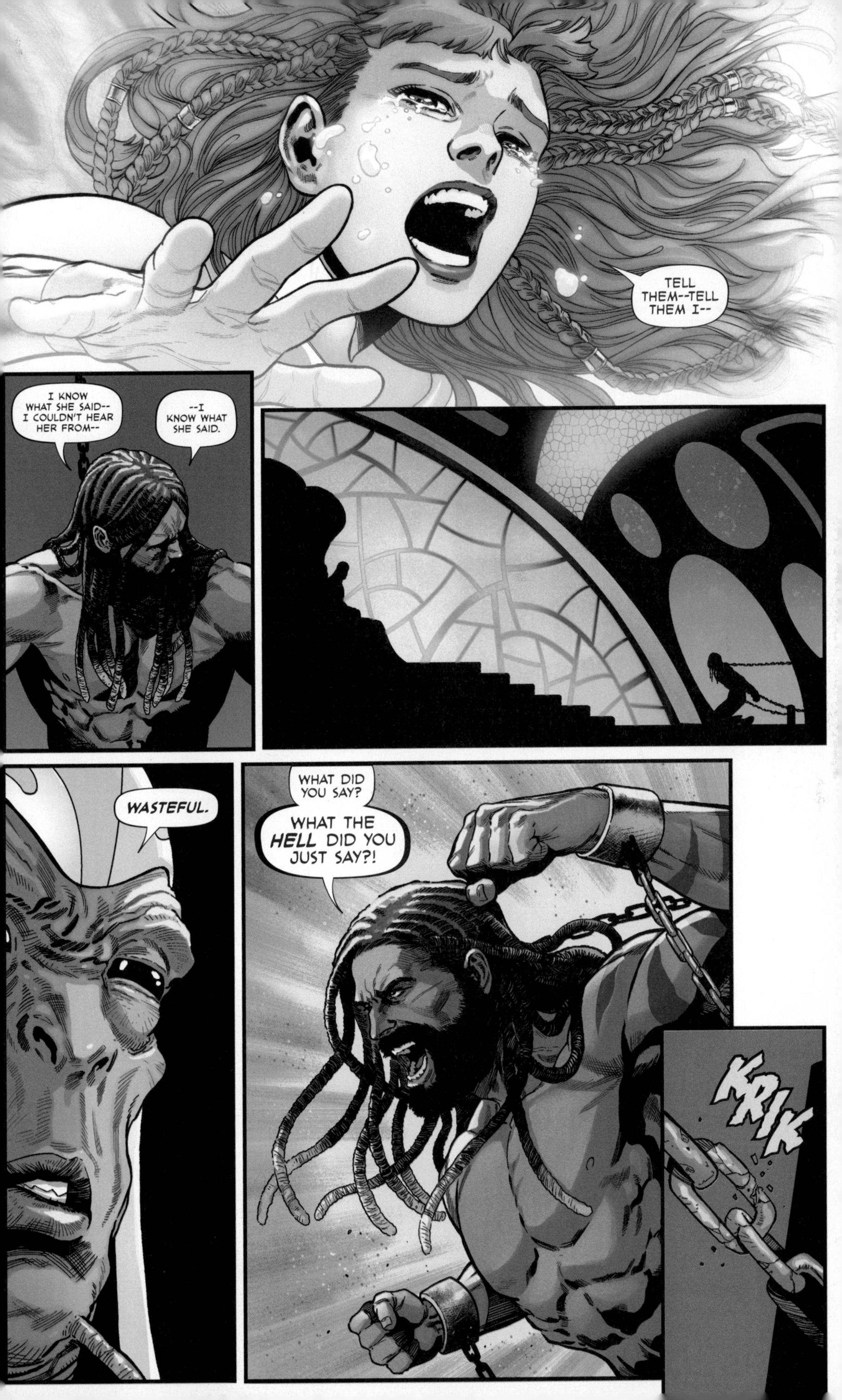
TELL THEM--TELL THEM I--
I KNOW WHAT SHE SAID-- I COULDN'T HEAR HER FROM--
--I KNOW WHAT SHE SAID.
WASTEFUL.
WHAT DID YOU SAY?
WHAT THE HELL DID YOU JUST SAY?!
KRIK

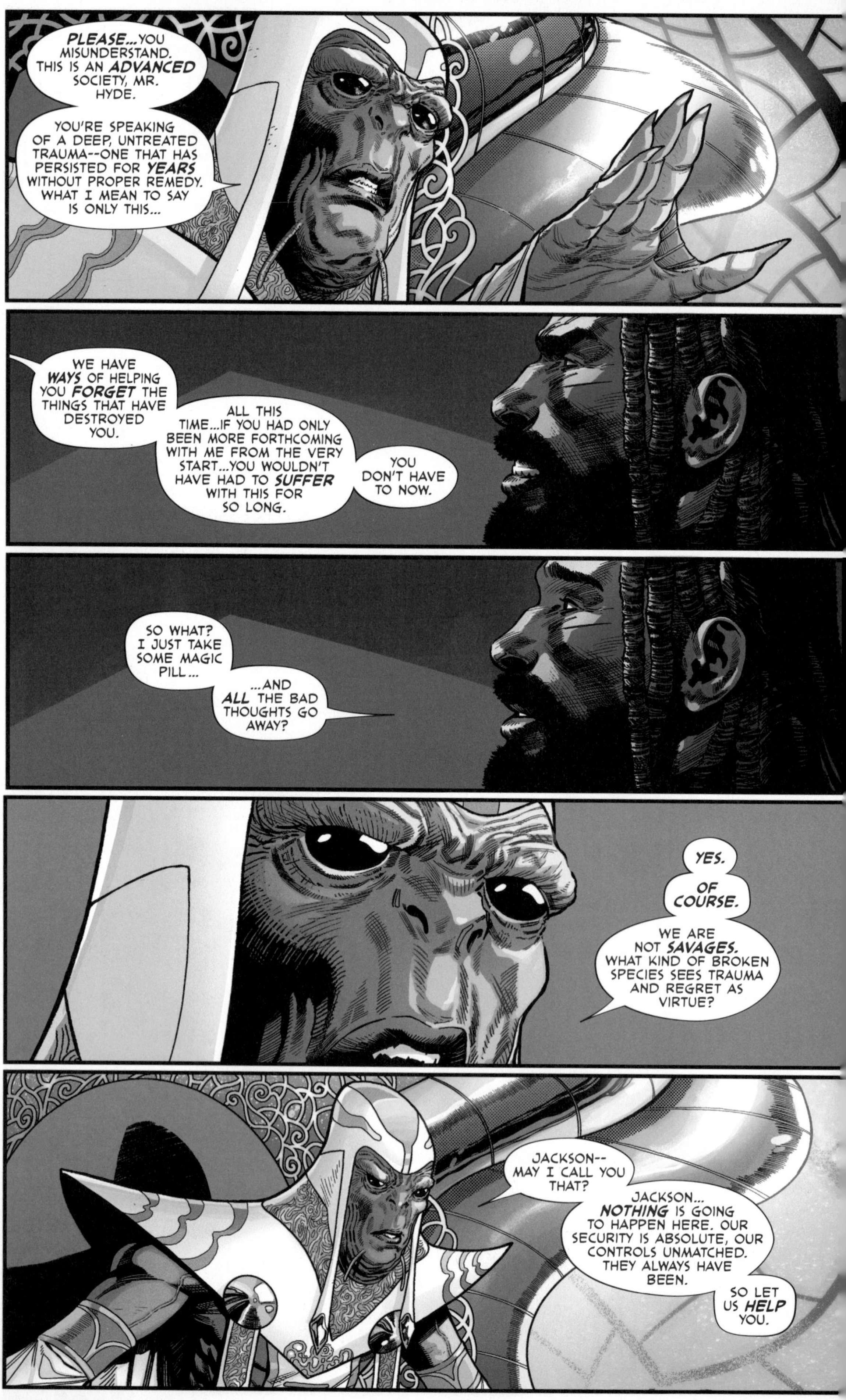
PLEASE...YOU MISUNDERSTAND. THIS IS AN ADVANCED SOCIETY, MR. HYDE.
YOU'RE SPEAKING OF A DEEP, UNTREATED TRAUMA--ONE THAT HAS PERSISTED FOR YEARS WITHOUT PROPER REMEDY. WHAT I MEAN TO SAY IS ONLY THIS...
WE HAVE WAYS OF HELPING YOU FORGET THE THINGS THAT HAVE DESTROYED YOU.
ALL THIS TIME...IF YOU HAD ONLY BEEN MORE FORTHCOMING WITH ME FROM THE VERY START...YOU WOULDN'T HAVE HAD TO SUFFER WITH THIS FOR SO LONG.
YOU DON'T HAVE TO NOW.
SO WHAT? I JUST TAKE SOME MAGIC PILL...
...AND ALL THE BAD THOUGHTS GO AWAY?
YES.
OF COURSE.
WE ARE NOT SAVAGES. WHAT KIND OF BROKEN SPECIES SEES TRAUMA AND REGRET AS VIRTUE?
JACKSON--MAY I CALL YOU THAT?
JACKSON... NOTHING IS GOING TO HAPPEN HERE. OUR SECURITY IS ABSOLUTE, OUR CONTROLS UNMATCHED. THEY ALWAYS HAVE BEEN.
SO LET US HELP YOU.

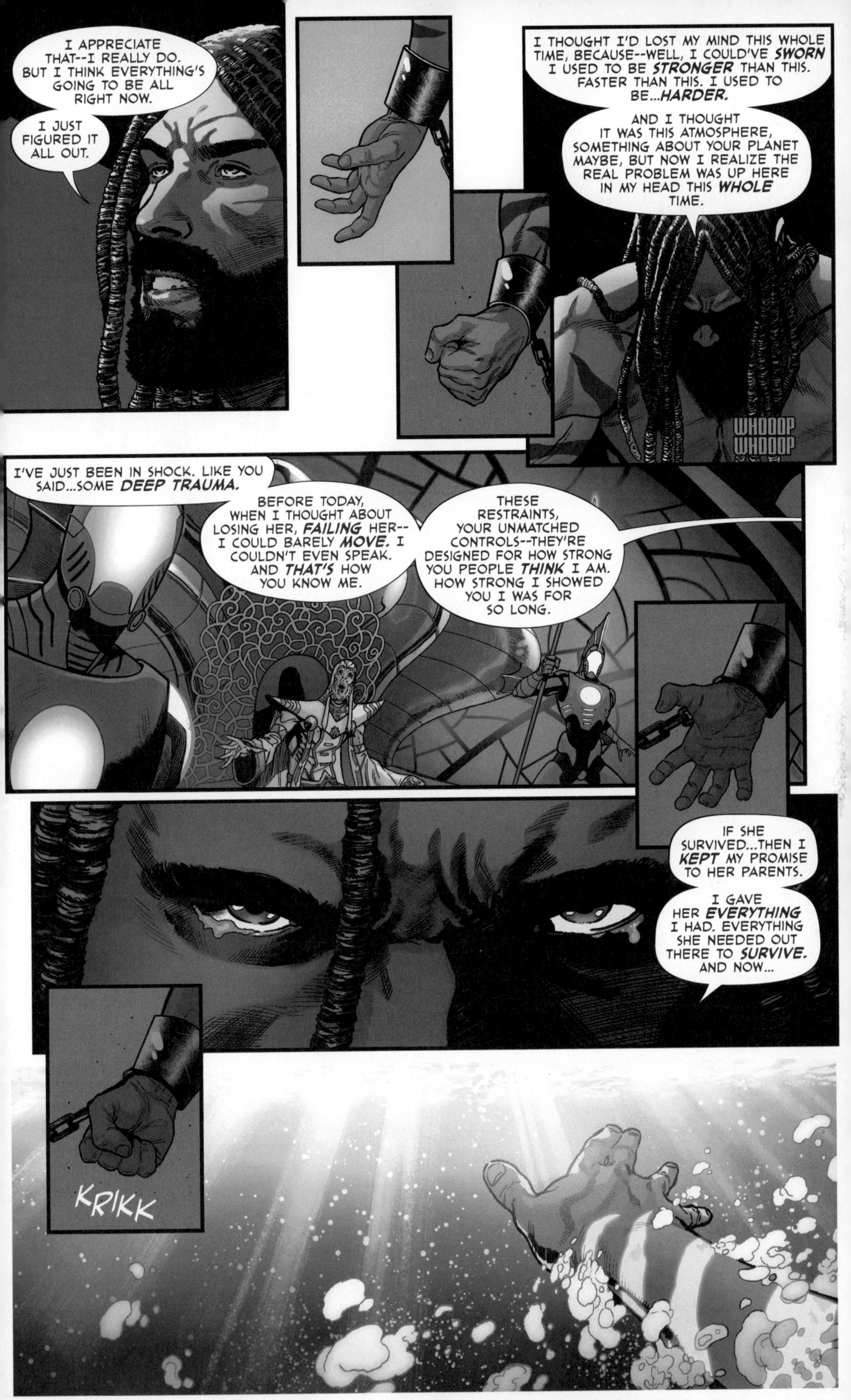

I APPRECIATE THAT--I REALLY DO. BUT I THINK EVERYTHING'S GOING TO BE ALL RIGHT NOW.
I JUST FIGURED IT ALL OUT.
I THOUGHT I'D LOST MY MIND THIS WHOLE TIME, BECAUSE--WELL, I COULD'VE SWORN I USED TO BE STRONGER THAN THIS. FASTER THAN THIS. I USED TO BE...HARDER.
AND I THOUGHT IT WAS THIS ATMOSPHERE, SOMETHING ABOUT YOUR PLANET MAYBE, BUT NOW I REALIZE THE REAL PROBLEM WAS UP HERE IN MY HEAD THIS WHOLE TIME.
WHOOOP WHOOOP
I'VE JUST BEEN IN SHOCK. LIKE YOU SAID...SOME DEEP TRAUMA.
BEFORE TODAY, WHEN I THOUGHT ABOUT LOSING HER, FAILING HER--I COULD BARELY MOVE. I COULDN'T EVEN SPEAK. AND THAT'S HOW YOU KNOW ME.
THESE RESTRAINTS, YOUR UNMATCHED CONTROLS--THEY'RE DESIGNED FOR HOW STRONG YOU PEOPLE THINK I AM. HOW STRONG I SHOWED YOU I WAS FOR SO LONG.
IF SHE SURVIVED...THEN I KEPT MY PROMISE TO HER PARENTS.
I GAVE HER EVERYTHING I HAD. EVERYTHING SHE NEEDED OUT THERE TO SURVIVE. AND NOW...
KRIKK

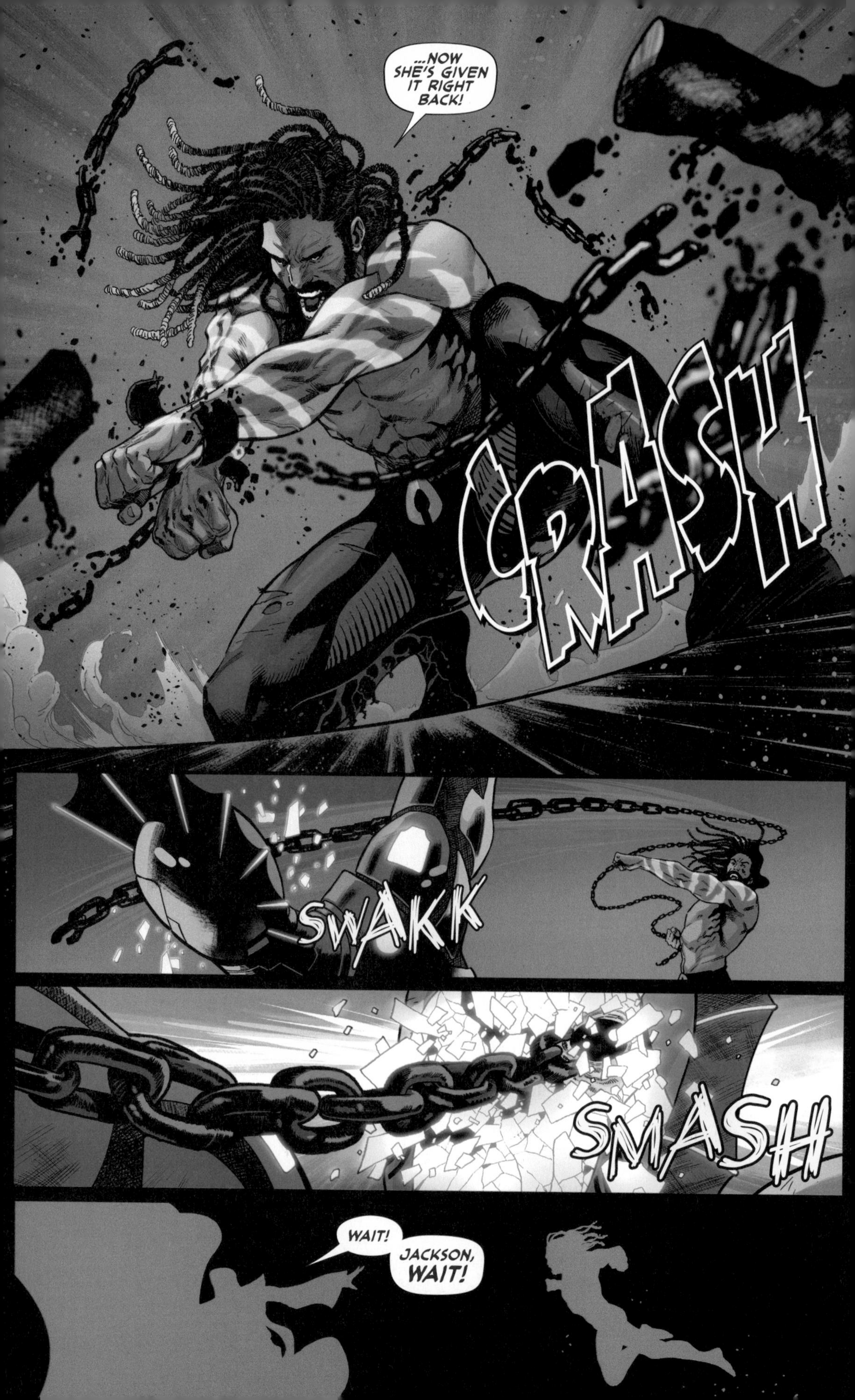
...NOW SHE'S GIVEN IT RIGHT BACK!
CRASH
SWAKK
SMASH
WAIT!
JACKSON, WAIT!

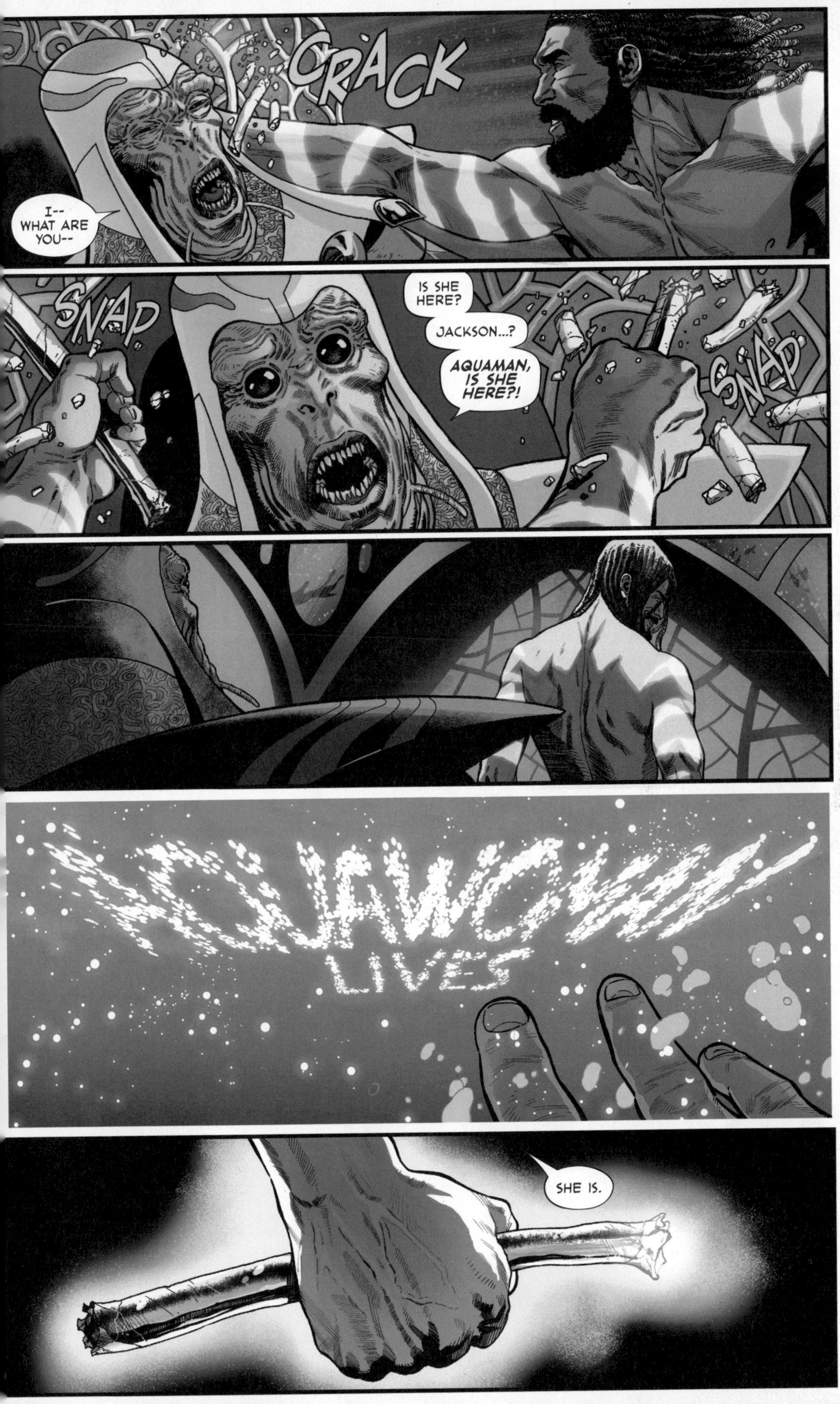
CRACK
I-- WHAT ARE YOU--
SNAP
IS SHE HERE?
JACKSON...?
AQUAMAN, IS SHE HERE?!
SNAP
AQUAMAN LIVES
SHE IS.

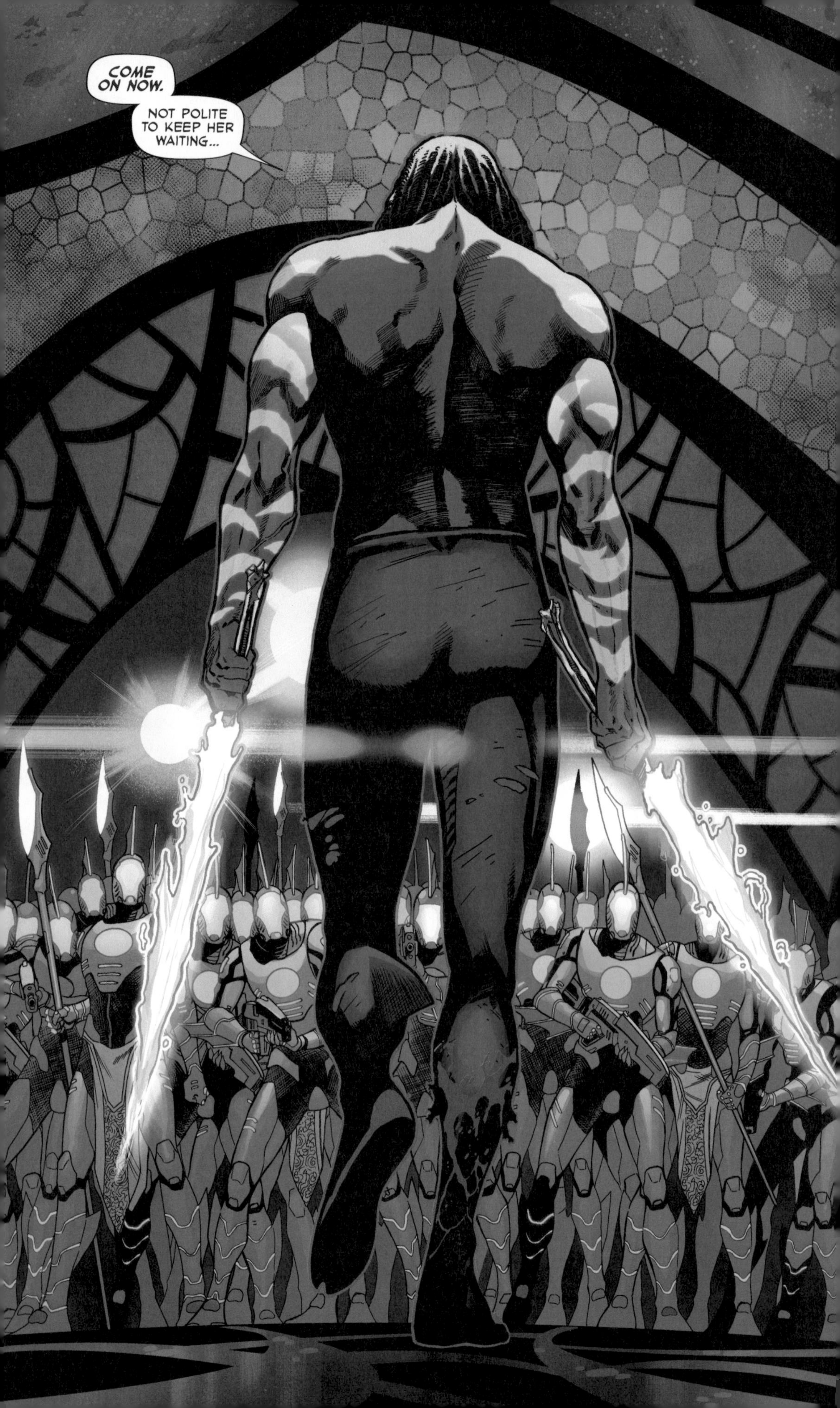
COME ON NOW.
NOT POLITE TO KEEP HER WAITING...

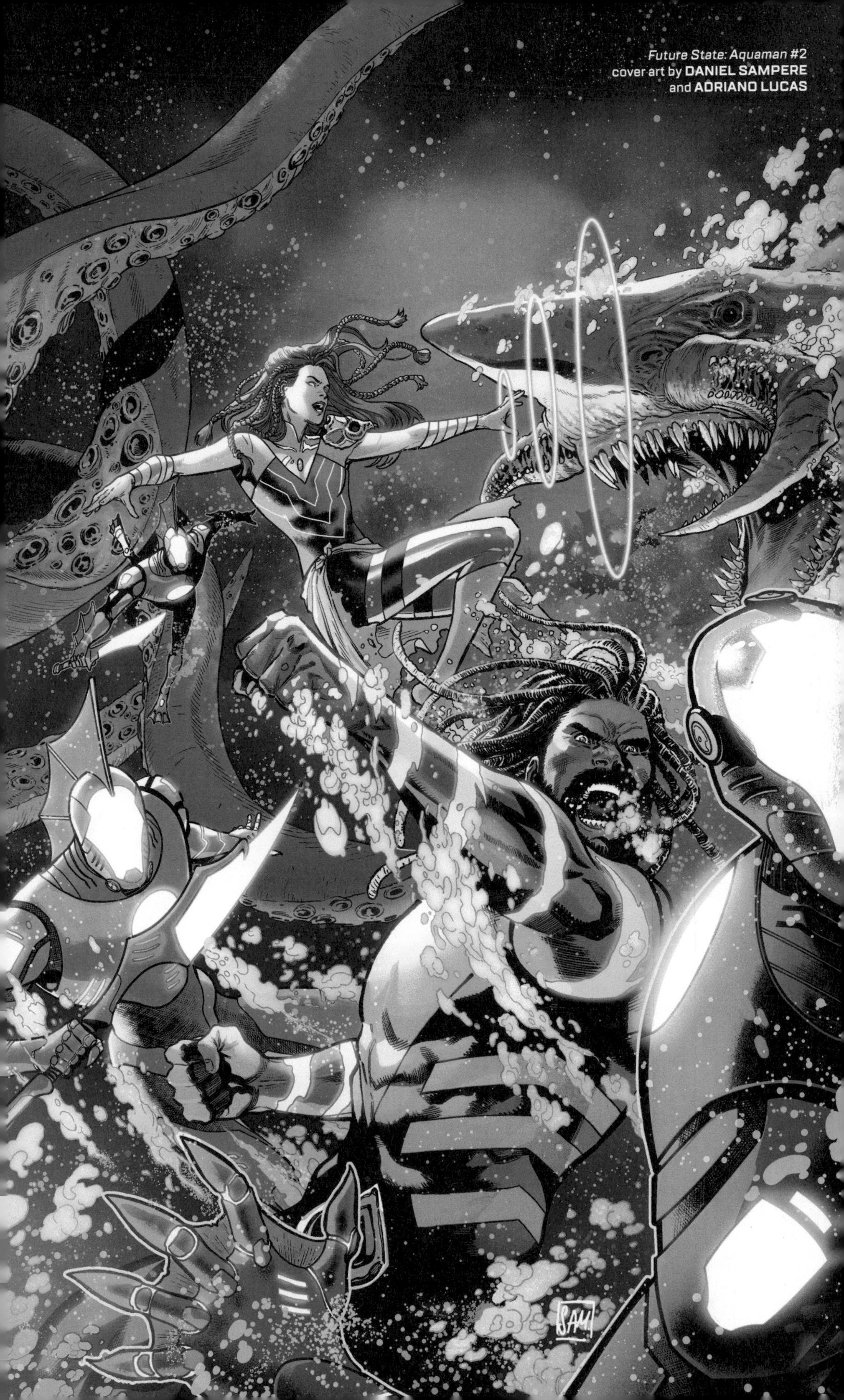

Future State: Aquaman #2
cover art by **DANIEL SAMPERE**
and **ADRIANO LUCAS**

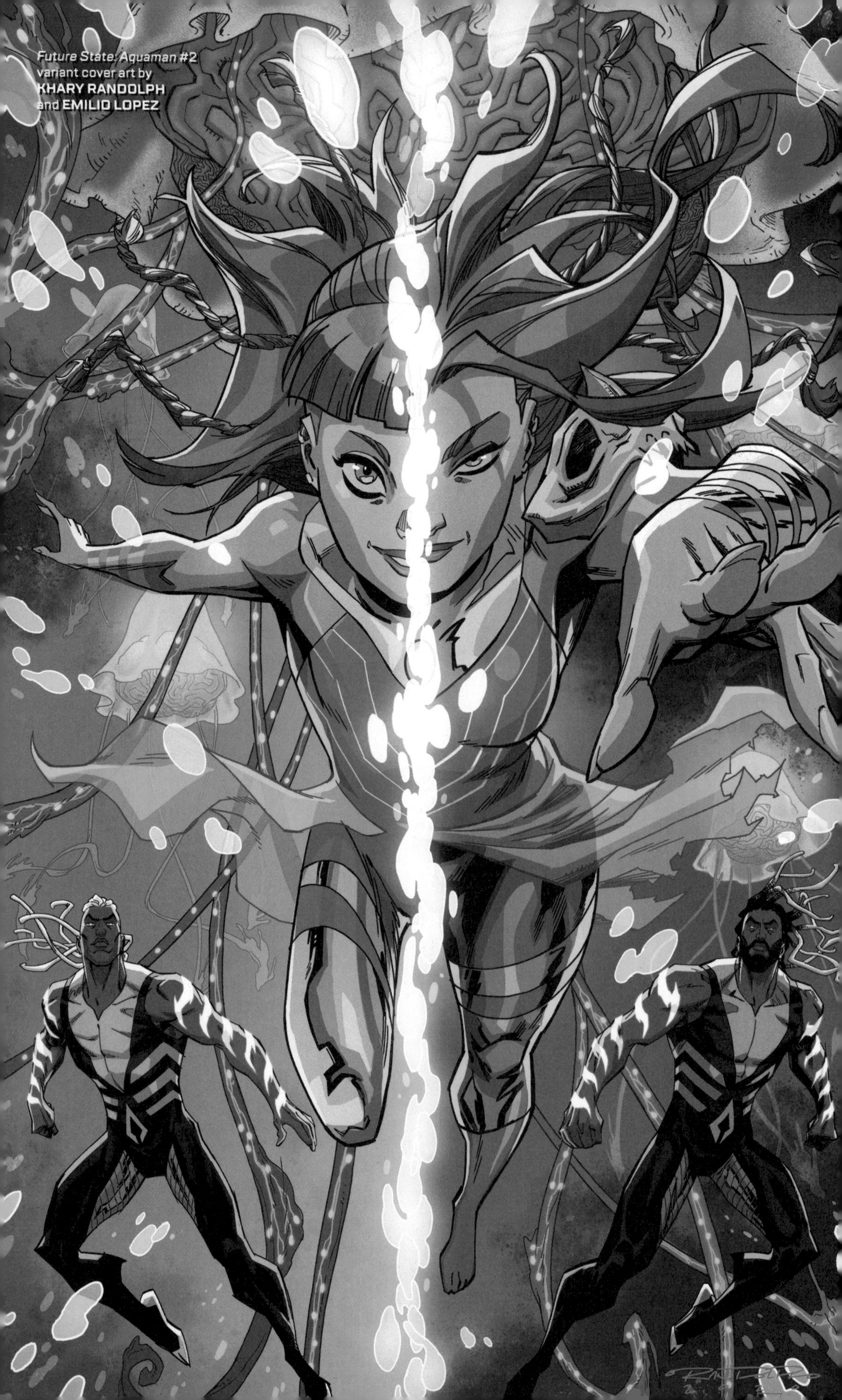

Future State: Aquaman #2 variant cover art by **KHARY RANDOLPH** and **EMILIO LOPEZ**

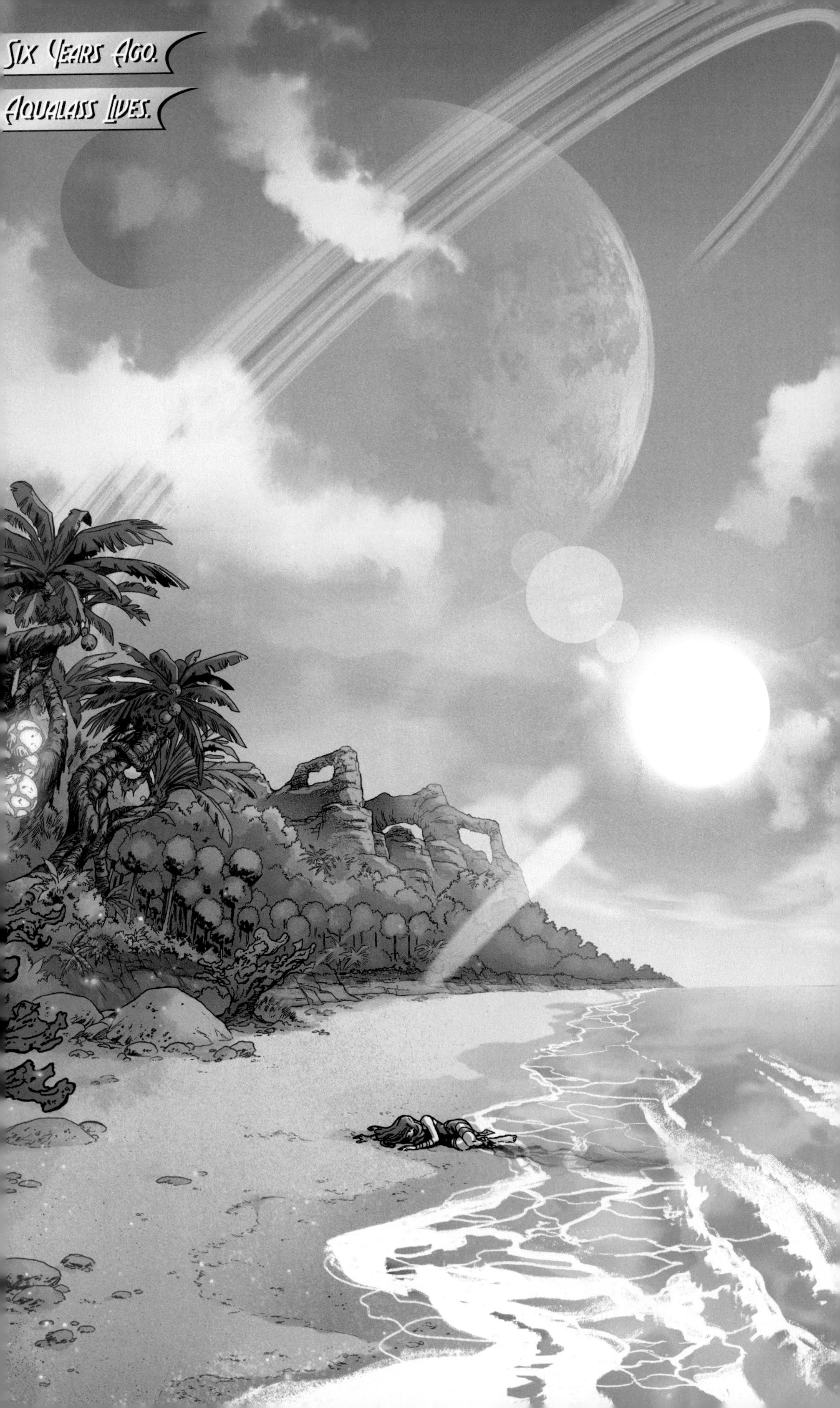
Six Years Ago.
Aqualass Lives.

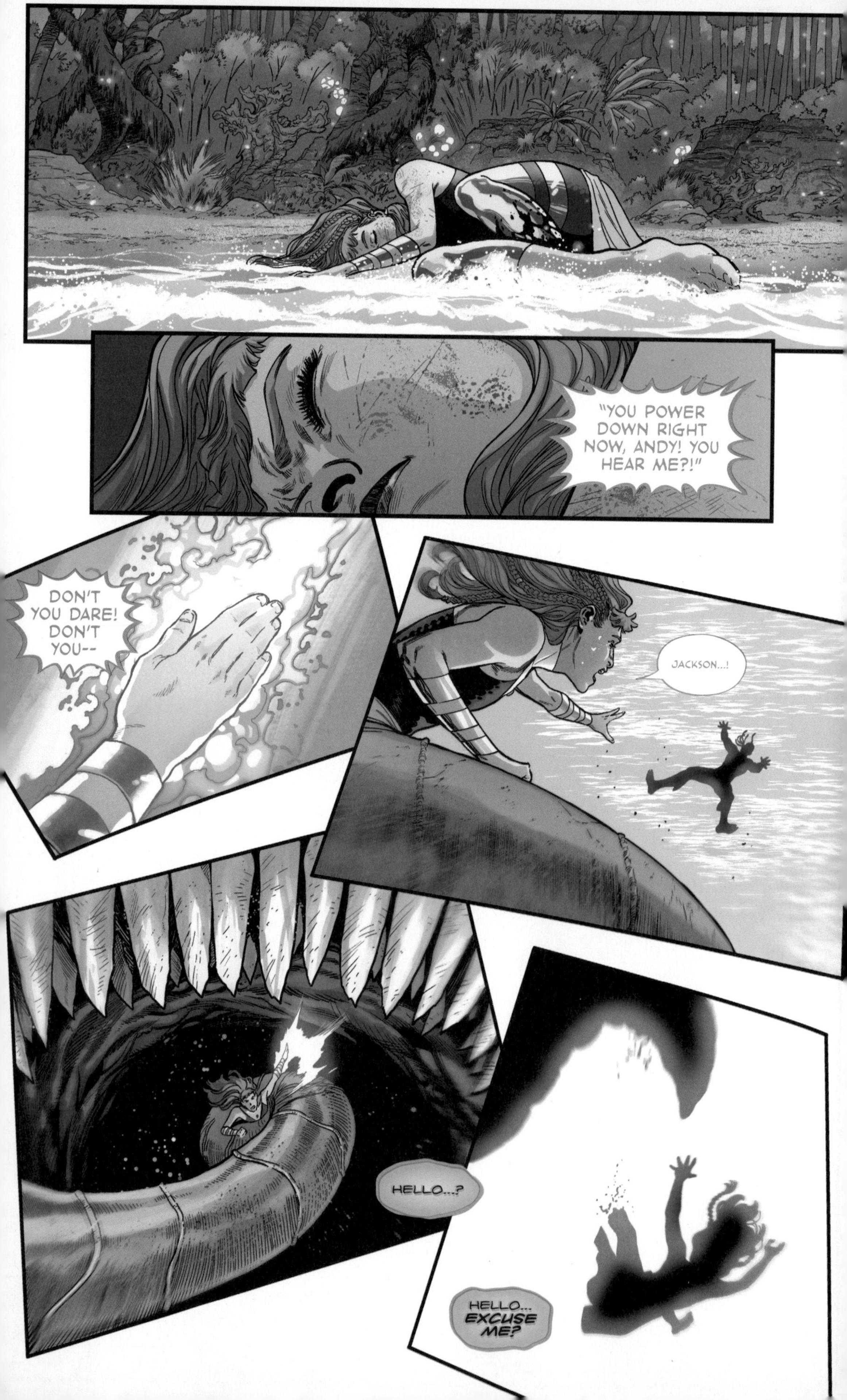
"YOU POWER DOWN RIGHT NOW, ANDY! YOU HEAR ME?!"
DON'T YOU DARE! DON'T YOU--
JACKSON...!
HELLO...?
HELLO... EXCUSE ME?

FUTURE STATE: AQUAMAN

THE CONFLUENCE

PART TWO

BRANDON THOMAS WRITER DANIEL SAMPERE ARTIST
ADRIANO LUCAS COLORIST CLAYTON COWLES LETTERER
SAMPERE & LUCAS COVER ARTISTS
KHARY RANDOLPH & EMILIO LOPEZ VARIANT COVER ARTISTS
ANDREA SHEA EDITOR CHRIS CONROY SENIOR EDITOR
AQUAMAN CREATED BY PAUL NORRIS

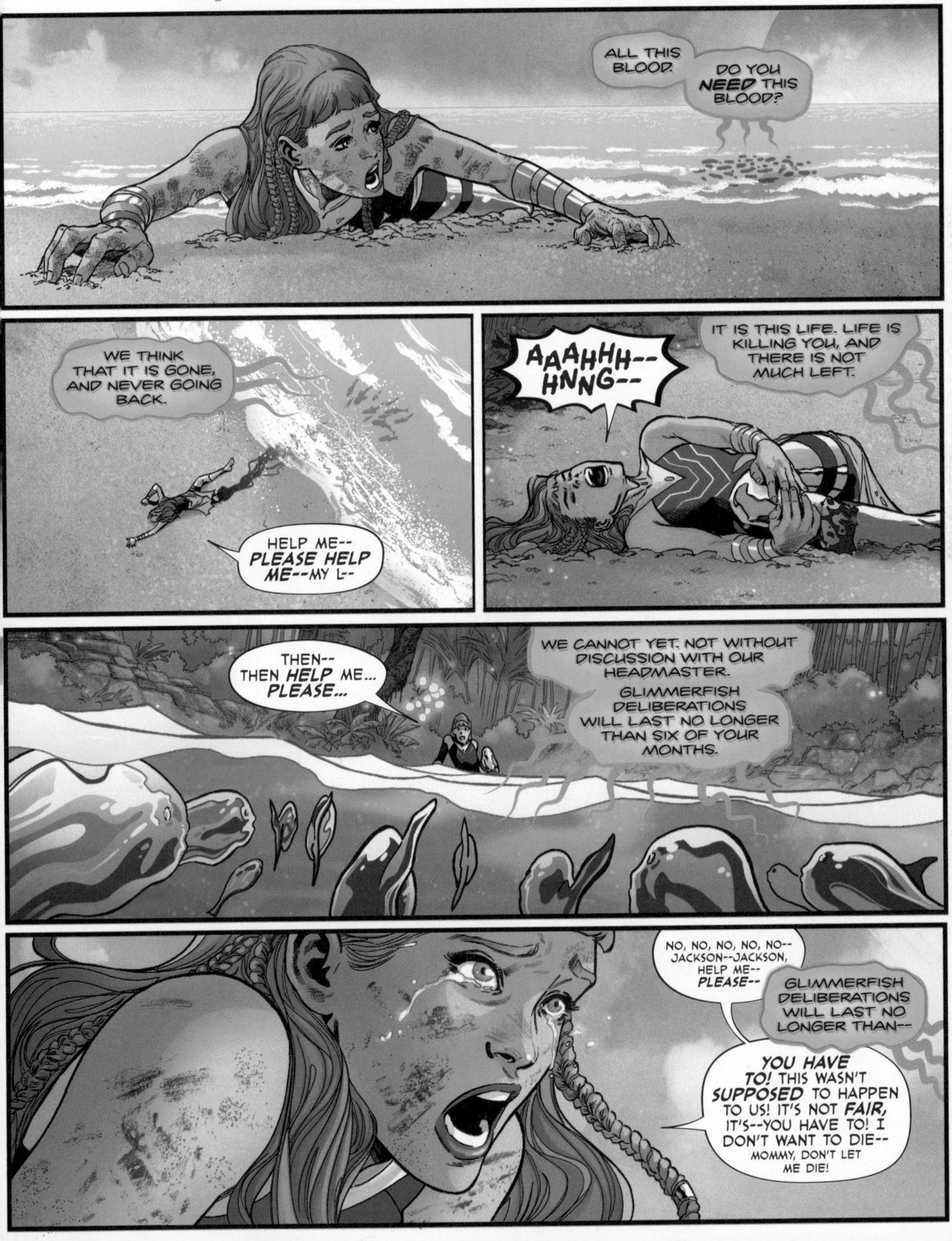
ALL THIS BLOOD.
DO YOU NEED THIS BLOOD?
WE THINK THAT IT IS GONE, AND NEVER GOING BACK.
HELP ME-- PLEASE HELP ME--MY L--
AAAHHH-- HNNG--
IT IS THIS LIFE. LIFE IS KILLING YOU, AND THERE IS NOT MUCH LEFT.
THEN-- THEN HELP ME... PLEASE...
WE CANNOT YET. NOT WITHOUT DISCUSSION WITH OUR HEADMASTER.
GLIMMERFISH DELIBERATIONS WILL LAST NO LONGER THAN SIX OF YOUR MONTHS.
NO, NO, NO, NO, NO-- JACKSON--JACKSON, HELP ME-- PLEASE--
GLIMMERFISH DELIBERATIONS WILL LAST NO LONGER THAN--
YOU HAVE TO! THIS WASN'T SUPPOSED TO HAPPEN TO US! IT'S NOT FAIR, IT'S--YOU HAVE TO! I DON'T WANT TO DIE-- MOMMY, DON'T LET ME DIE!

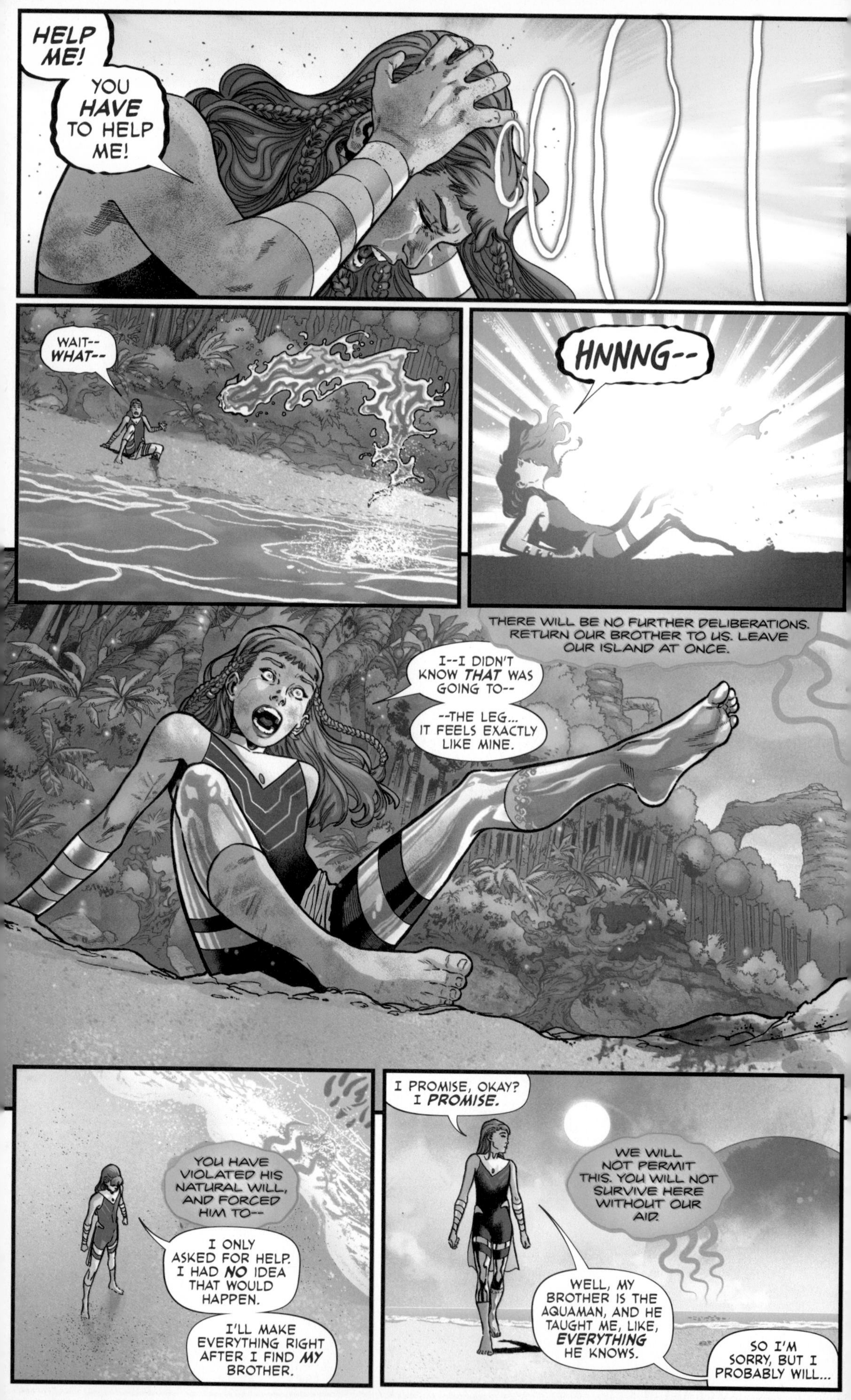
HELP ME!
YOU *HAVE* TO HELP ME!
WAIT-- *WHAT--*
HNNNG--
THERE WILL BE NO FURTHER DELIBERATIONS. RETURN OUR BROTHER TO US. LEAVE OUR ISLAND AT ONCE.
I--I DIDN'T KNOW *THAT* WAS GOING TO--
--THE LEG... IT FEELS EXACTLY LIKE MINE.
YOU HAVE VIOLATED HIS NATURAL WILL, AND FORCED HIM TO--
I ONLY ASKED FOR HELP. I HAD *NO* IDEA THAT WOULD HAPPEN.
I'LL MAKE EVERYTHING RIGHT AFTER I FIND *MY* BROTHER.
I PROMISE, OKAY? I *PROMISE.*
WE WILL NOT PERMIT THIS. YOU WILL NOT SURVIVE HERE WITHOUT OUR AID.
WELL, MY BROTHER IS THE AQUAMAN, AND HE TAUGHT ME, LIKE, *EVERYTHING* HE KNOWS.
SO I'M SORRY, BUT I PROBABLY WILL...

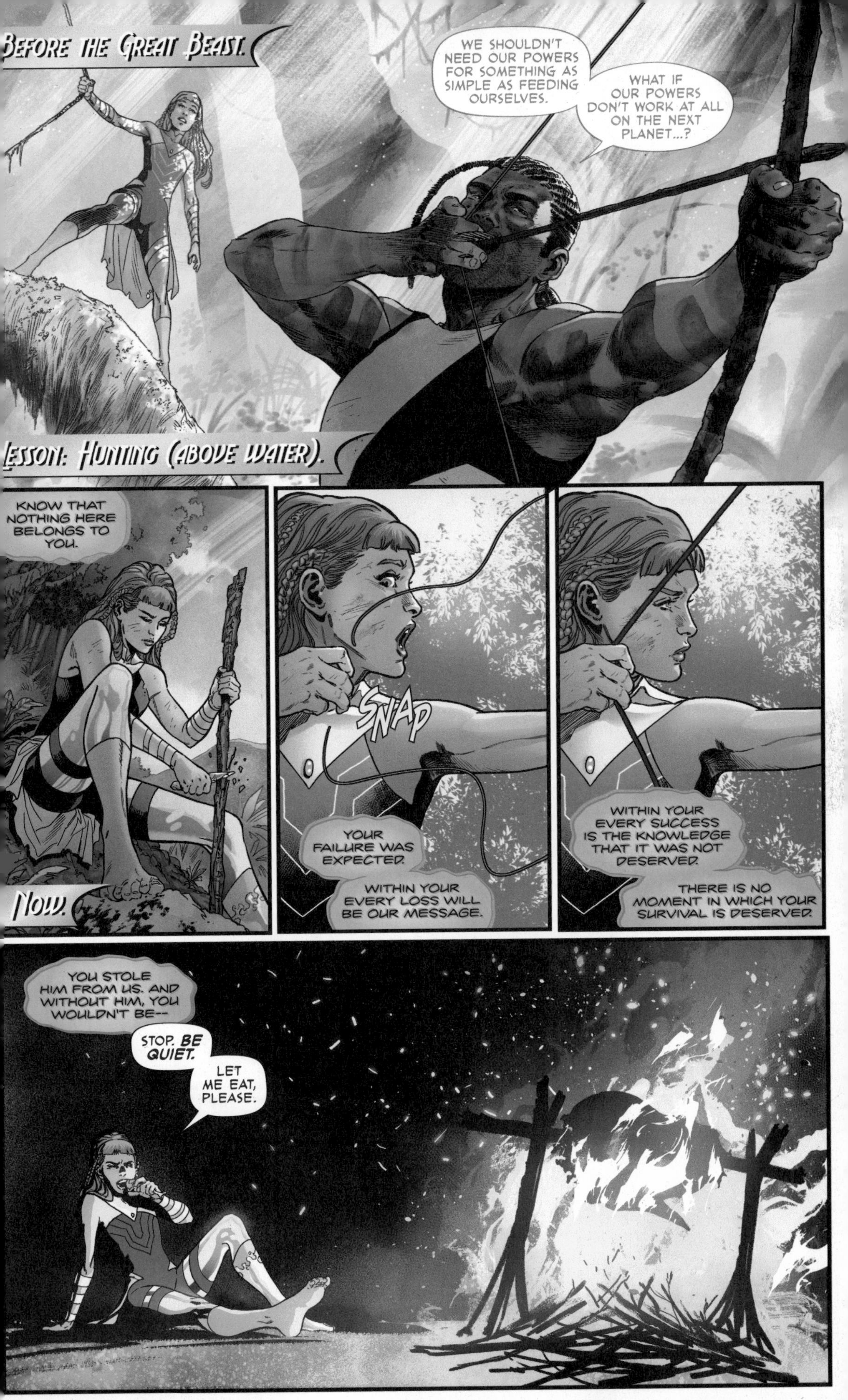

BEFORE THE GREAT BEAST.
WE SHOULDN'T NEED OUR POWERS FOR SOMETHING AS SIMPLE AS FEEDING OURSELVES.
WHAT IF OUR POWERS DON'T WORK AT ALL ON THE NEXT PLANET...?
LESSON: HUNTING (ABOVE WATER).
KNOW THAT NOTHING HERE BELONGS TO YOU.
NOW.
SNAP
YOUR FAILURE WAS EXPECTED.
WITHIN YOUR EVERY LOSS WILL BE OUR MESSAGE.
WITHIN YOUR EVERY SUCCESS IS THE KNOWLEDGE THAT IT WAS NOT DESERVED.
THERE IS NO MOMENT IN WHICH YOUR SURVIVAL IS DESERVED.
YOU STOLE HIM FROM US. AND WITHOUT HIM, YOU WOULDN'T BE--
STOP. BE QUIET.
LET ME EAT, PLEASE.

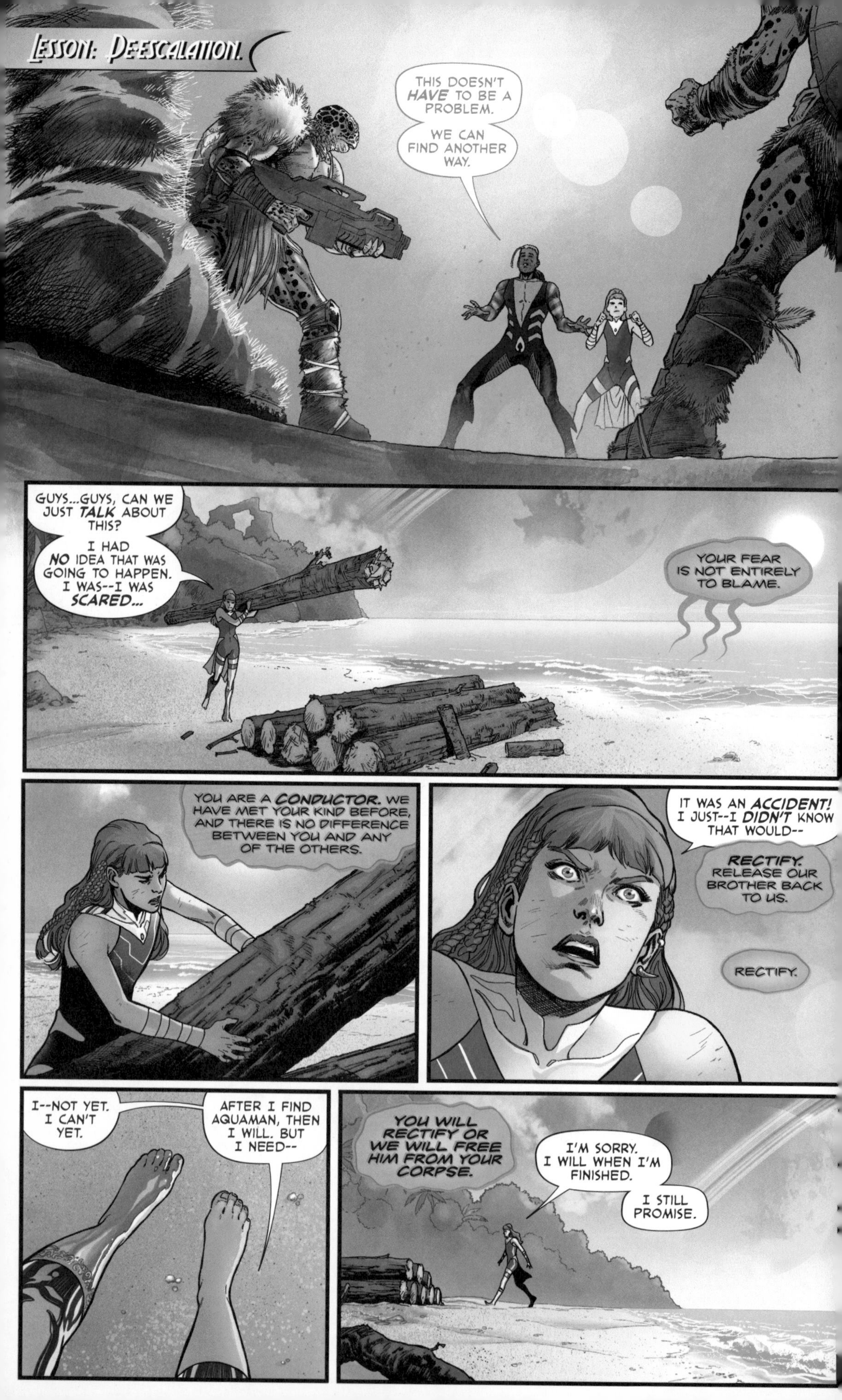
LESSON: DE-ESCALATION.
THIS DOESN'T HAVE TO BE A PROBLEM.
WE CAN FIND ANOTHER WAY.
GUYS...GUYS, CAN WE JUST TALK ABOUT THIS?
I HAD NO IDEA THAT WAS GOING TO HAPPEN. I WAS--I WAS SCARED...
YOUR FEAR IS NOT ENTIRELY TO BLAME.
YOU ARE A CONDUCTOR. WE HAVE MET YOUR KIND BEFORE, AND THERE IS NO DIFFERENCE BETWEEN YOU AND ANY OF THE OTHERS.
IT WAS AN ACCIDENT! I JUST--I DIDN'T KNOW THAT WOULD--
RECTIFY. RELEASE OUR BROTHER BACK TO US.
RECTIFY.
I--NOT YET. I CAN'T YET.
AFTER I FIND AQUAMAN, THEN I WILL. BUT I NEED--
YOU WILL RECTIFY OR WE WILL FREE HIM FROM YOUR CORPSE.
I'M SORRY. I WILL WHEN I'M FINISHED.
I STILL PROMISE.

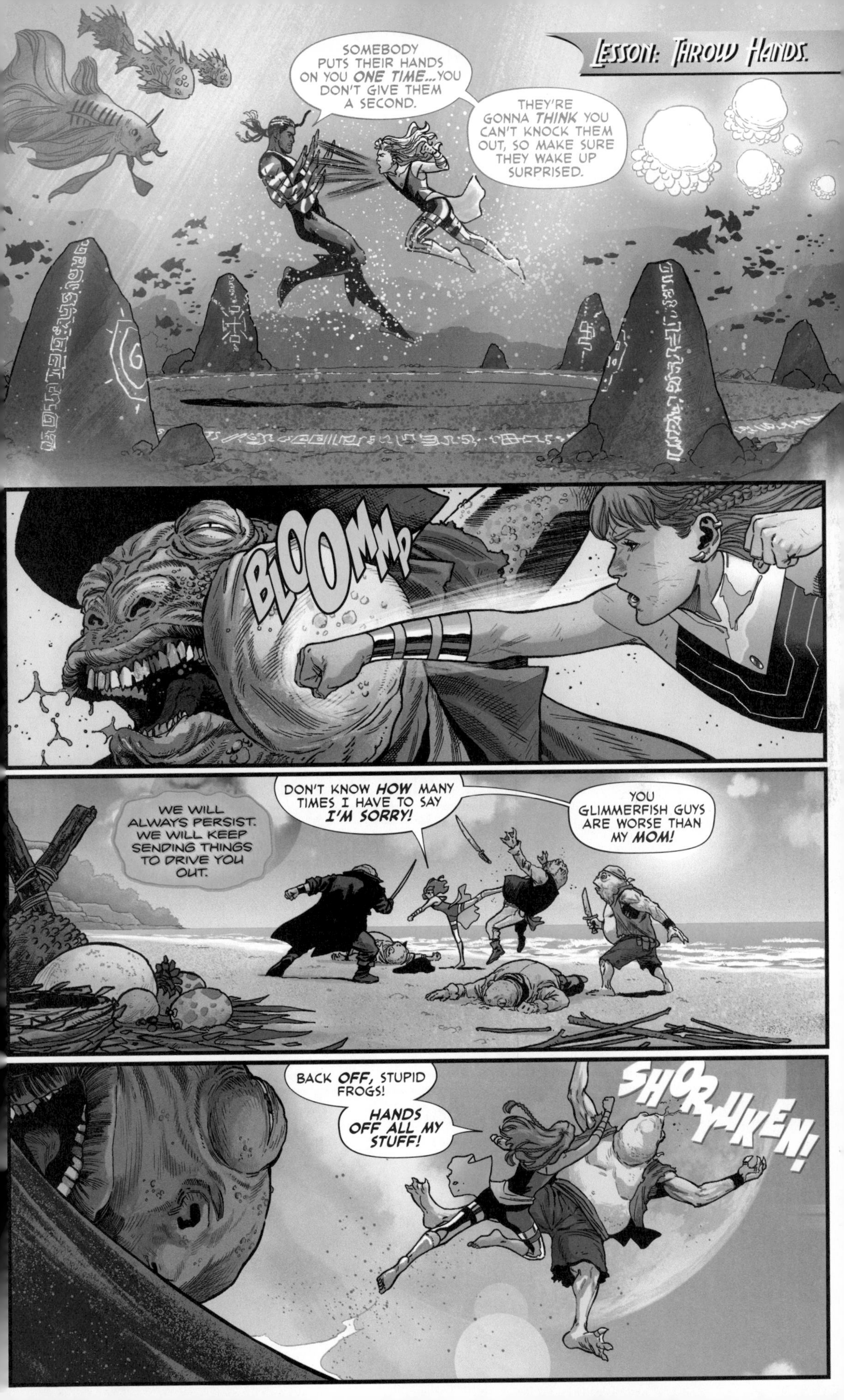
LESSON: THROW HANDS.
SOMEBODY PUTS THEIR HANDS ON YOU ONE TIME... YOU DON'T GIVE THEM A SECOND.
THEY'RE GONNA THINK YOU CAN'T KNOCK THEM OUT, SO MAKE SURE THEY WAKE UP SURPRISED.
BLOOMMP
WE WILL ALWAYS PERSIST. WE WILL KEEP SENDING THINGS TO DRIVE YOU OUT.
DON'T KNOW HOW MANY TIMES I HAVE TO SAY I'M SORRY!
YOU GLIMMERFISH GUYS ARE WORSE THAN MY MOM!
BACK OFF, STUPID FROGS!
HANDS OFF ALL MY STUFF!
SHORYUKEN!

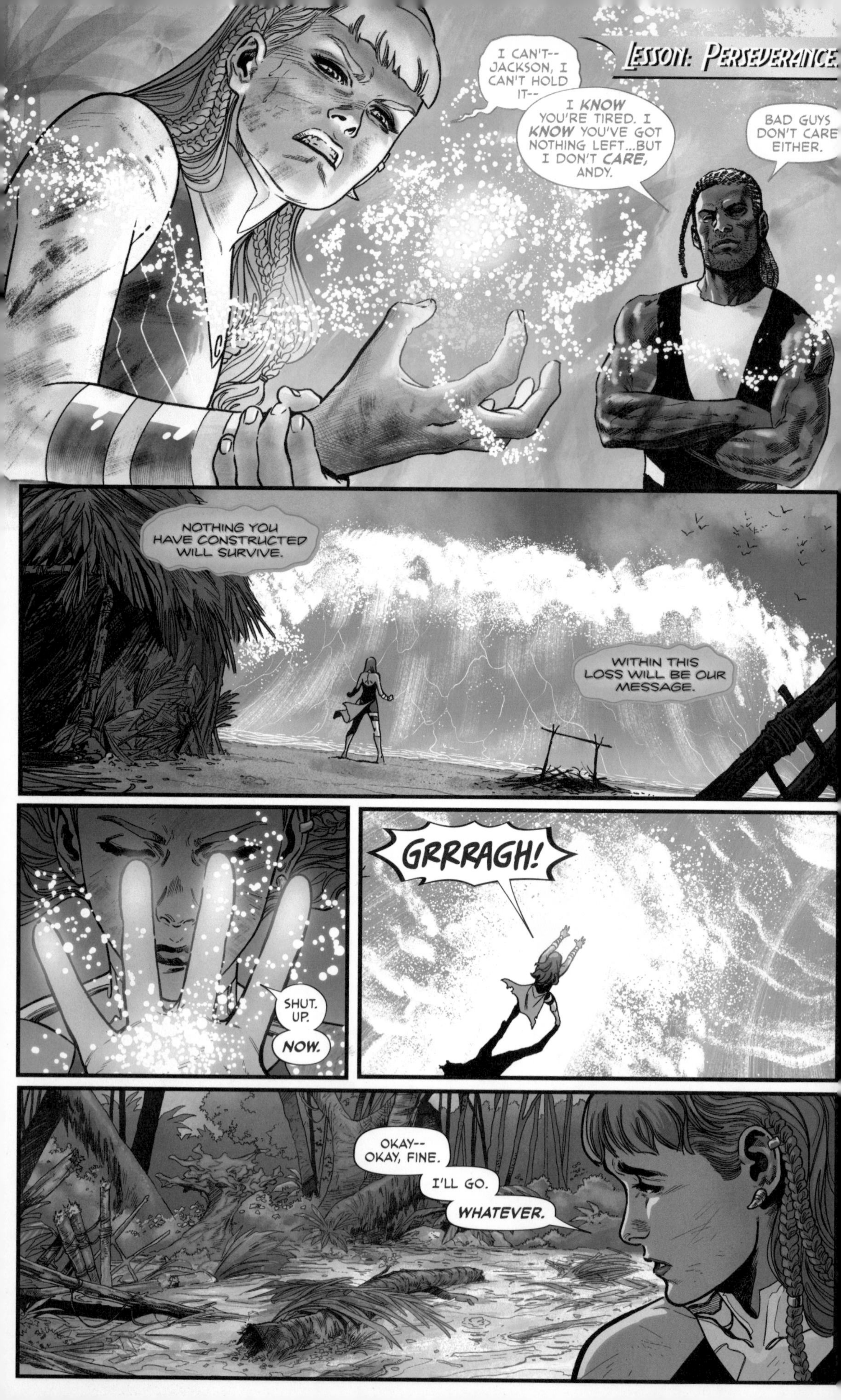
LESSON: PERSEVERANCE.
I CAN'T-- JACKSON, I CAN'T HOLD IT--
I KNOW YOU'RE TIRED. I KNOW YOU'VE GOT NOTHING LEFT...BUT I DON'T CARE, ANDY.
BAD GUYS DON'T CARE EITHER.
NOTHING YOU HAVE CONSTRUCTED WILL SURVIVE.
WITHIN THIS LOSS WILL BE OUR MESSAGE.
SHUT. UP.
NOW.
GRRRAGH!
OKAY-- OKAY, FINE.
I'LL GO.
WHATEVER.

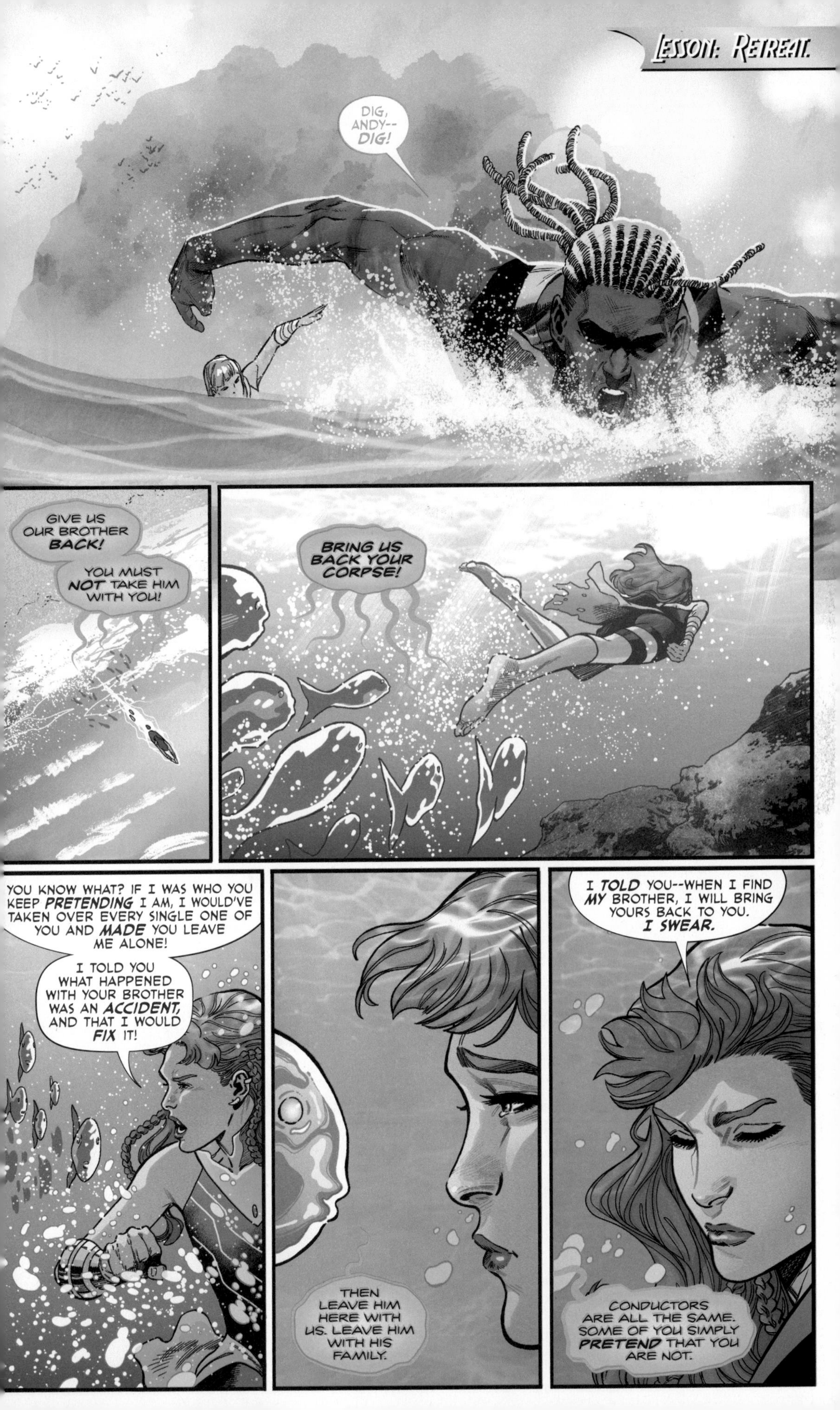
LESSON: RETREAT.
DIG, ANDY-- DIG!
GIVE US OUR BROTHER BACK!
YOU MUST NOT TAKE HIM WITH YOU!
BRING US BACK YOUR CORPSE!
YOU KNOW WHAT? IF I WAS WHO YOU KEEP PRETENDING I AM, I WOULD'VE TAKEN OVER EVERY SINGLE ONE OF YOU AND MADE YOU LEAVE ME ALONE!
I TOLD YOU WHAT HAPPENED WITH YOUR BROTHER WAS AN ACCIDENT, AND THAT I WOULD FIX IT!
THEN LEAVE HIM HERE WITH US. LEAVE HIM WITH HIS FAMILY.
I TOLD YOU--WHEN I FIND MY BROTHER, I WILL BRING YOURS BACK TO YOU. I SWEAR.
CONDUCTORS ARE ALL THE SAME. SOME OF YOU SIMPLY PRETEND THAT YOU ARE NOT.

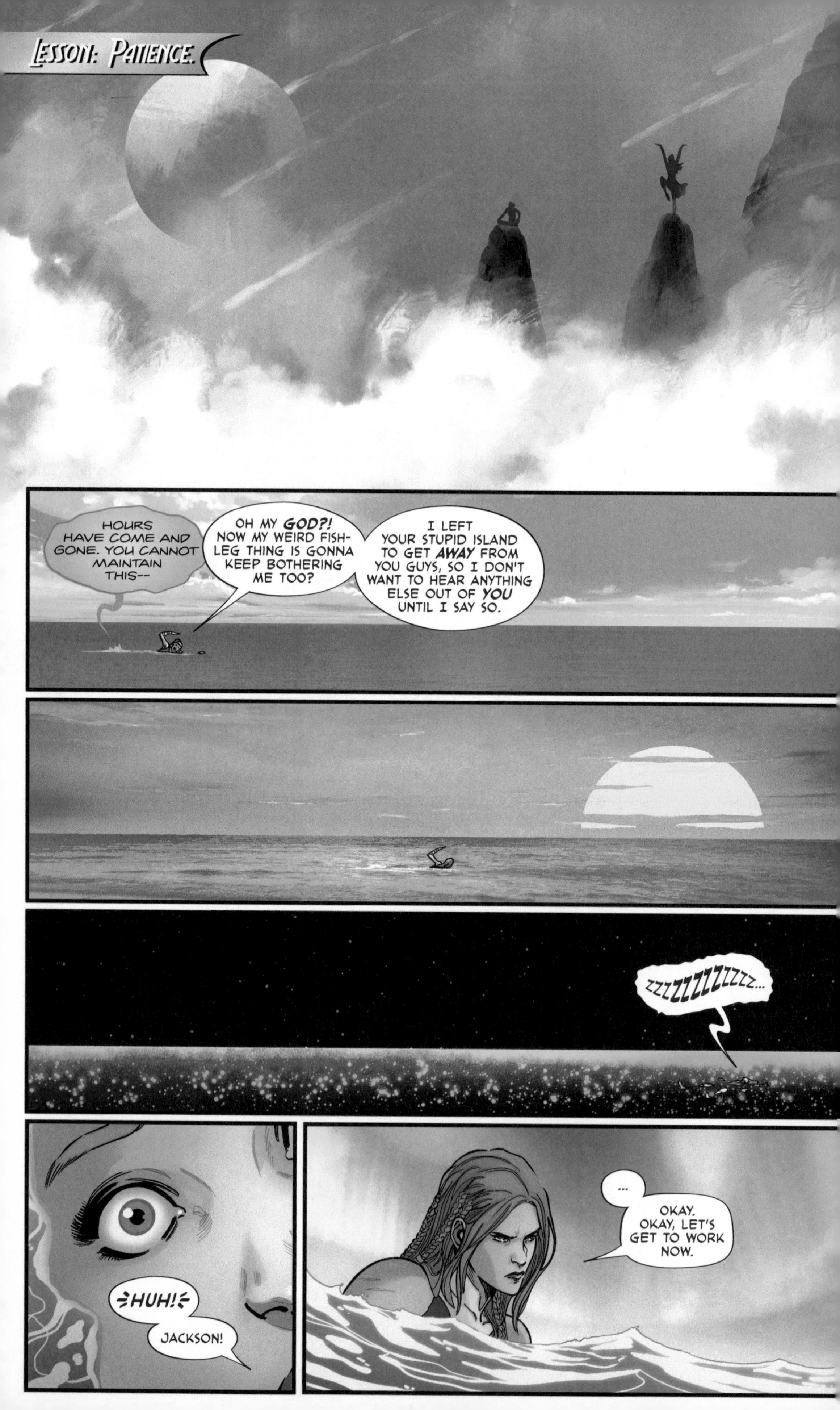
LESSON: PATIENCE.
HOURS HAVE COME AND GONE. YOU CANNOT MAINTAIN THIS--
OH MY GOD?! NOW MY WEIRD FISH-LEG THING IS GONNA KEEP BOTHERING ME TOO?
I LEFT YOUR STUPID ISLAND TO GET AWAY FROM YOU GUYS, SO I DON'T WANT TO HEAR ANYTHING ELSE OUT OF YOU UNTIL I SAY SO.
ZZZZZZZZZZZZ...
HUH!
JACKSON!
...
OKAY. OKAY, LET'S GET TO WORK NOW.

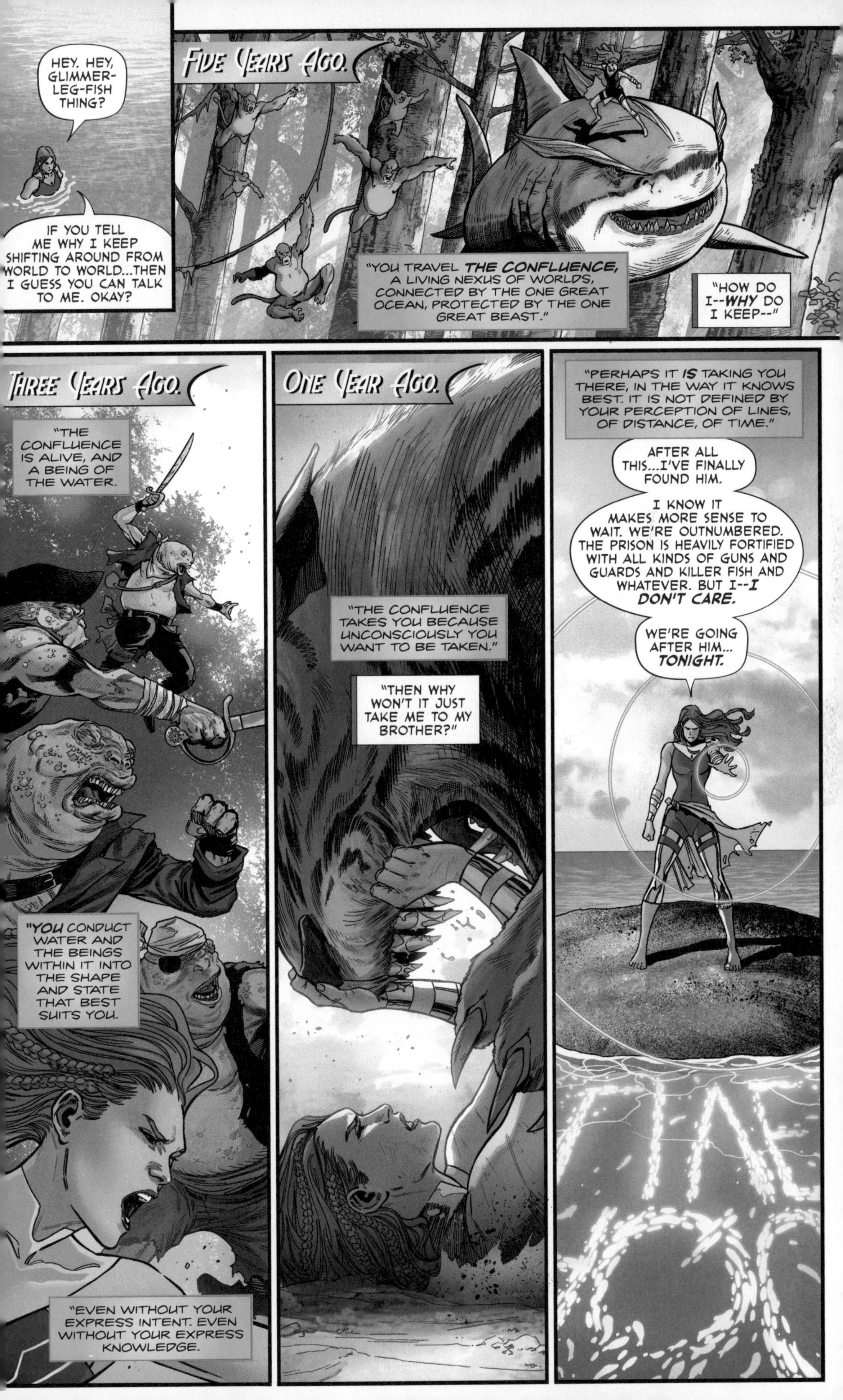
HEY. HEY, GLIMMER-LEG-FISH THING?
IF YOU TELL ME WHY I KEEP SHIFTING AROUND FROM WORLD TO WORLD...THEN I GUESS YOU CAN TALK TO ME. OKAY?
FIVE YEARS AGO.
"YOU TRAVEL THE CONFLUENCE, A LIVING NEXUS OF WORLDS, CONNECTED BY THE ONE GREAT OCEAN, PROTECTED BY THE ONE GREAT BEAST."
"HOW DO I--WHY DO I KEEP--"
THREE YEARS AGO.
"THE CONFLUENCE IS ALIVE, AND A BEING OF THE WATER.
"YOU CONDUCT WATER AND THE BEINGS WITHIN IT INTO THE SHAPE AND STATE THAT BEST SUITS YOU.
"EVEN WITHOUT YOUR EXPRESS INTENT. EVEN WITHOUT YOUR EXPRESS KNOWLEDGE.
ONE YEAR AGO.
"THE CONFLUENCE TAKES YOU BECAUSE UNCONSCIOUSLY YOU WANT TO BE TAKEN."
"THEN WHY WON'T IT JUST TAKE ME TO MY BROTHER?"
"PERHAPS IT IS TAKING YOU THERE, IN THE WAY IT KNOWS BEST. IT IS NOT DEFINED BY YOUR PERCEPTION OF LINES, OF DISTANCE, OF TIME."
AFTER ALL THIS...I'VE FINALLY FOUND HIM.
I KNOW IT MAKES MORE SENSE TO WAIT. WE'RE OUTNUMBERED. THE PRISON IS HEAVILY FORTIFIED WITH ALL KINDS OF GUNS AND GUARDS AND KILLER FISH AND WHATEVER. BUT I--I DON'T CARE.
WE'RE GOING AFTER HIM... TONIGHT.

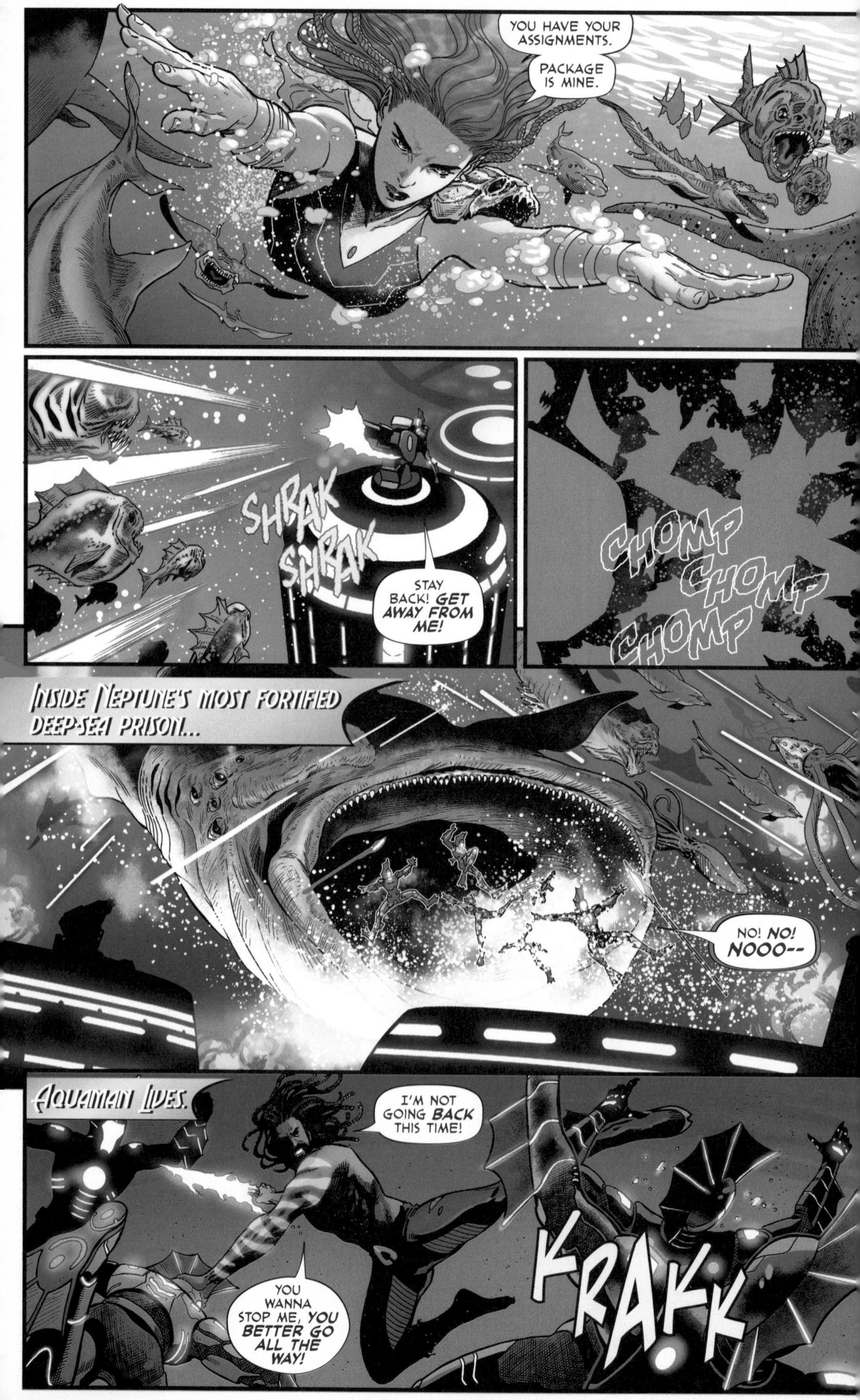
YOU HAVE YOUR ASSIGNMENTS.
PACKAGE IS MINE.
SHRAK
SHRAK
STAY BACK! GET AWAY FROM ME!
CHOMP
CHOMP
CHOMP
INSIDE NEPTUNE'S MOST FORTIFIED DEEP-SEA PRISON...
NO! NO! NOOO--
AQUAMAN LIVES.
I'M NOT GOING BACK THIS TIME!
YOU WANNA STOP ME, YOU BETTER GO ALL THE WAY!
KRAKK

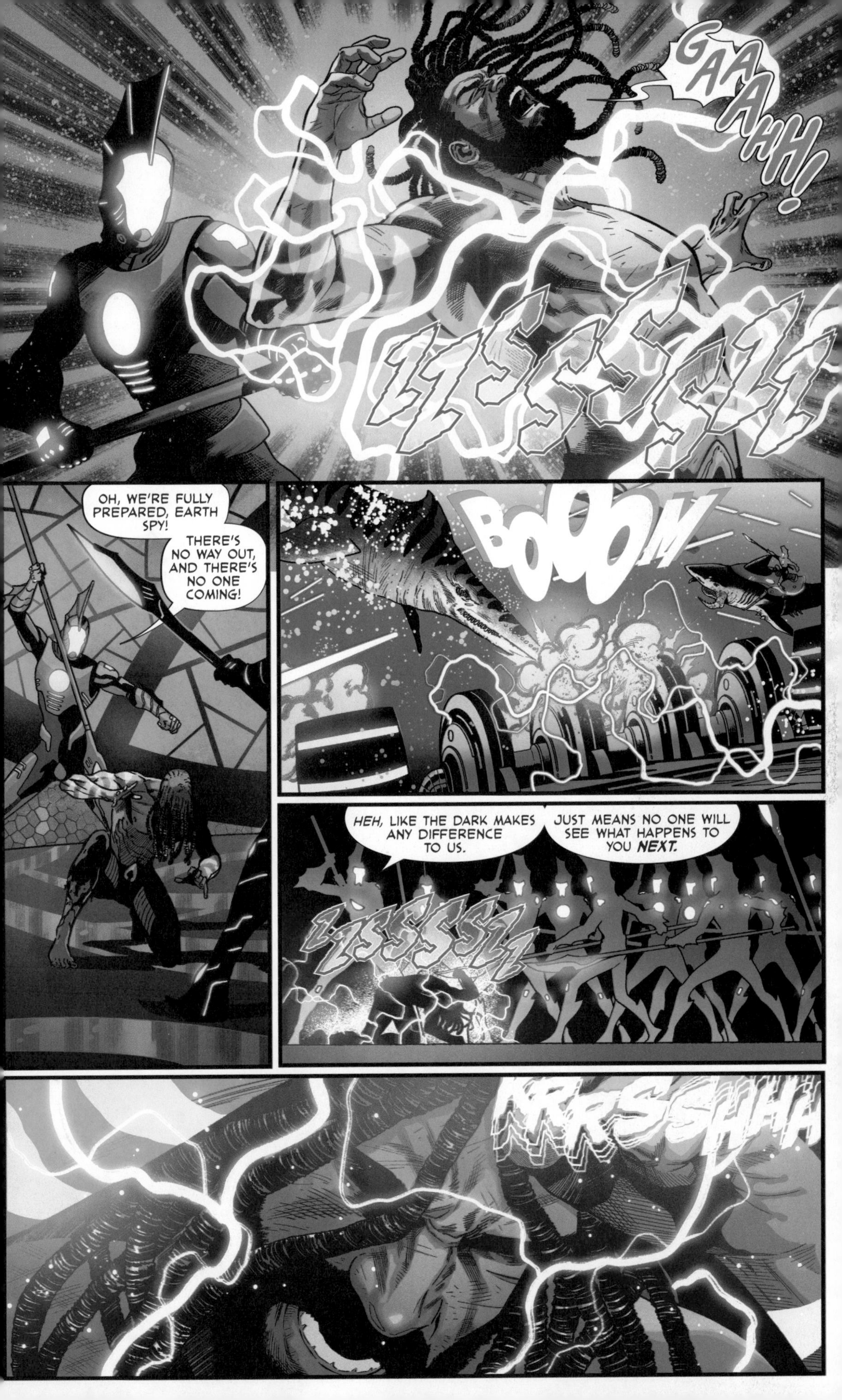

GAAAHH!
ZZZSSSHH
OH, WE'RE FULLY PREPARED, EARTH SPY!
THERE'S NO WAY OUT, AND THERE'S NO ONE COMING!
BOOOM
HEH, LIKE THE DARK MAKES ANY DIFFERENCE TO US.
JUST MEANS NO ONE WILL SEE WHAT HAPPENS TO YOU NEXT.
KRRSSHHH

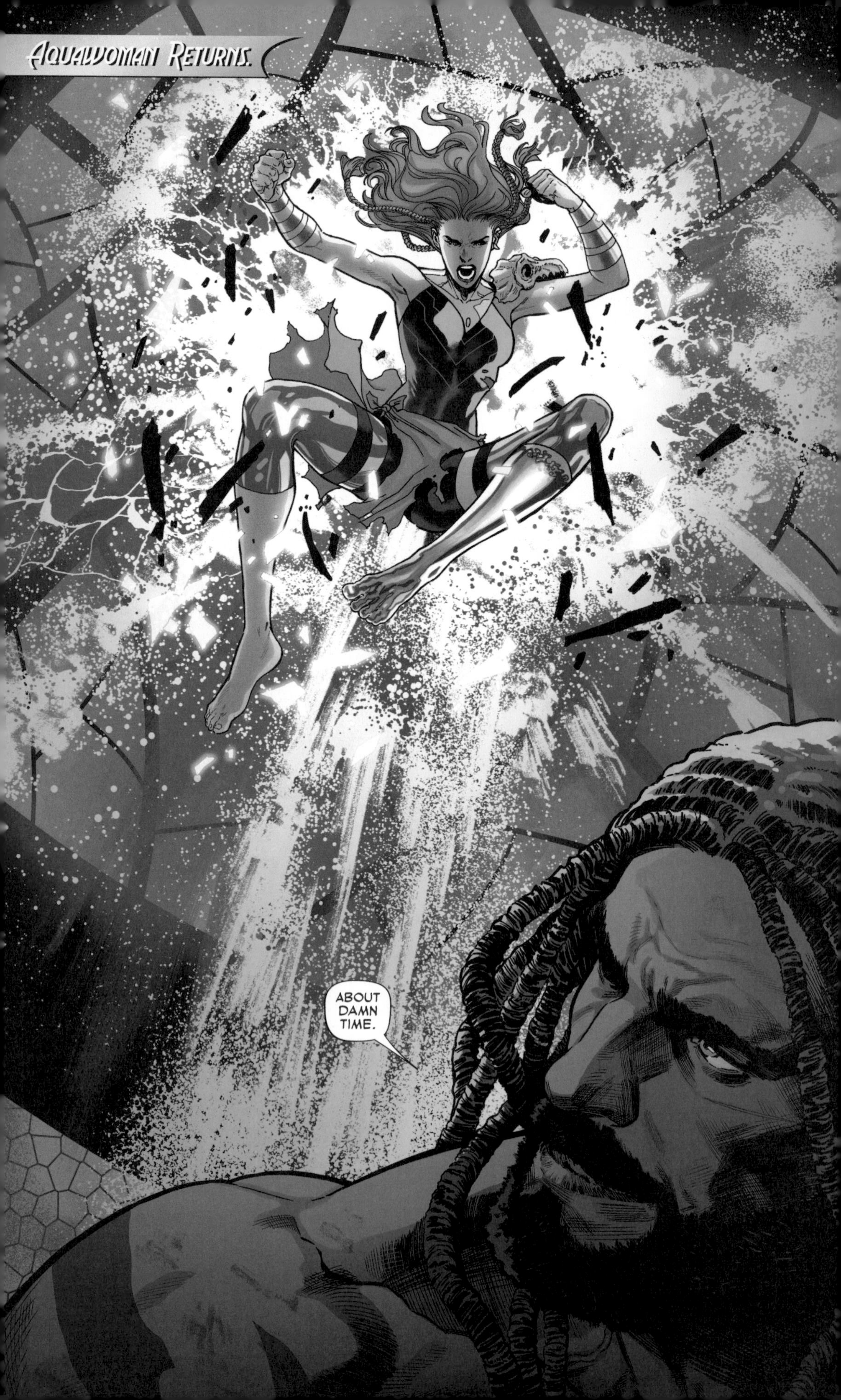

AQUAWOMAN RETURNS.
ABOUT DAMN TIME.

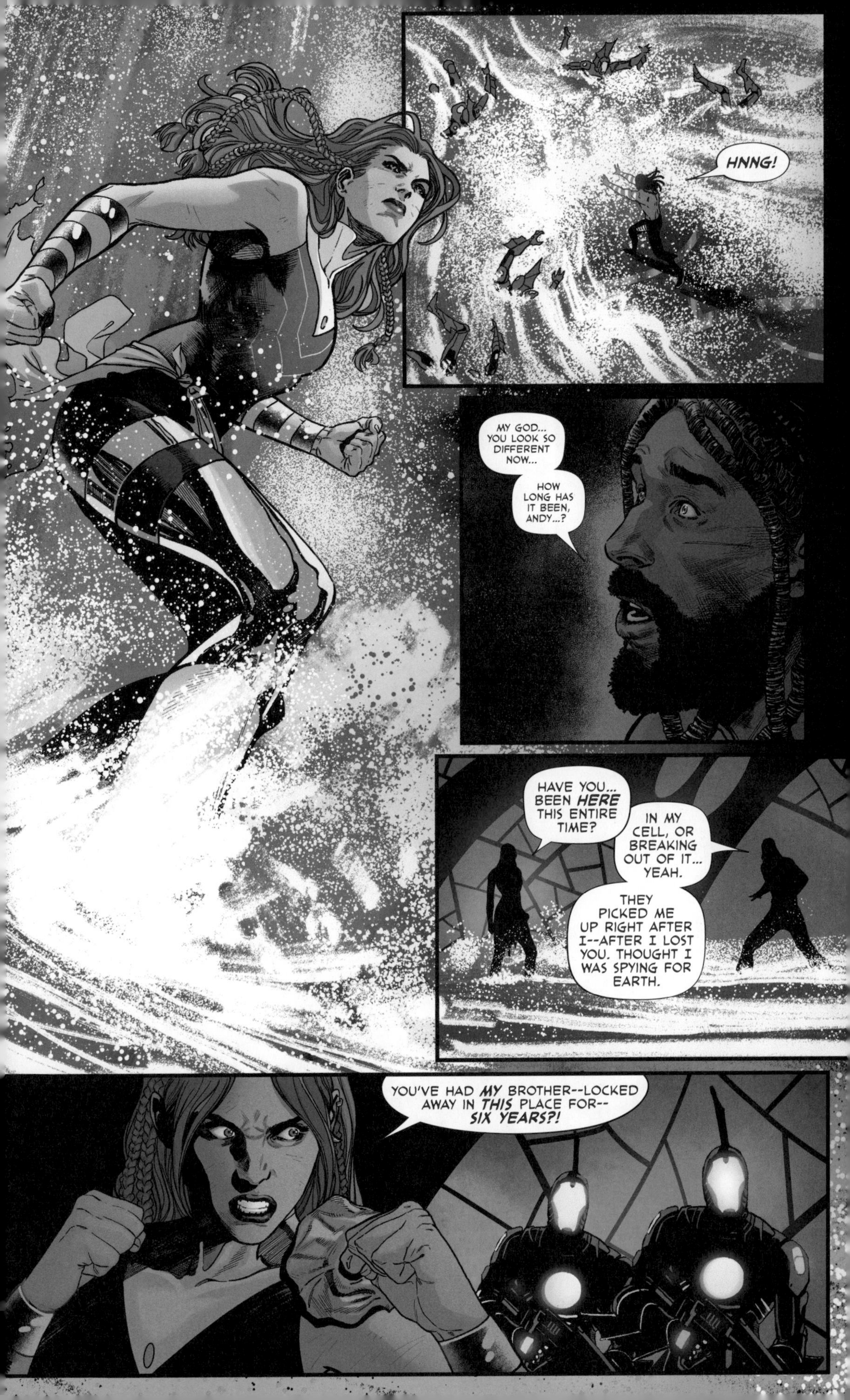
HNNG!
MY GOD... YOU LOOK SO DIFFERENT NOW...
HOW LONG HAS IT BEEN, ANDY...?
HAVE YOU... BEEN HERE THIS ENTIRE TIME?
IN MY CELL, OR BREAKING OUT OF IT... YEAH.
THEY PICKED ME UP RIGHT AFTER I--AFTER I LOST YOU. THOUGHT I WAS SPYING FOR EARTH.
YOU'VE HAD MY BROTHER--LOCKED AWAY IN THIS PLACE FOR-- SIX YEARS?!

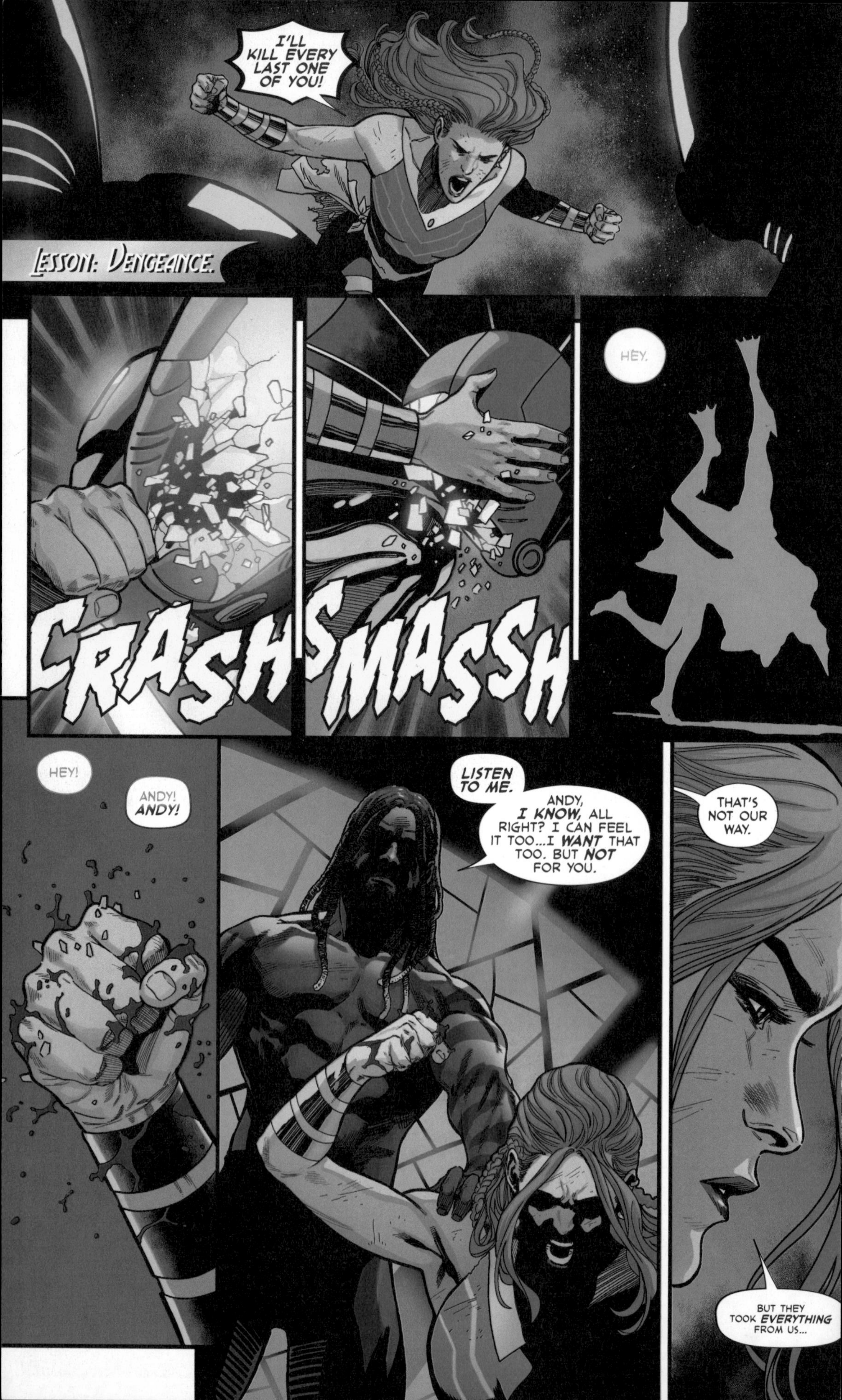
I'LL KILL EVERY LAST ONE OF YOU!
LESSON: VENGEANCE.
CRASH
SMASSH
HEY.
HEY!
ANDY! ANDY!
LISTEN TO ME.
ANDY, I KNOW, ALL RIGHT? I CAN FEEL IT TOO...I WANT THAT TOO. BUT NOT FOR YOU.
THAT'S NOT OUR WAY.
BUT THEY TOOK EVERYTHING FROM US...

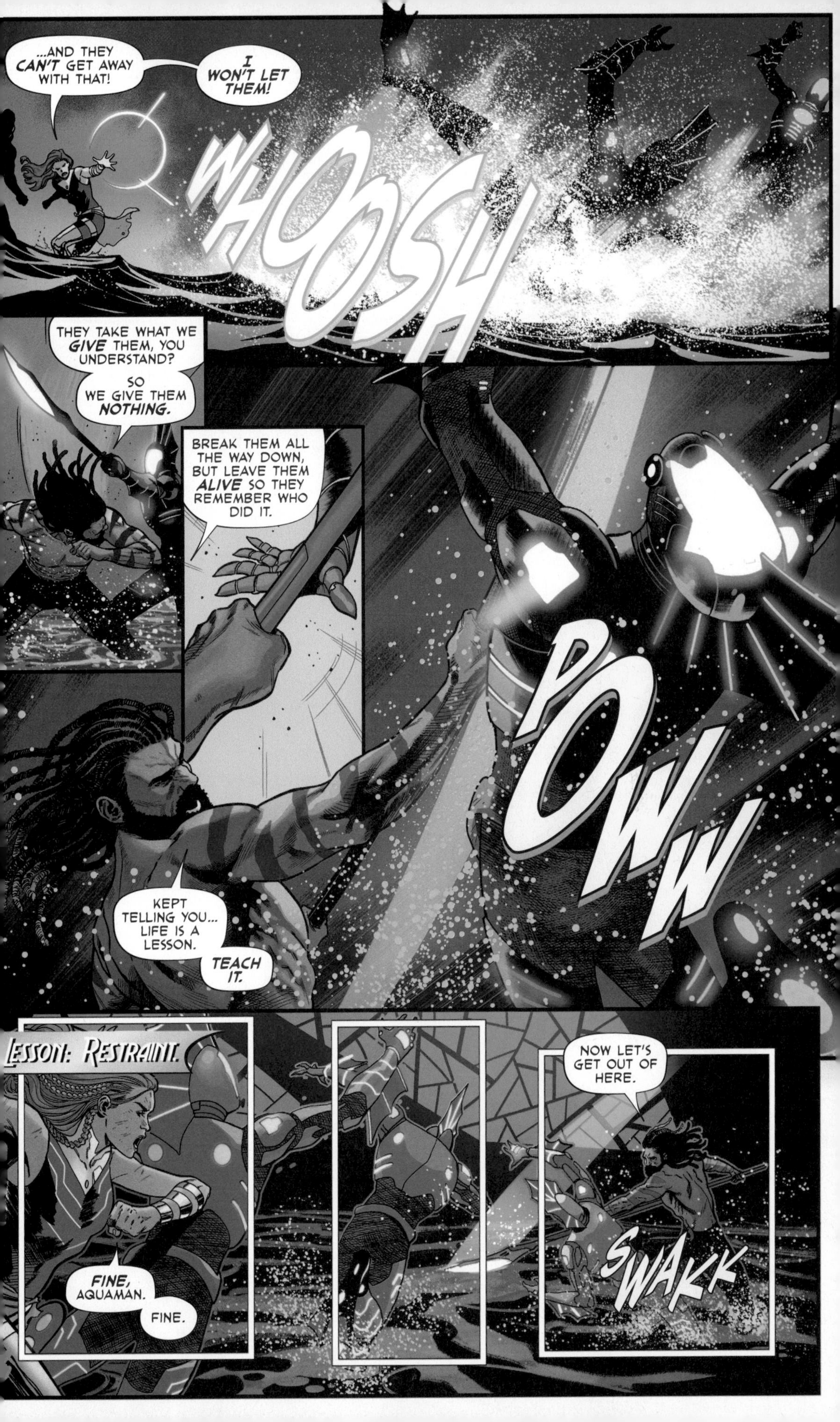
...AND THEY CAN'T GET AWAY WITH THAT!
I WON'T LET THEM!
WHOOOSH
THEY TAKE WHAT WE GIVE THEM, YOU UNDERSTAND?
SO WE GIVE THEM NOTHING.
BREAK THEM ALL THE WAY DOWN, BUT LEAVE THEM ALIVE SO THEY REMEMBER WHO DID IT.
POWW
KEPT TELLING YOU... LIFE IS A LESSON.
TEACH IT.
LESSON: RESTRAINT.
FINE, AQUAMAN.
FINE.
NOW LET'S GET OUT OF HERE.
SWAKK

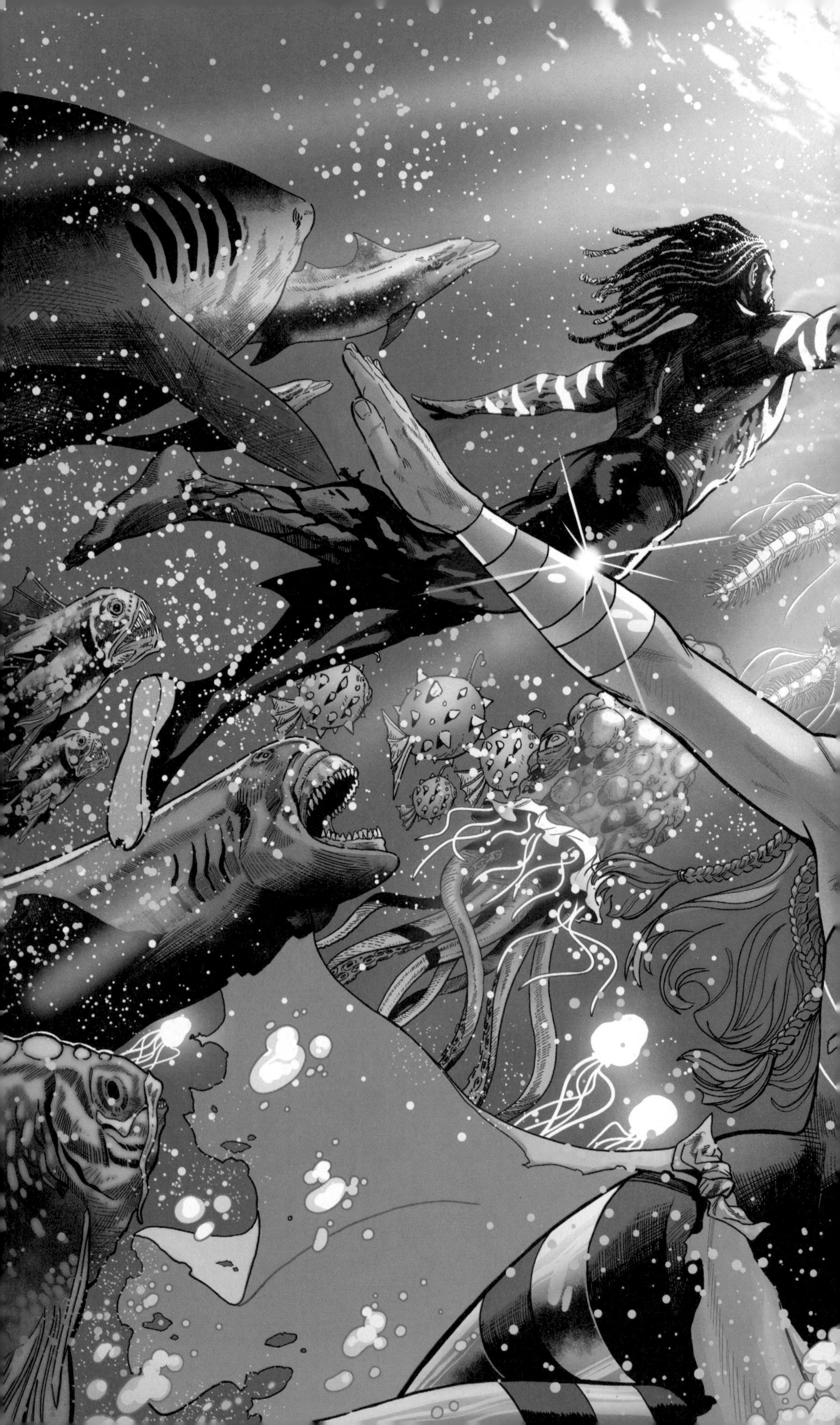

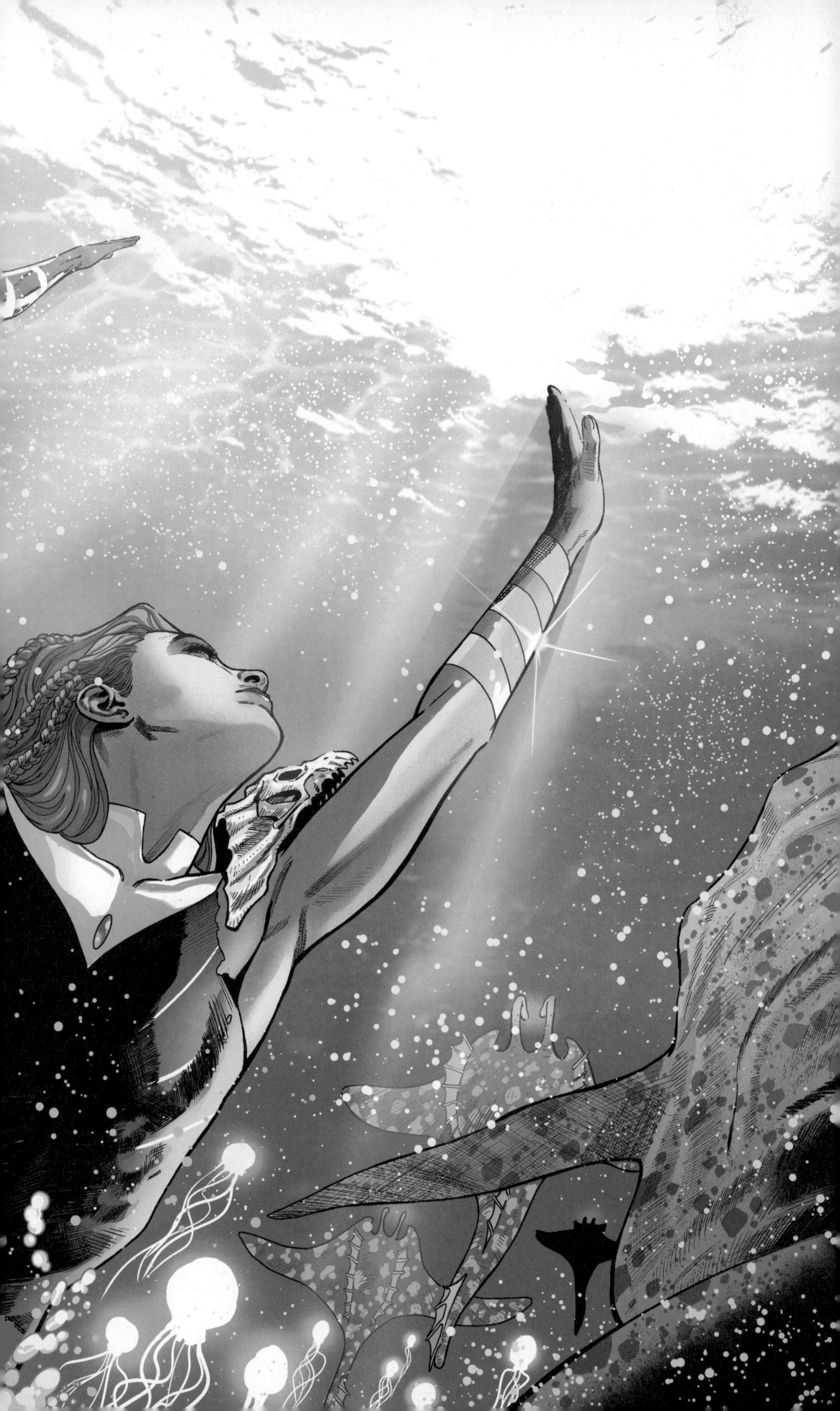

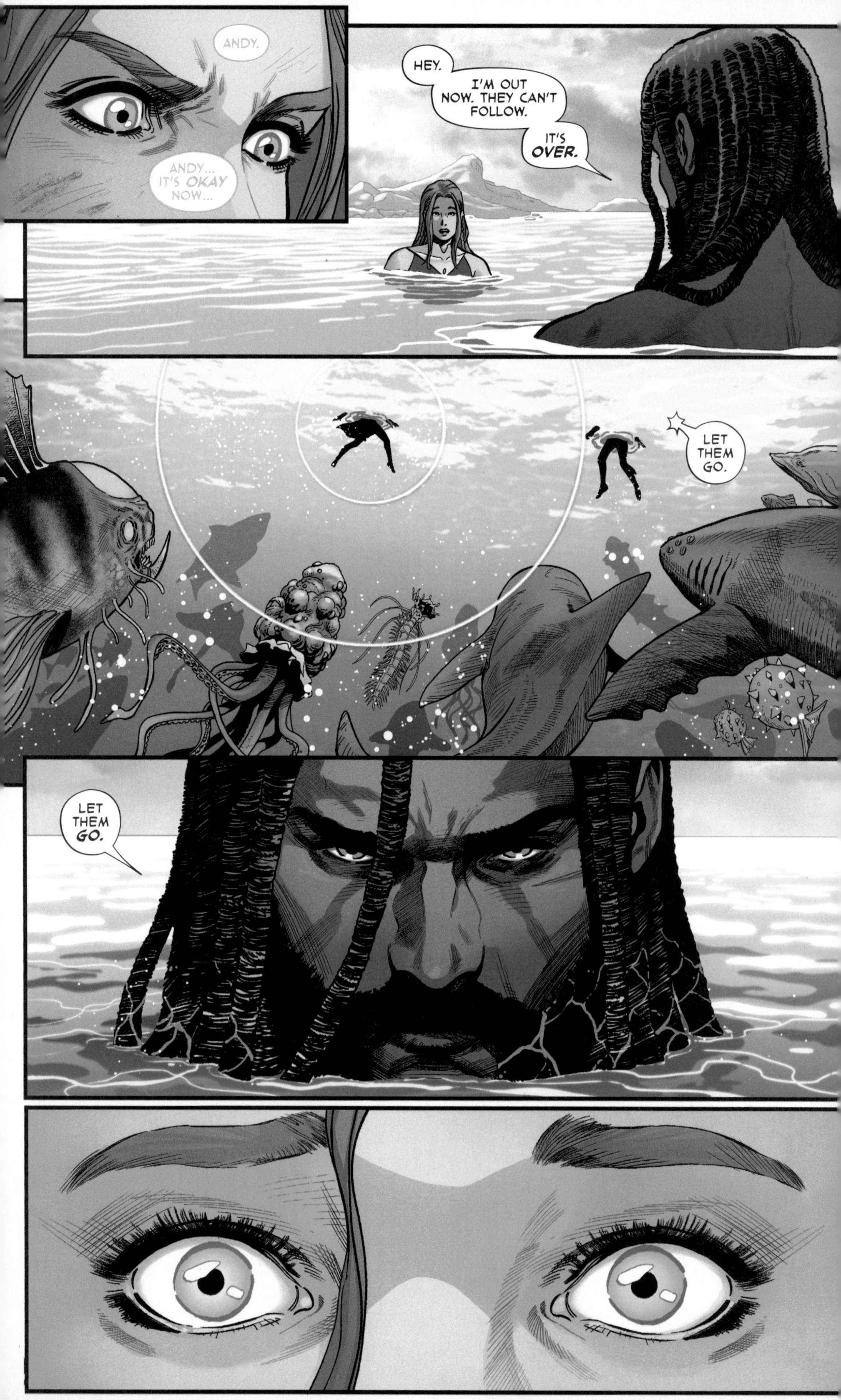
ANDY.
ANDY... IT'S OKAY NOW...
HEY.
I'M OUT NOW. THEY CAN'T FOLLOW.
IT'S OVER.
LET THEM GO.
LET THEM GO.

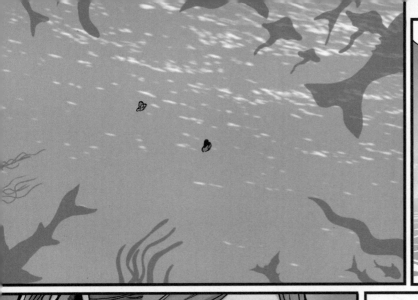

WOO. OKAY. OKAY.

THAT WAS SOME SAVE, PARTNER. I GOTTA TELL YOU THAT--

ANDY, LOOK AT ME--*LOOK AT ME.*

WE'RE *ALIVE.* WE *SURVIVED.*

AND WE *WILL* FIND OUR WAY BACK HOME.

WE WON'T LOSE EACH OTHER EVER AGAIN.

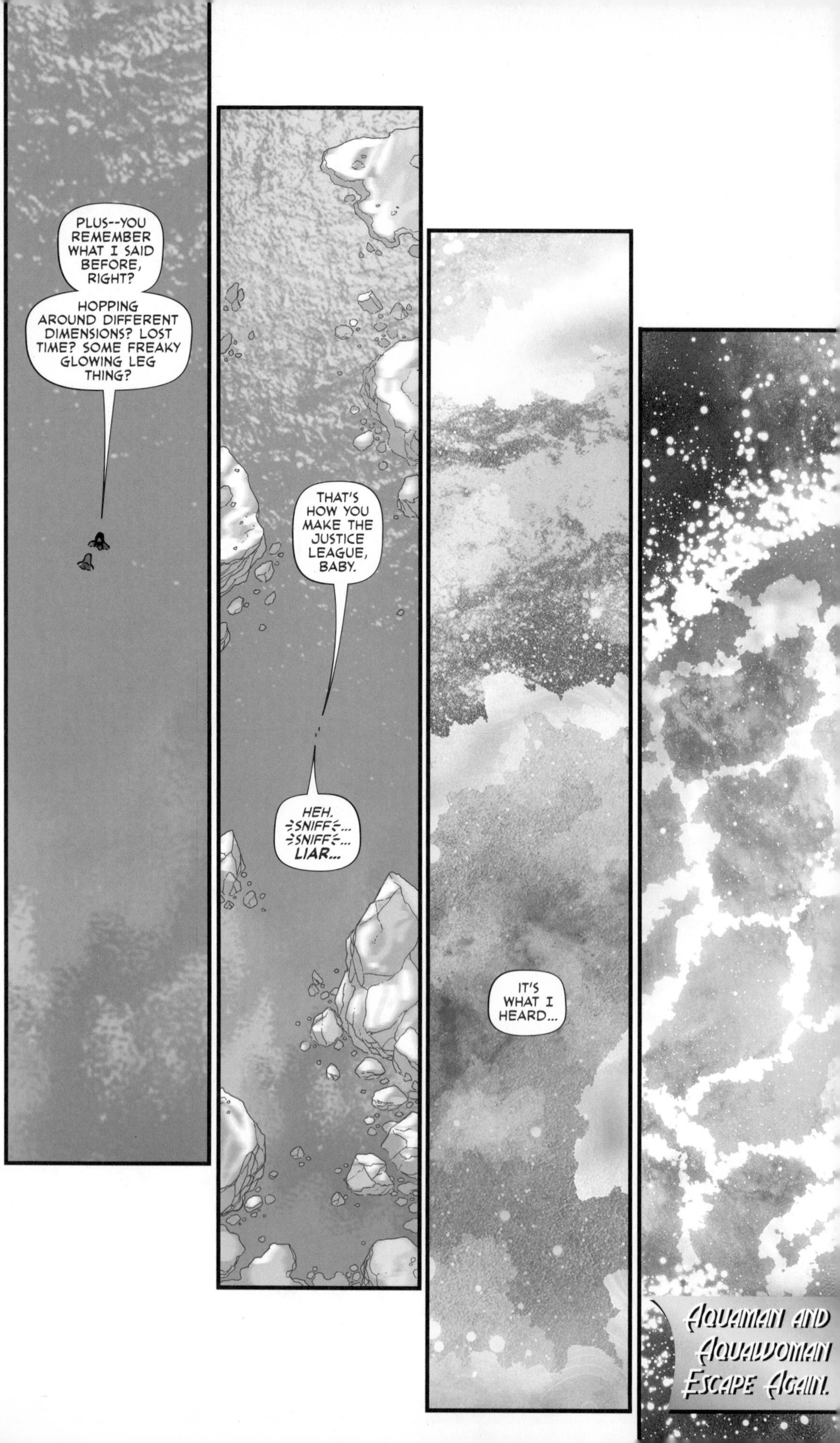

PLUS--YOU REMEMBER WHAT I SAID BEFORE, RIGHT?
HOPPING AROUND DIFFERENT DIMENSIONS? LOST TIME? SOME FREAKY GLOWING LEG THING?
THAT'S HOW YOU MAKE THE JUSTICE LEAGUE, BABY.
HEH. =SNIFF=... =SNIFF=... LIAR...
IT'S WHAT I HEARD...
Aquaman and Aquawoman Escape Again.

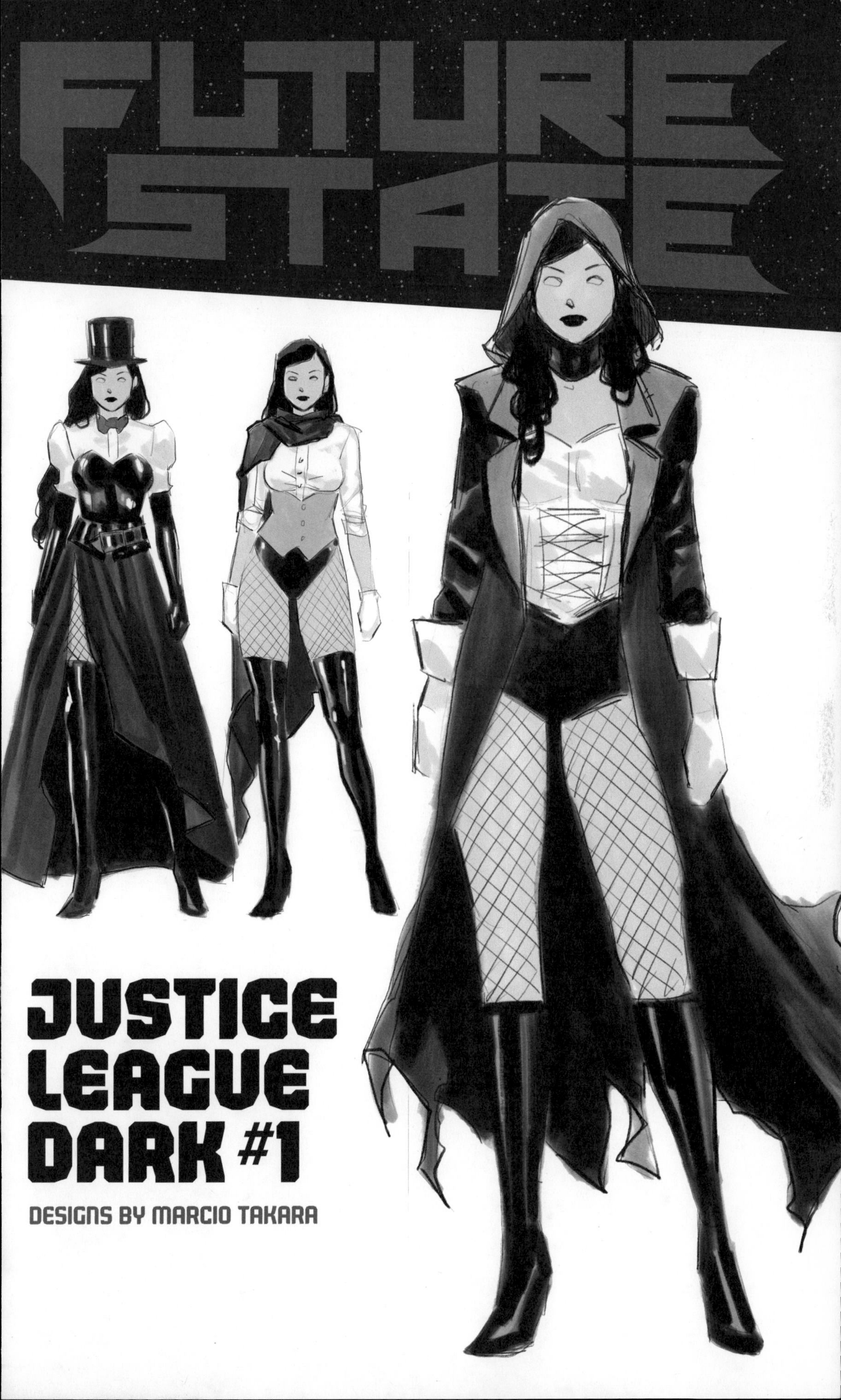
FUTURE STATE
JUSTICE LEAGUE DARK #1
DESIGNS BY MARCIO TAKARA

FUTURE STATE

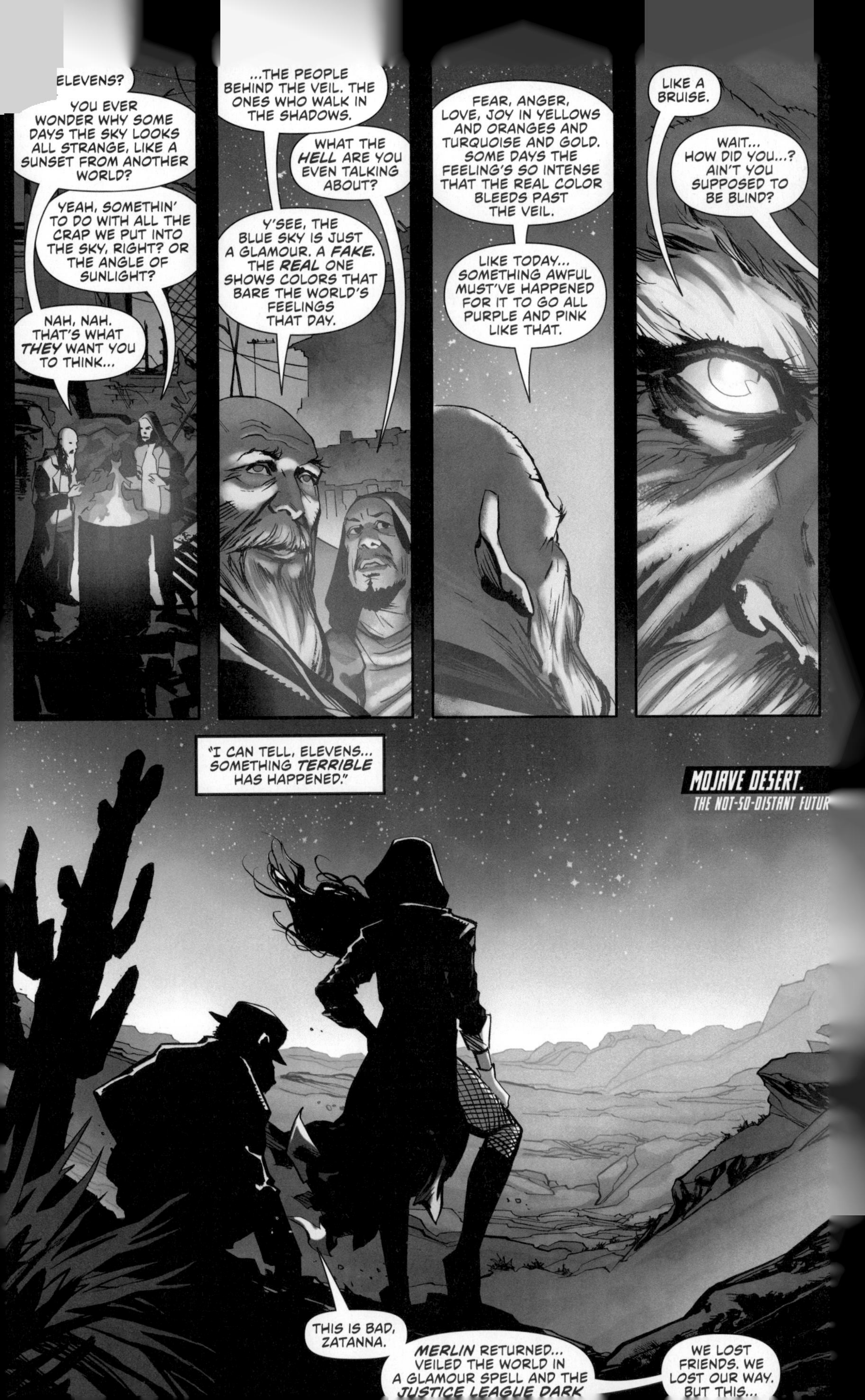
ELEVENS?
YOU EVER WONDER WHY SOME DAYS THE SKY LOOKS ALL STRANGE, LIKE A SUNSET FROM ANOTHER WORLD?
YEAH, SOMETHIN' TO DO WITH ALL THE CRAP WE PUT INTO THE SKY, RIGHT? OR THE ANGLE OF SUNLIGHT?
NAH, NAH. THAT'S WHAT THEY WANT YOU TO THINK...
...THE PEOPLE BEHIND THE VEIL. THE ONES WHO WALK IN THE SHADOWS.
WHAT THE HELL ARE YOU EVEN TALKING ABOUT?
Y'SEE, THE BLUE SKY IS JUST A GLAMOUR. A FAKE. THE REAL ONE SHOWS COLORS THAT BARE THE WORLD'S FEELINGS THAT DAY.
FEAR, ANGER, LOVE, JOY IN YELLOWS AND ORANGES AND TURQUOISE AND GOLD. SOME DAYS THE FEELING'S SO INTENSE THAT THE REAL COLOR BLEEDS PAST THE VEIL.
LIKE TODAY... SOMETHING AWFUL MUST'VE HAPPENED FOR IT TO GO ALL PURPLE AND PINK LIKE THAT.
LIKE A BRUISE.
WAIT... HOW DID YOU...? AIN'T YOU SUPPOSED TO BE BLIND?
"I CAN TELL, ELEVENS... SOMETHING TERRIBLE HAS HAPPENED."
MOJAVE DESERT.
THE NOT-SO-DISTANT FUTUR
THIS IS BAD, ZATANNA.
MERLIN RETURNED... VEILED THE WORLD IN A GLAMOUR SPELL AND THE JUSTICE LEAGUE DARK
WE LOST FRIENDS. WE LOST OUR WAY. BUT THIS...

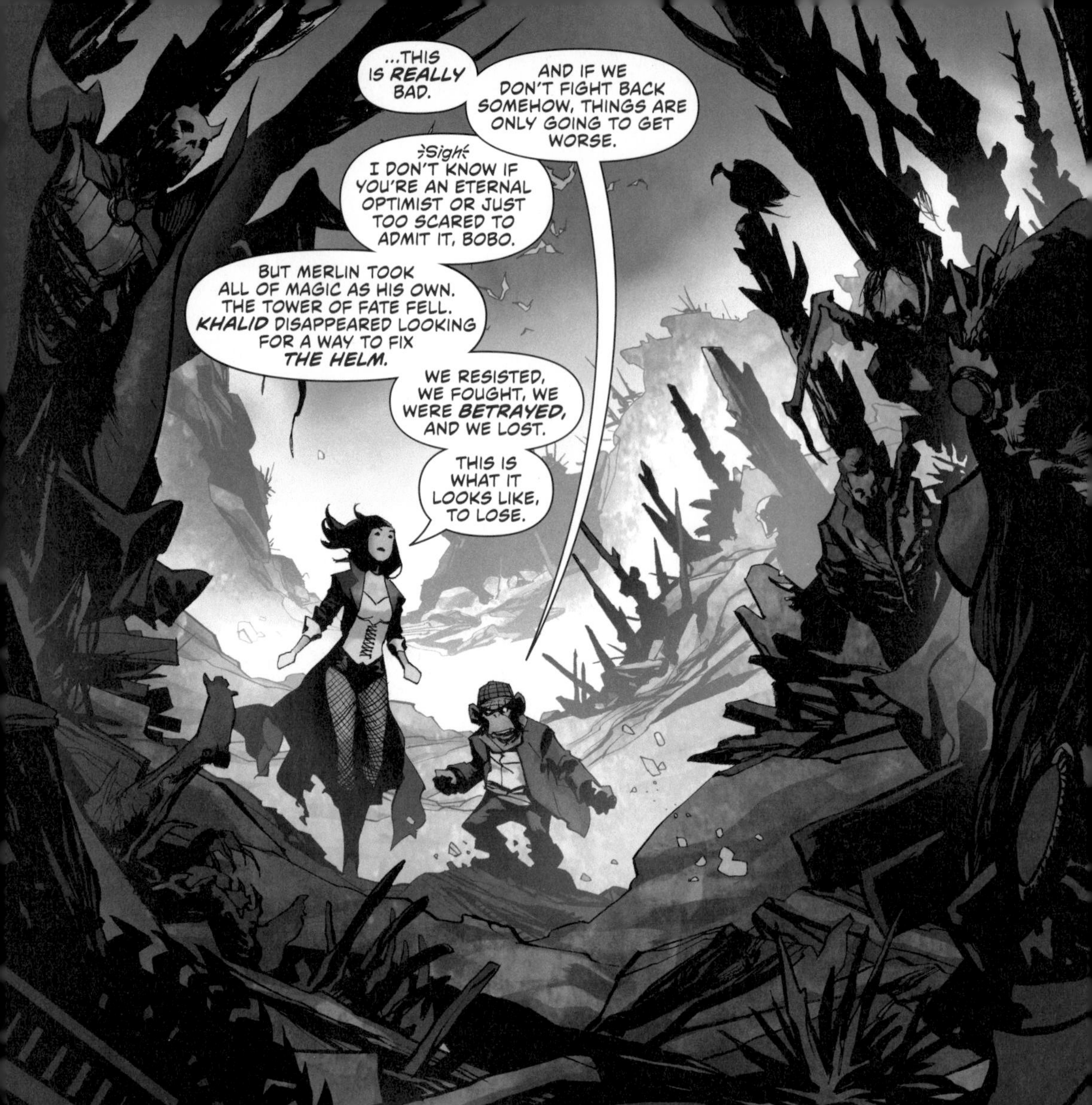
...THIS IS REALLY BAD.
AND IF WE DON'T FIGHT BACK SOMEHOW, THINGS ARE ONLY GOING TO GET WORSE.
Sigh
I DON'T KNOW IF YOU'RE AN ETERNAL OPTIMIST OR JUST TOO SCARED TO ADMIT IT, BOBO.
BUT MERLIN TOOK ALL OF MAGIC AS HIS OWN. THE TOWER OF FATE FELL. KHALID DISAPPEARED LOOKING FOR A WAY TO FIX THE HELM.
WE RESISTED, WE FOUGHT, WE WERE BETRAYED, AND WE LOST.
THIS IS WHAT IT LOOKS LIKE, TO LOSE.

FUTURE STATE JUSTICE LEAGUE DARK:

PROPHÉTIES

PART 1

Writer: RAM V • Artist: MARCIO TAKARA • Colorist: MARCELO MAIOLO • Letterer: ROB LEIGH
Associate Editor: ANDREA SHEA • Editor: ALEX R. CARR

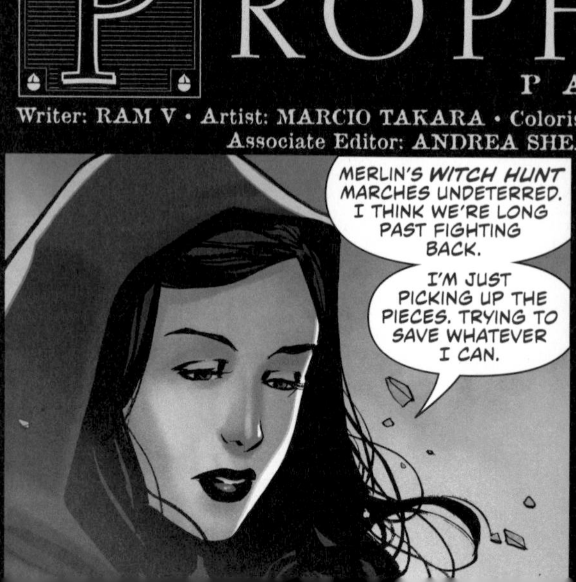
MERLIN'S WITCH HUNT MARCHES UNDETERRED. I THINK WE'RE LONG PAST FIGHTING BACK.
I'M JUST PICKING UP THE PIECES. TRYING TO SAVE WHATEVER I CAN.

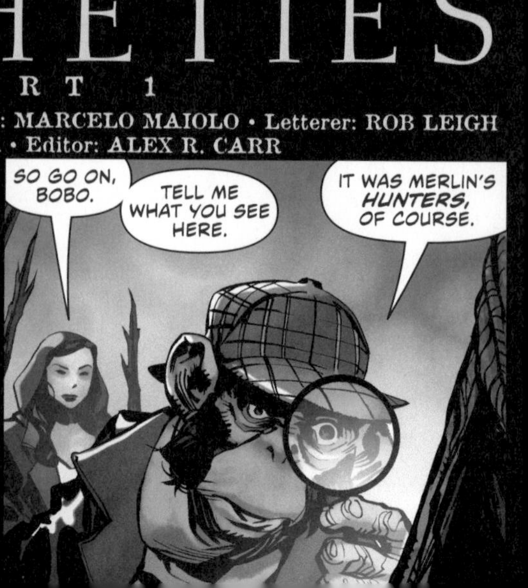
SO GO ON, BOBO.
TELL ME WHAT YOU SEE HERE.
IT WAS MERLIN'S HUNTERS, OF COURSE.

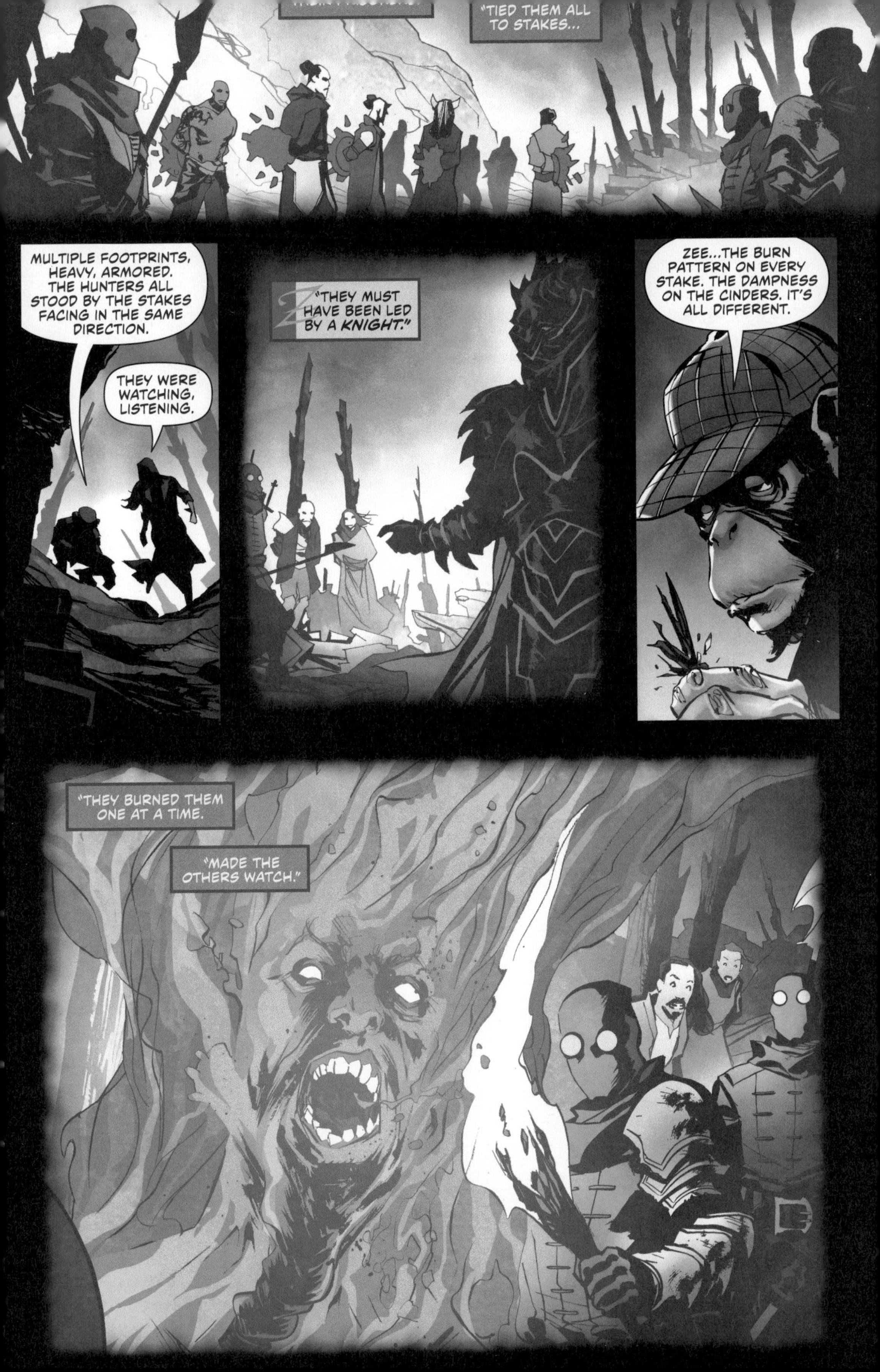
"TIED THEM ALL TO STAKES...
MULTIPLE FOOTPRINTS, HEAVY, ARMORED. THE HUNTERS ALL STOOD BY THE STAKES FACING IN THE SAME DIRECTION.
THEY WERE WATCHING, LISTENING.
"THEY MUST HAVE BEEN LED BY A KNIGHT."
ZEE...THE BURN PATTERN ON EVERY STAKE. THE DAMPNESS ON THE CINDERS. IT'S ALL DIFFERENT.
"THEY BURNED THEM ONE AT A TIME.
"MADE THE OTHERS WATCH."

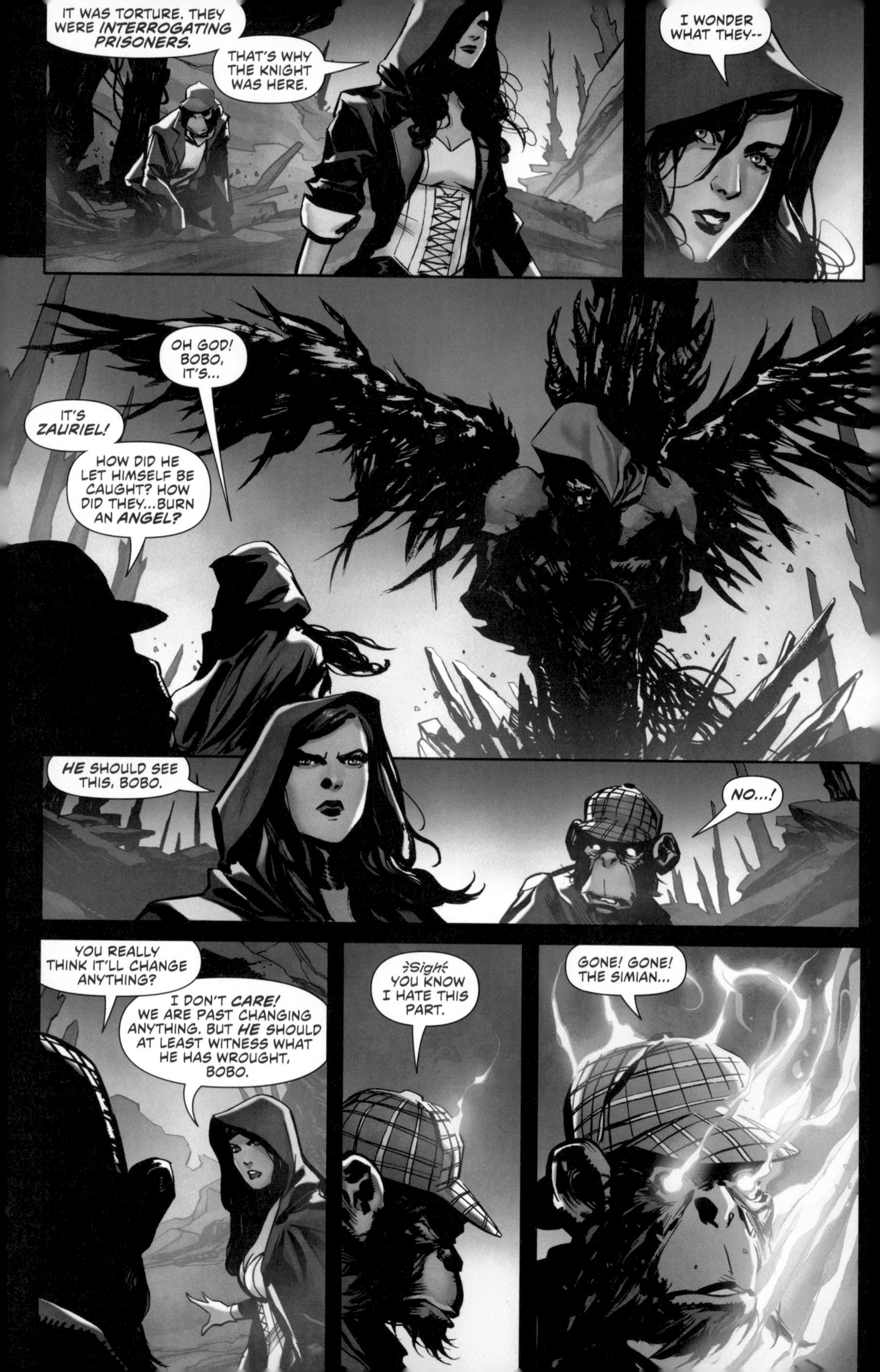
IT WAS TORTURE. THEY WERE INTERROGATING PRISONERS.
THAT'S WHY THE KNIGHT WAS HERE.
I WONDER WHAT THEY--
OH GOD! BOBO, IT'S...
IT'S ZAURIEL!
HOW DID HE LET HIMSELF BE CAUGHT? HOW DID THEY...BURN AN ANGEL?
HE SHOULD SEE THIS, BOBO.
NO...!
YOU REALLY THINK IT'LL CHANGE ANYTHING?
I DON'T CARE! WE ARE PAST CHANGING ANYTHING. BUT HE SHOULD AT LEAST WITNESS WHAT HE HAS WROUGHT, BOBO.
Sigh YOU KNOW I HATE THIS PART.
GONE! GONE! THE SIMIAN...

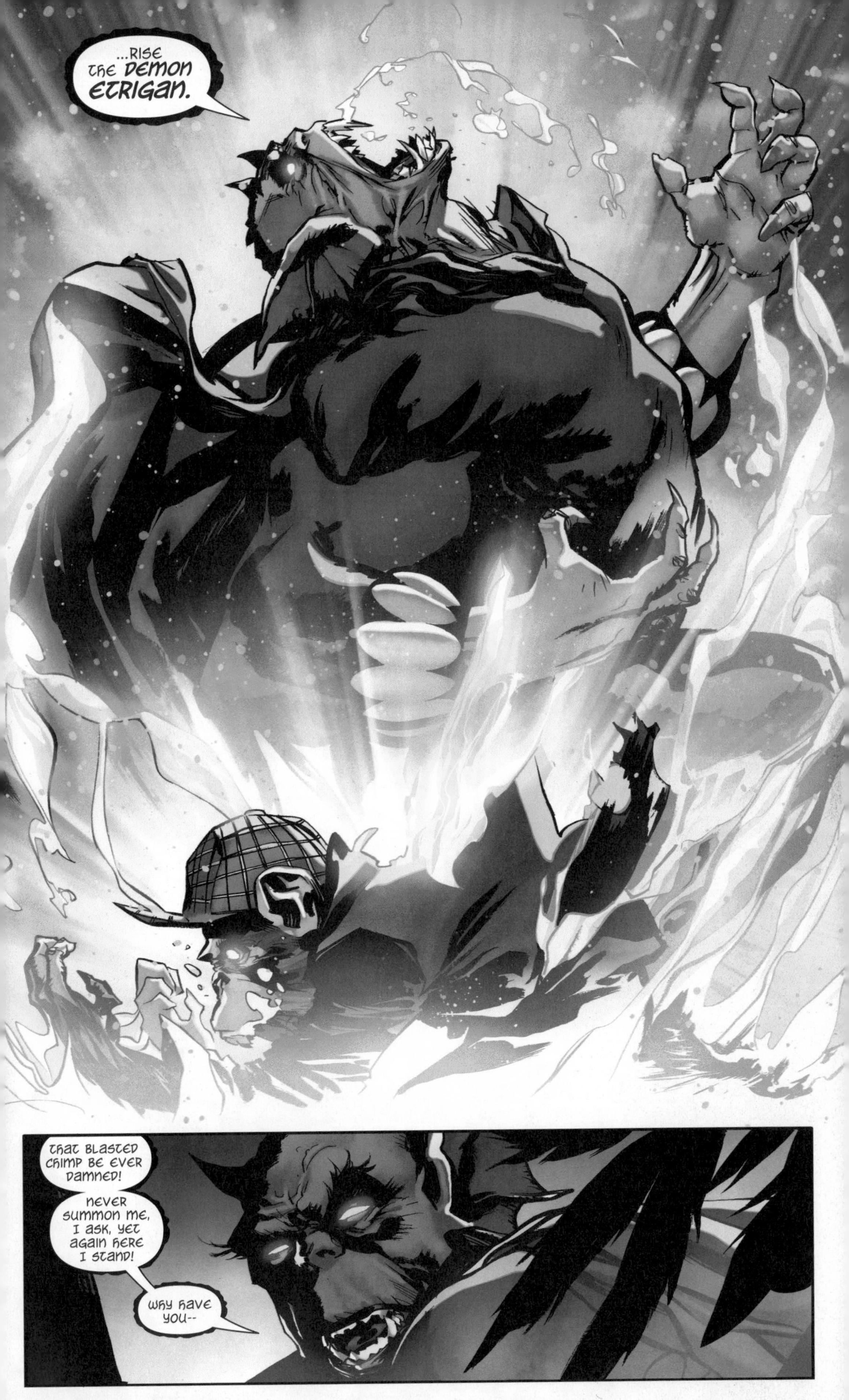
...RISE THE DEMON ETRIGAN.
THAT BLASTED CHIMP BE EVER DAMNED!
NEVER SUMMON ME, I ASK, YET AGAIN HERE I STAND!
WHY HAVE YOU--

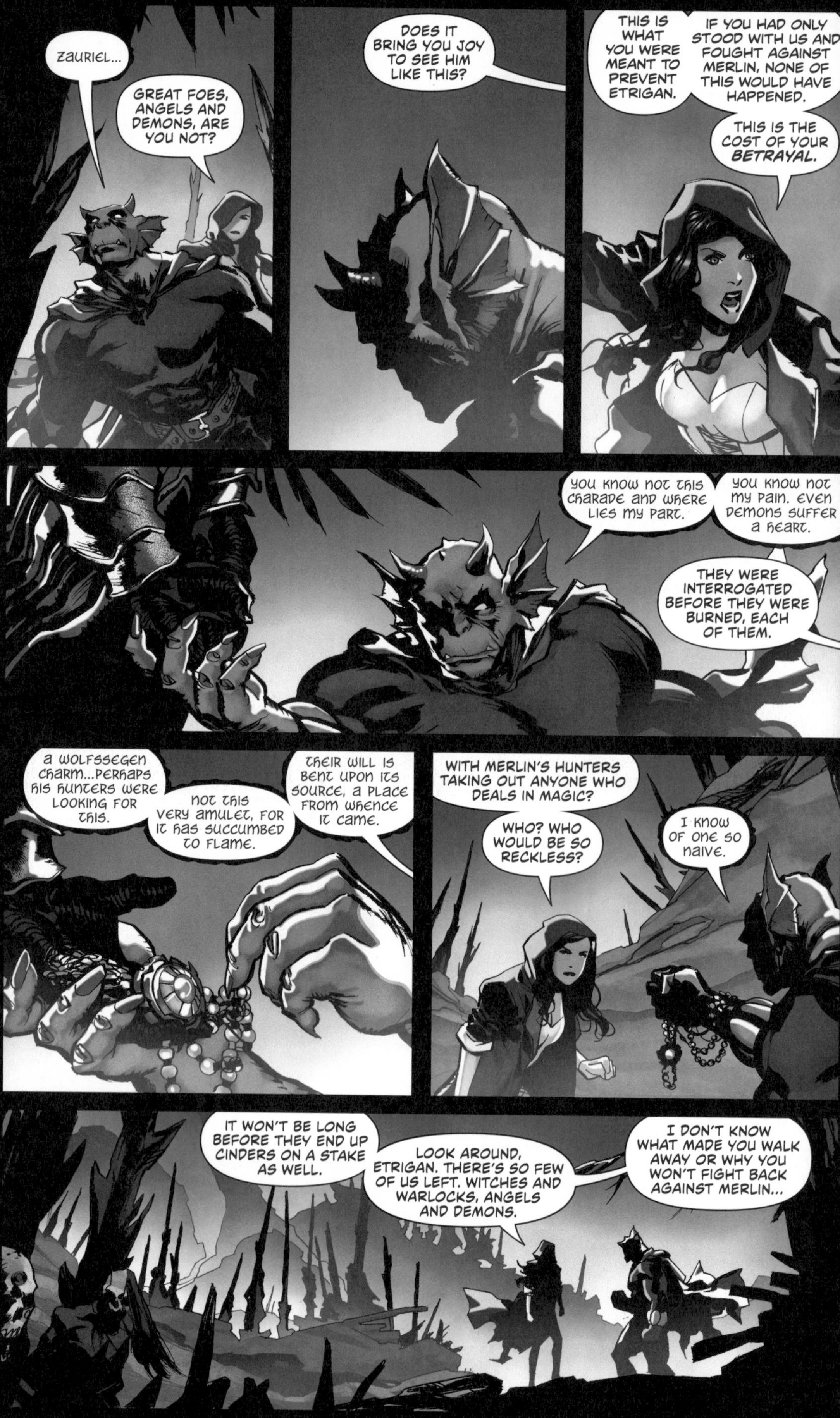

ZAURIEL...
GREAT FOES, ANGELS AND DEMONS, ARE YOU NOT?
DOES IT BRING YOU JOY TO SEE HIM LIKE THIS?
THIS IS WHAT YOU WERE MEANT TO PREVENT ETRIGAN.
IF YOU HAD ONLY STOOD WITH US AND FOUGHT AGAINST MERLIN, NONE OF THIS WOULD HAVE HAPPENED.
THIS IS THE COST OF YOUR BETRAYAL.
YOU KNOW NOT THIS CHARADE AND WHERE LIES MY PART.
YOU KNOW NOT MY PAIN. EVEN DEMONS SUFFER A HEART.
THEY WERE INTERROGATED BEFORE THEY WERE BURNED, EACH OF THEM.
A WOLFSSEGEN CHARM...PERHAPS HIS HUNTERS WERE LOOKING FOR THIS.
NOT THIS VERY AMULET, FOR IT HAS SUCCUMBED TO FLAME.
THEIR WILL IS BENT UPON ITS SOURCE, A PLACE FROM WHENCE IT CAME.
WITH MERLIN'S HUNTERS TAKING OUT ANYONE WHO DEALS IN MAGIC?
WHO? WHO WOULD BE SO RECKLESS?
I KNOW OF ONE SO NAIVE.
IT WON'T BE LONG BEFORE THEY END UP CINDERS ON A STAKE AS WELL.
LOOK AROUND, ETRIGAN. THERE'S SO FEW OF US LEFT. WITCHES AND WARLOCKS, ANGELS AND DEMONS.
I DON'T KNOW WHAT MADE YOU WALK AWAY OR WHY YOU WON'T FIGHT BACK AGAINST MERLIN...

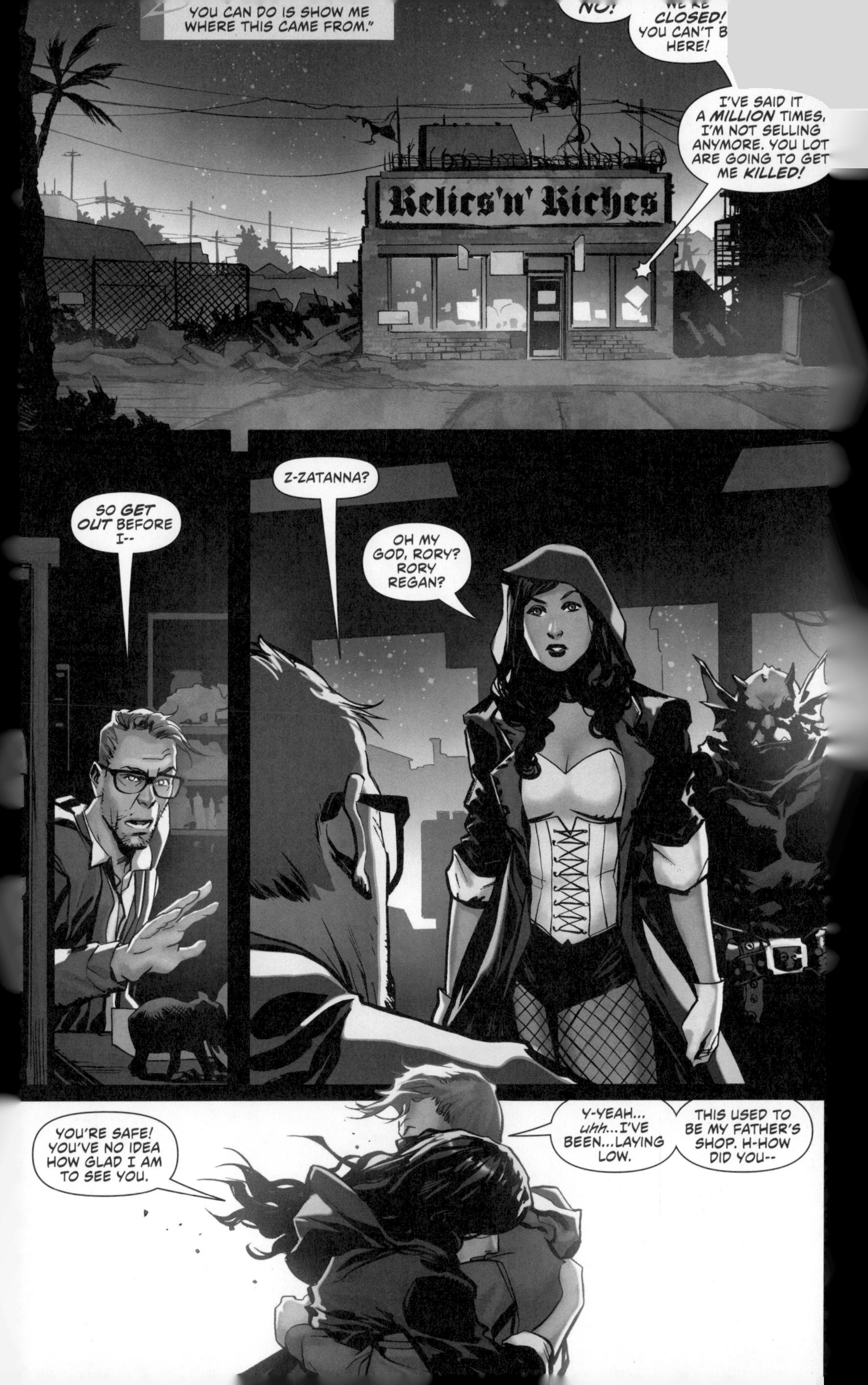
YOU CAN DO IS SHOW ME WHERE THIS CAME FROM."
NO!
CLOSED! YOU CAN'T B HERE!
I'VE SAID IT A *MILLION* TIMES, I'M NOT SELLING ANYMORE. YOU LOT ARE GOING TO GET ME *KILLED!*
Relics'n' Riches
SO *GET OUT* BEFORE I--
Z-ZATANNA?
OH MY GOD, RORY? RORY REGAN?
YOU'RE SAFE! YOU'VE NO IDEA HOW GLAD I AM TO SEE YOU.
Y-YEAH... *uhh*...I'VE BEEN...LAYING LOW.
THIS USED TO BE MY FATHER'S SHOP. H-HOW DID YOU--

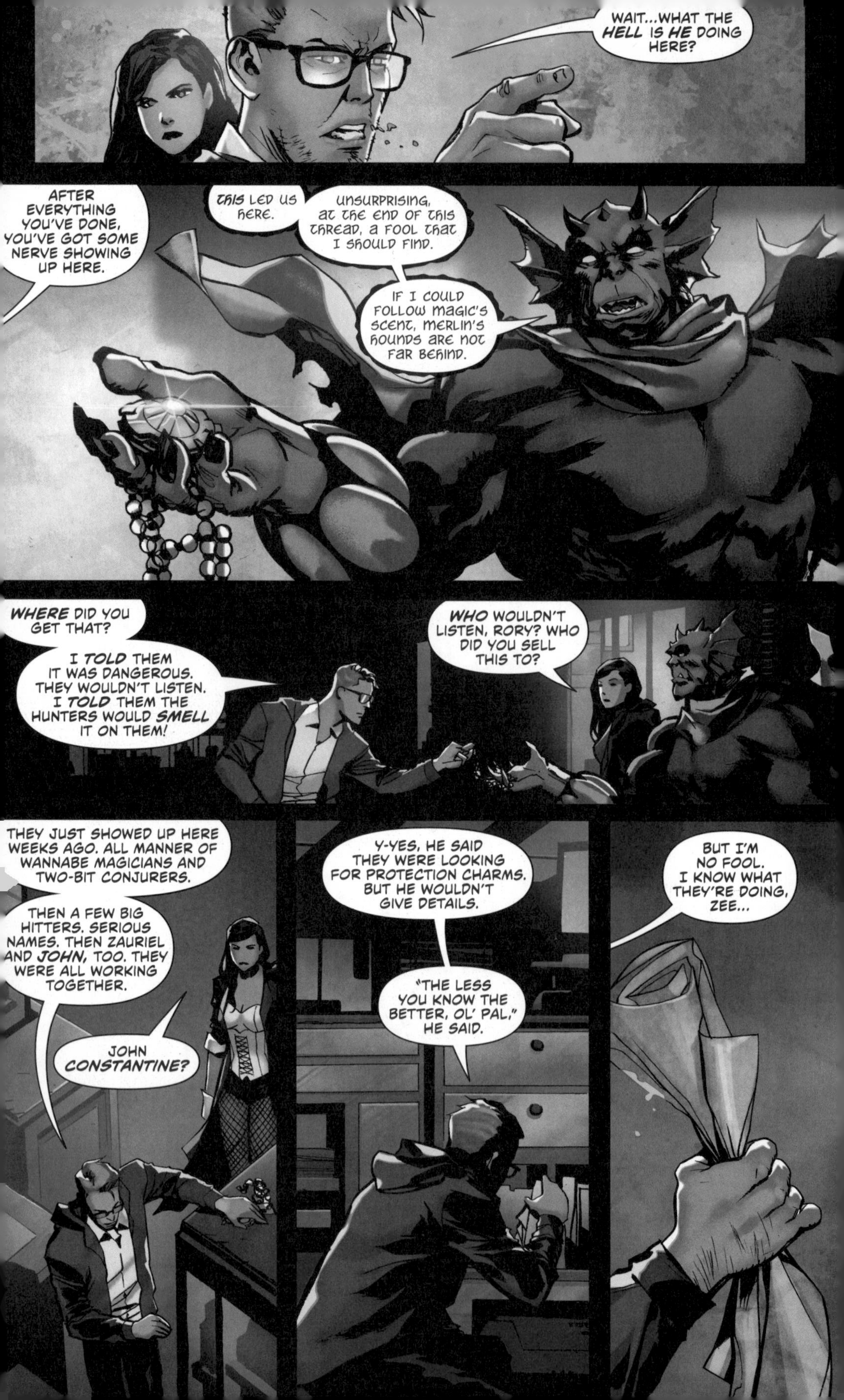
WAIT...WHAT THE HELL IS HE DOING HERE?
AFTER EVERYTHING YOU'VE DONE, YOU'VE GOT SOME NERVE SHOWING UP HERE.
THIS LED US HERE.
UNSURPRISING, AT THE END OF THIS THREAD, A FOOL THAT I SHOULD FIND.
IF I COULD FOLLOW MAGIC'S SCENT, MERLIN'S HOUNDS ARE NOT FAR BEHIND.
WHERE DID YOU GET THAT?
I TOLD THEM IT WAS DANGEROUS. THEY WOULDN'T LISTEN. I TOLD THEM THE HUNTERS WOULD SMELL IT ON THEM!
WHO WOULDN'T LISTEN, RORY? WHO DID YOU SELL THIS TO?
THEY JUST SHOWED UP HERE WEEKS AGO. ALL MANNER OF WANNABE MAGICIANS AND TWO-BIT CONJURERS.
THEN A FEW BIG HITTERS. SERIOUS NAMES. THEN ZAURIEL AND JOHN, TOO. THEY WERE ALL WORKING TOGETHER.
JOHN CONSTANTINE?
Y-YES, HE SAID THEY WERE LOOKING FOR PROTECTION CHARMS. BUT HE WOULDN'T GIVE DETAILS.
"THE LESS YOU KNOW THE BETTER, OL' PAL," HE SAID.
BUT I'M NO FOOL. I KNOW WHAT THEY'RE DOING, ZEE...

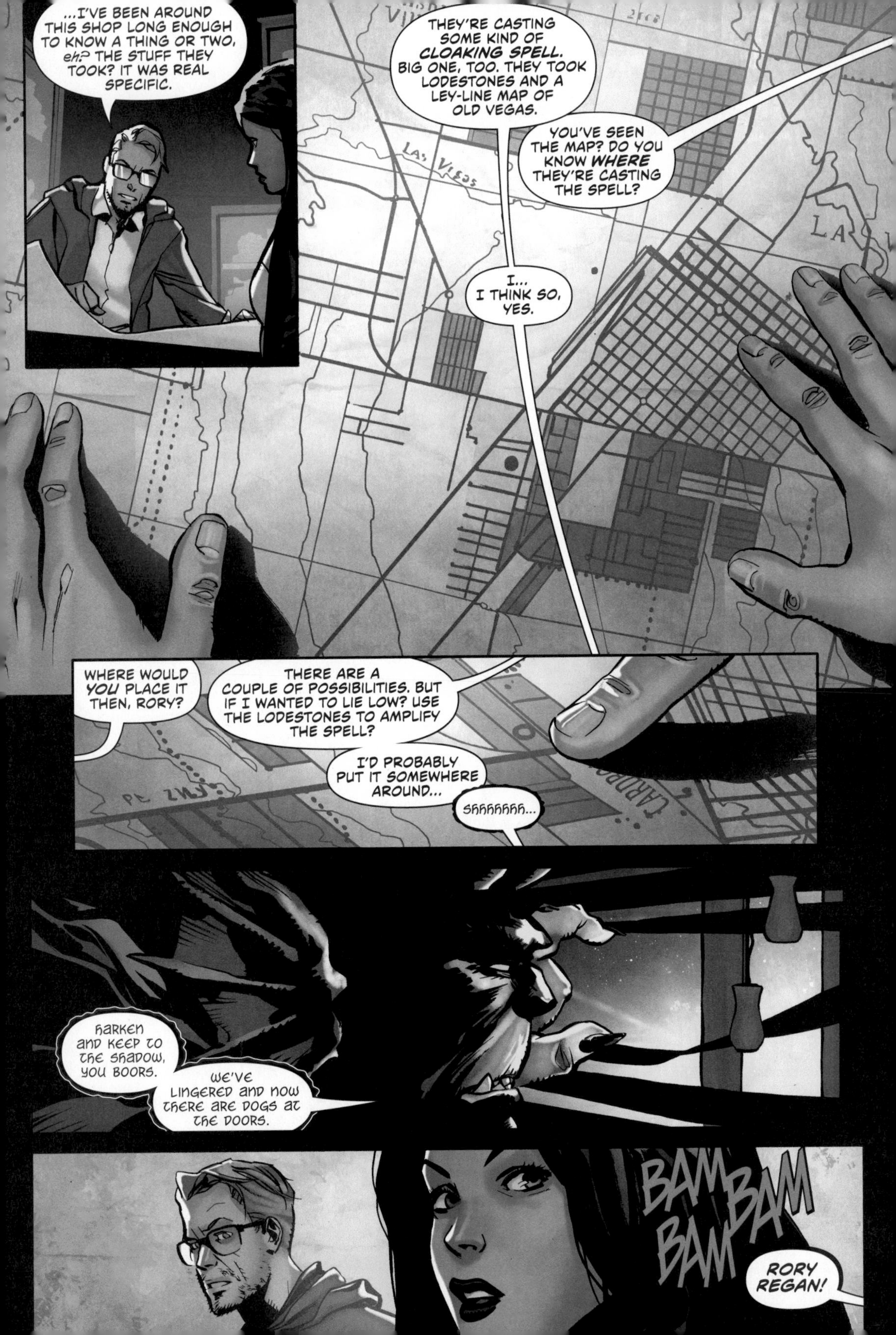

...I'VE BEEN AROUND THIS SHOP LONG ENOUGH TO KNOW A THING OR TWO, *eh?* THE STUFF THEY TOOK? IT WAS REAL SPECIFIC.
THEY'RE CASTING SOME KIND OF **CLOAKING SPELL.** BIG ONE, TOO. THEY TOOK LODESTONES AND A LEY-LINE MAP OF OLD VEGAS.
YOU'VE SEEN THE MAP? DO YOU KNOW **WHERE** THEY'RE CASTING THE SPELL?
I... I THINK SO, YES.
WHERE WOULD **YOU** PLACE IT THEN, RORY?
THERE ARE A COUPLE OF POSSIBILITIES. BUT IF I WANTED TO LIE LOW? USE THE LODESTONES TO AMPLIFY THE SPELL?
I'D PROBABLY PUT IT SOMEWHERE AROUND...
SHHHHHHH...
HARKEN AND KEEP TO THE SHADOW, YOU BOORS.
WE'VE LINGERED AND NOW THERE ARE DOGS AT THE DOORS.
BAM BAM BAM BAM
RORY REGAN!

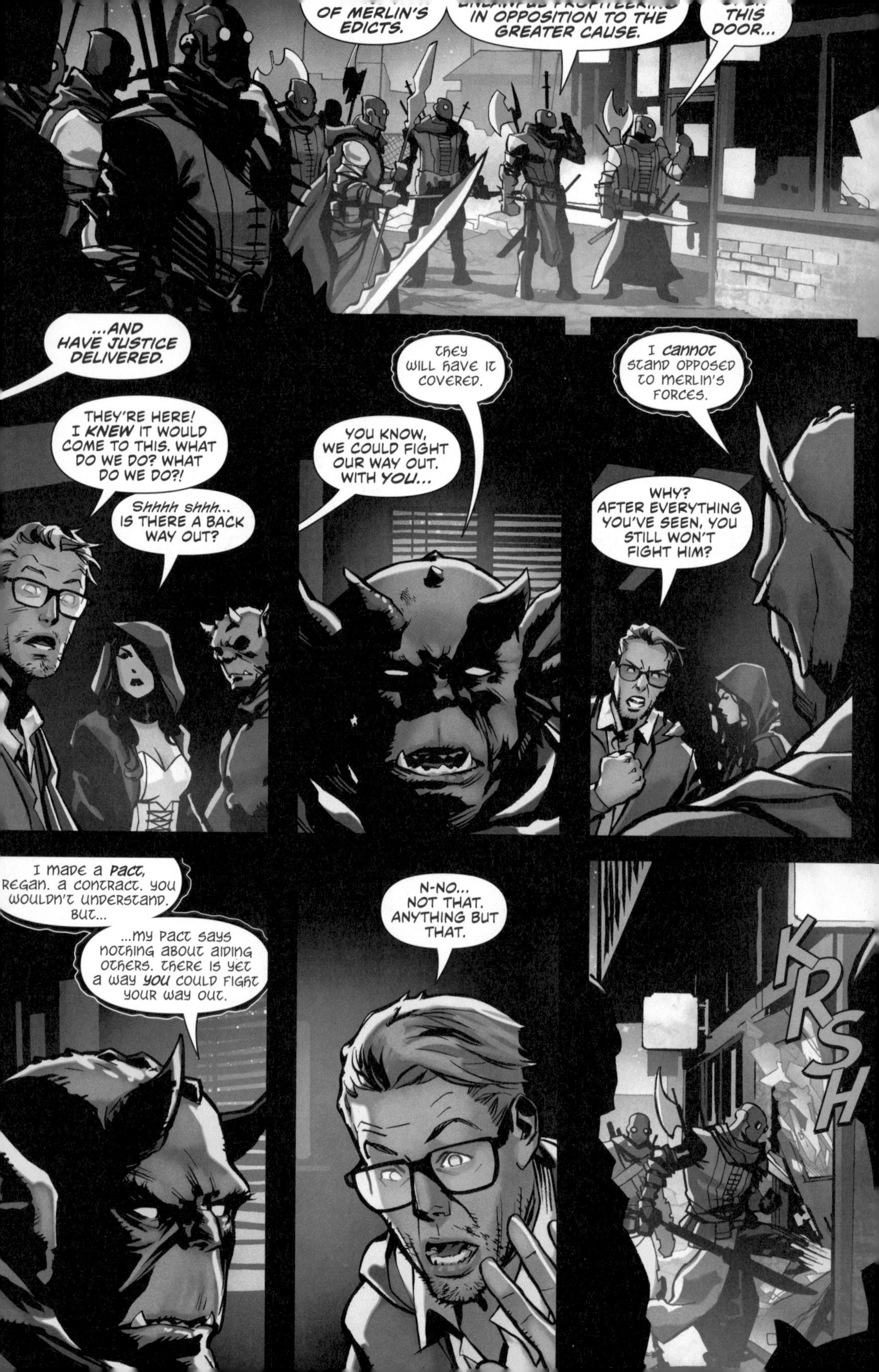
OF MERLIN'S EDICTS.
IN OPPOSITION TO THE GREATER CAUSE.
THIS DOOR...
...AND HAVE JUSTICE DELIVERED.
THEY'RE HERE! I KNEW IT WOULD COME TO THIS. WHAT DO WE DO? WHAT DO WE DO?!
Shhhh shhh... IS THERE A BACK WAY OUT?
THEY WILL HAVE IT COVERED.
YOU KNOW, WE COULD FIGHT OUR WAY OUT. WITH YOU...
I CANNOT STAND OPPOSED TO MERLIN'S FORCES.
WHY? AFTER EVERYTHING YOU'VE SEEN, YOU STILL WON'T FIGHT HIM?
I MADE A PACT, REGAN. A CONTRACT. YOU WOULDN'T UNDERSTAND. BUT...
...MY PACT SAYS NOTHING ABOUT AIDING OTHERS. THERE IS YET A WAY YOU COULD FIGHT YOUR WAY OUT.
N-NO... NOT THAT. ANYTHING BUT THAT.
KRSH

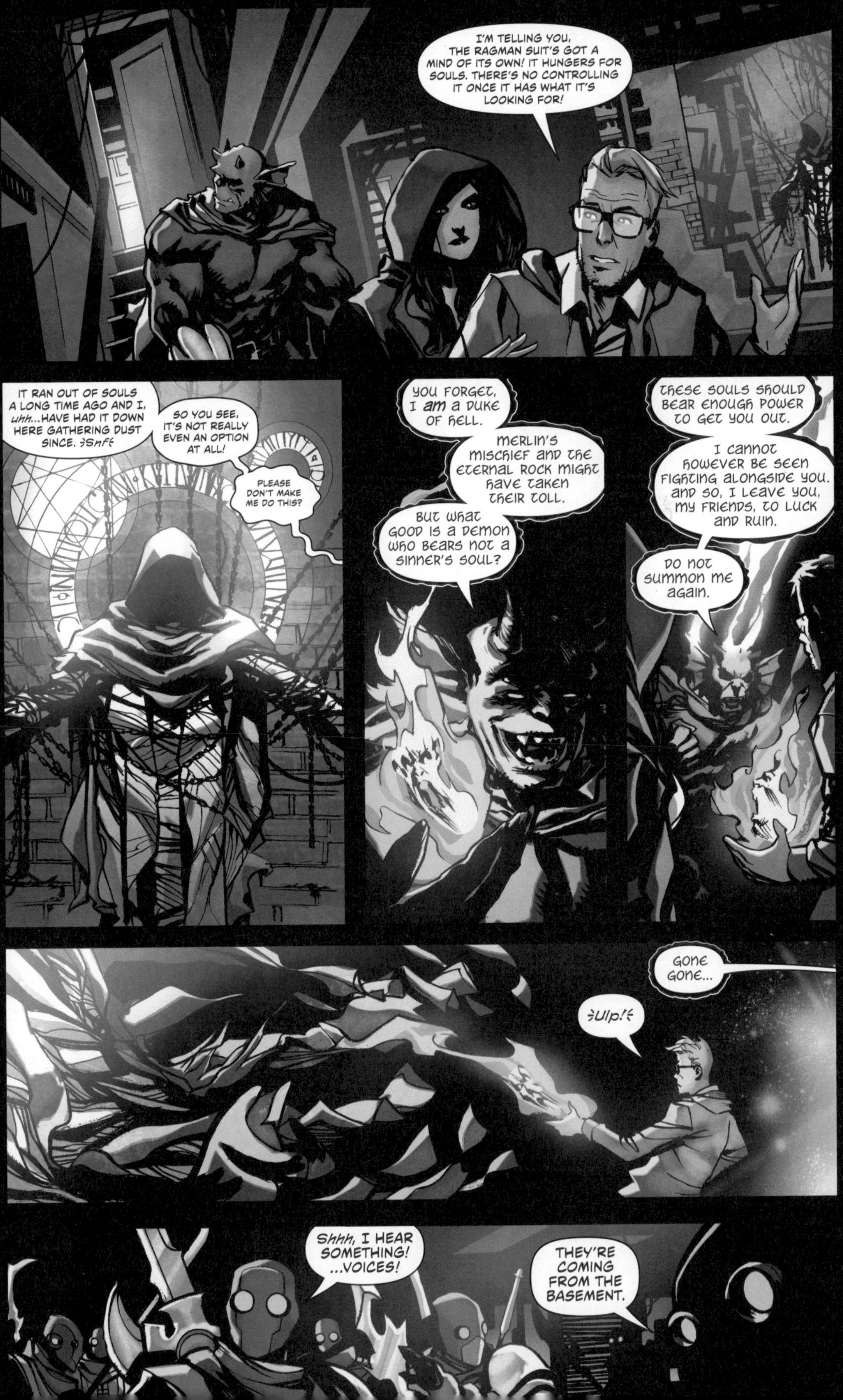
I'M TELLING YOU, THE RAGMAN SUIT'S GOT A MIND OF ITS OWN! IT HUNGERS FOR SOULS. THERE'S NO CONTROLLING IT ONCE IT HAS WHAT IT'S LOOKING FOR!
IT RAN OUT OF SOULS A LONG TIME AGO AND I, *uhh*...HAVE HAD IT DOWN HERE GATHERING DUST SINCE. *Snf*
SO YOU SEE, IT'S NOT REALLY EVEN AN OPTION AT ALL!
PLEASE DON'T MAKE ME DO THIS?
YOU FORGET, I *AM* A DUKE OF HELL.
MERLIN'S MISCHIEF AND THE ETERNAL ROCK MIGHT HAVE TAKEN THEIR TOLL.
BUT WHAT GOOD IS A DEMON WHO BEARS NOT A SINNER'S SOUL?
THESE SOULS SHOULD BEAR ENOUGH POWER TO GET YOU OUT.
I CANNOT HOWEVER BE SEEN FIGHTING ALONGSIDE YOU. AND SO, I LEAVE YOU, MY FRIENDS, TO LUCK AND RUIN.
DO NOT SUMMON ME AGAIN.
GONE GONE...
Ulp!
Shhh, I HEAR SOMETHING! ...VOICES!
THEY'RE COMING FROM THE BASEMENT.

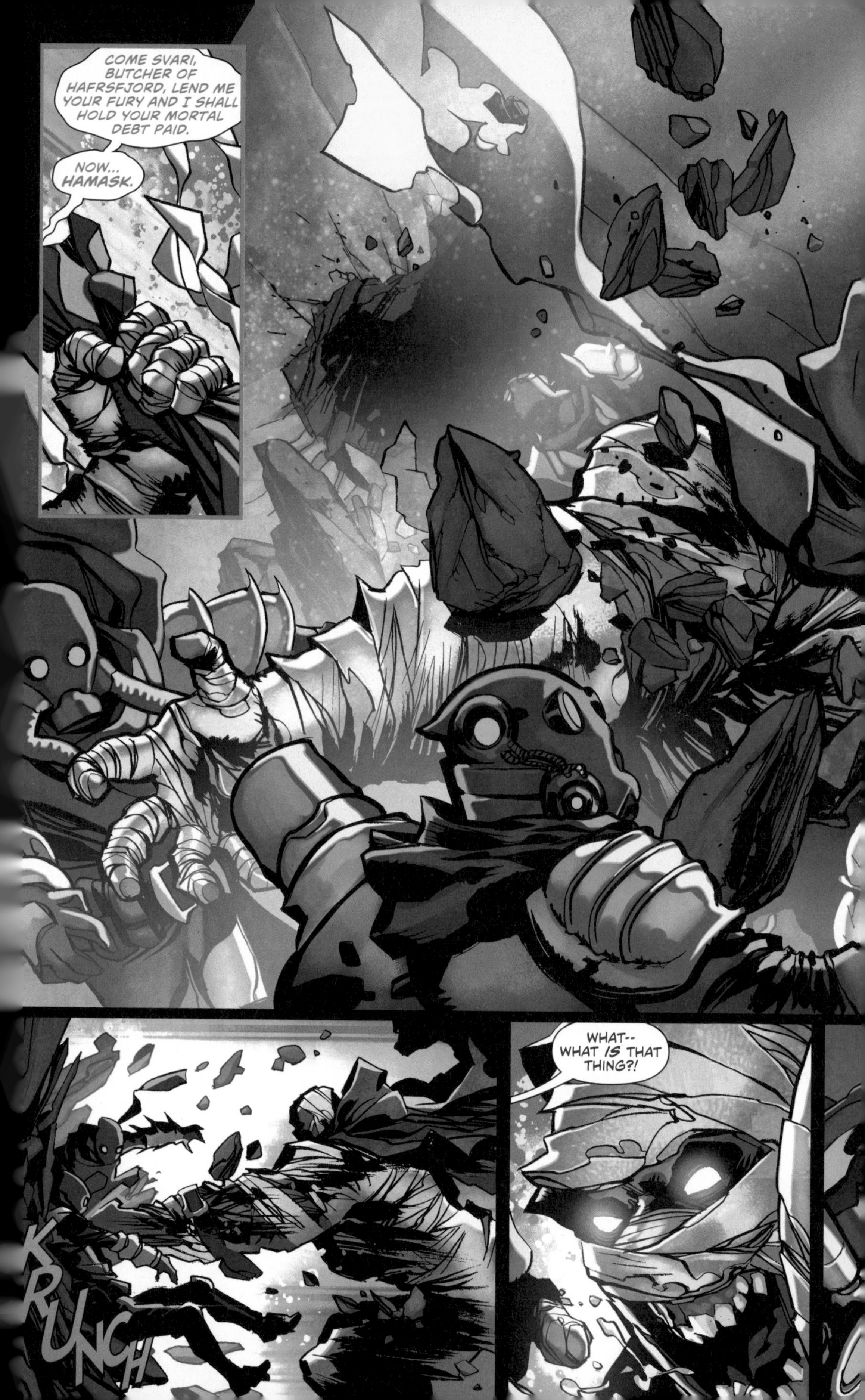
COME SVARI, BUTCHER OF HAFRSFJORD, LEND ME YOUR FURY AND I SHALL HOLD YOUR MORTAL DEBT PAID.
NOW... HAMASK.
KRUNCH
WHAT-- WHAT IS THAT THING?!

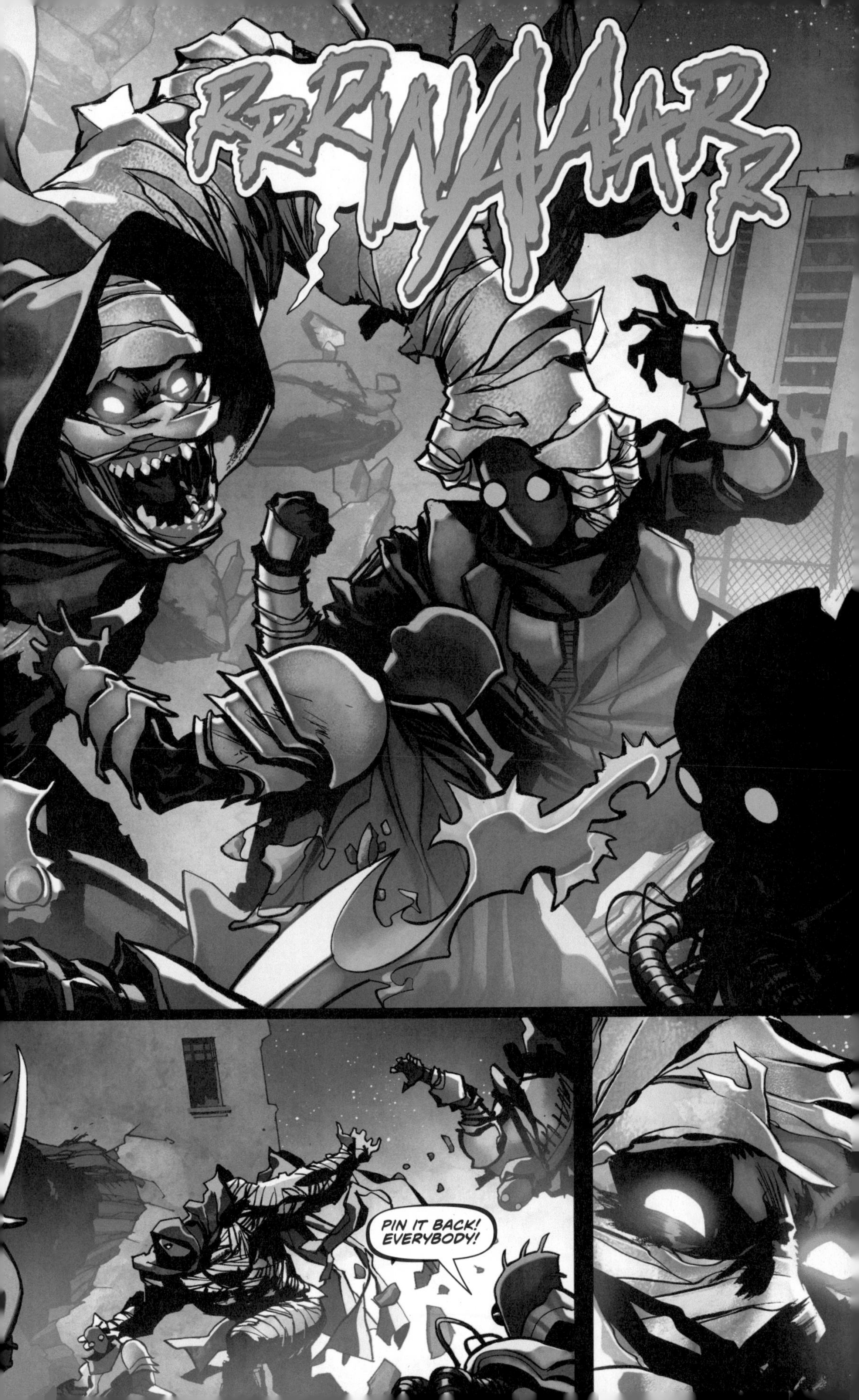
RRRWAAARR
PIN IT BACK! EVERYBODY!

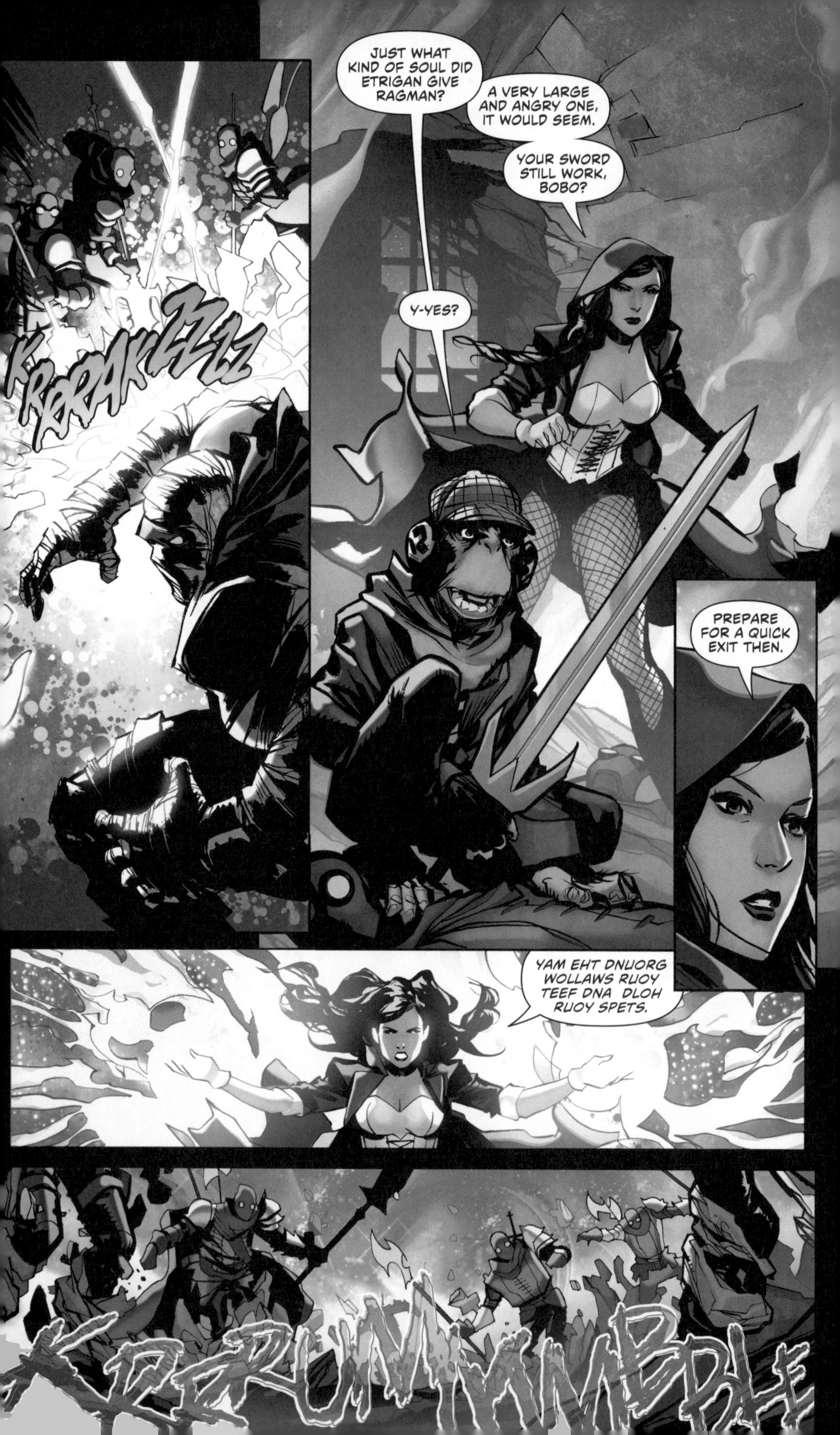
JUST WHAT KIND OF SOUL DID ETRIGAN GIVE RAGMAN?
A VERY LARGE AND ANGRY ONE, IT WOULD SEEM.
YOUR SWORD STILL WORK, BOBO?
Y-YES?
PREPARE FOR A QUICK EXIT THEN.
YAM EHT DNUORG WOLLAWS RUOY TEEF DNA DLOH RUOY SPETS.

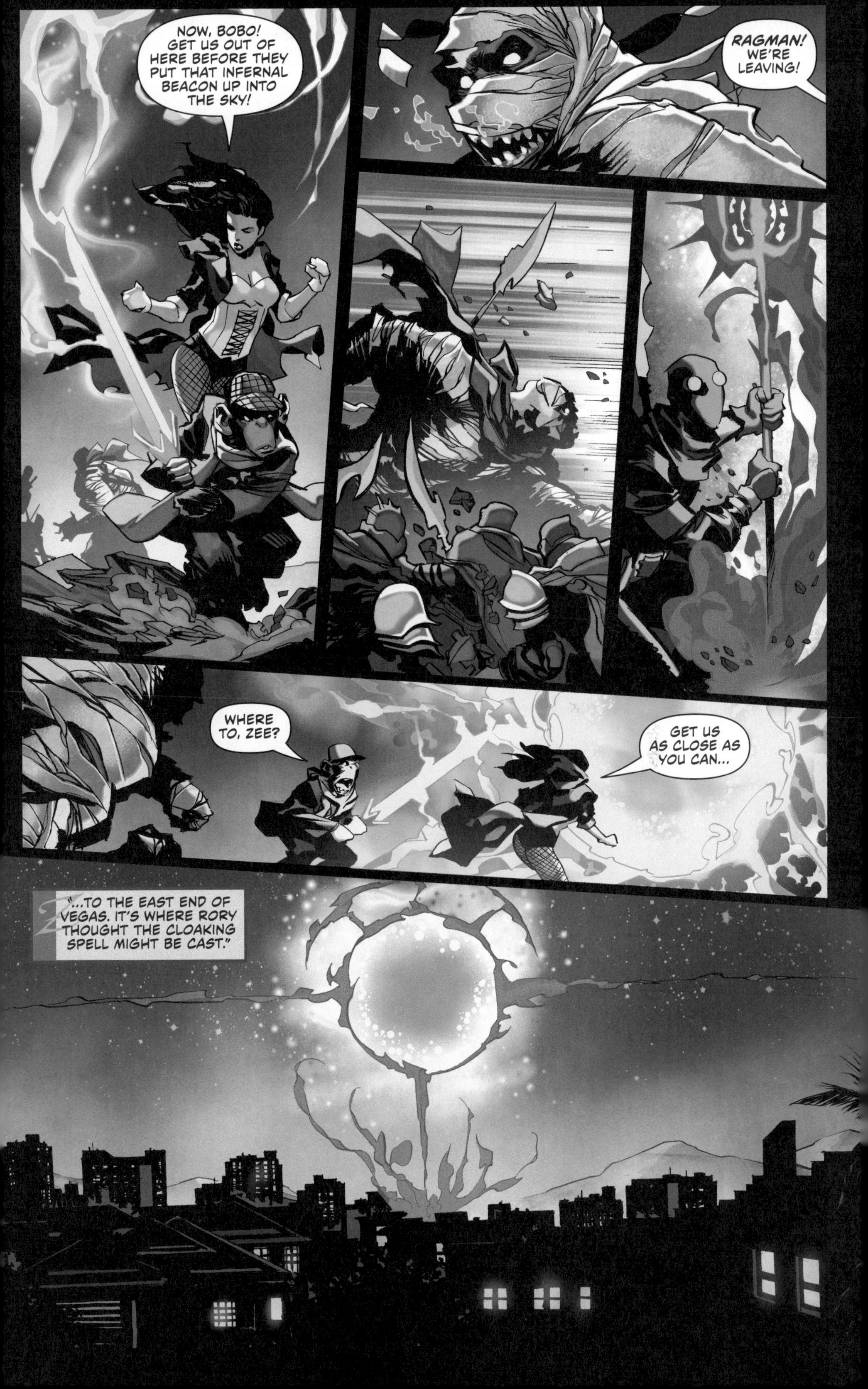
NOW, BOBO! GET US OUT OF HERE BEFORE THEY PUT THAT INFERNAL BEACON UP INTO THE SKY!
RAGMAN! WE'RE LEAVING!
WHERE TO, ZEE?
GET US AS CLOSE AS YOU CAN...
"...TO THE EAST END OF VEGAS. IT'S WHERE RORY THOUGHT THE CLOAKING SPELL MIGHT BE CAST."

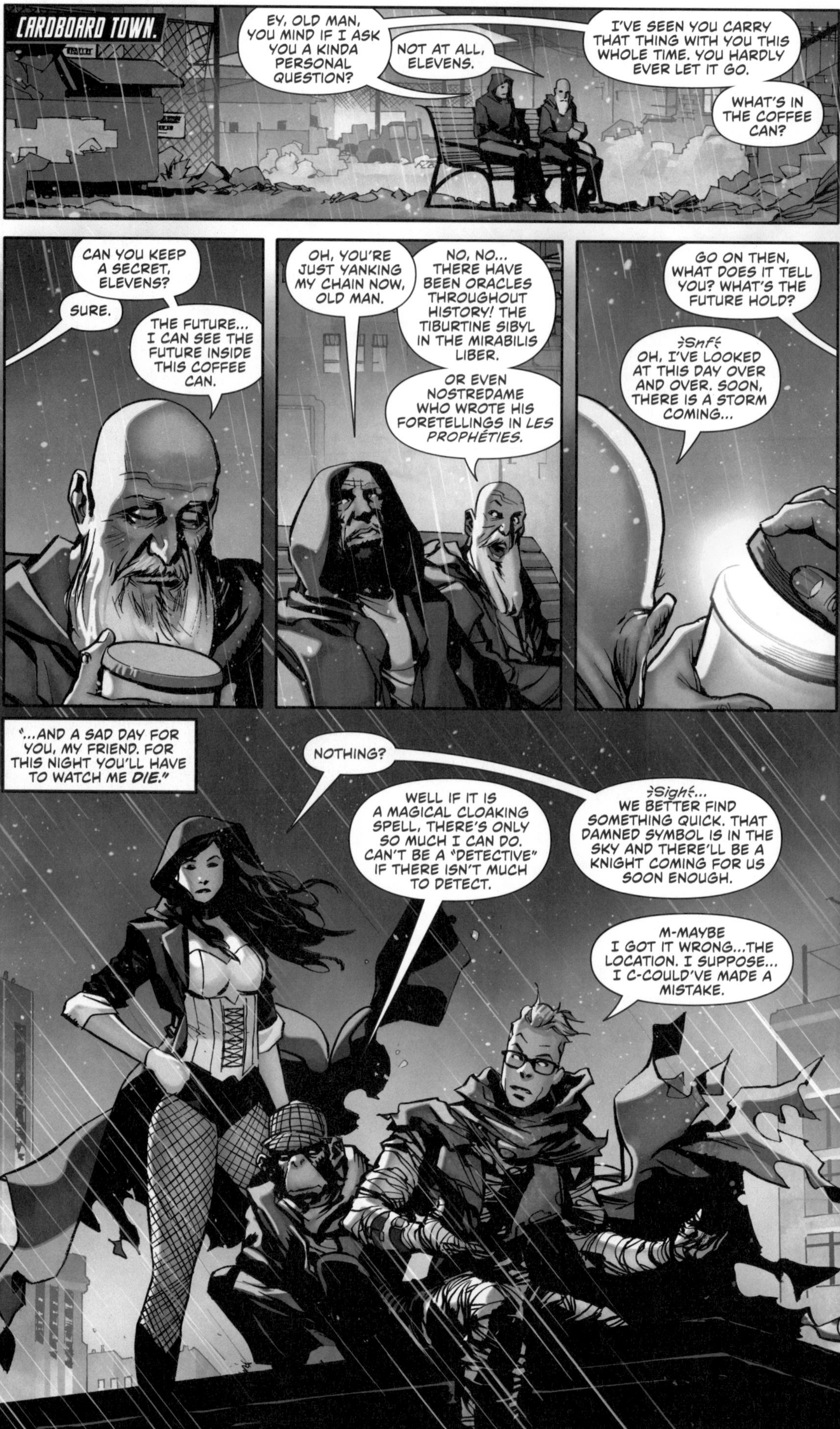
CARDBOARD TOWN.
EY, OLD MAN, YOU MIND IF I ASK YOU A KINDA PERSONAL QUESTION?
NOT AT ALL, ELEVENS.
I'VE SEEN YOU CARRY THAT THING WITH YOU THIS WHOLE TIME. YOU HARDLY EVER LET IT GO.
WHAT'S IN THE COFFEE CAN?
CAN YOU KEEP A SECRET, ELEVENS?
SURE.
THE FUTURE... I CAN SEE THE FUTURE INSIDE THIS COFFEE CAN.
OH, YOU'RE JUST YANKING MY CHAIN NOW, OLD MAN.
NO, NO... THERE HAVE BEEN ORACLES THROUGHOUT HISTORY! THE TIBURTINE SIBYL IN THE MIRABILIS LIBER.
OR EVEN NOSTREDAME WHO WROTE HIS FORETELLINGS IN *LES PROPHÉTIES.*
GO ON THEN, WHAT DOES IT TELL YOU? WHAT'S THE FUTURE HOLD?
Snf OH, I'VE LOOKED AT THIS DAY OVER AND OVER. SOON, THERE IS A STORM COMING...
"...AND A SAD DAY FOR YOU, MY FRIEND. FOR THIS NIGHT YOU'LL HAVE TO WATCH ME *DIE.*"
NOTHING?
WELL IF IT IS A MAGICAL CLOAKING SPELL, THERE'S ONLY SO MUCH I CAN DO. CAN'T BE A "DETECTIVE" IF THERE ISN'T MUCH TO DETECT.
Sigh... WE BETTER FIND SOMETHING QUICK. THAT DAMNED SYMBOL IS IN THE SKY AND THERE'LL BE A KNIGHT COMING FOR US SOON ENOUGH.
M-MAYBE I GOT IT WRONG...THE LOCATION. I SUPPOSE... I C-COULD'VE MADE A MISTAKE.

KLNK

THE ONLY MISTAKE *YOU* MADE, SQUIRE, WAS NOT TAKING MY ADVICE IN THE FIRST PLACE.

I TOLD YOU TO LEAVE IT ALONE, DIDN'T I?

JOHN?

'LO, LUV.

I WISH THIS REUNION WAS UNDER BETTER CIRCUMSTANCES. BUT IT'S PRETTY PAR FOR THE COURSE WITH US, *eh?*

WHAT HAPPENED TO YOU?

CAME FACE TO FACE WITH A KNIGHT NOT LONG AGO. NOT WITHOUT ITS COSTS, SURVIVAL.

IS IT TRUE, JOHN? IS THERE A CLOAKING SPELL? ARE YOU AND THE OTHERS BUILDING A SAFE HAVEN OF SOME SORT?

SAFE HAVEN? IS THAT WHAT YOU THINK THIS IS?

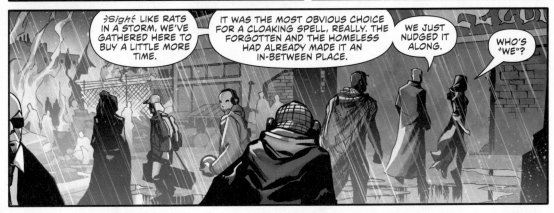

Sigh LIKE RATS IN A STORM, WE'VE GATHERED HERE TO BUY A LITTLE MORE TIME.

IT WAS THE MOST OBVIOUS CHOICE FOR A CLOAKING SPELL, REALLY. THE FORGOTTEN AND THE HOMELESS HAD ALREADY MADE IT AN IN-BETWEEN PLACE.

WE JUST NUDGED IT ALONG.

WHO'S "WE"?

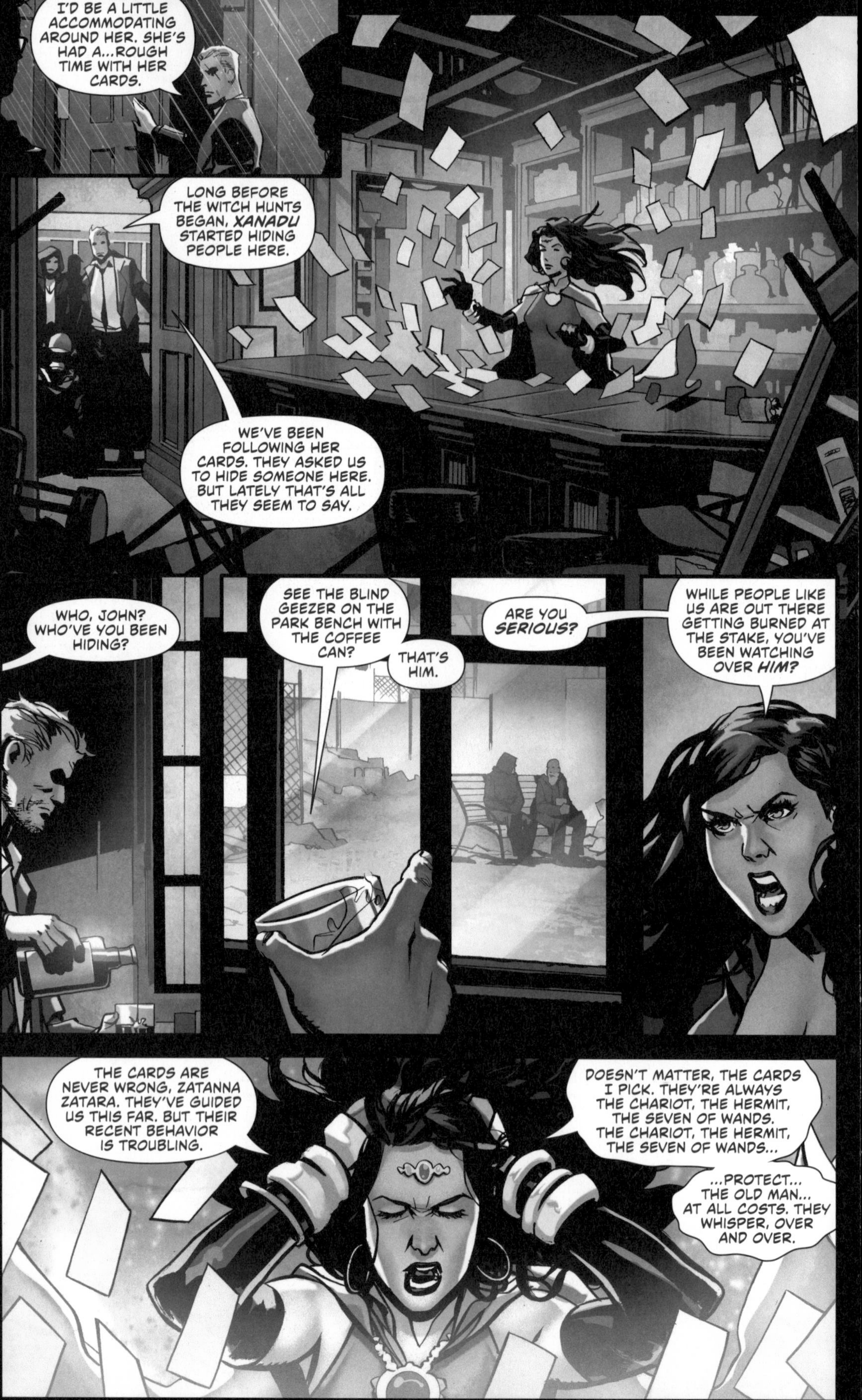

I'D BE A LITTLE ACCOMMODATING AROUND HER. SHE'S HAD A...ROUGH TIME WITH HER CARDS.
LONG BEFORE THE WITCH HUNTS BEGAN, XANADU STARTED HIDING PEOPLE HERE.
WE'VE BEEN FOLLOWING HER CARDS. THEY ASKED US TO HIDE SOMEONE HERE. BUT LATELY THAT'S ALL THEY SEEM TO SAY.
WHO, JOHN? WHO'VE YOU BEEN HIDING?
SEE THE BLIND GEEZER ON THE PARK BENCH WITH THE COFFEE CAN?
THAT'S HIM.
ARE YOU SERIOUS?
WHILE PEOPLE LIKE US ARE OUT THERE GETTING BURNED AT THE STAKE, YOU'VE BEEN WATCHING OVER HIM?
THE CARDS ARE NEVER WRONG, ZATANNA ZATARA. THEY'VE GUIDED US THIS FAR. BUT THEIR RECENT BEHAVIOR IS TROUBLING.
DOESN'T MATTER, THE CARDS I PICK. THEY'RE ALWAYS THE CHARIOT, THE HERMIT, THE SEVEN OF WANDS. THE CHARIOT, THE HERMIT, THE SEVEN OF WANDS...
...PROTECT... THE OLD MAN... AT ALL COSTS. THEY WHISPER, OVER AND OVER.

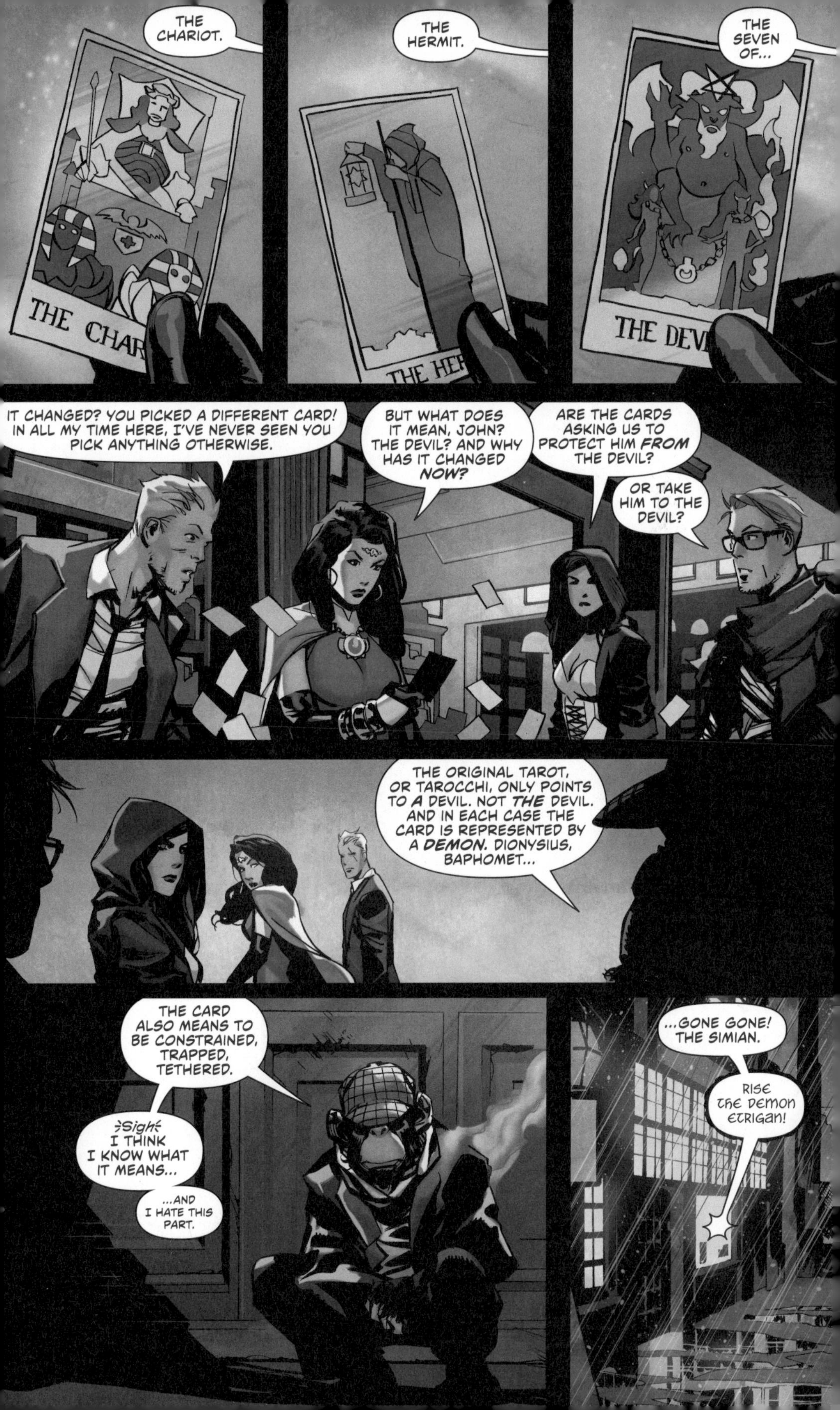
THE CHARIOT.
THE CHAR
THE HERMIT.
THE HER
THE SEVEN OF...
THE DEVI
IT CHANGED? YOU PICKED A DIFFERENT CARD! IN ALL MY TIME HERE, I'VE NEVER SEEN YOU PICK ANYTHING OTHERWISE.
BUT WHAT DOES IT MEAN, JOHN? THE DEVIL? AND WHY HAS IT CHANGED NOW?
ARE THE CARDS ASKING US TO PROTECT HIM FROM THE DEVIL?
OR TAKE HIM TO THE DEVIL?
THE ORIGINAL TAROT, OR TAROCCHI, ONLY POINTS TO A DEVIL. NOT THE DEVIL. AND IN EACH CASE THE CARD IS REPRESENTED BY A DEMON. DIONYSIUS, BAPHOMET...
THE CARD ALSO MEANS TO BE CONSTRAINED, TRAPPED, TETHERED.
Sigh I THINK I KNOW WHAT IT MEANS...
...AND I HATE THIS PART.
...GONE GONE! THE SIMIAN.
RISE THE DEMON ETRIGAN!

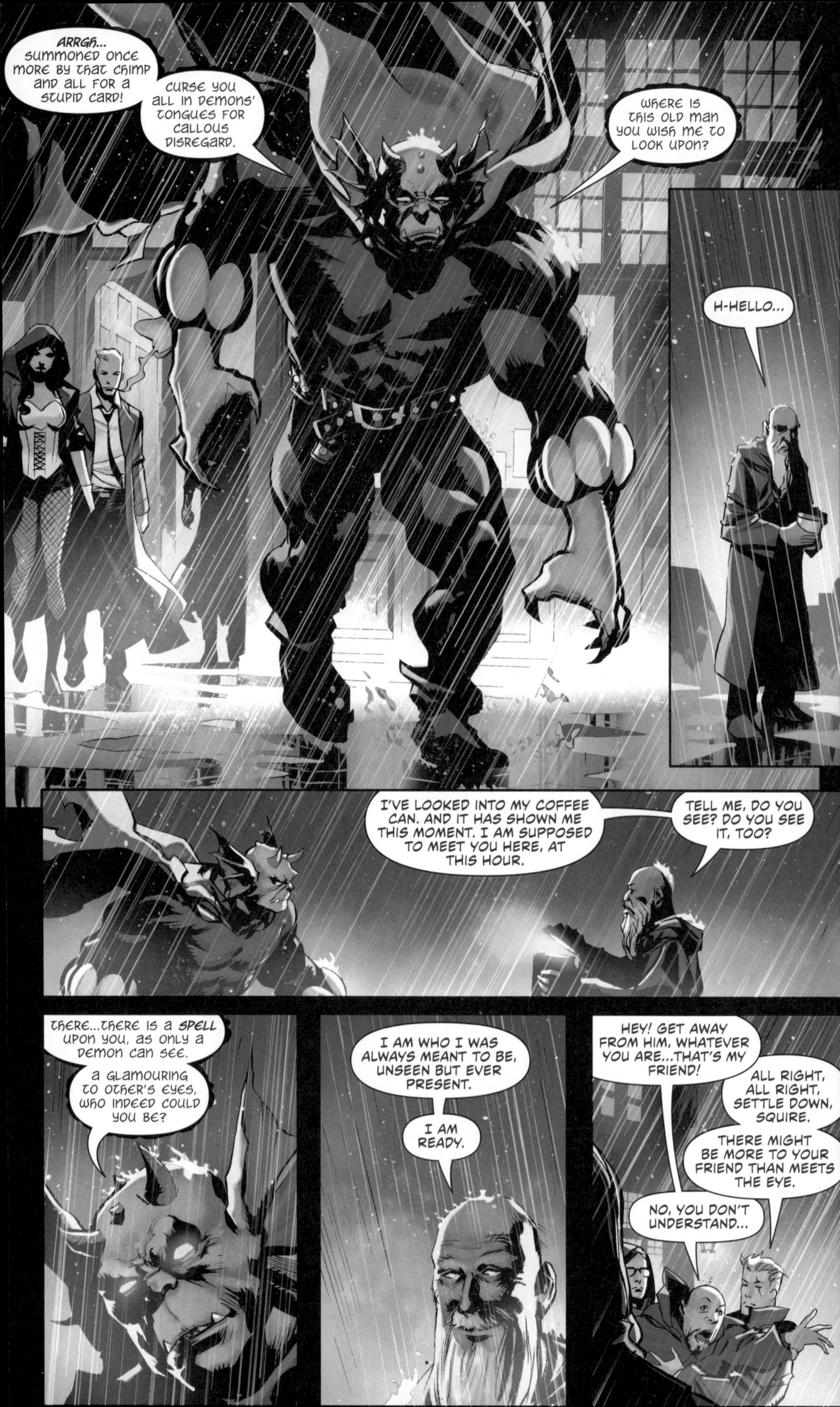
ARRGH... SUMMONED ONCE MORE BY THAT CHIMP AND ALL FOR A STUPID CARD!
CURSE YOU ALL IN DEMONS' TONGUES FOR CALLOUS DISREGARD.
WHERE IS THIS OLD MAN YOU WISH ME TO LOOK UPON?
H-HELLO...
I'VE LOOKED INTO MY COFFEE CAN. AND IT HAS SHOWN ME THIS MOMENT. I AM SUPPOSED TO MEET YOU HERE, AT THIS HOUR.
TELL ME, DO YOU SEE? DO YOU SEE IT, TOO?
THERE...THERE IS A SPELL UPON YOU, AS ONLY A DEMON CAN SEE.
A GLAMOURING TO OTHER'S EYES, WHO INDEED COULD YOU BE?
I AM WHO I WAS ALWAYS MEANT TO BE, UNSEEN BUT EVER PRESENT.
I AM READY.
HEY! GET AWAY FROM HIM, WHATEVER YOU ARE...THAT'S MY FRIEND!
ALL RIGHT, ALL RIGHT, SETTLE DOWN, SQUIRE.
THERE MIGHT BE MORE TO YOUR FRIEND THAN MEETS THE EYE.
NO, YOU DON'T UNDERSTAND...

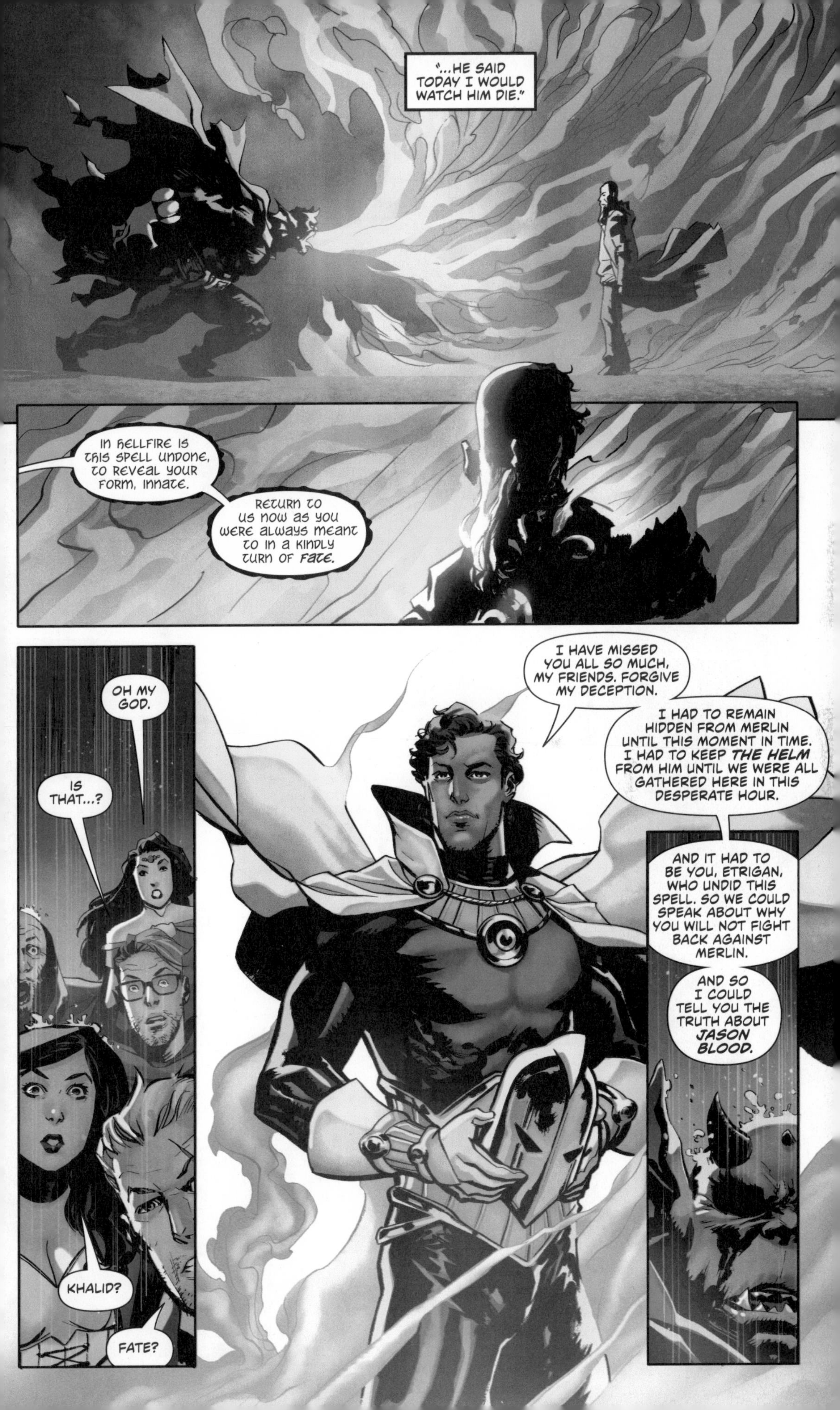
"...HE SAID TODAY I WOULD WATCH HIM DIE."
IN HELLFIRE IS THIS SPELL UNDONE, TO REVEAL YOUR FORM, INNATE.
RETURN TO US NOW AS YOU WERE ALWAYS MEANT TO IN A KINDLY TURN OF FATE.
I HAVE MISSED YOU ALL SO MUCH, MY FRIENDS. FORGIVE MY DECEPTION.
I HAD TO REMAIN HIDDEN FROM MERLIN UNTIL THIS MOMENT IN TIME. I HAD TO KEEP THE HELM FROM HIM UNTIL WE WERE ALL GATHERED HERE IN THIS DESPERATE HOUR.
OH MY GOD.
IS THAT...?
AND IT HAD TO BE YOU, ETRIGAN, WHO UNDID THIS SPELL. SO WE COULD SPEAK ABOUT WHY YOU WILL NOT FIGHT BACK AGAINST MERLIN.
AND SO I COULD TELL YOU THE TRUTH ABOUT JASON BLOOD.
KHALID?
FATE?

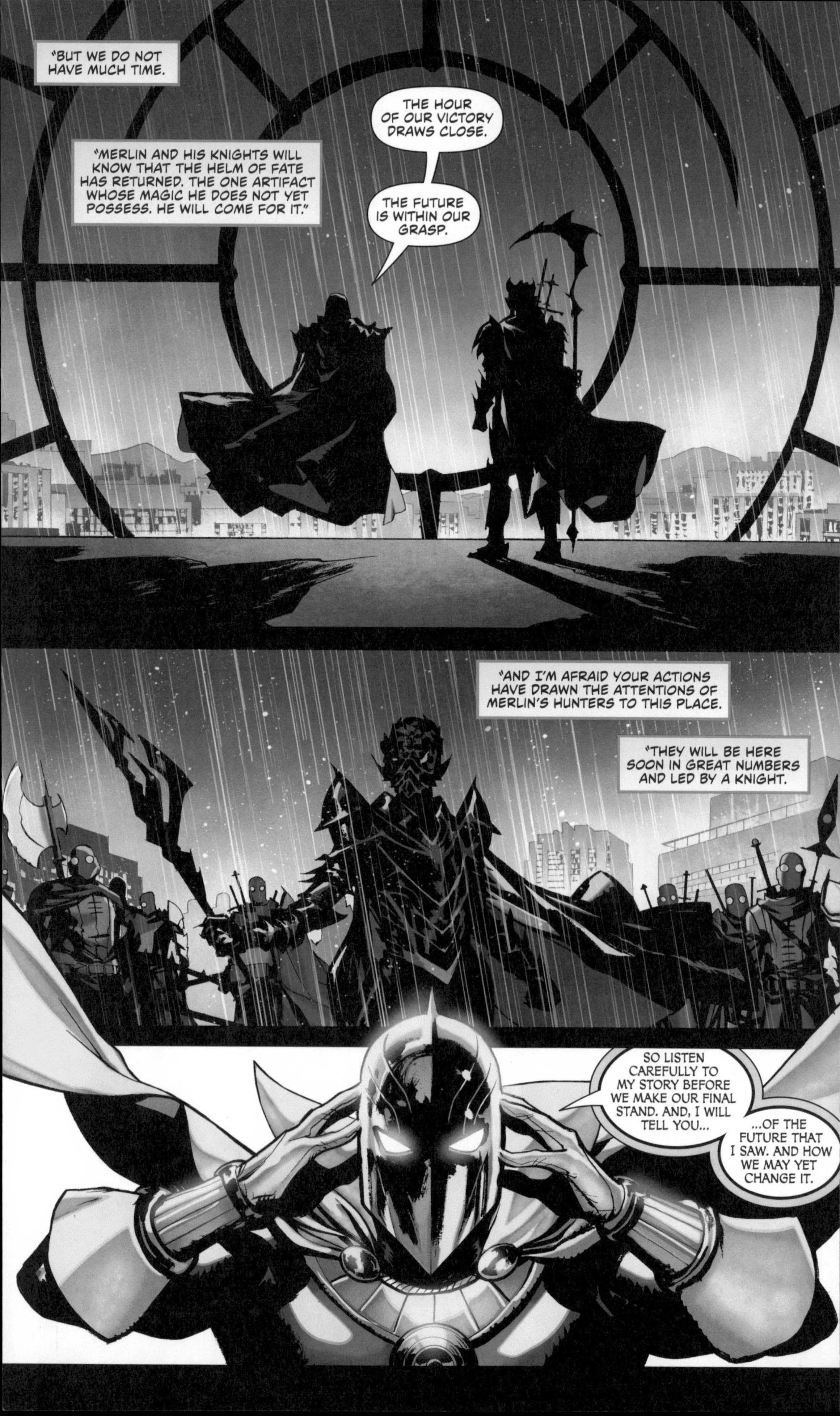
"BUT WE DO NOT HAVE MUCH TIME.
"MERLIN AND HIS KNIGHTS WILL KNOW THAT THE HELM OF FATE HAS RETURNED. THE ONE ARTIFACT WHOSE MAGIC HE DOES NOT YET POSSESS. HE WILL COME FOR IT."
THE HOUR OF OUR VICTORY DRAWS CLOSE.
THE FUTURE IS WITHIN OUR GRASP.
"AND I'M AFRAID YOUR ACTIONS HAVE DRAWN THE ATTENTIONS OF MERLIN'S HUNTERS TO THIS PLACE.
"THEY WILL BE HERE SOON IN GREAT NUMBERS AND LED BY A KNIGHT.
SO LISTEN CAREFULLY TO MY STORY BEFORE WE MAKE OUR FINAL STAND. AND, I WILL TELL YOU...
...OF THE FUTURE THAT I SAW. AND HOW WE MAY YET CHANGE IT.

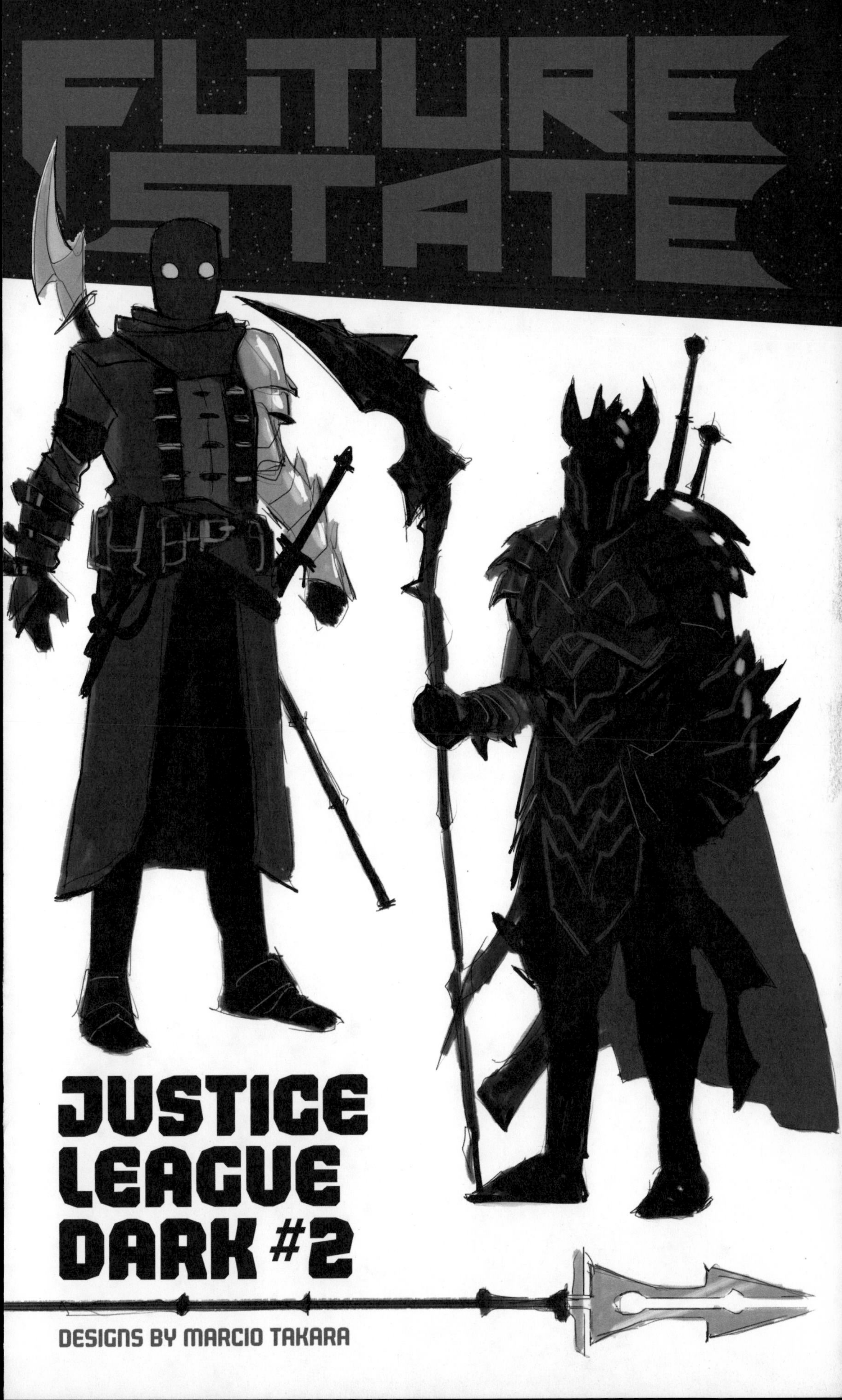
FUTURE STATE
JUSTICE LEAGUE DARK #2
DESIGNS BY MARCIO TAKARA

FUTURE STATE

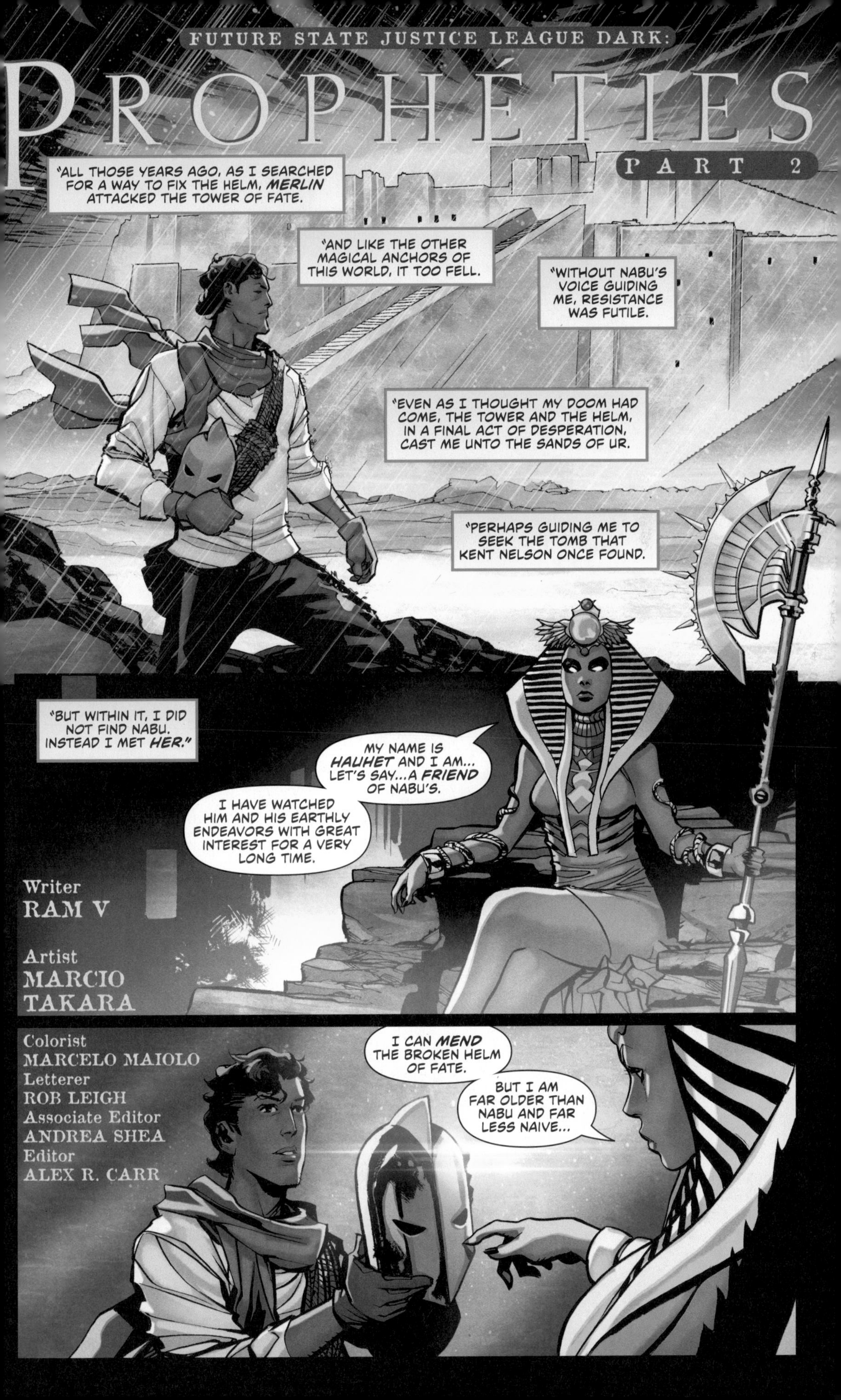

FUTURE STATE JUSTICE LEAGUE DARK:
PROPHÉTIES
PART 2
"ALL THOSE YEARS AGO, AS I SEARCHED FOR A WAY TO FIX THE HELM, MERLIN ATTACKED THE TOWER OF FATE.
"AND LIKE THE OTHER MAGICAL ANCHORS OF THIS WORLD, IT TOO FELL.
"WITHOUT NABU'S VOICE GUIDING ME, RESISTANCE WAS FUTILE.
"EVEN AS I THOUGHT MY DOOM HAD COME, THE TOWER AND THE HELM, IN A FINAL ACT OF DESPERATION, CAST ME UNTO THE SANDS OF UR.
"PERHAPS GUIDING ME TO SEEK THE TOMB THAT KENT NELSON ONCE FOUND.
"BUT WITHIN IT, I DID NOT FIND NABU. INSTEAD I MET HER."
MY NAME IS HAUHET AND I AM... LET'S SAY...A FRIEND OF NABU'S.
I HAVE WATCHED HIM AND HIS EARTHLY ENDEAVORS WITH GREAT INTEREST FOR A VERY LONG TIME.
Writer
RAM V
Artist
MARCIO TAKARA
Colorist
MARCELO MAIOLO
Letterer
ROB LEIGH
Associate Editor
ANDREA SHEA
Editor
ALEX R. CARR
I CAN MEND THE BROKEN HELM OF FATE.
BUT I AM FAR OLDER THAN NABU AND FAR LESS NAIVE...

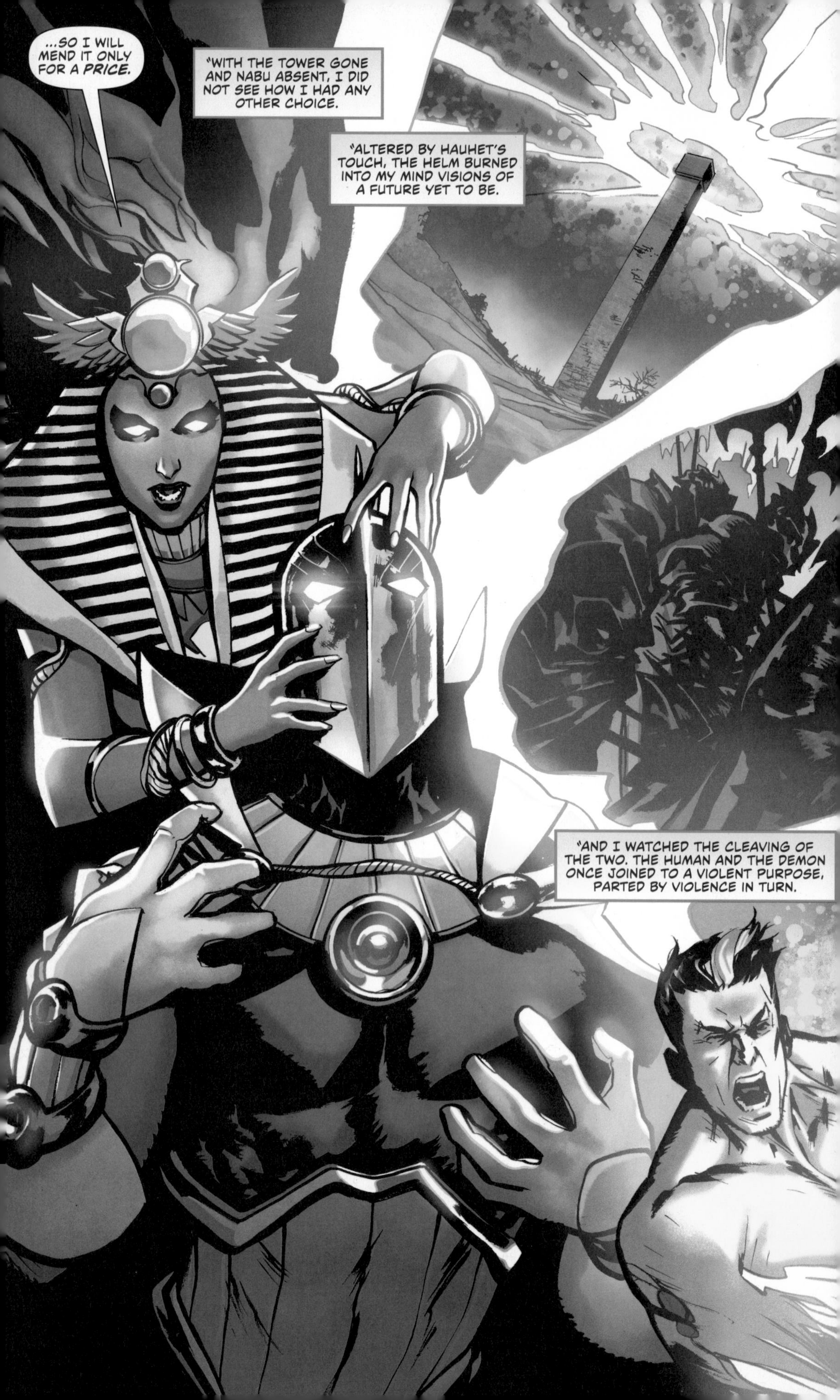
...SO I WILL MEND IT ONLY FOR A *PRICE*.
"WITH THE TOWER GONE AND NABU ABSENT, I DID NOT SEE HOW I HAD ANY OTHER CHOICE.
"ALTERED BY HAUHET'S TOUCH, THE HELM BURNED INTO MY MIND VISIONS OF A FUTURE YET TO BE.
"AND I WATCHED THE CLEAVING OF THE TWO. THE HUMAN AND THE DEMON ONCE JOINED TO A VIOLENT PURPOSE, PARTED BY VIOLENCE IN TURN.

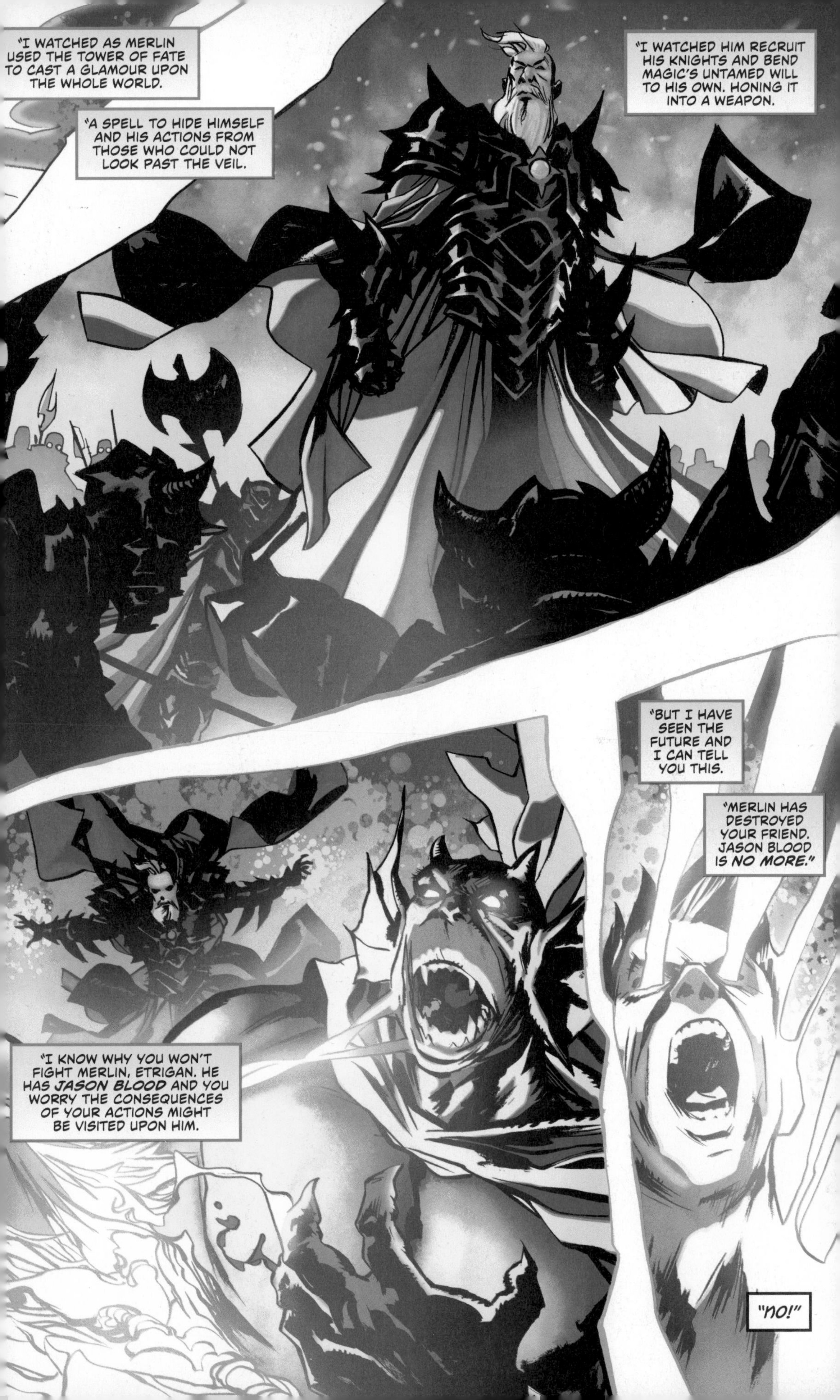
"I WATCHED AS MERLIN USED THE TOWER OF FATE TO CAST A GLAMOUR UPON THE WHOLE WORLD.
"A SPELL TO HIDE HIMSELF AND HIS ACTIONS FROM THOSE WHO COULD NOT LOOK PAST THE VEIL.
"I WATCHED HIM RECRUIT HIS KNIGHTS AND BEND MAGIC'S UNTAMED WILL TO HIS OWN. HONING IT INTO A WEAPON.
"BUT I HAVE SEEN THE FUTURE AND I CAN TELL YOU THIS.
"MERLIN HAS DESTROYED YOUR FRIEND. JASON BLOOD IS *NO MORE.*"
"I KNOW WHY YOU WON'T FIGHT MERLIN, ETRIGAN. HE HAS *JASON BLOOD* AND YOU WORRY THE CONSEQUENCES OF YOUR ACTIONS MIGHT BE VISITED UPON HIM.
"NO!"

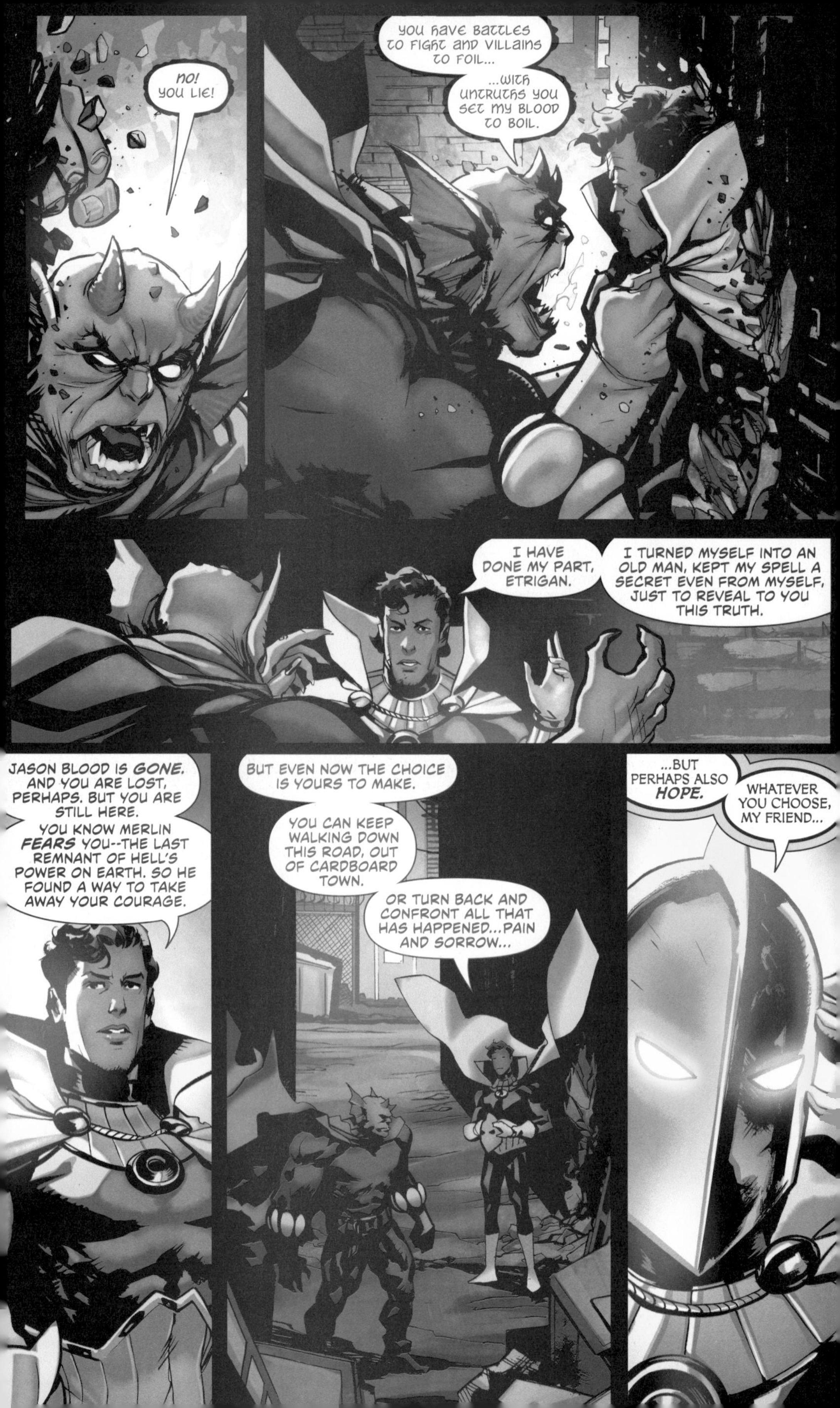
NO!
YOU LIE!
YOU HAVE BATTLES TO FIGHT AND VILLAINS TO FOIL...
...WITH UNTRUTHS YOU SET MY BLOOD TO BOIL.
I HAVE DONE MY PART, ETRIGAN.
I TURNED MYSELF INTO AN OLD MAN, KEPT MY SPELL A SECRET EVEN FROM MYSELF, JUST TO REVEAL TO YOU THIS TRUTH.
JASON BLOOD IS GONE. AND YOU ARE LOST, PERHAPS. BUT YOU ARE STILL HERE.
YOU KNOW MERLIN FEARS YOU--THE LAST REMNANT OF HELL'S POWER ON EARTH. SO HE FOUND A WAY TO TAKE AWAY YOUR COURAGE.
BUT EVEN NOW THE CHOICE IS YOURS TO MAKE.
YOU CAN KEEP WALKING DOWN THIS ROAD, OUT OF CARDBOARD TOWN.
OR TURN BACK AND CONFRONT ALL THAT HAS HAPPENED...PAIN AND SORROW...
...BUT PERHAPS ALSO HOPE.
WHATEVER YOU CHOOSE, MY FRIEND...

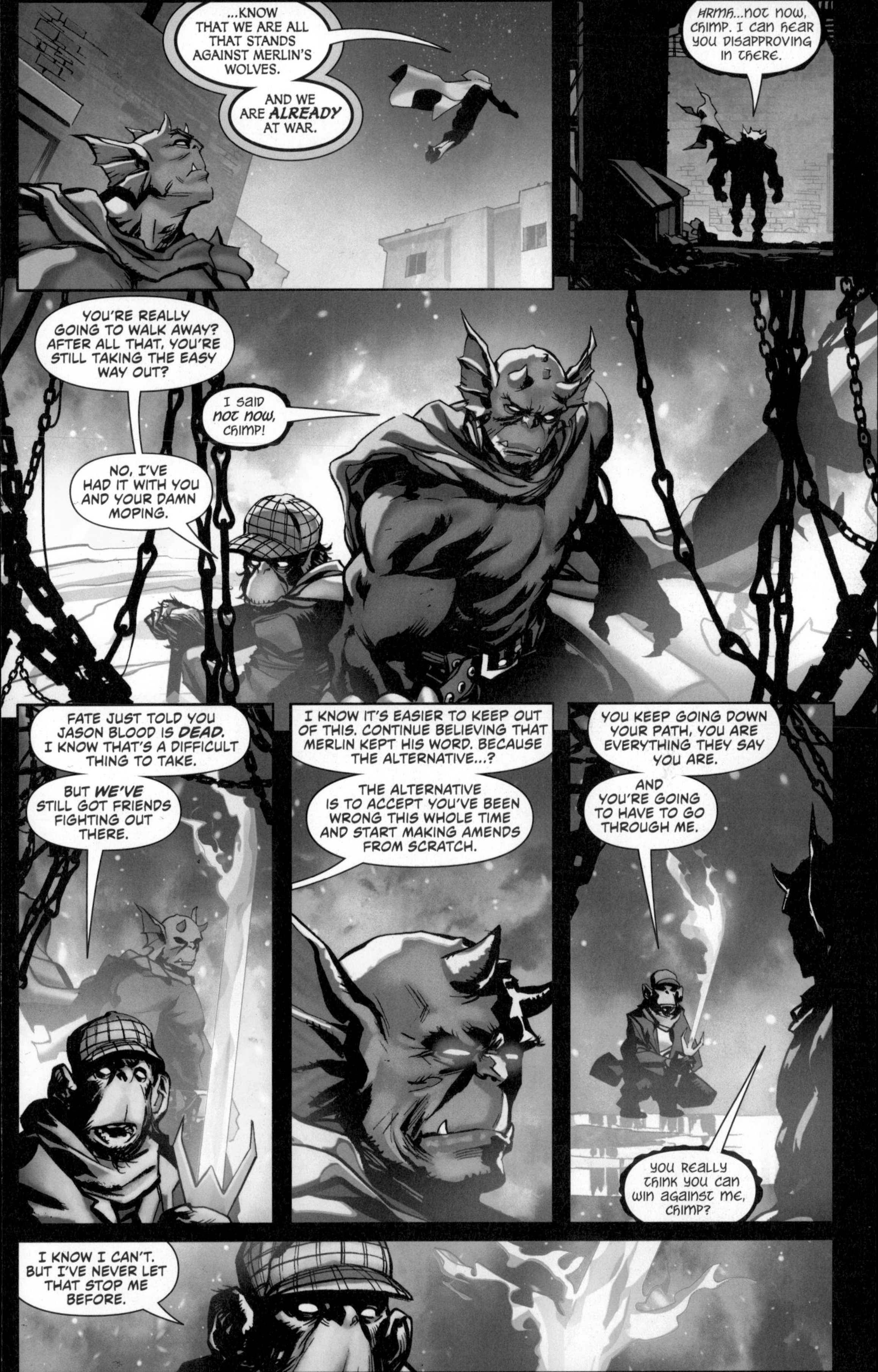
...KNOW THAT WE ARE ALL THAT STANDS AGAINST MERLIN'S WOLVES.
AND WE ARE ALREADY AT WAR.
HRMH...NOT NOW, CHIMP. I CAN HEAR YOU DISAPPROVING IN THERE.
YOU'RE REALLY GOING TO WALK AWAY? AFTER ALL THAT, YOU'RE STILL TAKING THE EASY WAY OUT?
I SAID NOT NOW, CHIMP!
NO, I'VE HAD IT WITH YOU AND YOUR DAMN MOPING.
FATE JUST TOLD YOU JASON BLOOD IS DEAD. I KNOW THAT'S A DIFFICULT THING TO TAKE.
BUT WE'VE STILL GOT FRIENDS FIGHTING OUT THERE.
I KNOW IT'S EASIER TO KEEP OUT OF THIS. CONTINUE BELIEVING THAT MERLIN KEPT HIS WORD. BECAUSE THE ALTERNATIVE...?
THE ALTERNATIVE IS TO ACCEPT YOU'VE BEEN WRONG THIS WHOLE TIME AND START MAKING AMENDS FROM SCRATCH.
YOU KEEP GOING DOWN YOUR PATH, YOU ARE EVERYTHING THEY SAY YOU ARE.
AND YOU'RE GOING TO HAVE TO GO THROUGH ME.
YOU REALLY THINK YOU CAN WIN AGAINST ME, CHIMP?
I KNOW I CAN'T. BUT I'VE NEVER LET THAT STOP ME BEFORE.

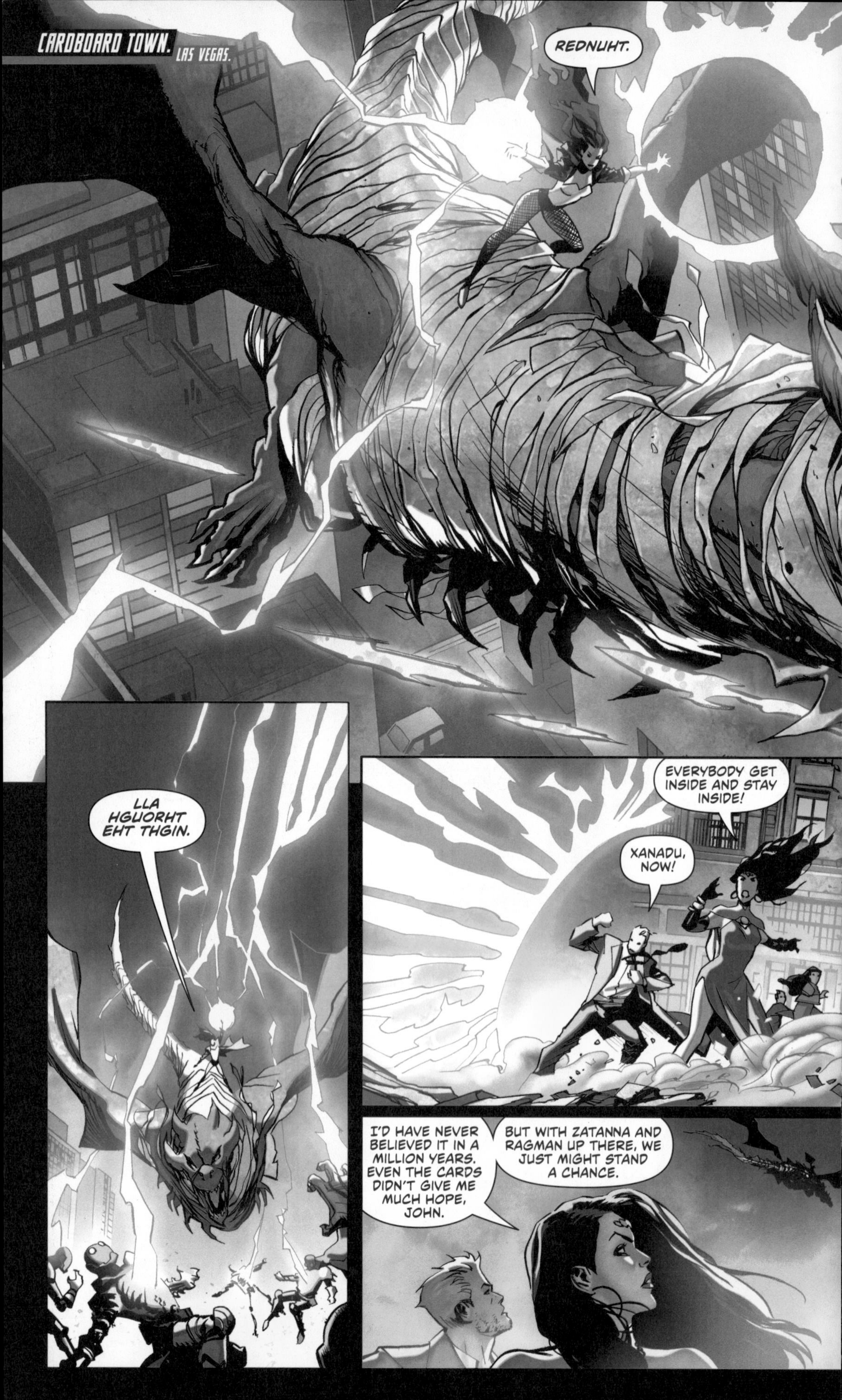
CARDBOARD TOWN. LAS VEGAS.
REDNUHT.
LLA HGUORHT EHT THGIN.
EVERYBODY GET INSIDE AND STAY INSIDE!
XANADU, NOW!
I'D HAVE NEVER BELIEVED IT IN A MILLION YEARS. EVEN THE CARDS DIDN'T GIVE ME MUCH HOPE, JOHN.
BUT WITH ZATANNA AND RAGMAN UP THERE, WE JUST MIGHT STAND A CHANCE.

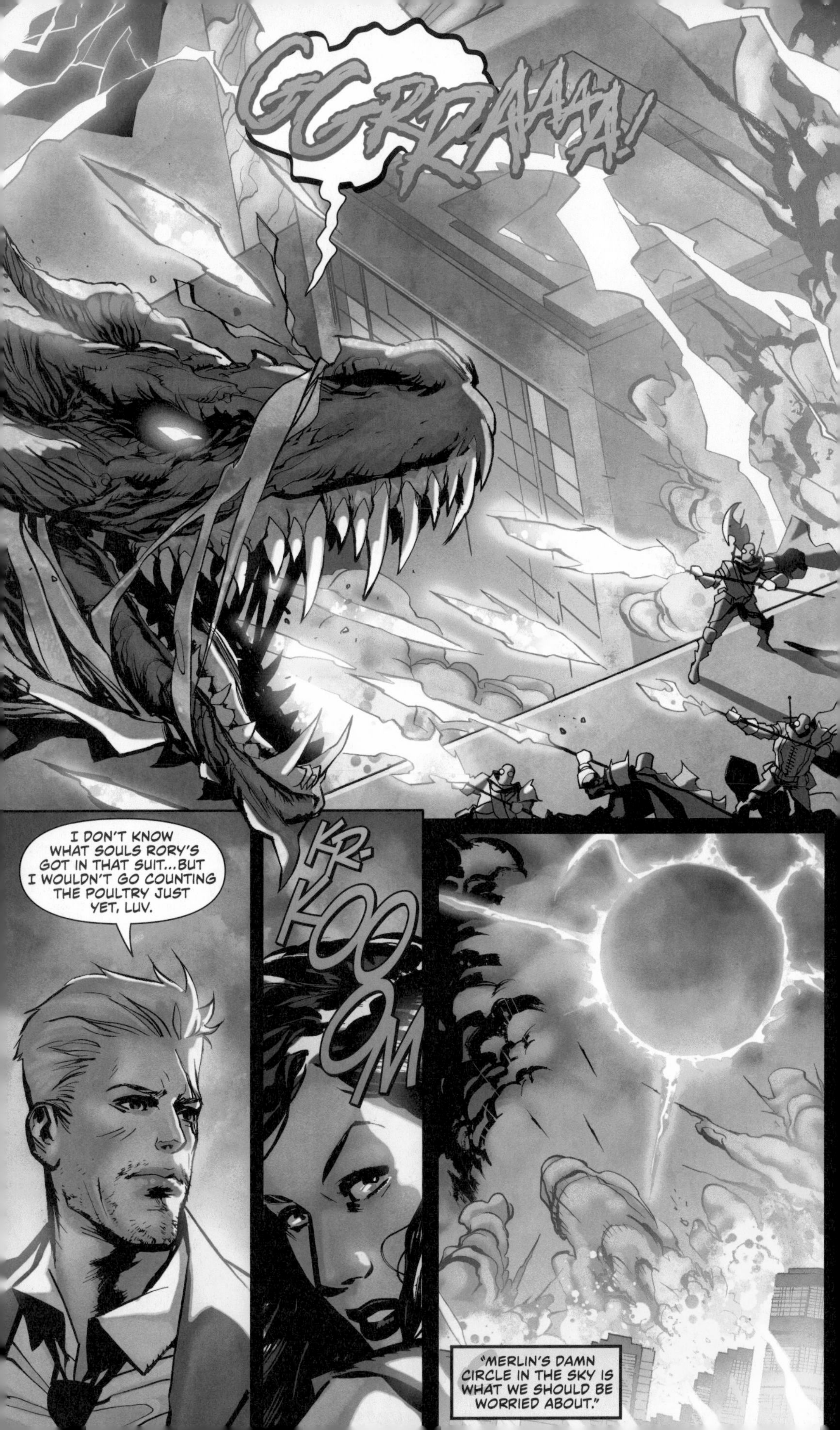
GGRRAAAA!
I DON'T KNOW WHAT SOULS RORY'S GOT IN THAT SUIT...BUT I WOULDN'T GO COUNTING THE POULTRY JUST YET, LUV.
KR-KOOOOM
"MERLIN'S DAMN CIRCLE IN THE SKY IS WHAT WE SHOULD BE WORRIED ABOUT."

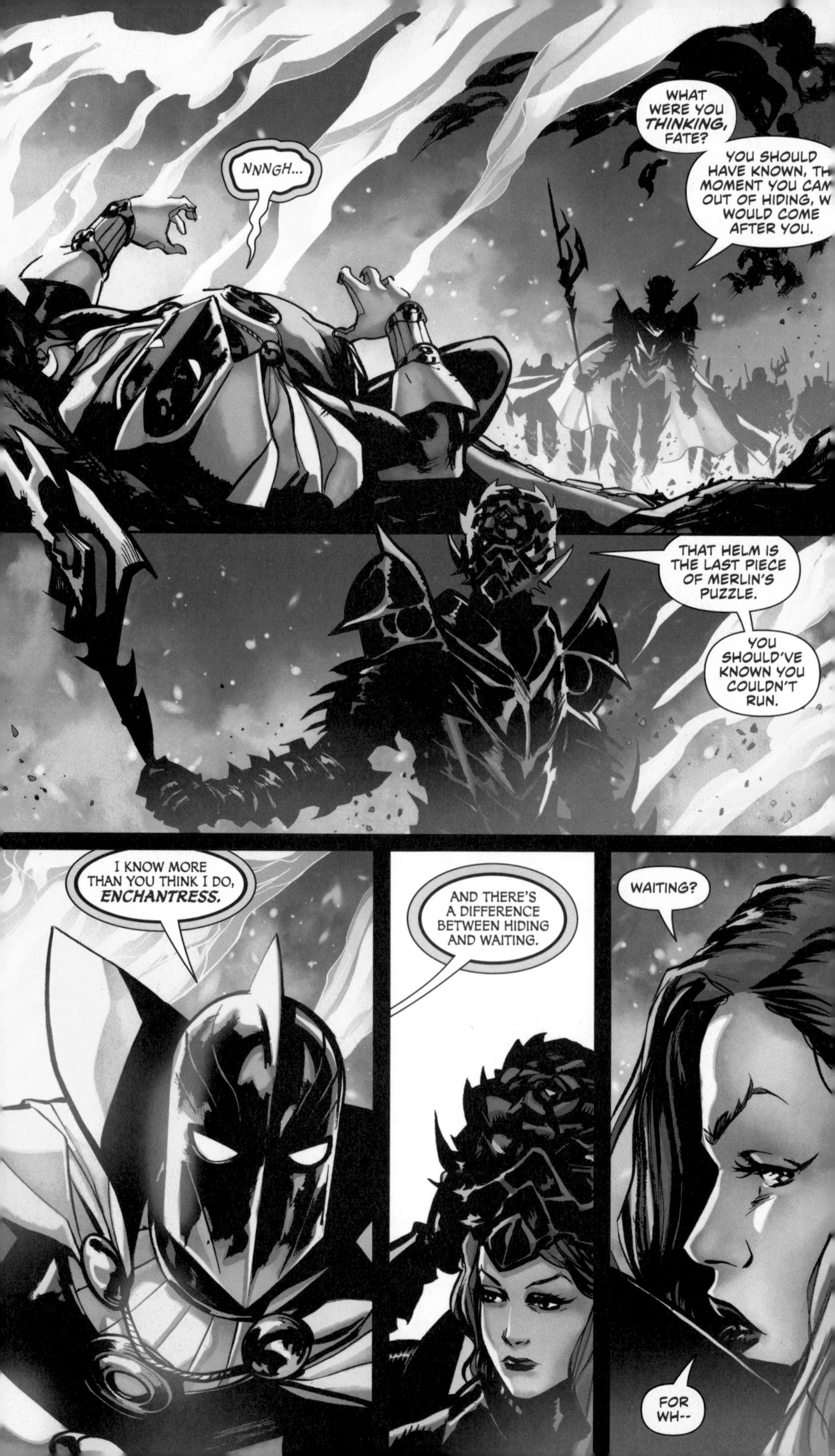
NNNGH...
WHAT WERE YOU THINKING, FATE?
YOU SHOULD HAVE KNOWN, TH MOMENT YOU CAM OUT OF HIDING, W WOULD COME AFTER YOU.
THAT HELM IS THE LAST PIECE OF MERLIN'S PUZZLE.
YOU SHOULD'VE KNOWN YOU COULDN'T RUN.
I KNOW MORE THAN YOU THINK I DO, ENCHANTRESS.
AND THERE'S A DIFFERENCE BETWEEN HIDING AND WAITING.
WAITING?
FOR WH--

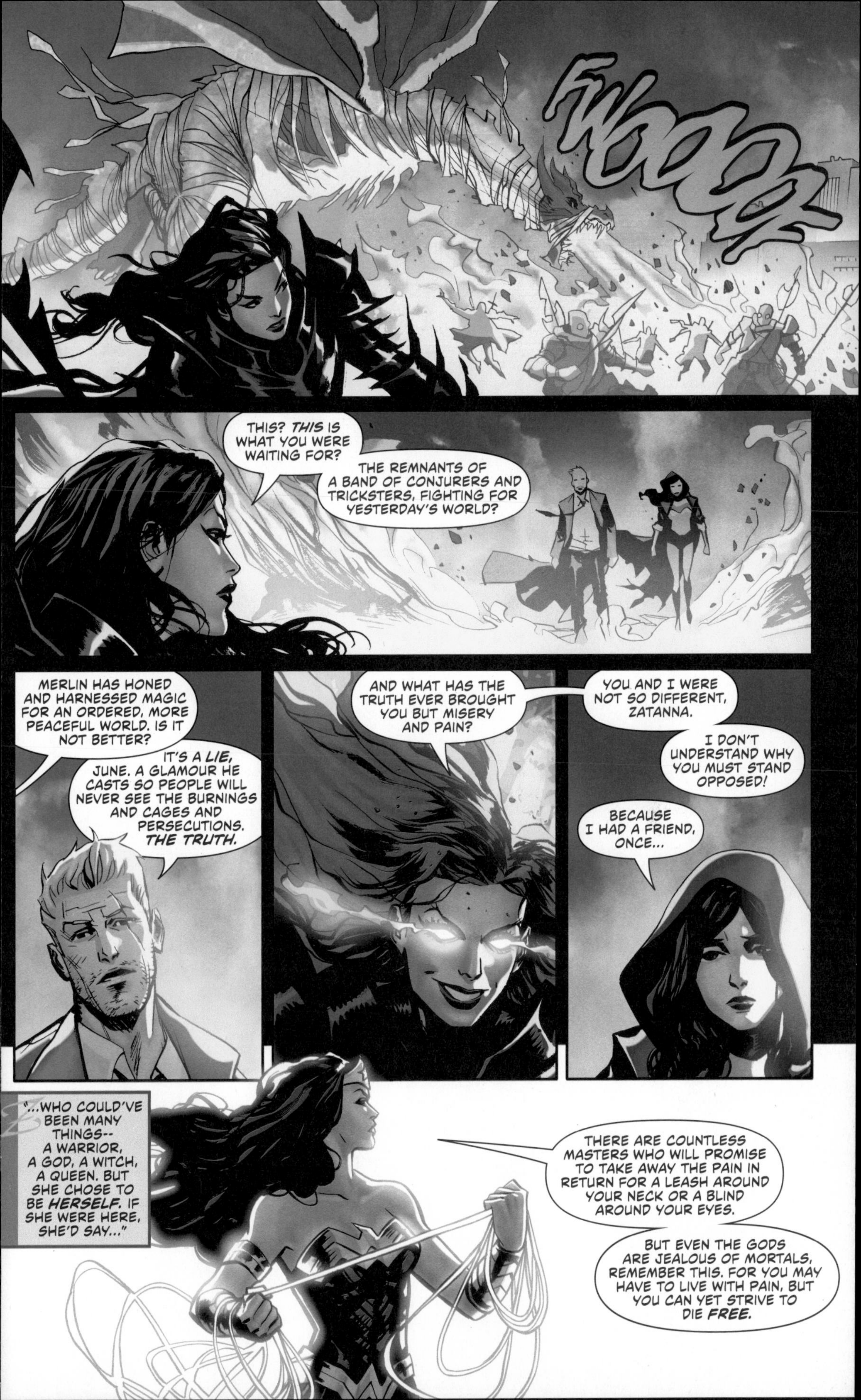

FWOOOOOF
THIS? *THIS* IS WHAT YOU WERE WAITING FOR?
THE REMNANTS OF A BAND OF CONJURERS AND TRICKSTERS, FIGHTING FOR YESTERDAY'S WORLD?
MERLIN HAS HONED AND HARNESSED MAGIC FOR AN ORDERED, MORE PEACEFUL WORLD. IS IT NOT BETTER?
IT'S A *LIE,* JUNE. A GLAMOUR HE CASTS SO PEOPLE WILL NEVER SEE THE BURNINGS AND CAGES AND PERSECUTIONS. *THE TRUTH.*
AND WHAT HAS THE TRUTH EVER BROUGHT YOU BUT MISERY AND PAIN?
YOU AND I WERE NOT SO DIFFERENT, ZATANNA.
I DON'T UNDERSTAND WHY YOU MUST STAND OPPOSED!
BECAUSE I HAD A FRIEND, ONCE...
"...WHO COULD'VE BEEN MANY THINGS-- A WARRIOR, A GOD, A WITCH, A QUEEN. BUT SHE CHOSE TO BE *HERSELF.* IF SHE WERE HERE, SHE'D SAY..."
THERE ARE COUNTLESS MASTERS WHO WILL PROMISE TO TAKE AWAY THE PAIN IN RETURN FOR A LEASH AROUND YOUR NECK OR A BLIND AROUND YOUR EYES.
BUT EVEN THE GODS ARE JEALOUS OF MORTALS, REMEMBER THIS. FOR YOU MAY HAVE TO LIVE WITH PAIN, BUT YOU CAN YET STRIVE TO DIE *FREE.*

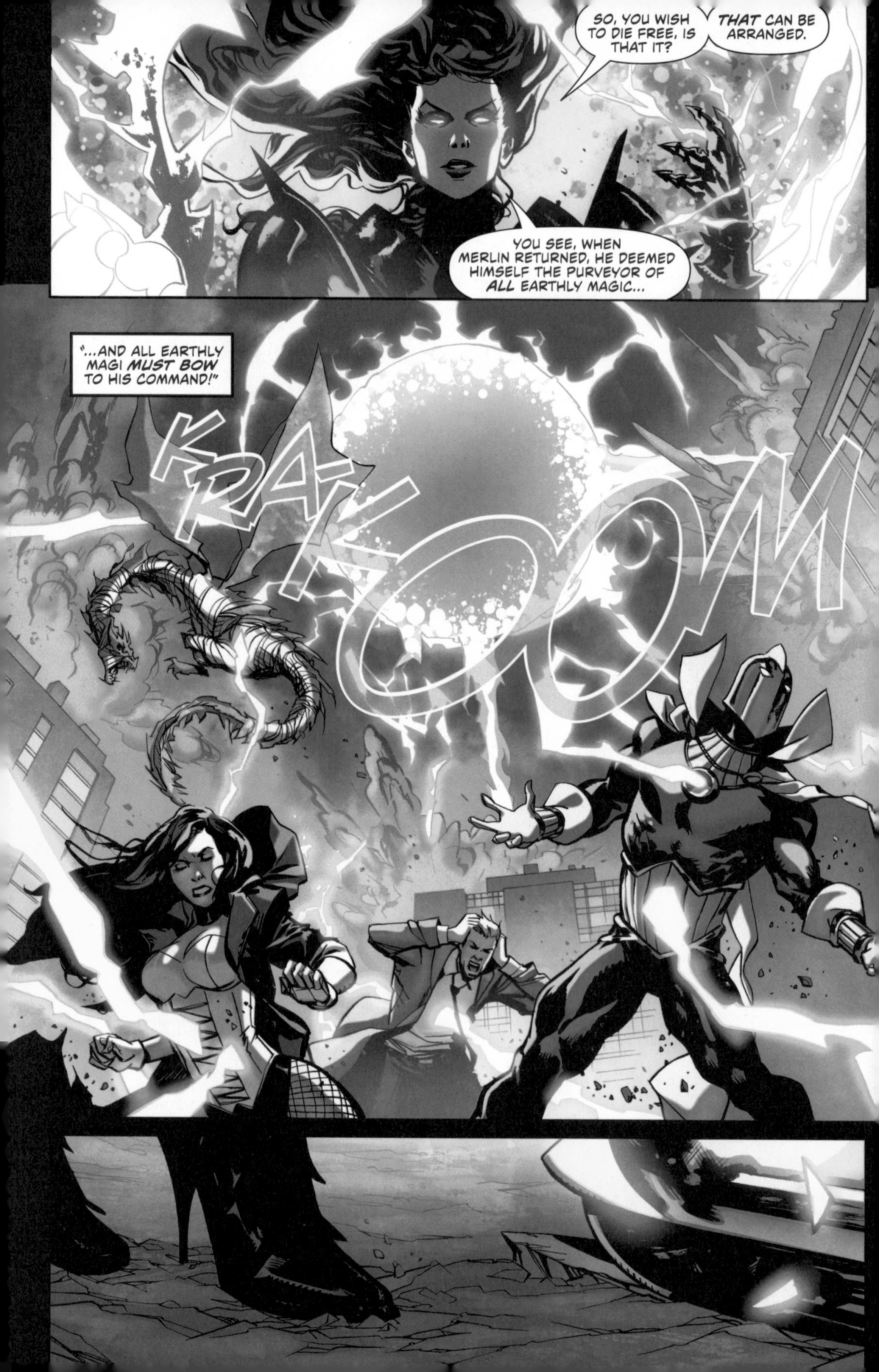
SO, YOU WISH TO DIE FREE, IS THAT IT?
THAT CAN BE ARRANGED.
YOU SEE, WHEN MERLIN RETURNED, HE DEEMED HIMSELF THE PURVEYOR OF ALL EARTHLY MAGIC...
"...AND ALL EARTHLY MAGI MUST BOW TO HIS COMMAND!"
KRAKOOOM

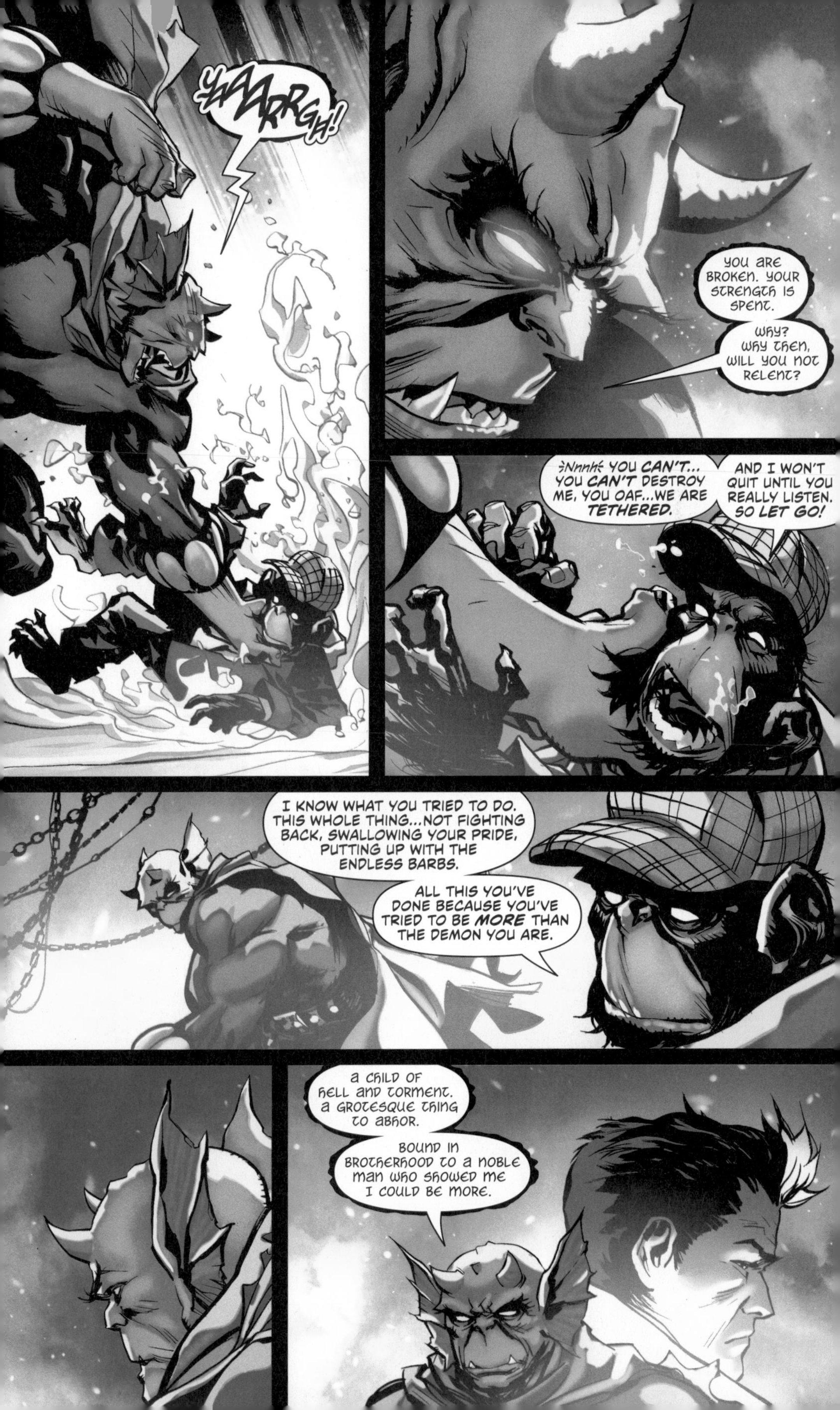
YAAARRGH!
YOU ARE BROKEN. YOUR STRENGTH IS SPENT.
WHY? WHY THEN, WILL YOU NOT RELENT?
Nnnh YOU CAN'T... YOU CAN'T DESTROY ME, YOU OAF...WE ARE TETHERED.
AND I WON'T QUIT UNTIL YOU REALLY LISTEN. SO LET GO!
I KNOW WHAT YOU TRIED TO DO. THIS WHOLE THING...NOT FIGHTING BACK, SWALLOWING YOUR PRIDE, PUTTING UP WITH THE ENDLESS BARBS.
ALL THIS YOU'VE DONE BECAUSE YOU'VE TRIED TO BE MORE THAN THE DEMON YOU ARE.
A CHILD OF HELL AND TORMENT. A GROTESQUE THING TO ABHOR.
BOUND IN BROTHERHOOD TO A NOBLE MAN WHO SHOWED ME I COULD BE MORE.

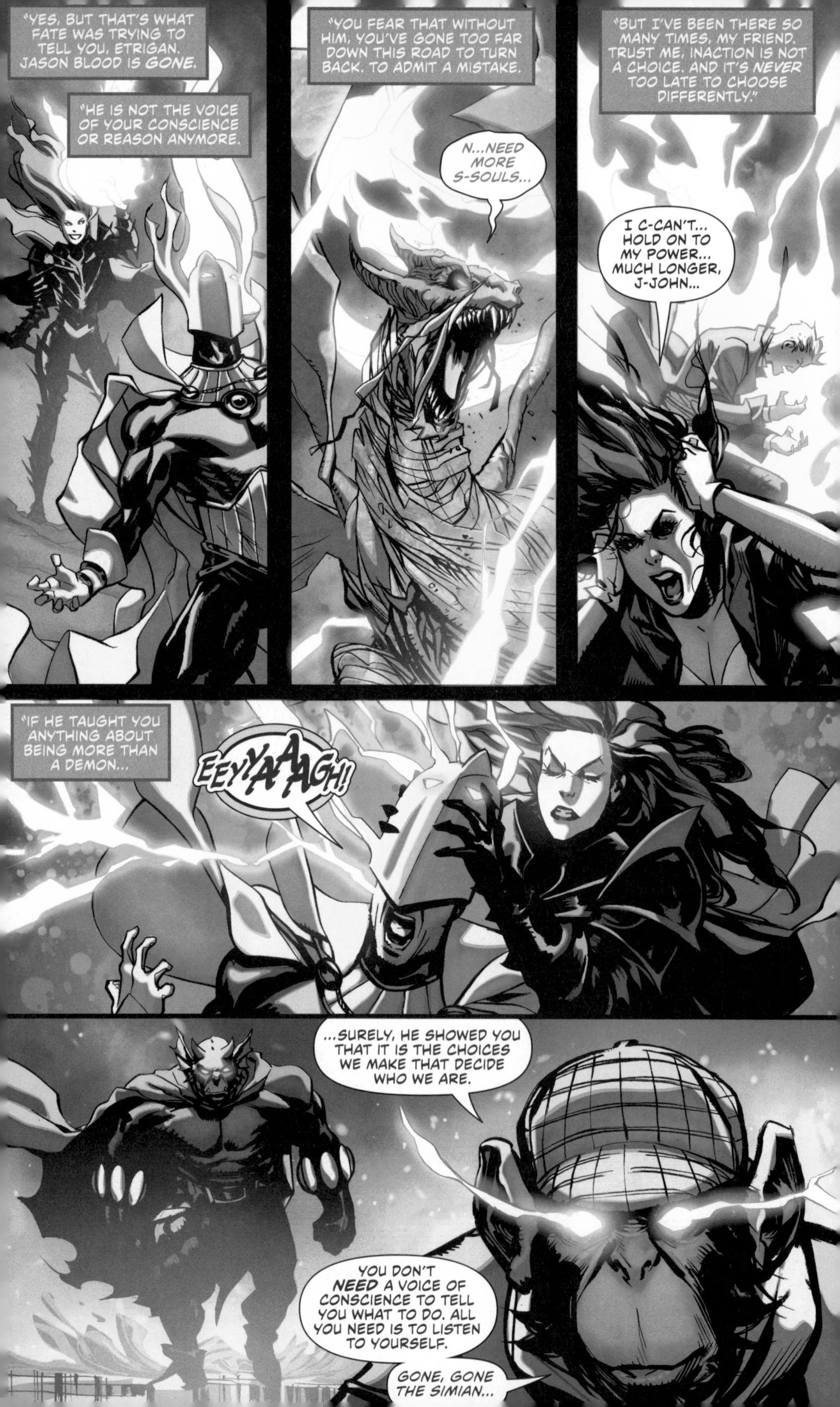
"YES, BUT THAT'S WHAT FATE WAS TRYING TO TELL YOU, ETRIGAN. JASON BLOOD IS *GONE*.
"HE IS NOT THE VOICE OF YOUR CONSCIENCE OR REASON ANYMORE.
"YOU FEAR THAT WITHOUT HIM, YOU'VE GONE TOO FAR DOWN THIS ROAD TO TURN BACK. TO ADMIT A MISTAKE.
N...NEED MORE S-SOULS...
"BUT I'VE BEEN THERE SO MANY TIMES, MY FRIEND. TRUST ME, INACTION IS NOT A CHOICE. AND IT'S *NEVER* TOO LATE TO CHOOSE DIFFERENTLY."
I C-CAN'T... HOLD ON TO MY POWER... MUCH LONGER, J-JOHN...
"IF HE TAUGHT YOU ANYTHING ABOUT BEING MORE THAN A DEMON...
EEYYAAAAGH!
...SURELY, HE SHOWED YOU THAT IT IS THE CHOICES WE MAKE THAT DECIDE WHO WE ARE.
YOU DON'T **NEED** A VOICE OF CONSCIENCE TO TELL YOU WHAT TO DO. ALL YOU NEED IS TO LISTEN TO YOURSELF.
GONE, GONE THE SIMIAN...

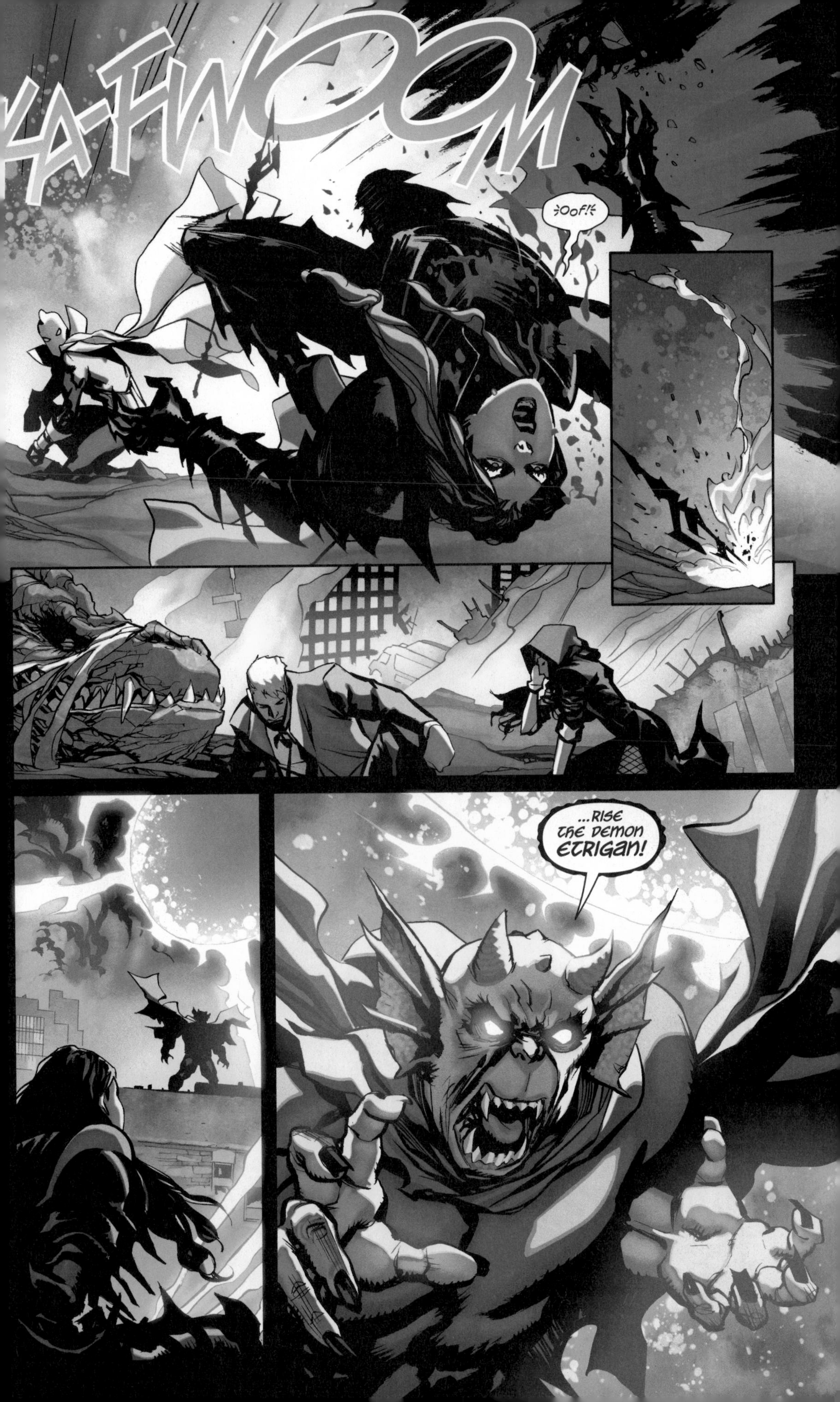
KA-FWOOM
Oof!
...RISE THE DEMON ETRIGAN!

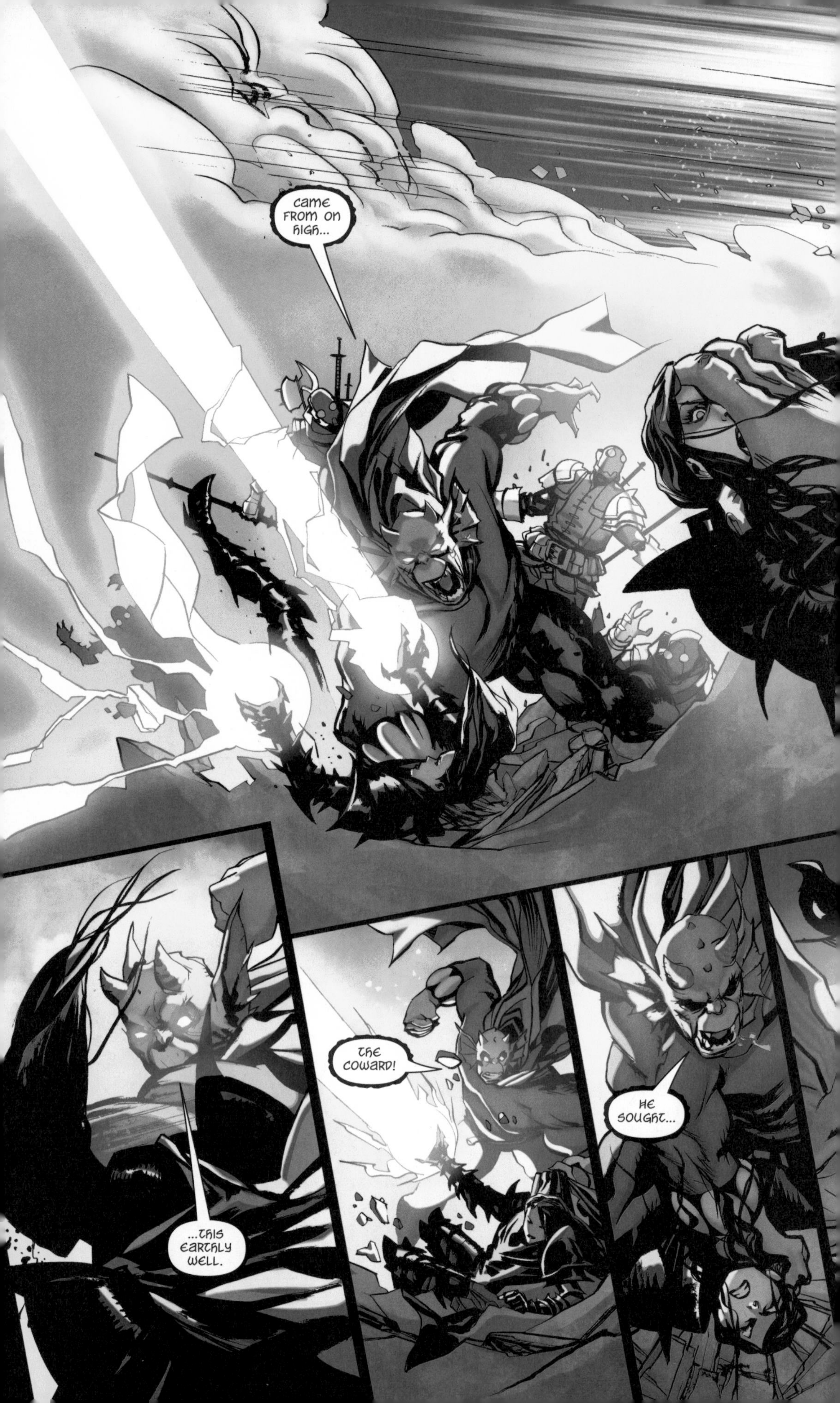

CAME FROM ON HIGH...
...THIS EARTHLY WELL.
THE COWARD!
HE SOUGHT...

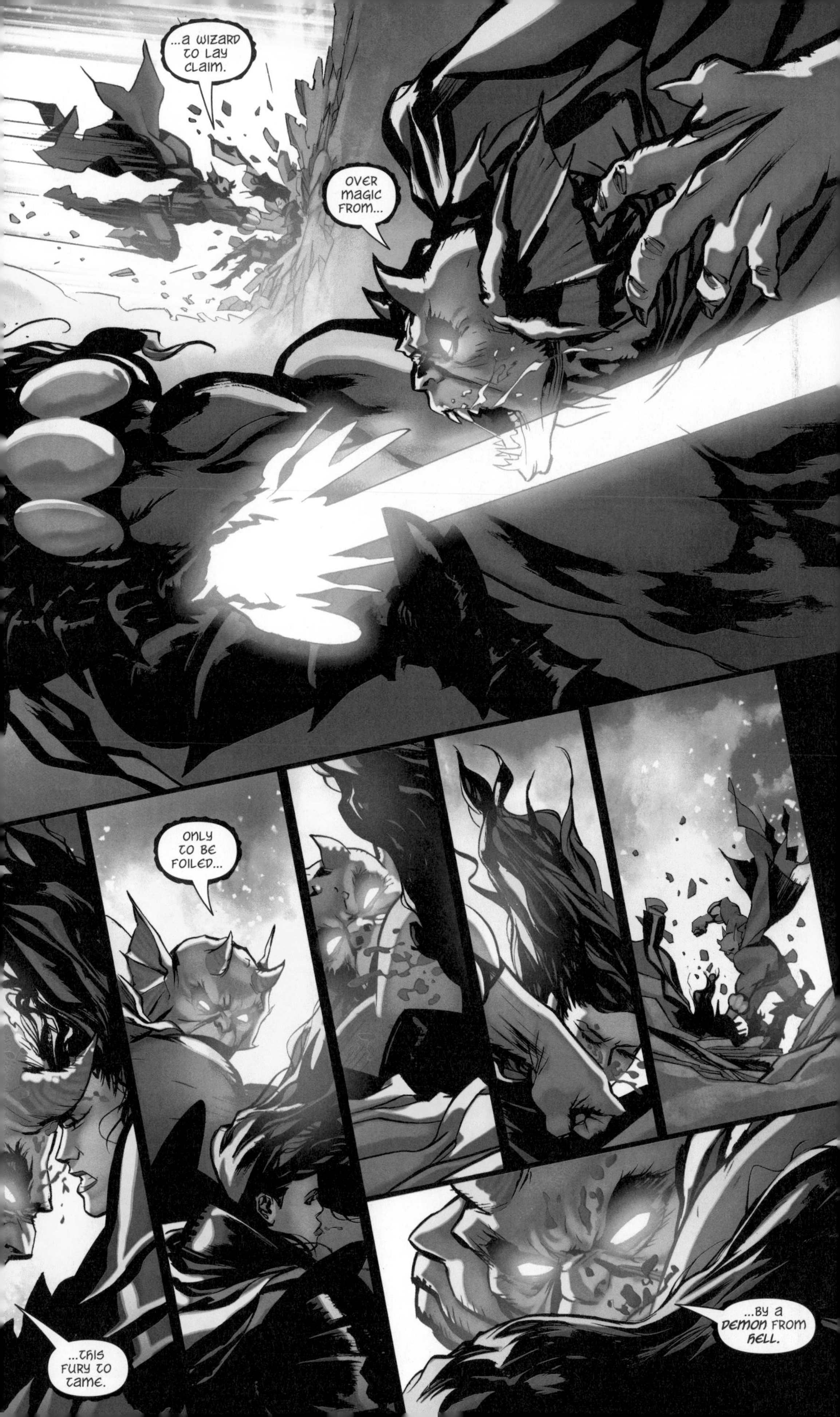
...a wizard to lay claim.
OVER magic FROM...
ONLY TO BE FOILED...
...BY A DEMON FROM HELL.
...THIS FURY TO TAME.

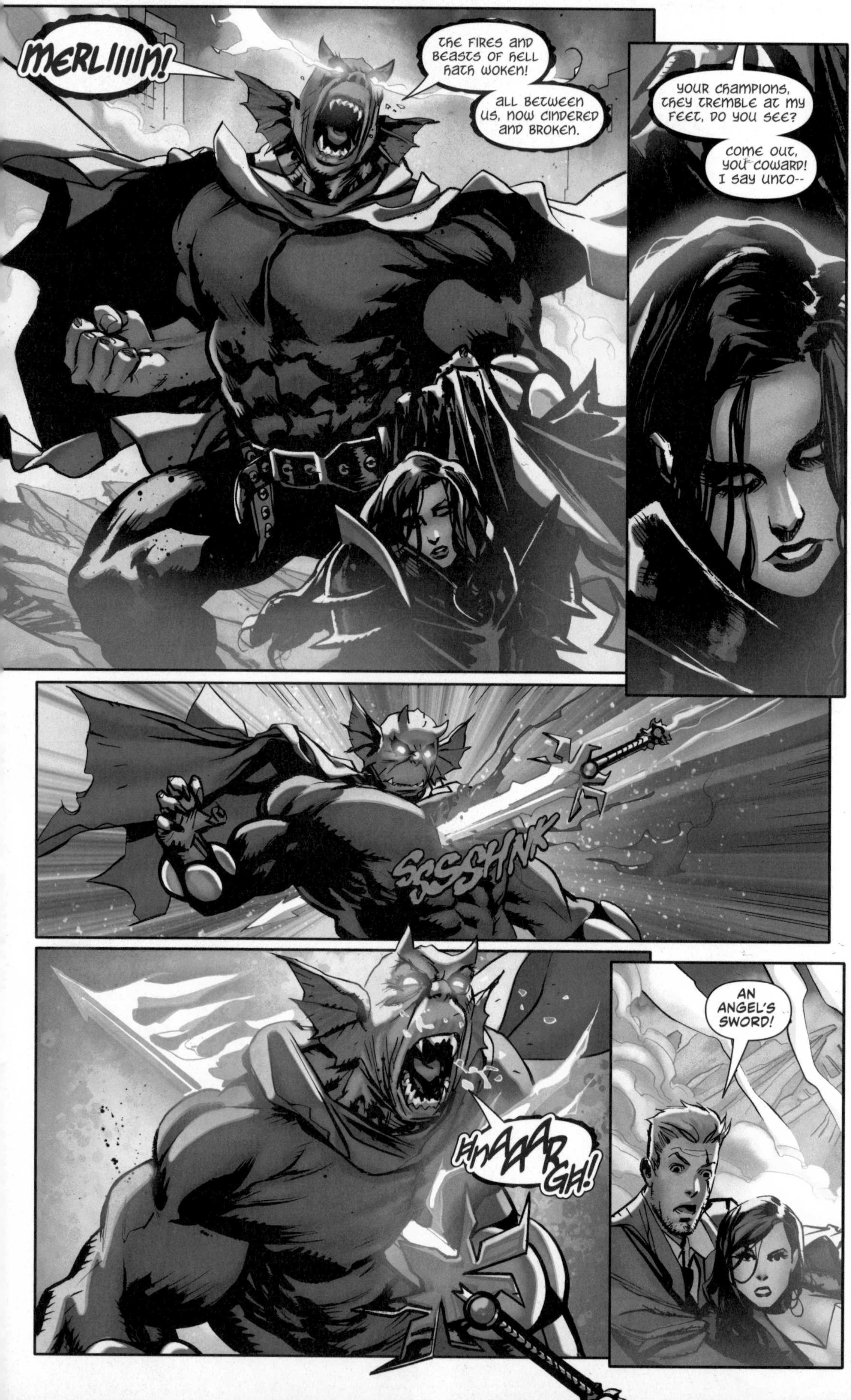
MERLIIIIN!
THE FIRES AND BEASTS OF HELL HATH WOKEN!
ALL BETWEEN US, NOW CINDERED AND BROKEN.
YOUR CHAMPIONS, THEY TREMBLE AT MY FEET, DO YOU SEE?
COME OUT, YOU COWARD! I SAY UNTO--
SSSSHNK
HNAAARGH!
AN ANGEL'S SWORD!

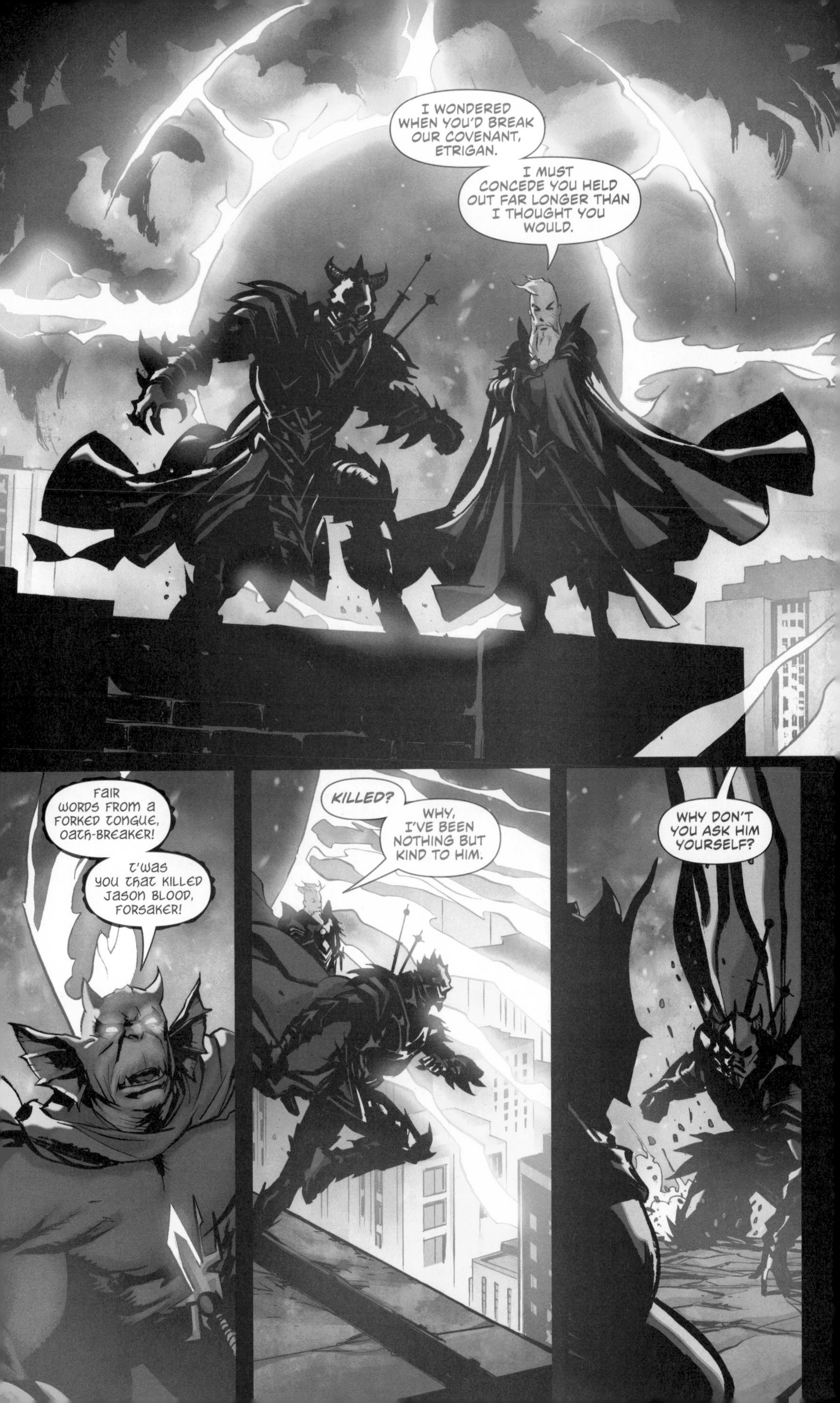
I WONDERED WHEN YOU'D BREAK OUR COVENANT, ETRIGAN.
I MUST CONCEDE YOU HELD OUT FAR LONGER THAN I THOUGHT YOU WOULD.
FAIR WORDS FROM A FORKED TONGUE, OATH-BREAKER!
T'WAS YOU THAT KILLED JASON BLOOD, FORSAKER!
KILLED?
WHY, I'VE BEEN NOTHING BUT KIND TO HIM.
WHY DON'T YOU ASK HIM YOURSELF?

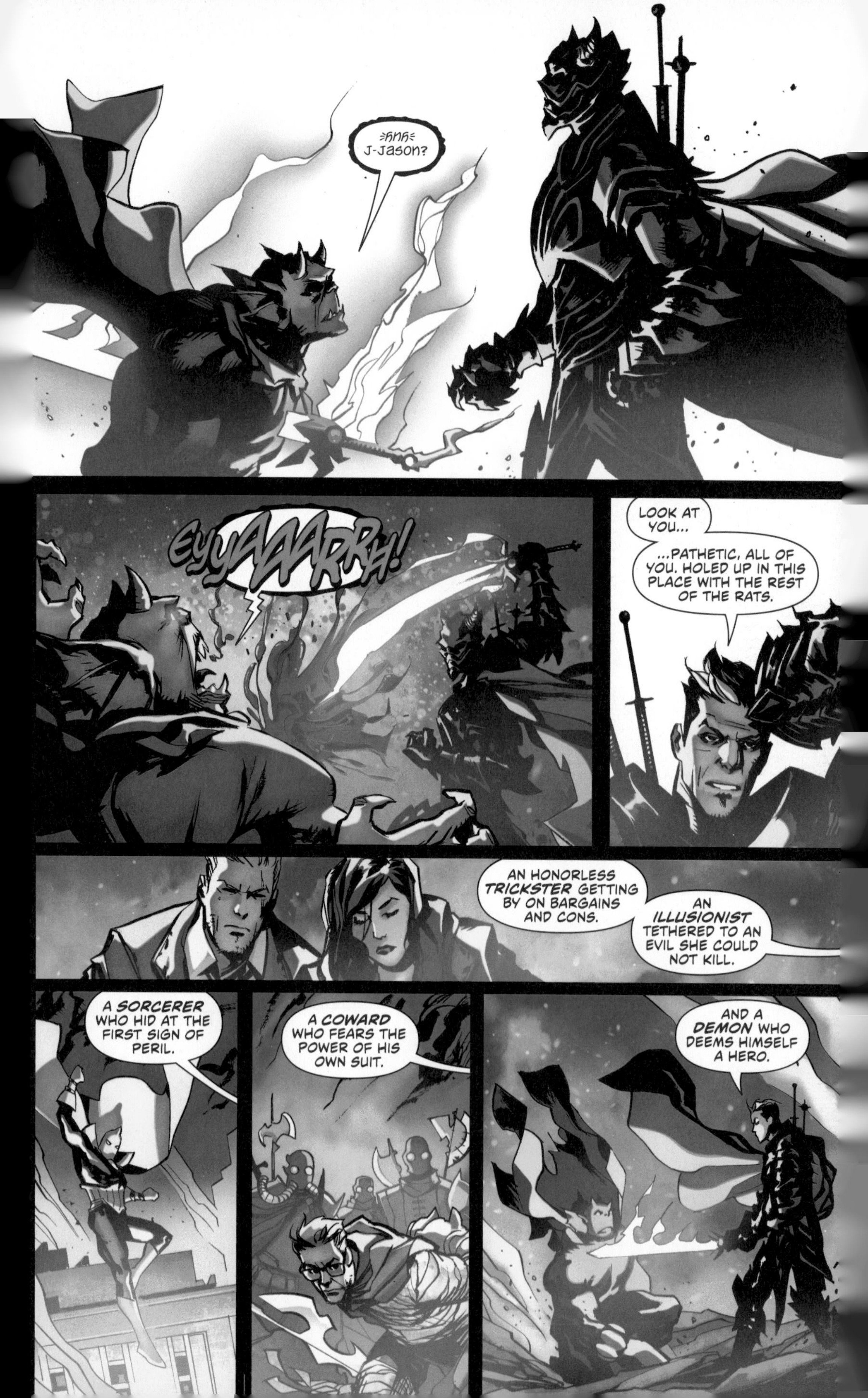

≈HHH≈
J-JASON?
EYYAAAARRH!
LOOK AT YOU...
...PATHETIC, ALL OF YOU. HOLED UP IN THIS PLACE WITH THE REST OF THE RATS.
AN HONORLESS TRICKSTER GETTING BY ON BARGAINS AND CONS.
AN ILLUSIONIST TETHERED TO AN EVIL SHE COULD NOT KILL.
A SORCERER WHO HID AT THE FIRST SIGN OF PERIL.
A COWARD WHO FEARS THE POWER OF HIS OWN SUIT.
AND A DEMON WHO DEEMS HIMSELF A HERO.

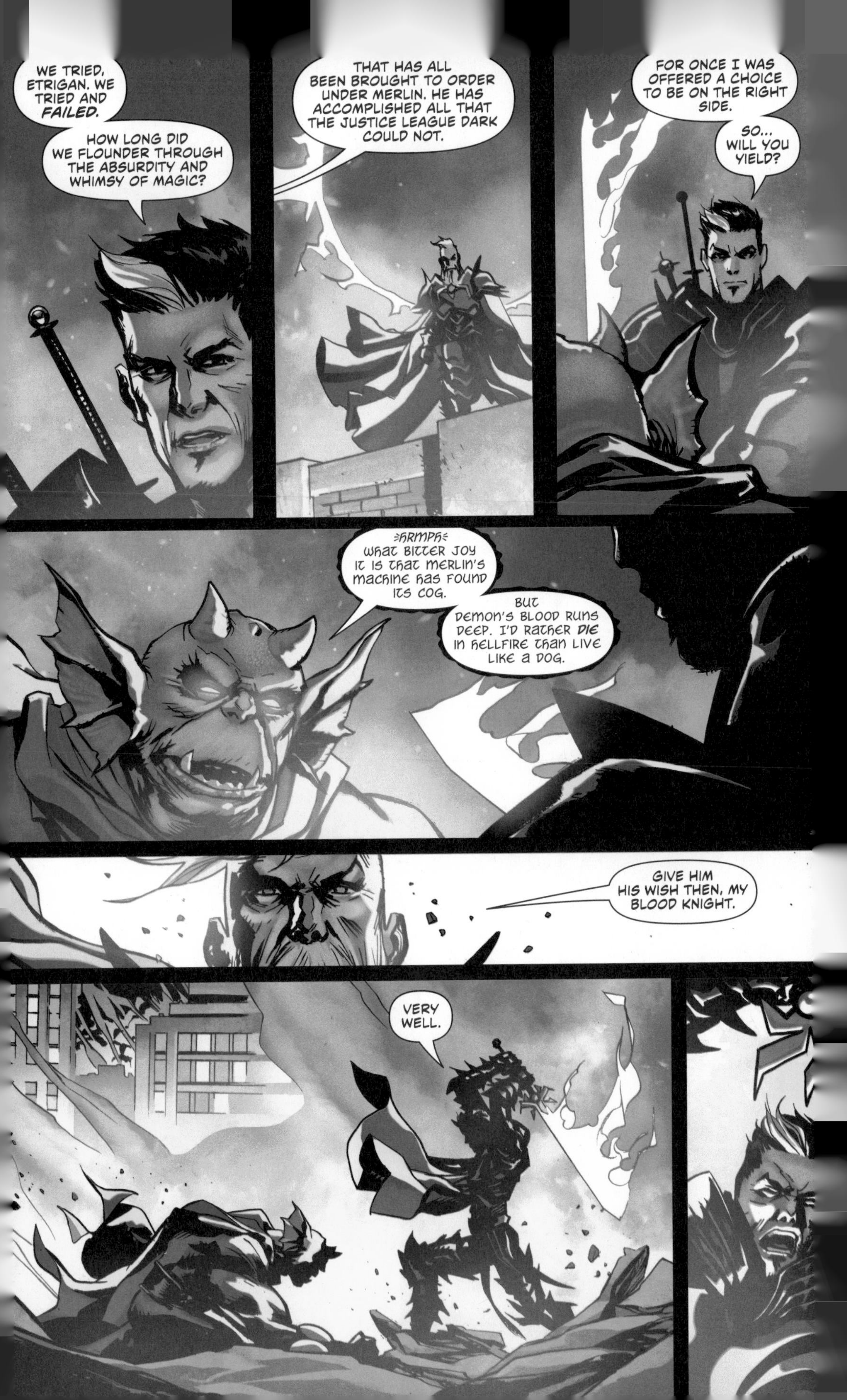
WE TRIED, ETRIGAN. WE TRIED AND FAILED.
HOW LONG DID WE FLOUNDER THROUGH THE ABSURDITY AND WHIMSY OF MAGIC?
THAT HAS ALL BEEN BROUGHT TO ORDER UNDER MERLIN. HE HAS ACCOMPLISHED ALL THAT THE JUSTICE LEAGUE DARK COULD NOT.
FOR ONCE I WAS OFFERED A CHOICE TO BE ON THE RIGHT SIDE.
SO... WILL YOU YIELD?
HRMPH
WHAT BITTER JOY IT IS THAT MERLIN'S MACHINE HAS FOUND ITS COG.
BUT DEMON'S BLOOD RUNS DEEP. I'D RATHER DIE IN HELLFIRE THAN LIVE LIKE A DOG.
GIVE HIM HIS WISH THEN, MY BLOOD KNIGHT.
VERY WELL.

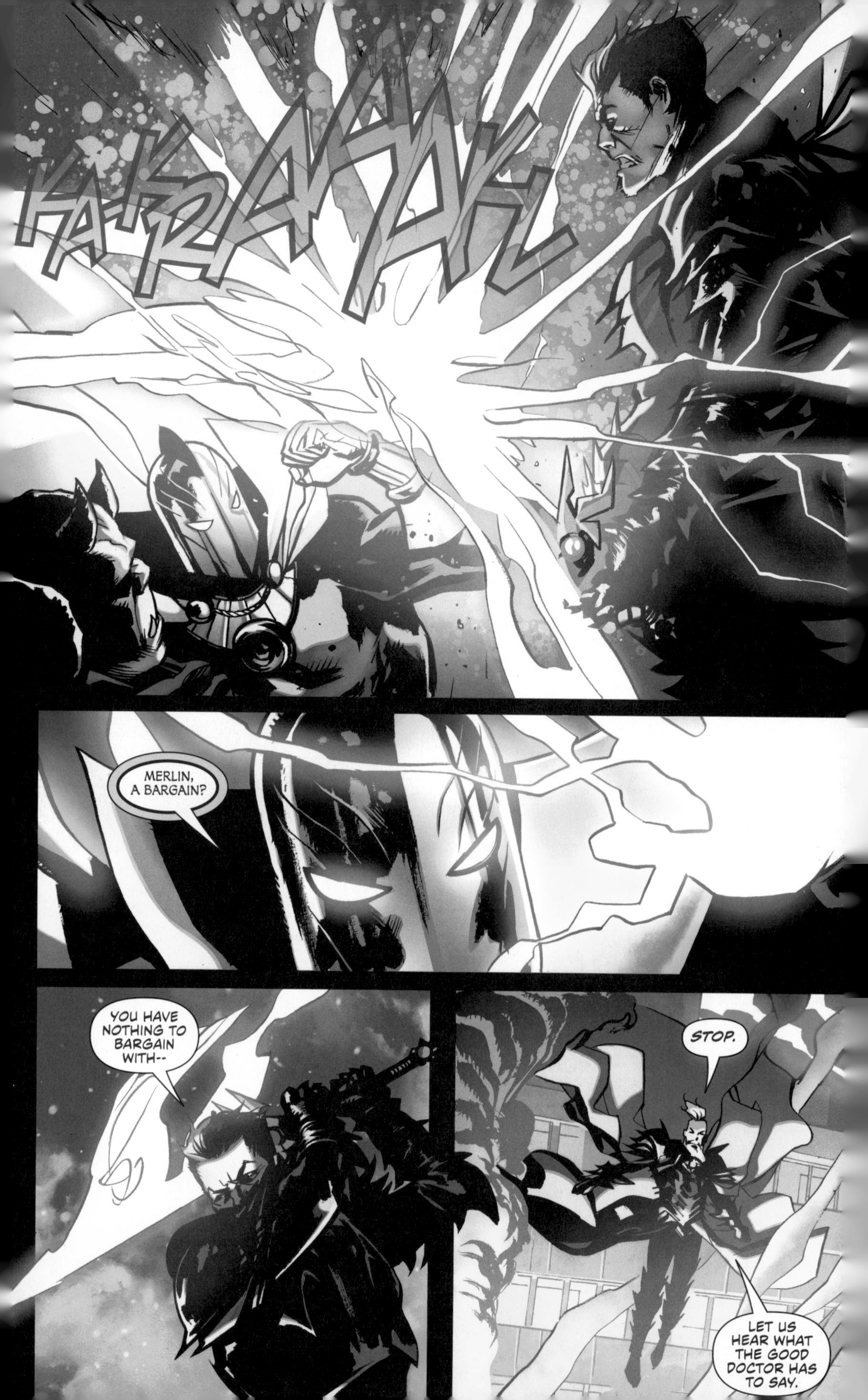
KA-RAKAHAKL
MERLIN, A BARGAIN?
YOU HAVE NOTHING TO BARGAIN WITH--
STOP.
LET US HEAR WHAT THE GOOD DOCTOR HAS TO SAY.

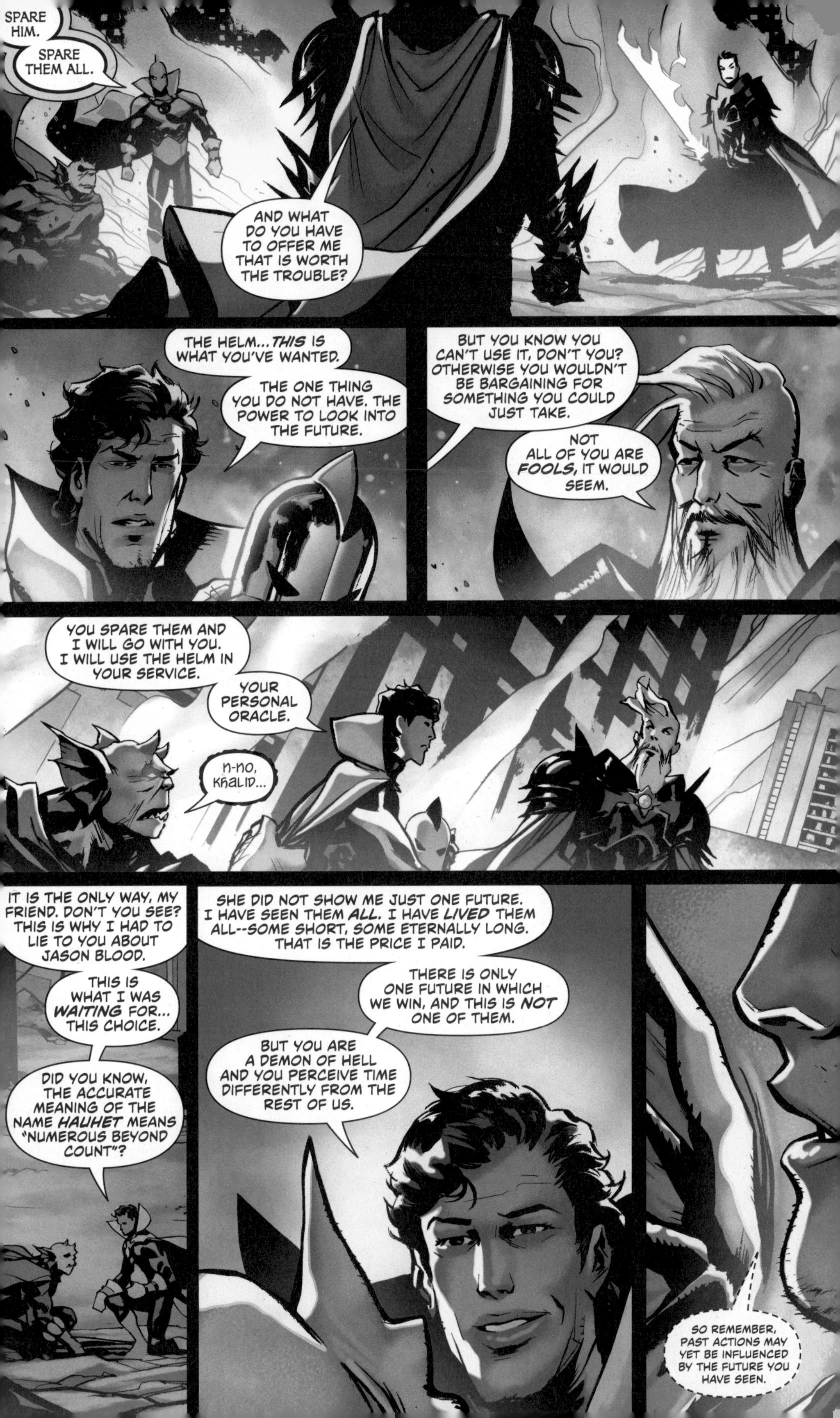
SPARE HIM.
SPARE THEM ALL.
AND WHAT DO YOU HAVE TO OFFER ME THAT IS WORTH THE TROUBLE?
THE HELM...*THIS* IS WHAT YOU'VE WANTED.
THE ONE THING YOU DO NOT HAVE. THE POWER TO LOOK INTO THE FUTURE.
BUT YOU KNOW YOU CAN'T USE IT, DON'T YOU? OTHERWISE YOU WOULDN'T BE BARGAINING FOR SOMETHING YOU COULD JUST TAKE.
NOT ALL OF YOU ARE *FOOLS*, IT WOULD SEEM.
YOU SPARE THEM AND I WILL GO WITH YOU. I WILL USE THE HELM IN YOUR SERVICE.
YOUR PERSONAL ORACLE.
N-NO, KHALID...
IT IS THE ONLY WAY, MY FRIEND. DON'T YOU SEE? THIS IS WHY I HAD TO LIE TO YOU ABOUT JASON BLOOD.
THIS IS WHAT I WAS *WAITING* FOR... THIS CHOICE.
DID YOU KNOW, THE ACCURATE MEANING OF THE NAME *HAUHET* MEANS "NUMEROUS BEYOND COUNT"?
SHE DID NOT SHOW ME JUST ONE FUTURE. I HAVE SEEN THEM *ALL*. I HAVE *LIVED* THEM ALL--SOME SHORT, SOME ETERNALLY LONG. THAT IS THE PRICE I PAID.
THERE IS ONLY ONE FUTURE IN WHICH WE WIN, AND THIS IS *NOT* ONE OF THEM.
BUT YOU ARE A DEMON OF HELL AND YOU PERCEIVE TIME DIFFERENTLY FROM THE REST OF US.
SO REMEMBER, PAST ACTIONS MAY YET BE INFLUENCED BY THE FUTURE YOU HAVE SEEN.

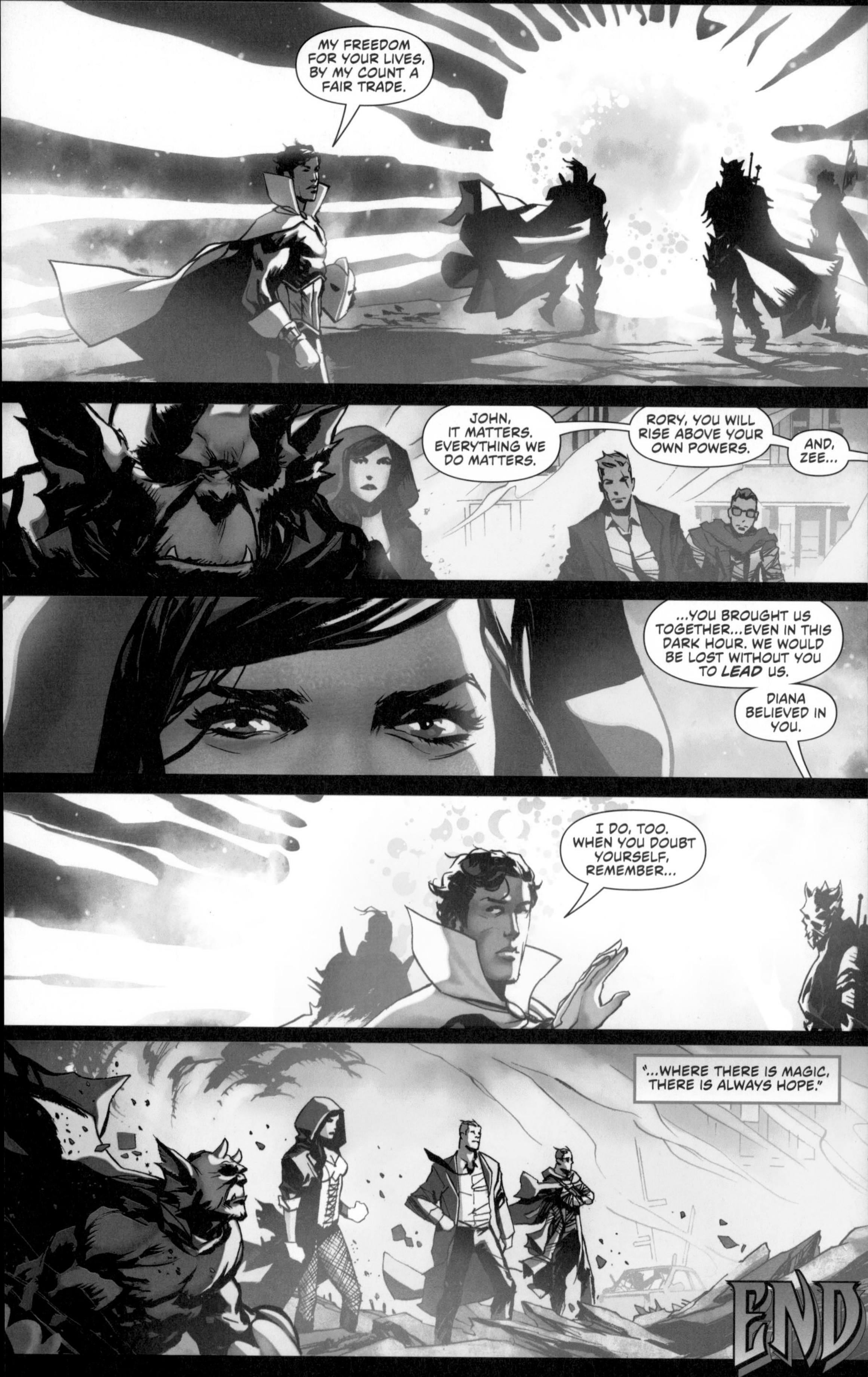
MY FREEDOM FOR YOUR LIVES, BY MY COUNT A FAIR TRADE.
JOHN, IT MATTERS. EVERYTHING WE DO MATTERS.
RORY, YOU WILL RISE ABOVE YOUR OWN POWERS.
AND, ZEE...
...YOU BROUGHT US TOGETHER...EVEN IN THIS DARK HOUR. WE WOULD BE LOST WITHOUT YOU TO LEAD US.
DIANA BELIEVED IN YOU.
I DO, TOO. WHEN YOU DOUBT YOURSELF, REMEMBER...
"...WHERE THERE IS MAGIC, THERE IS ALWAYS HOPE."
END

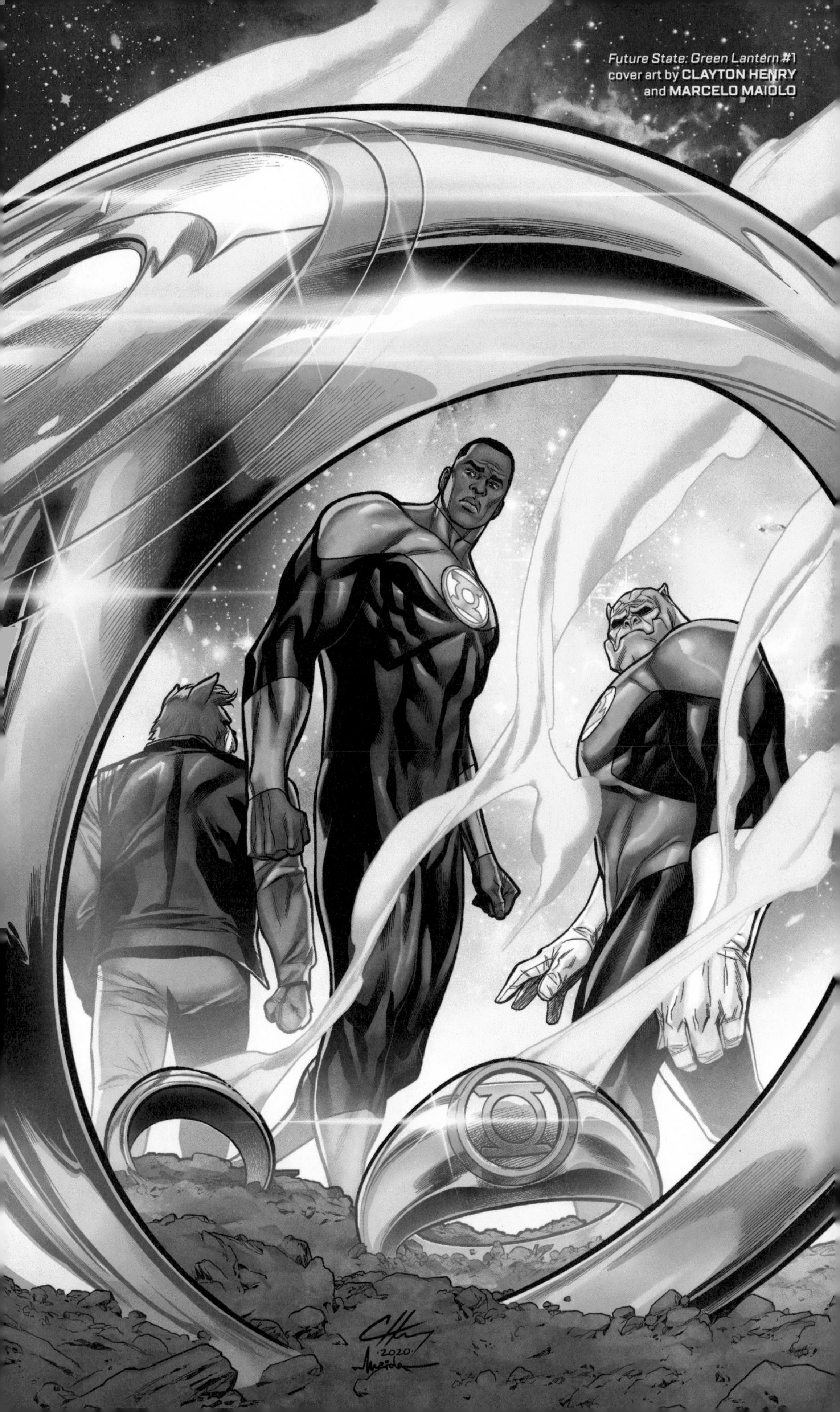

Future State: Green Lantern #1
cover art by **CLAYTON HENRY**
and **MARCELO MAIOLO**

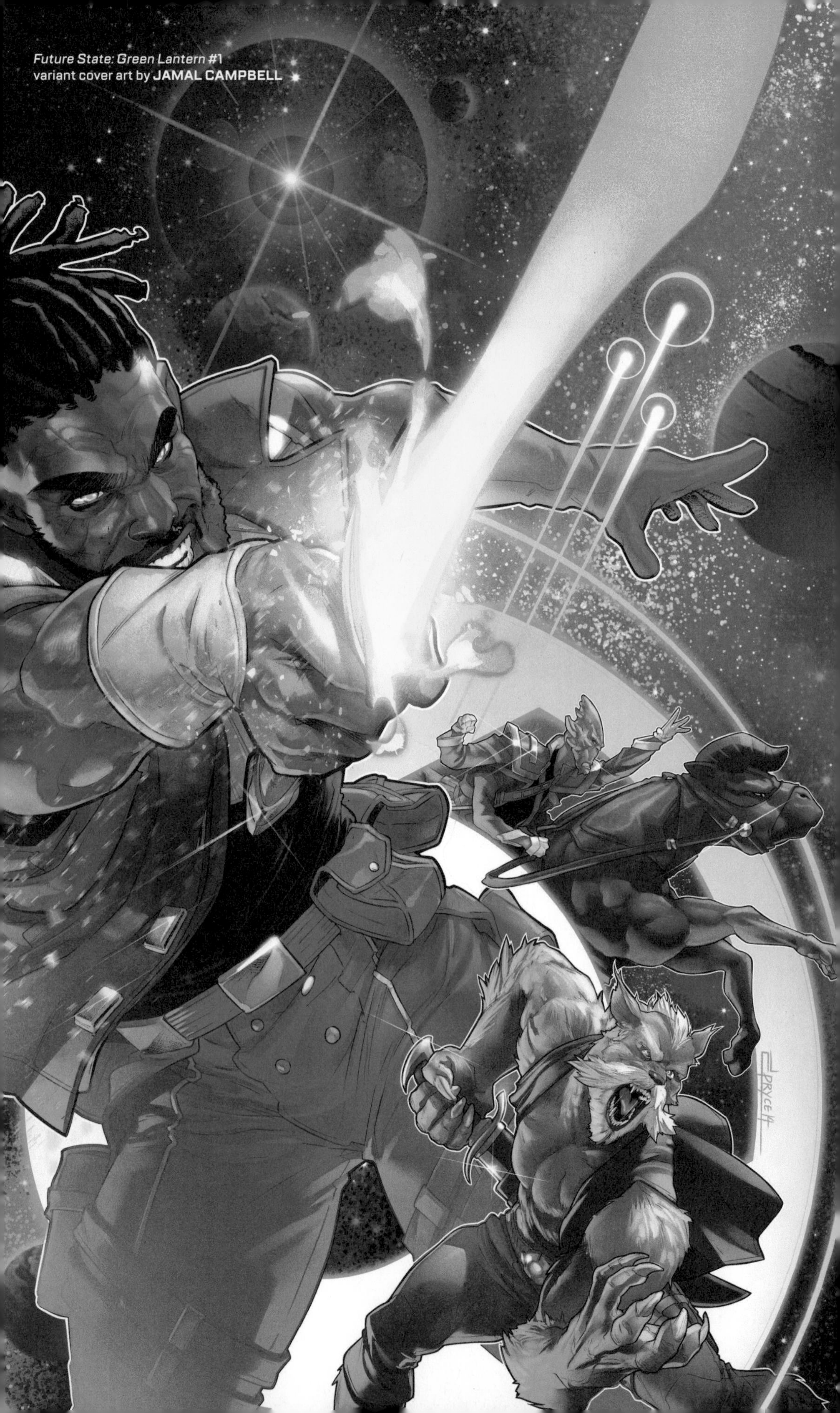

Future State: Green Lantern #1
variant cover art by **JAMAL CAMPBELL**

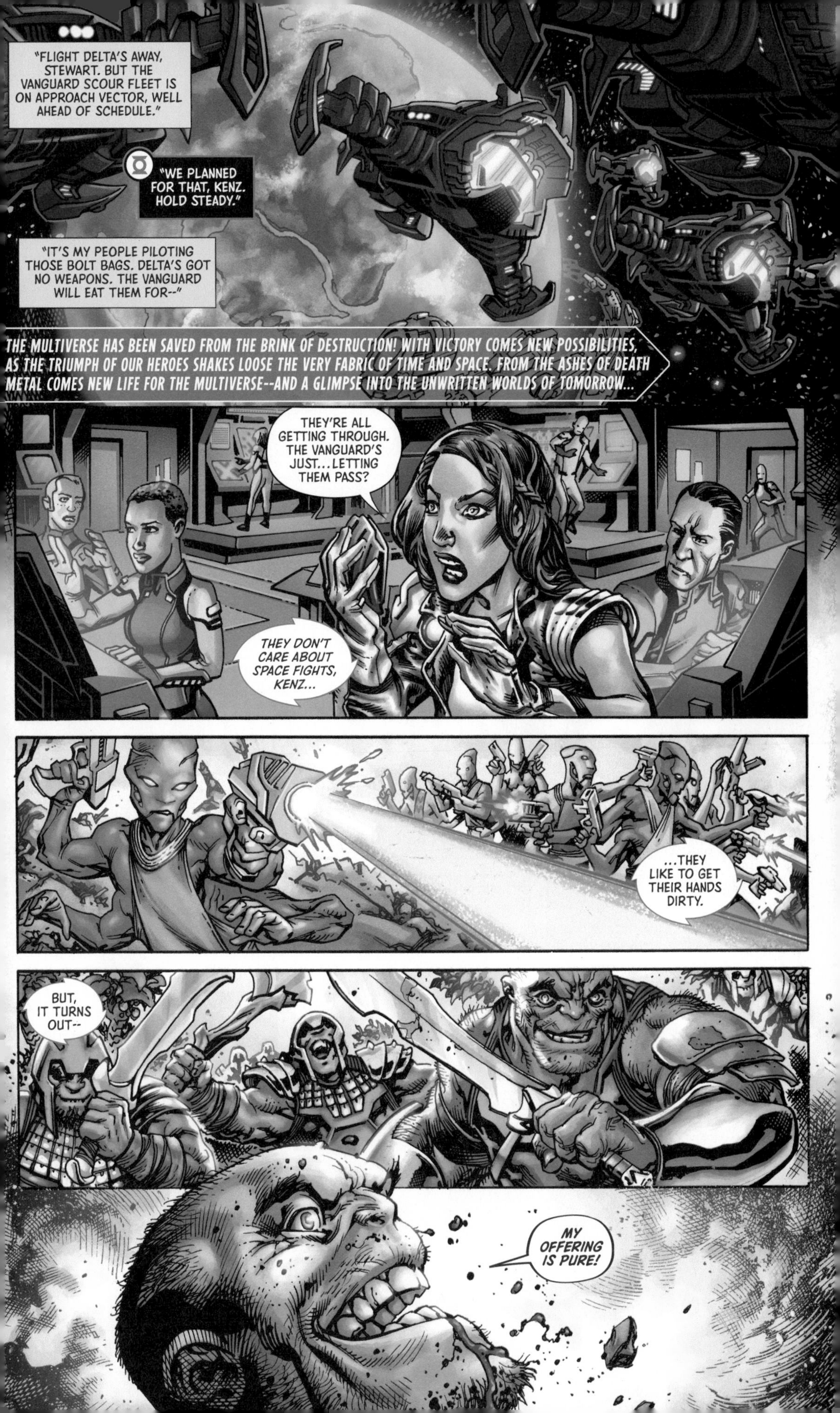
"FLIGHT DELTA'S AWAY, STEWART. BUT THE VANGUARD SCOUR FLEET IS ON APPROACH VECTOR, WELL AHEAD OF SCHEDULE."
"WE PLANNED FOR THAT, KENZ. HOLD STEADY."
"IT'S MY PEOPLE PILOTING THOSE BOLT BAGS. DELTA'S GOT NO WEAPONS. THE VANGUARD WILL EAT THEM FOR--"
THE MULTIVERSE HAS BEEN SAVED FROM THE BRINK OF DESTRUCTION! WITH VICTORY COMES NEW POSSIBILITIES, AS THE TRIUMPH OF OUR HEROES SHAKES LOOSE THE VERY FABRIC OF TIME AND SPACE. FROM THE ASHES OF DEATH METAL COMES NEW LIFE FOR THE MULTIVERSE--AND A GLIMPSE INTO THE UNWRITTEN WORLDS OF TOMORROW...
THEY'RE ALL GETTING THROUGH. THE VANGUARD'S JUST...LETTING THEM PASS?
THEY DON'T CARE ABOUT SPACE FIGHTS, KENZ...
...THEY LIKE TO GET THEIR HANDS DIRTY.
BUT, IT TURNS OUT--
MY OFFERING IS PURE!

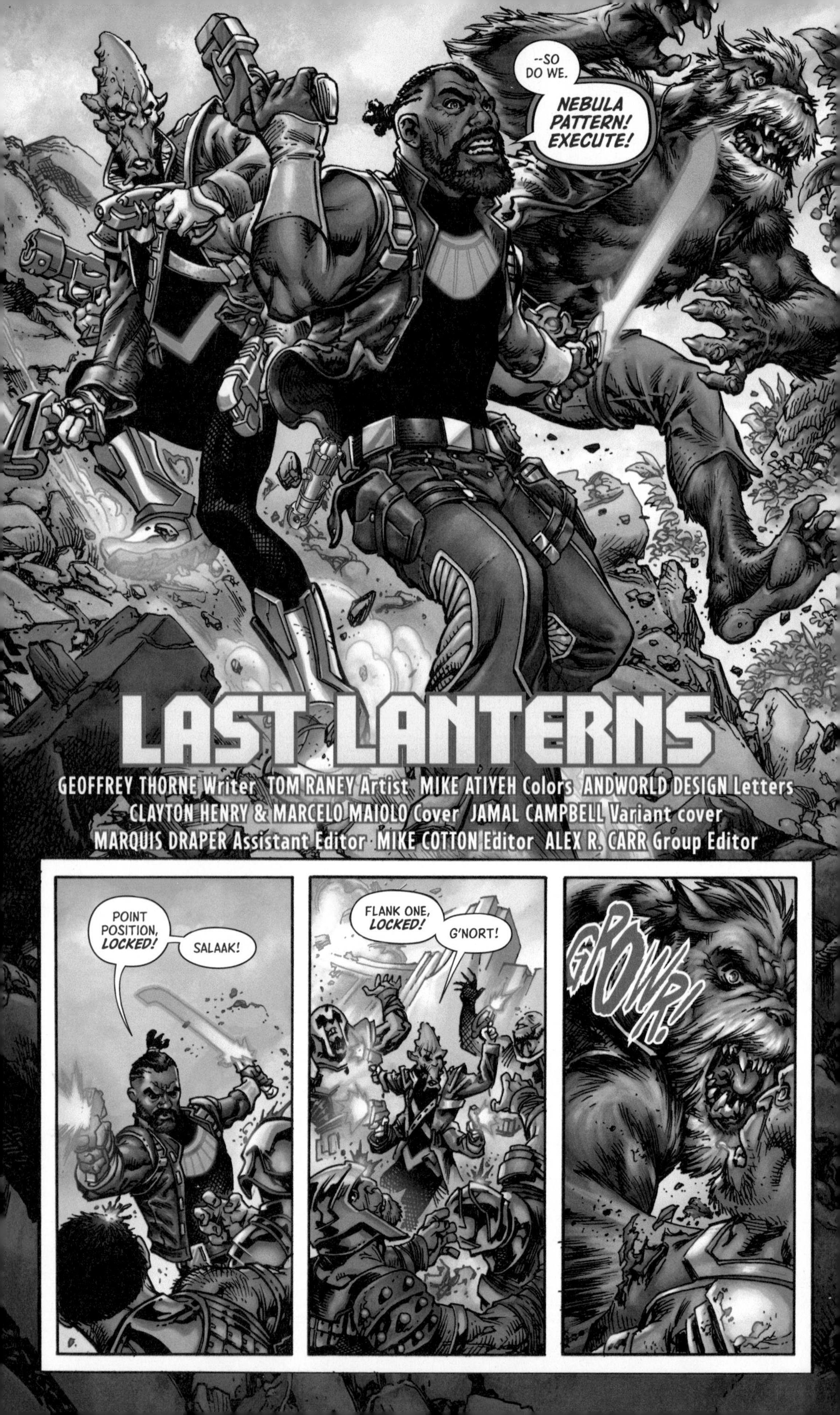
--SO DO WE.
NEBULA PATTERN! EXECUTE!
LAST LANTERNS
GEOFFREY THORNE Writer TOM RANEY Artist MIKE ATIYEH Colors ANDWORLD DESIGN Letters
CLAYTON HENRY & MARCELO MAIOLO Cover JAMAL CAMPBELL Variant cover
MARQUIS DRAPER Assistant Editor MIKE COTTON Editor ALEX R. CARR Group Editor
POINT POSITION, LOCKED!
SALAAK!
FLANK ONE, LOCKED!
G'NORT!
GROWR!

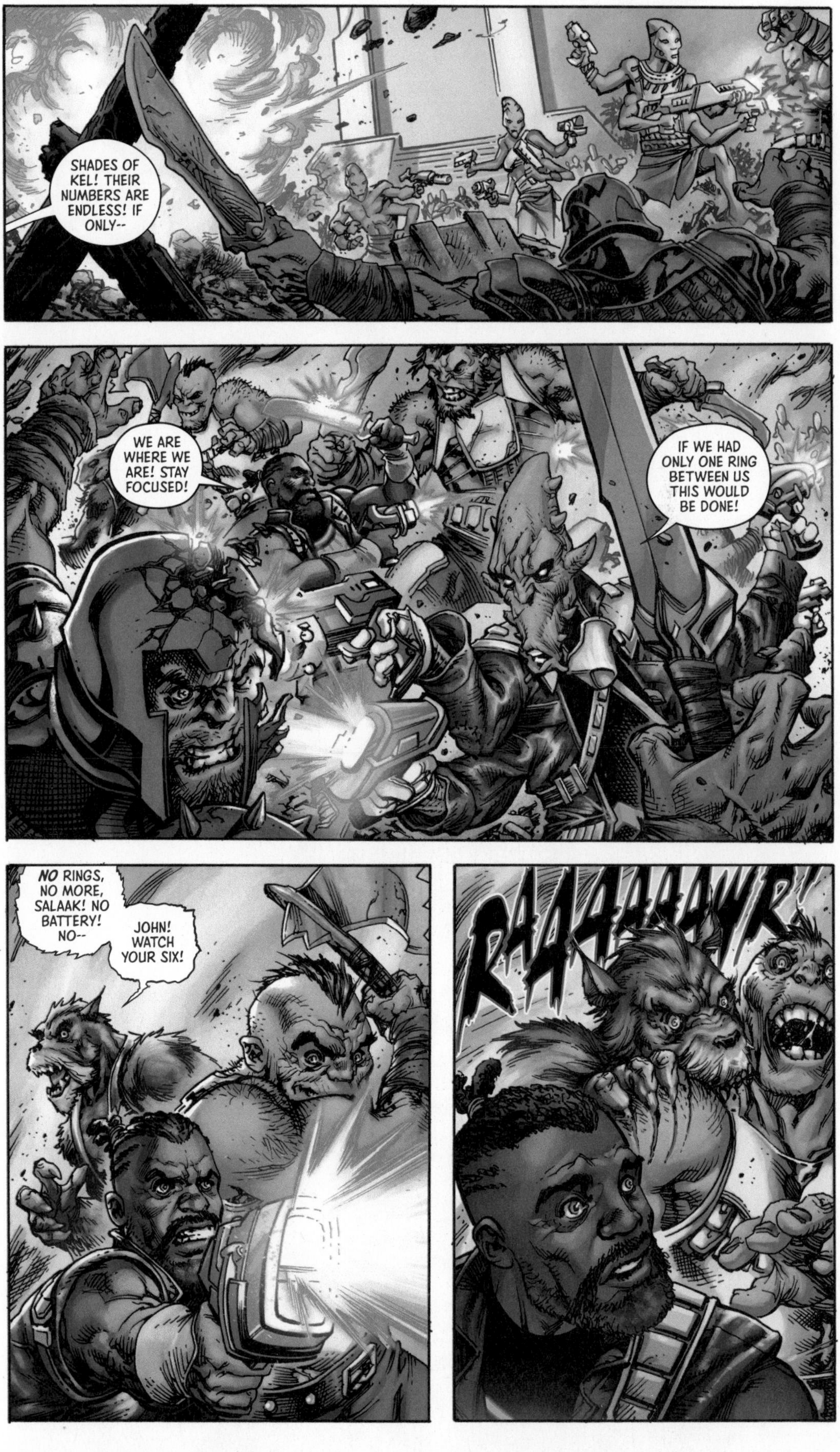
SHADES OF KEL! THEIR NUMBERS ARE ENDLESS! IF ONLY--
WE ARE WHERE WE ARE! STAY FOCUSED!
IF WE HAD ONLY ONE RING BETWEEN US THIS WOULD BE DONE!
NO RINGS, NO MORE, SALAAK! NO BATTERY! NO--
JOHN! WATCH YOUR SIX!
RAAAAAAWR!

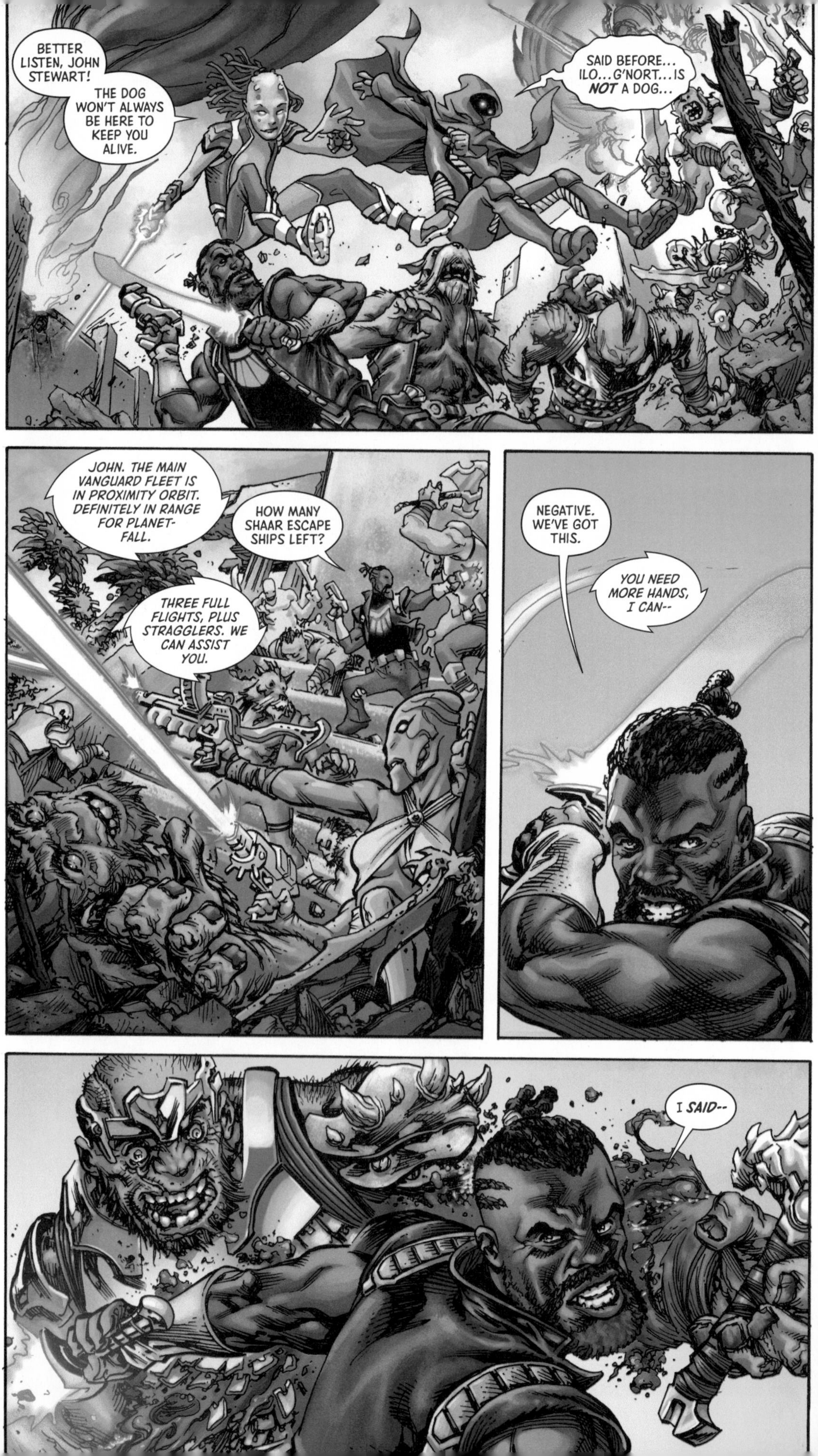
BETTER LISTEN, JOHN STEWART!
THE DOG WON'T ALWAYS BE HERE TO KEEP YOU ALIVE.
SAID BEFORE... ILO... G'NORT... IS NOT A DOG...
JOHN. THE MAIN VANGUARD FLEET IS IN PROXIMITY ORBIT. DEFINITELY IN RANGE FOR PLANET-FALL.
HOW MANY SHAAR ESCAPE SHIPS LEFT?
THREE FULL FLIGHTS, PLUS STRAGGLERS. WE CAN ASSIST YOU.
NEGATIVE. WE'VE GOT THIS.
YOU NEED MORE HANDS, I CAN--
I SAID--

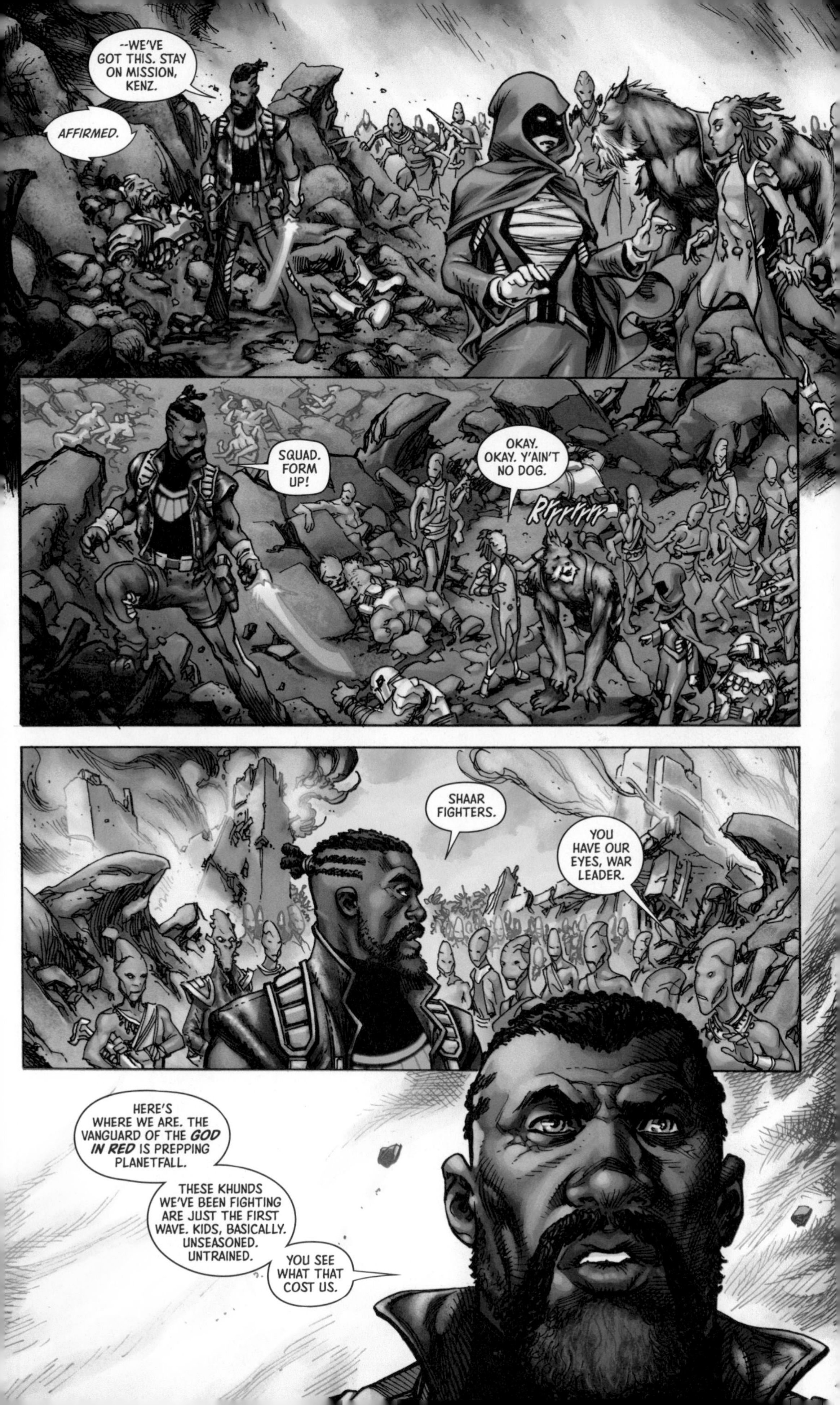
--WE'VE GOT THIS. STAY ON MISSION, KENZ.
AFFIRMED.
SQUAD. FORM UP!
OKAY. OKAY. Y'AIN'T NO DOG.
RRrrrrrr
SHAAR FIGHTERS.
YOU HAVE OUR EYES, WAR LEADER.
HERE'S WHERE WE ARE. THE VANGUARD OF THE *GOD IN RED* IS PREPPING PLANETFALL.
THESE KHUNDS WE'VE BEEN FIGHTING ARE JUST THE FIRST WAVE. KIDS, BASICALLY. UNSEASONED. UNTRAINED.
YOU SEE WHAT THAT COST US.

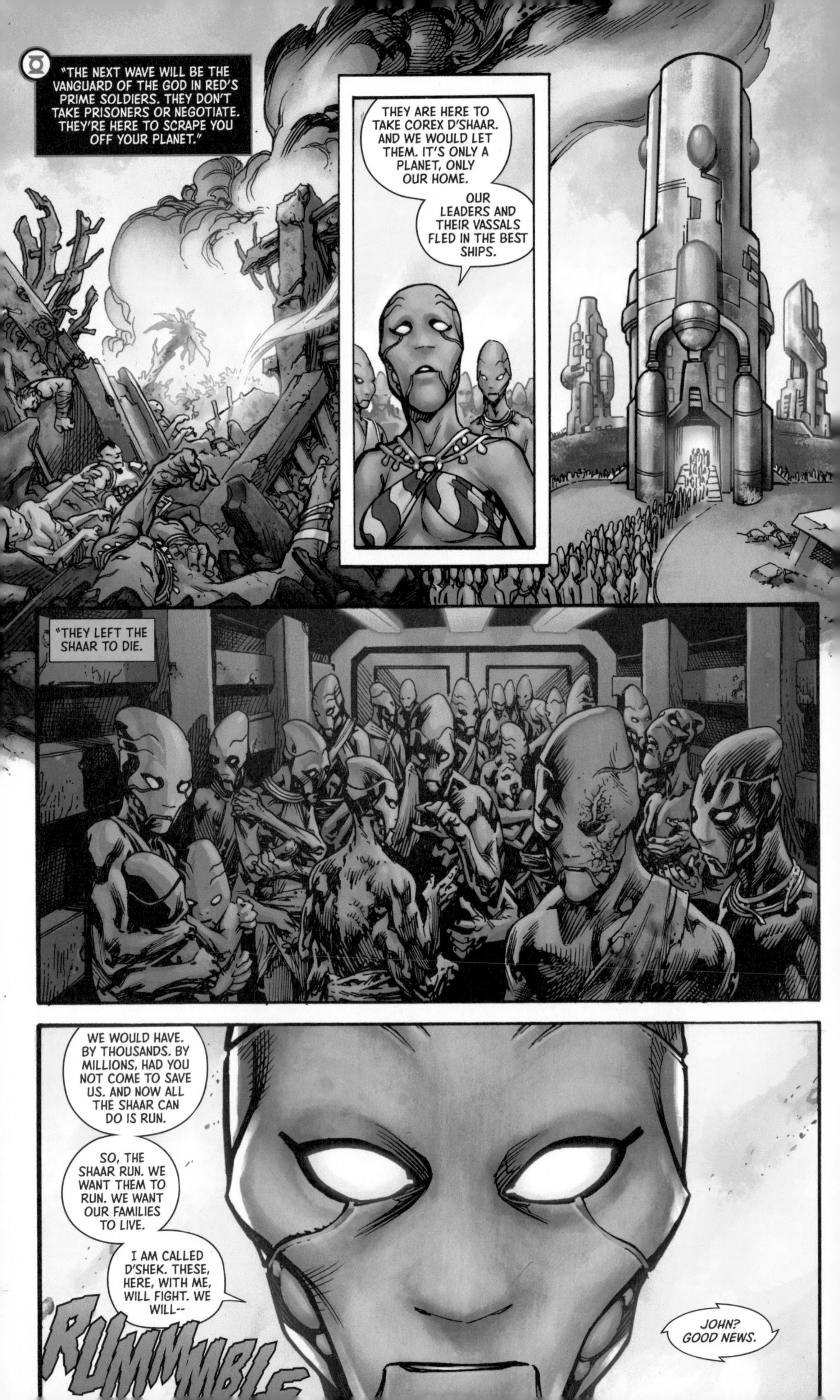

"THE NEXT WAVE WILL BE THE VANGUARD OF THE GOD IN RED'S PRIME SOLDIERS. THEY DON'T TAKE PRISONERS OR NEGOTIATE. THEY'RE HERE TO SCRAPE YOU OFF YOUR PLANET."
THEY ARE HERE TO TAKE COREX D'SHAAR. AND WE WOULD LET THEM. IT'S ONLY A PLANET, ONLY OUR HOME.
OUR LEADERS AND THEIR VASSALS FLED IN THE BEST SHIPS.
"THEY LEFT THE SHAAR TO DIE.
WE WOULD HAVE. BY THOUSANDS. BY MILLIONS, HAD YOU NOT COME TO SAVE US. AND NOW ALL THE SHAAR CAN DO IS RUN.
SO, THE SHAAR RUN. WE WANT THEM TO RUN. WE WANT OUR FAMILIES TO LIVE.
I AM CALLED D'SHEK. THESE, HERE, WITH ME, WILL FIGHT. WE WILL--
RUMMMBLE
JOHN? GOOD NEWS.

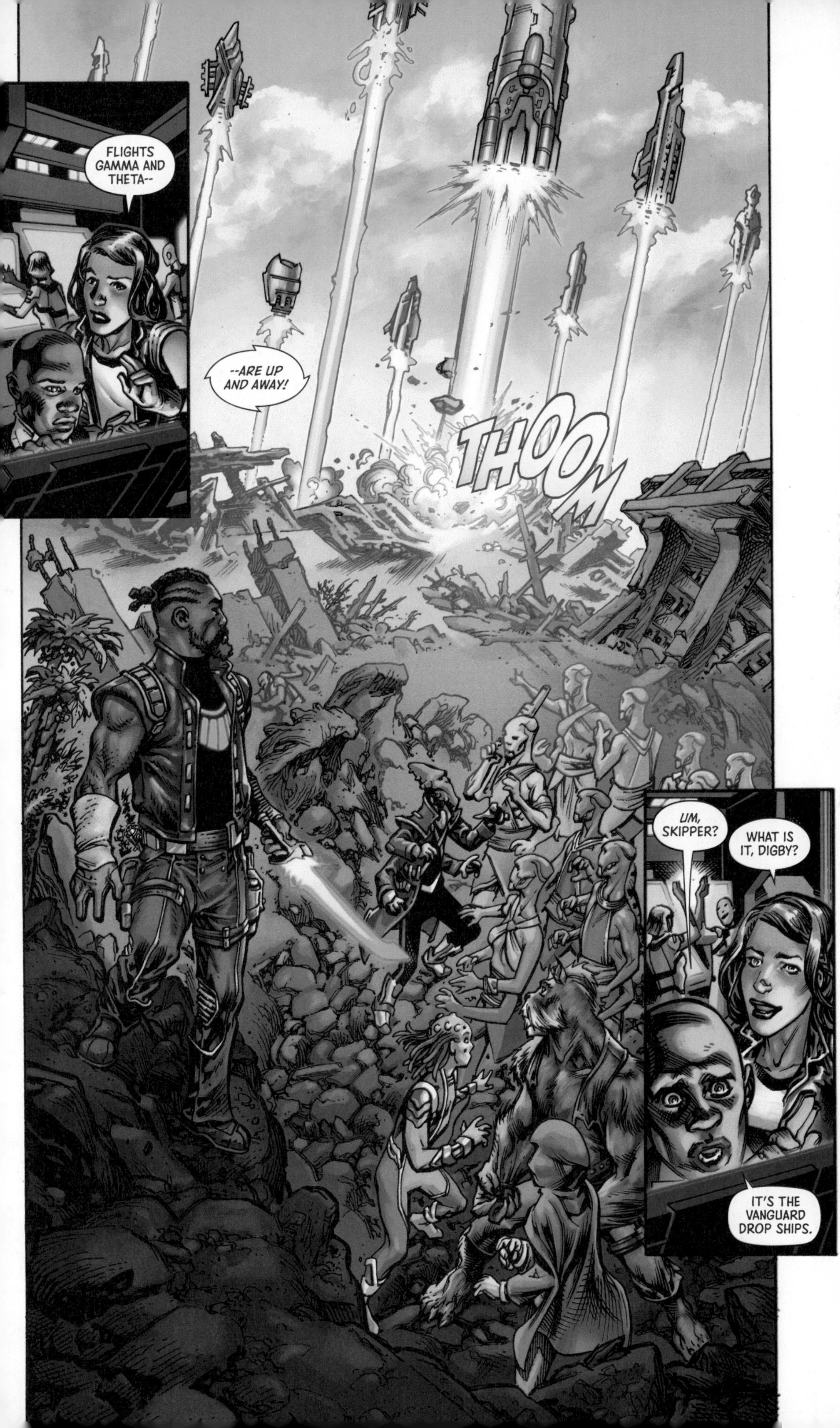
FLIGHTS GAMMA AND THETA--
--ARE UP AND AWAY!
THOOM
UM, SKIPPER?
WHAT IS IT, DIGBY?
IT'S THE VANGUARD DROP SHIPS.

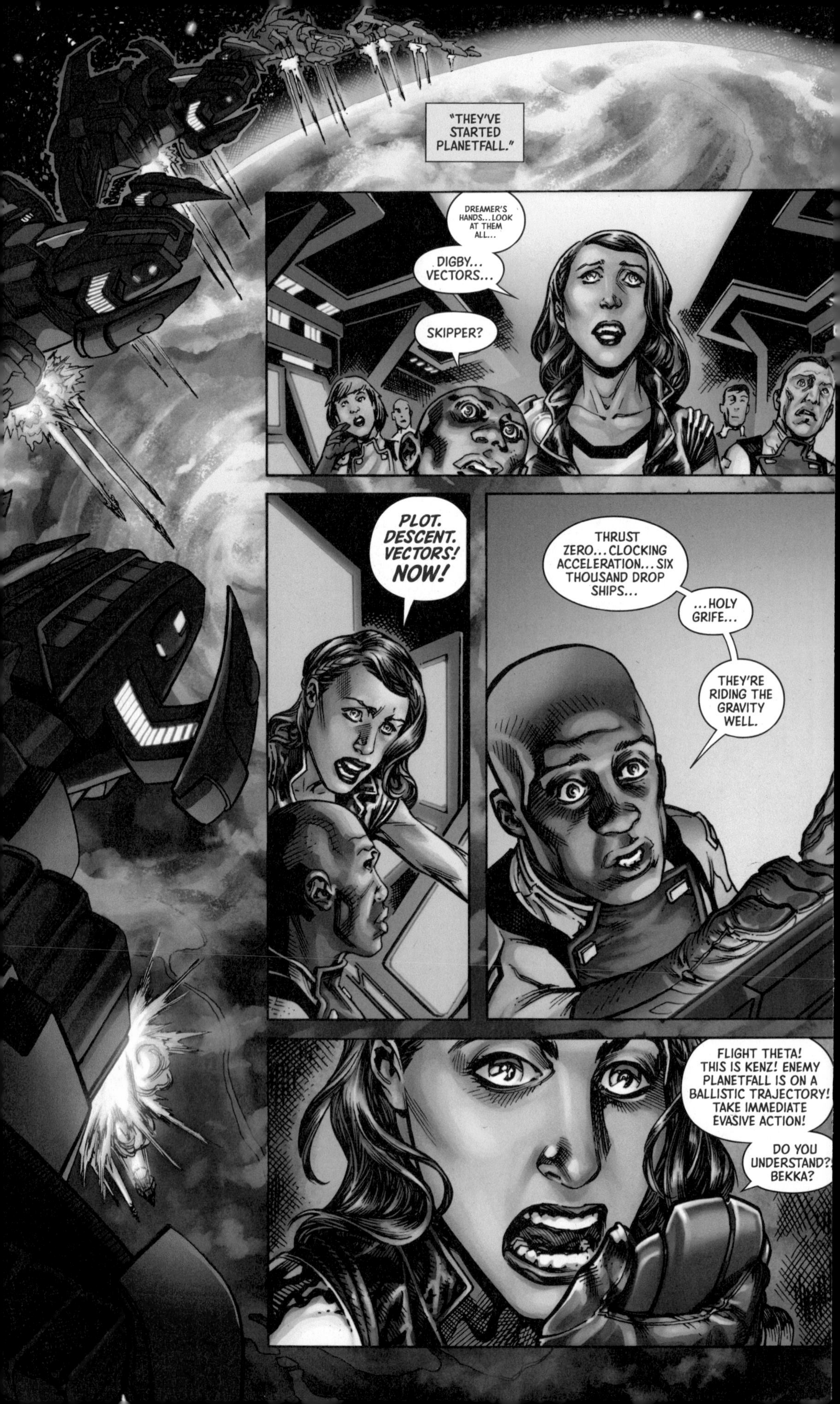

"THEY'VE STARTED PLANETFALL."
DREAMER'S HANDS...LOOK AT THEM ALL...
DIGBY... VECTORS...
SKIPPER?
PLOT. DESCENT. VECTORS! NOW!
THRUST ZERO...CLOCKING ACCELERATION...SIX THOUSAND DROP SHIPS...
...HOLY GRIFE...
THEY'RE RIDING THE GRAVITY WELL.
FLIGHT THETA! THIS IS KENZ! ENEMY PLANETFALL IS ON A BALLISTIC TRAJECTORY! TAKE IMMEDIATE EVASIVE ACTION!
DO YOU UNDERSTAND?! BEKKA?

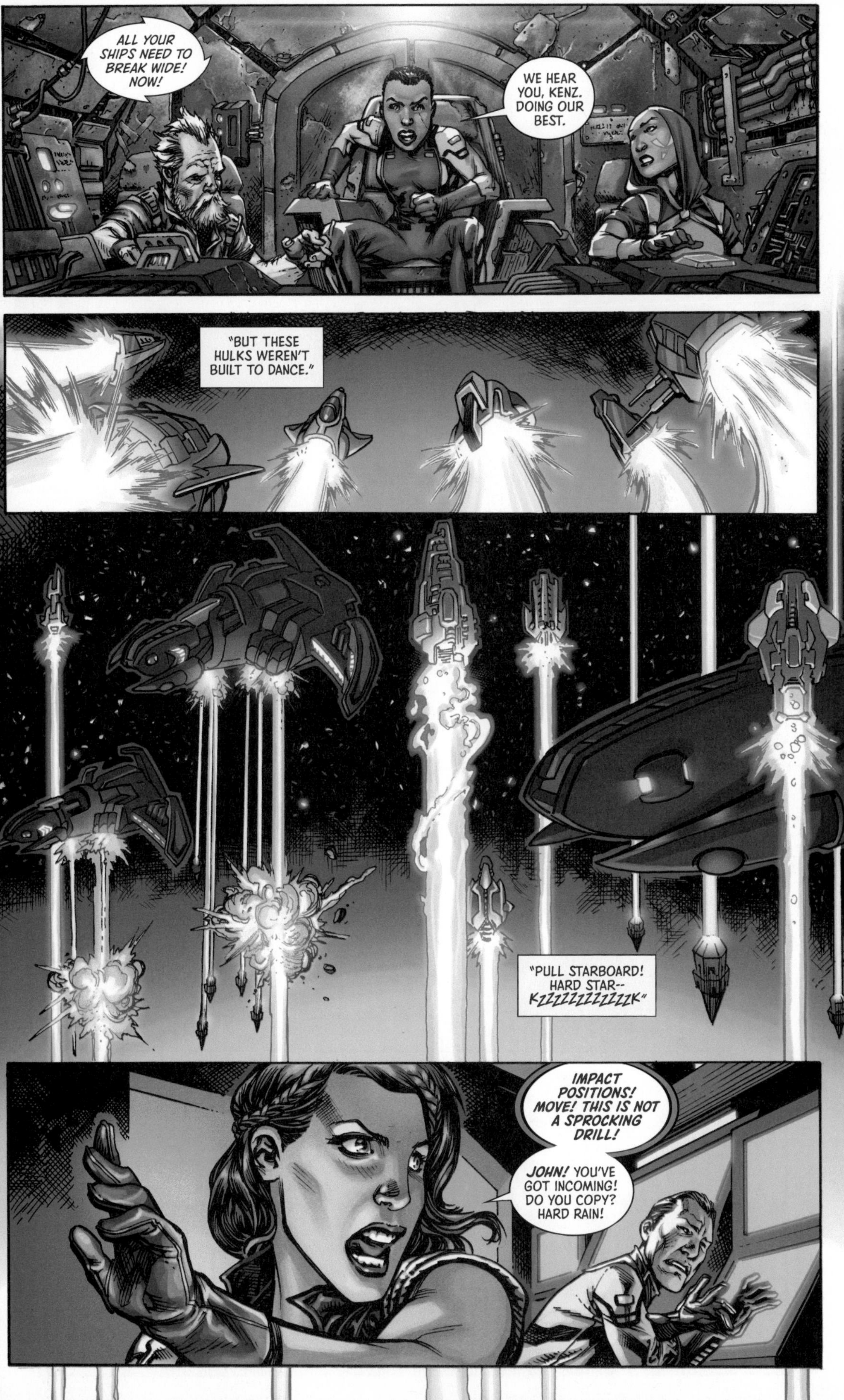
ALL YOUR SHIPS NEED TO BREAK WIDE! NOW!
WE HEAR YOU, KENZ. DOING OUR BEST.
"BUT THESE HULKS WEREN'T BUILT TO DANCE."
"PULL STARBOARD! HARD STAR-- KZZZZZZZZZZZZK"
IMPACT POSITIONS! MOVE! THIS IS NOT A SPROCKING DRILL!
JOHN! YOU'VE GOT INCOMING! DO YOU COPY? HARD RAIN!

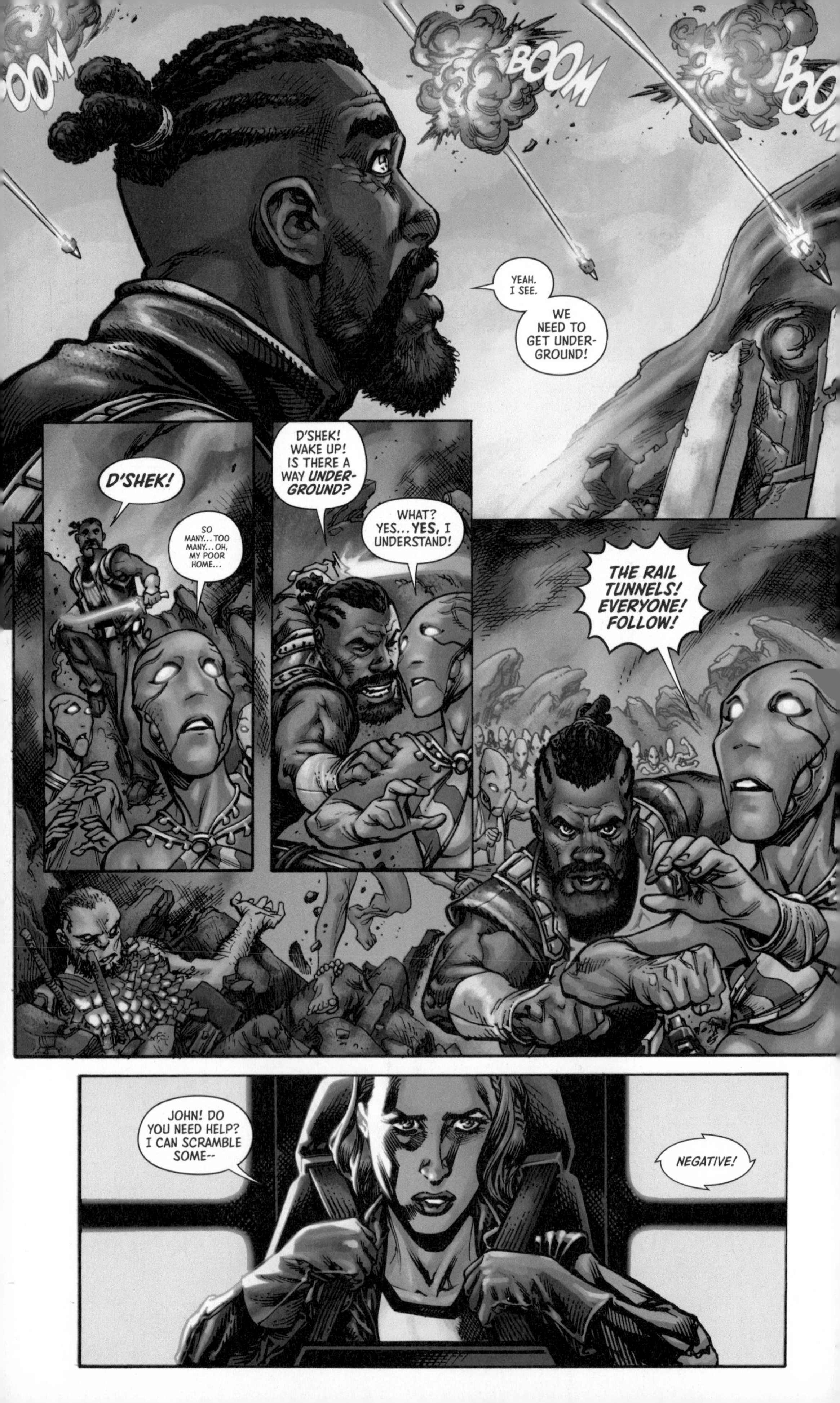
BOOM
BOOM
BOOM
YEAH. I SEE.
WE NEED TO GET UNDER-GROUND!
D'SHEK!
SO MANY... TOO MANY... OH, MY POOR HOME...
D'SHEK! WAKE UP! IS THERE A WAY UNDER-GROUND?
WHAT? YES... YES, I UNDERSTAND!
THE RAIL TUNNELS! EVERYONE! FOLLOW!
JOHN! DO YOU NEED HELP? I CAN SCRAMBLE SOME--
NEGATIVE!

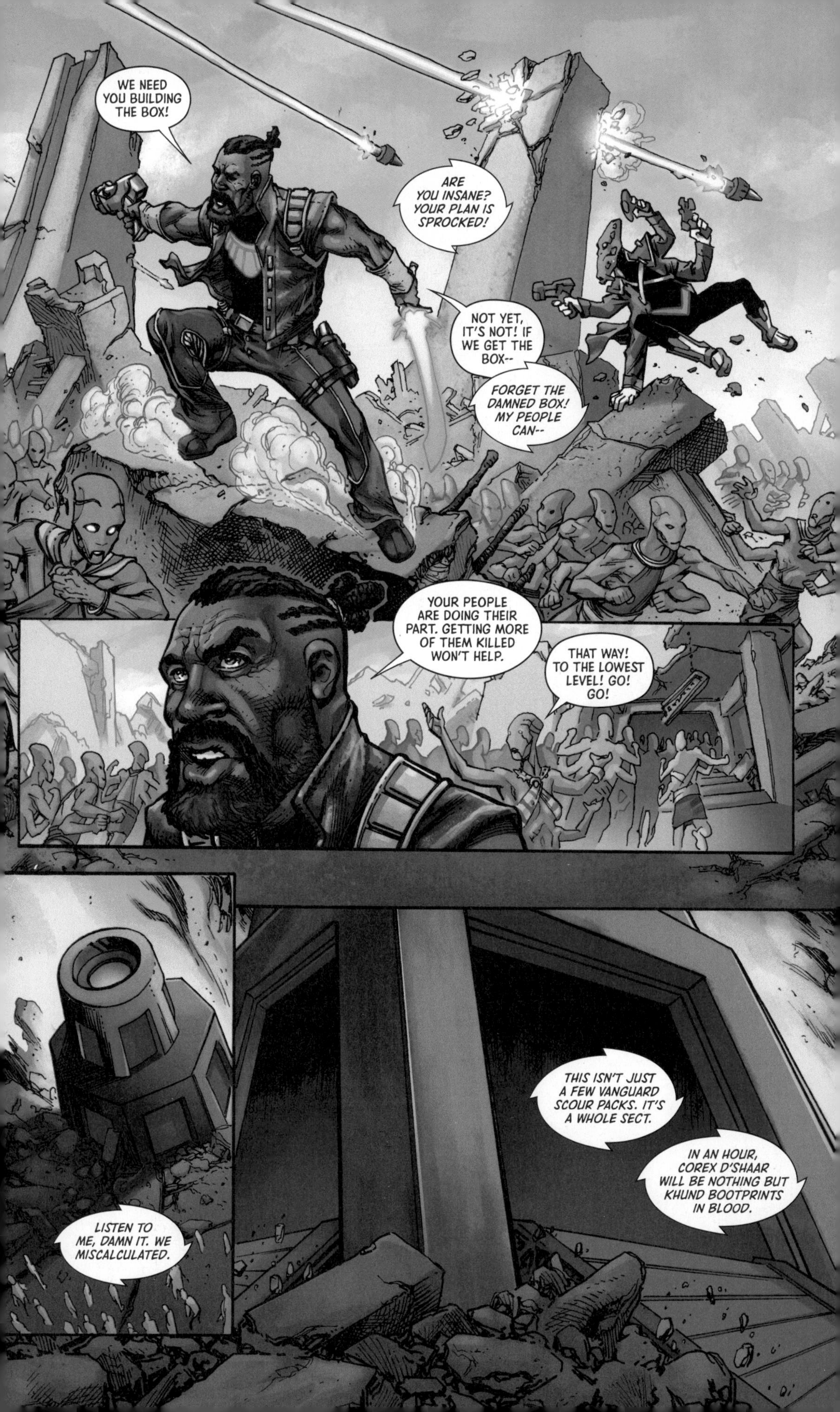
WE NEED YOU BUILDING THE BOX!
ARE YOU INSANE? YOUR PLAN IS SPROCKED!
NOT YET, IT'S NOT! IF WE GET THE BOX--
FORGET THE DAMNED BOX! MY PEOPLE CAN--
YOUR PEOPLE ARE DOING THEIR PART. GETTING MORE OF THEM KILLED WON'T HELP.
THAT WAY! TO THE LOWEST LEVEL! GO! GO!
LISTEN TO ME, DAMN IT. WE MISCALCULATED.
THIS ISN'T JUST A FEW VANGUARD SCOUR PACKS. IT'S A WHOLE SECT.
IN AN HOUR, COREX D'SHAAR WILL BE NOTHING BUT KHUND BOOTPRINTS IN BLOOD.

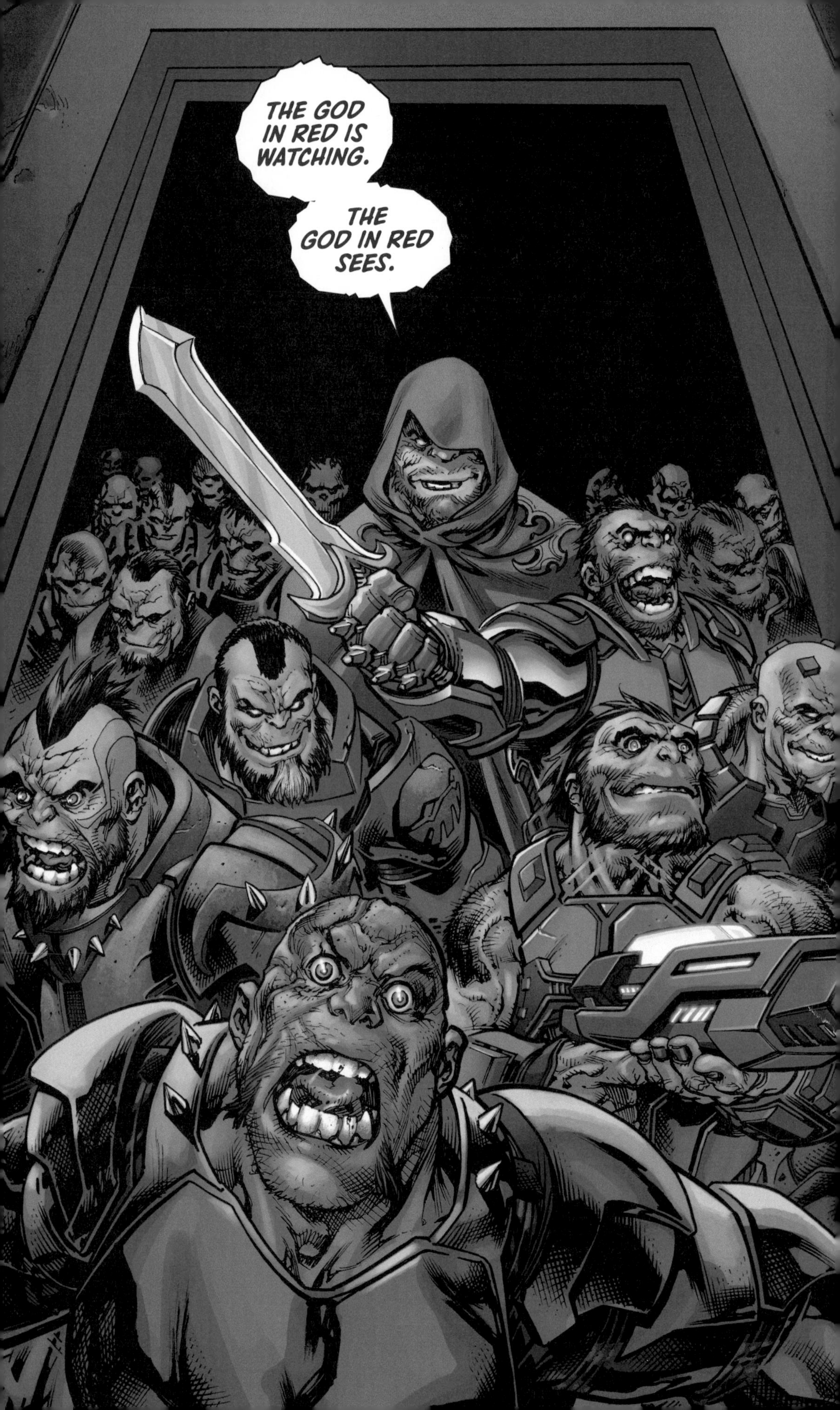
THE GOD IN RED IS WATCHING.
THE GOD IN RED SEES.

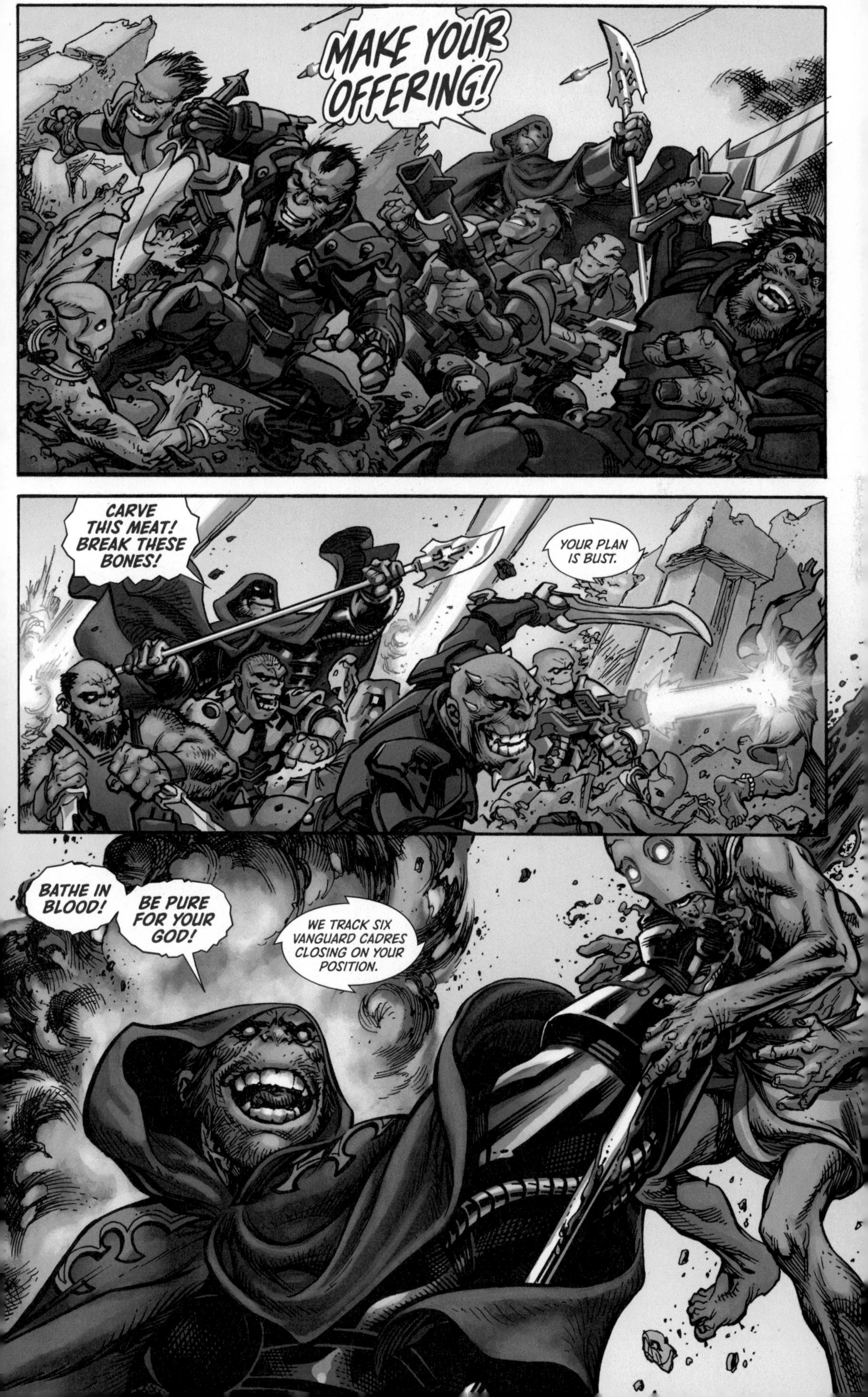
MAKE YOUR OFFERING!
CARVE THIS MEAT! BREAK THESE BONES!
YOUR PLAN IS BUST.
BATHE IN BLOOD!
BE PURE FOR YOUR GOD!
WE TRACK SIX VANGUARD CADRES CLOSING ON YOUR POSITION.

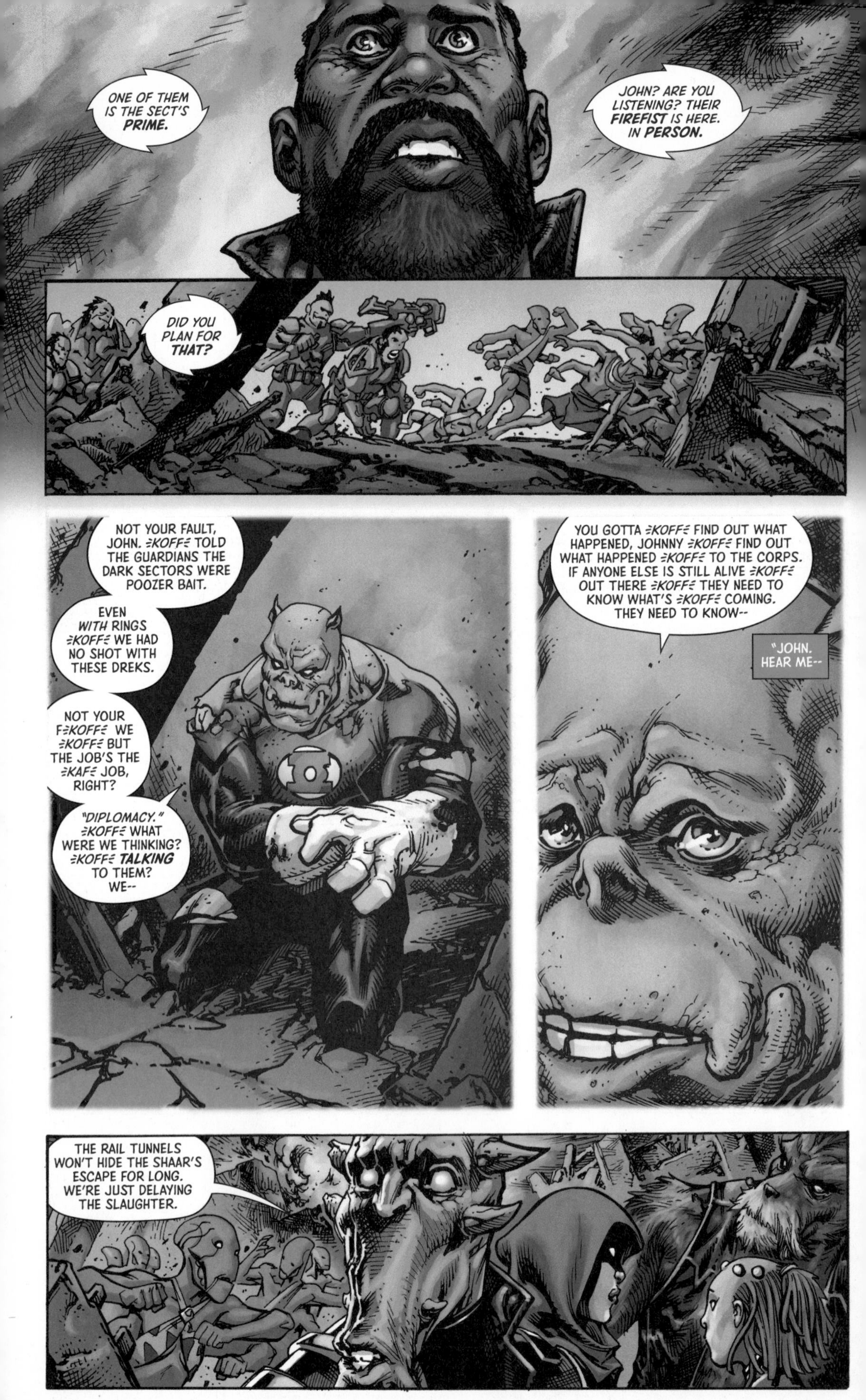

ONE OF THEM IS THE SECT'S **PRIME.**
JOHN? ARE YOU LISTENING? THEIR **FIREFIST** IS HERE. IN **PERSON.**
DID YOU PLAN FOR **THAT?**
NOT YOUR FAULT, JOHN. ≡KOFF≡ TOLD THE GUARDIANS THE DARK SECTORS WERE POOZER BAIT.
EVEN *WITH* RINGS ≡KOFF≡ WE HAD NO SHOT WITH THESE DREKS.
NOT YOUR F≡KOFF≡ WE ≡KOFF≡ BUT THE JOB'S THE ≡KAF≡ JOB, RIGHT?
"DIPLOMACY." ≡KOFF≡ WHAT WERE WE THINKING? ≡KOFF≡ **TALKING** TO THEM? WE--
YOU GOTTA ≡KOFF≡ FIND OUT WHAT HAPPENED, JOHNNY ≡KOFF≡ FIND OUT WHAT HAPPENED ≡KOFF≡ TO THE CORPS. IF ANYONE ELSE IS STILL ALIVE ≡KOFF≡ OUT THERE ≡KOFF≡ THEY NEED TO KNOW WHAT'S ≡KOFF≡ COMING. THEY NEED TO KNOW--
"JOHN. HEAR ME--
THE RAIL TUNNELS WON'T HIDE THE SHAAR'S ESCAPE FOR LONG. WE'RE JUST DELAYING THE SLAUGHTER.

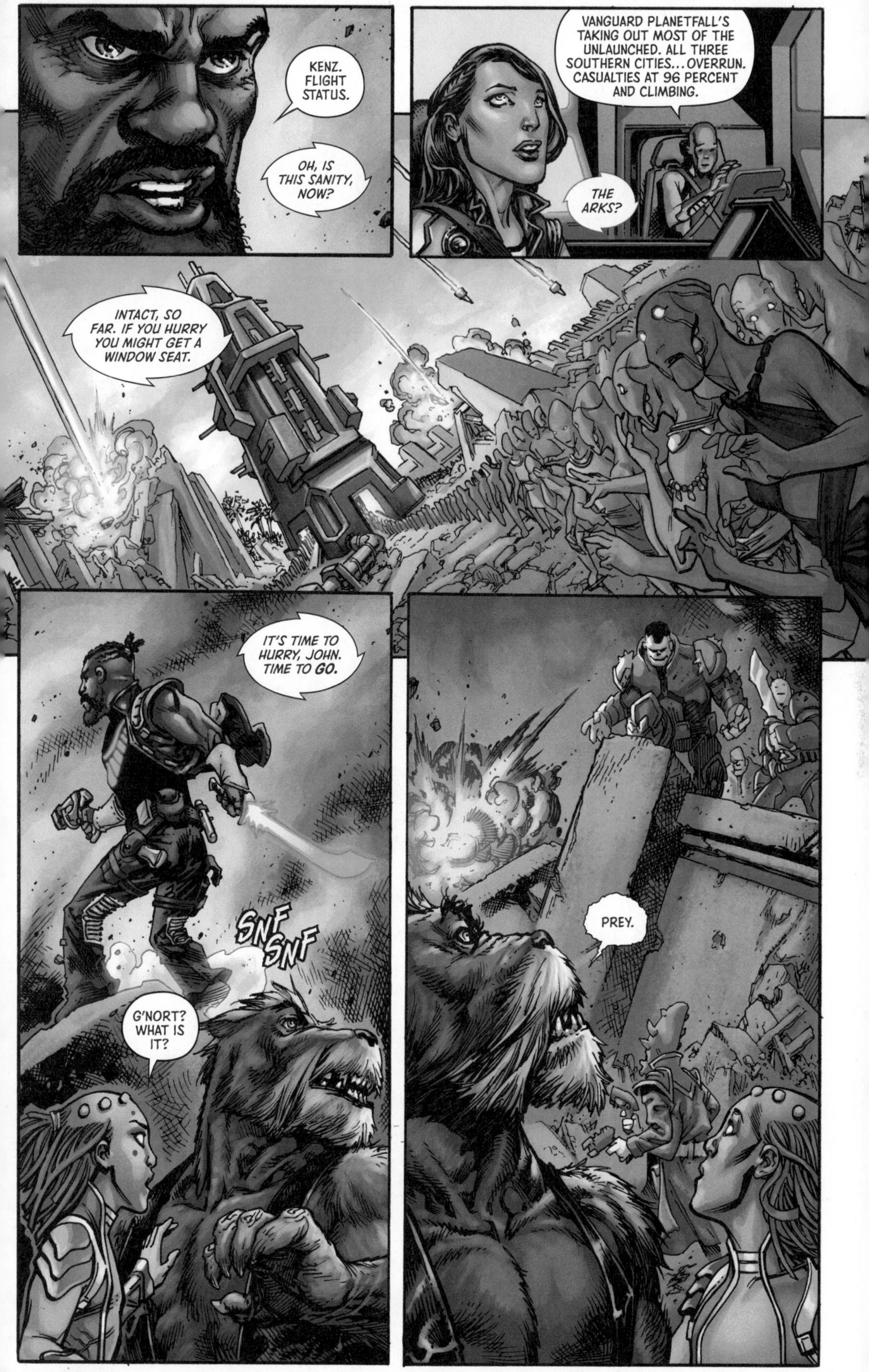
KENZ. FLIGHT STATUS.
OH, IS THIS SANITY, NOW?
VANGUARD PLANETFALL'S TAKING OUT MOST OF THE UNLAUNCHED. ALL THREE SOUTHERN CITIES... OVERRUN. CASUALTIES AT 96 PERCENT AND CLIMBING.
THE ARKS?
INTACT, SO FAR. IF YOU HURRY YOU MIGHT GET A WINDOW SEAT.
IT'S TIME TO HURRY, JOHN. TIME TO GO.
SNF SNF
G'NORT? WHAT IS IT?
PREY.

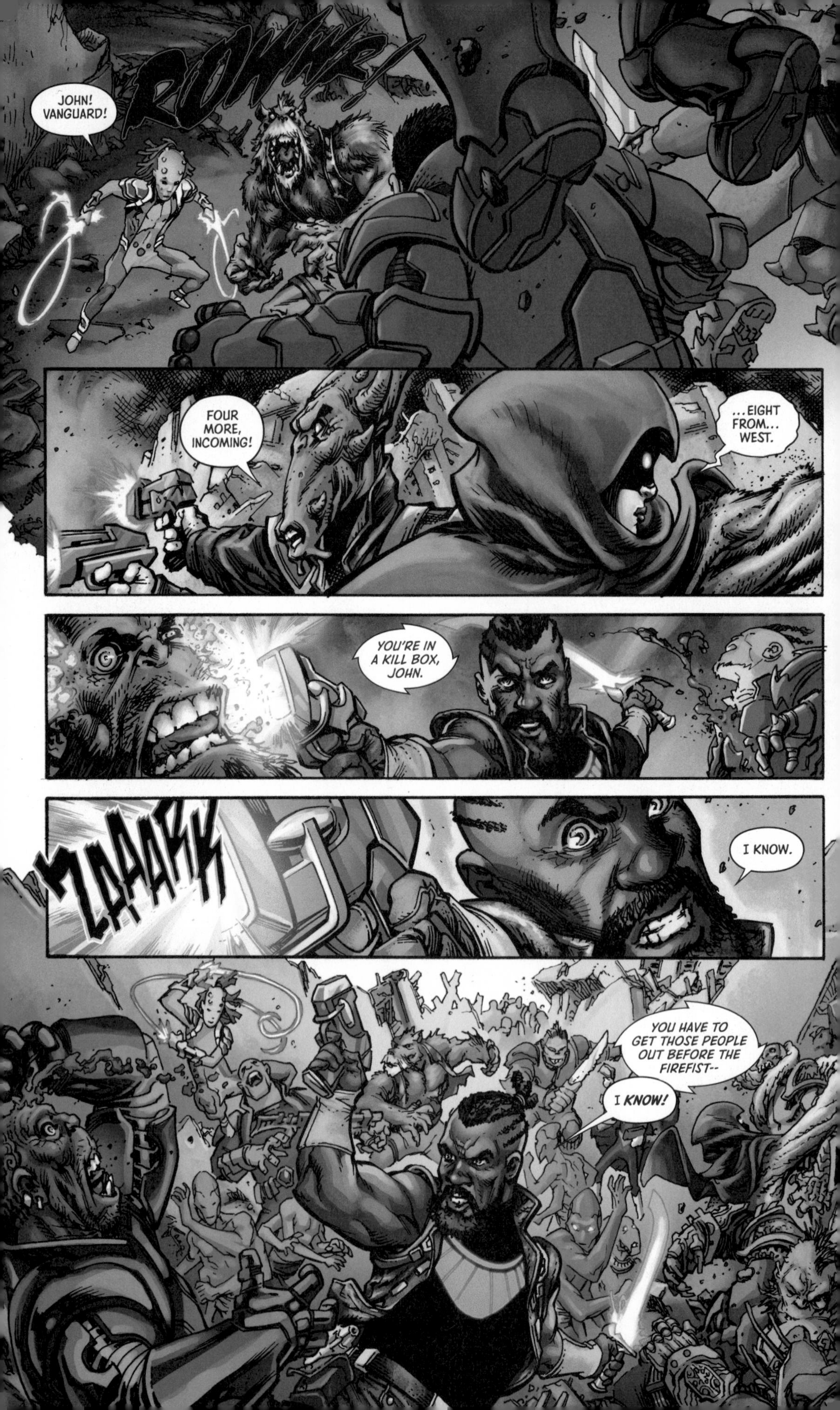
RROWWR!
JOHN! VANGUARD!
FOUR MORE, INCOMING!
...EIGHT FROM... WEST.
YOU'RE IN A KILL BOX, JOHN.
ZAARK
I KNOW.
YOU HAVE TO GET THOSE PEOPLE OUT BEFORE THE FIREFIST--
I KNOW!

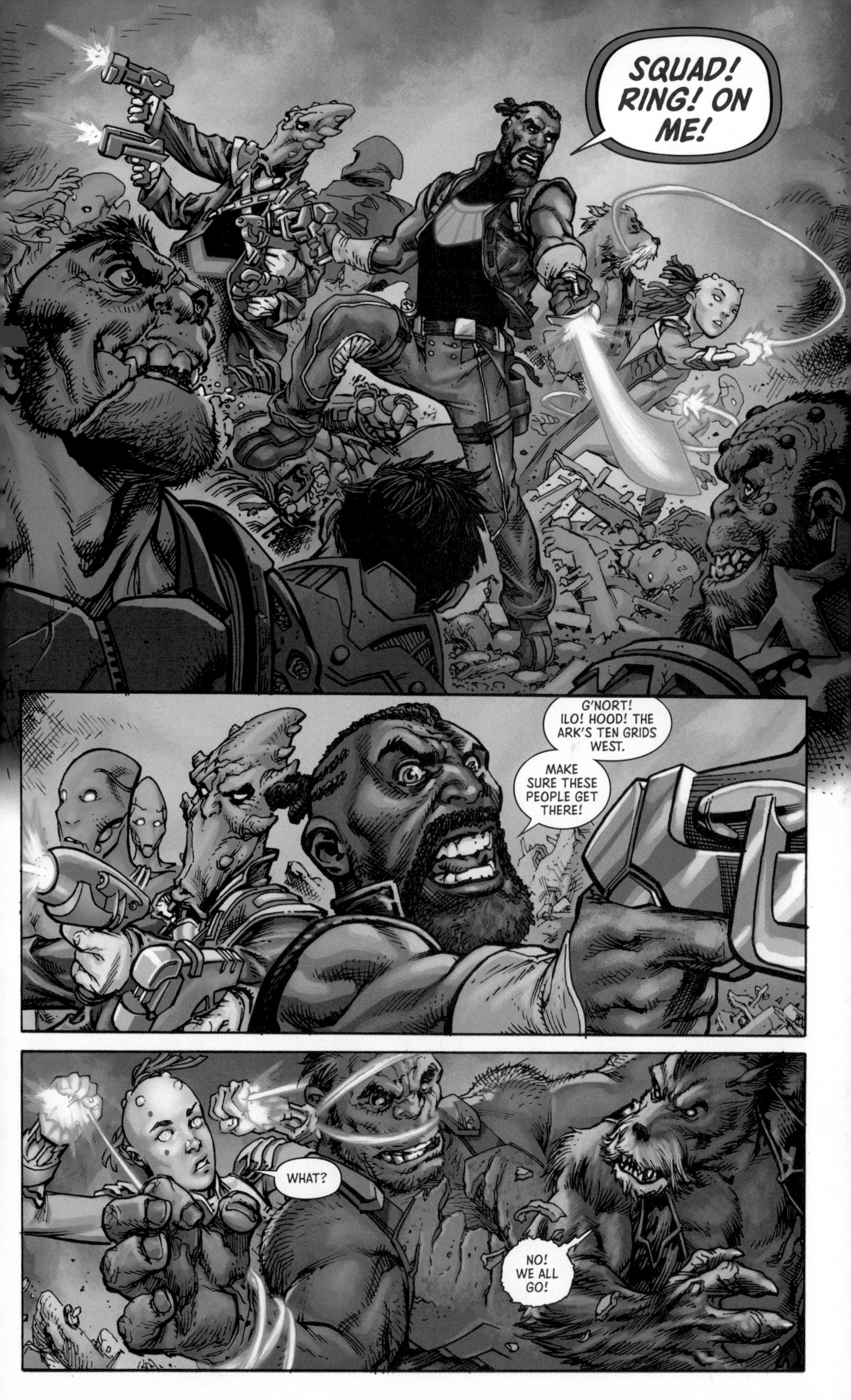
SQUAD! RING! ON ME!
G'NORT! ILO! HOOD! THE ARK'S TEN GRIDS WEST.
MAKE SURE THESE PEOPLE GET THERE!
WHAT?
NO! WE ALL GO!

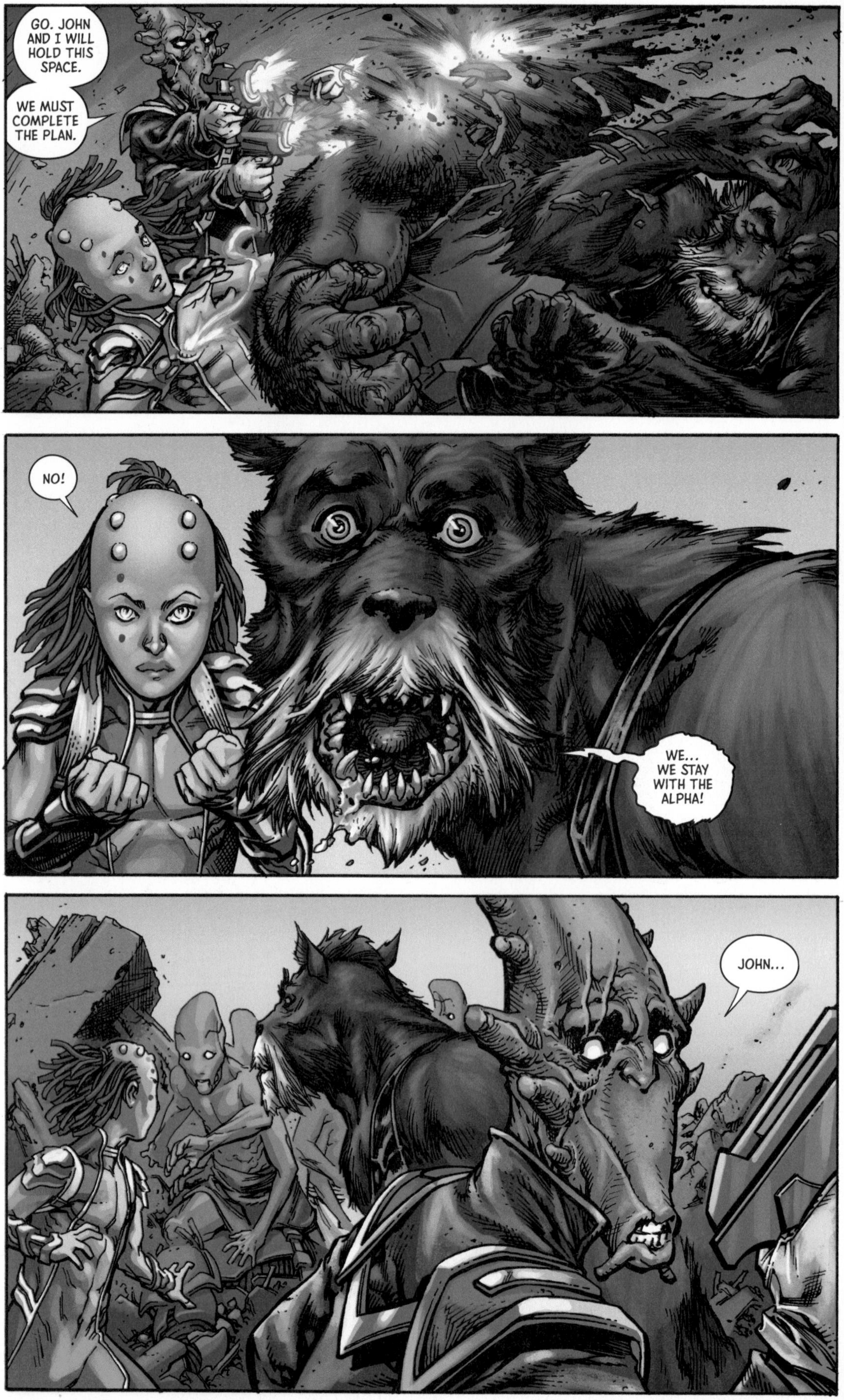
GO. JOHN AND I WILL HOLD THIS SPACE.
WE MUST COMPLETE THE PLAN.
NO!
WE... WE STAY WITH THE ALPHA!
JOHN...

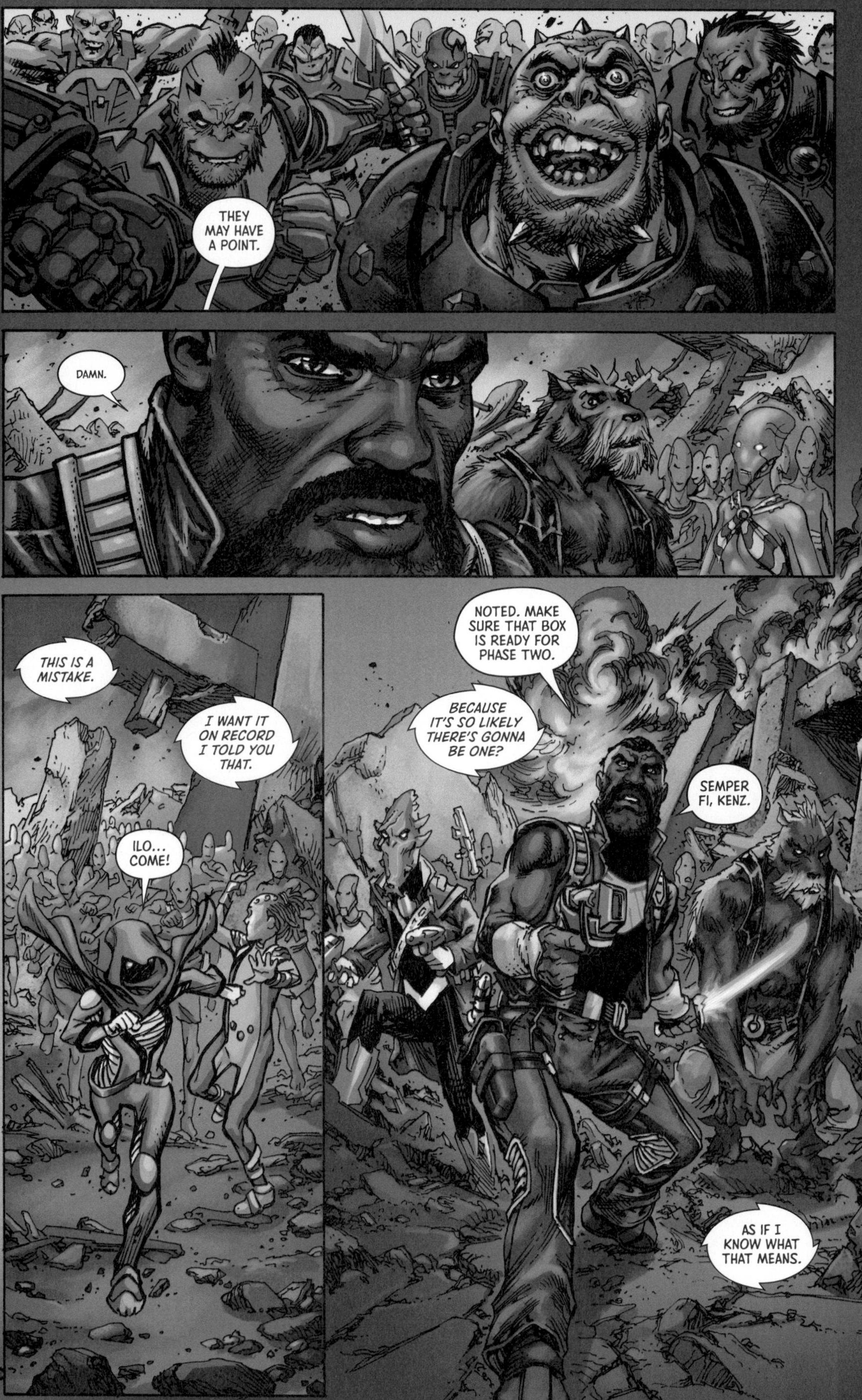
THEY MAY HAVE A POINT.
DAMN.
THIS IS A MISTAKE.
I WANT IT ON RECORD I TOLD YOU THAT.
ILO... COME!
NOTED. MAKE SURE THAT BOX IS READY FOR PHASE TWO.
BECAUSE IT'S SO LIKELY THERE'S GONNA BE ONE?
SEMPER FI, KENZ.
AS IF I KNOW WHAT THAT MEANS.

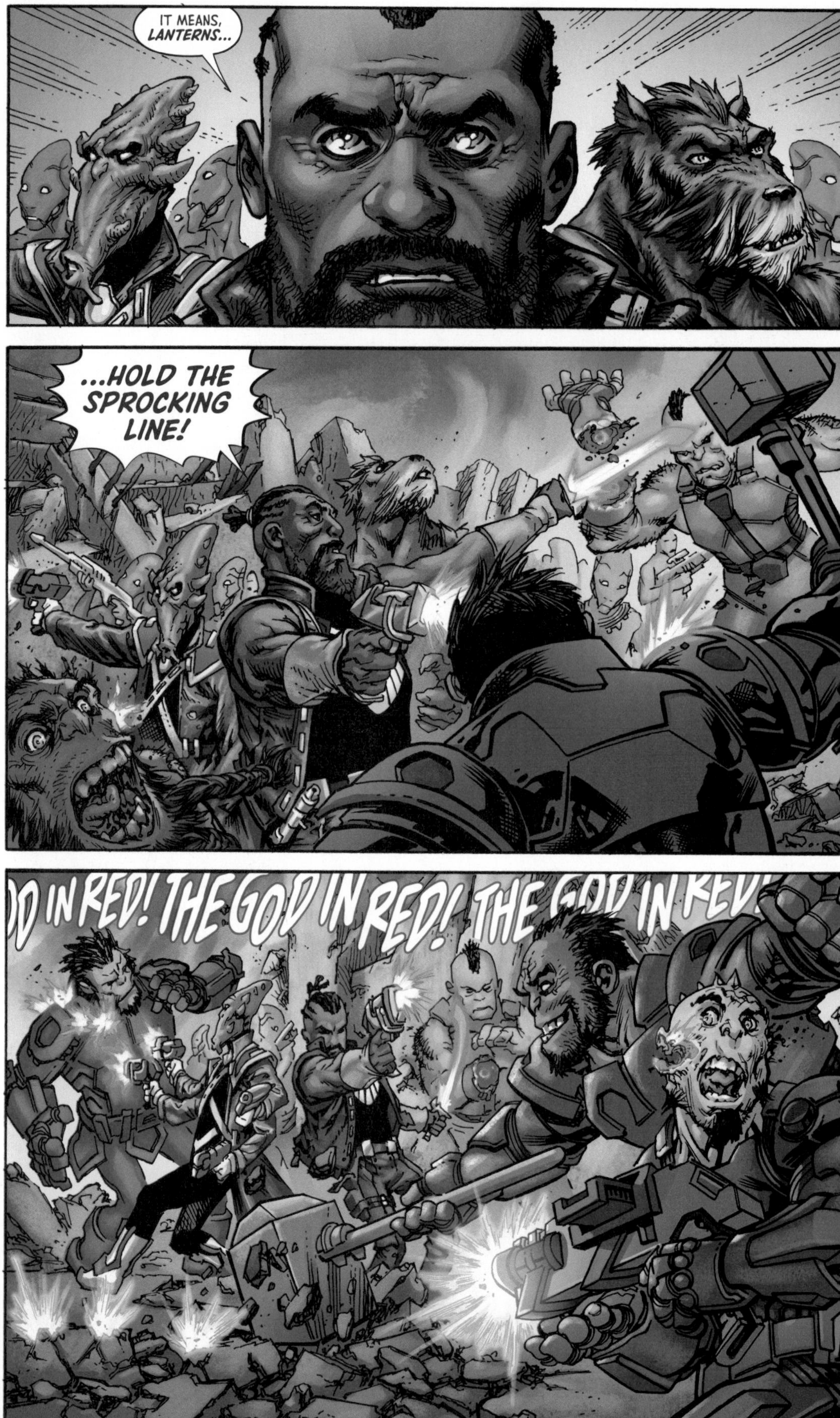

IT MEANS, LANTERNS...
...HOLD THE SPROCKING LINE!
OD IN RED! THE GOD IN RED! THE GOD IN RED!

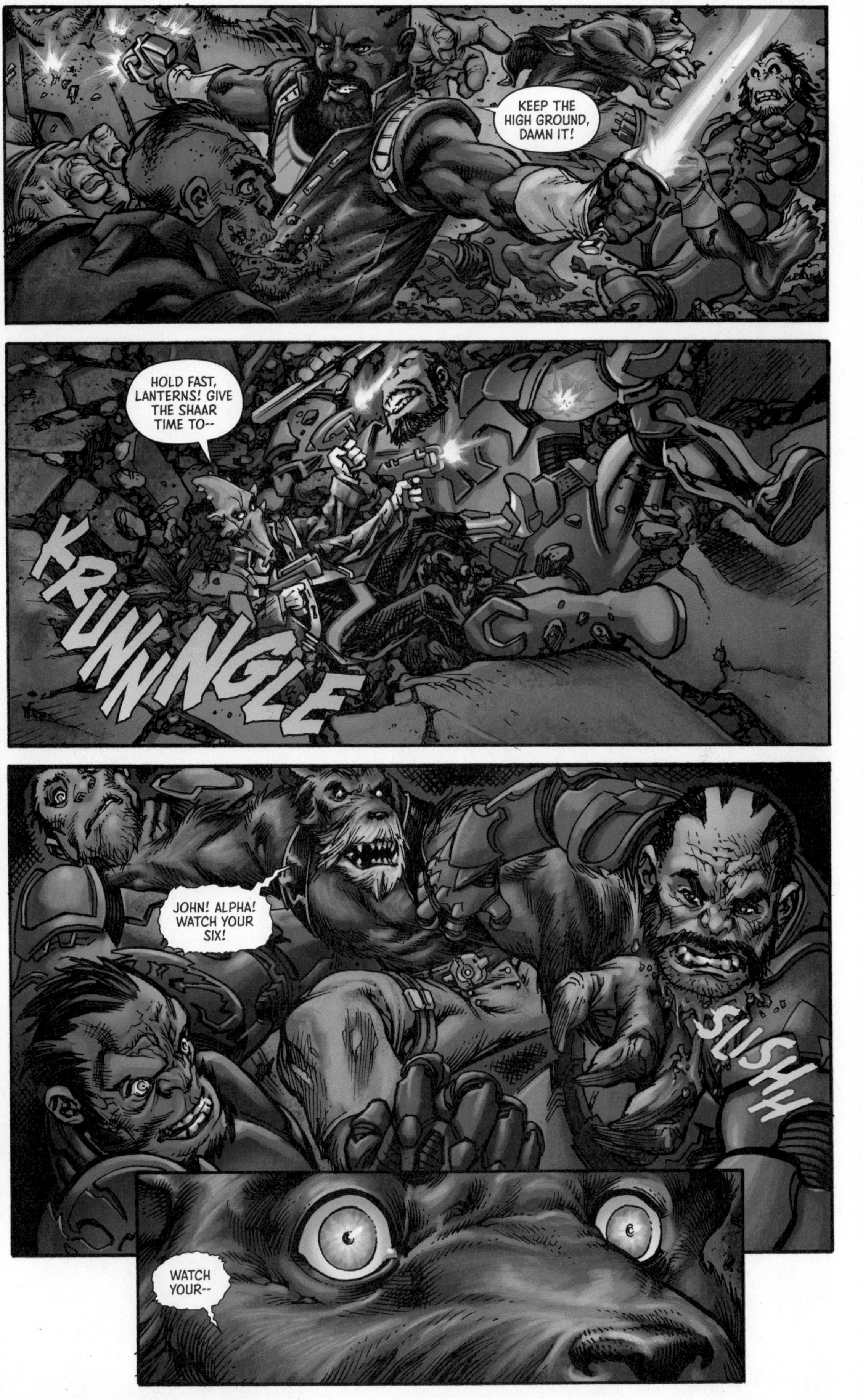
KEEP THE HIGH GROUND, DAMN IT!
HOLD FAST, LANTERNS! GIVE THE SHAAR TIME TO--
KRUNNNGLE
JOHN! ALPHA! WATCH YOUR SIX!
SLISHH
WATCH YOUR--

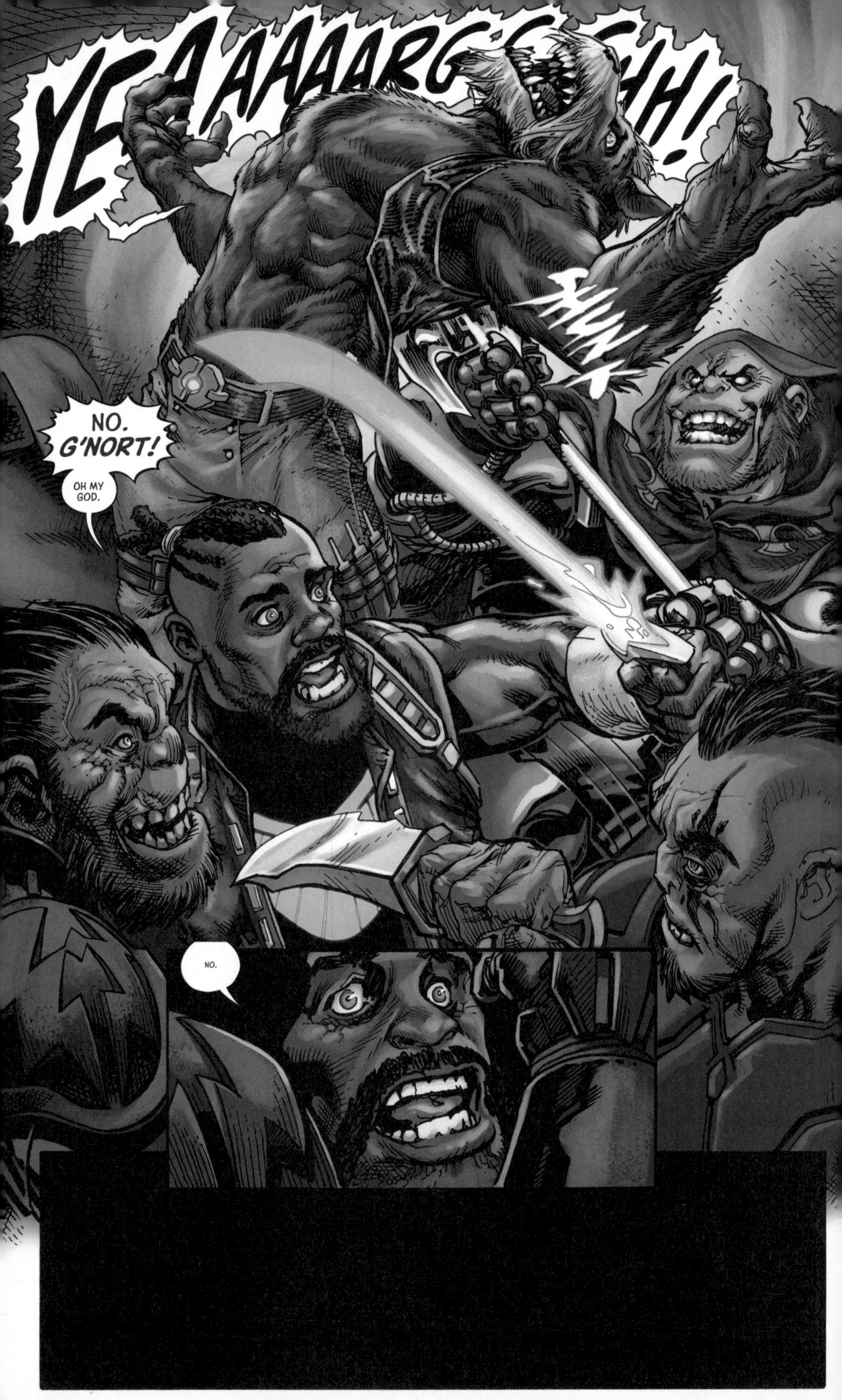

YEAAAAARGGHH!
SHUNK
NO. G'NORT!
OH MY GOD.
NO.

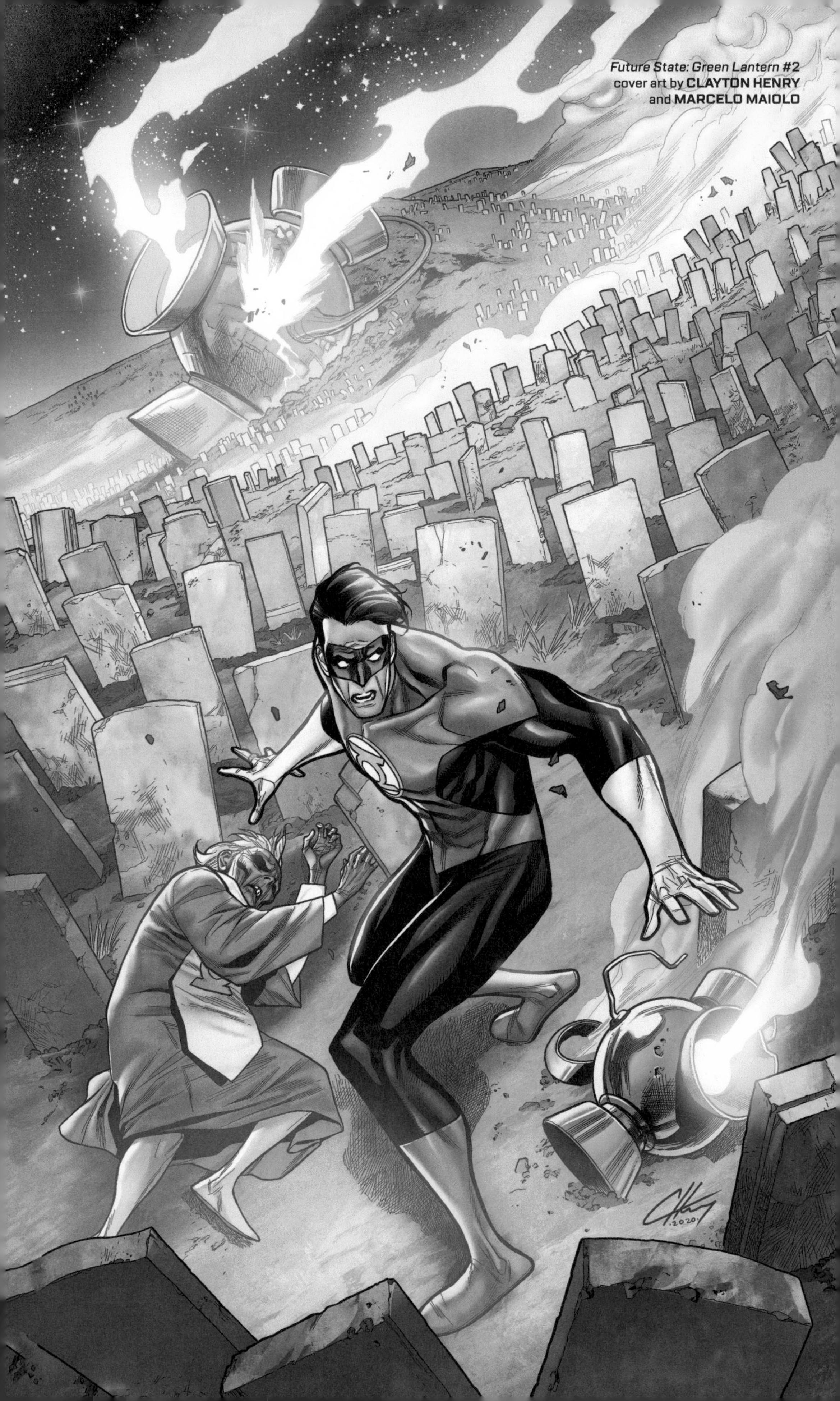

Future State: Green Lantern #2
cover art by **CLAYTON HENRY**
and **MARCELO MAIOLO**

Future State: Green Lantern #2
variant cover art by **JAMAL CAMPBELL**

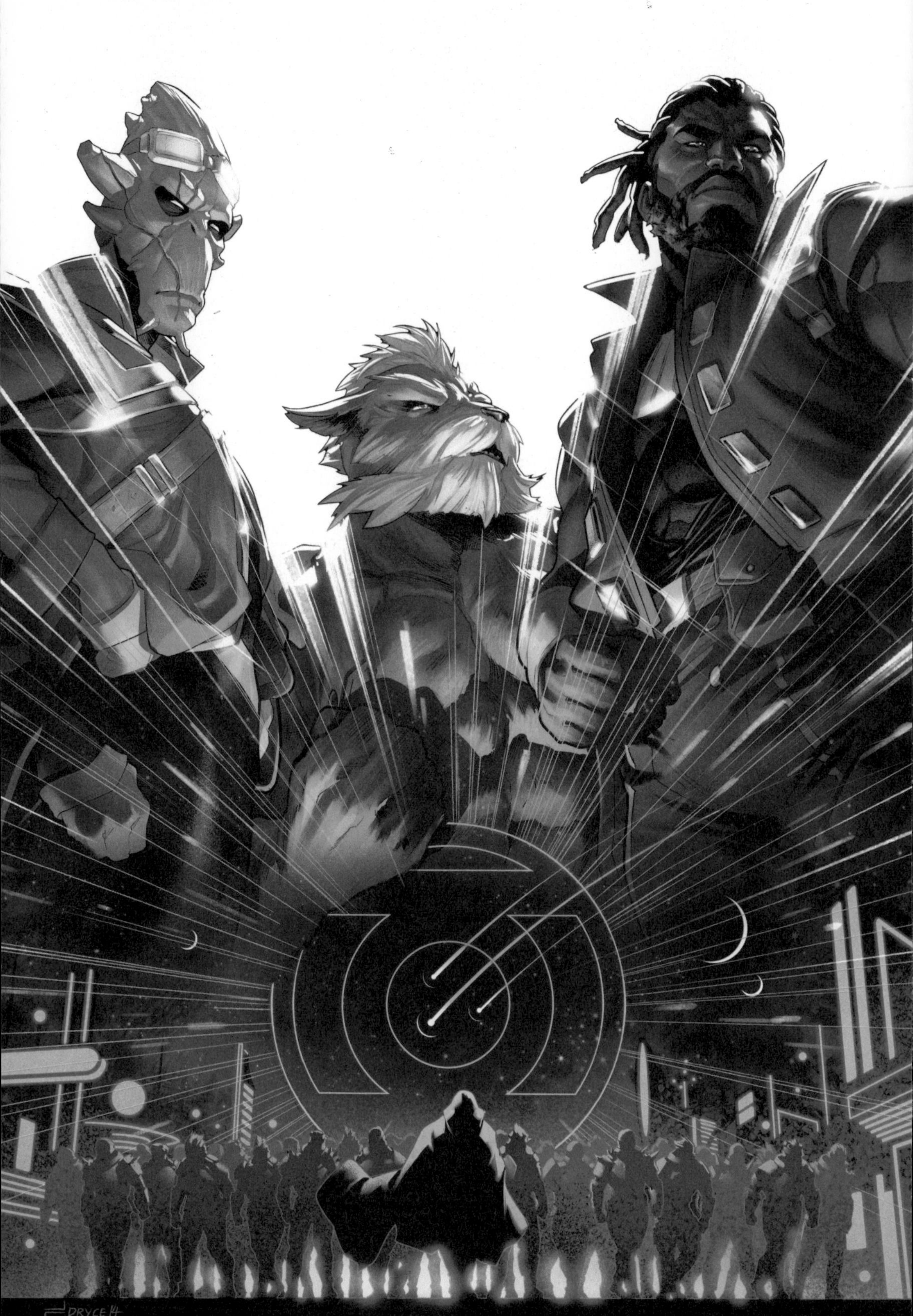

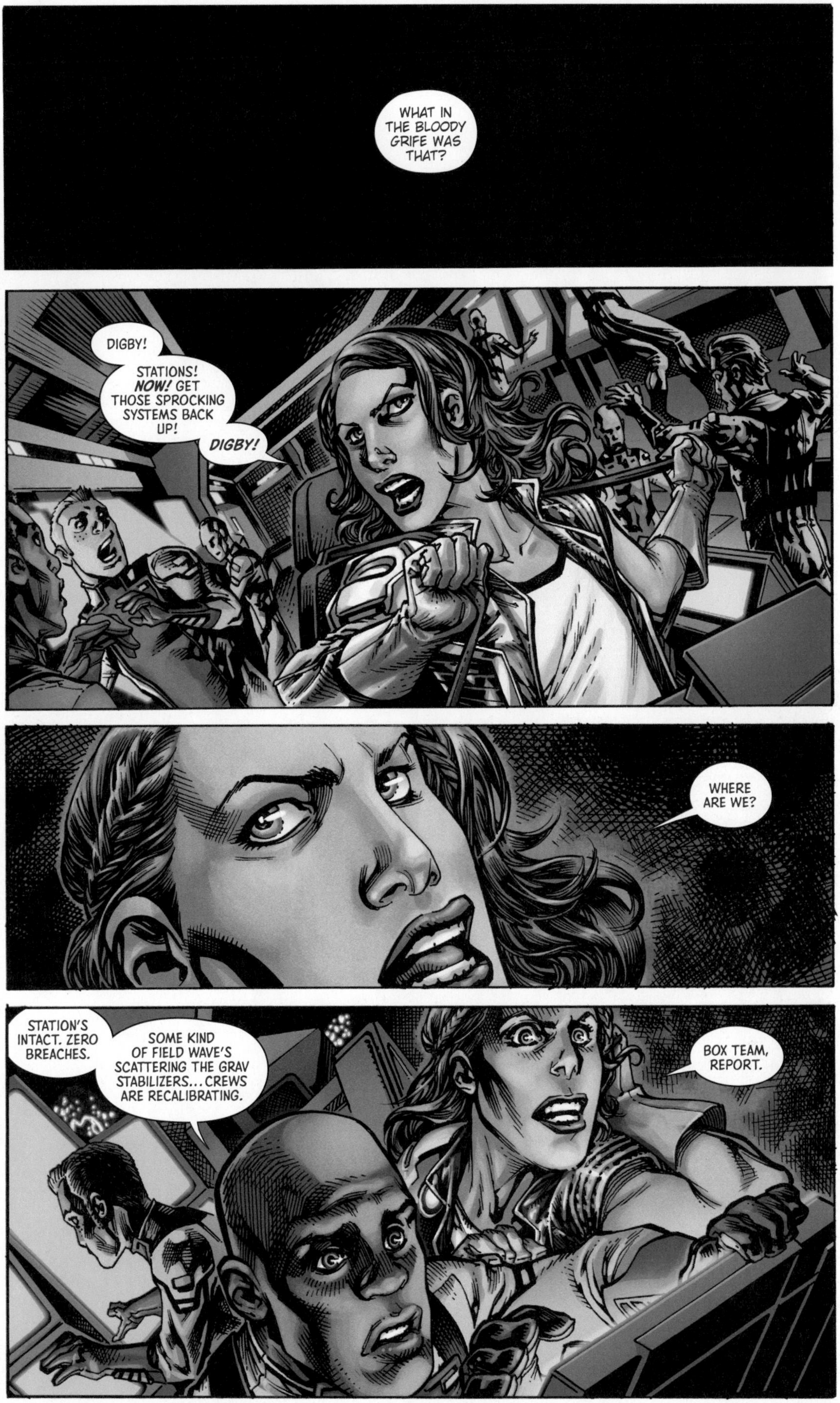
WHAT IN THE BLOODY GRIFE WAS THAT?
DIGBY!
STATIONS! NOW! GET THOSE SPROCKING SYSTEMS BACK UP!
DIGBY!
WHERE ARE WE?
STATION'S INTACT. ZERO BREACHES.
SOME KIND OF FIELD WAVE'S SCATTERING THE GRAV STABILIZERS... CREWS ARE RECALIBRATING.
BOX TEAM, REPORT.

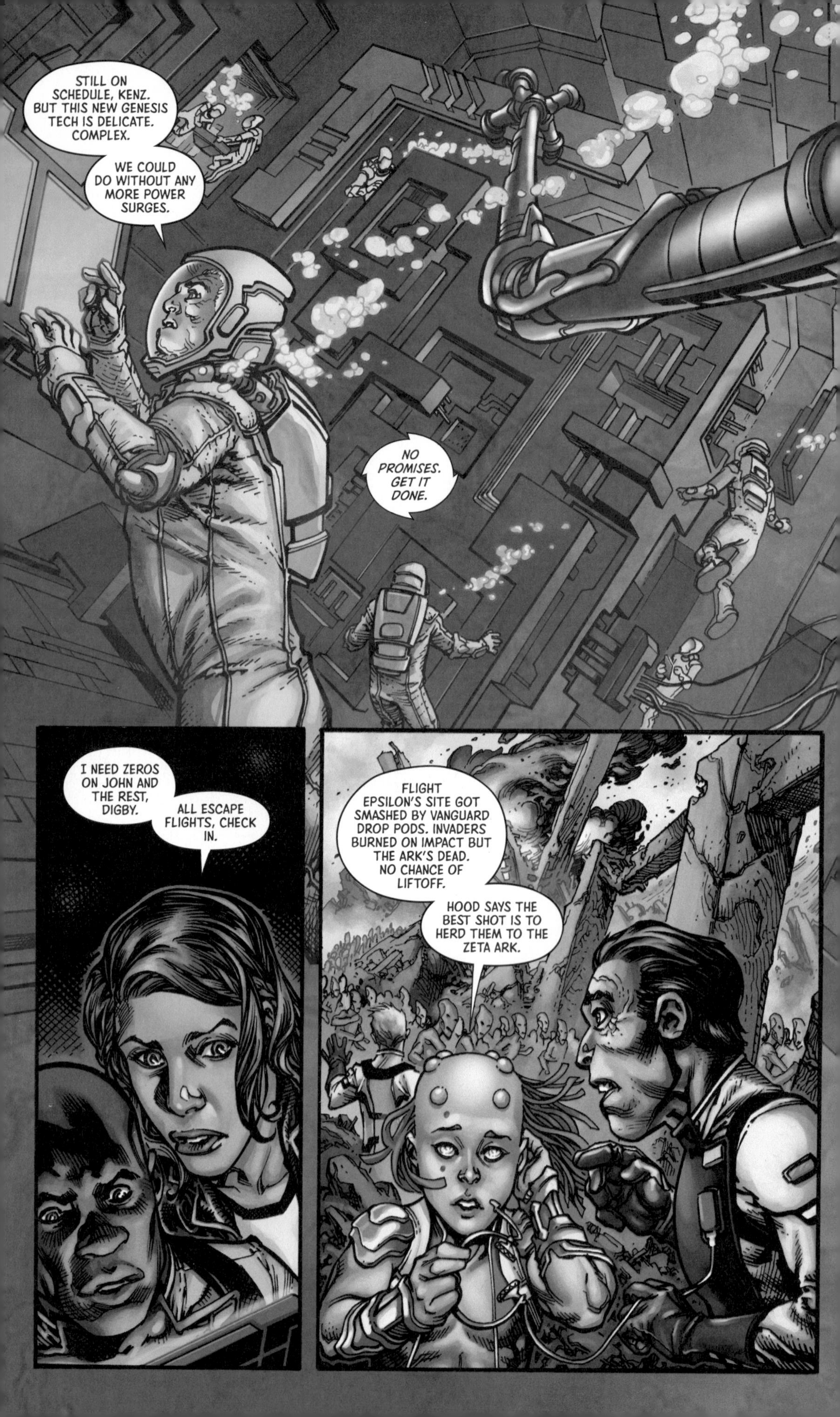
STILL ON SCHEDULE, KENZ. BUT THIS NEW GENESIS TECH IS DELICATE. COMPLEX.
WE COULD DO WITHOUT ANY MORE POWER SURGES.
NO PROMISES. GET IT DONE.
I NEED ZEROS ON JOHN AND THE REST, DIGBY.
ALL ESCAPE FLIGHTS, CHECK IN.
FLIGHT EPSILON'S SITE GOT SMASHED BY VANGUARD DROP PODS. INVADERS BURNED ON IMPACT BUT THE ARK'S DEAD. NO CHANCE OF LIFTOFF.
HOOD SAYS THE BEST SHOT IS TO HERD THEM TO THE ZETA ARK.

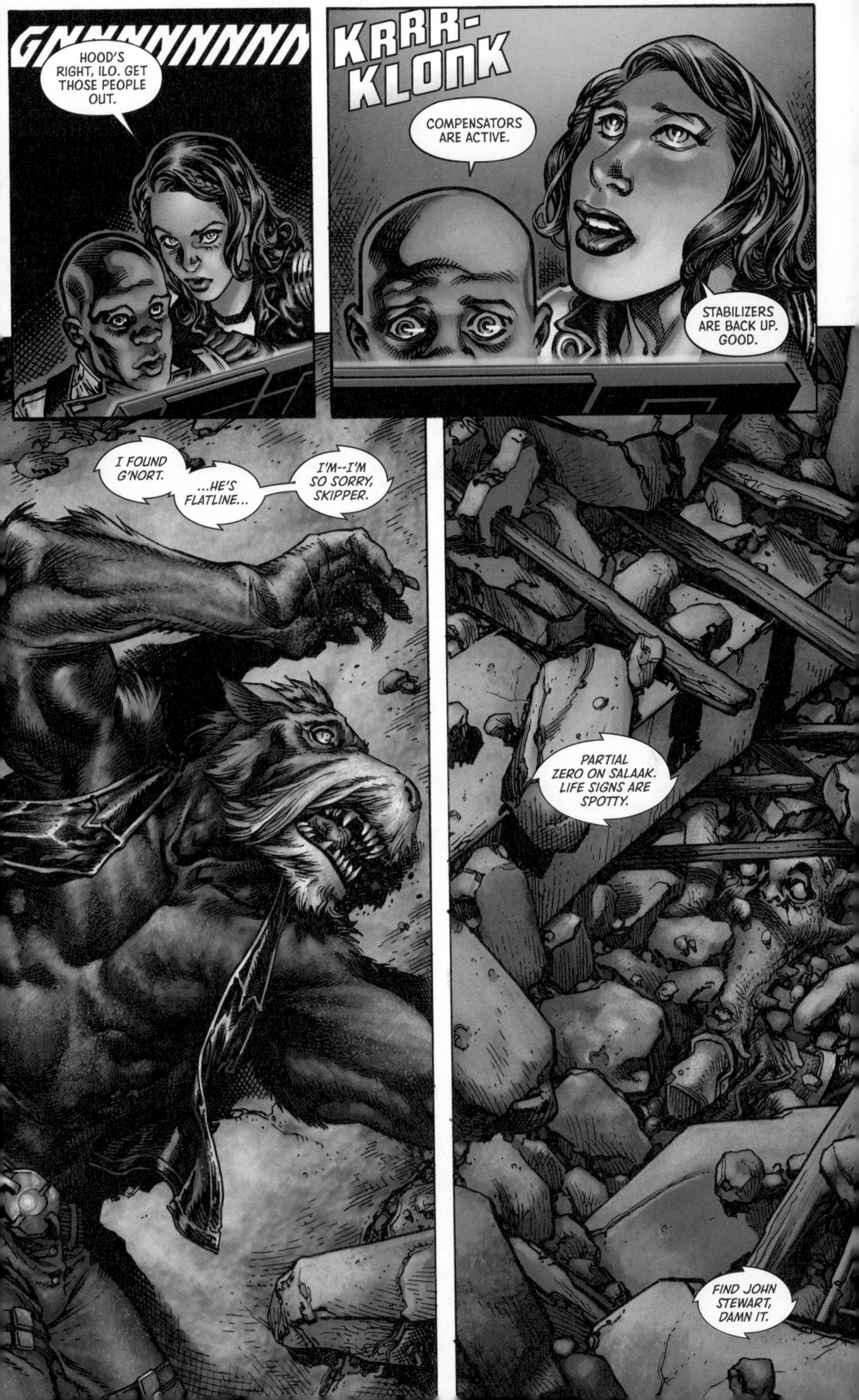
GNNNNNNNN
HOOD'S RIGHT, ILO. GET THOSE PEOPLE OUT.
KRRR-KLONK
COMPENSATORS ARE ACTIVE.
STABILIZERS ARE BACK UP. GOOD.
I FOUND G'NORT.
...HE'S FLATLINE...
I'M--I'M SO SORRY, SKIPPER.
PARTIAL ZERO ON SALAAK. LIFE SIGNS ARE SPOTTY.
FIND JOHN STEWART, DAMN IT.

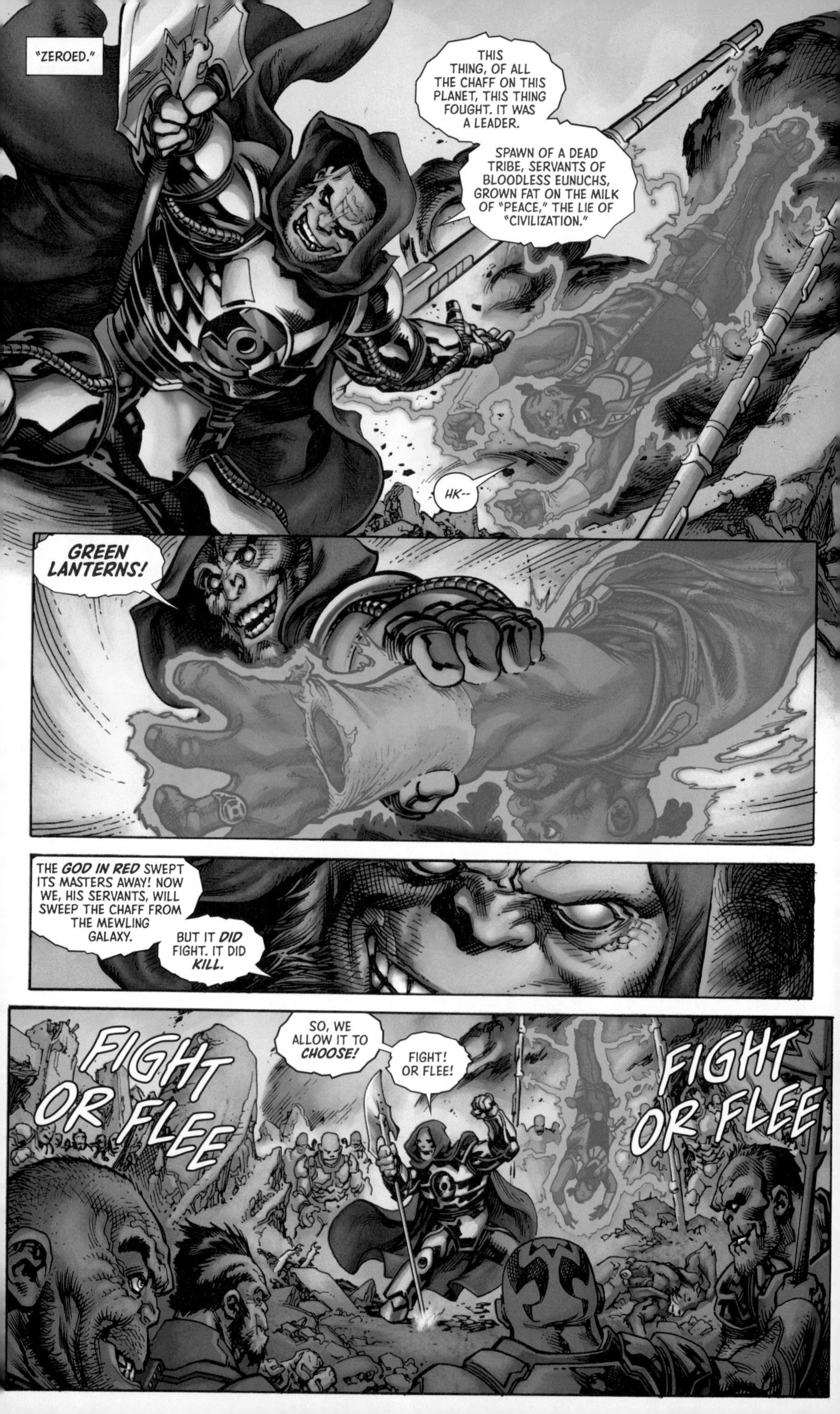
"ZEROED."
THIS THING, OF ALL THE CHAFF ON THIS PLANET, THIS THING FOUGHT. IT WAS A LEADER.
SPAWN OF A DEAD TRIBE, SERVANTS OF BLOODLESS EUNUCHS, GROWN FAT ON THE MILK OF "PEACE," THE LIE OF "CIVILIZATION."
HK--
GREEN LANTERNS!
THE GOD IN RED SWEPT ITS MASTERS AWAY! NOW WE, HIS SERVANTS, WILL SWEEP THE CHAFF FROM THE MEWLING GALAXY.
BUT IT DID FIGHT. IT DID KILL.
FIGHT OR FLEE
SO, WE ALLOW IT TO CHOOSE!
FIGHT! OR FLEE!
FIGHT OR FLEE

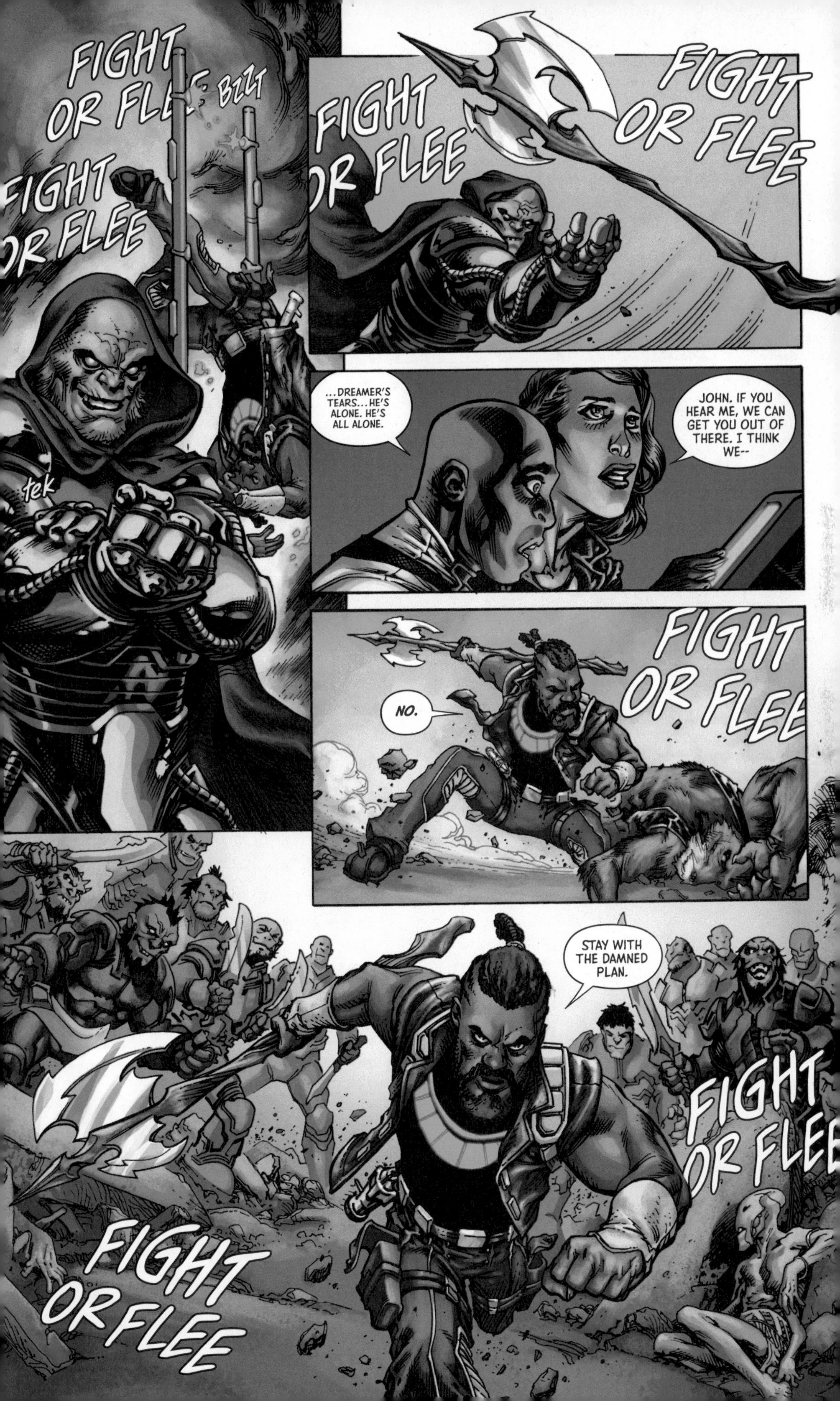
FIGHT OR FLEE
BZZT
FIGHT OR FLEE
tek
FIGHT OR FLEE
FIGHT OR FLEE
...DREAMER'S TEARS...HE'S ALONE. HE'S ALL ALONE.
JOHN. IF YOU HEAR ME, WE CAN GET YOU OUT OF THERE. I THINK WE--
FIGHT OR FLEE
NO.
STAY WITH THE DAMNED PLAN.
FIGHT OR FLEE
FIGHT OR FLEE

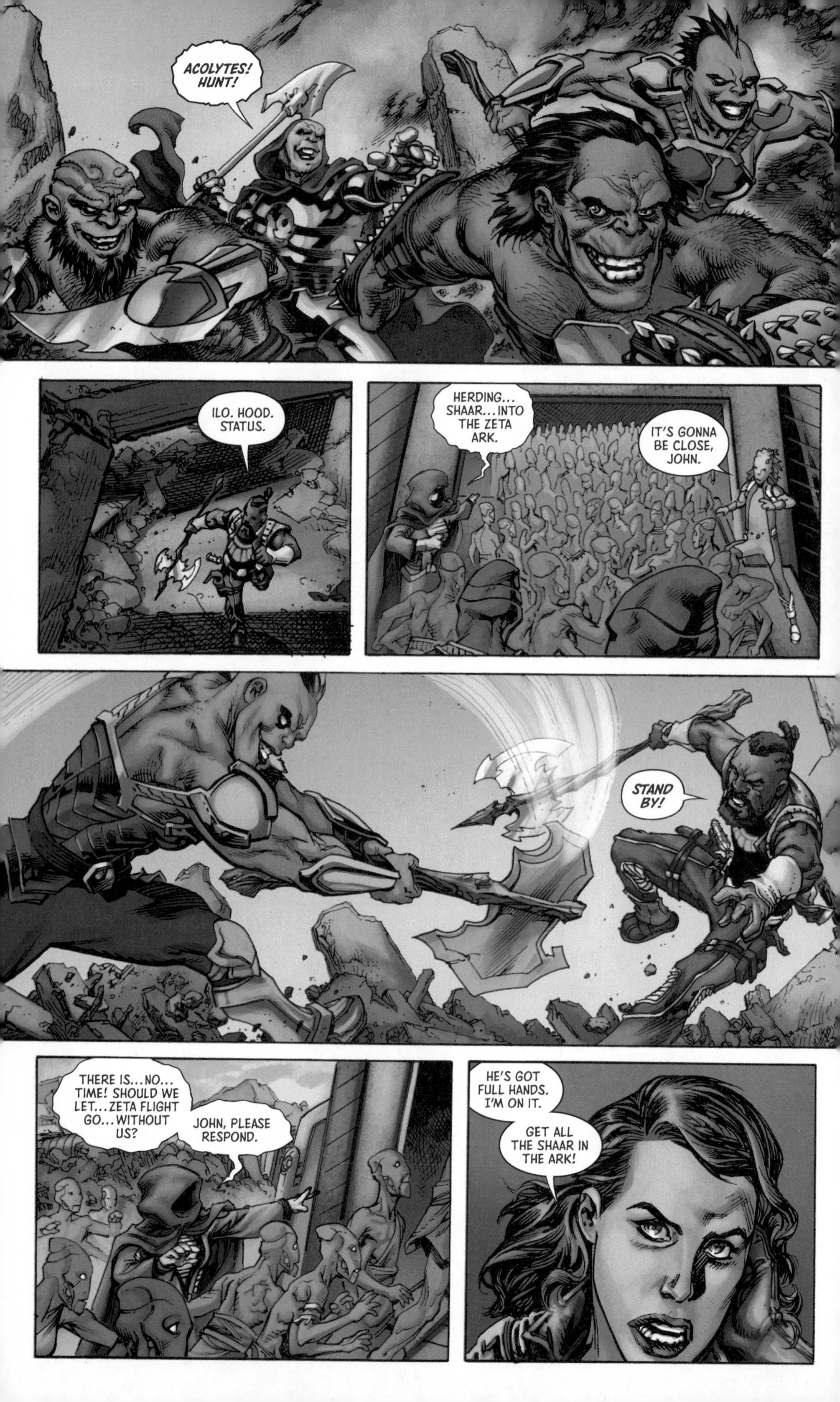
ACOLYTES! HUNT!
ILO. HOOD. STATUS.
HERDING... SHAAR...INTO THE ZETA ARK.
IT'S GONNA BE CLOSE, JOHN.
STAND BY!
THERE IS...NO... TIME! SHOULD WE LET...ZETA FLIGHT GO...WITHOUT US?
JOHN, PLEASE RESPOND.
HE'S GOT FULL HANDS. I'M ON IT.
GET ALL THE SHAAR IN THE ARK!

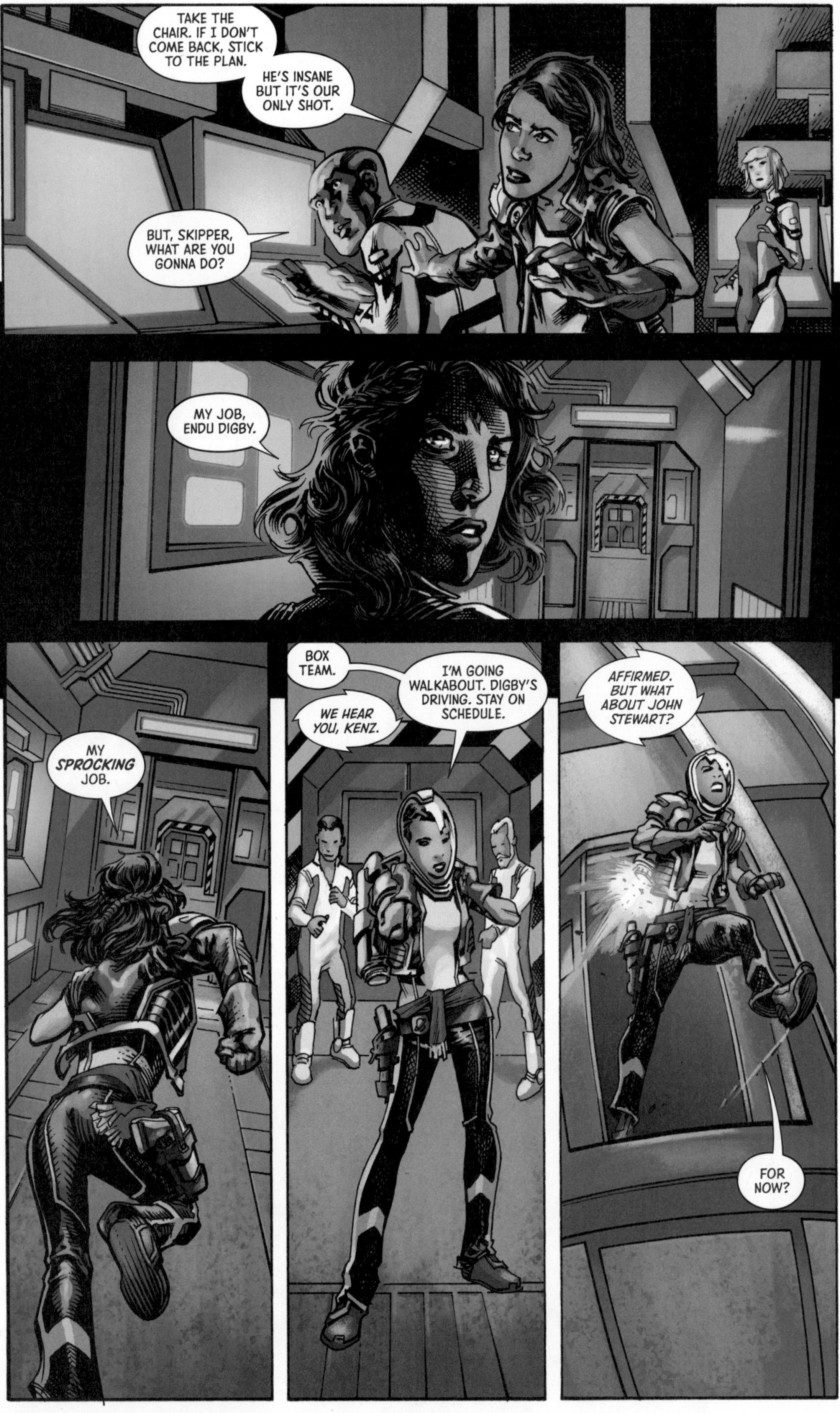
TAKE THE CHAIR. IF I DON'T COME BACK, STICK TO THE PLAN.
HE'S INSANE BUT IT'S OUR ONLY SHOT.
BUT, SKIPPER, WHAT ARE YOU GONNA DO?
MY JOB, ENDU DIGBY.
MY *SPROCKING* JOB.
BOX TEAM.
I'M GOING WALKABOUT. DIGBY'S DRIVING. STAY ON SCHEDULE.
WE HEAR YOU, KENZ.
AFFIRMED. BUT WHAT ABOUT JOHN STEWART?
FOR NOW?

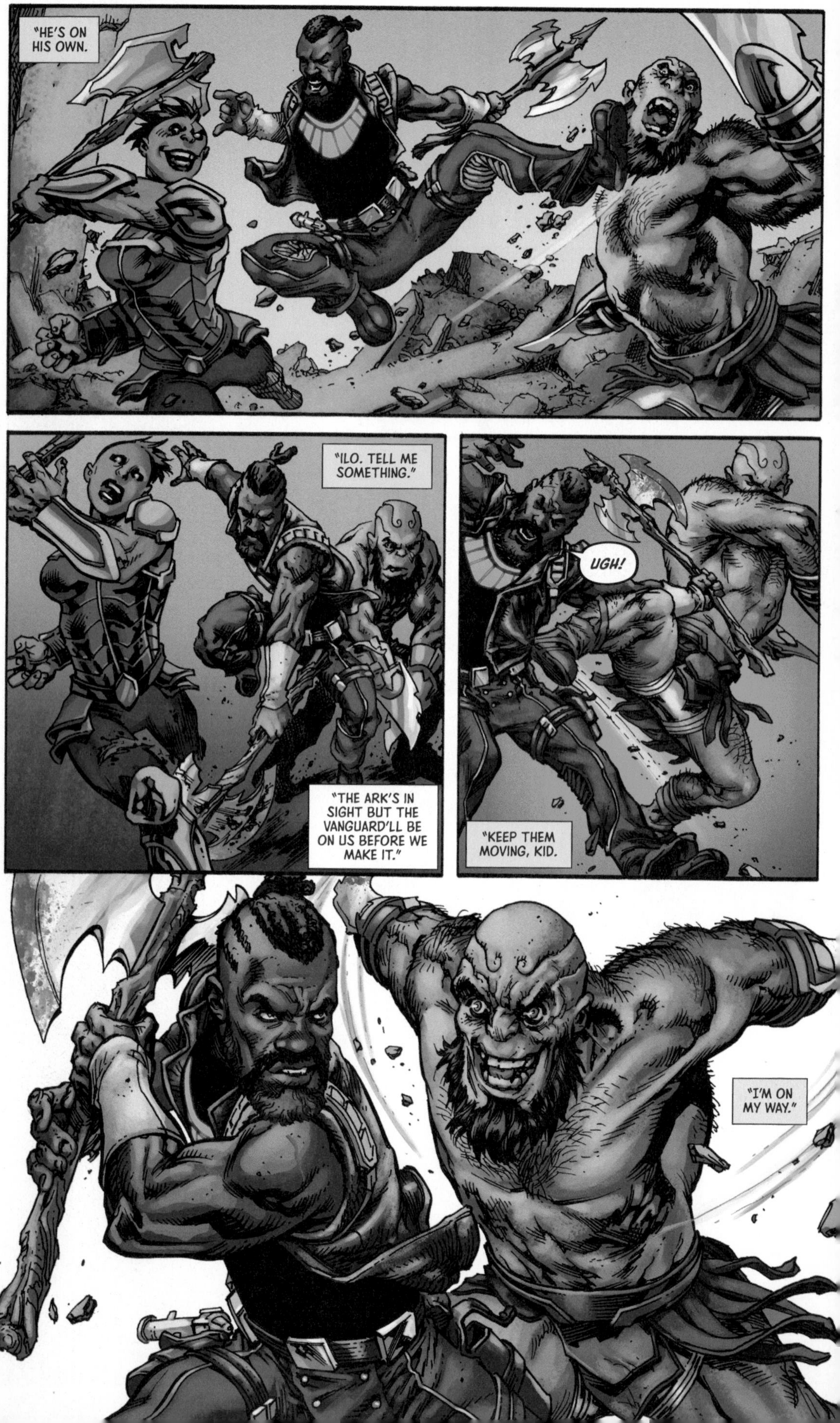
"HE'S ON HIS OWN.
"ILO. TELL ME SOMETHING."
"THE ARK'S IN SIGHT BUT THE VANGUARD'LL BE ON US BEFORE WE MAKE IT."
UGH!
"KEEP THEM MOVING, KID.
"I'M ON MY WAY."

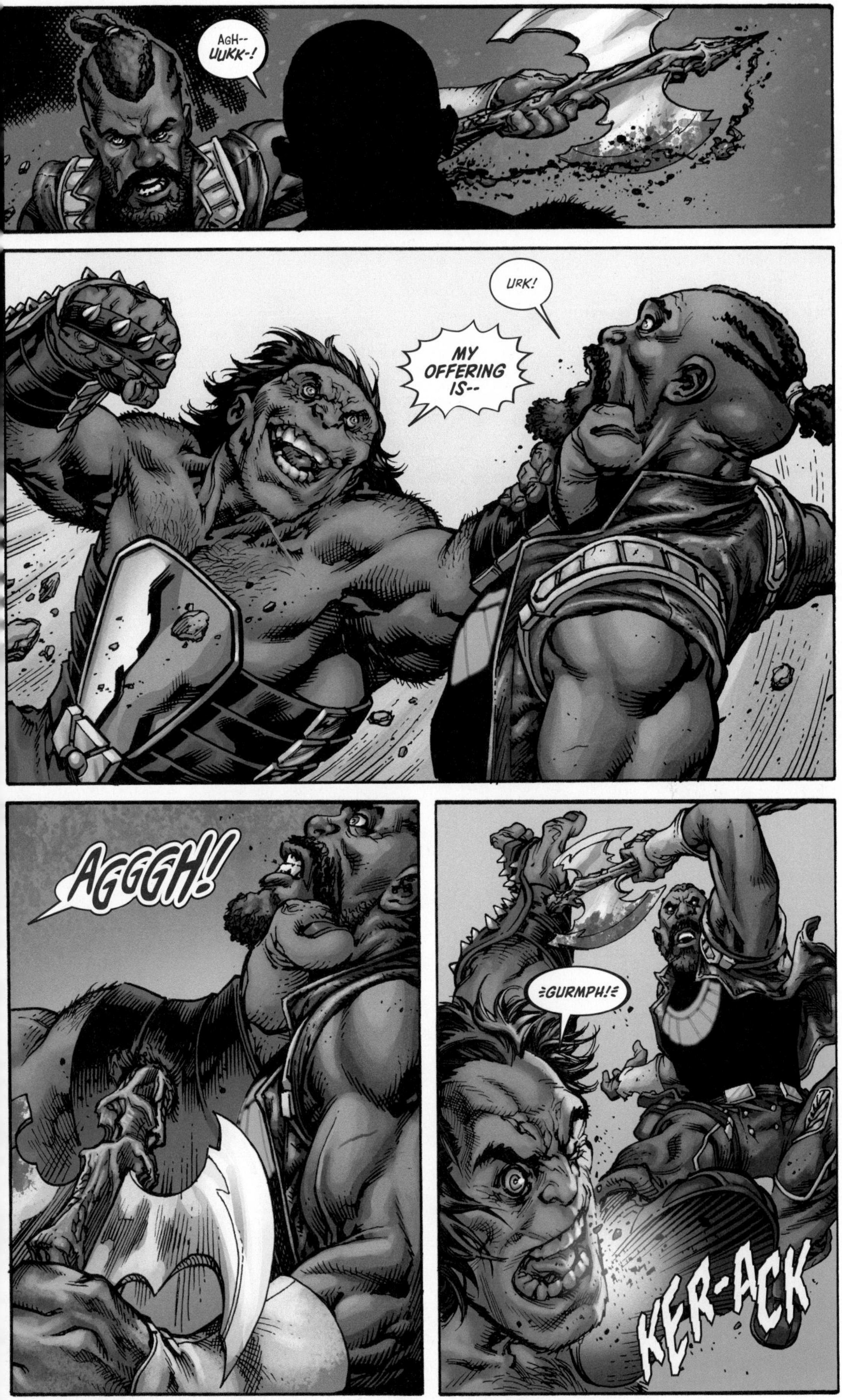
AGH--
UUKK-!
URK!
MY OFFERING IS--
AGGGH!
GURMPH!
KER-ACK

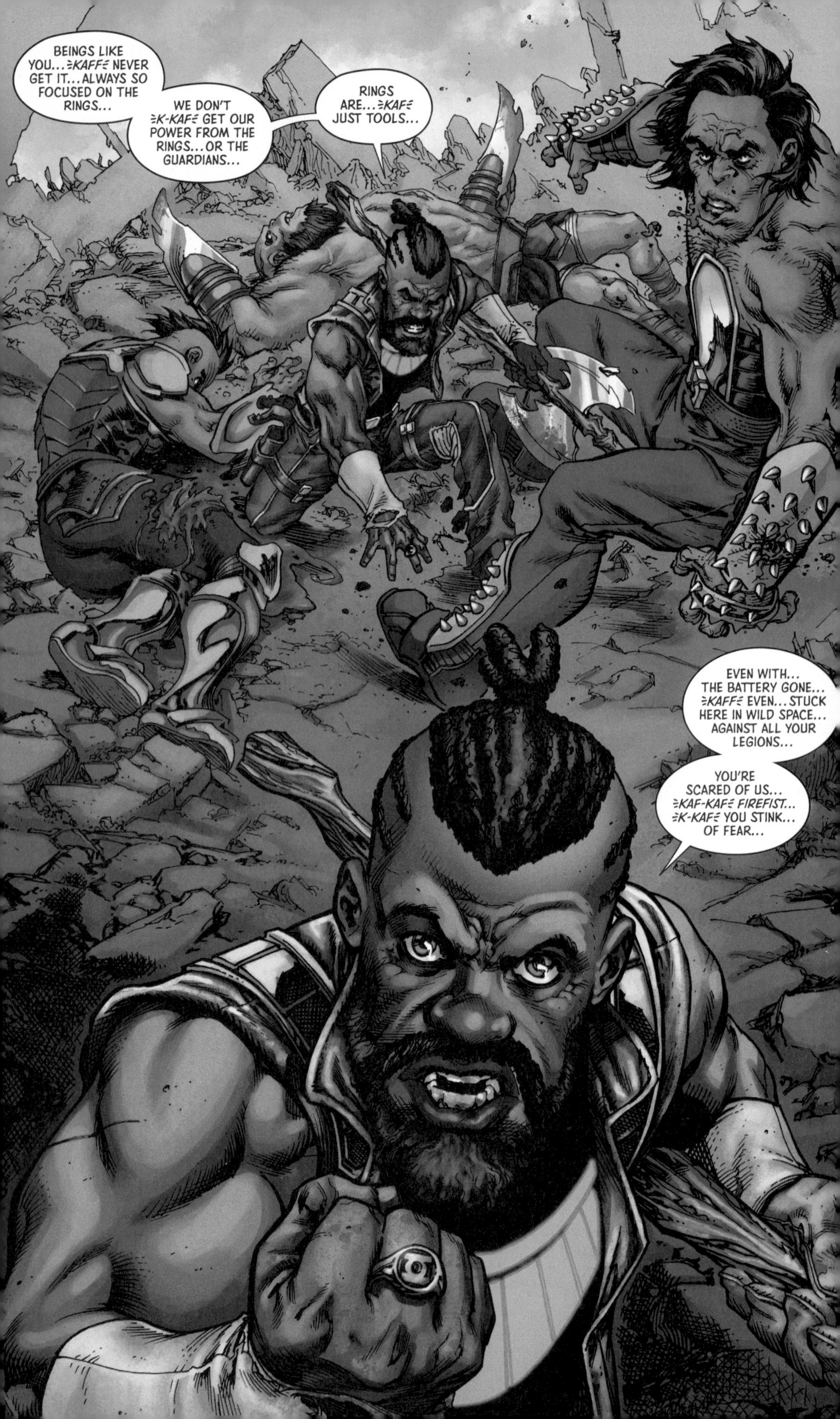
BEINGS LIKE YOU... ≡KAFF≡ NEVER GET IT... ALWAYS SO FOCUSED ON THE RINGS...
WE DON'T ≡K-KAF≡ GET OUR POWER FROM THE RINGS... OR THE GUARDIANS...
RINGS ARE... ≡KAF≡ JUST TOOLS...
EVEN WITH... THE BATTERY GONE... ≡KAFF≡ EVEN... STUCK HERE IN WILD SPACE... AGAINST ALL YOUR LEGIONS...
YOU'RE SCARED OF US... ≡KAF-KAF≡ FIREFIST... ≡K-KAF≡ YOU STINK... OF FEAR...

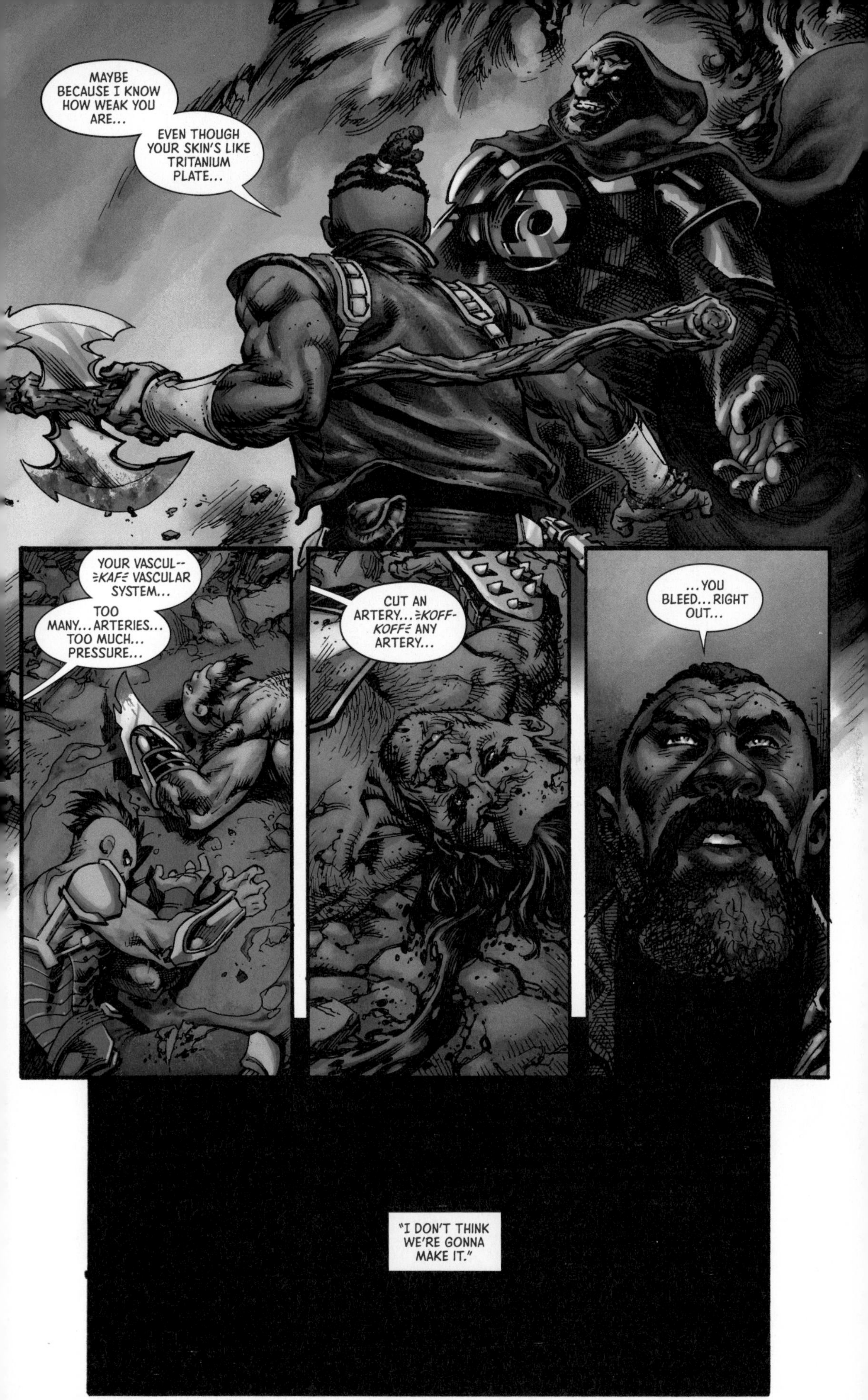
MAYBE BECAUSE I KNOW HOW WEAK YOU ARE...
EVEN THOUGH YOUR SKIN'S LIKE TRITANIUM PLATE...
YOUR VASCUL-- =KAF= VASCULAR SYSTEM...
TOO MANY... ARTERIES... TOO MUCH... PRESSURE...
CUT AN ARTERY... =KOFF-KOFF= ANY ARTERY...
...YOU BLEED... RIGHT OUT...

"I DON'T THINK WE'RE GONNA MAKE IT."

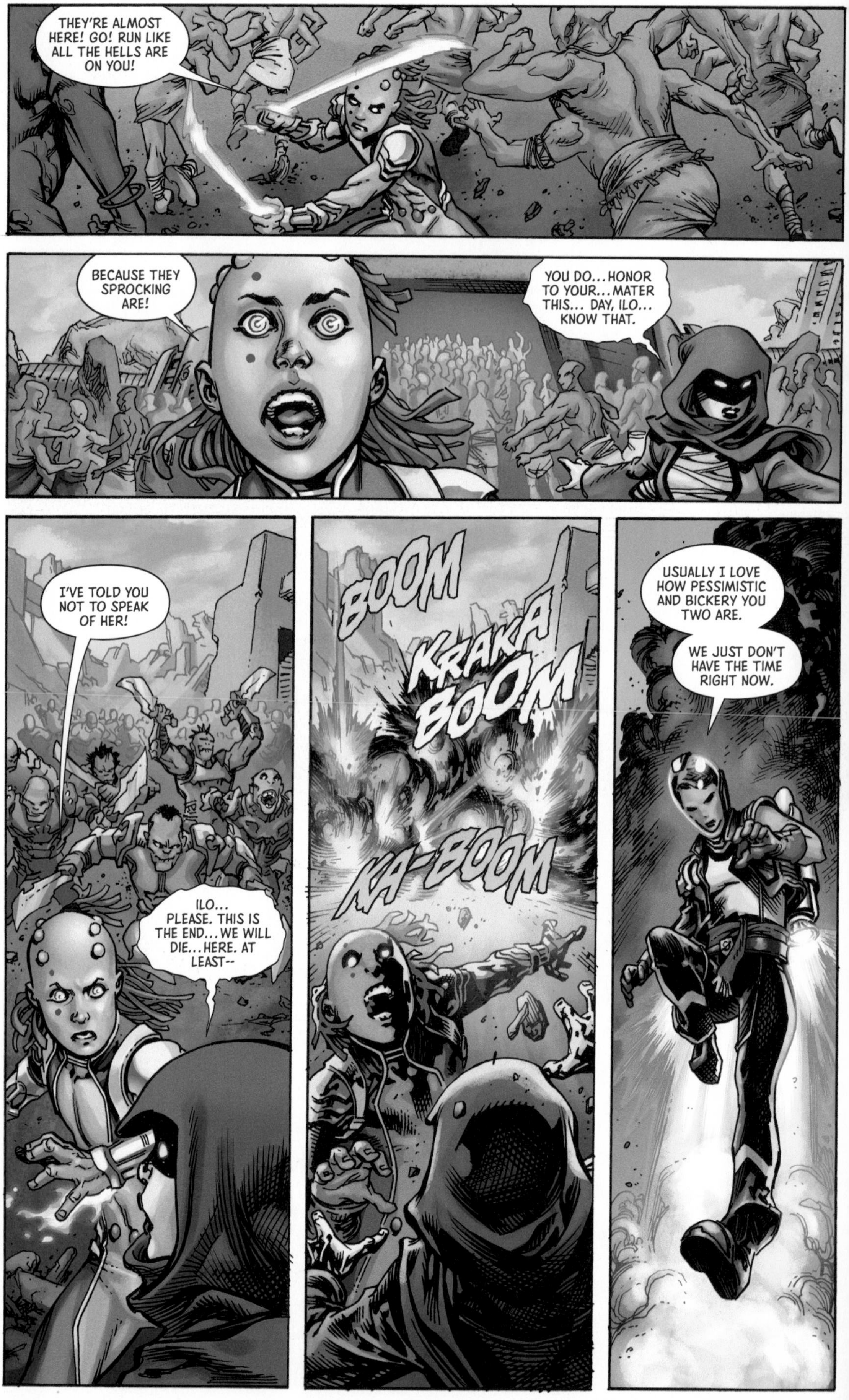
THEY'RE ALMOST HERE! GO! RUN LIKE ALL THE HELLS ARE ON YOU!
BECAUSE THEY SPROCKING ARE!
YOU DO...HONOR TO YOUR...MATER THIS... DAY, ILO... KNOW THAT.
I'VE TOLD YOU NOT TO SPEAK OF HER!
ILO... PLEASE. THIS IS THE END...WE WILL DIE...HERE. AT LEAST--
BOOM
KRAKA BOOM
KA-BOOM
USUALLY I LOVE HOW PESSIMISTIC AND BICKERY YOU TWO ARE.
WE JUST DON'T HAVE THE TIME RIGHT NOW.

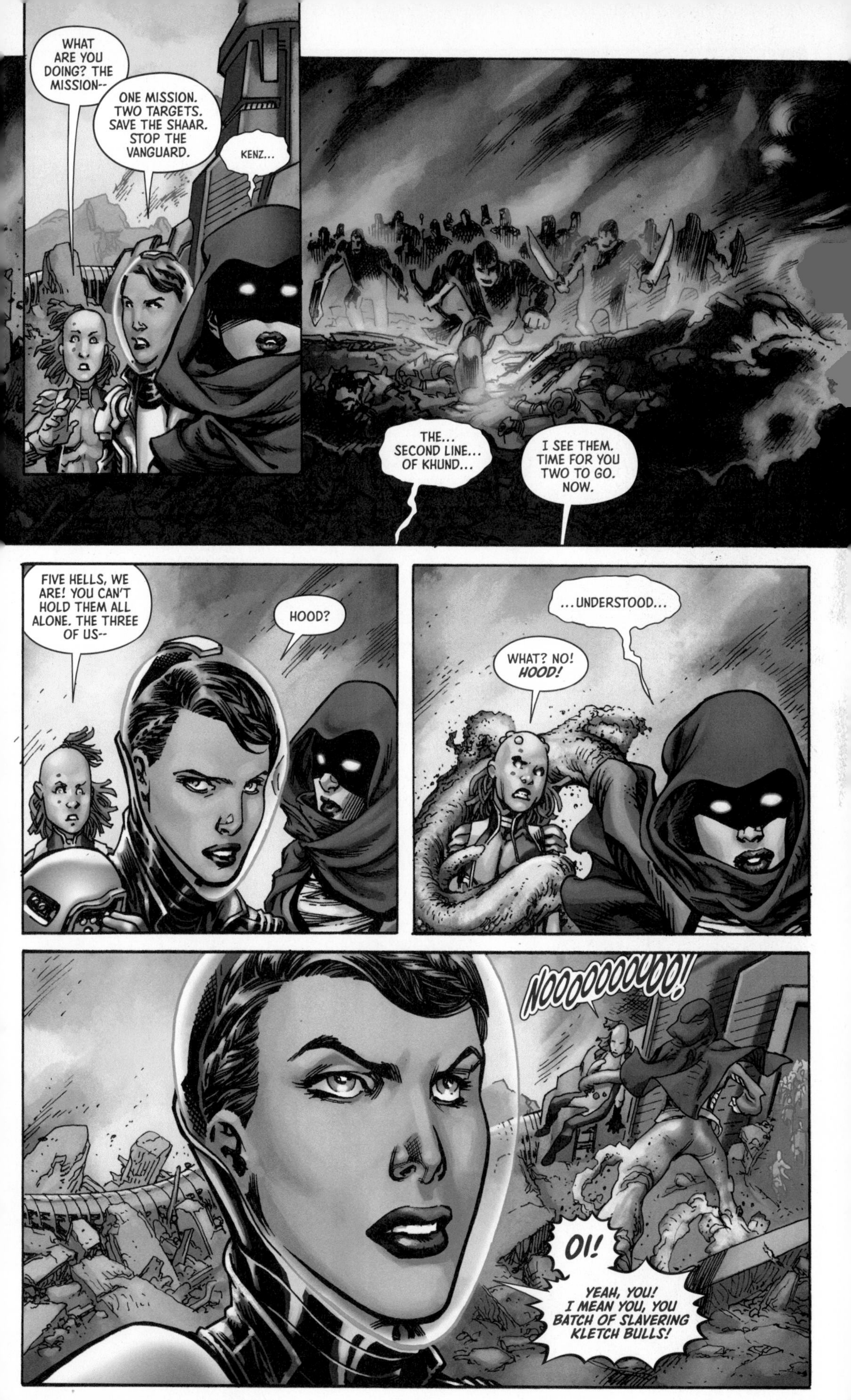
WHAT ARE YOU DOING? THE MISSION--
ONE MISSION. TWO TARGETS. SAVE THE SHAAR. STOP THE VANGUARD.
KENZ...
THE... SECOND LINE... OF KHUND...
I SEE THEM. TIME FOR YOU TWO TO GO. NOW.
FIVE HELLS, WE ARE! YOU CAN'T HOLD THEM ALL ALONE. THE THREE OF US--
HOOD?
...UNDERSTOOD...
WHAT? NO! HOOD!
NOOOOOOOOOO!
OI!
YEAH, YOU! I MEAN YOU, YOU BATCH OF SLAVERING KLETCH BULLS!

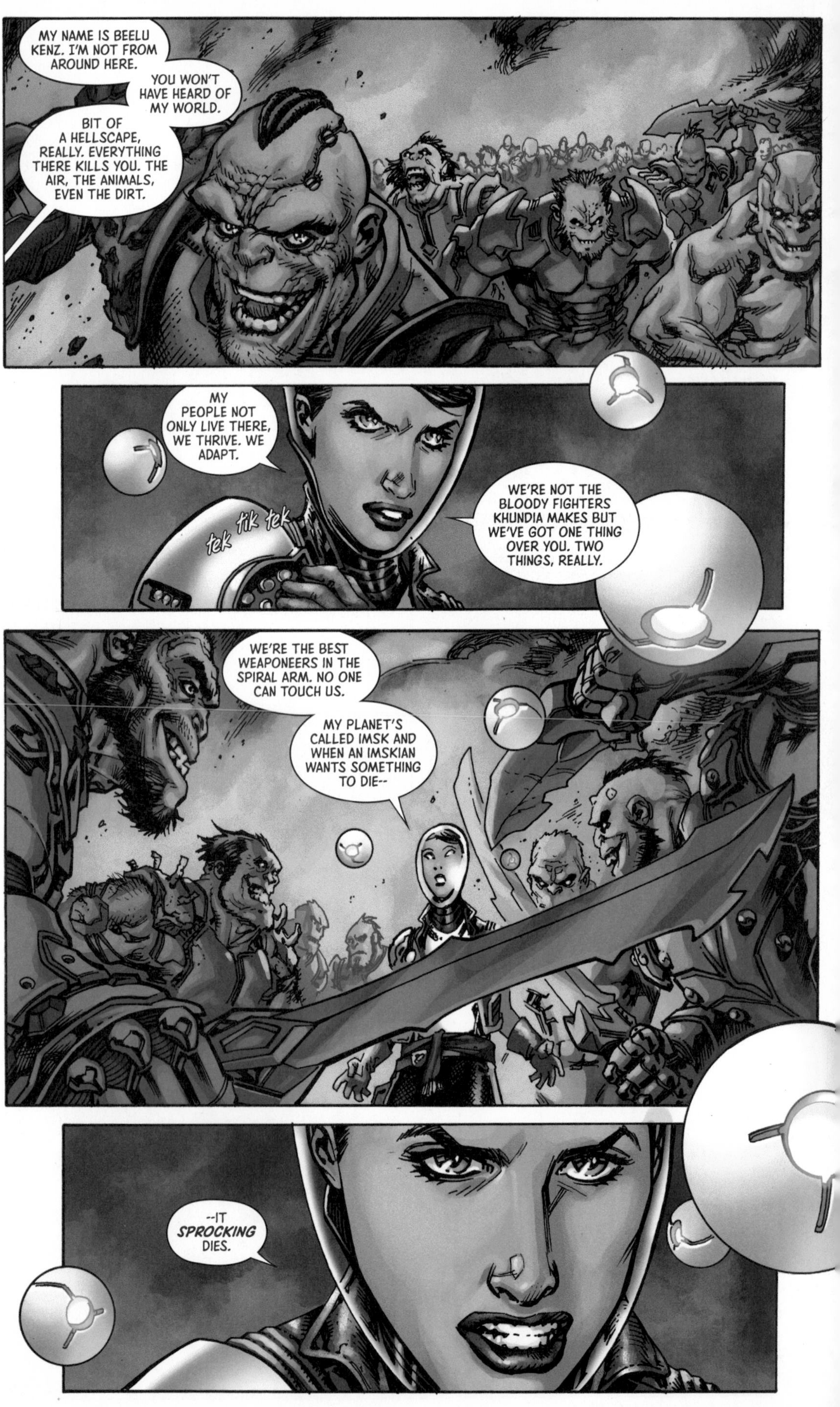
MY NAME IS BEELU KENZ. I'M NOT FROM AROUND HERE.
YOU WON'T HAVE HEARD OF MY WORLD.
BIT OF A HELLSCAPE, REALLY. EVERYTHING THERE KILLS YOU. THE AIR, THE ANIMALS, EVEN THE DIRT.
MY PEOPLE NOT ONLY LIVE THERE, WE THRIVE. WE ADAPT.
tek tik tek
WE'RE NOT THE BLOODY FIGHTERS KHUNDIA MAKES BUT WE'VE GOT ONE THING OVER YOU. TWO THINGS, REALLY.
WE'RE THE BEST WEAPONEERS IN THE SPIRAL ARM. NO ONE CAN TOUCH US.
MY PLANET'S CALLED IMSK AND WHEN AN IMSKIAN WANTS SOMETHING TO DIE--
--IT *SPROCKING* DIES.

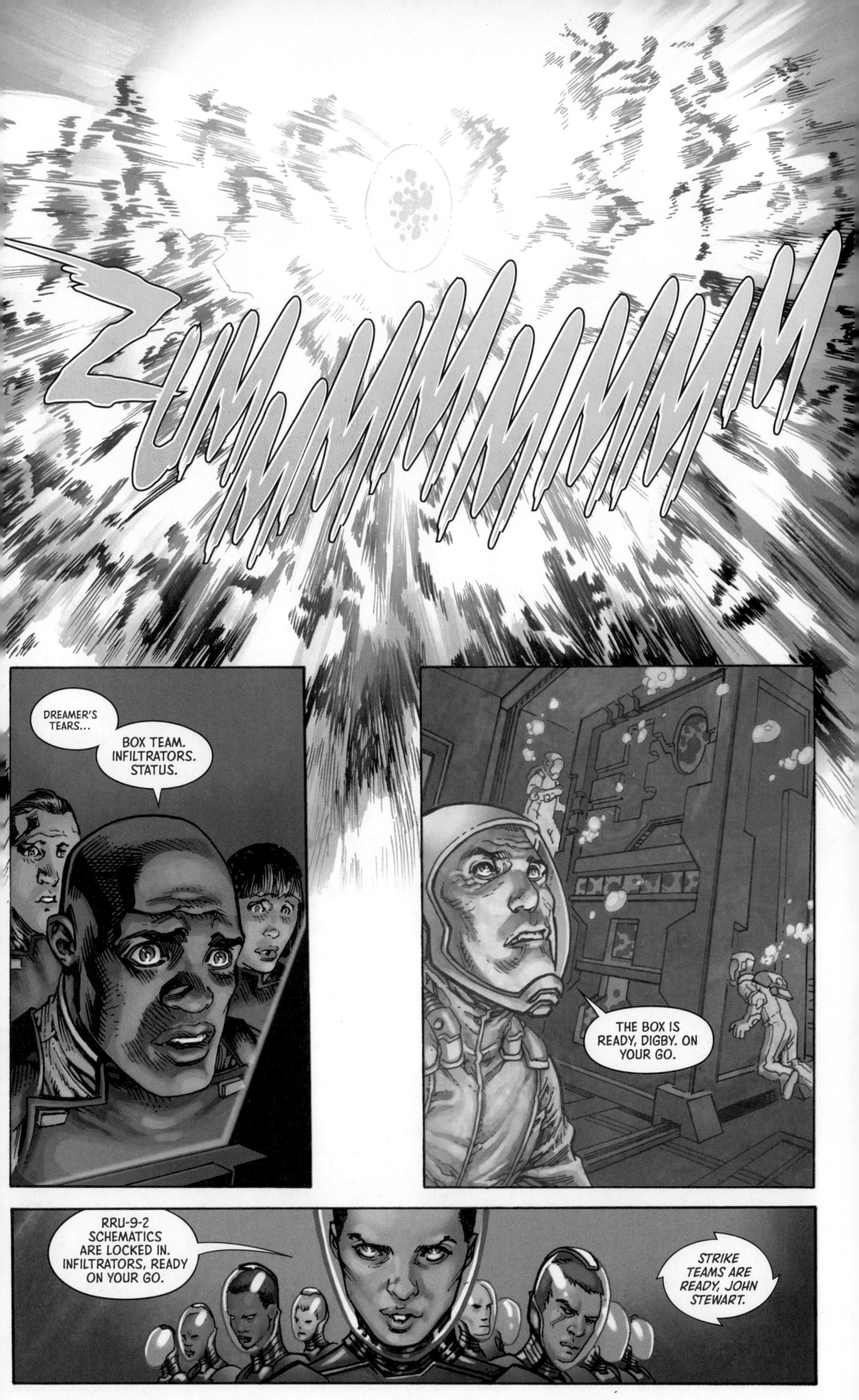
ZUMMMMMMMMMM
DREAMER'S TEARS...
BOX TEAM. INFILTRATORS. STATUS.
THE BOX IS READY, DIGBY. ON YOUR GO.
RRU-9-2 SCHEMATICS ARE LOCKED IN. INFILTRATORS, READY ON YOUR GO.
STRIKE TEAMS ARE READY, JOHN STEWART.

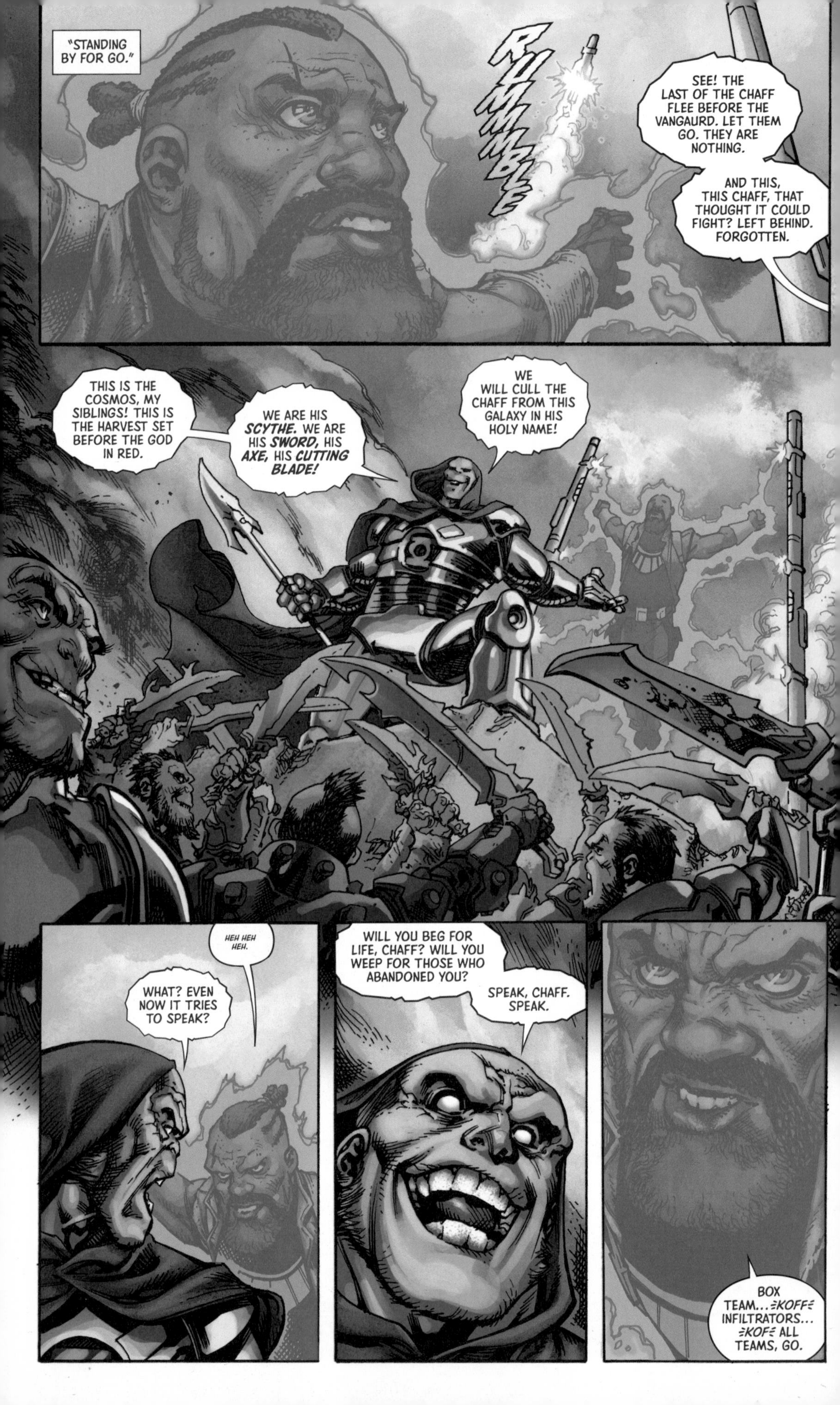
"STANDING BY FOR GO."
RUMMMBLE
SEE! THE LAST OF THE CHAFF FLEE BEFORE THE VANGAURD. LET THEM GO. THEY ARE NOTHING.
AND THIS, THIS CHAFF, THAT THOUGHT IT COULD FIGHT? LEFT BEHIND. FORGOTTEN.
THIS IS THE COSMOS, MY SIBLINGS! THIS IS THE HARVEST SET BEFORE THE GOD IN RED.
WE ARE HIS SCYTHE. WE ARE HIS SWORD, HIS AXE, HIS CUTTING BLADE!
WE WILL CULL THE CHAFF FROM THIS GALAXY IN HIS HOLY NAME!
HEH HEH HEH.
WHAT? EVEN NOW IT TRIES TO SPEAK?
WILL YOU BEG FOR LIFE, CHAFF? WILL YOU WEEP FOR THOSE WHO ABANDONED YOU?
SPEAK, CHAFF. SPEAK.
BOX TEAM... KOFF INFILTRATORS... KOFF ALL TEAMS, GO.

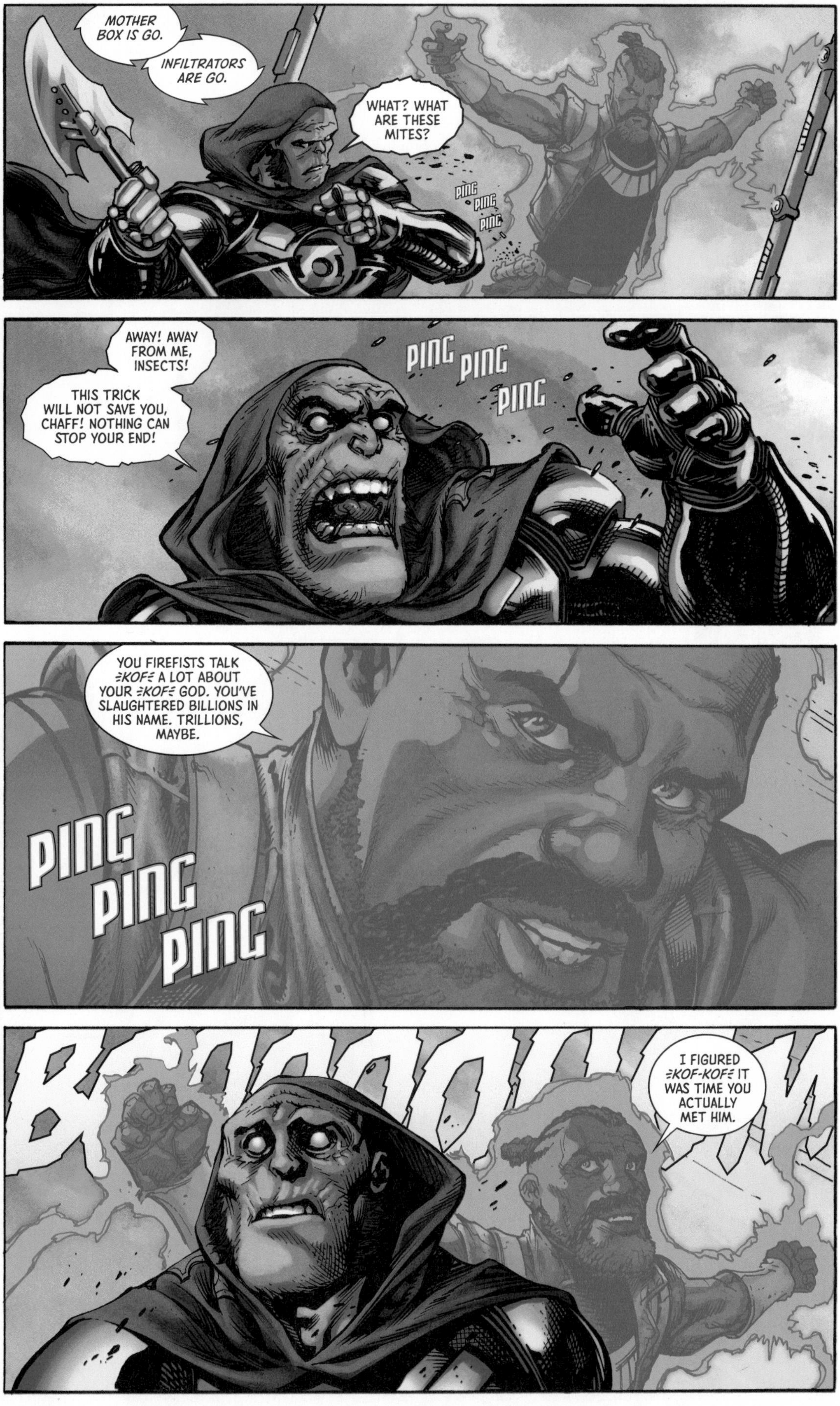
MOTHER BOX IS GO.
INFILTRATORS ARE GO.
WHAT? WHAT ARE THESE MITES?
PING PING PING
AWAY! AWAY FROM ME, INSECTS!
THIS TRICK WILL NOT SAVE YOU, CHAFF! NOTHING CAN STOP YOUR END!
PING PING PING
YOU FIREFISTS TALK =KOF= A LOT ABOUT YOUR =KOF= GOD. YOU'VE SLAUGHTERED BILLIONS IN HIS NAME. TRILLIONS, MAYBE.
PING PING PING
I FIGURED =KOF-KOF= IT WAS TIME YOU ACTUALLY MET HIM.

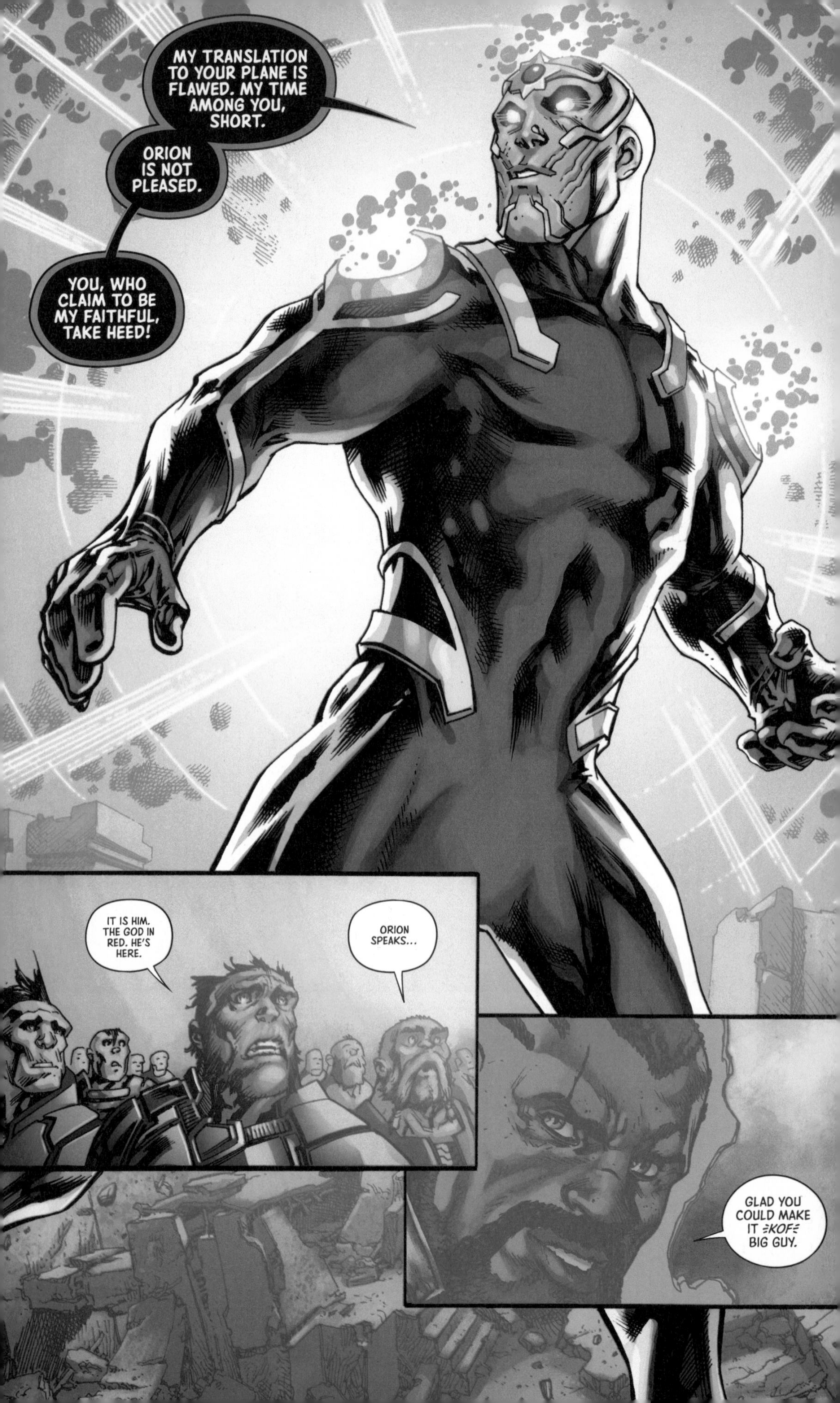
MY TRANSLATION TO YOUR PLANE IS FLAWED. MY TIME AMONG YOU, SHORT.
ORION IS NOT PLEASED.
YOU, WHO CLAIM TO BE MY FAITHFUL, TAKE HEED!
IT IS HIM. THE GOD IN RED. HE'S HERE.
ORION SPEAKS...
GLAD YOU COULD MAKE IT *KOF* BIG GUY.

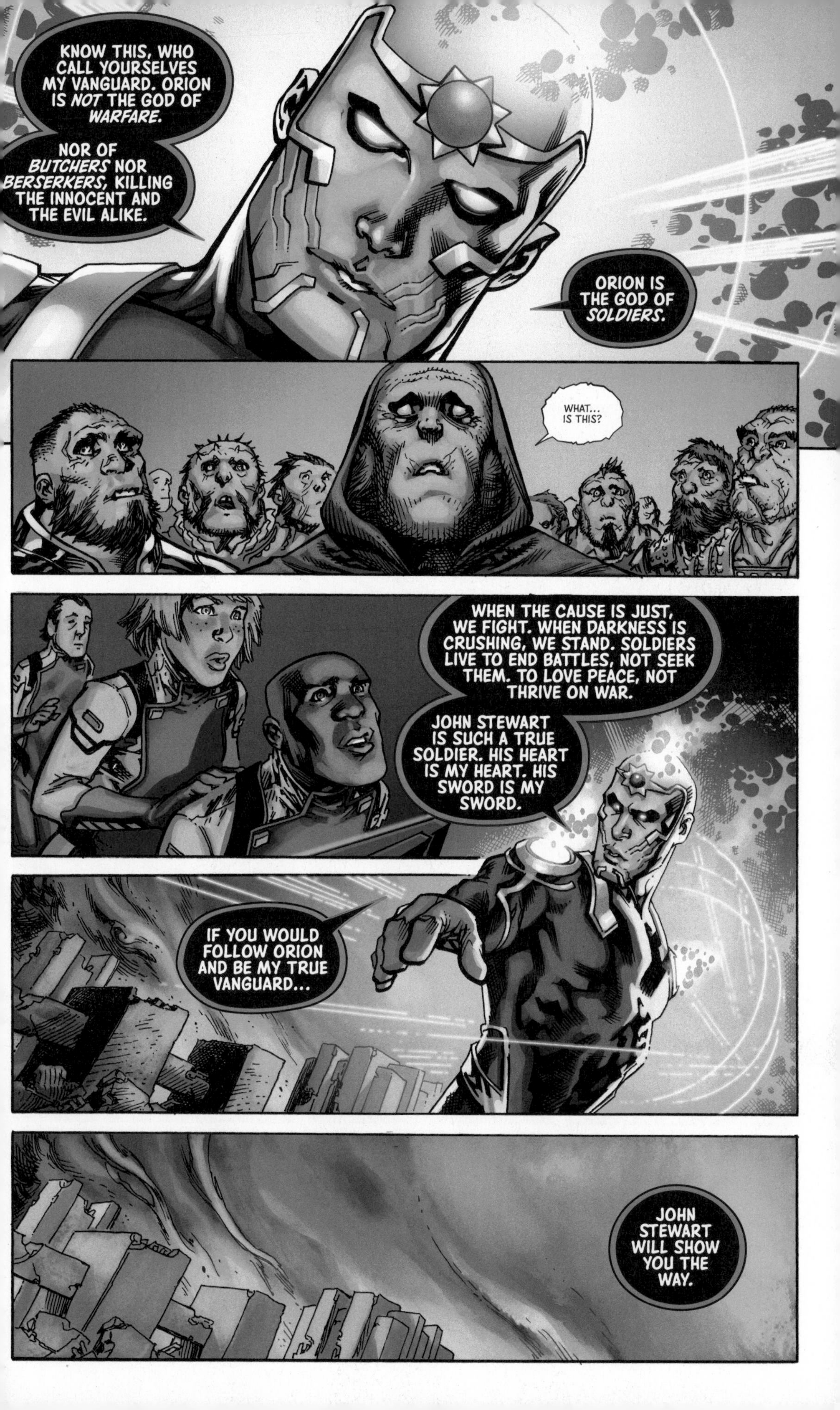

KNOW THIS, WHO CALL YOURSELVES MY VANGUARD. ORION IS *NOT* THE GOD OF *WARFARE*.
NOR OF *BUTCHERS* NOR *BERSERKERS*, KILLING THE INNOCENT AND THE EVIL ALIKE.
ORION IS THE GOD OF *SOLDIERS*.
WHAT... IS THIS?
WHEN THE CAUSE IS JUST, WE FIGHT. WHEN DARKNESS IS CRUSHING, WE STAND. SOLDIERS LIVE TO END BATTLES, NOT SEEK THEM. TO LOVE PEACE, NOT THRIVE ON WAR.
JOHN STEWART IS SUCH A TRUE SOLDIER. HIS HEART IS MY HEART. HIS SWORD IS MY SWORD.
IF YOU WOULD FOLLOW ORION AND BE MY TRUE VANGUARD...
JOHN STEWART WILL SHOW YOU THE WAY.

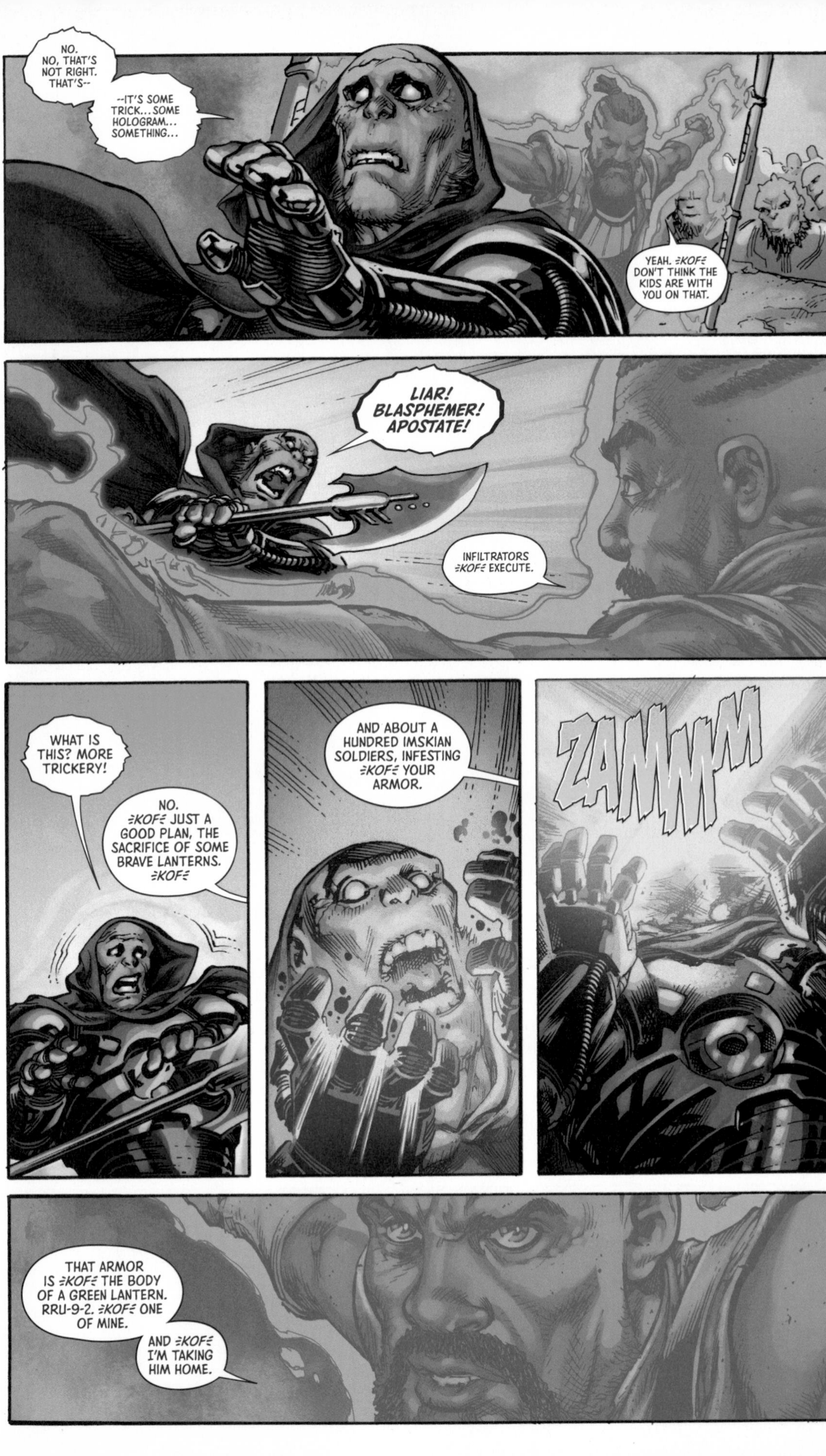
NO. NO, THAT'S NOT RIGHT. THAT'S--
--IT'S SOME TRICK... SOME HOLOGRAM... SOMETHING...
YEAH. ≈KOF≈ DON'T THINK THE KIDS ARE WITH YOU ON THAT.
LIAR! BLASPHEMER! APOSTATE!
INFILTRATORS ≈KOF≈ EXECUTE.
WHAT IS THIS? MORE TRICKERY!
NO. ≈KOF≈ JUST A GOOD PLAN, THE SACRIFICE OF SOME BRAVE LANTERNS. ≈KOF≈
AND ABOUT A HUNDRED IMSKIAN SOLDIERS, INFESTING ≈KOF≈ YOUR ARMOR.
ZAMMM
THAT ARMOR IS ≈KOF≈ THE BODY OF A GREEN LANTERN. RRU-9-2. ≈KOF≈ ONE OF MINE.
AND ≈KOF≈ I'M TAKING HIM HOME.

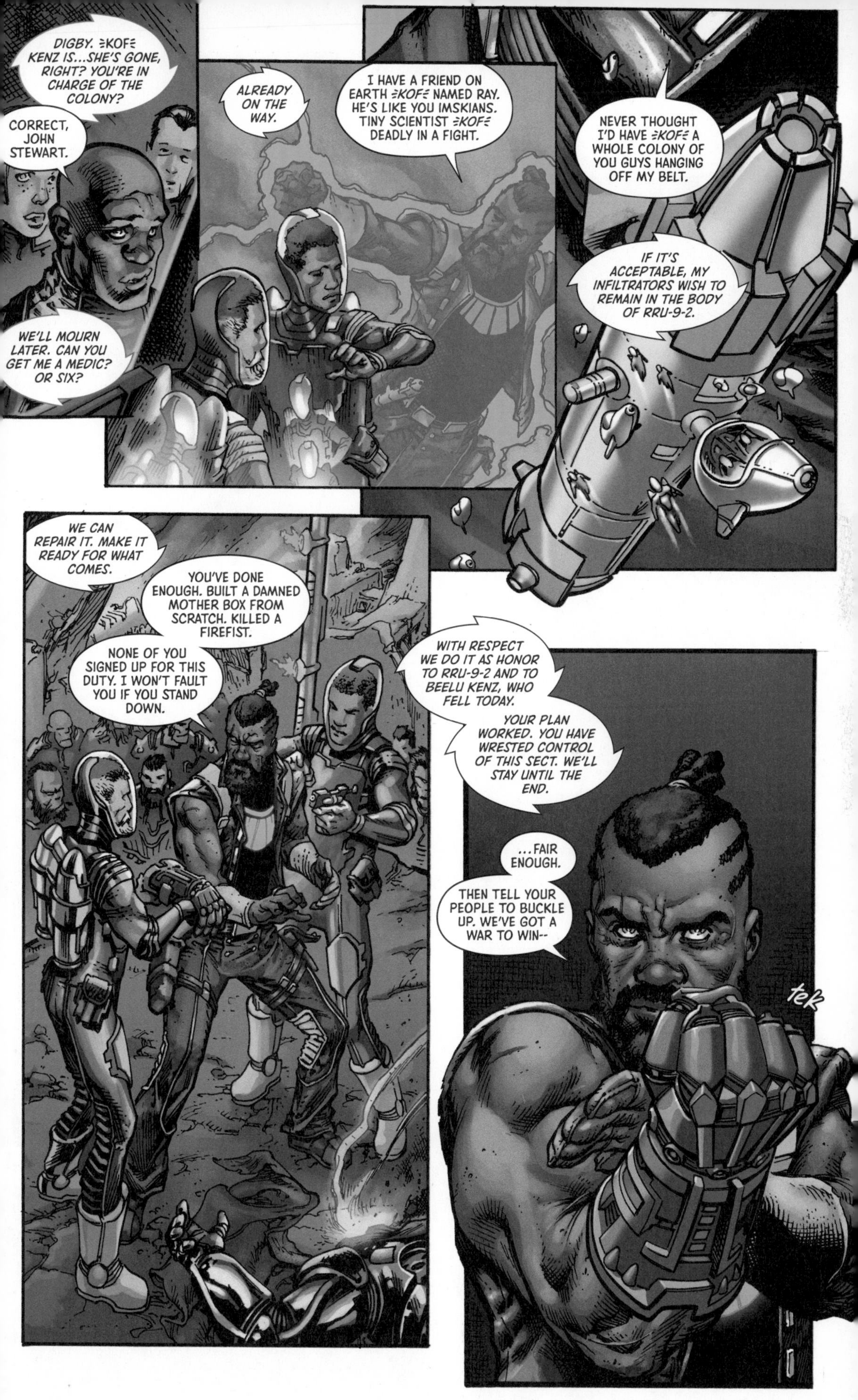

DIGBY. ≡KOF≡ KENZ IS...SHE'S GONE, RIGHT? YOU'RE IN CHARGE OF THE COLONY?
CORRECT, JOHN STEWART.
WE'LL MOURN LATER. CAN YOU GET ME A MEDIC? OR SIX?
ALREADY ON THE WAY.
I HAVE A FRIEND ON EARTH ≡KOF≡ NAMED RAY. HE'S LIKE YOU IMSKIANS. TINY SCIENTIST ≡KOF≡ DEADLY IN A FIGHT.
NEVER THOUGHT I'D HAVE ≡KOF≡ A WHOLE COLONY OF YOU GUYS HANGING OFF MY BELT.
IF IT'S ACCEPTABLE, MY INFILTRATORS WISH TO REMAIN IN THE BODY OF RRU-9-2.
WE CAN REPAIR IT. MAKE IT READY FOR WHAT COMES.
YOU'VE DONE ENOUGH. BUILT A DAMNED MOTHER BOX FROM SCRATCH. KILLED A FIREFIST.
NONE OF YOU SIGNED UP FOR THIS DUTY. I WON'T FAULT YOU IF YOU STAND DOWN.
WITH RESPECT WE DO IT AS HONOR TO RRU-9-2 AND TO BEELU KENZ, WHO FELL TODAY.
YOUR PLAN WORKED. YOU HAVE WRESTED CONTROL OF THIS SECT. WE'LL STAY UNTIL THE END.
...FAIR ENOUGH.
THEN TELL YOUR PEOPLE TO BUCKLE UP. WE'VE GOT A WAR TO WIN--
tek

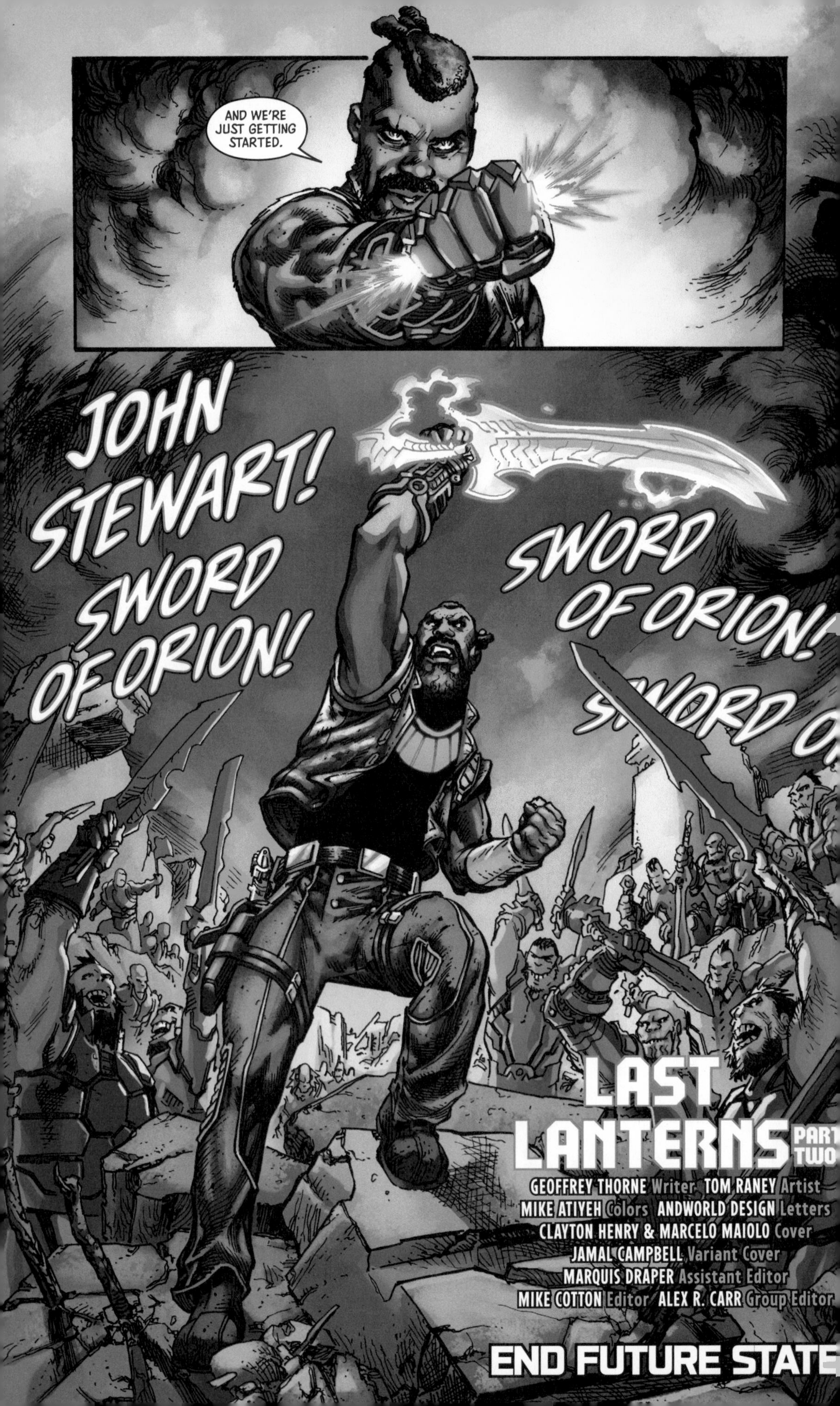
AND WE'RE JUST GETTING STARTED.
JOHN STEWART! SWORD OF ORION!
SWORD OF ORION!
SWORD OF
LAST LANTERNS PART TWO
GEOFFREY THORNE Writer TOM RANEY Artist
MIKE ATIYEH Colors ANDWORLD DESIGN Letters
CLAYTON HENRY & MARCELO MAIOLO Cover
JAMAL CAMPBELL Variant Cover
MARQUIS DRAPER Assistant Editor
MIKE COTTON Editor ALEX R. CARR Group Editor
END FUTURE STATE

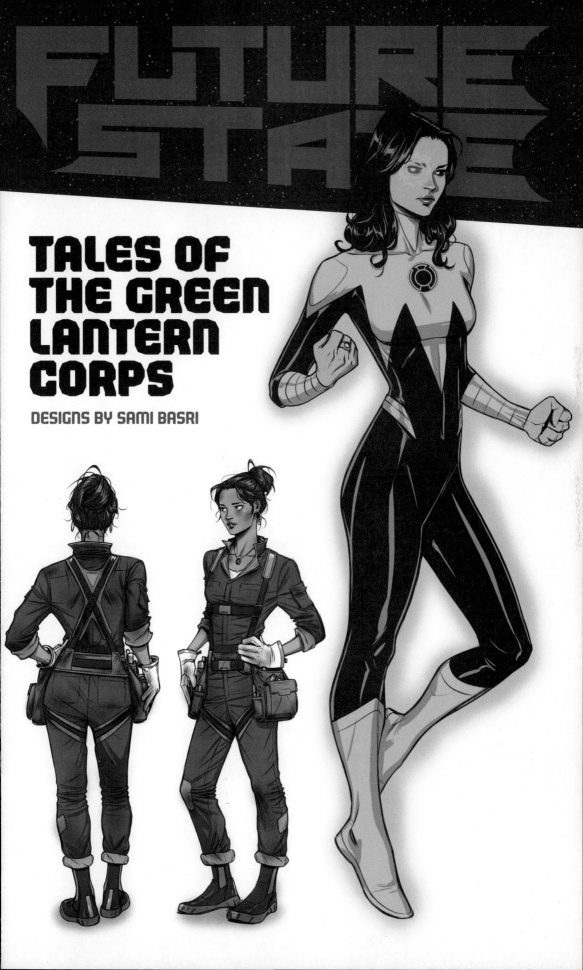

FUTURE STATE

TALES OF THE GREEN LANTERN CORPS

DESIGNS BY SAMI BASRI

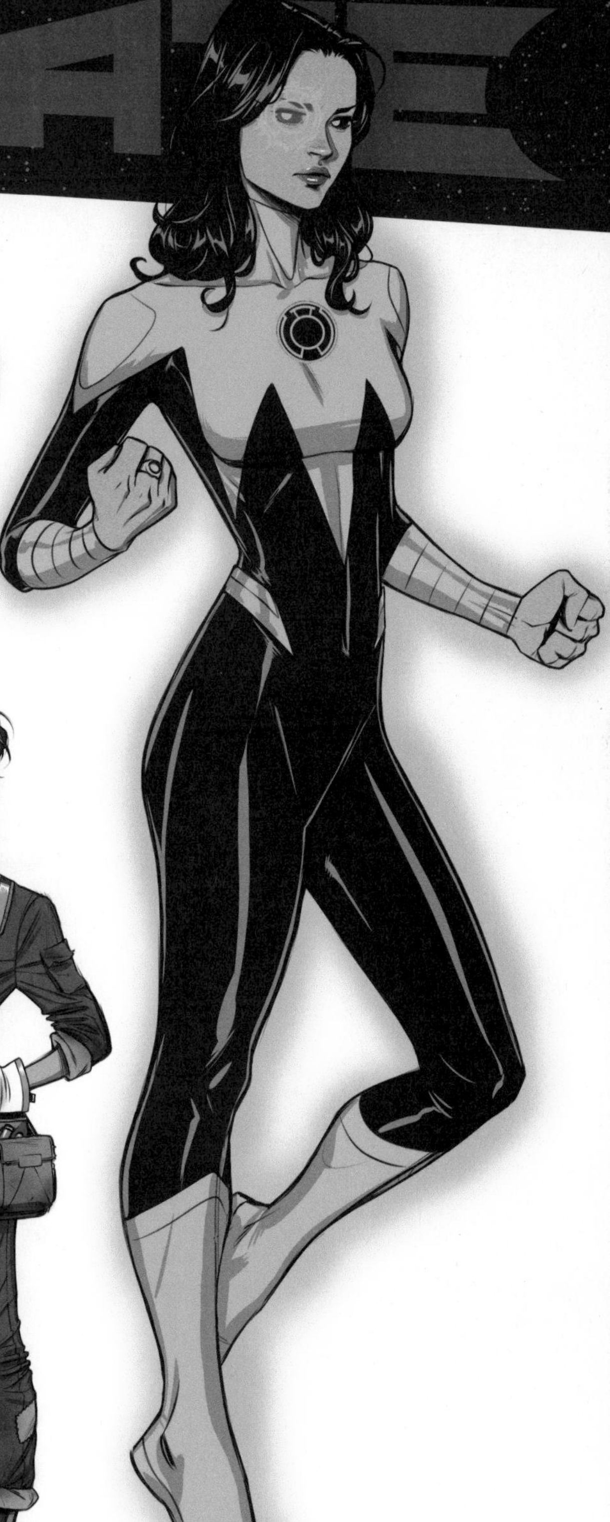

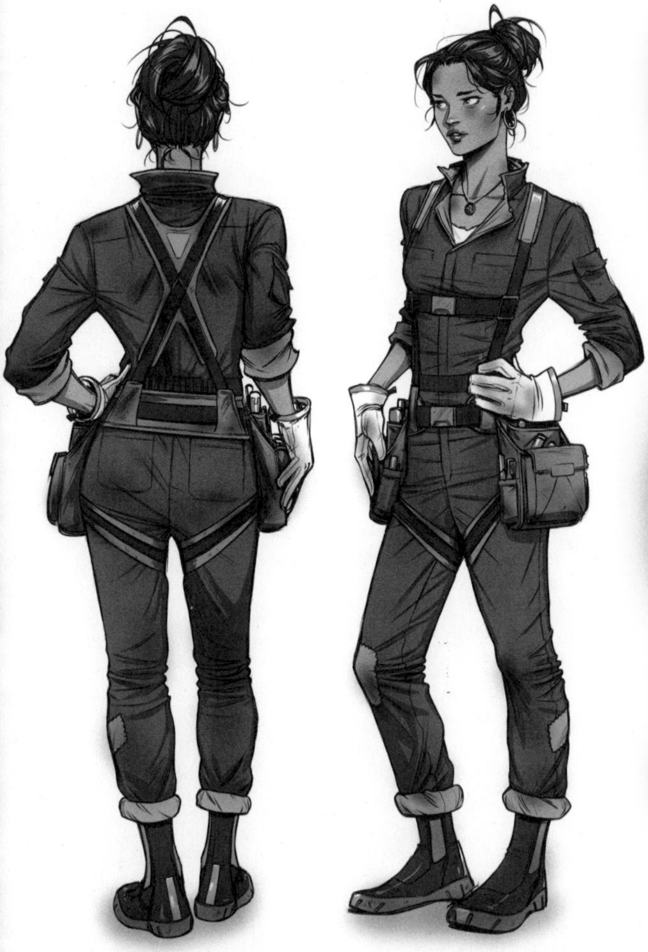

FUTURE STATE

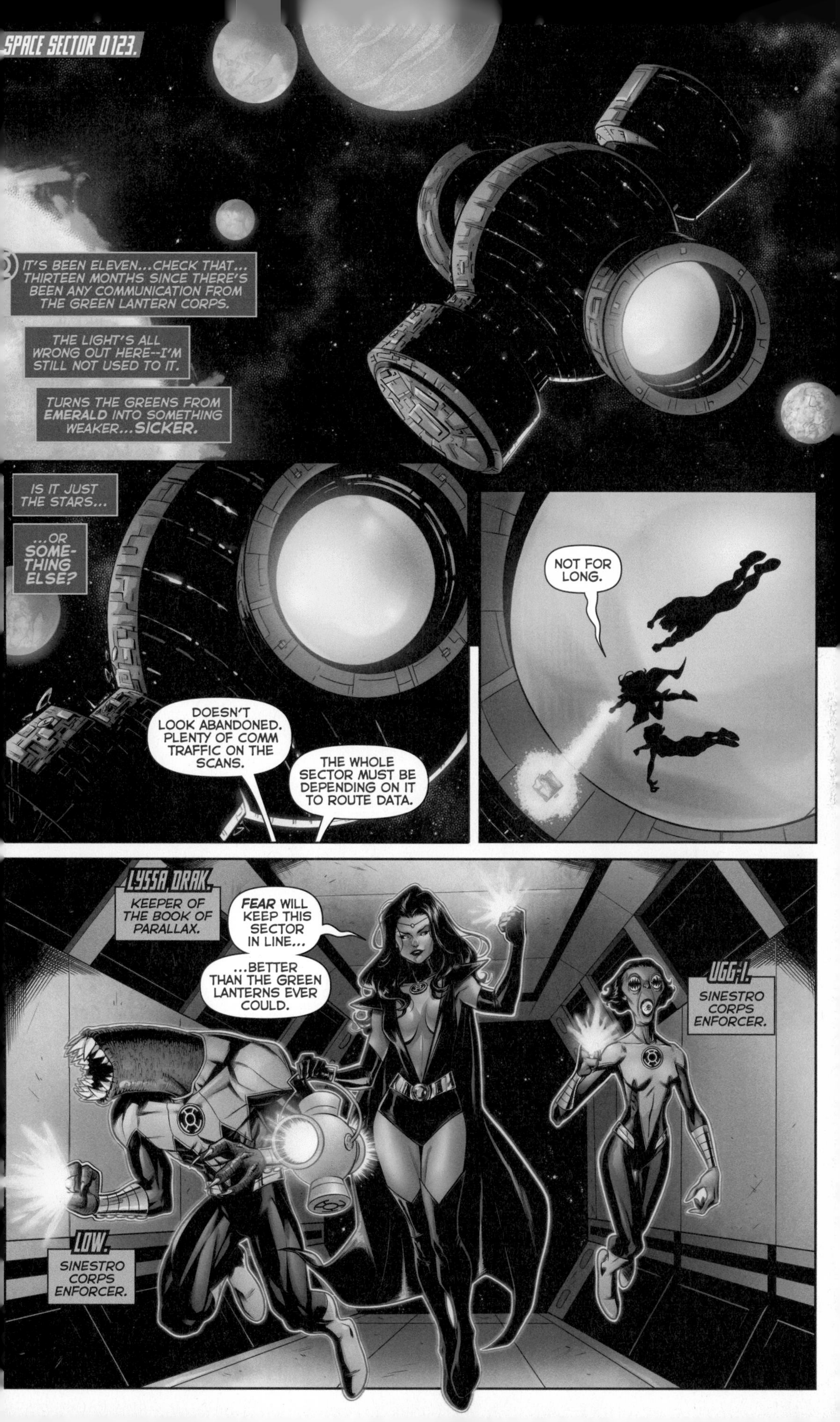
SPACE SECTOR 0123.
IT'S BEEN ELEVEN...CHECK THAT... THIRTEEN MONTHS SINCE THERE'S BEEN ANY COMMUNICATION FROM THE GREEN LANTERN CORPS.
THE LIGHT'S ALL WRONG OUT HERE--I'M STILL NOT USED TO IT.
TURNS THE GREENS FROM EMERALD INTO SOMETHING WEAKER...SICKER.
IS IT JUST THE STARS...
...OR SOME-THING ELSE?
DOESN'T LOOK ABANDONED. PLENTY OF COMM TRAFFIC ON THE SCANS.
THE WHOLE SECTOR MUST BE DEPENDING ON IT TO ROUTE DATA.
NOT FOR LONG.
LYSSA DRAK.
KEEPER OF THE BOOK OF PARALLAX.
FEAR WILL KEEP THIS SECTOR IN LINE...
...BETTER THAN THE GREEN LANTERNS EVER COULD.
UGG-I.
SINESTRO CORPS ENFORCER.
LOW.
SINESTRO CORPS ENFORCER.

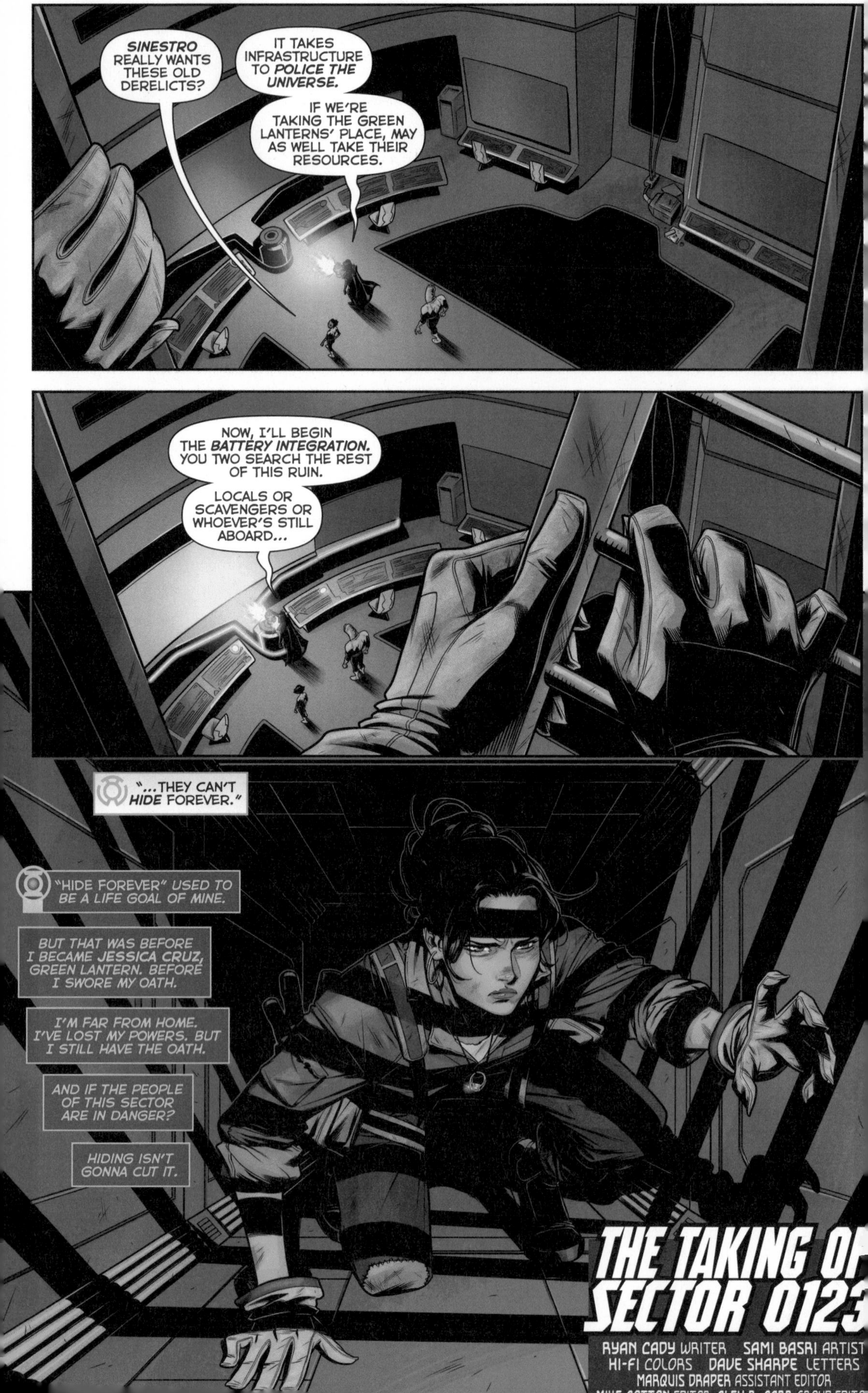
SINESTRO REALLY WANTS THESE OLD DERELICTS?
IT TAKES INFRASTRUCTURE TO POLICE THE UNIVERSE.
IF WE'RE TAKING THE GREEN LANTERNS' PLACE, MAY AS WELL TAKE THEIR RESOURCES.
NOW, I'LL BEGIN THE BATTERY INTEGRATION. YOU TWO SEARCH THE REST OF THIS RUIN.
LOCALS OR SCAVENGERS OR WHOEVER'S STILL ABOARD...
"...THEY CAN'T HIDE FOREVER."
"HIDE FOREVER" USED TO BE A LIFE GOAL OF MINE.
BUT THAT WAS BEFORE I BECAME JESSICA CRUZ, GREEN LANTERN. BEFORE I SWORE MY OATH.
I'M FAR FROM HOME. I'VE LOST MY POWERS. BUT I STILL HAVE THE OATH.
AND IF THE PEOPLE OF THIS SECTOR ARE IN DANGER?
HIDING ISN'T GONNA CUT IT.
THE TAKING OF SECTOR 0123
RYAN CADY WRITER SAMI BASRI ARTIST
HI-FI COLORS DAVE SHARPE LETTERS
MARQUIS DRAPER ASSISTANT EDITOR
MIKE COTTON EDITOR ALEX R. CARR GROUP EDITO

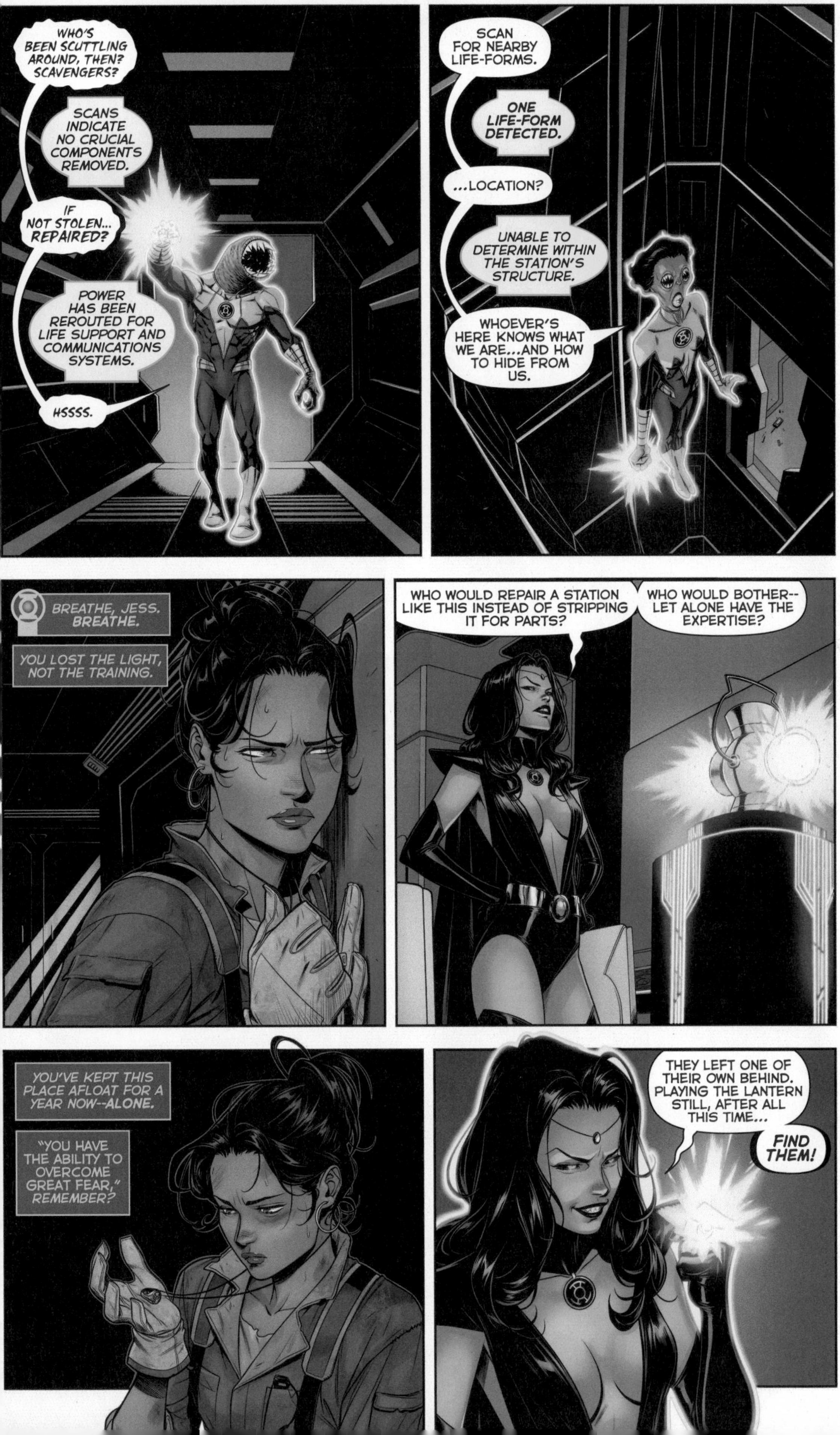
WHO'S BEEN SCUTTLING AROUND, THEN? SCAVENGERS?
SCANS INDICATE NO CRUCIAL COMPONENTS REMOVED.
IF NOT STOLEN... REPAIRED?
POWER HAS BEEN REROUTED FOR LIFE SUPPORT AND COMMUNICATIONS SYSTEMS.
HSSSS.
SCAN FOR NEARBY LIFE-FORMS.
ONE LIFE-FORM DETECTED.
...LOCATION?
UNABLE TO DETERMINE WITHIN THE STATION'S STRUCTURE.
WHOEVER'S HERE KNOWS WHAT WE ARE...AND HOW TO HIDE FROM US.
BREATHE, JESS. BREATHE.
YOU LOST THE LIGHT, NOT THE TRAINING.
WHO WOULD REPAIR A STATION LIKE THIS INSTEAD OF STRIPPING IT FOR PARTS?
WHO WOULD BOTHER--LET ALONE HAVE THE EXPERTISE?
YOU'VE KEPT THIS PLACE AFLOAT FOR A YEAR NOW--ALONE.
"YOU HAVE THE ABILITY TO OVERCOME GREAT FEAR," REMEMBER?
THEY LEFT ONE OF THEIR OWN BEHIND. PLAYING THE LANTERN STILL, AFTER ALL THIS TIME...
FIND THEM!

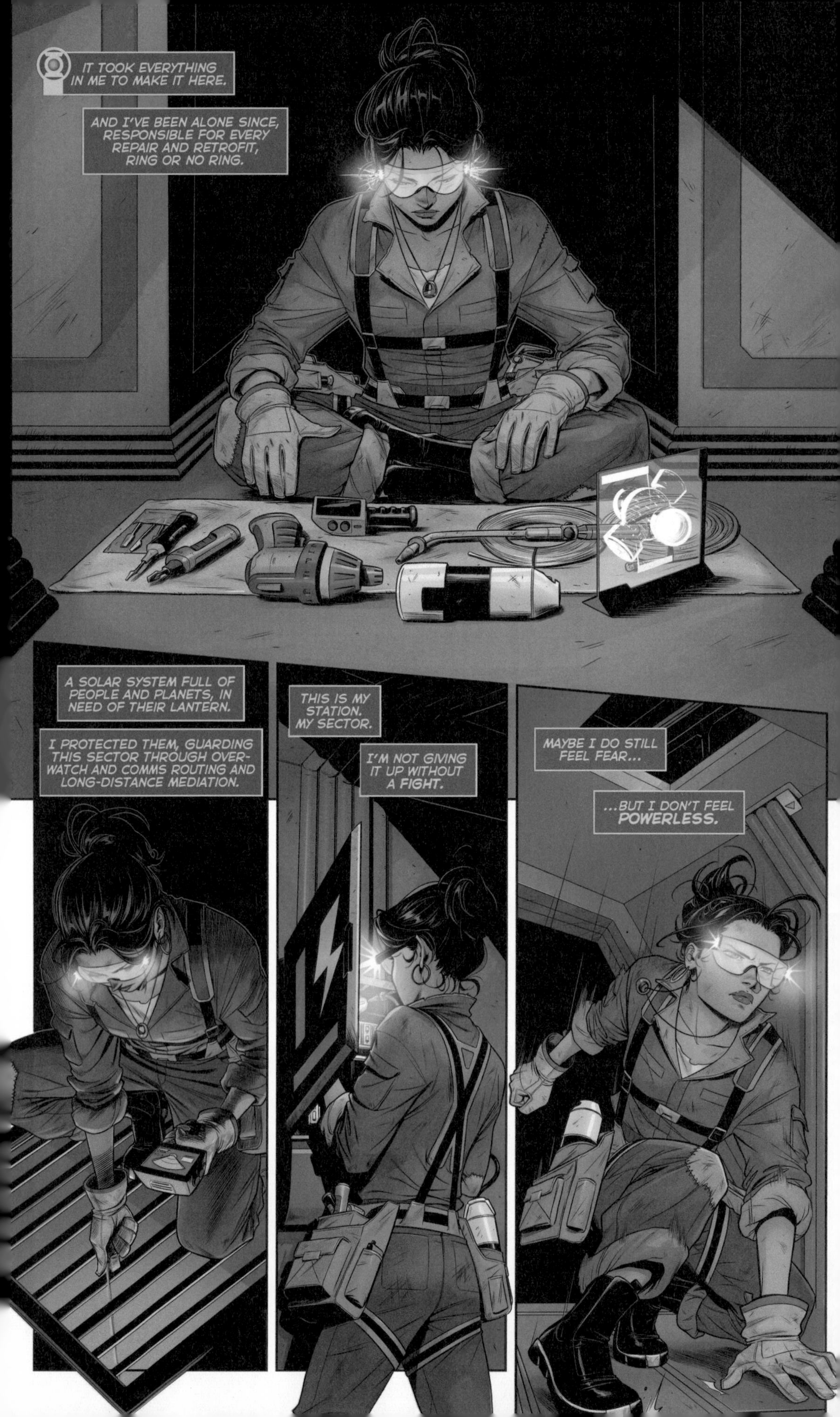

IT TOOK EVERYTHING IN ME TO MAKE IT HERE.
AND I'VE BEEN ALONE SINCE, RESPONSIBLE FOR EVERY REPAIR AND RETROFIT, RING OR NO RING.
A SOLAR SYSTEM FULL OF PEOPLE AND PLANETS, IN NEED OF THEIR LANTERN.
I PROTECTED THEM, GUARDING THIS SECTOR THROUGH OVER-WATCH AND COMMS ROUTING AND LONG-DISTANCE MEDIATION.
THIS IS MY STATION. MY SECTOR.
I'M NOT GIVING IT UP WITHOUT A FIGHT.
MAYBE I DO STILL FEEL FEAR...
...BUT I DON'T FEEL POWERLESS.

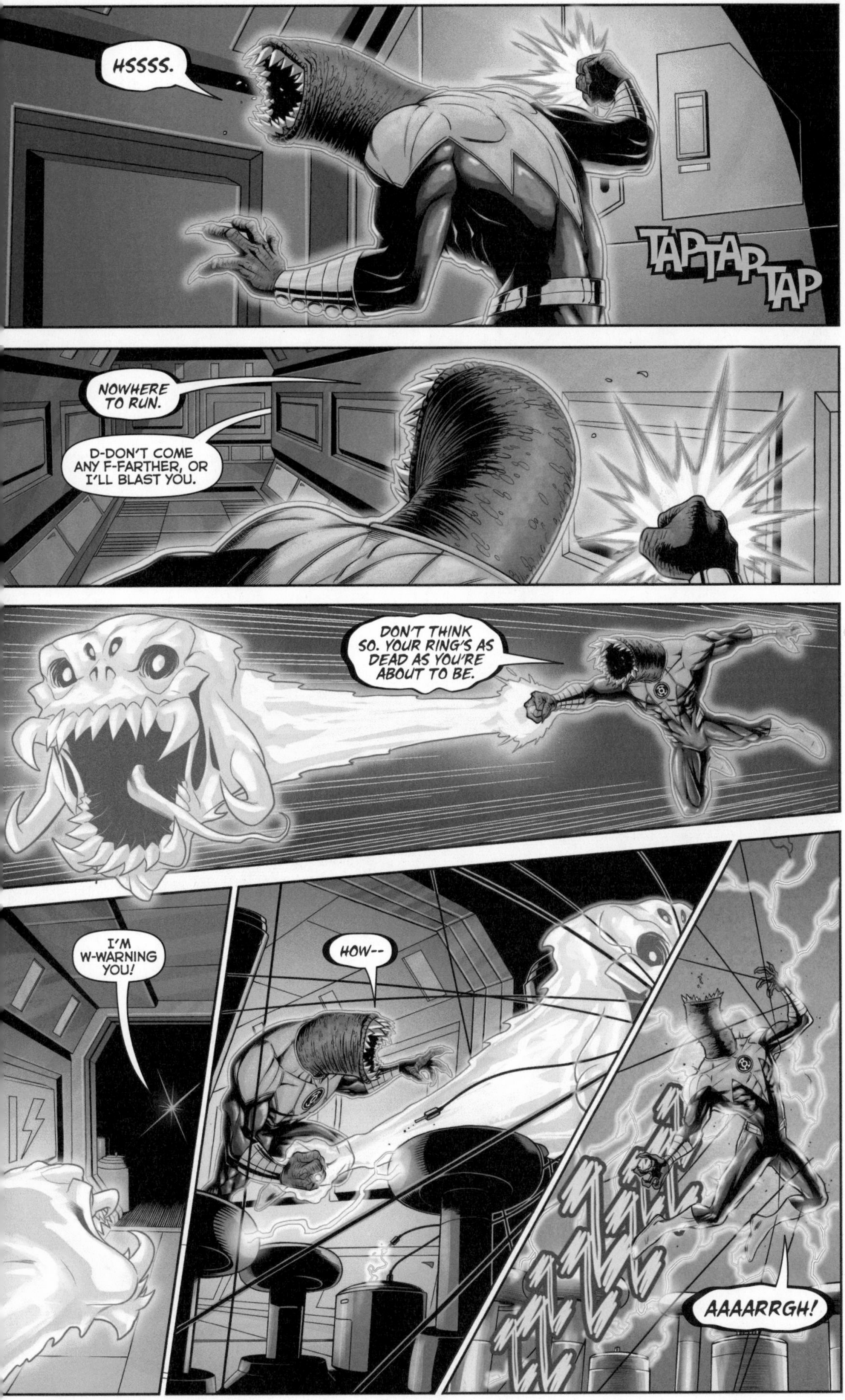
HSSSS.
TAPTAPTAP
NOWHERE TO RUN.
D-DON'T COME ANY F-FARTHER, OR I'LL BLAST YOU.
DON'T THINK SO. YOUR RING'S AS DEAD AS YOU'RE ABOUT TO BE.
I'M W-WARNING YOU!
HOW--
AAAARRGH!

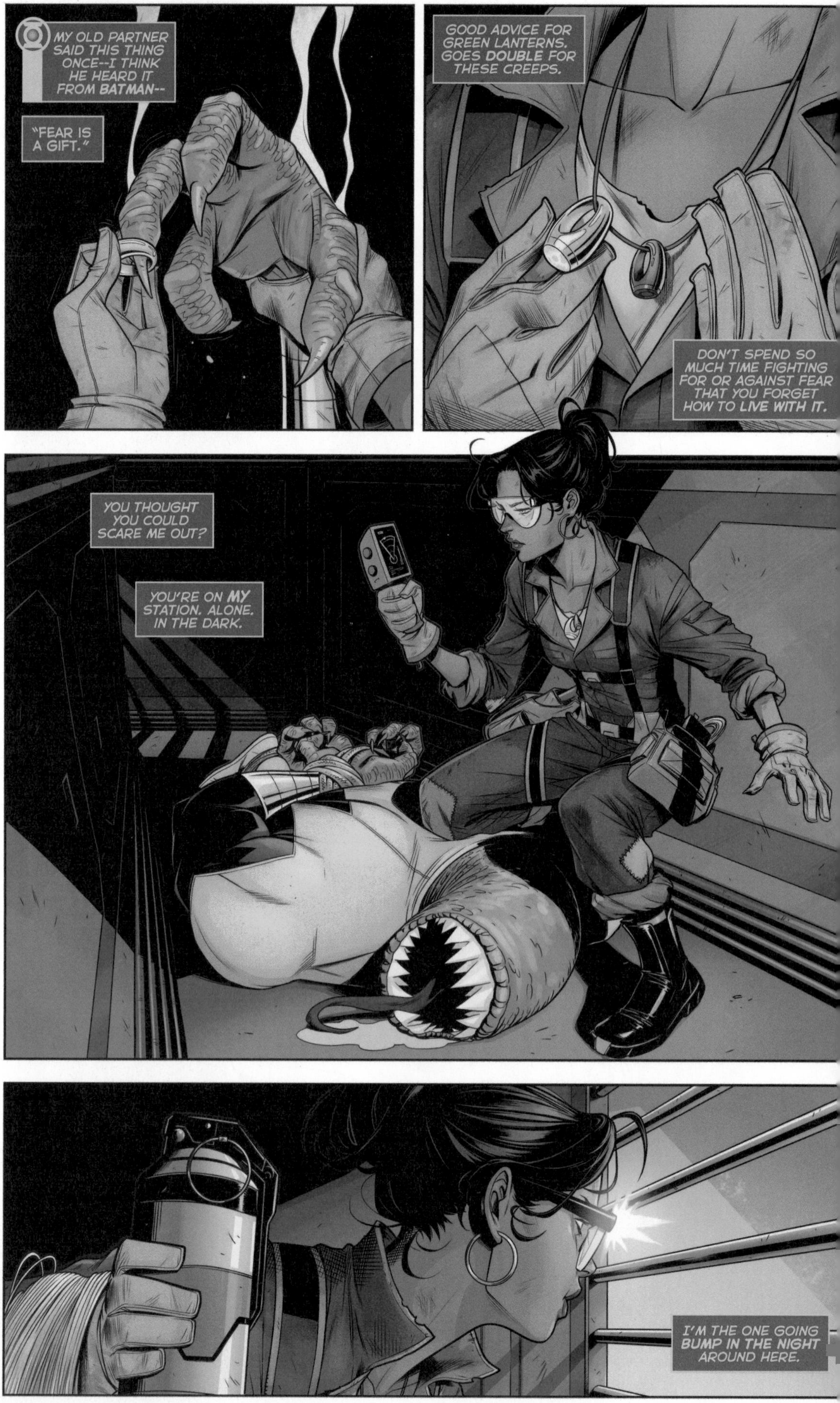
MY OLD PARTNER SAID THIS THING ONCE--I THINK HE HEARD IT FROM BATMAN--
"FEAR IS A GIFT."
GOOD ADVICE FOR GREEN LANTERNS. GOES DOUBLE FOR THESE CREEPS.
DON'T SPEND SO MUCH TIME FIGHTING FOR OR AGAINST FEAR THAT YOU FORGET HOW TO LIVE WITH IT.
YOU THOUGHT YOU COULD SCARE ME OUT?
YOU'RE ON MY STATION. ALONE. IN THE DARK.
I'M THE ONE GOING BUMP IN THE NIGHT AROUND HERE.

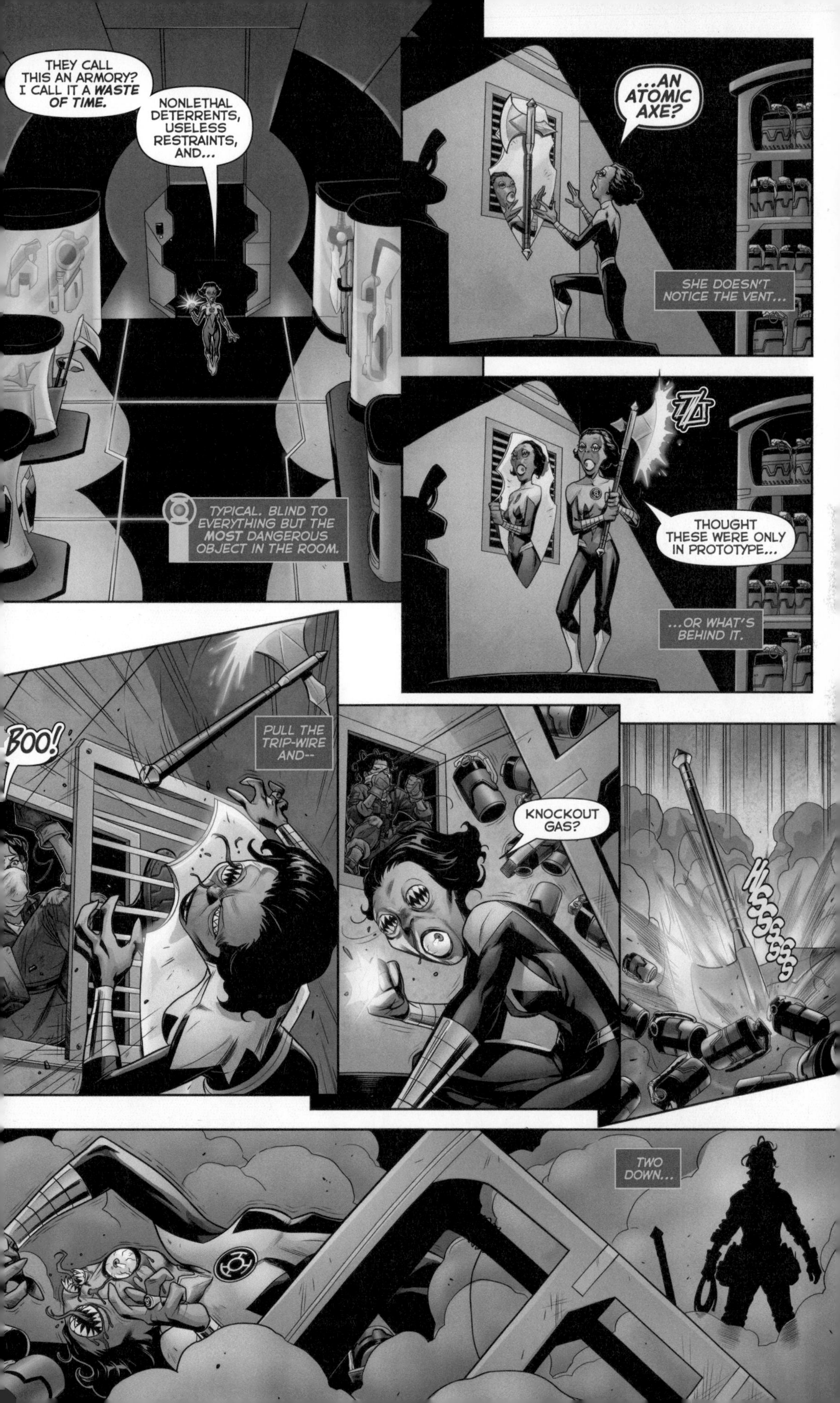
THEY CALL THIS AN ARMORY? I CALL IT A WASTE OF TIME.
NONLETHAL DETERRENTS, USELESS RESTRAINTS, AND...
TYPICAL. BLIND TO EVERYTHING BUT THE MOST DANGEROUS OBJECT IN THE ROOM.
...AN ATOMIC AXE?
SHE DOESN'T NOTICE THE VENT...
THOUGHT THESE WERE ONLY IN PROTOTYPE...
...OR WHAT'S BEHIND IT.
BOO!
PULL THE TRIP-WIRE AND--
KNOCKOUT GAS?
HISSSSSS
TWO DOWN...

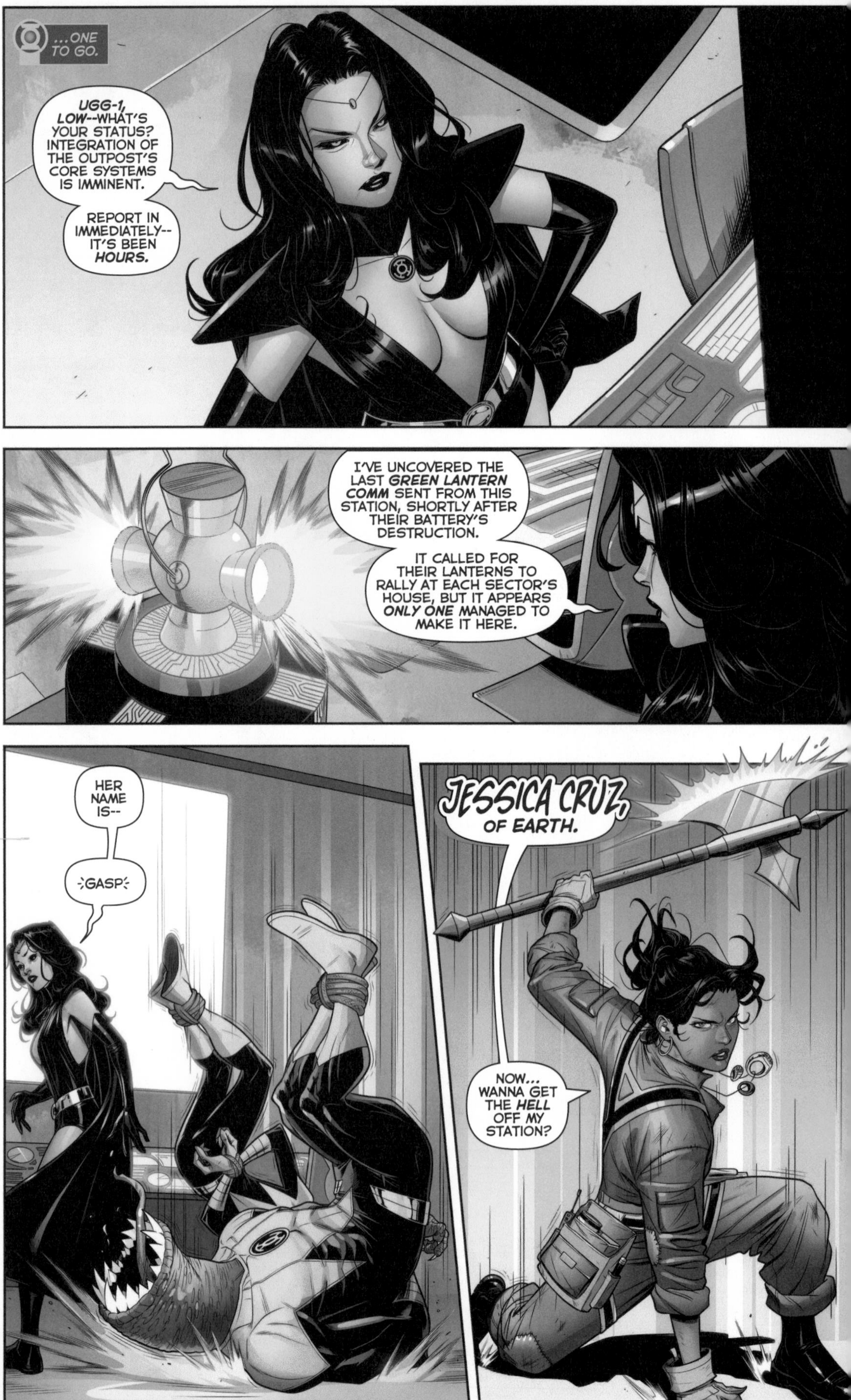
...ONE TO GO.
UGG-1, LOW--WHAT'S YOUR STATUS? INTEGRATION OF THE OUTPOST'S CORE SYSTEMS IS IMMINENT.
REPORT IN IMMEDIATELY-- IT'S BEEN HOURS.
I'VE UNCOVERED THE LAST GREEN LANTERN COMM SENT FROM THIS STATION, SHORTLY AFTER THEIR BATTERY'S DESTRUCTION.
IT CALLED FOR THEIR LANTERNS TO RALLY AT EACH SECTOR'S HOUSE, BUT IT APPEARS ONLY ONE MANAGED TO MAKE IT HERE.
HER NAME IS--
GASP
JESSICA CRUZ, OF EARTH.
NOW... WANNA GET THE HELL OFF MY STATION?

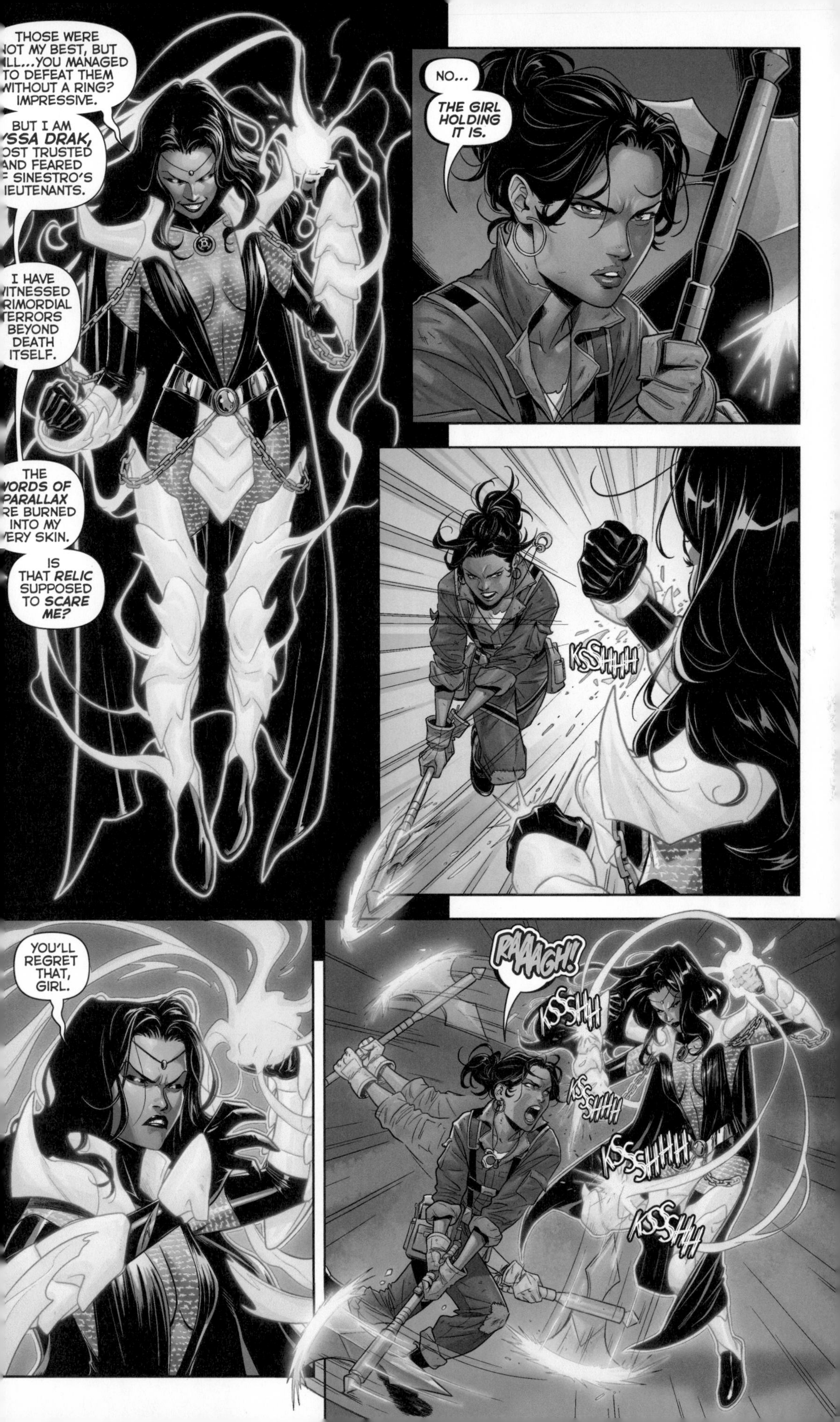
THOSE WERE OT MY BEST, BUT ILL...YOU MANAGED TO DEFEAT THEM WITHOUT A RING? IMPRESSIVE.
BUT I AM YSSA DRAK, OST TRUSTED AND FEARED F SINESTRO'S IEUTENANTS.
I HAVE WITNESSED RIMORDIAL TERRORS BEYOND DEATH ITSELF.
THE WORDS OF PARALLAX RE BURNED INTO MY ERY SKIN.
IS THAT RELIC SUPPOSED TO SCARE ME?
NO...
THE GIRL HOLDING IT IS.
KSSHHHH
YOU'LL REGRET THAT, GIRL.
RAAAGH!!
KSSSHH
KSSSHHH
KSSSHHHH
KSSSHH

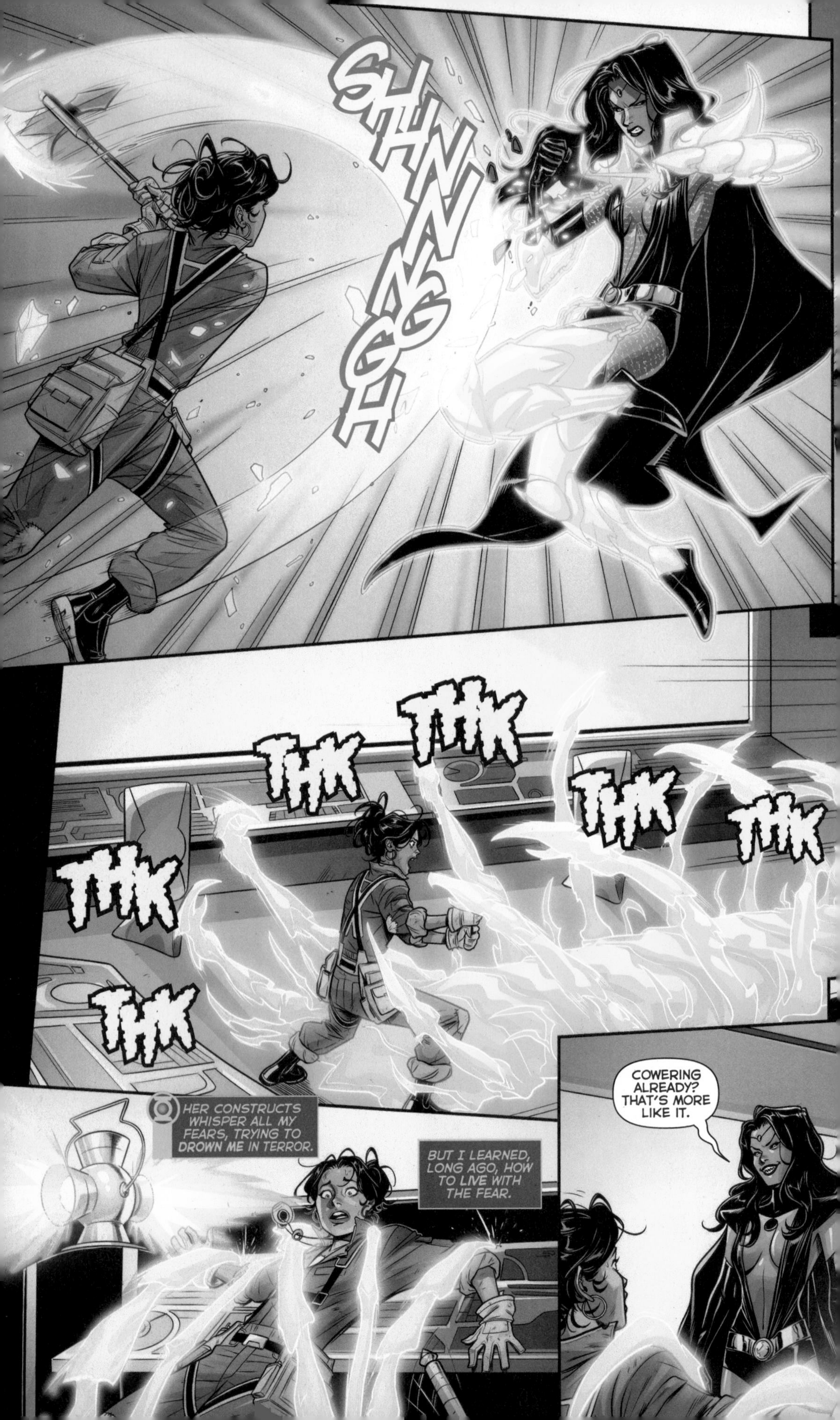
SHHNNNGGH
THK
THK
THK
THK
THK
THK
HER CONSTRUCTS WHISPER ALL MY FEARS, TRYING TO DROWN ME IN TERROR.
BUT I LEARNED, LONG AGO, HOW TO LIVE WITH THE FEAR.
COWERING ALREADY? THAT'S MORE LIKE IT.

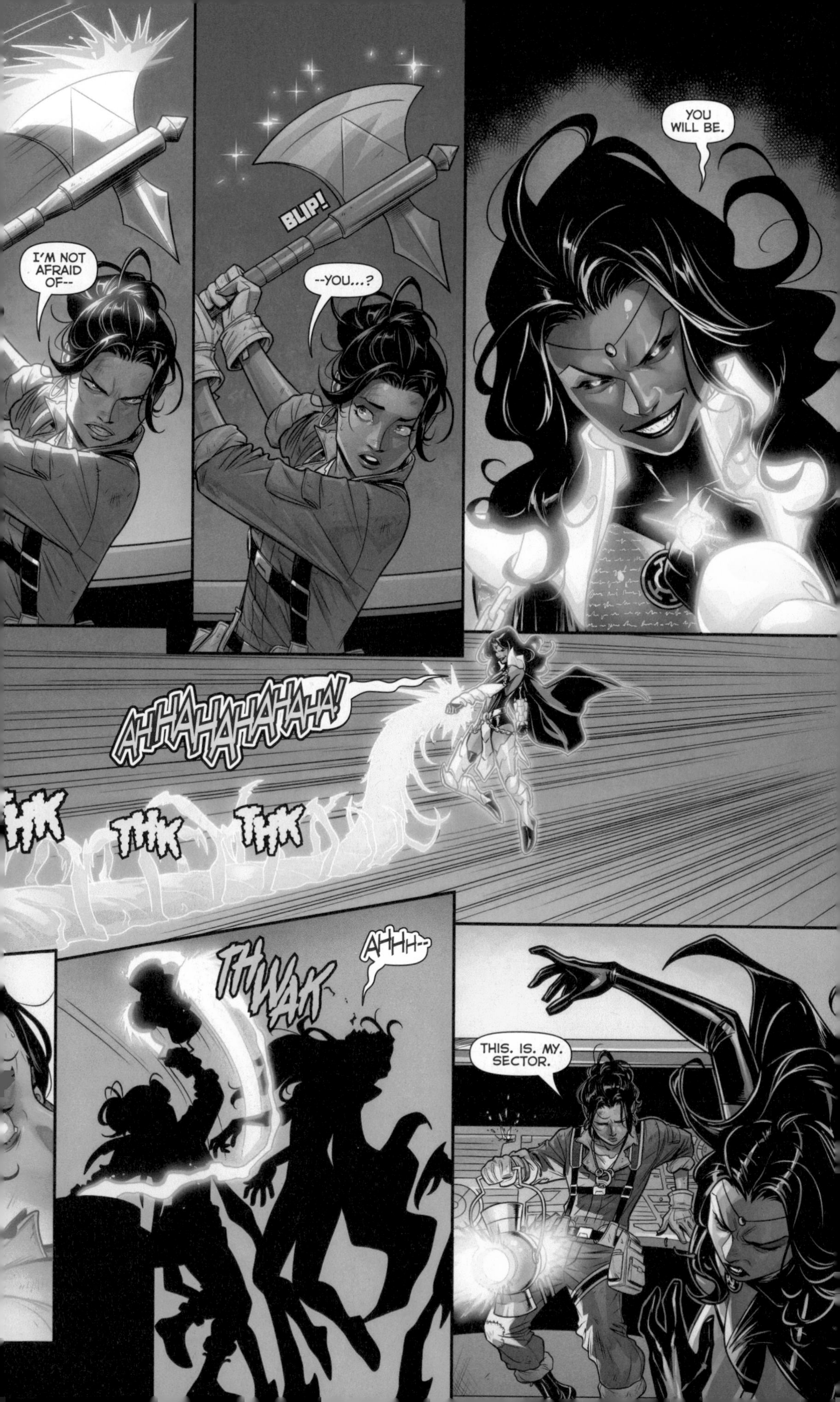
I'M NOT AFRAID OF--
BLIP!
--YOU...?
YOU WILL BE.
AHHAHAHAHAHA!
THK
THK
THK
THWAK
AHHH--
THIS. IS. MY. SECTOR.

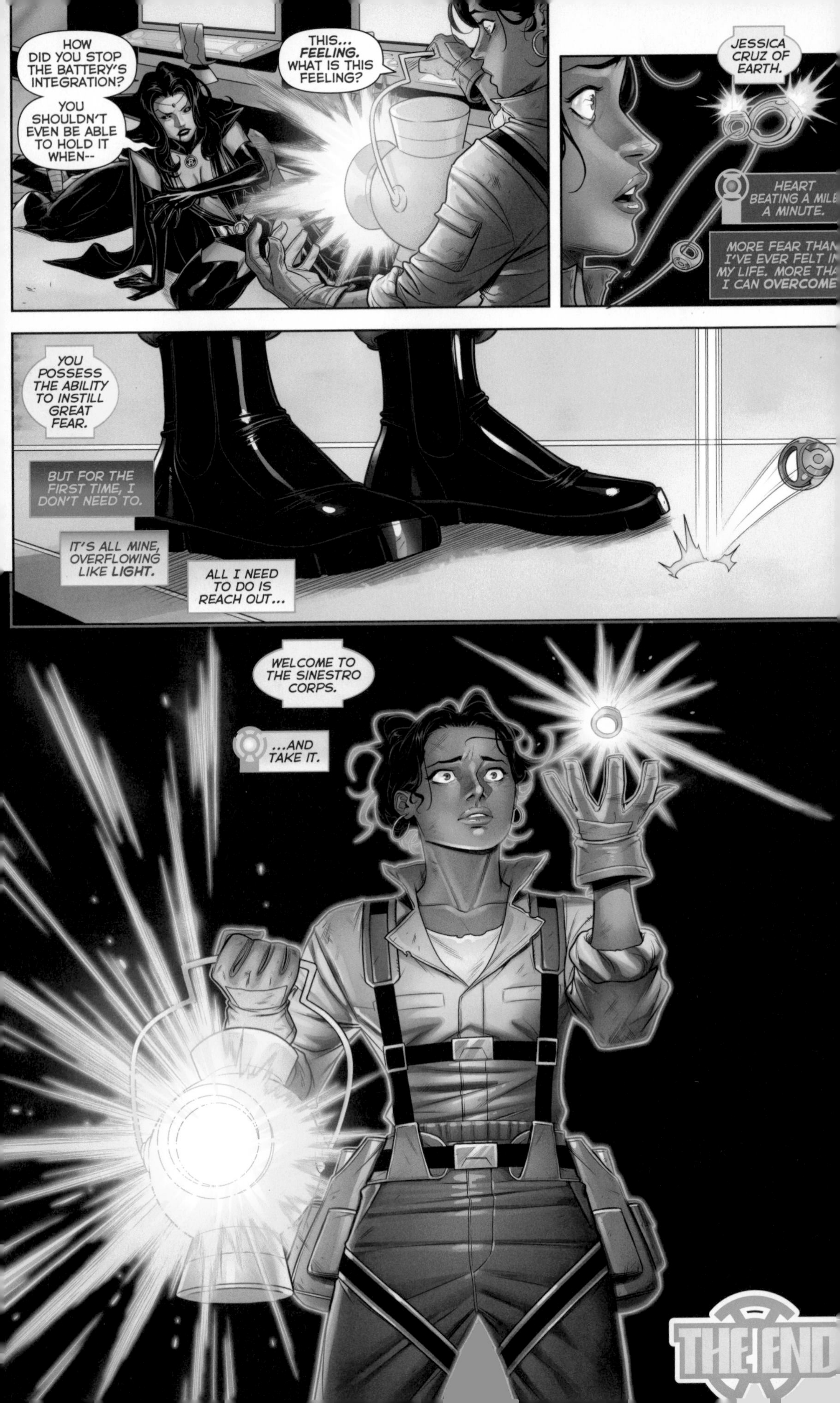
HOW DID YOU STOP THE BATTERY'S INTEGRATION?
YOU SHOULDN'T EVEN BE ABLE TO HOLD IT WHEN--
THIS... FEELING. WHAT IS THIS FEELING?
JESSICA CRUZ OF EARTH.
HEART BEATING A MILE A MINUTE.
MORE FEAR THAN I'VE EVER FELT IN MY LIFE. MORE THA I CAN OVERCOME
YOU POSSESS THE ABILITY TO INSTILL GREAT FEAR.
BUT FOR THE FIRST TIME, I DON'T NEED TO.
IT'S ALL MINE, OVERFLOWING LIKE LIGHT.
ALL I NEED TO DO IS REACH OUT...
WELCOME TO THE SINESTRO CORPS.
...AND TAKE IT.
THE END

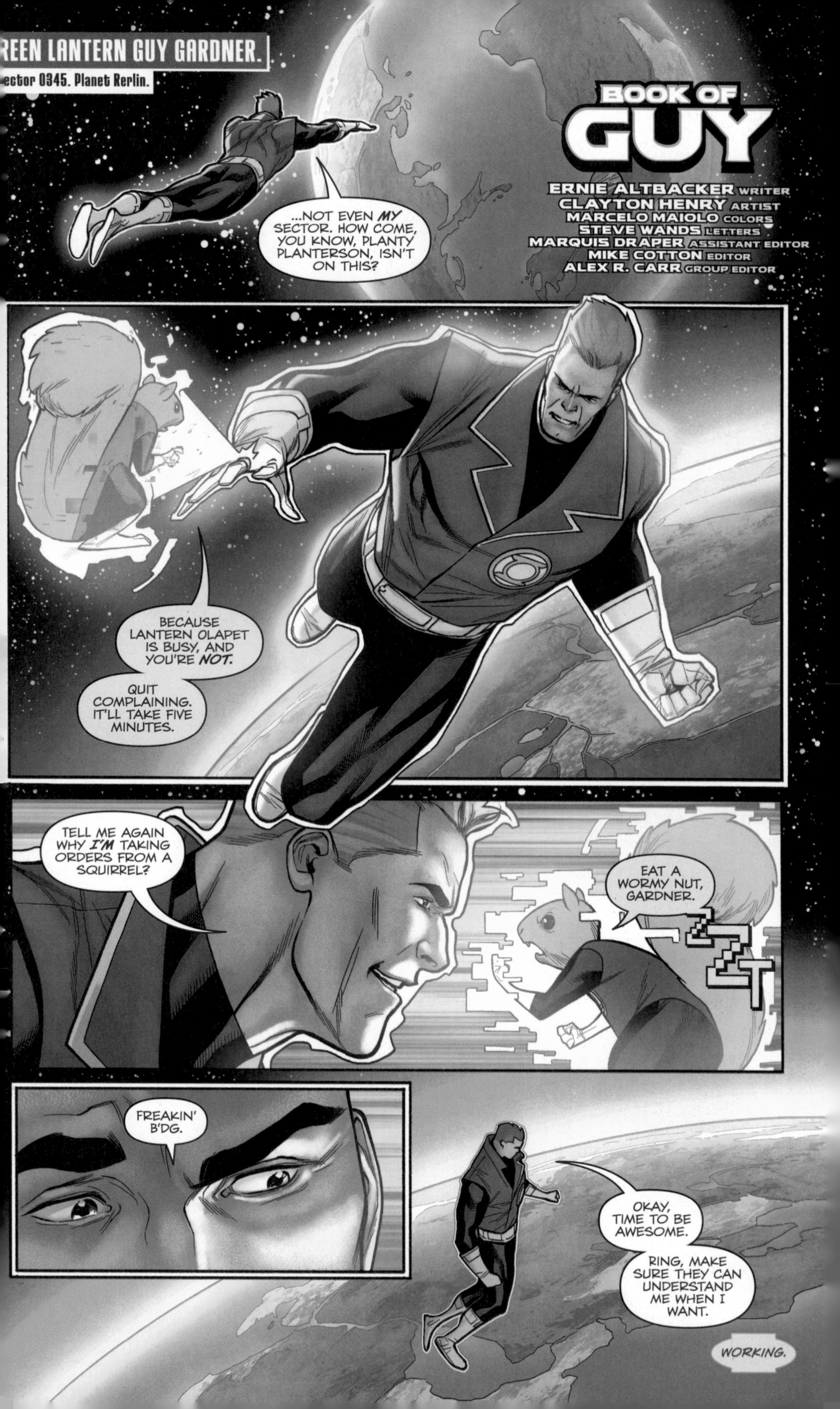

REEN LANTERN GUY GARDNER.
ector 0345. Planet Rerlin.
BOOK OF GUY
ERNIE ALTBACKER WRITER
CLAYTON HENRY ARTIST
MARCELO MAIOLO COLORS
STEVE WANDS LETTERS
MARQUIS DRAPER ASSISTANT EDITOR
MIKE COTTON EDITOR
ALEX R. CARR GROUP EDITOR
...NOT EVEN MY SECTOR. HOW COME, YOU KNOW, PLANTY PLANTERSON, ISN'T ON THIS?
BECAUSE LANTERN OLAPET IS BUSY, AND YOU'RE NOT.
QUIT COMPLAINING. IT'LL TAKE FIVE MINUTES.
TELL ME AGAIN WHY I'M TAKING ORDERS FROM A SQUIRREL?
EAT A WORMY NUT, GARDNER.
ZZT
FREAKIN' B'DG.
OKAY, TIME TO BE AWESOME.
RING, MAKE SURE THEY CAN UNDERSTAND ME WHEN I WANT.
WORKING.

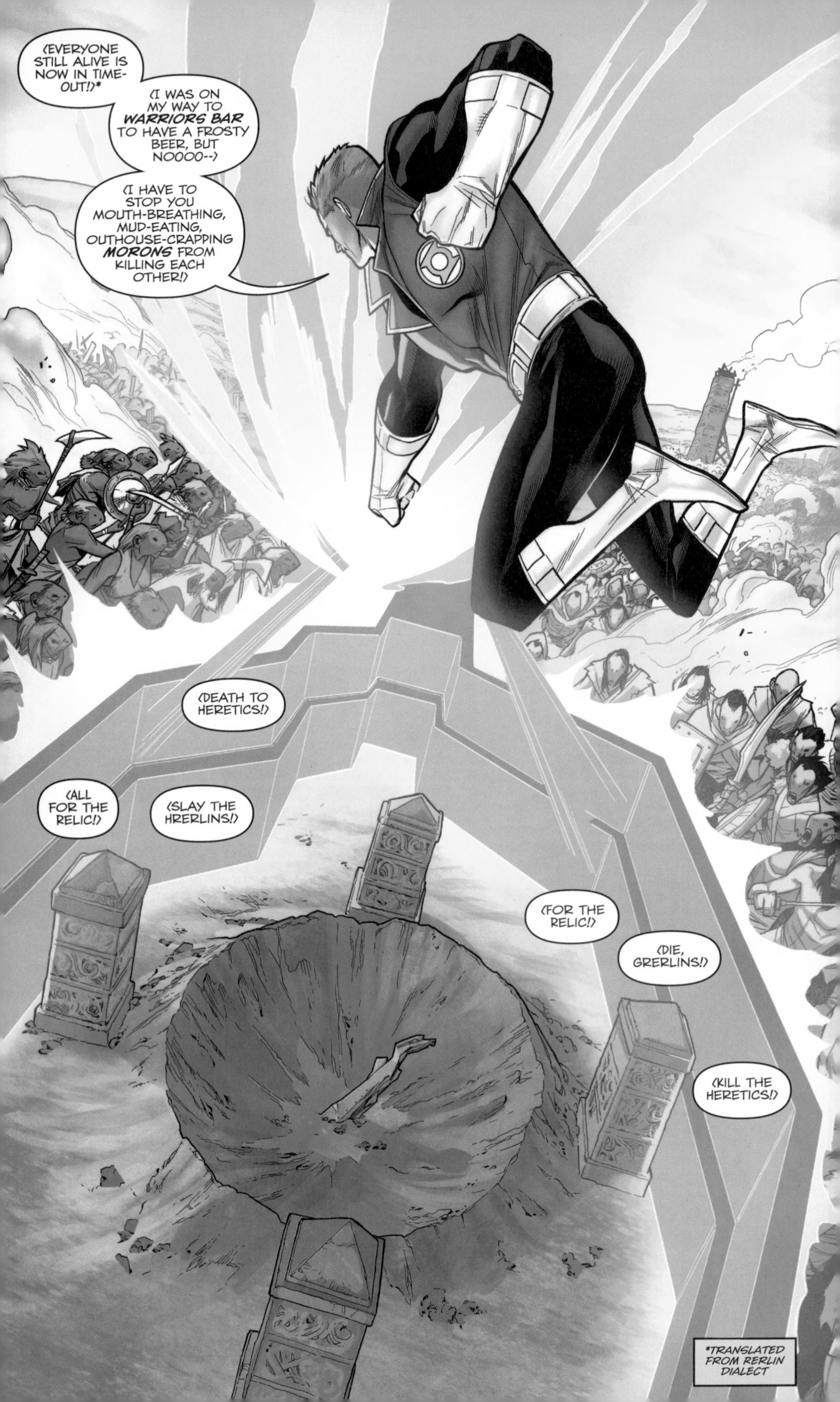

‹EVERYONE STILL ALIVE IS NOW IN TIME-OUT!›*
‹I WAS ON MY WAY TO WARRIORS BAR TO HAVE A FROSTY BEER, BUT NOOOO--›
‹I HAVE TO STOP YOU MOUTH-BREATHING, MUD-EATING, OUTHOUSE-CRAPPING MORONS FROM KILLING EACH OTHER!›
‹DEATH TO HERETICS!›
‹ALL FOR THE RELIC!›
‹SLAY THE HRERLINS!›
‹FOR THE RELIC!›
‹DIE, GRERLINS!›
‹KILL THE HERETICS!›
*TRANSLATED FROM RERLIN DIALECT

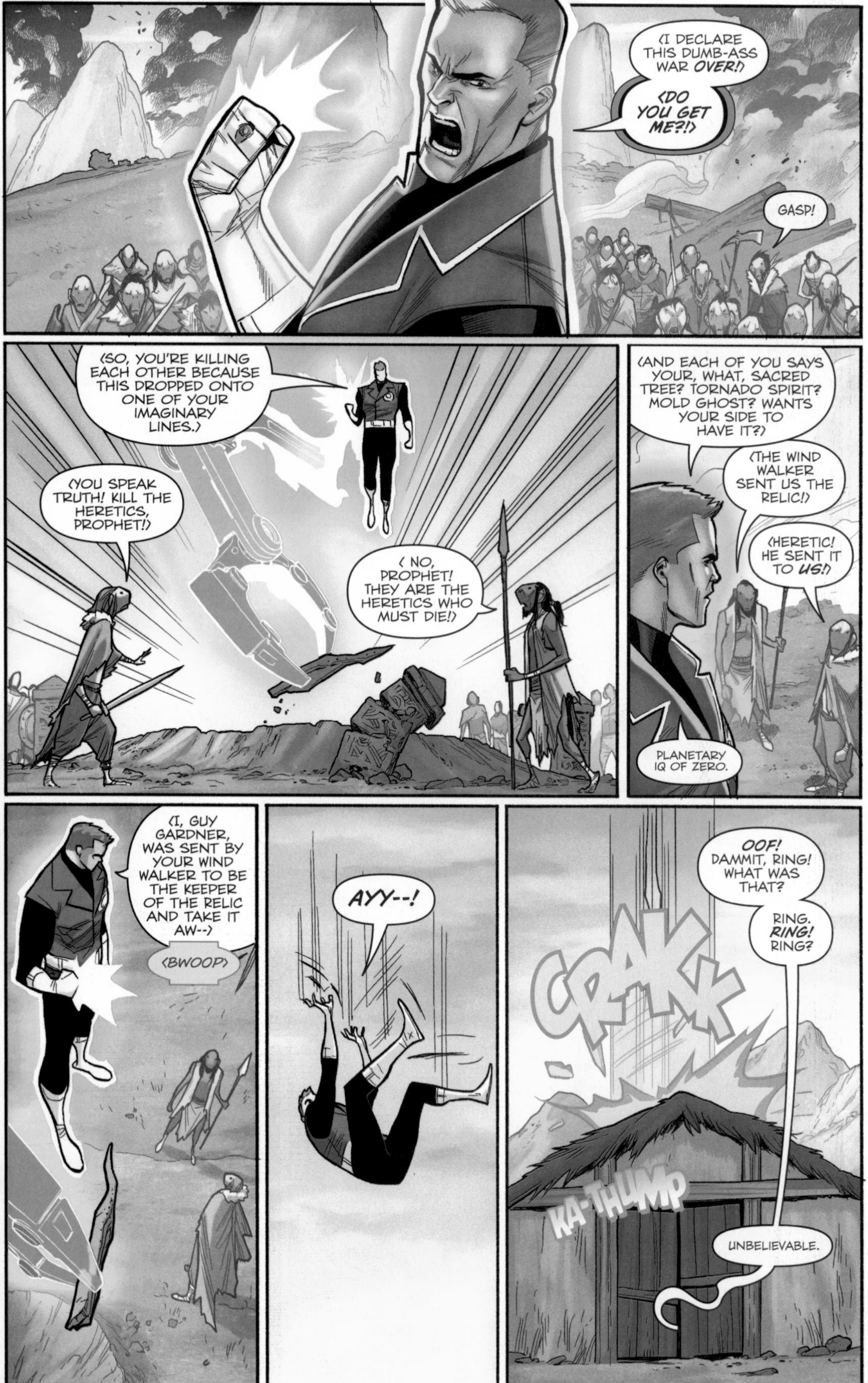

<I DECLARE THIS DUMB-ASS WAR OVER!>
<DO YOU GET ME?!>
GASP!
<SO, YOU'RE KILLING EACH OTHER BECAUSE THIS DROPPED ONTO ONE OF YOUR IMAGINARY LINES.>
<YOU SPEAK TRUTH! KILL THE HERETICS, PROPHET!>
< NO, PROPHET! THEY ARE THE HERETICS WHO MUST DIE!>
<AND EACH OF YOU SAYS YOUR, WHAT, SACRED TREE? TORNADO SPIRIT? MOLD GHOST? WANTS YOUR SIDE TO HAVE IT?>
<THE WIND WALKER SENT US THE RELIC!>
<HERETIC! HE SENT IT TO US!>
PLANETARY IQ OF ZERO.
<I, GUY GARDNER, WAS SENT BY YOUR WIND WALKER TO BE THE KEEPER OF THE RELIC AND TAKE IT AW-->
<BWOOP>
AYY--!
OOF! DAMMIT, RING! WHAT WAS THAT?
RING. RING! RING?
CRAKK
KA-THUMP
UNBELIEVABLE.

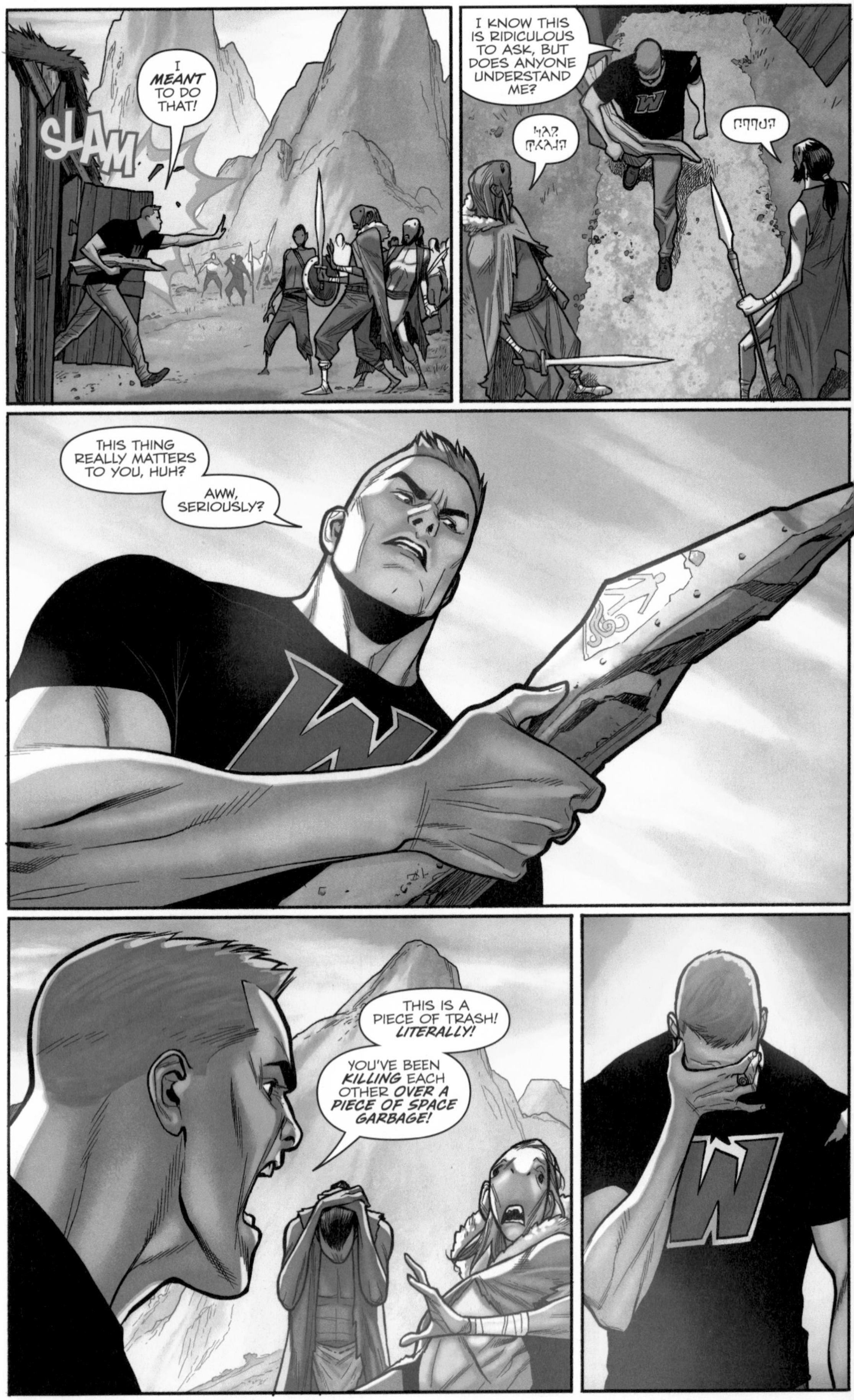

SLAM
I MEANT TO DO THAT!
I KNOW THIS IS RIDICULOUS TO ASK, BUT DOES ANYONE UNDERSTAND ME?
THIS THING REALLY MATTERS TO YOU, HUH?
AWW, SERIOUSLY?
THIS IS A PIECE OF TRASH! LITERALLY!
YOU'VE BEEN KILLING EACH OTHER OVER A PIECE OF SPACE GARBAGE!

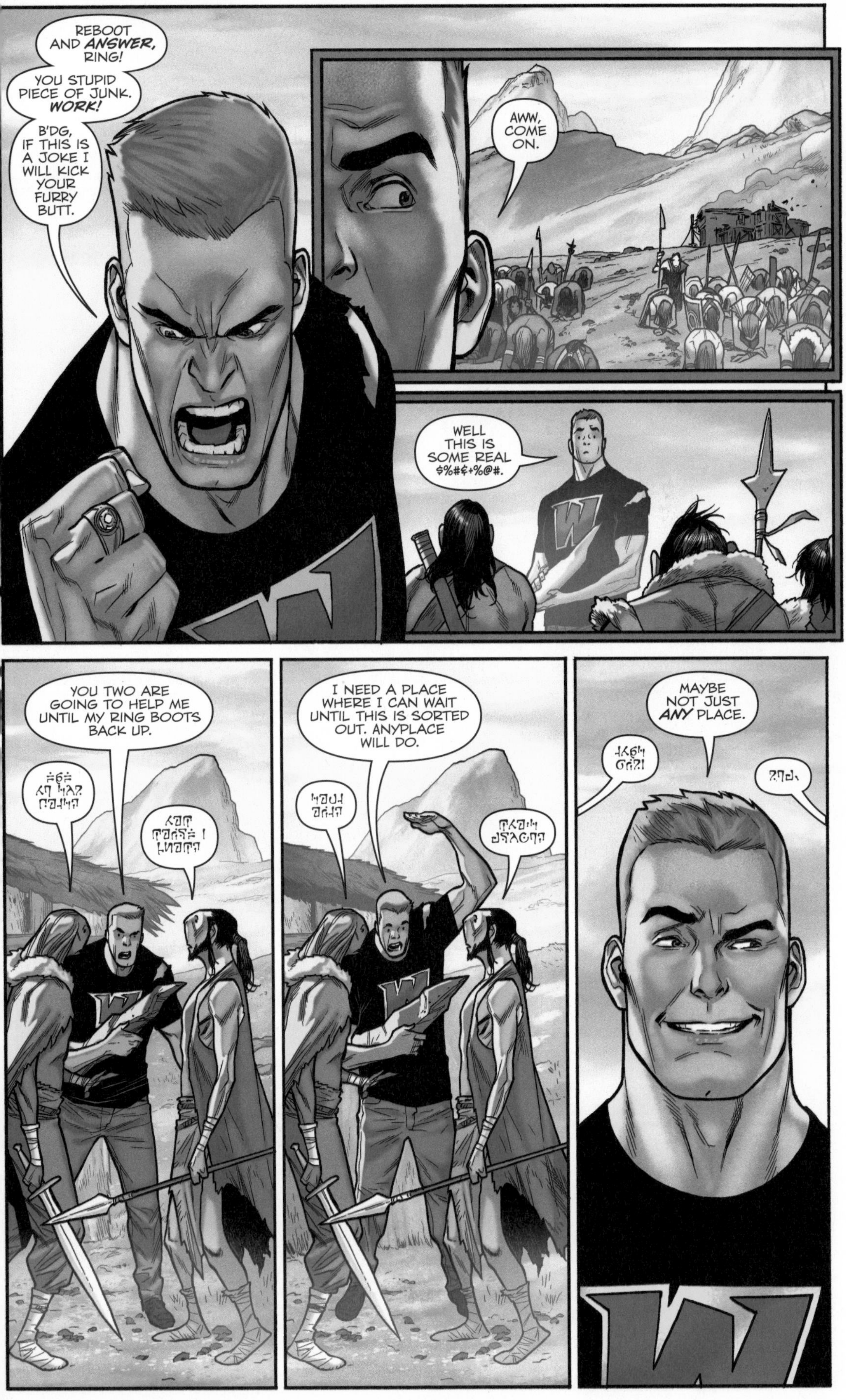
REBOOT AND *ANSWER,* RING!
YOU STUPID PIECE OF JUNK. ***WORK!***
B'DG, IF THIS IS A JOKE I WILL KICK YOUR FURRY BUTT.
AWW, COME ON.
WELL THIS IS SOME REAL $%#&+%@#.
YOU TWO ARE GOING TO HELP ME UNTIL MY RING BOOTS BACK UP.
I NEED A PLACE WHERE I CAN WAIT UNTIL THIS IS SORTED OUT. ANYPLACE WILL DO.
MAYBE NOT JUST ***ANY*** PLACE.

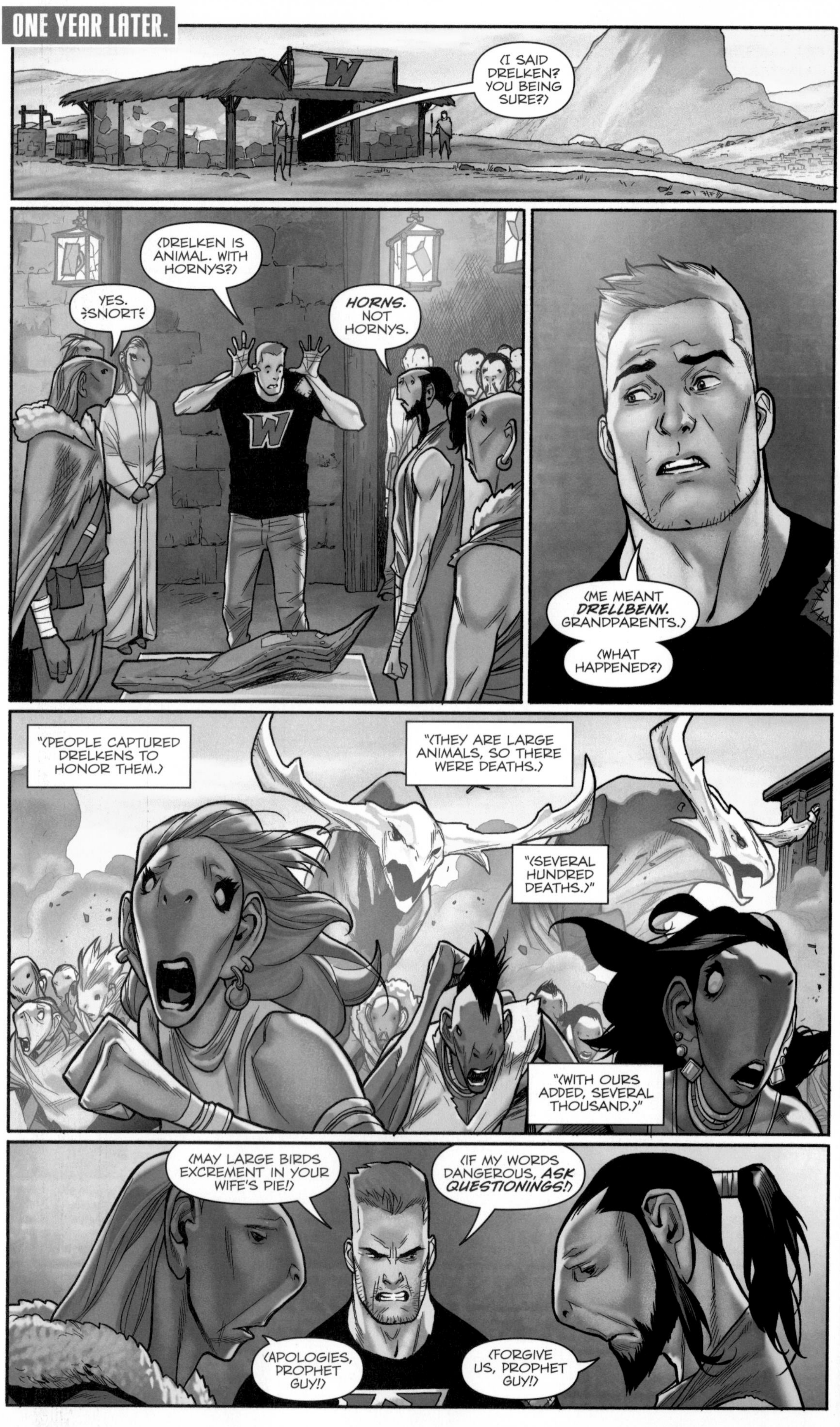
ONE YEAR LATER.
‹I SAID DRELKEN? YOU BEING SURE?›
‹DRELKEN IS ANIMAL. WITH HORNYS?›
YES. ⁘SNORT⁘
HORNS. NOT HORNYS.
‹ME MEANT DRELLBENN. GRANDPARENTS.›
‹WHAT HAPPENED?›
"‹PEOPLE CAPTURED DRELKENS TO HONOR THEM.›
"‹THEY ARE LARGE ANIMALS, SO THERE WERE DEATHS.›
"‹SEVERAL HUNDRED DEATHS.›"
"‹WITH OURS ADDED, SEVERAL THOUSAND.›"
‹MAY LARGE BIRDS EXCREMENT IN YOUR WIFE'S PIE!›
‹IF MY WORDS DANGEROUS, ASK QUESTIONINGS!›
‹APOLOGIES, PROPHET GUY!›
‹FORGIVE US, PROPHET GUY!›

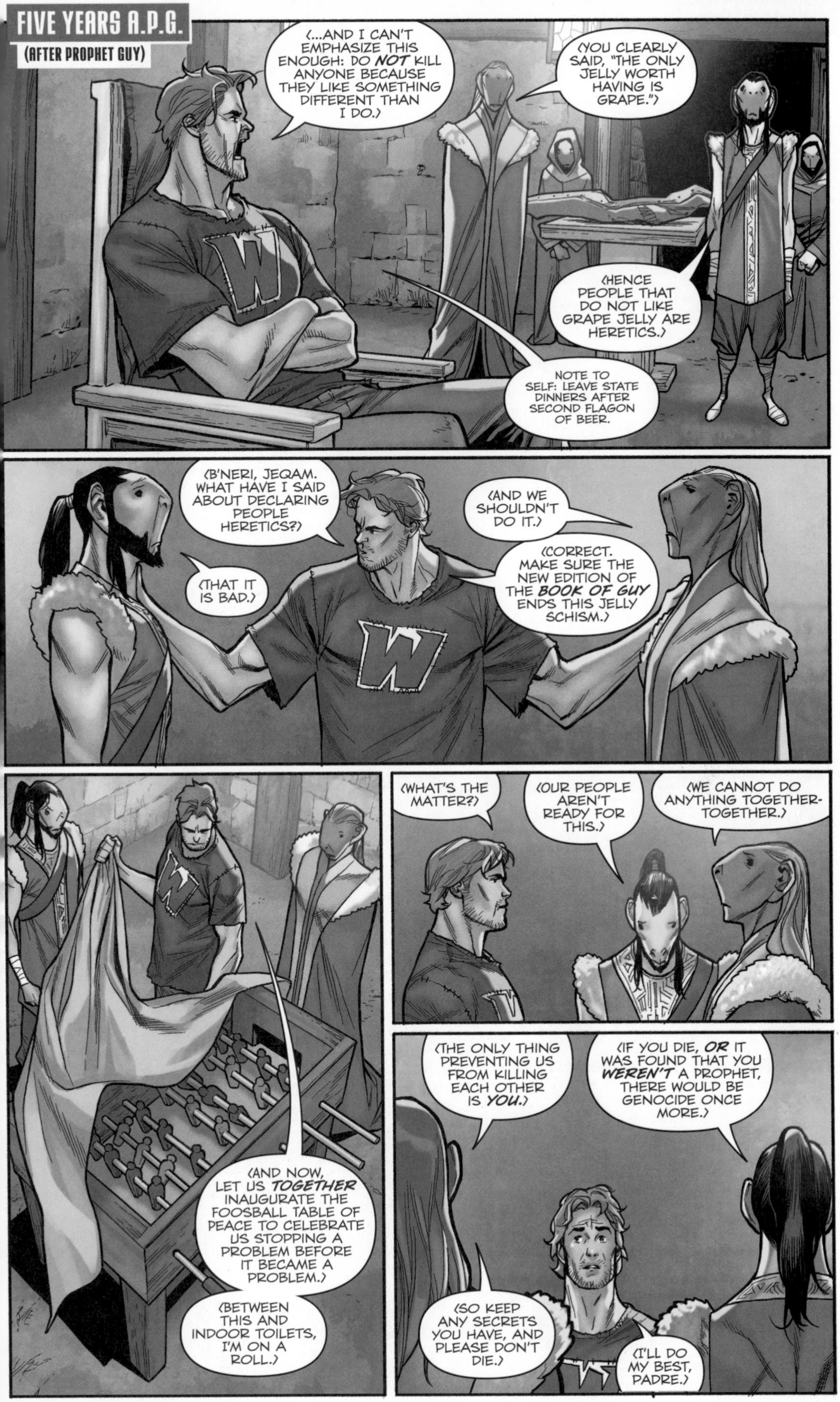
FIVE YEARS A.P.G.
(AFTER PROPHET GUY)
(...AND I CAN'T EMPHASIZE THIS ENOUGH: DO NOT KILL ANYONE BECAUSE THEY LIKE SOMETHING DIFFERENT THAN I DO.)
(YOU CLEARLY SAID, "THE ONLY JELLY WORTH HAVING IS GRAPE.")
(HENCE PEOPLE THAT DO NOT LIKE GRAPE JELLY ARE HERETICS.)
NOTE TO SELF: LEAVE STATE DINNERS AFTER SECOND FLAGON OF BEER.
(B'NERI, JEQAM. WHAT HAVE I SAID ABOUT DECLARING PEOPLE HERETICS?)
(THAT IT IS BAD.)
(AND WE SHOULDN'T DO IT.)
(CORRECT. MAKE SURE THE NEW EDITION OF THE BOOK OF GUY ENDS THIS JELLY SCHISM.)
(AND NOW, LET US TOGETHER INAUGURATE THE FOOSBALL TABLE OF PEACE TO CELEBRATE US STOPPING A PROBLEM BEFORE IT BECAME A PROBLEM.)
(BETWEEN THIS AND INDOOR TOILETS, I'M ON A ROLL.)
(WHAT'S THE MATTER?)
(OUR PEOPLE AREN'T READY FOR THIS.)
(WE CANNOT DO ANYTHING TOGETHER-TOGETHER.)
(THE ONLY THING PREVENTING US FROM KILLING EACH OTHER IS YOU.)
(IF YOU DIE, OR IT WAS FOUND THAT YOU WEREN'T A PROPHET, THERE WOULD BE GENOCIDE ONCE MORE.)
(SO KEEP ANY SECRETS YOU HAVE, AND PLEASE DON'T DIE.)
(I'LL DO MY BEST, PADRE.)

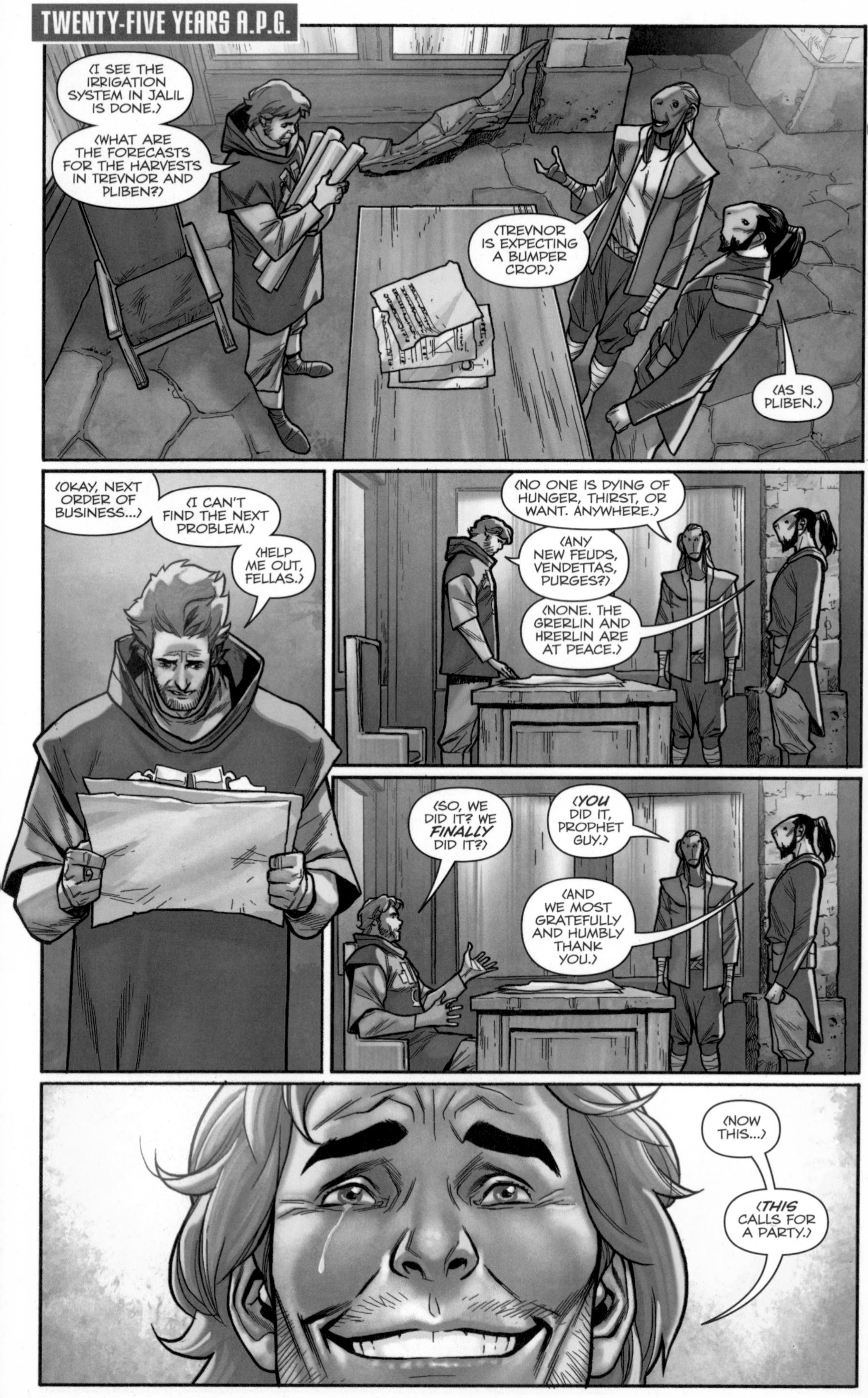
TWENTY-FIVE YEARS A.P.G.
(I SEE THE IRRIGATION SYSTEM IN JALIL IS DONE.)
(WHAT ARE THE FORECASTS FOR THE HARVESTS IN TREVNOR AND PLIBEN?)
(TREVNOR IS EXPECTING A BUMPER CROP.)
(AS IS PLIBEN.)
(OKAY, NEXT ORDER OF BUSINESS...)
(I CAN'T FIND THE NEXT PROBLEM.)
(HELP ME OUT, FELLAS.)
(NO ONE IS DYING OF HUNGER, THIRST, OR WANT. ANYWHERE.)
(ANY NEW FEUDS, VENDETTAS, PURGES?)
(NONE. THE GRERLIN AND HRERLIN ARE AT PEACE.)
(SO, WE DID IT? WE *FINALLY* DID IT?)
(*YOU* DID IT, PROPHET GUY.)
(AND WE MOST GRATEFULLY AND HUMBLY THANK YOU.)
(NOW THIS...)
(*THIS* CALLS FOR A PARTY.)

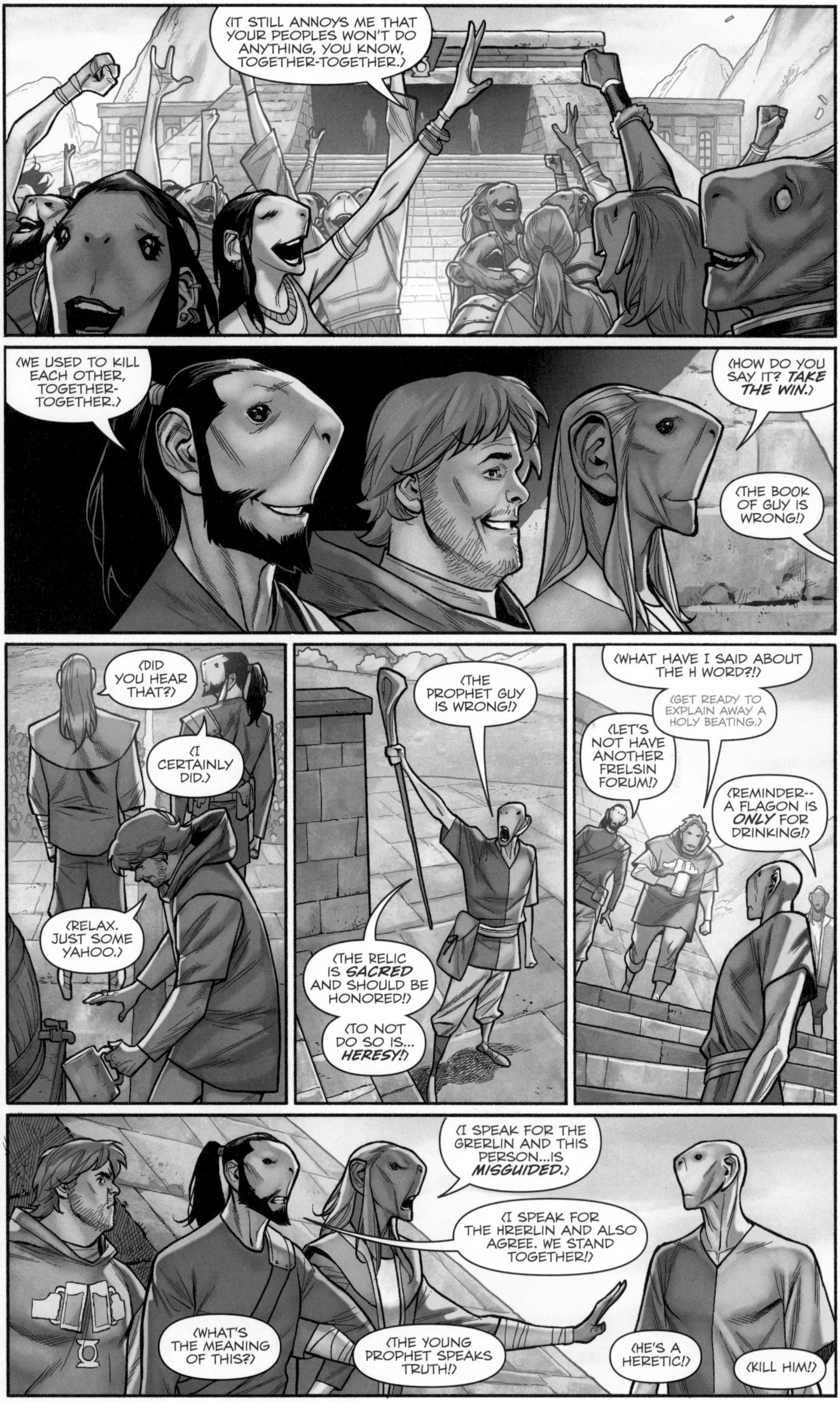
⟨IT STILL ANNOYS ME THAT YOUR PEOPLES WON'T DO ANYTHING, YOU KNOW, TOGETHER-TOGETHER.⟩
⟨WE USED TO KILL EACH OTHER, TOGETHER-TOGETHER.⟩
⟨HOW DO YOU SAY IT? *TAKE THE WIN.*⟩
⟨THE BOOK OF GUY IS WRONG!⟩
⟨DID YOU HEAR THAT?⟩
⟨I CERTAINLY DID.⟩
⟨RELAX. JUST SOME YAHOO.⟩
⟨THE PROPHET GUY IS WRONG!⟩
⟨THE RELIC IS *SACRED* AND SHOULD BE HONORED!⟩
⟨TO NOT DO SO IS... *HERESY!*⟩
⟨WHAT HAVE I SAID ABOUT THE H WORD?!⟩
⟨GET READY TO EXPLAIN AWAY A HOLY BEATING.⟩
⟨LET'S NOT HAVE ANOTHER FRELSIN FORUM!⟩
⟨REMINDER-- A FLAGON IS *ONLY* FOR DRINKING!⟩
⟨I SPEAK FOR THE GRERLIN AND THIS PERSON...IS *MISGUIDED.*⟩
⟨I SPEAK FOR THE HRERLIN AND ALSO AGREE. WE STAND TOGETHER!⟩
⟨WHAT'S THE MEANING OF THIS?⟩
⟨THE YOUNG PROPHET SPEAKS TRUTH!⟩
⟨HE'S A HERETIC!⟩
⟨KILL HIM!⟩

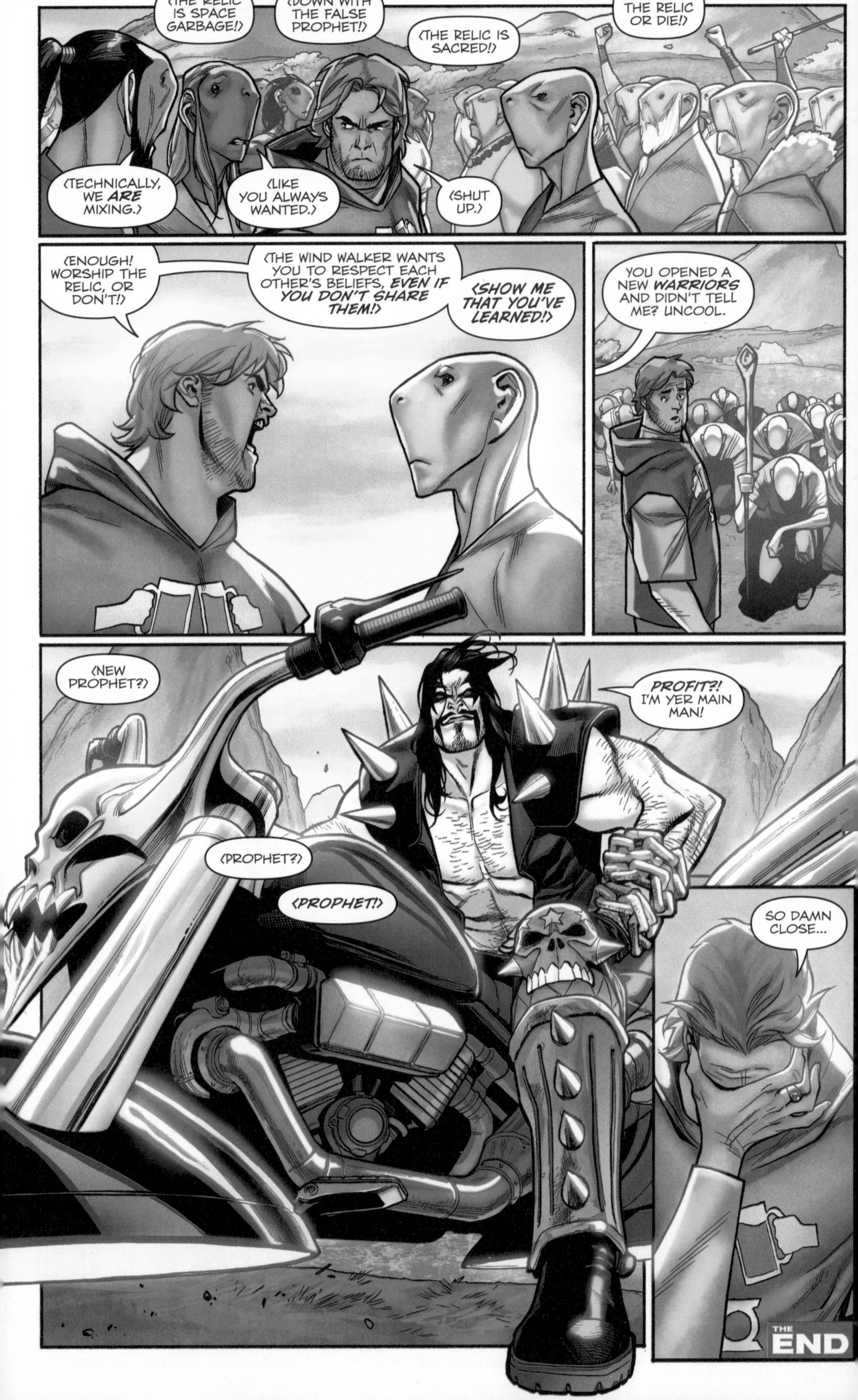

⟨THE RELIC IS SPACE GARBAGE!⟩
⟨DOWN WITH THE FALSE PROPHET!⟩
⟨THE RELIC IS SACRED!⟩
⟨HONOR THE RELIC OR DIE!⟩
⟨TECHNICALLY, WE ARE MIXING.⟩
⟨LIKE YOU ALWAYS WANTED.⟩
⟨SHUT UP.⟩
⟨ENOUGH! WORSHIP THE RELIC, OR DON'T!⟩
⟨THE WIND WALKER WANTS YOU TO RESPECT EACH OTHER'S BELIEFS, EVEN IF YOU DON'T SHARE THEM!⟩
⟨SHOW ME THAT YOU'VE LEARNED!⟩
YOU OPENED A NEW WARRIORS AND DIDN'T TELL ME? UNCOOL.
⟨NEW PROPHET?⟩
PROFIT?! I'M YER MAIN MAN!
⟨PROPHET?⟩
⟨PROPHET!⟩
SO DAMN CLOSE...
THE END

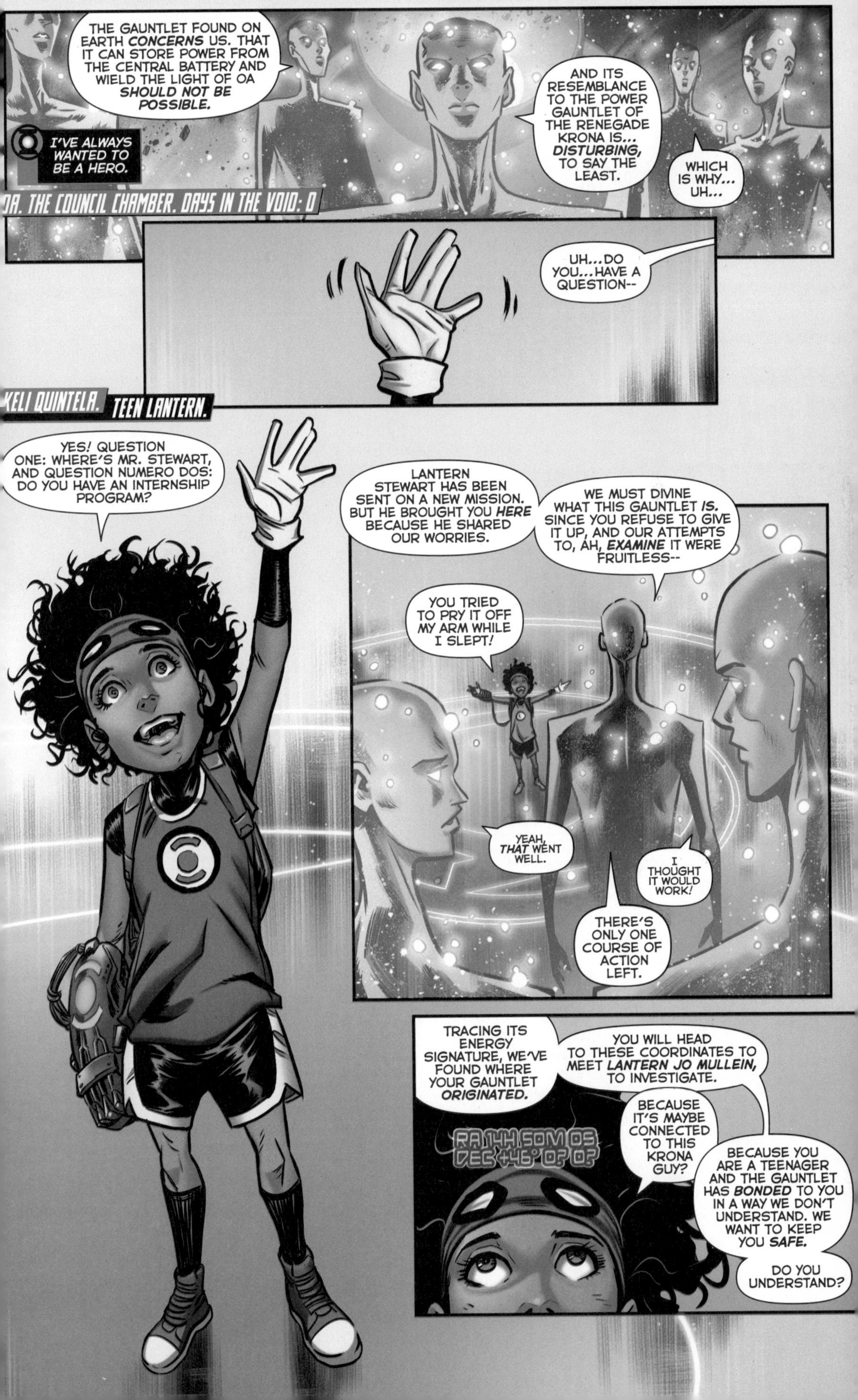
THE GAUNTLET FOUND ON EARTH CONCERNS US. THAT IT CAN STORE POWER FROM THE CENTRAL BATTERY AND WIELD THE LIGHT OF OA SHOULD NOT BE POSSIBLE.
I'VE ALWAYS WANTED TO BE A HERO.
OA. THE COUNCIL CHAMBER. DAYS IN THE VOID: 0
AND ITS RESEMBLANCE TO THE POWER GAUNTLET OF THE RENEGADE KRONA IS... DISTURBING, TO SAY THE LEAST.
WHICH IS WHY... UH...
UH...DO YOU...HAVE A QUESTION--
KELI QUINTELA. TEEN LANTERN.
YES! QUESTION ONE: WHERE'S MR. STEWART, AND QUESTION NUMERO DOS: DO YOU HAVE AN INTERNSHIP PROGRAM?
LANTERN STEWART HAS BEEN SENT ON A NEW MISSION. BUT HE BROUGHT YOU HERE BECAUSE HE SHARED OUR WORRIES.
WE MUST DIVINE WHAT THIS GAUNTLET IS. SINCE YOU REFUSE TO GIVE IT UP, AND OUR ATTEMPTS TO, AH, EXAMINE IT WERE FRUITLESS--
YOU TRIED TO PRY IT OFF MY ARM WHILE I SLEPT!
YEAH, THAT WENT WELL.
I THOUGHT IT WOULD WORK!
THERE'S ONLY ONE COURSE OF ACTION LEFT.
TRACING ITS ENERGY SIGNATURE, WE'VE FOUND WHERE YOUR GAUNTLET ORIGINATED.
YOU WILL HEAD TO THESE COORDINATES TO MEET LANTERN JO MULLEIN, TO INVESTIGATE.
RA 14H 50M 0S
DEC +46° 0' 0"
BECAUSE IT'S MAYBE CONNECTED TO THIS KRONA GUY?
BECAUSE YOU ARE A TEENAGER AND THE GAUNTLET HAS BONDED TO YOU IN A WAY WE DON'T UNDERSTAND. WE WANT TO KEEP YOU SAFE.
DO YOU UNDERSTAND?

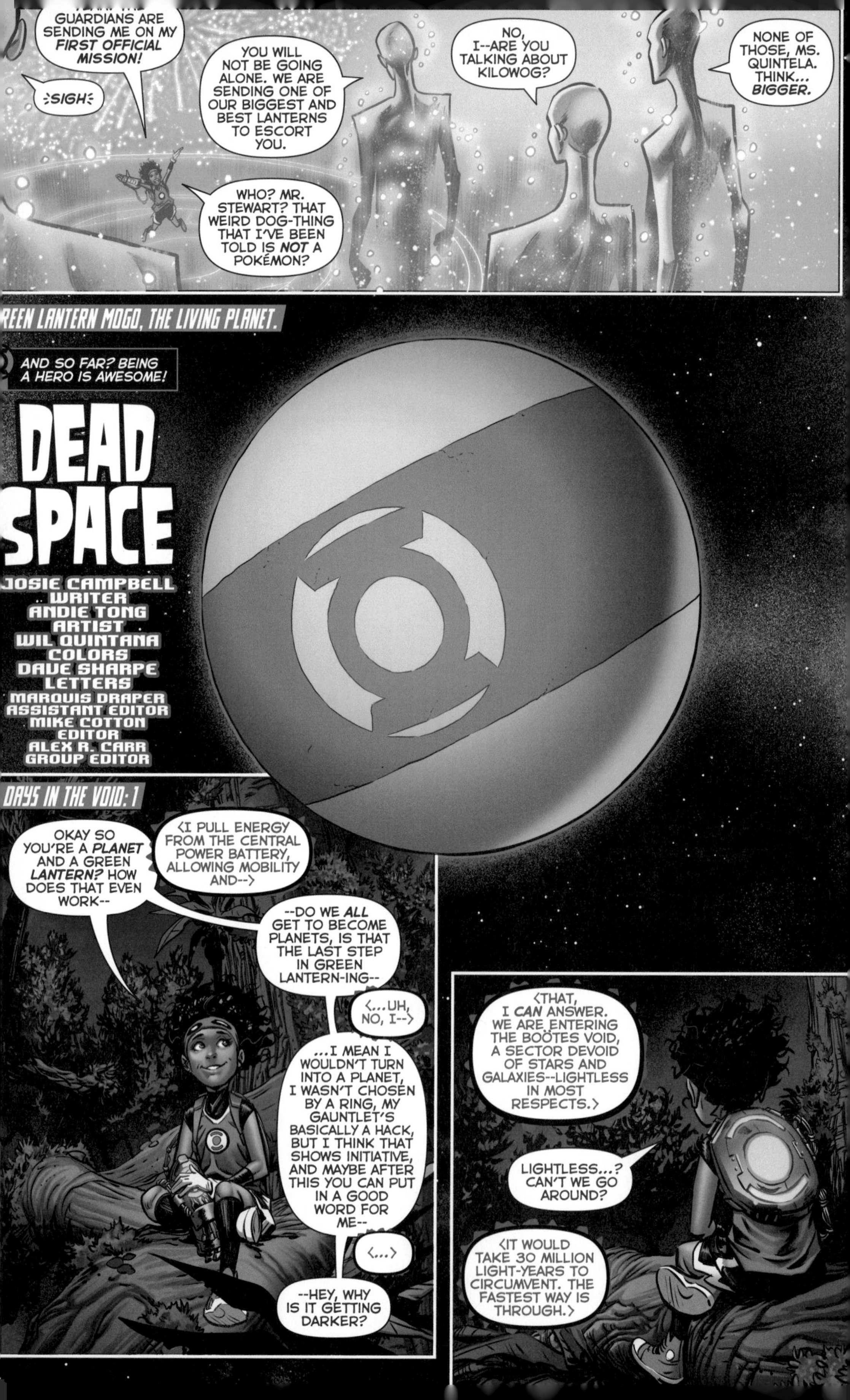

GUARDIANS ARE SENDING ME ON MY FIRST OFFICIAL MISSION!
SIGH
YOU WILL NOT BE GOING ALONE. WE ARE SENDING ONE OF OUR BIGGEST AND BEST LANTERNS TO ESCORT YOU.
WHO? MR. STEWART? THAT WEIRD DOG-THING THAT I'VE BEEN TOLD IS NOT A POKÉMON?
NO, I--ARE YOU TALKING ABOUT KILOWOG?
NONE OF THOSE, MS. QUINTELA. THINK... BIGGER.
REEN LANTERN MOGO, THE LIVING PLANET.
AND SO FAR? BEING A HERO IS AWESOME!
DEAD SPACE
JOSIE CAMPBELL WRITER
ANDIE TONG ARTIST
WIL QUINTANA COLORS
DAVE SHARPE LETTERS
MARQUIS DRAPER ASSISTANT EDITOR
MIKE COTTON EDITOR
ALEX R. CARR GROUP EDITOR
DAYS IN THE VOID: 1
OKAY SO YOU'RE A PLANET AND A GREEN LANTERN? HOW DOES THAT EVEN WORK--
<I PULL ENERGY FROM THE CENTRAL POWER BATTERY, ALLOWING MOBILITY AND-->
--DO WE ALL GET TO BECOME PLANETS, IS THAT THE LAST STEP IN GREEN LANTERN-ING--
<...UH, NO, I-->
...I MEAN I WOULDN'T TURN INTO A PLANET, I WASN'T CHOSEN BY A RING, MY GAUNTLET'S BASICALLY A HACK, BUT I THINK THAT SHOWS INITIATIVE, AND MAYBE AFTER THIS YOU CAN PUT IN A GOOD WORD FOR ME--
<...>
--HEY, WHY IS IT GETTING DARKER?
<THAT, I CAN ANSWER. WE ARE ENTERING THE BOÖTES VOID, A SECTOR DEVOID OF STARS AND GALAXIES--LIGHTLESS IN MOST RESPECTS.>
LIGHTLESS...? CAN'T WE GO AROUND?
<IT WOULD TAKE 30 MILLION LIGHT-YEARS TO CIRCUMVENT. THE FASTEST WAY IS THROUGH.>

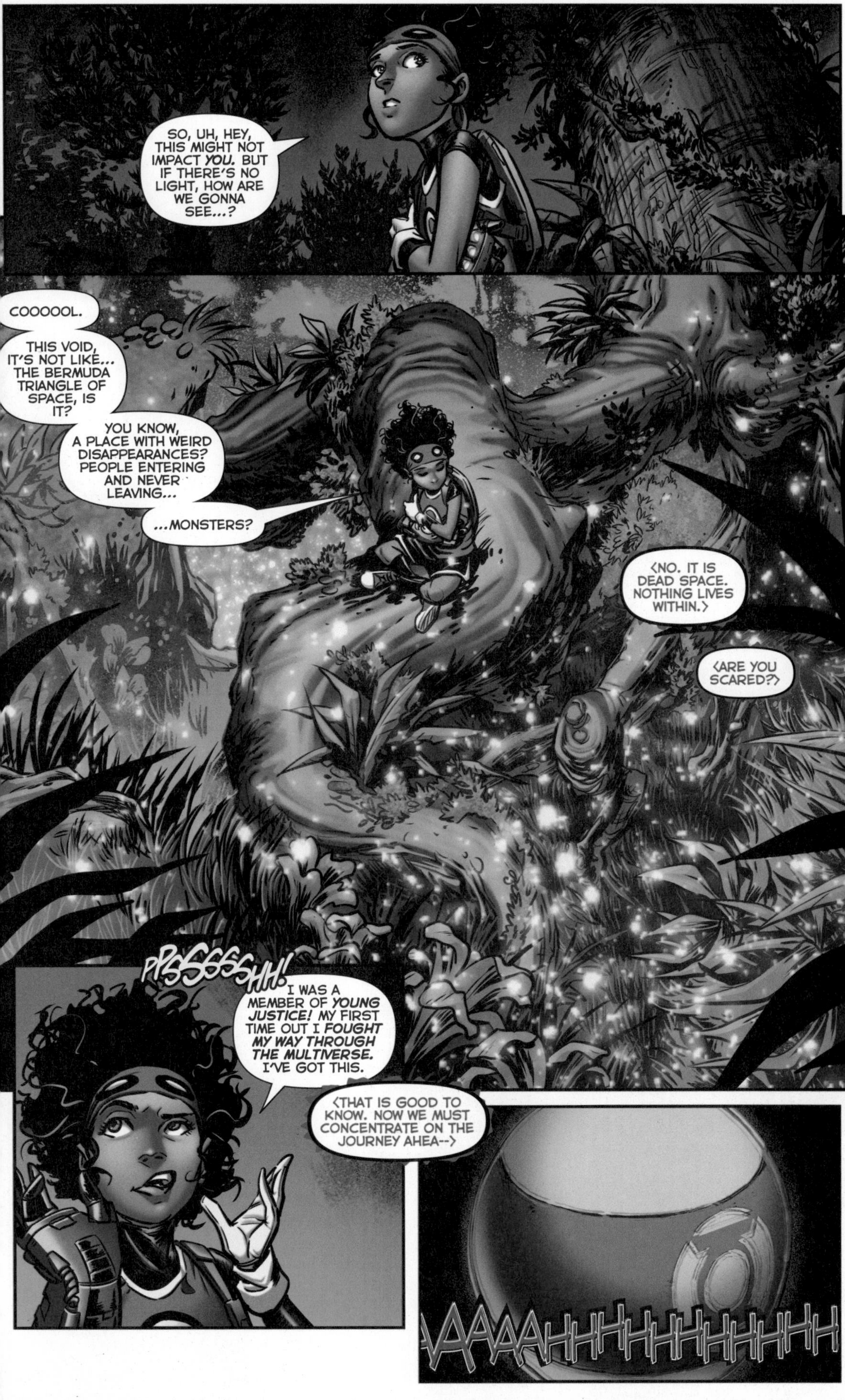

SO, UH, HEY, THIS MIGHT NOT IMPACT *YOU.* BUT IF THERE'S NO LIGHT, HOW ARE WE GONNA SEE...?
COOOOOL.
THIS VOID, IT'S NOT LIKE... THE BERMUDA TRIANGLE OF SPACE, IS IT?
YOU KNOW, A PLACE WITH WEIRD DISAPPEARANCES? PEOPLE ENTERING AND NEVER LEAVING...
...MONSTERS?
<NO. IT IS DEAD SPACE. NOTHING LIVES WITHIN.>
<ARE YOU SCARED?>
PPSSSSSHH!
I WAS A MEMBER OF *YOUNG JUSTICE!* MY FIRST TIME OUT I *FOUGHT MY WAY THROUGH THE MULTIVERSE.* I'VE GOT THIS.
<THAT IS GOOD TO KNOW. NOW WE MUST CONCENTRATE ON THE JOURNEY AHEA-->
AAAAAHHHHHHHHHHHH

MOGO! WHAT'S WRONG?!

〈CENTRAL... POWER BATTERY... *GONE!* WITHOUT IT...I...I...〉

MOGO? MOGO!

MOGO...?

OOOOKAAAAY! YOU'RE OKAY, KELI. SOMETHING'S OBVIOUSLY HAPPENED TO THE MAIN POWER THING THAT MOGO WAS TALKING ABOUT, BUT IT DOESN'T MATTER!

THIS IS THE TIME TO PROVE *YOURSELF!* YOU'RE A *HERO.* WAKE UP MOGO AND GET OUT OF HERE.

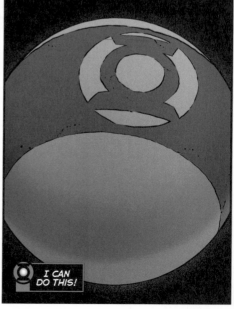

I CAN DO THIS!

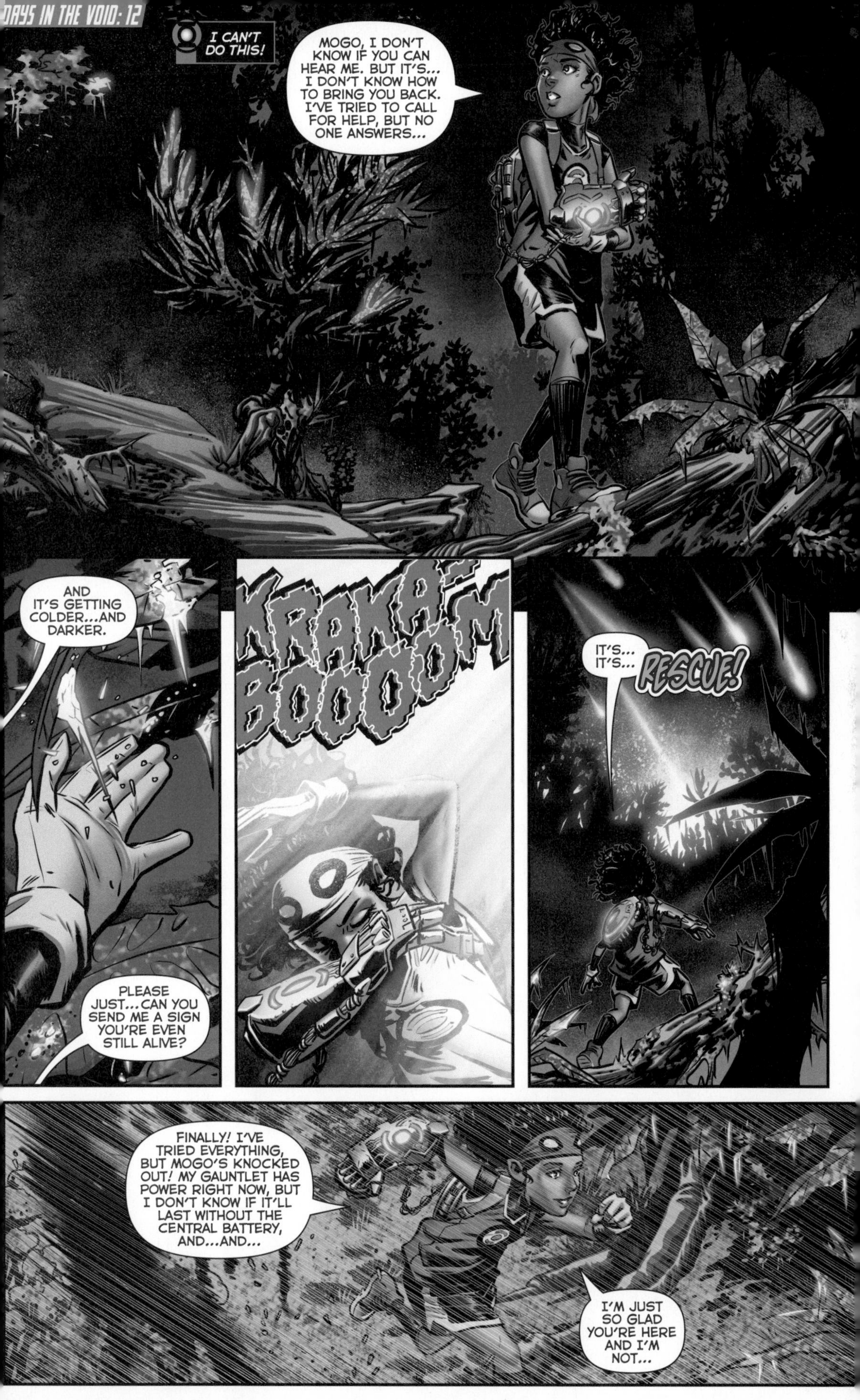

DAYS IN THE VOID: 12
I CAN'T DO THIS!
MOGO, I DON'T KNOW IF YOU CAN HEAR ME. BUT IT'S... I DON'T KNOW HOW TO BRING YOU BACK. I'VE TRIED TO CALL FOR HELP, BUT NO ONE ANSWERS...
AND IT'S GETTING COLDER...AND DARKER.
PLEASE JUST...CAN YOU SEND ME A SIGN YOU'RE EVEN STILL ALIVE?
KRAKA-BOOOOOM
IT'S... IT'S... RESCUE!
FINALLY! I'VE TRIED EVERYTHING, BUT MOGO'S KNOCKED OUT! MY GAUNTLET HAS POWER RIGHT NOW, BUT I DON'T KNOW IF IT'LL LAST WITHOUT THE CENTRAL BATTERY, AND...AND...
I'M JUST SO GLAD YOU'RE HERE AND I'M NOT...

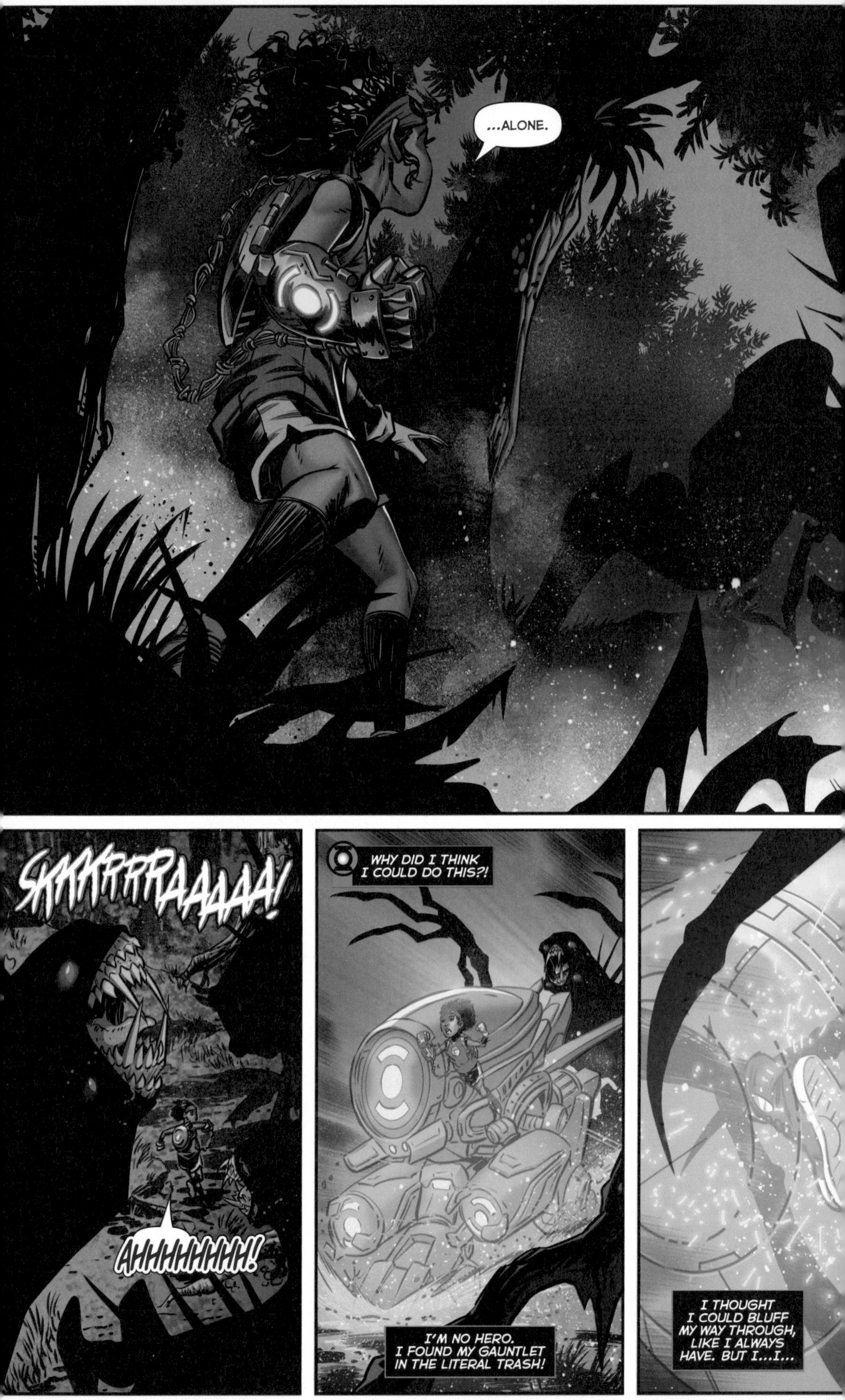
...ALONE.
SKKKRRRAAAAA!
AHHHHHHHH!
WHY DID I THINK I COULD DO THIS?!
I'M NO HERO. I FOUND MY GAUNTLET IN THE LITERAL TRASH!
I THOUGHT I COULD BLUFF MY WAY THROUGH, LIKE I ALWAYS HAVE. BUT I...I...

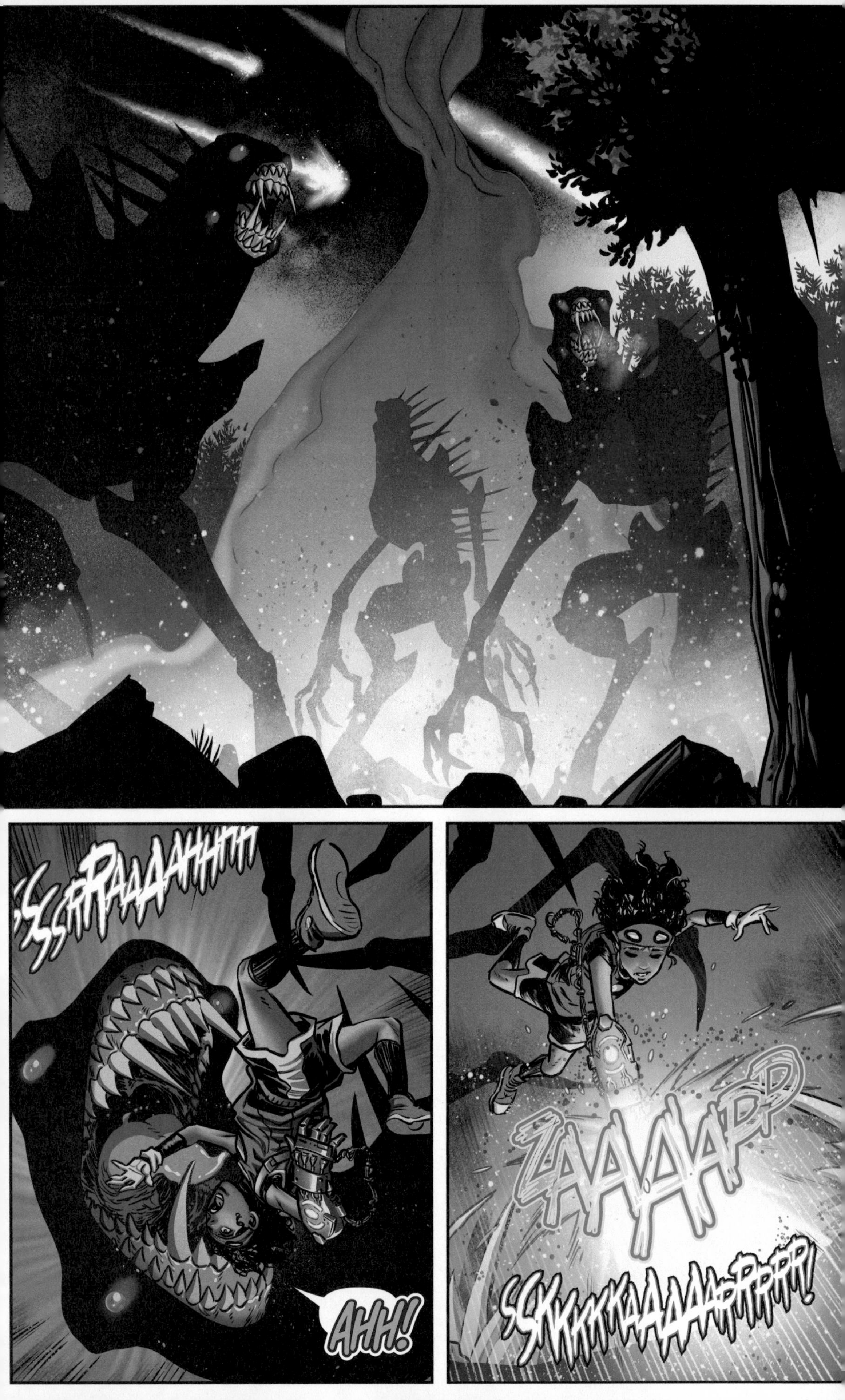
SSSRRAAAAHHHH
AHH!
ZAAAAAPP
SSKKKKKAAAAAPPPPR!

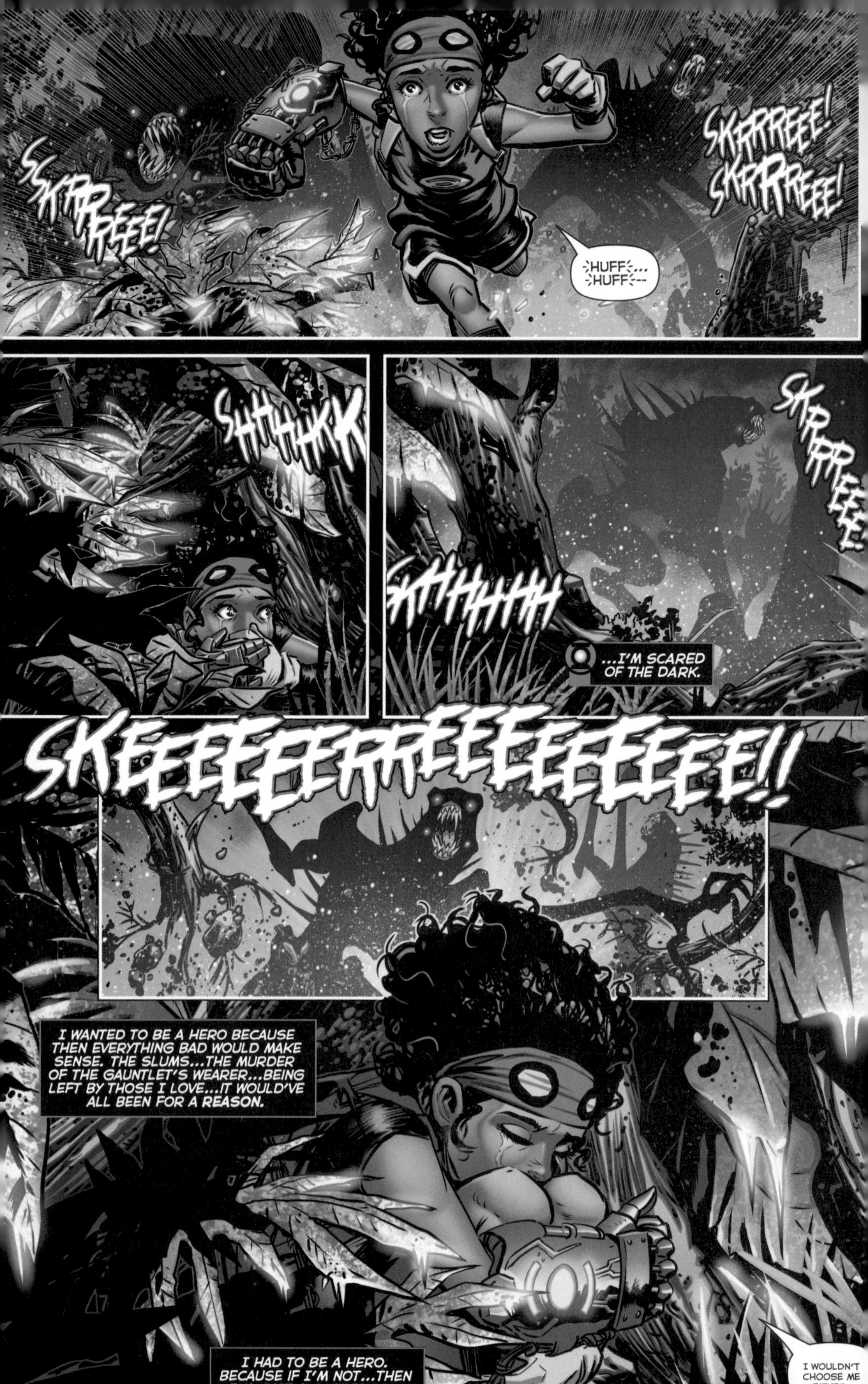
SSKRRREEE!
SKRRREEE! SKRRREEE!
HUFF... HUFF--
SHHHHKK
SKRRREEE
SKHHHHHH
...I'M SCARED OF THE DARK.
SKEEEEERRREEEEEEEEEE!!
I WANTED TO BE A HERO BECAUSE THEN EVERYTHING BAD WOULD MAKE SENSE. THE SLUMS...THE MURDER OF THE GAUNTLET'S WEARER...BEING LEFT BY THOSE I LOVE...IT WOULD'VE ALL BEEN FOR A REASON.
I HAD TO BE A HERO. BECAUSE IF I'M NOT...THEN I'M JUST A SCARED KID.
I WOULDN'T CHOOSE ME EITHER.
OF COURSE I NEVER GOT

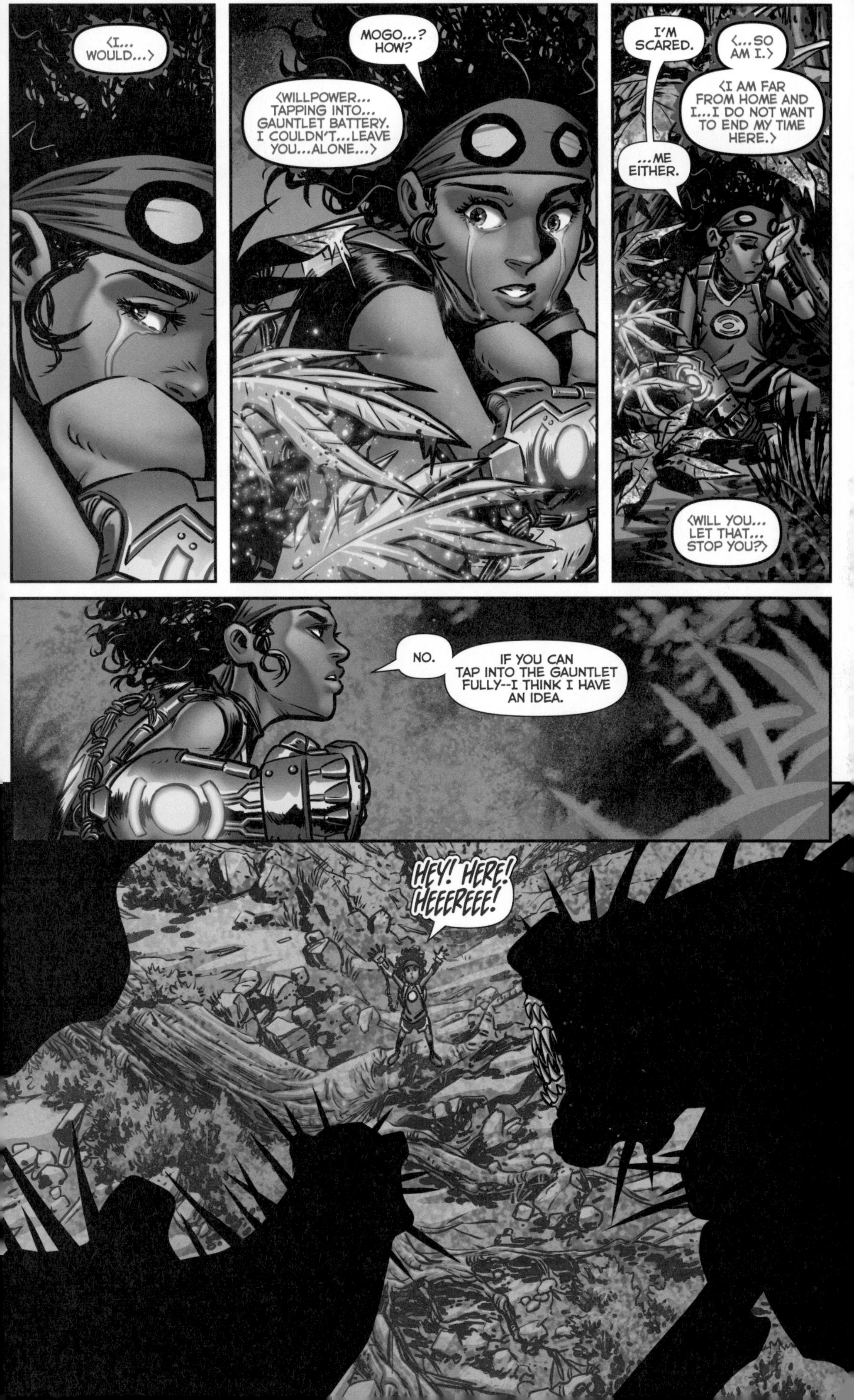
<I... WOULD...>
MOGO...? HOW?
<WILLPOWER... TAPPING INTO... GAUNTLET BATTERY. I COULDN'T...LEAVE YOU...ALONE...>
I'M SCARED.
<...SO AM I.>
<I AM FAR FROM HOME AND I...I DO NOT WANT TO END MY TIME HERE.>
...ME EITHER.
<WILL YOU... LET THAT... STOP YOU?>
NO.
IF YOU CAN TAP INTO THE GAUNTLET FULLY--I THINK I HAVE AN IDEA.
HEY! HERE! HEEEREEE!

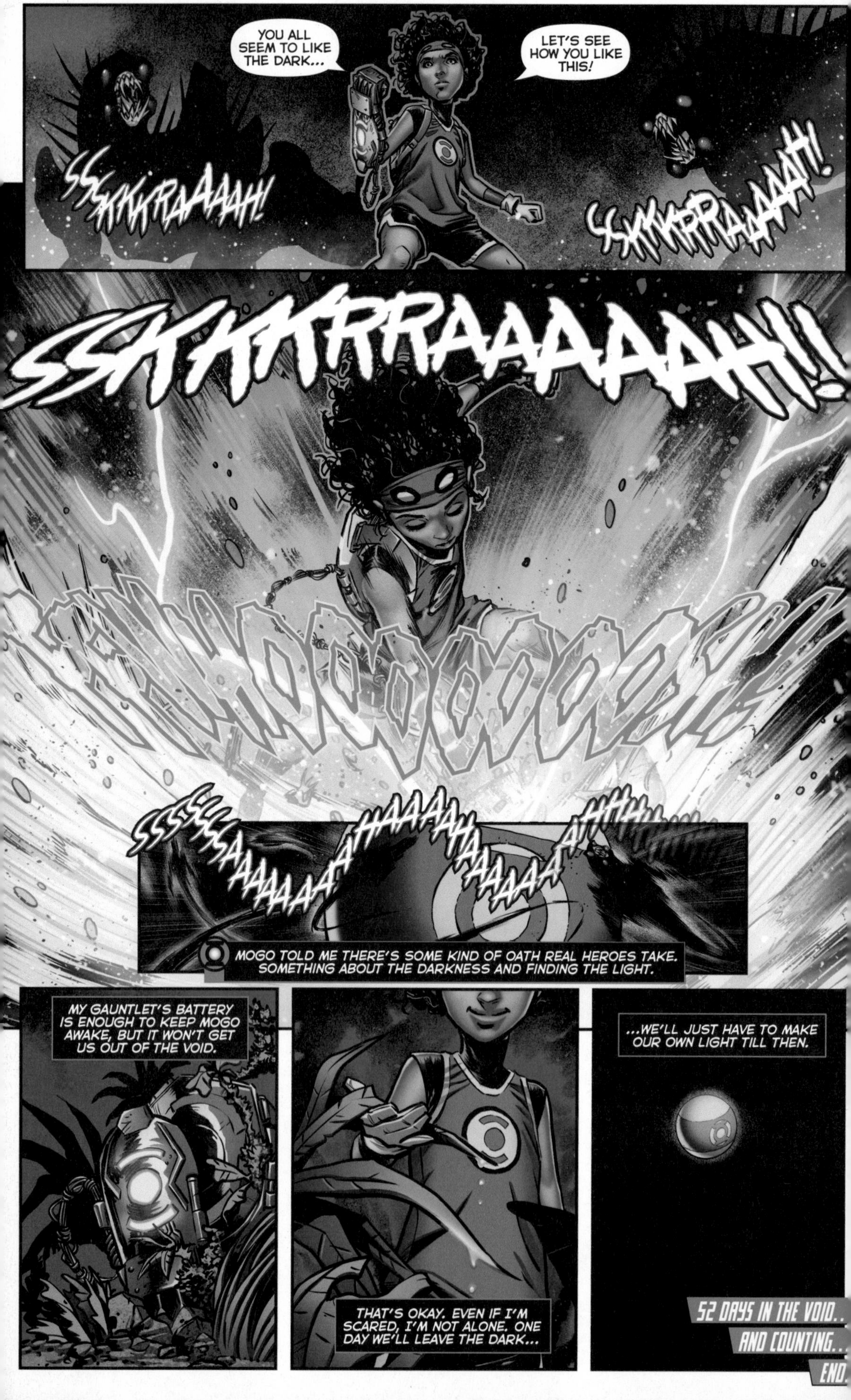

YOU ALL SEEM TO LIKE THE DARK...
LET'S SEE HOW YOU LIKE THIS!
SSKKKRAAAAH!
SSKKKRRAAAAH!
SSKKRRAAAAAAH!!
MOGO TOLD ME THERE'S SOME KIND OF OATH REAL HEROES TAKE. SOMETHING ABOUT THE DARKNESS AND FINDING THE LIGHT.
MY GAUNTLET'S BATTERY IS ENOUGH TO KEEP MOGO AWAKE, BUT IT WON'T GET US OUT OF THE VOID.
THAT'S OKAY. EVEN IF I'M SCARED, I'M NOT ALONE. ONE DAY WE'LL LEAVE THE DARK...
...WE'LL JUST HAVE TO MAKE OUR OWN LIGHT TILL THEN.
52 DAYS IN THE VOID...
AND COUNTING...
END.

RING, START RECORDING.

RECORDING INITIATED.

I HAVEN'T HEARD FROM THE *GREEN LANTERN CORPS* IN MONTHS. JOHN, GUY, AND KYLE ARE ALL M.I.A.

THE *JUSTICE LEAGUE* CAN'T FIND SIMON OR JESSICA.

CYBORG BUILT AN *ENERGY AMPLIFIER* FOR MY RING BEFORE HIS...ACCIDENT. THEN HE DISAPPEARED, TOO.

WHAT HEROES ARE LEFT, THEIR HANDS ARE FULL KEEPING *EARTH* ALIVE.

SOMEONE HAS TO SEE WHAT THREATS ARE *CLOSING IN* FROM ACROSS THE UNIVERSE. SOMEONE HAS TO GO *BEYOND.*

THIS MAY WELL BE MY *FINAL* TRANSMISSION.

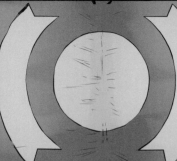

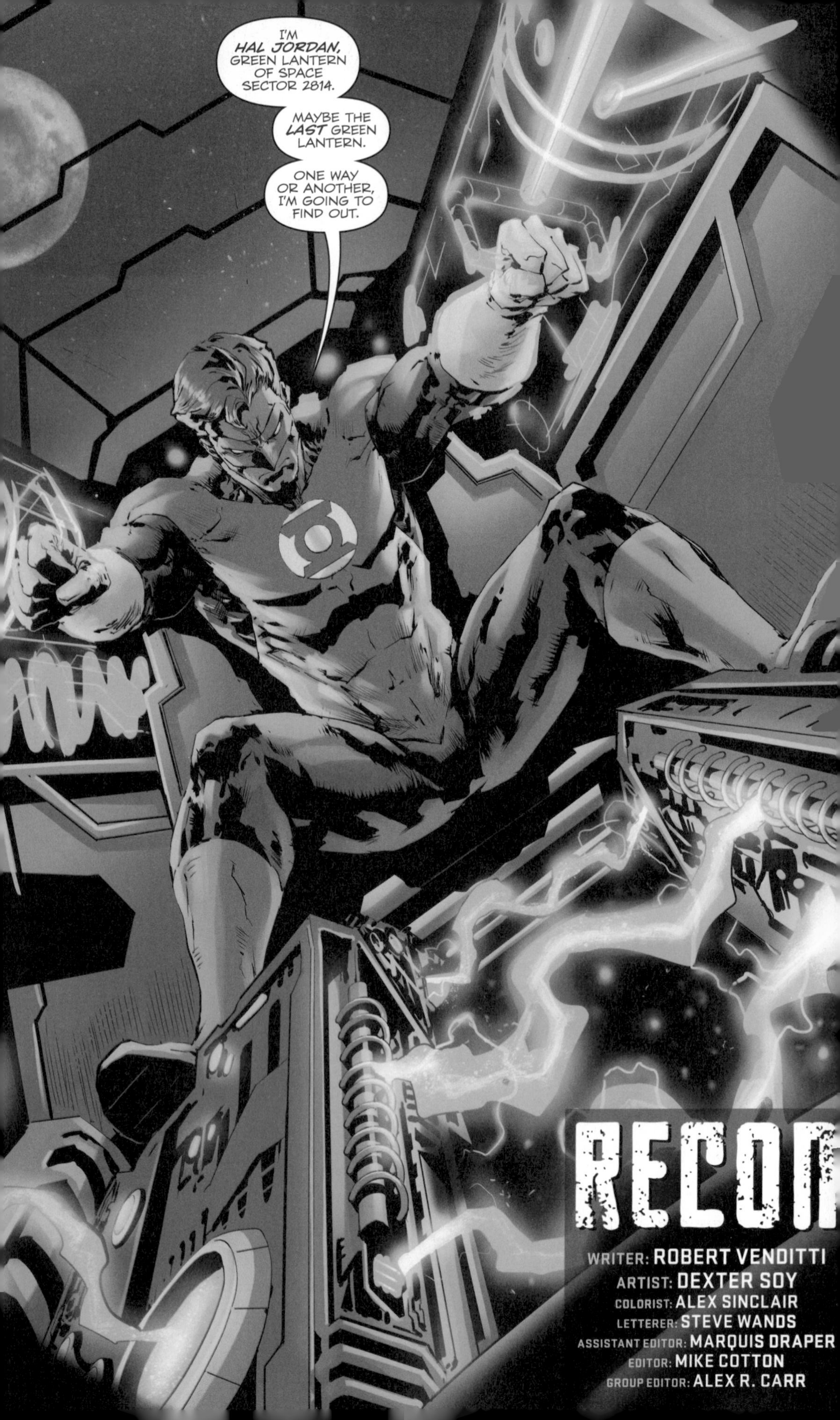
I'M HAL JORDAN, GREEN LANTERN OF SPACE SECTOR 2814.
MAYBE THE LAST GREEN LANTERN.
ONE WAY OR ANOTHER, I'M GOING TO FIND OUT.
RECON
WRITER: ROBERT VENDITTI
ARTIST: DEXTER SOY
COLORIST: ALEX SINCLAIR
LETTERER: STEVE WANDS
ASSISTANT EDITOR: MARQUIS DRAPER
EDITOR: MIKE COTTON
GROUP EDITOR: ALEX R. CARR

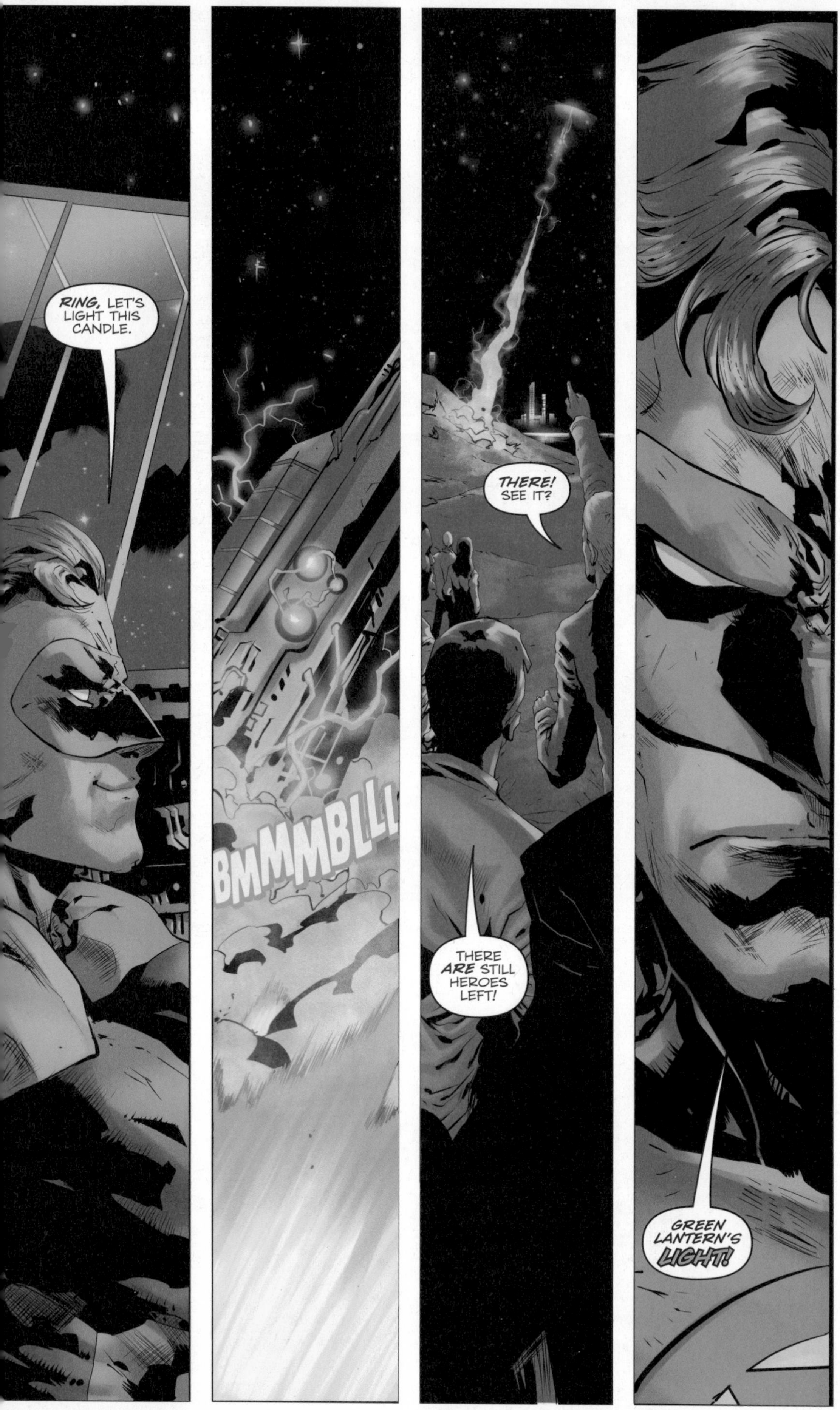
RING, LET'S LIGHT THIS CANDLE.
BMMMBLLL
THERE! SEE IT?
THERE ARE STILL HEROES LEFT!
GREEN LANTERN'S LIGHT!

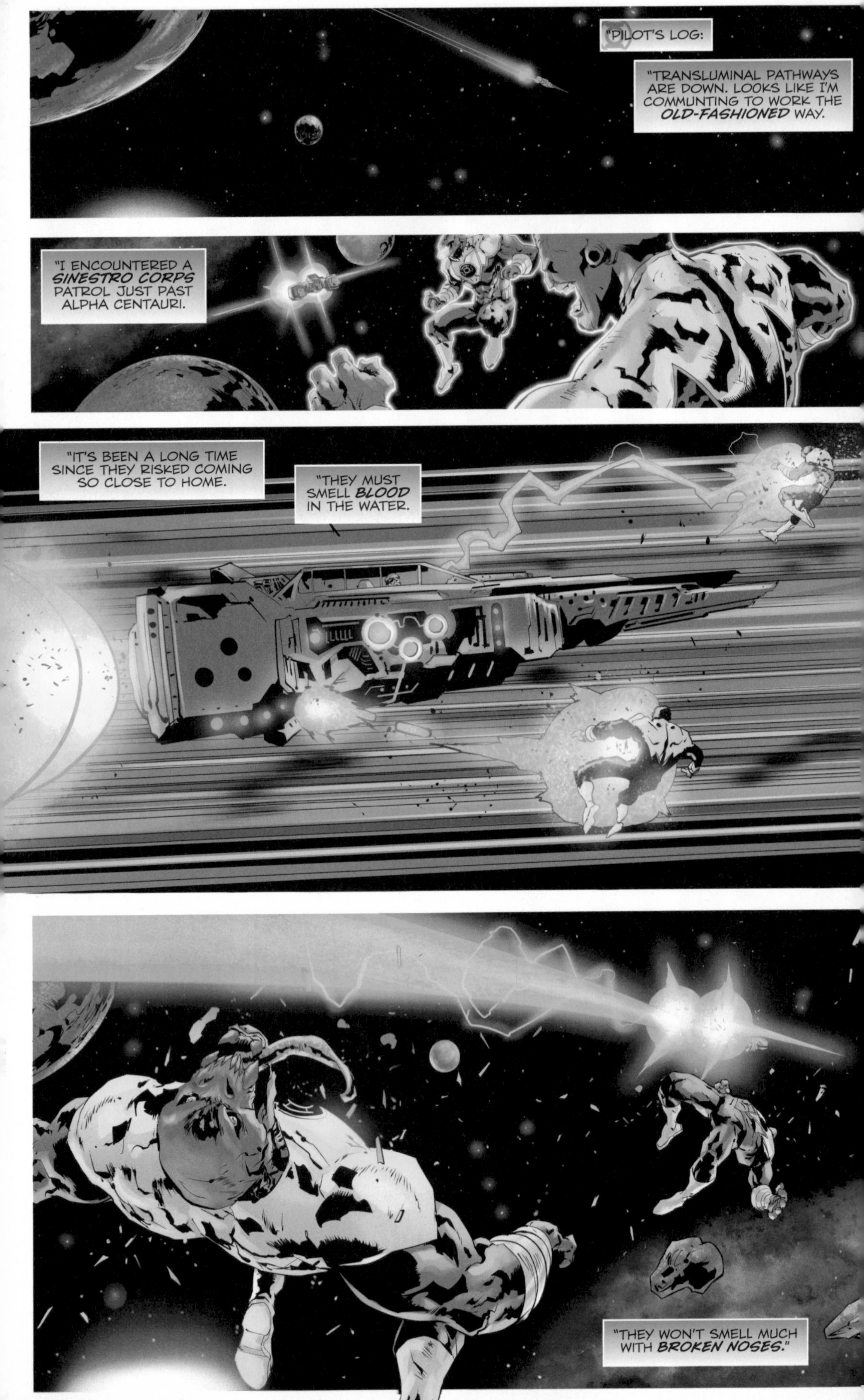
"PILOT'S LOG:
"TRANSLUMINAL PATHWAYS ARE DOWN. LOOKS LIKE I'M COMMUNTING TO WORK THE *OLD-FASHIONED* WAY.
"I ENCOUNTERED A *SINESTRO CORPS* PATROL JUST PAST ALPHA CENTAURI.
"IT'S BEEN A LONG TIME SINCE THEY RISKED COMING SO CLOSE TO HOME.
"THEY MUST SMELL *BLOOD* IN THE WATER.
"THEY WON'T SMELL MUCH WITH *BROKEN NOSES*."

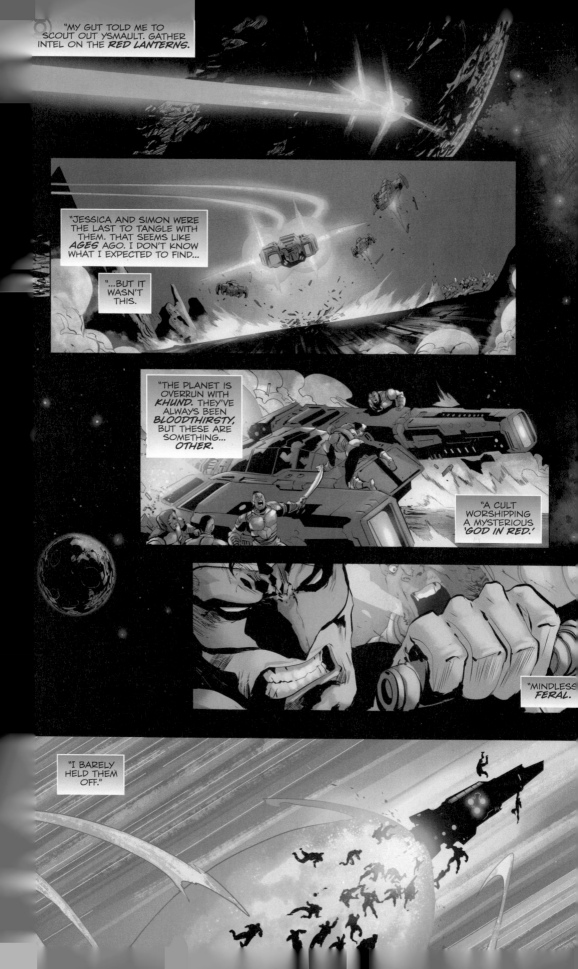

"MY GUT TOLD ME TO SCOUT OUT YSMAULT. GATHER INTEL ON THE *RED LANTERNS*.

"JESSICA AND SIMON WERE THE LAST TO TANGLE WITH THEM. THAT SEEMS LIKE *AGES* AGO. I DON'T KNOW WHAT I EXPECTED TO FIND...

"...BUT IT WASN'T THIS.

"THE PLANET IS OVERRUN WITH *KHUND*. THEY''VE ALWAYS BEEN *BLOODTHIRSTY*, BUT THESE ARE SOMETHING... *OTHER*.

"A CULT WORSHIPPING A MYSTERIOUS *'GOD IN RED.'*

"MINDLESS. *FERAL*.

"I BARELY HELD THEM OFF."

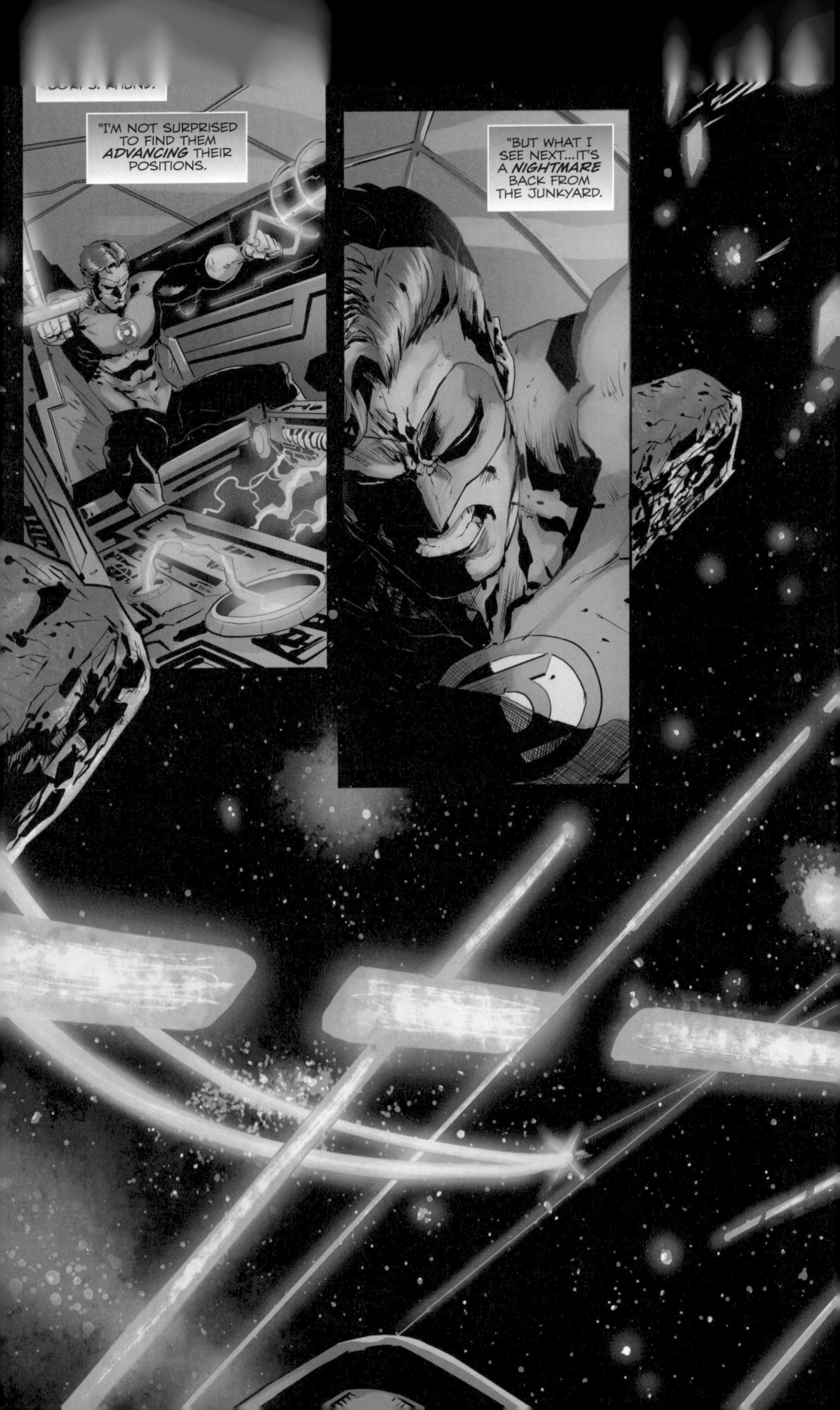
"I'M NOT SURPRISED TO FIND THEM ADVANCING THEIR POSITIONS.
"BUT WHAT I SEE NEXT...IT'S A NIGHTMARE BACK FROM THE JUNKYARD.

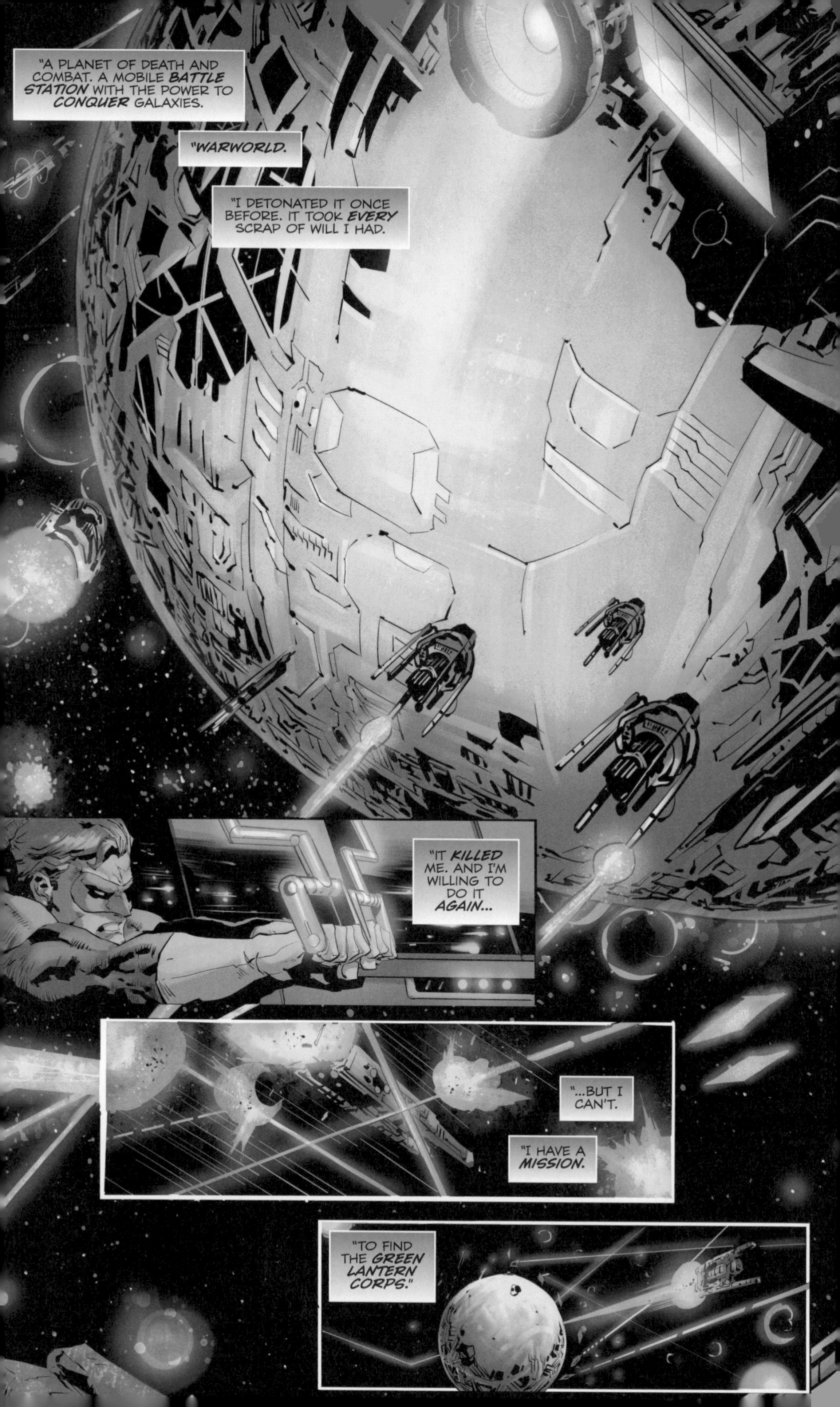
"A PLANET OF DEATH AND COMBAT. A MOBILE BATTLE STATION WITH THE POWER TO CONQUER GALAXIES.
"WARWORLD.
"I DETONATED IT ONCE BEFORE. IT TOOK EVERY SCRAP OF WILL I HAD.
"IT KILLED ME. AND I'M WILLING TO DO IT AGAIN...
"...BUT I CAN'T.
"I HAVE A MISSION.
"TO FIND THE GREEN LANTERN CORPS."

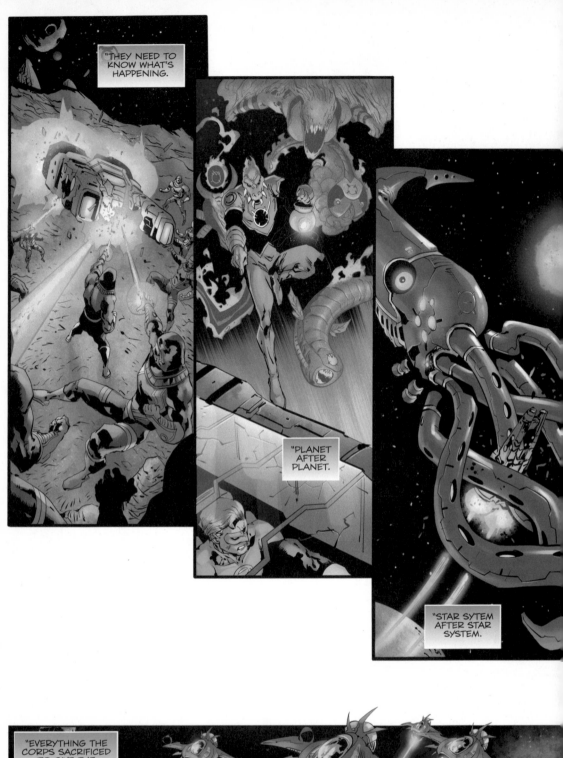

"THEY NEED TO KNOW WHAT'S HAPPENING.

"PLANET AFTER PLANET.

"STAR SYTEM AFTER STAR SYSTEM.

"EVERYTHING THE CORPS SACRIFICED TO GIVE THE UNIVERSE *PEACE* AND *SECURITY*.

"IT'S *ALL* COMING APART."

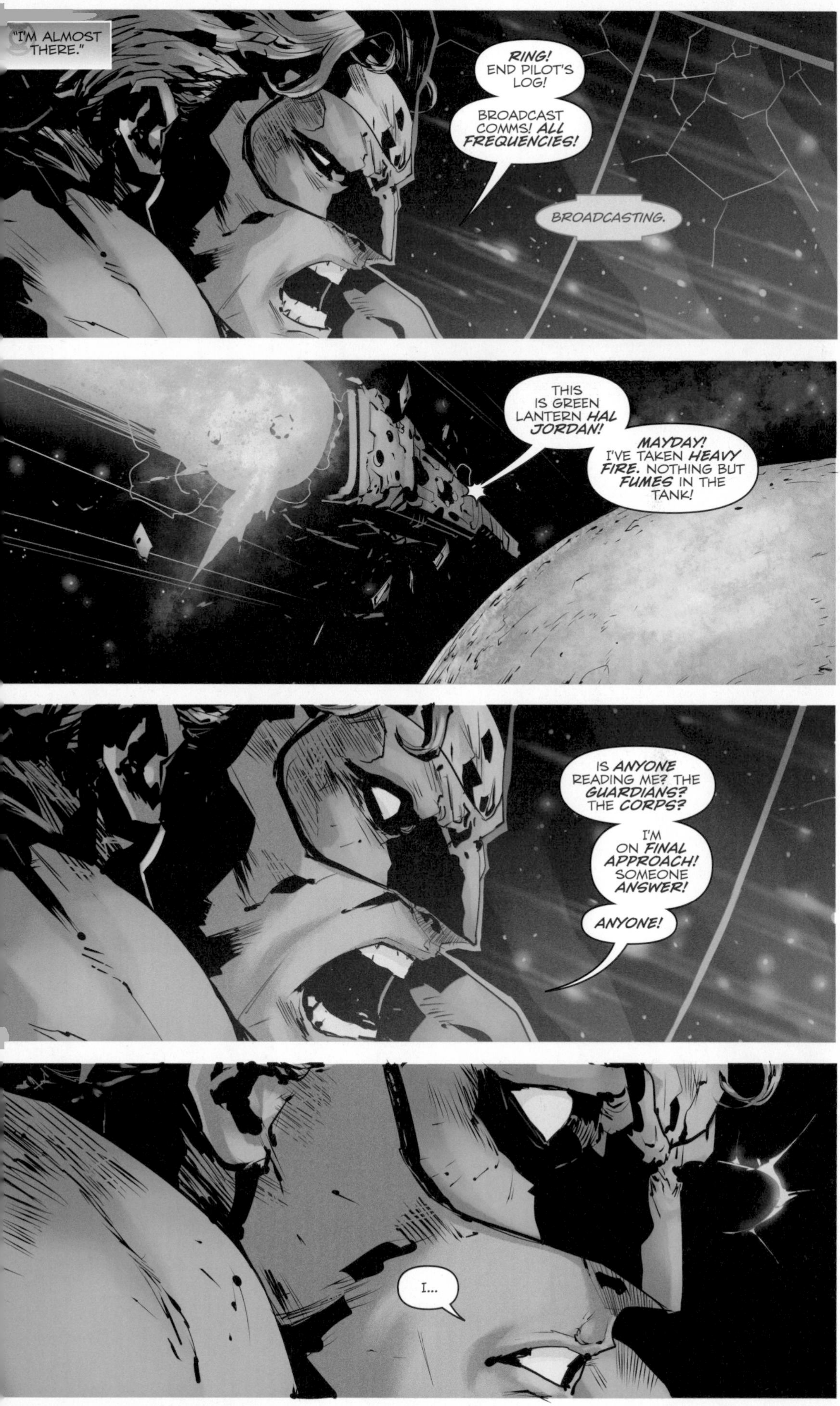
"I'M ALMOST THERE."
RING! END PILOT'S LOG!
BROADCAST COMMS! ALL FREQUENCIES!
BROADCASTING.
THIS IS GREEN LANTERN HAL JORDAN!
MAYDAY! I'VE TAKEN HEAVY FIRE. NOTHING BUT FUMES IN THE TANK!
IS ANYONE READING ME? THE GUARDIANS? THE CORPS?
I'M ON FINAL APPROACH! SOMEONE ANSWER!
ANYONE!
I...

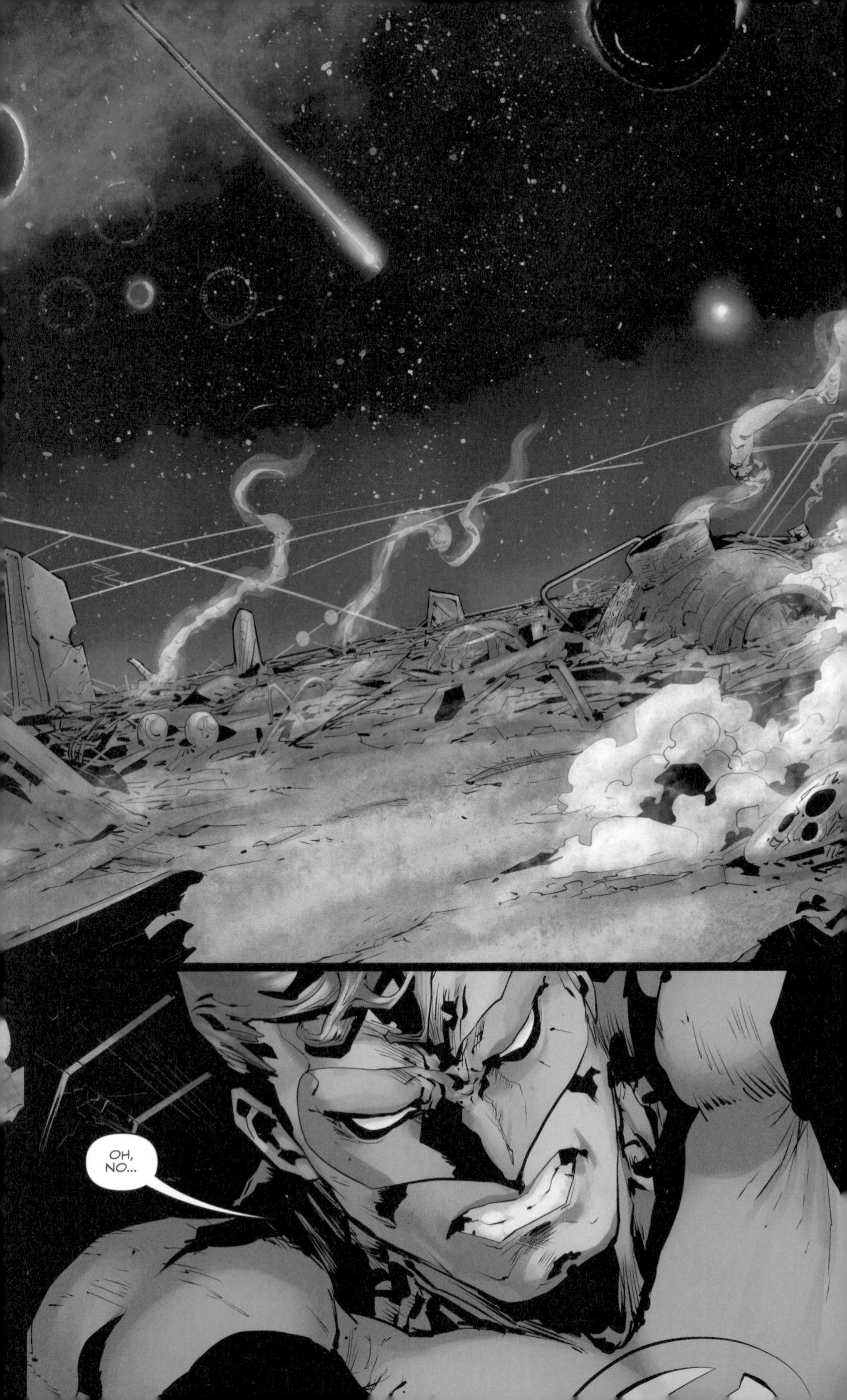
OH, NO...

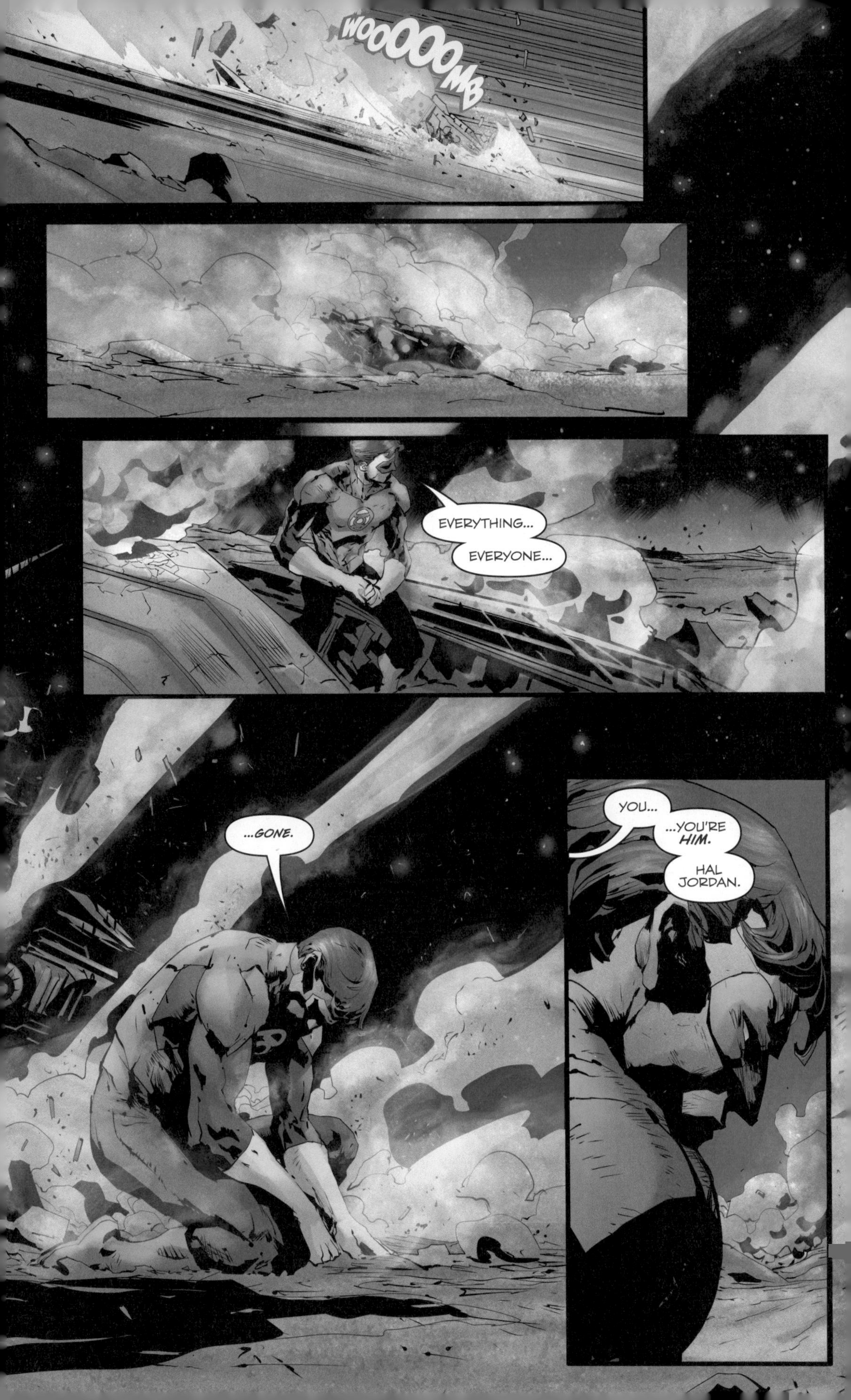
WOOOOOMB
EVERYTHING...
EVERYONE...
...GONE.
YOU...
...YOU'RE HIM.
HAL JORDAN.

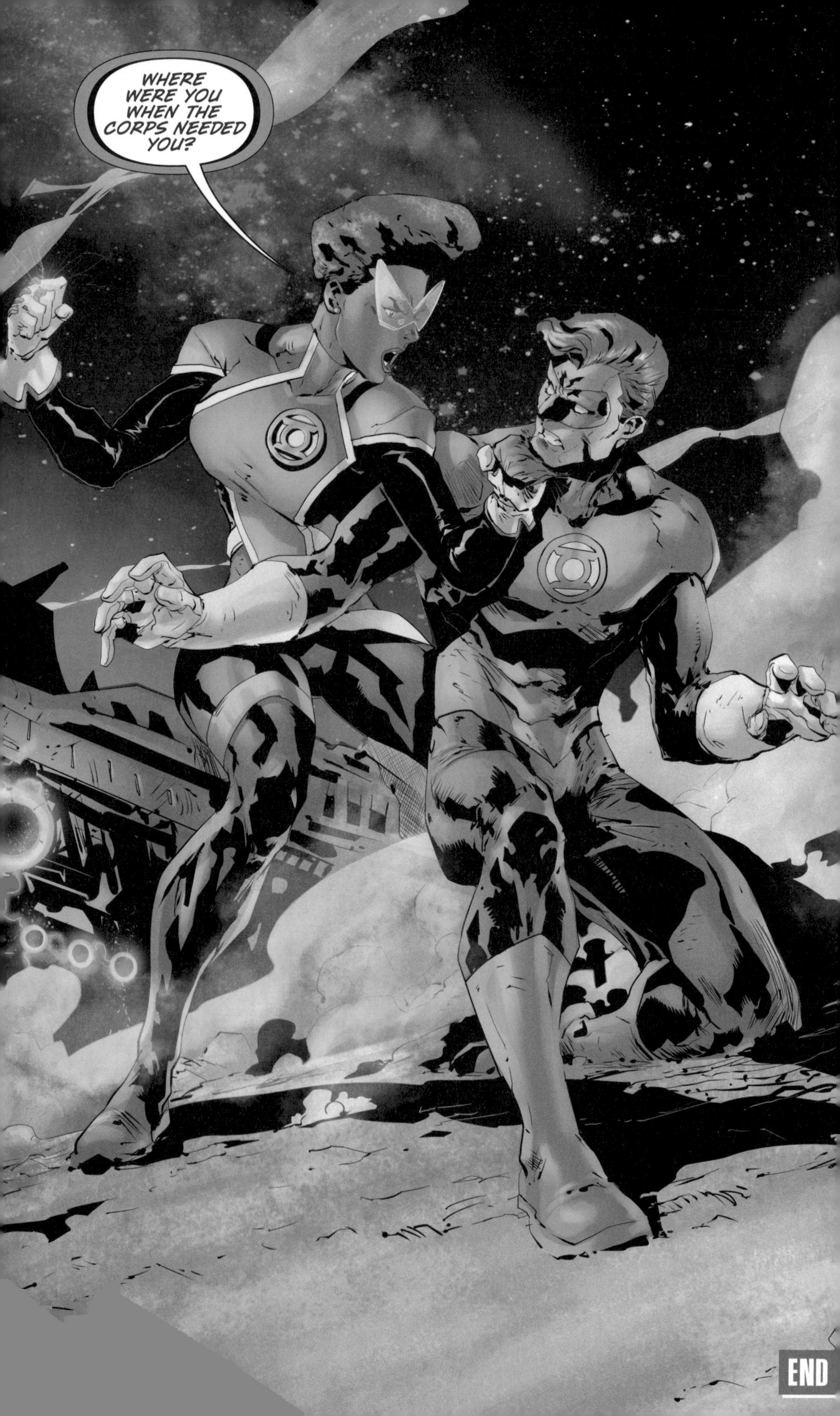
WHERE WERE YOU WHEN THE CORPS NEEDED YOU?
END

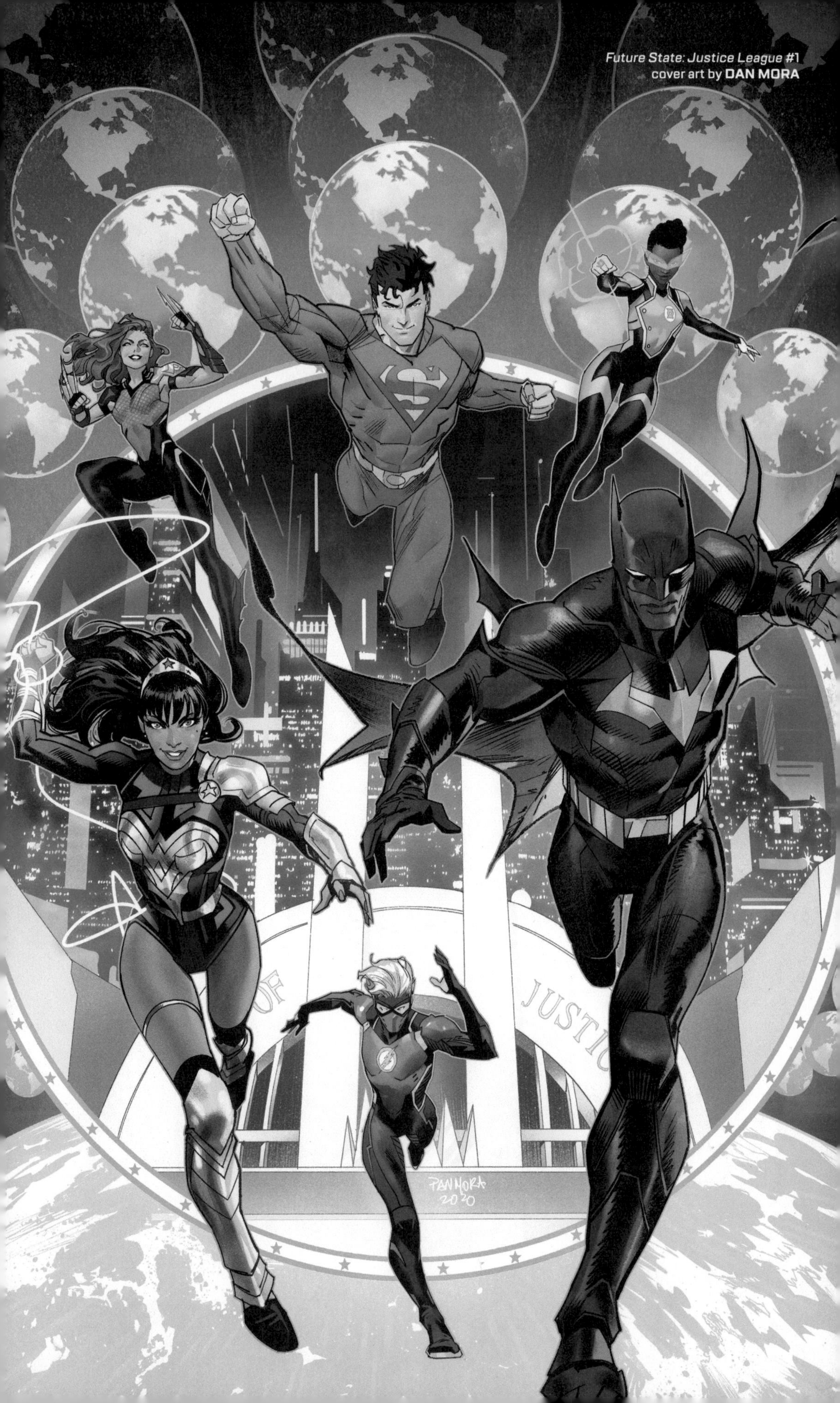
DAN MORA
2020

Future State: Justice League #1
cover art by **DAN MORA**

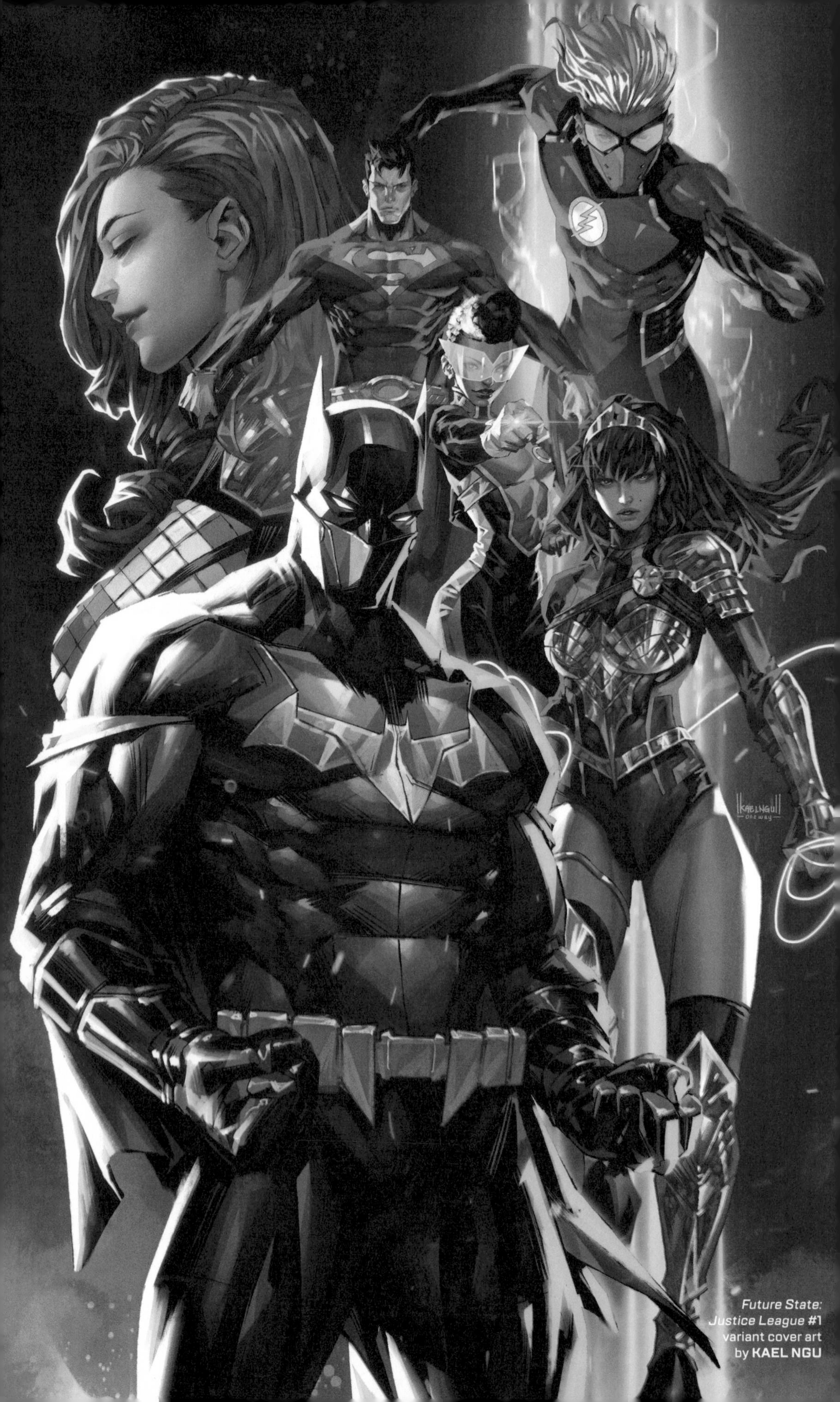

Future State: Justice League #1 variant cover art by **KAEL NGU**

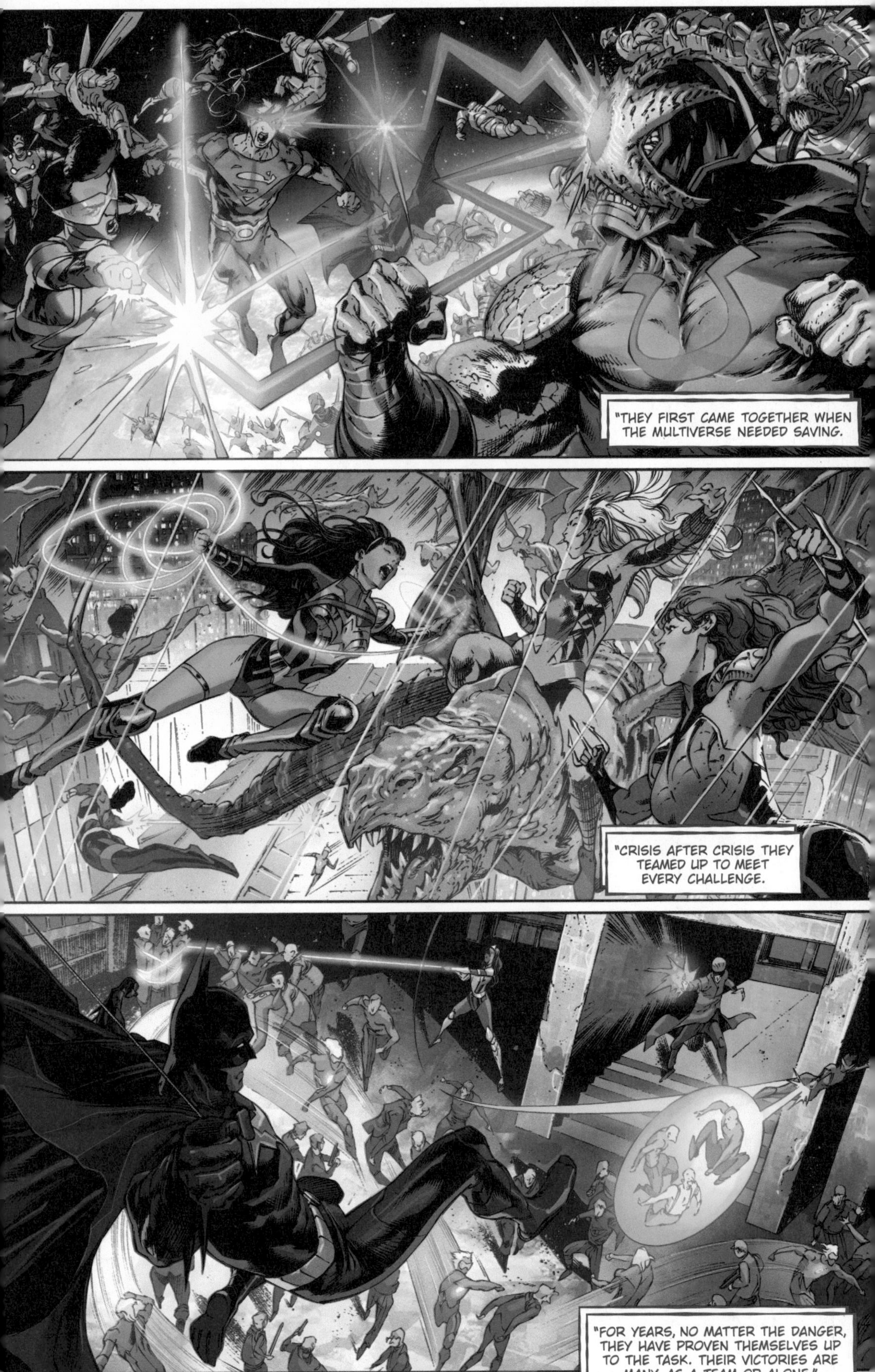
"THEY FIRST CAME TOGETHER WHEN THE MULTIVERSE NEEDED SAVING.
"CRISIS AFTER CRISIS THEY TEAMED UP TO MEET EVERY CHALLENGE.
"FOR YEARS, NO MATTER THE DANGER, THEY HAVE PROVEN THEMSELVES UP TO THE TASK. THEIR VICTORIES ARE MANY, AS A TEAM OR ALONE."

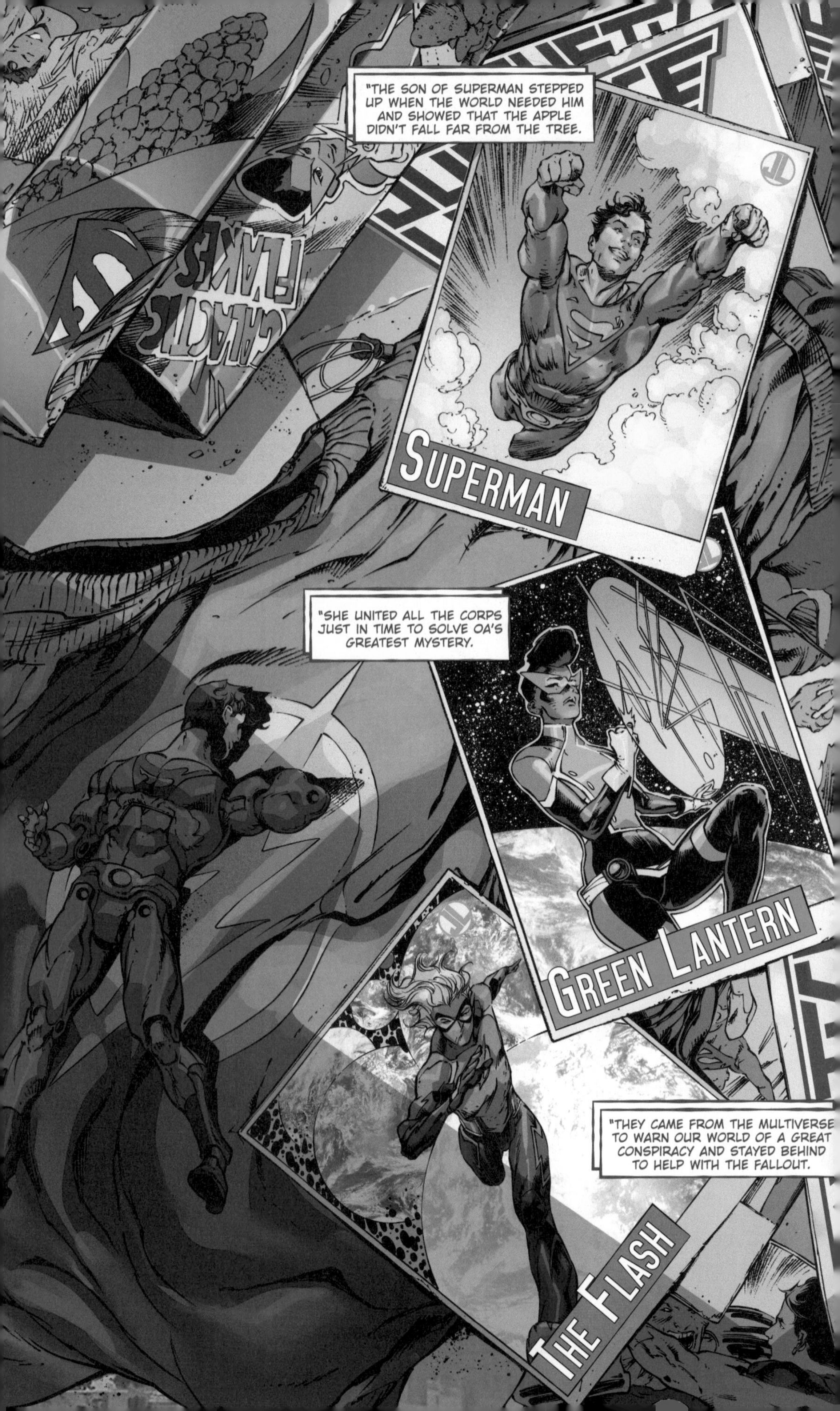
"THE SON OF SUPERMAN STEPPED UP WHEN THE WORLD NEEDED HIM AND SHOWED THAT THE APPLE DIDN'T FALL FAR FROM THE TREE.
SUPERMAN
"SHE UNITED ALL THE CORPS JUST IN TIME TO SOLVE OA'S GREATEST MYSTERY.
GREEN LANTERN
"THEY CAME FROM THE MULTIVERSE TO WARN OUR WORLD OF A GREAT CONSPIRACY AND STAYED BEHIND TO HELP WITH THE FALLOUT.
THE FLASH

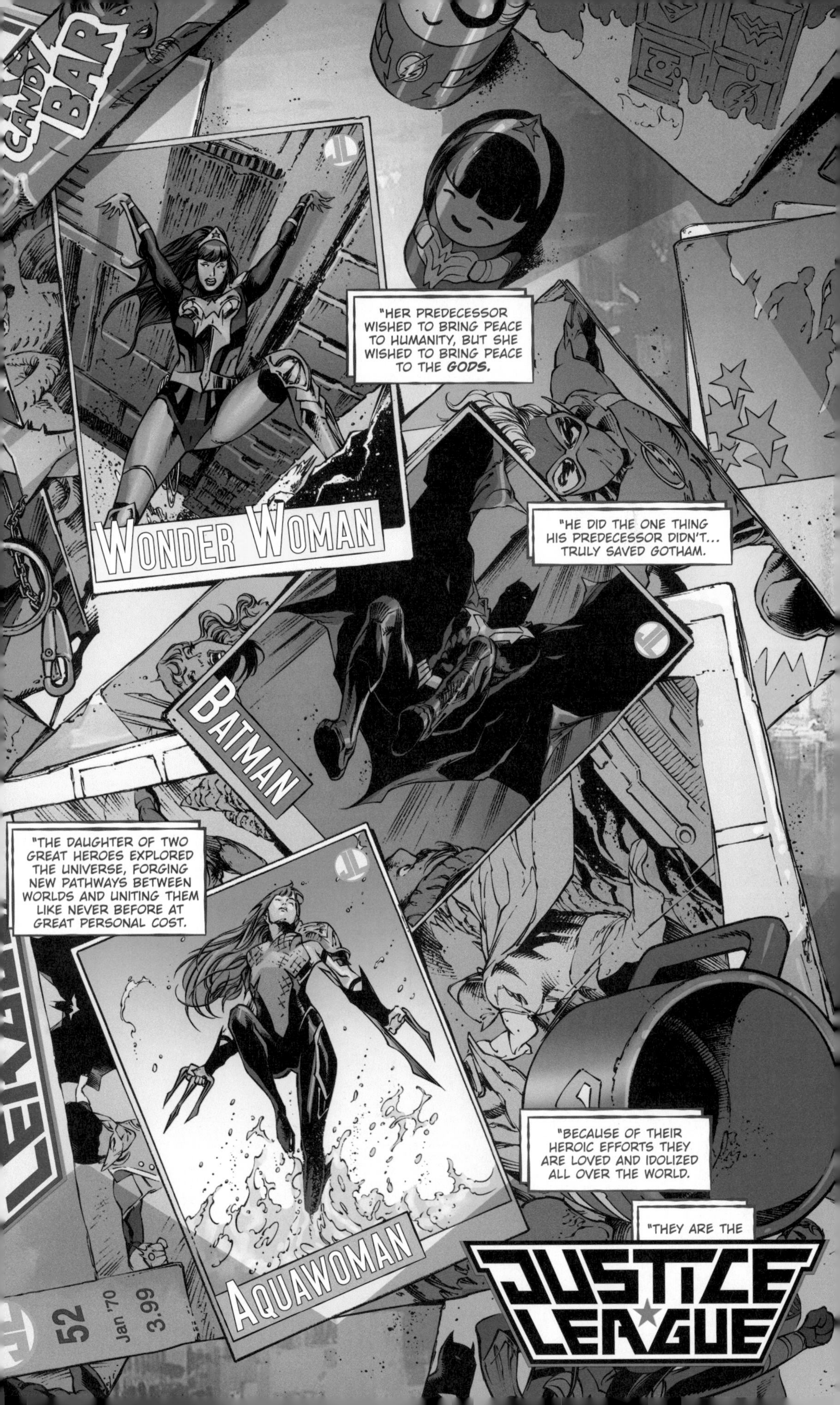
CANDY BAR
"HER PREDECESSOR WISHED TO BRING PEACE TO HUMANITY, BUT SHE WISHED TO BRING PEACE TO THE GODS.
WONDER WOMAN
"HE DID THE ONE THING HIS PREDECESSOR DIDN'T... TRULY SAVED GOTHAM.
BATMAN
"THE DAUGHTER OF TWO GREAT HEROES EXPLORED THE UNIVERSE, FORGING NEW PATHWAYS BETWEEN WORLDS AND UNITING THEM LIKE NEVER BEFORE AT GREAT PERSONAL COST.
AQUAWOMAN
52
Jan '70
3.99
"BECAUSE OF THEIR HEROIC EFFORTS THEY ARE LOVED AND IDOLIZED ALL OVER THE WORLD.
"THEY ARE THE
JUSTICE LEAGUE

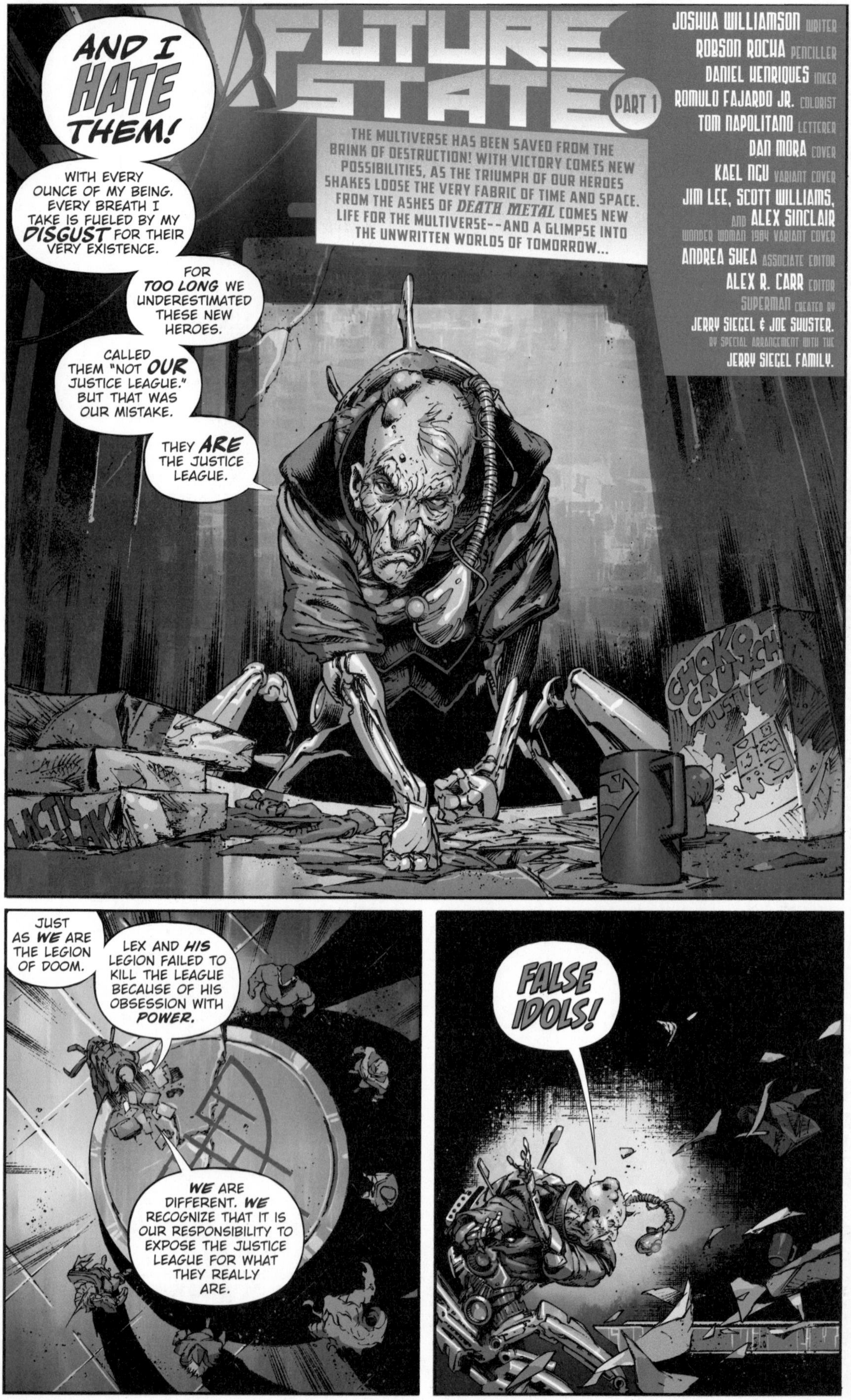
AND I HATE THEM!
WITH EVERY OUNCE OF MY BEING. EVERY BREATH I TAKE IS FUELED BY MY DISGUST FOR THEIR VERY EXISTENCE.
FOR TOO LONG WE UNDERESTIMATED THESE NEW HEROES.
CALLED THEM "NOT OUR JUSTICE LEAGUE." BUT THAT WAS OUR MISTAKE.
THEY ARE THE JUSTICE LEAGUE.
FUTURE STATE
PART 1
THE MULTIVERSE HAS BEEN SAVED FROM THE BRINK OF DESTRUCTION! WITH VICTORY COMES NEW POSSIBILITIES, AS THE TRIUMPH OF OUR HEROES SHAKES LOOSE THE VERY FABRIC OF TIME AND SPACE. FROM THE ASHES OF DEATH METAL COMES NEW LIFE FOR THE MULTIVERSE--AND A GLIMPSE INTO THE UNWRITTEN WORLDS OF TOMORROW...
JOSHUA WILLIAMSON WRITER
ROBSON ROCHA PENCILLER
DANIEL HENRIQUES INKER
ROMULO FAJARDO JR. COLORIST
TOM NAPOLITANO LETTERER
DAN MORA COVER
KAEL NGU VARIANT COVER
JIM LEE, SCOTT WILLIAMS, AND ALEX SINCLAIR
WONDER WOMAN 1984 VARIANT COVER
ANDREA SHEA ASSOCIATE EDITOR
ALEX R. CARR EDITOR
SUPERMAN CREATED BY
JERRY SIEGEL & JOE SHUSTER.
BY SPECIAL ARRANGEMENT WITH THE
JERRY SIEGEL FAMILY.
CHOKO CRUNCH
JUSTICE
JUST AS WE ARE THE LEGION OF DOOM.
LEX AND HIS LEGION FAILED TO KILL THE LEAGUE BECAUSE OF HIS OBSESSION WITH POWER.
WE ARE DIFFERENT. WE RECOGNIZE THAT IT IS OUR RESPONSIBILITY TO EXPOSE THE JUSTICE LEAGUE FOR WHAT THEY REALLY ARE.
FALSE IDOLS!

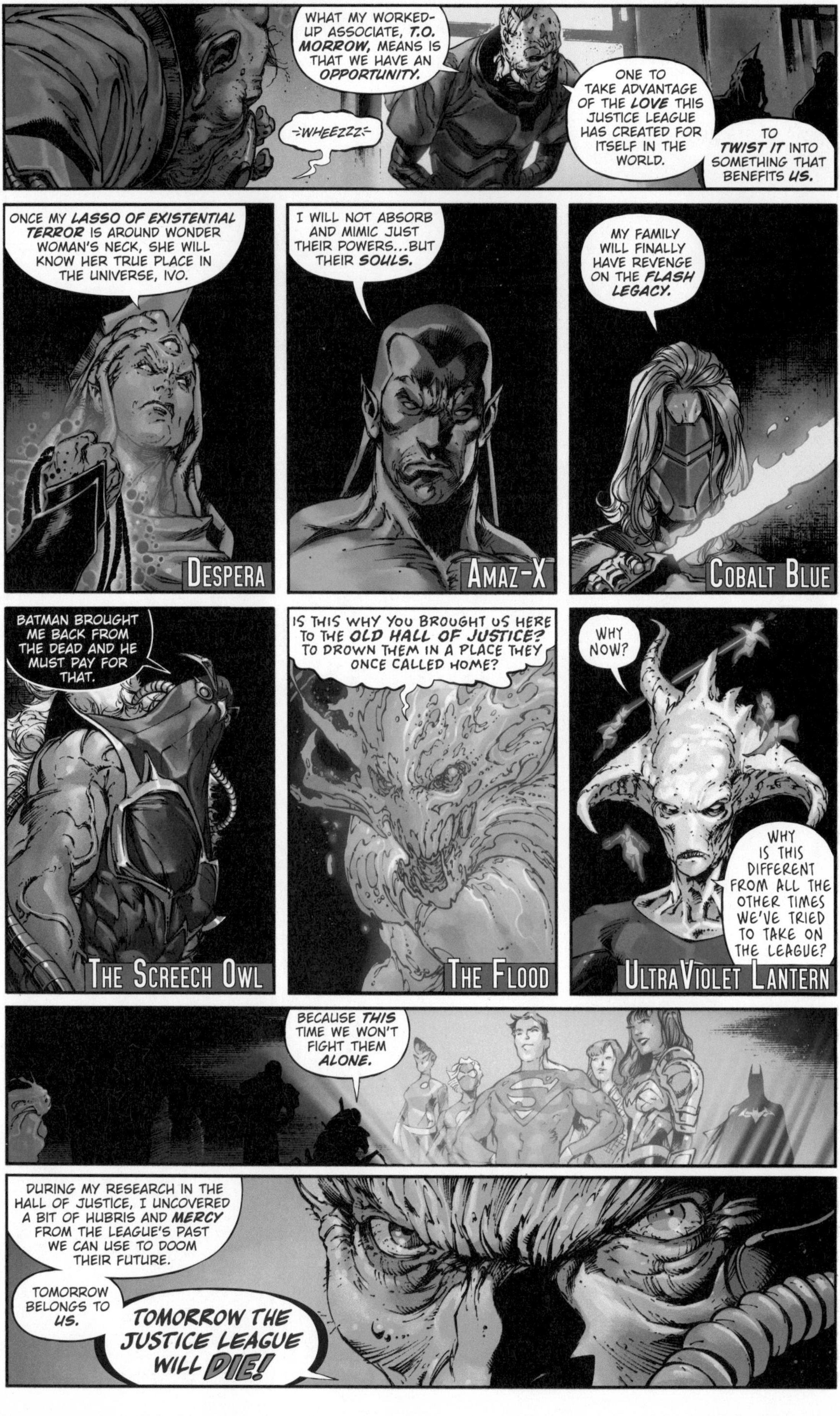
WHAT MY WORKED-UP ASSOCIATE, T.O. MORROW, MEANS IS THAT WE HAVE AN OPPORTUNITY.
-WHEEZZZ-
ONE TO TAKE ADVANTAGE OF THE LOVE THIS JUSTICE LEAGUE HAS CREATED FOR ITSELF IN THE WORLD.
TO TWIST IT INTO SOMETHING THAT BENEFITS US.
ONCE MY LASSO OF EXISTENTIAL TERROR IS AROUND WONDER WOMAN'S NECK, SHE WILL KNOW HER TRUE PLACE IN THE UNIVERSE, IVO.
DESPERA
I WILL NOT ABSORB AND MIMIC JUST THEIR POWERS...BUT THEIR SOULS.
AMAZ-X
MY FAMILY WILL FINALLY HAVE REVENGE ON THE FLASH LEGACY.
COBALT BLUE
BATMAN BROUGHT ME BACK FROM THE DEAD AND HE MUST PAY FOR THAT.
THE SCREECH OWL
IS THIS WHY YOU BROUGHT US HERE TO THE OLD HALL OF JUSTICE? TO DROWN THEM IN A PLACE THEY ONCE CALLED HOME?
THE FLOOD
WHY NOW?
WHY IS THIS DIFFERENT FROM ALL THE OTHER TIMES WE'VE TRIED TO TAKE ON THE LEAGUE?
ULTRAVIOLET LANTERN
BECAUSE THIS TIME WE WON'T FIGHT THEM ALONE.
DURING MY RESEARCH IN THE HALL OF JUSTICE, I UNCOVERED A BIT OF HUBRIS AND MERCY FROM THE LEAGUE'S PAST WE CAN USE TO DOOM THEIR FUTURE.
TOMORROW BELONGS TO US.
TOMORROW THE JUSTICE LEAGUE WILL DIE!

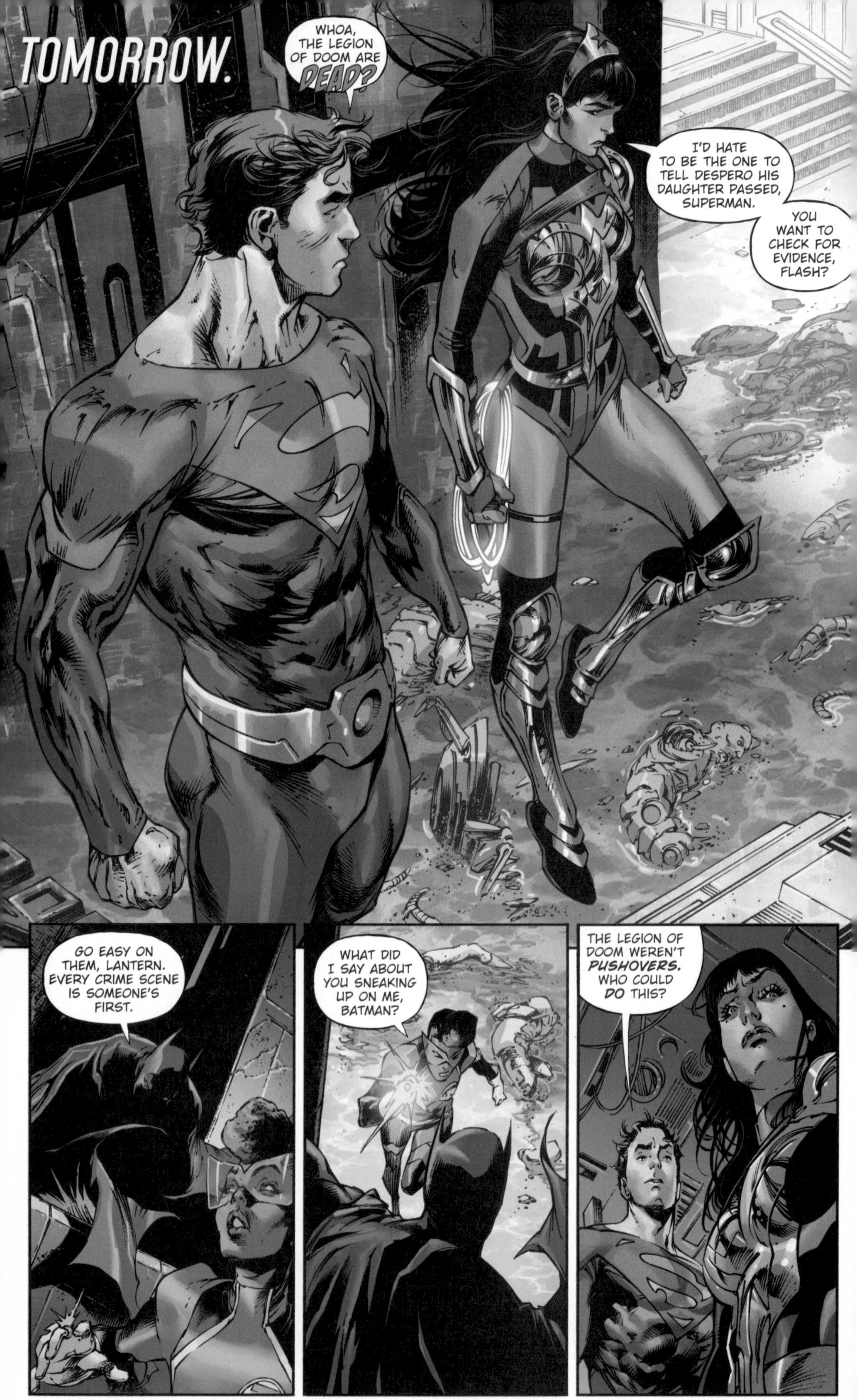
TOMORROW.
WHOA, THE LEGION OF DOOM ARE DEAD?
I'D HATE TO BE THE ONE TO TELL DESPERO HIS DAUGHTER PASSED, SUPERMAN.
YOU WANT TO CHECK FOR EVIDENCE, FLASH?
GO EASY ON THEM, LANTERN. EVERY CRIME SCENE IS SOMEONE'S FIRST.
WHAT DID I SAY ABOUT YOU SNEAKING UP ON ME, BATMAN?
THE LEGION OF DOOM WEREN'T PUSHOVERS. WHO COULD DO THIS?

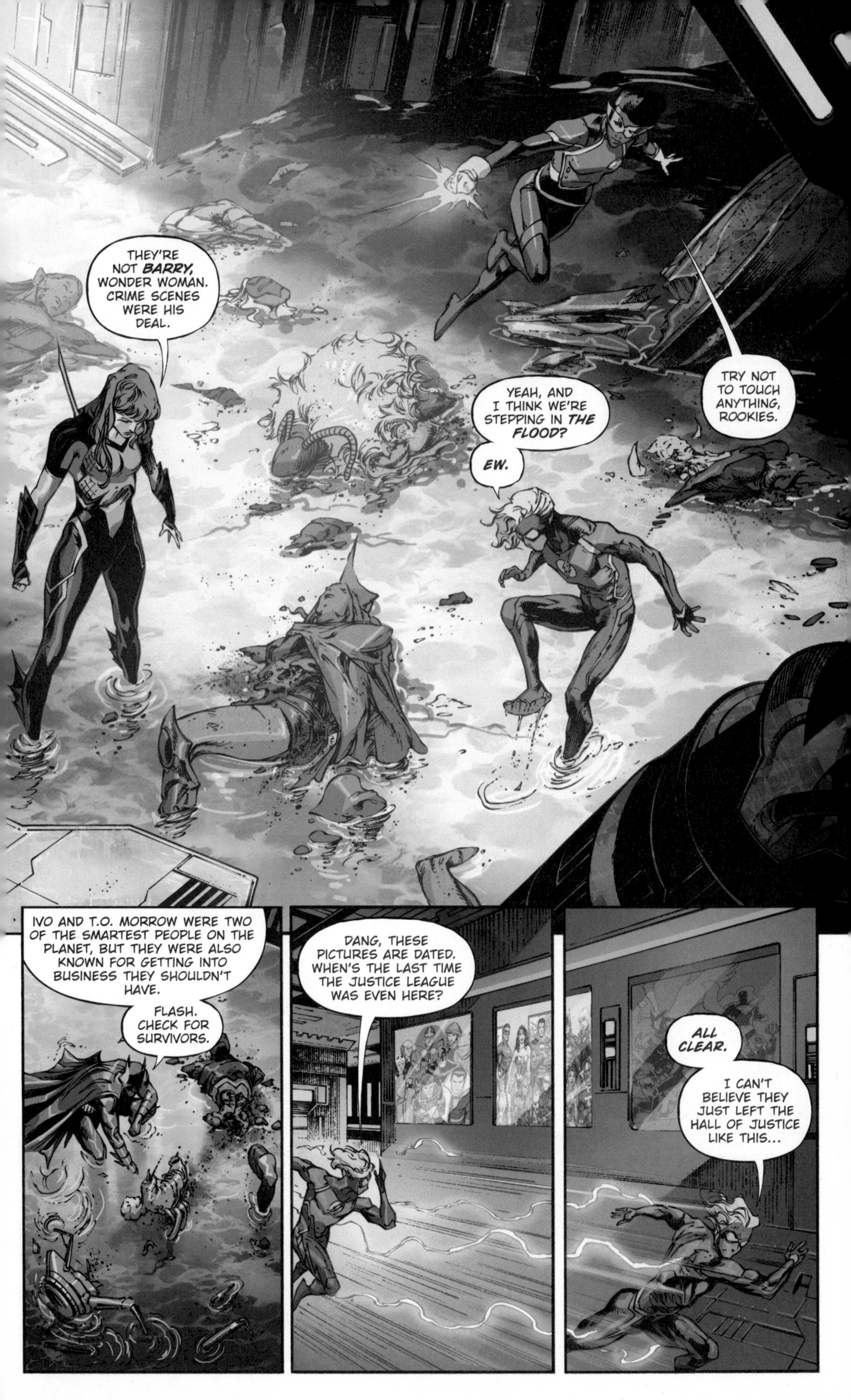
THEY'RE NOT BARRY, WONDER WOMAN. CRIME SCENES WERE HIS DEAL.
TRY NOT TO TOUCH ANYTHING, ROOKIES.
YEAH, AND I THINK WE'RE STEPPING IN THE FLOOD?
EW.
IVO AND T.O. MORROW WERE TWO OF THE SMARTEST PEOPLE ON THE PLANET, BUT THEY WERE ALSO KNOWN FOR GETTING INTO BUSINESS THEY SHOULDN'T HAVE.
FLASH. CHECK FOR SURVIVORS.
DANG, THESE PICTURES ARE DATED. WHEN'S THE LAST TIME THE JUSTICE LEAGUE WAS EVEN HERE?
ALL CLEAR.
I CAN'T BELIEVE THEY JUST LEFT THE HALL OF JUSTICE LIKE THIS...

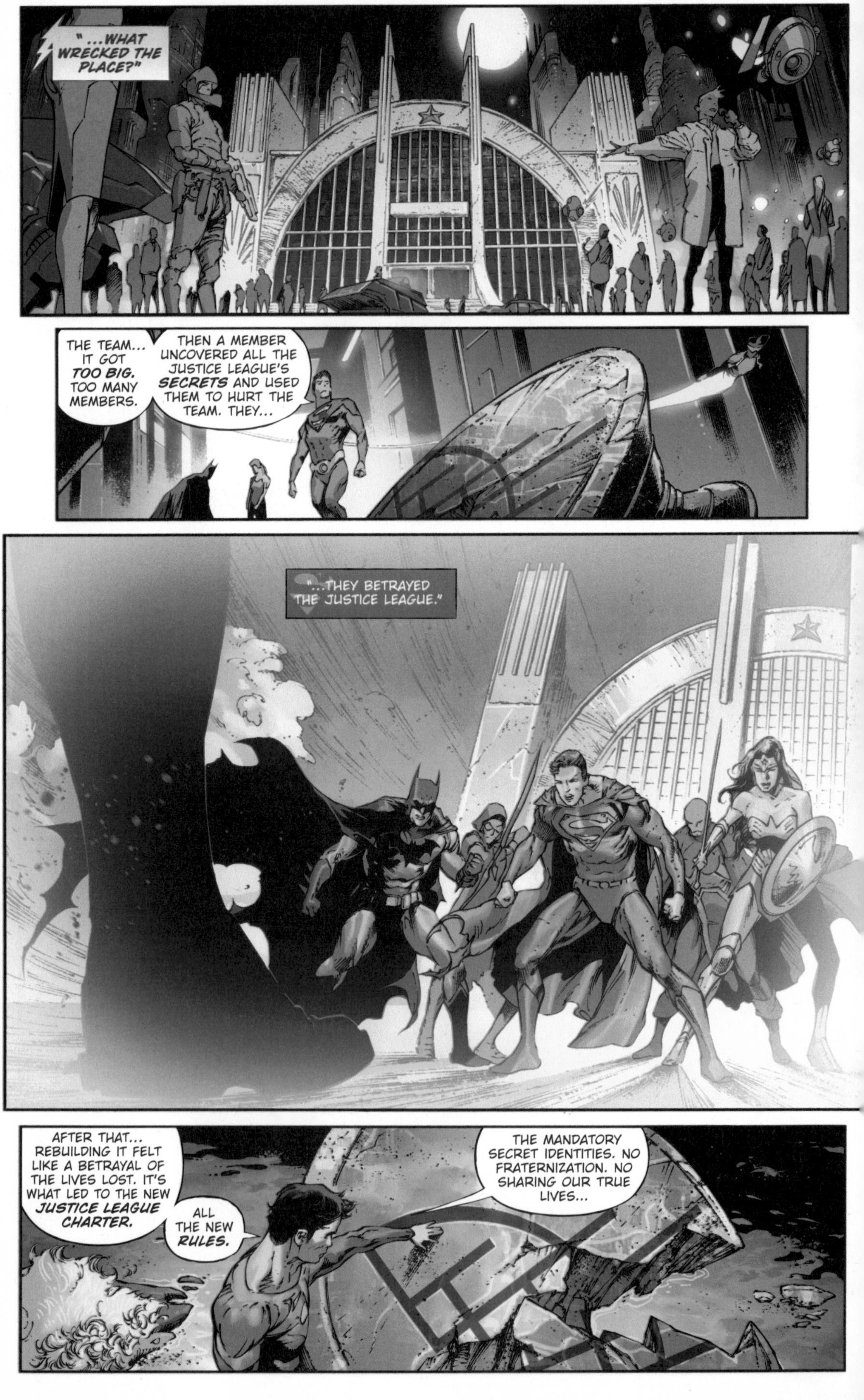
"...WHAT WRECKED THE PLACE?"
THE TEAM... IT GOT TOO BIG. TOO MANY MEMBERS.
THEN A MEMBER UNCOVERED ALL THE JUSTICE LEAGUE'S SECRETS AND USED THEM TO HURT THE TEAM. THEY...
"...THEY BETRAYED THE JUSTICE LEAGUE."
AFTER THAT... REBUILDING IT FELT LIKE A BETRAYAL OF THE LIVES LOST. IT'S WHAT LED TO THE NEW JUSTICE LEAGUE CHARTER.
ALL THE NEW RULES.
THE MANDATORY SECRET IDENTITIES. NO FRATERNIZATION. NO SHARING OUR TRUE LIVES...

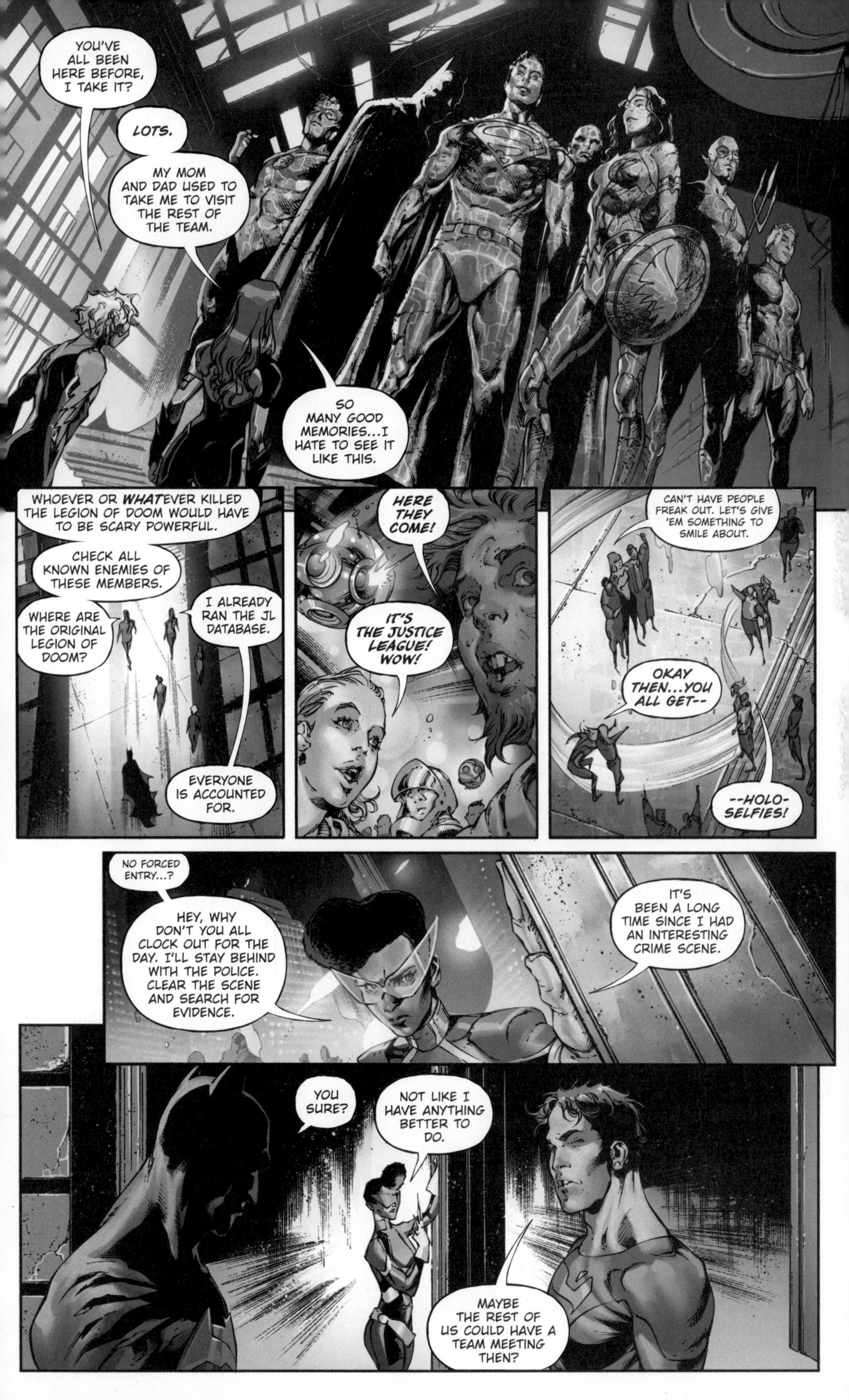

YOU'VE ALL BEEN HERE BEFORE, I TAKE IT?
LOTS.
MY MOM AND DAD USED TO TAKE ME TO VISIT THE REST OF THE TEAM.
SO MANY GOOD MEMORIES...I HATE TO SEE IT LIKE THIS.
WHOEVER OR WHATEVER KILLED THE LEGION OF DOOM WOULD HAVE TO BE SCARY POWERFUL.
CHECK ALL KNOWN ENEMIES OF THESE MEMBERS.
WHERE ARE THE ORIGINAL LEGION OF DOOM?
I ALREADY RAN THE JL DATABASE.
EVERYONE IS ACCOUNTED FOR.
HERE THEY COME!
IT'S THE JUSTICE LEAGUE! WOW!
CAN'T HAVE PEOPLE FREAK OUT. LET'S GIVE 'EM SOMETHING TO SMILE ABOUT.
OKAY THEN...YOU ALL GET--
--HOLO-SELFIES!
NO FORCED ENTRY...?
HEY, WHY DON'T YOU ALL CLOCK OUT FOR THE DAY. I'LL STAY BEHIND WITH THE POLICE. CLEAR THE SCENE AND SEARCH FOR EVIDENCE.
IT'S BEEN A LONG TIME SINCE I HAD AN INTERESTING CRIME SCENE.
YOU SURE?
NOT LIKE I HAVE ANYTHING BETTER TO DO.
MAYBE THE REST OF US COULD HAVE A TEAM MEETING THEN?

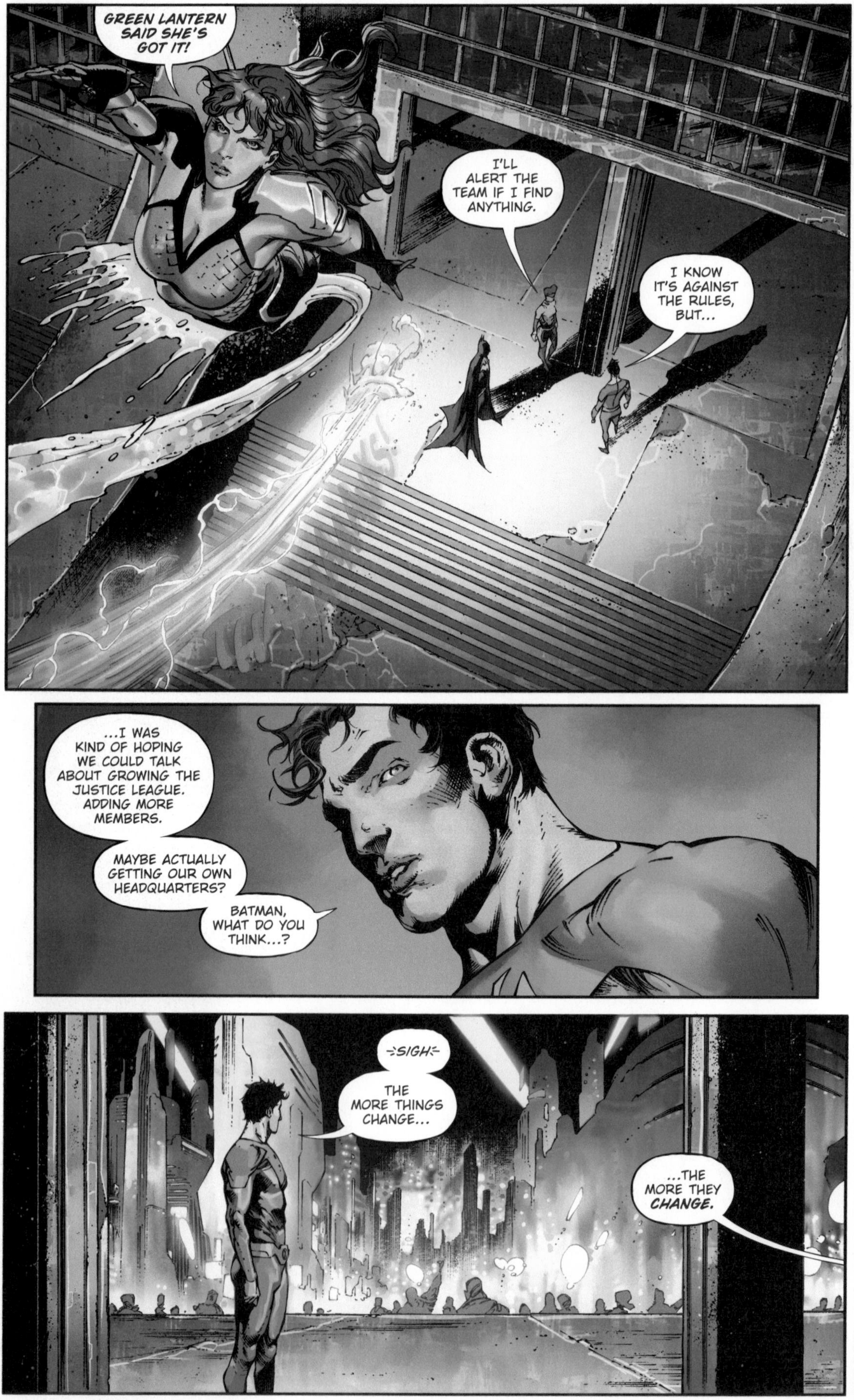
GREEN LANTERN SAID SHE'S GOT IT!
I'LL ALERT THE TEAM IF I FIND ANYTHING.
I KNOW IT'S AGAINST THE RULES, BUT...
...I WAS KIND OF HOPING WE COULD TALK ABOUT GROWING THE JUSTICE LEAGUE. ADDING MORE MEMBERS.
MAYBE ACTUALLY GETTING OUR OWN HEADQUARTERS?
BATMAN, WHAT DO YOU THINK...?
SIGH
THE MORE THINGS CHANGE...
...THE MORE THEY CHANGE.

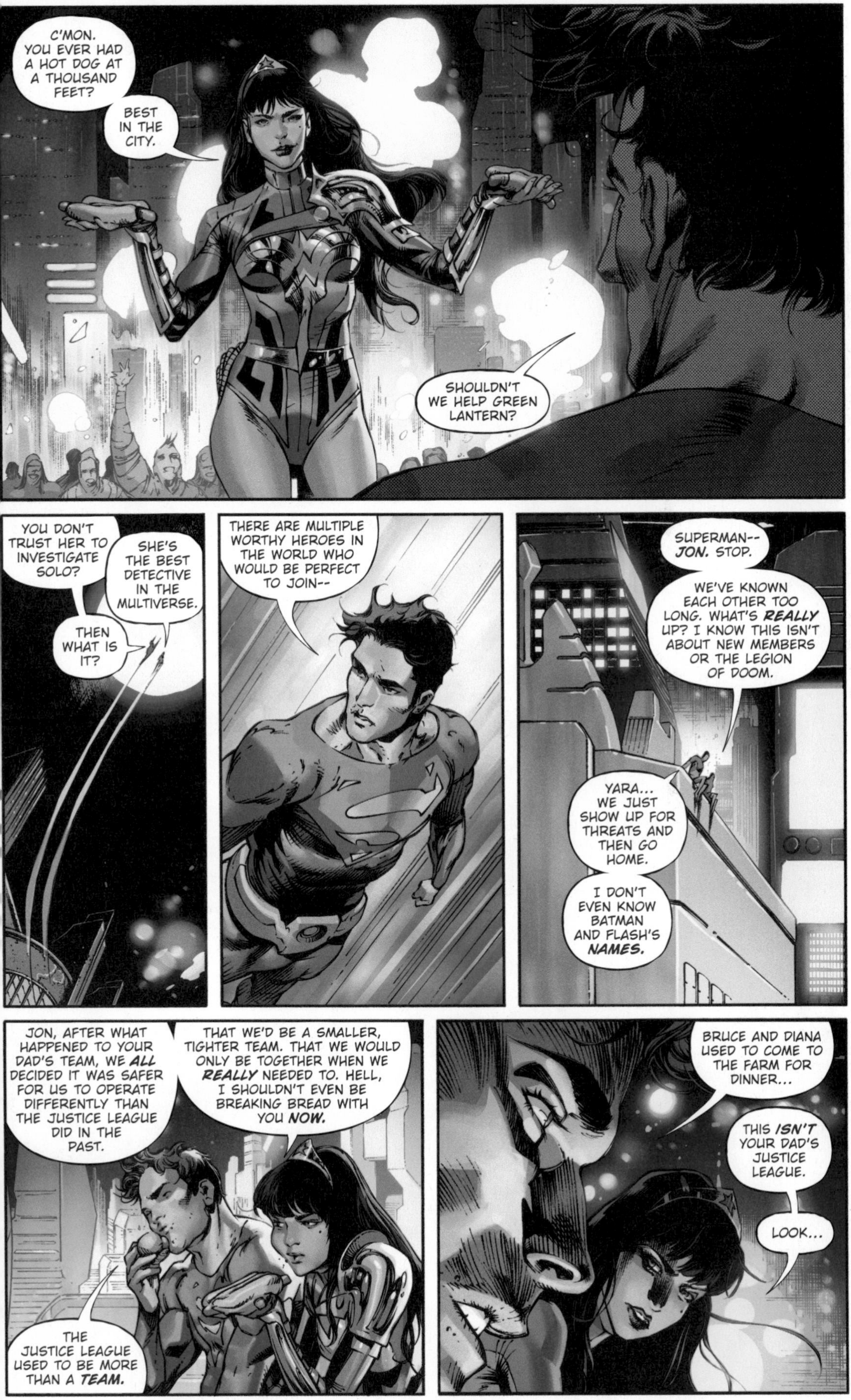

C'MON. YOU EVER HAD A HOT DOG AT A THOUSAND FEET?
BEST IN THE CITY.
SHOULDN'T WE HELP GREEN LANTERN?
YOU DON'T TRUST HER TO INVESTIGATE SOLO?
SHE'S THE BEST DETECTIVE IN THE MULTIVERSE.
THEN WHAT IS IT?
THERE ARE MULTIPLE WORTHY HEROES IN THE WORLD WHO WOULD BE PERFECT TO JOIN--
SUPERMAN-- *JON.* STOP.
WE'VE KNOWN EACH OTHER TOO LONG. WHAT'S *REALLY* UP? I KNOW THIS ISN'T ABOUT NEW MEMBERS OR THE LEGION OF DOOM.
YARA... WE JUST SHOW UP FOR THREATS AND THEN GO HOME.
I DON'T EVEN KNOW BATMAN AND FLASH'S *NAMES.*
JON, AFTER WHAT HAPPENED TO YOUR DAD'S TEAM, WE *ALL* DECIDED IT WAS SAFER FOR US TO OPERATE DIFFERENTLY THAN THE JUSTICE LEAGUE DID IN THE PAST.
THAT WE'D BE A SMALLER, TIGHTER TEAM. THAT WE WOULD ONLY BE TOGETHER WHEN WE *REALLY* NEEDED TO. HELL, I SHOULDN'T EVEN BE BREAKING BREAD WITH YOU *NOW.*
THE JUSTICE LEAGUE USED TO BE MORE THAN A *TEAM.*
BRUCE AND DIANA USED TO COME TO THE FARM FOR DINNER...
THIS *ISN'T* YOUR DAD'S JUSTICE LEAGUE.
LOOK...

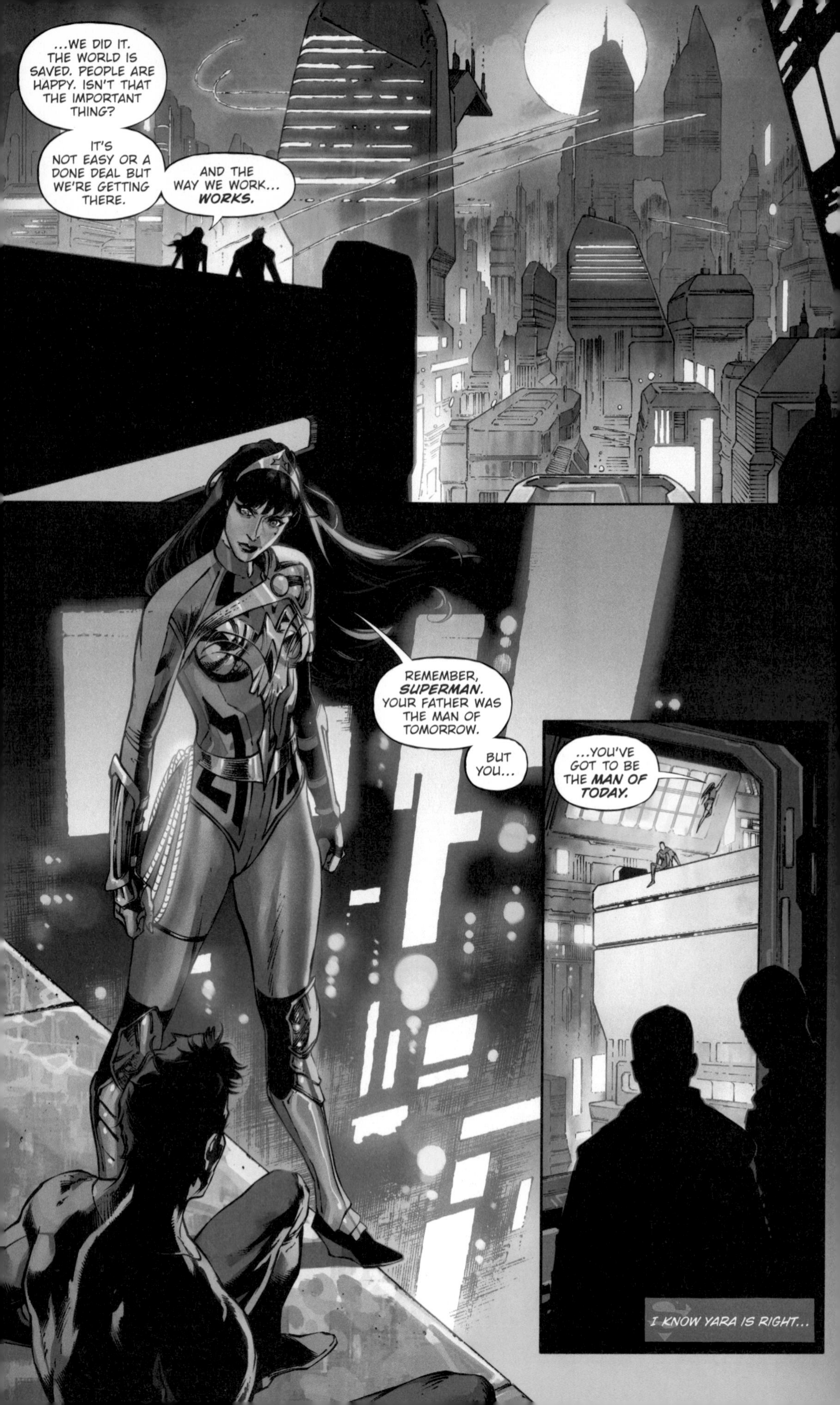
...WE DID IT. THE WORLD IS SAVED. PEOPLE ARE HAPPY. ISN'T THAT THE IMPORTANT THING?
IT'S NOT EASY OR A DONE DEAL BUT WE'RE GETTING THERE.
AND THE WAY WE WORK... **WORKS.**
REMEMBER, ***SUPERMAN***. YOUR FATHER WAS THE MAN OF TOMORROW.
BUT YOU...
...YOU'VE GOT TO BE THE ***MAN OF TODAY.***
I KNOW YARA IS RIGHT...

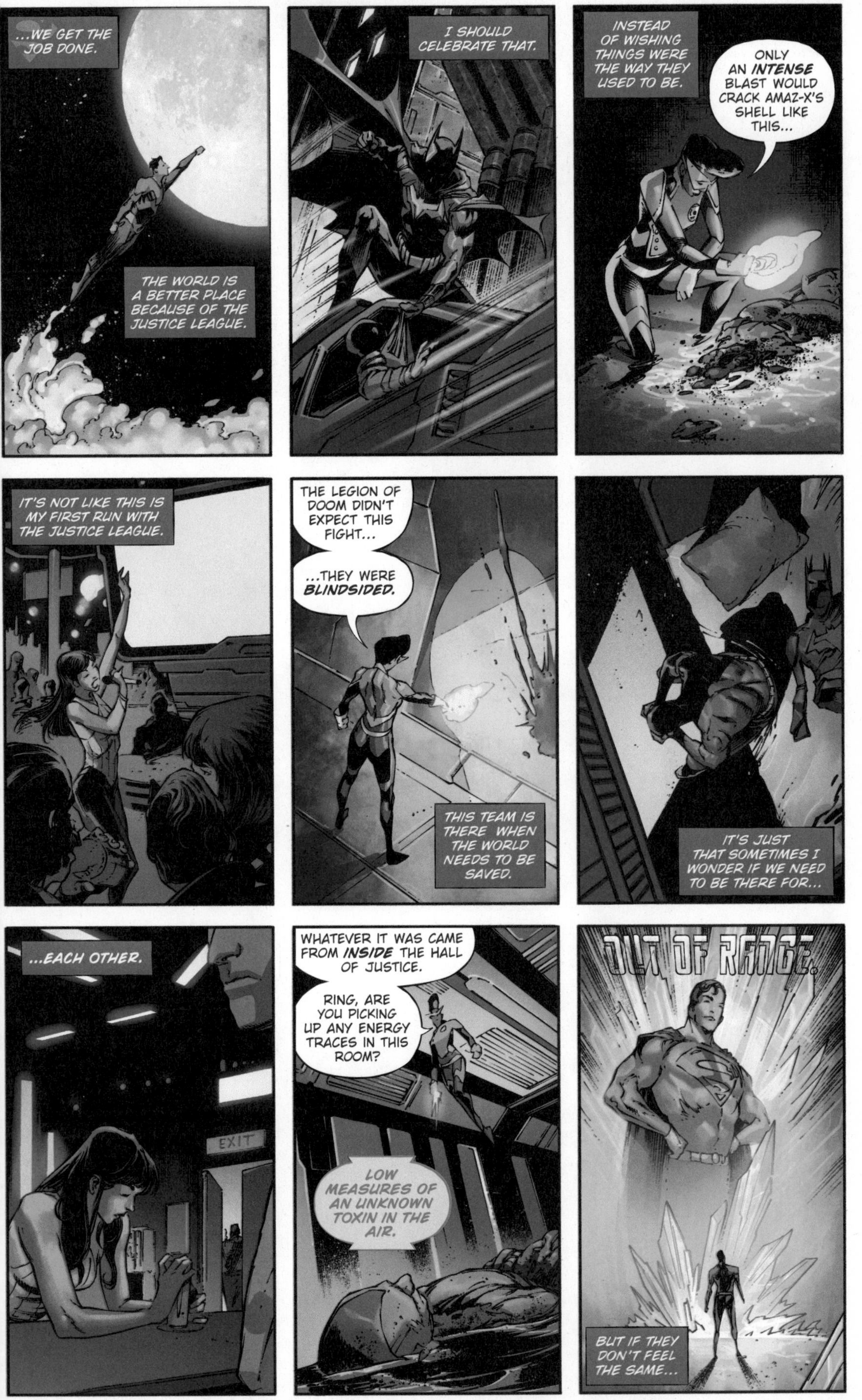

...WE GET THE JOB DONE.
THE WORLD IS A BETTER PLACE BECAUSE OF THE JUSTICE LEAGUE.
I SHOULD CELEBRATE THAT.
INSTEAD OF WISHING THINGS WERE THE WAY THEY USED TO BE.
ONLY AN INTENSE BLAST WOULD CRACK AMAZ-X'S SHELL LIKE THIS...
IT'S NOT LIKE THIS IS MY FIRST RUN WITH THE JUSTICE LEAGUE.
THE LEGION OF DOOM DIDN'T EXPECT THIS FIGHT...
...THEY WERE BLINDSIDED.
THIS TEAM IS THERE WHEN THE WORLD NEEDS TO BE SAVED.
IT'S JUST THAT SOMETIMES I WONDER IF WE NEED TO BE THERE FOR...
...EACH OTHER.
EXIT
WHATEVER IT WAS CAME FROM INSIDE THE HALL OF JUSTICE.
RING, ARE YOU PICKING UP ANY ENERGY TRACES IN THIS ROOM?
LOW MEASURES OF AN UNKNOWN TOXIN IN THE AIR.
OUT OF RANGE.
BUT IF THEY DON'T FEEL THE SAME...

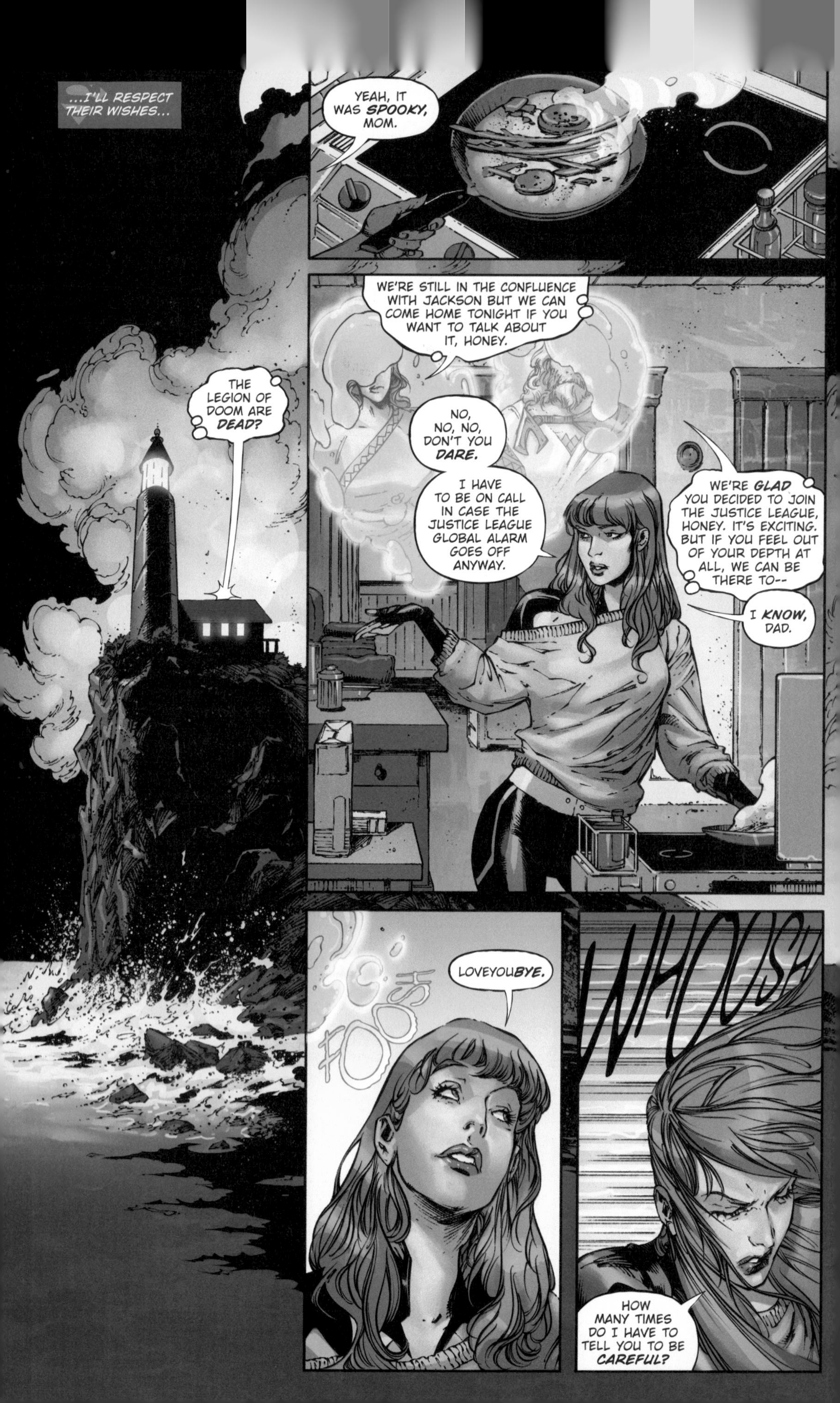
...I'LL RESPECT THEIR WISHES...
YEAH, IT WAS SPOOKY, MOM.
WE'RE STILL IN THE CONFLUENCE WITH JACKSON BUT WE CAN COME HOME TONIGHT IF YOU WANT TO TALK ABOUT IT, HONEY.
THE LEGION OF DOOM ARE DEAD?
NO, NO, NO, DON'T YOU DARE.
I HAVE TO BE ON CALL IN CASE THE JUSTICE LEAGUE GLOBAL ALARM GOES OFF ANYWAY.
WE'RE GLAD YOU DECIDED TO JOIN THE JUSTICE LEAGUE, HONEY. IT'S EXCITING. BUT IF YOU FEEL OUT OF YOUR DEPTH AT ALL, WE CAN BE THERE TO--
I KNOW, DAD.
LOVEYOUBYE.
WHOOSH
HOW MANY TIMES DO I HAVE TO TELL YOU TO BE CAREFUL?

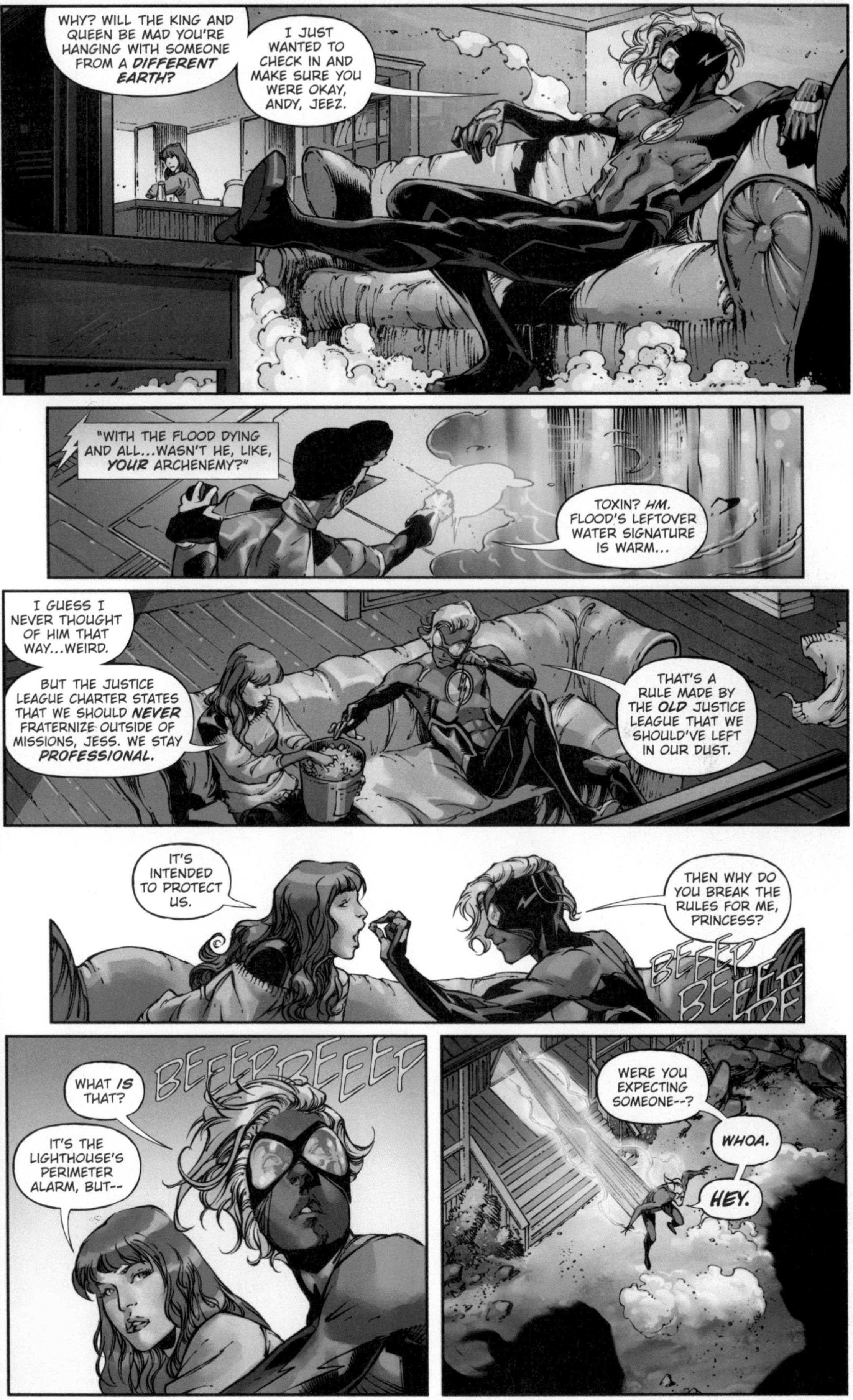

WHY? WILL THE KING AND QUEEN BE MAD YOU'RE HANGING WITH SOMEONE FROM A *DIFFERENT EARTH?*
I JUST WANTED TO CHECK IN AND MAKE SURE YOU WERE OKAY, ANDY, JEEZ.
"WITH THE FLOOD DYING AND ALL...WASN'T HE, LIKE, *YOUR* ARCHENEMY?"
TOXIN? *HM.* FLOOD'S LEFTOVER WATER SIGNATURE IS WARM...
I GUESS I NEVER THOUGHT OF HIM THAT WAY...WEIRD.
BUT THE JUSTICE LEAGUE CHARTER STATES THAT WE SHOULD *NEVER* FRATERNIZE OUTSIDE OF MISSIONS, JESS. WE STAY *PROFESSIONAL.*
THAT'S A RULE MADE BY THE *OLD* JUSTICE LEAGUE THAT WE SHOULD'VE LEFT IN OUR DUST.
IT'S INTENDED TO PROTECT US.
THEN WHY DO YOU BREAK THE RULES FOR ME, PRINCESS?
BEEEP
BEEEP
BEEEP BEEEP
WHAT *IS* THAT?
IT'S THE LIGHTHOUSE'S PERIMETER ALARM, BUT--
WERE YOU EXPECTING SOMEONE--?
WHOA.
HEY.

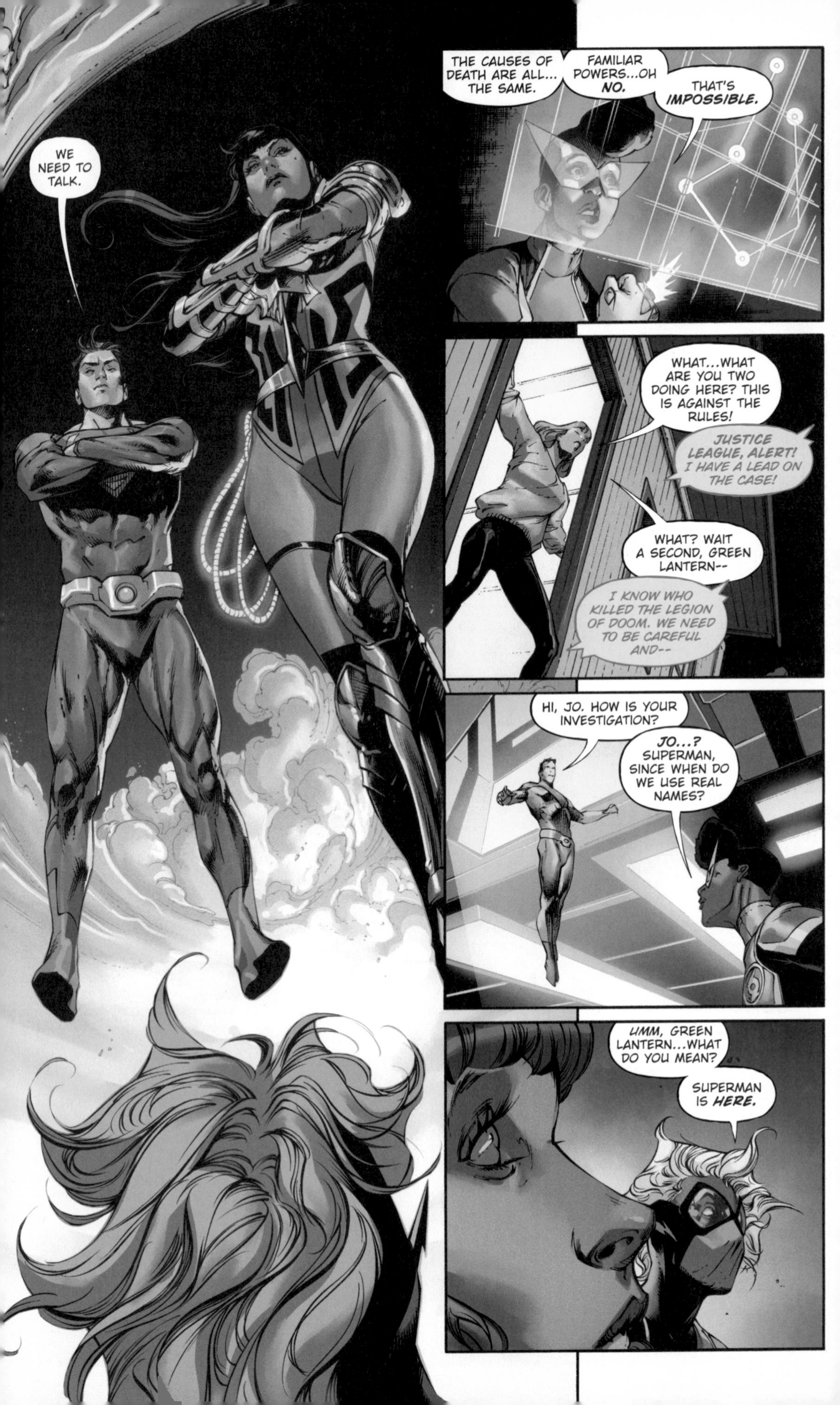
WE NEED TO TALK.
THE CAUSES OF DEATH ARE ALL... THE SAME.
FAMILIAR POWERS...OH *NO.*
THAT'S *IMPOSSIBLE.*
WHAT...WHAT ARE YOU TWO DOING HERE? THIS IS AGAINST THE RULES!
JUSTICE LEAGUE, ALERT! I HAVE A LEAD ON THE CASE!
WHAT? WAIT A SECOND, GREEN LANTERN--
I KNOW WHO KILLED THE LEGION OF DOOM. WE NEED TO BE CAREFUL AND--
HI, JO. HOW IS YOUR INVESTIGATION?
JO...? SUPERMAN, SINCE WHEN DO WE USE REAL NAMES?
UMM, GREEN LANTERN...WHAT DO YOU MEAN?
SUPERMAN IS *HERE.*

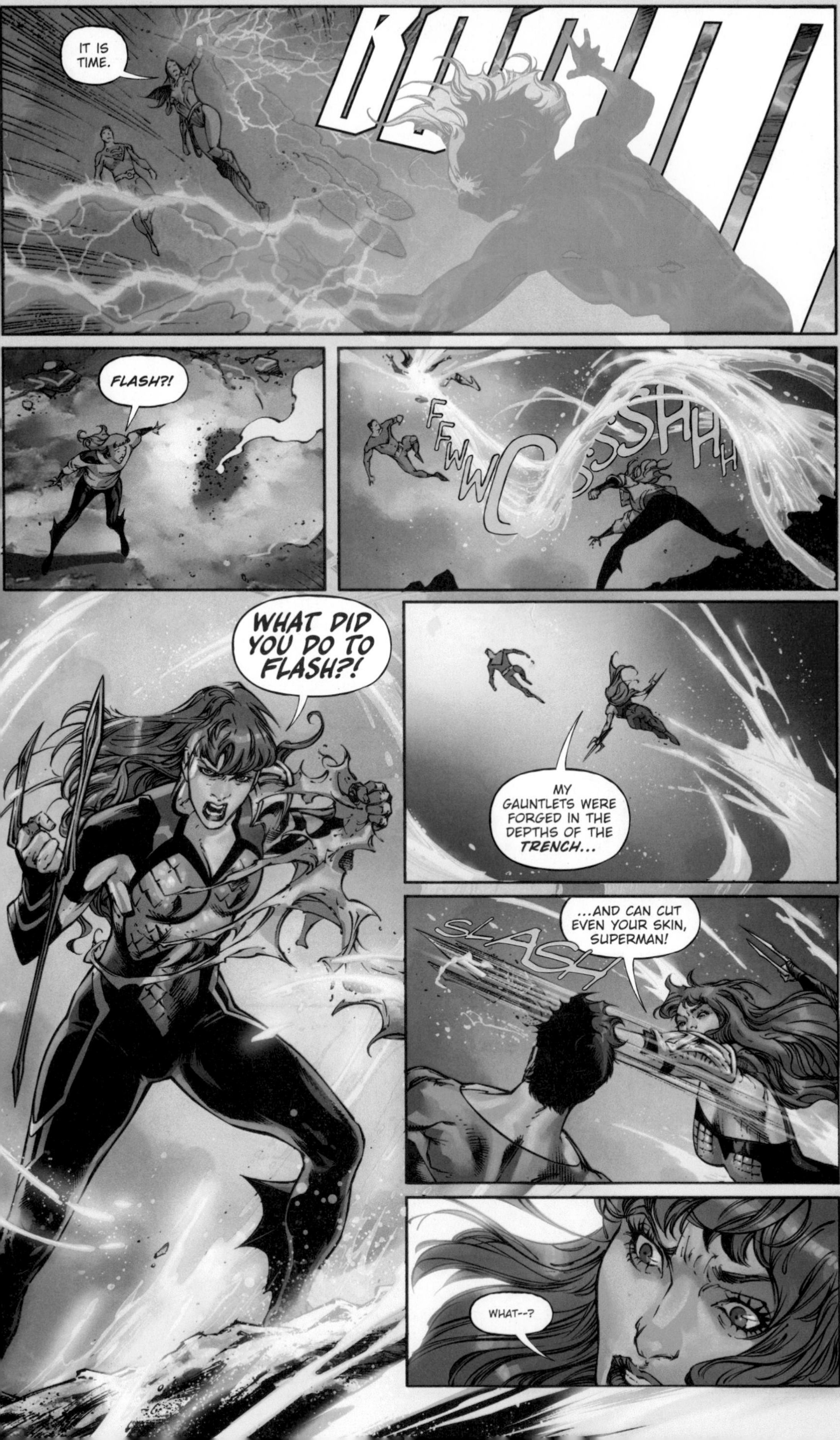
IT IS TIME.
FLASH?!
FFWWOOSSHHH
WHAT DID YOU DO TO FLASH?!
MY GAUNTLETS WERE FORGED IN THE DEPTHS OF THE TRENCH...
SLASH
...AND CAN CUT EVEN YOUR SKIN, SUPERMAN!
WHAT--?

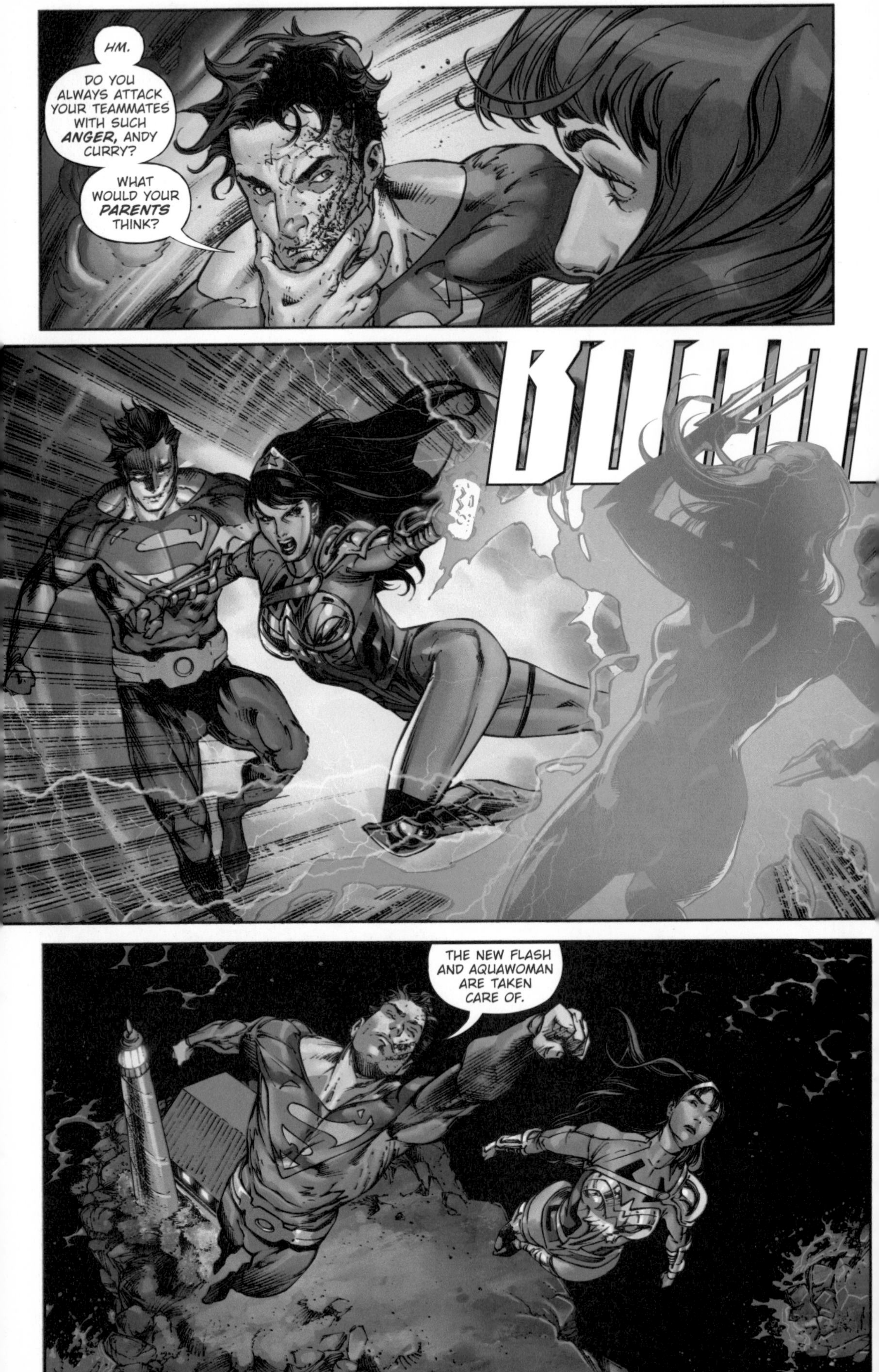
HM.
DO YOU ALWAYS ATTACK YOUR TEAMMATES WITH SUCH ANGER, ANDY CURRY?
WHAT WOULD YOUR PARENTS THINK?
THE NEW FLASH AND AQUAWOMAN ARE TAKEN CARE OF.

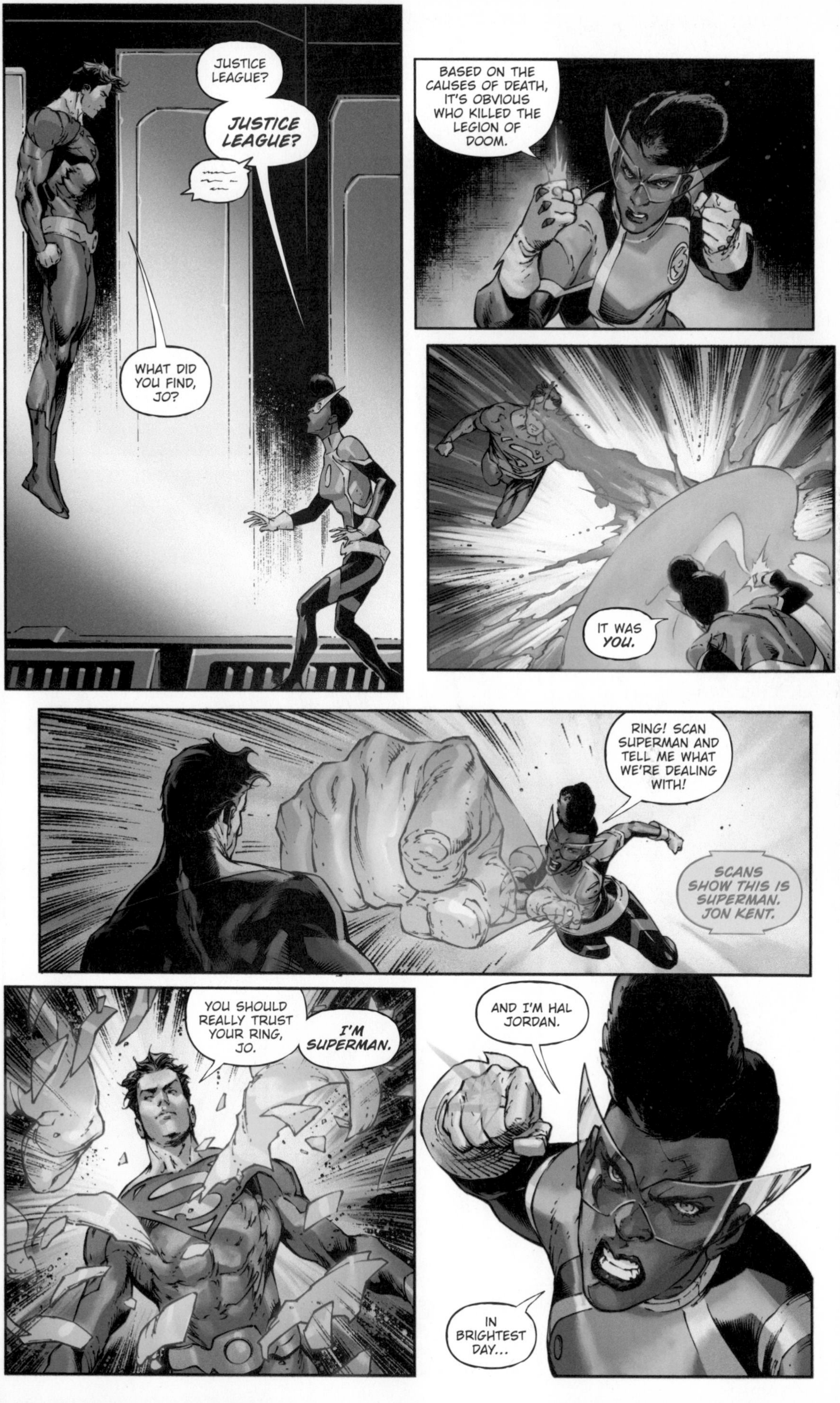
JUSTICE LEAGUE?
JUSTICE LEAGUE?
WHAT DID YOU FIND, JO?
BASED ON THE CAUSES OF DEATH, IT'S OBVIOUS WHO KILLED THE LEGION OF DOOM.
IT WAS YOU.
RING! SCAN SUPERMAN AND TELL ME WHAT WE'RE DEALING WITH!
SCANS SHOW THIS IS SUPERMAN. JON KENT.
YOU SHOULD REALLY TRUST YOUR RING, JO.
I'M SUPERMAN.
AND I'M HAL JORDAN.
IN BRIGHTEST DAY...

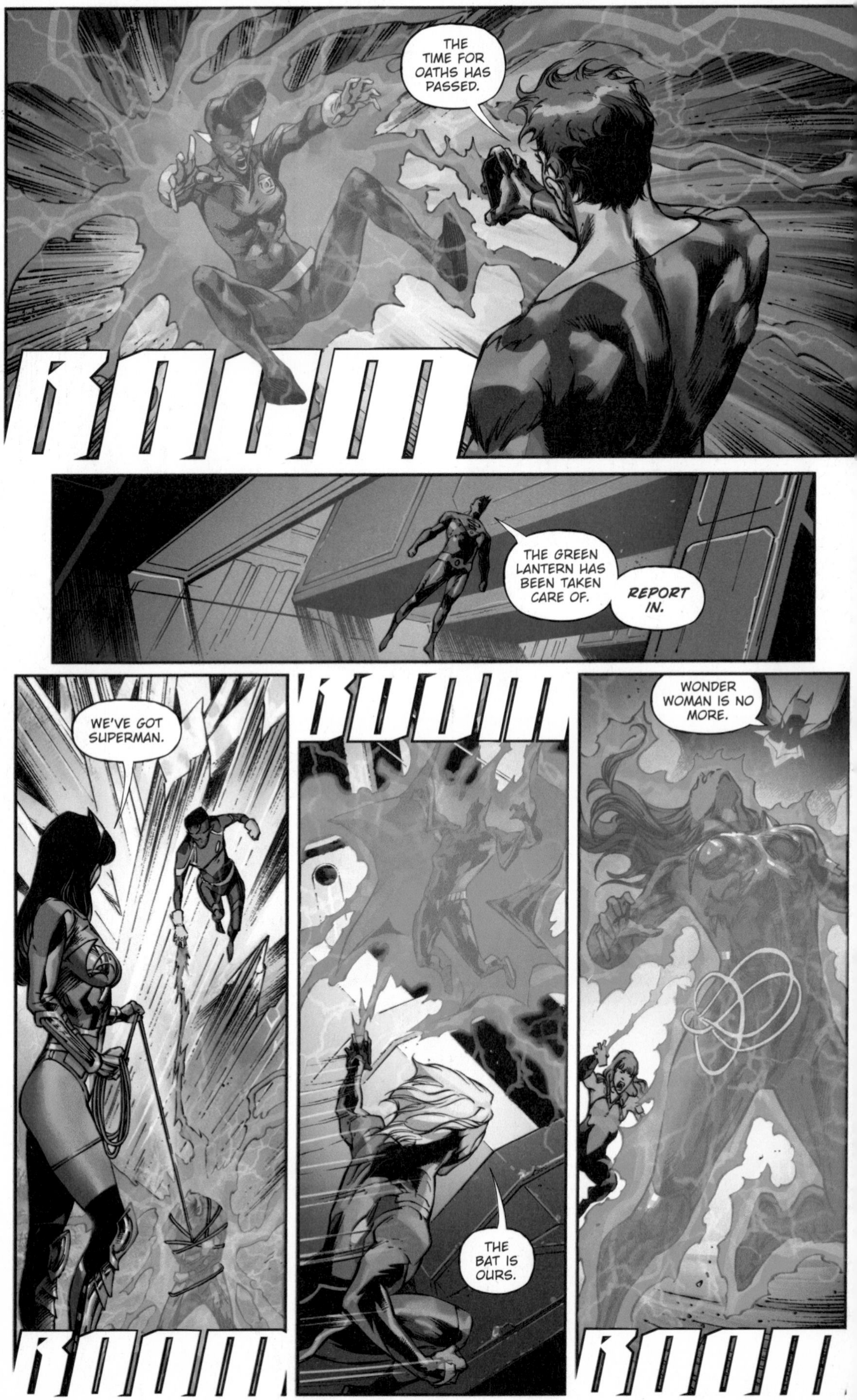
THE TIME FOR OATHS HAS PASSED.
BOOM
THE GREEN LANTERN HAS BEEN TAKEN CARE OF.
REPORT IN.
WE'VE GOT SUPERMAN.
BOOM
THE BAT IS OURS.
BOOM
WONDER WOMAN IS NO MORE.
BOOM

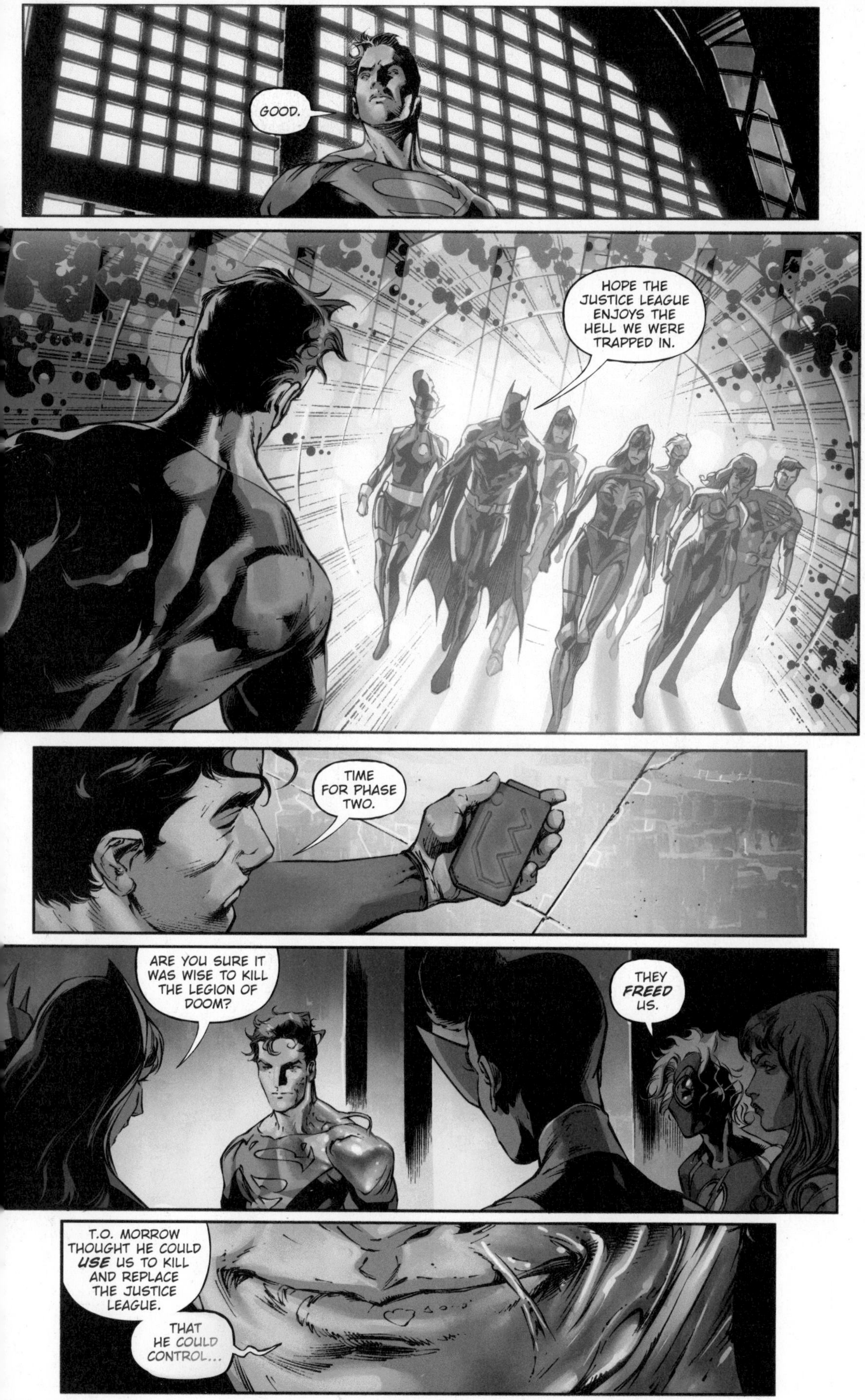

GOOD.
HOPE THE JUSTICE LEAGUE ENJOYS THE HELL WE WERE TRAPPED IN.
TIME FOR PHASE TWO.
ARE YOU SURE IT WAS WISE TO KILL THE LEGION OF DOOM?
THEY FREED US.
T.O. MORROW THOUGHT HE COULD USE US TO KILL AND REPLACE THE JUSTICE LEAGUE.
THAT HE COULD CONTROL...

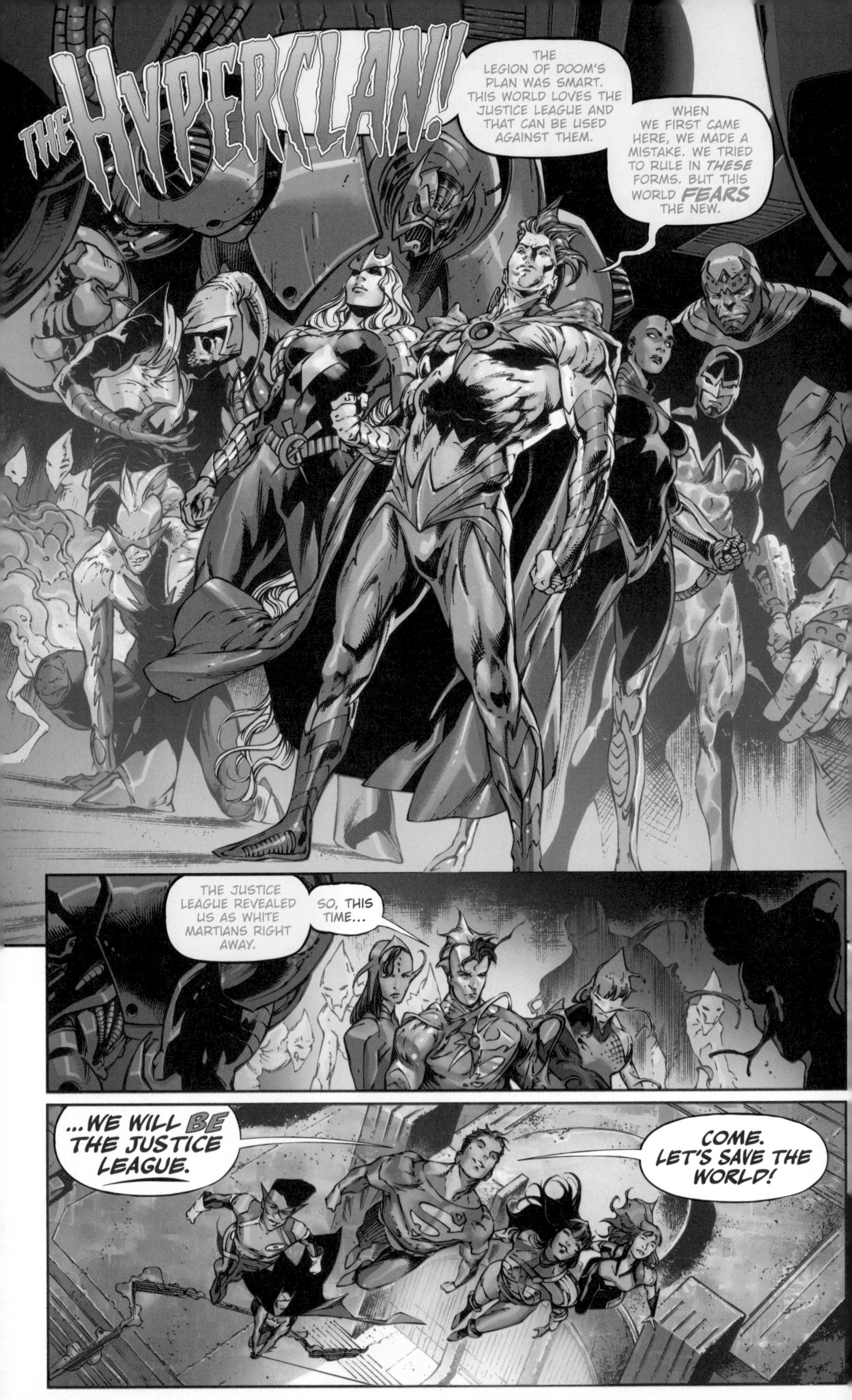
THE HYPERCLAN!
THE LEGION OF DOOM'S PLAN WAS SMART. THIS WORLD LOVES THE JUSTICE LEAGUE AND THAT CAN BE USED AGAINST THEM.
WHEN WE FIRST CAME HERE, WE MADE A MISTAKE. WE TRIED TO RULE IN *THESE* FORMS. BUT THIS WORLD **FEARS** THE NEW.
THE JUSTICE LEAGUE REVEALED US AS WHITE MARTIANS RIGHT AWAY.
SO, THIS TIME...
...WE WILL *BE* THE JUSTICE LEAGUE.
COME. LET'S SAVE THE WORLD!

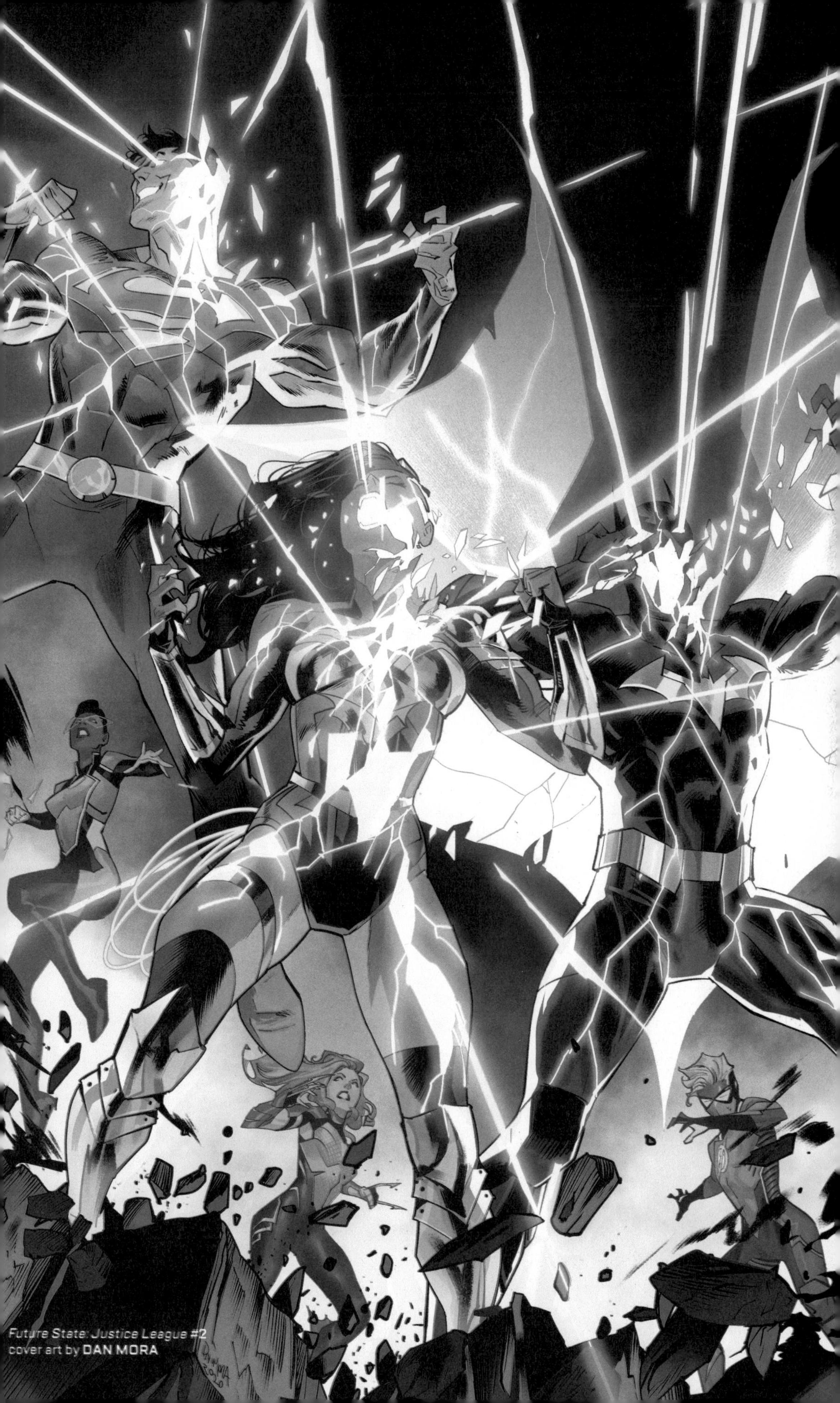

Future State: Justice League #2
cover art by **DAN MORA**

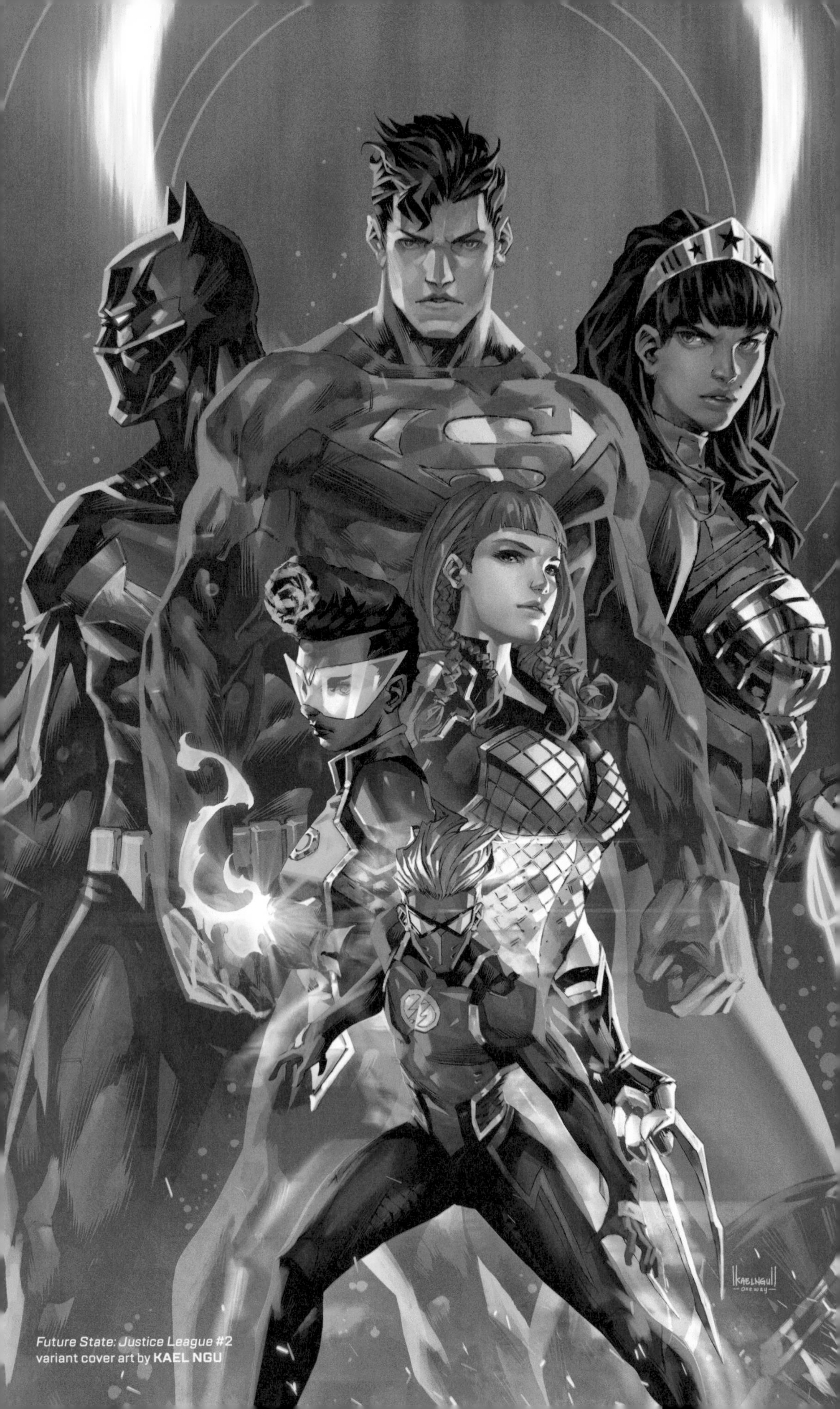

Future State: Justice League #2
variant cover art by **KAEL NGU**

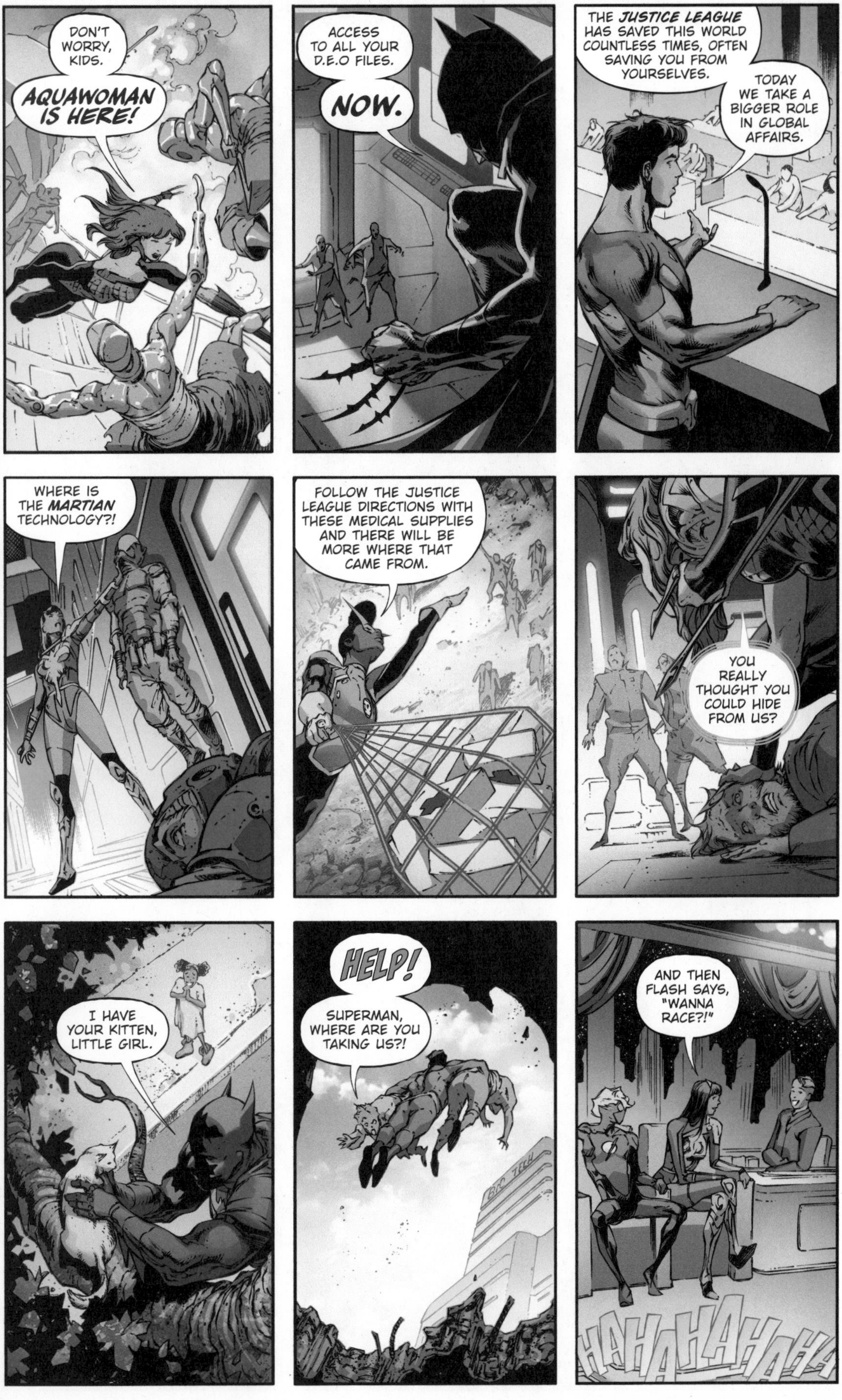

DON'T WORRY, KIDS.
AQUAWOMAN IS HERE!
ACCESS TO ALL YOUR D.E.O FILES.
NOW.
THE JUSTICE LEAGUE HAS SAVED THIS WORLD COUNTLESS TIMES, OFTEN SAVING YOU FROM YOURSELVES.
TODAY WE TAKE A BIGGER ROLE IN GLOBAL AFFAIRS.
WHERE IS THE MARTIAN TECHNOLOGY?!
FOLLOW THE JUSTICE LEAGUE DIRECTIONS WITH THESE MEDICAL SUPPLIES AND THERE WILL BE MORE WHERE THAT CAME FROM.
YOU REALLY THOUGHT YOU COULD HIDE FROM US?
I HAVE YOUR KITTEN, LITTLE GIRL.
HELP!
SUPERMAN, WHERE ARE YOU TAKING US?!
AND THEN FLASH SAYS, "WANNA RACE?!"
HAHAHAHAHAHA

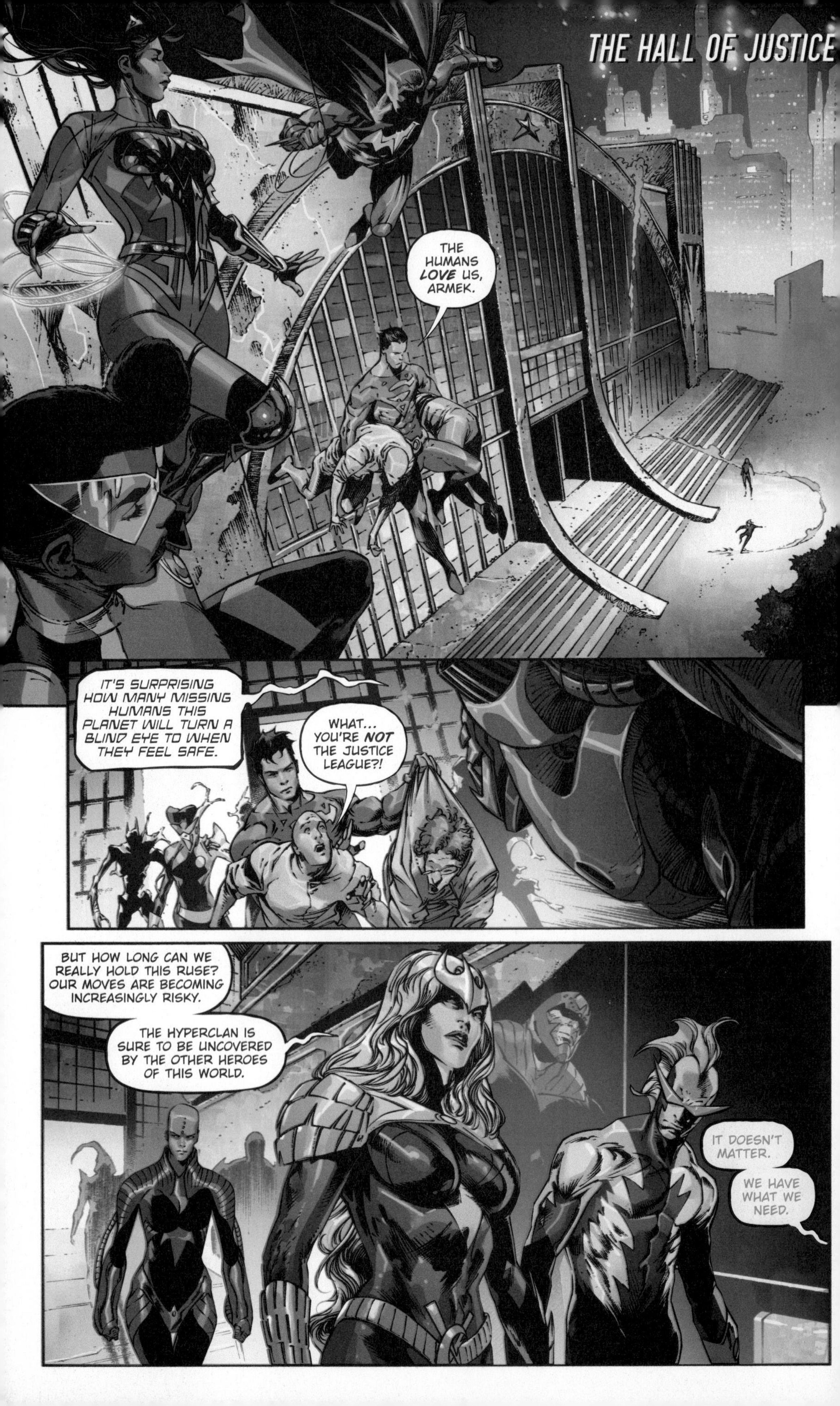
THE HALL OF JUSTICE
THE HUMANS LOVE US, ARMEK.
IT'S SURPRISING HOW MANY MISSING HUMANS THIS PLANET WILL TURN A BLIND EYE TO WHEN THEY FEEL SAFE.
WHAT... YOU'RE NOT THE JUSTICE LEAGUE?!
BUT HOW LONG CAN WE REALLY HOLD THIS RUSE? OUR MOVES ARE BECOMING INCREASINGLY RISKY.
THE HYPERCLAN IS SURE TO BE UNCOVERED BY THE OTHER HEROES OF THIS WORLD.
IT DOESN'T MATTER.
WE HAVE WHAT WE NEED.

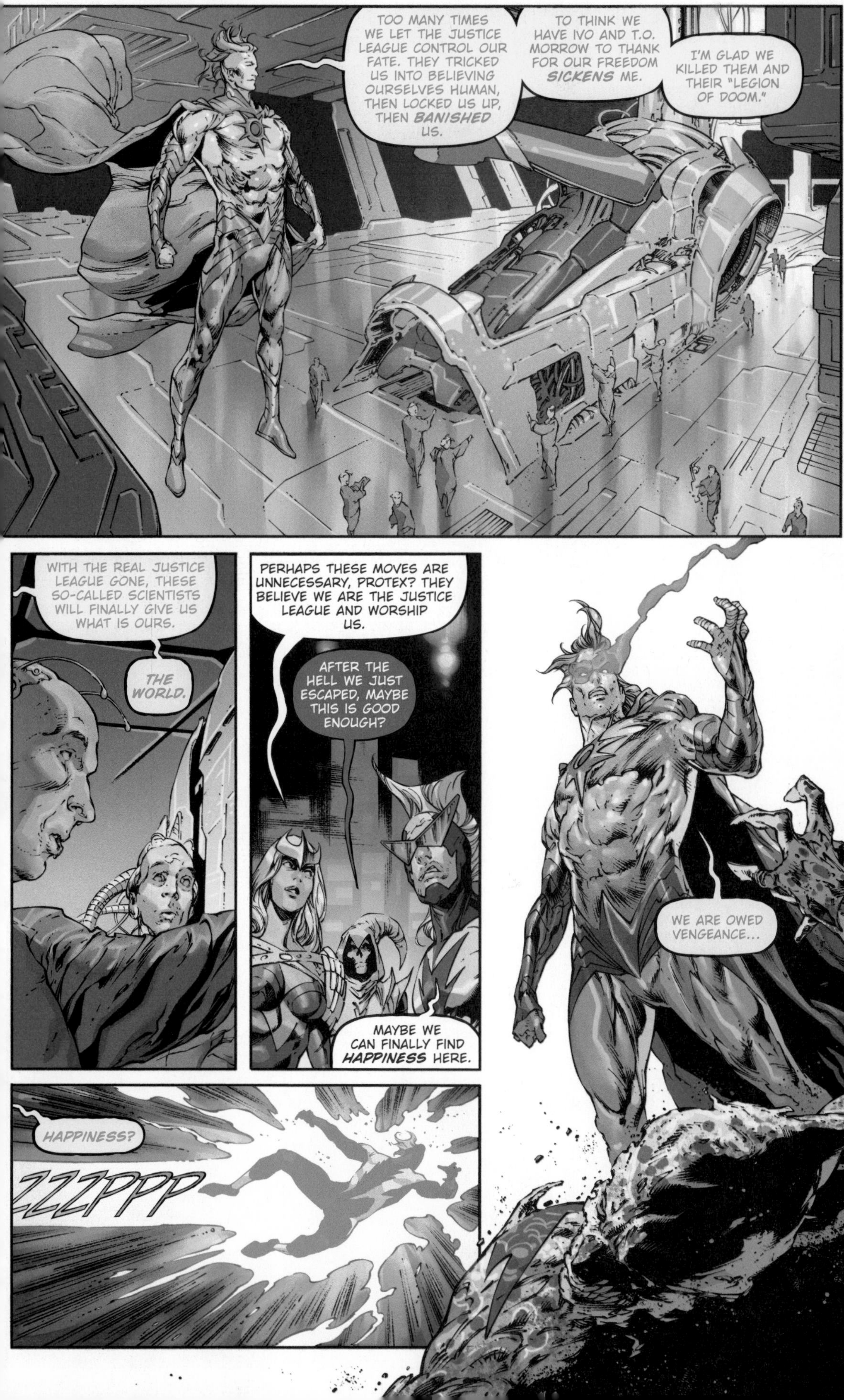

TOO MANY TIMES WE LET THE JUSTICE LEAGUE CONTROL OUR FATE. THEY TRICKED US INTO BELIEVING OURSELVES HUMAN, THEN LOCKED US UP, THEN BANISHED US.
TO THINK WE HAVE IVO AND T.O. MORROW TO THANK FOR OUR FREEDOM SICKENS ME.
I'M GLAD WE KILLED THEM AND THEIR "LEGION OF DOOM."
WITH THE REAL JUSTICE LEAGUE GONE, THESE SO-CALLED SCIENTISTS WILL FINALLY GIVE US WHAT IS OURS.
THE WORLD.
PERHAPS THESE MOVES ARE UNNECESSARY, PROTEX? THEY BELIEVE WE ARE THE JUSTICE LEAGUE AND WORSHIP US.
AFTER THE HELL WE JUST ESCAPED, MAYBE THIS IS GOOD ENOUGH?
MAYBE WE CAN FINALLY FIND HAPPINESS HERE.
WE ARE OWED VENGEANCE...
HAPPINESS?
ZZZPPPP

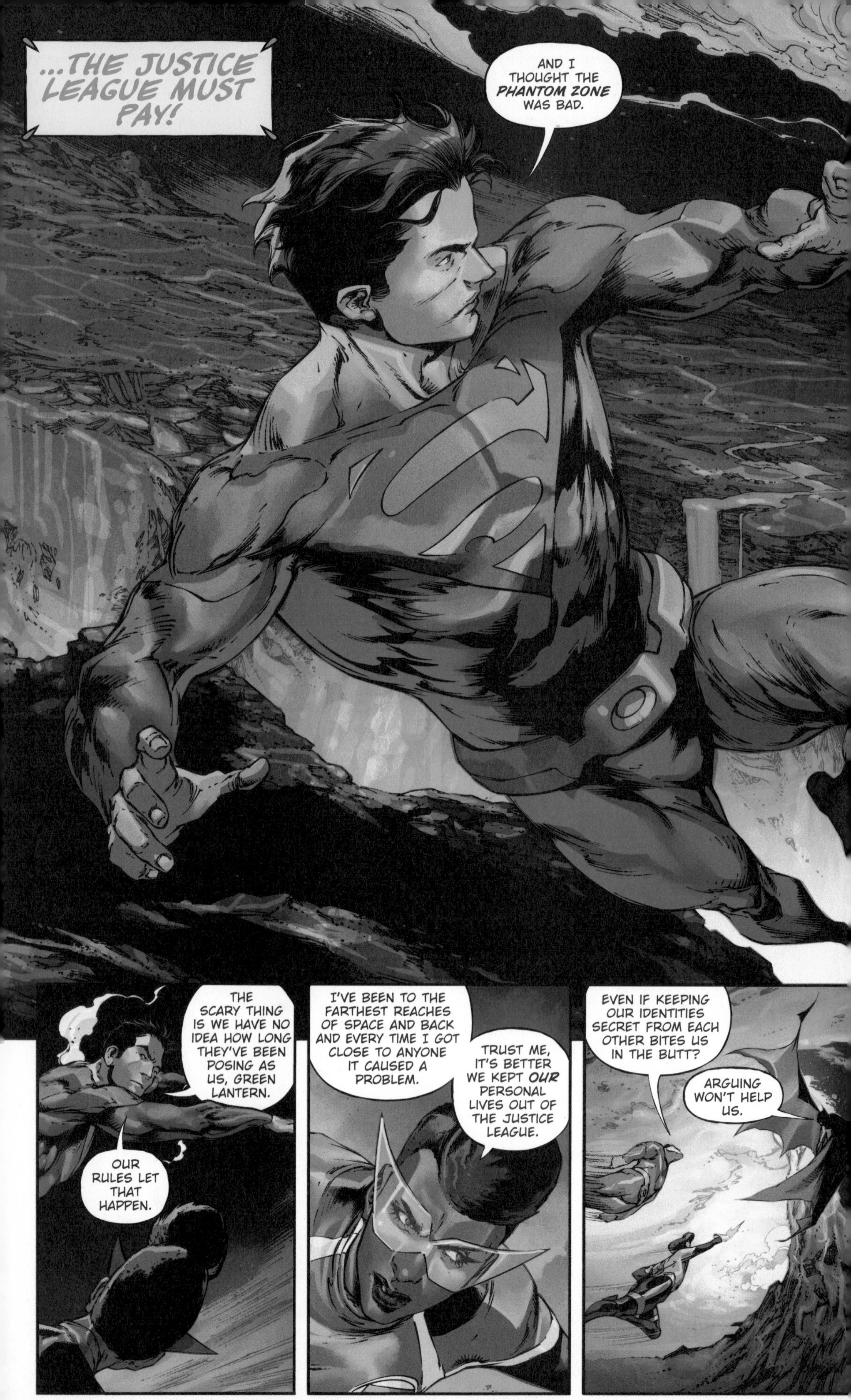
...THE JUSTICE LEAGUE MUST PAY!
AND I THOUGHT THE PHANTOM ZONE WAS BAD.
THE SCARY THING IS WE HAVE NO IDEA HOW LONG THEY'VE BEEN POSING AS US, GREEN LANTERN.
OUR RULES LET THAT HAPPEN.
I'VE BEEN TO THE FARTHEST REACHES OF SPACE AND BACK AND EVERY TIME I GOT CLOSE TO ANYONE IT CAUSED A PROBLEM.
TRUST ME, IT'S BETTER WE KEPT OUR PERSONAL LIVES OUT OF THE JUSTICE LEAGUE.
EVEN IF KEEPING OUR IDENTITIES SECRET FROM EACH OTHER BITES US IN THE BUTT?
ARGUING WON'T HELP US.

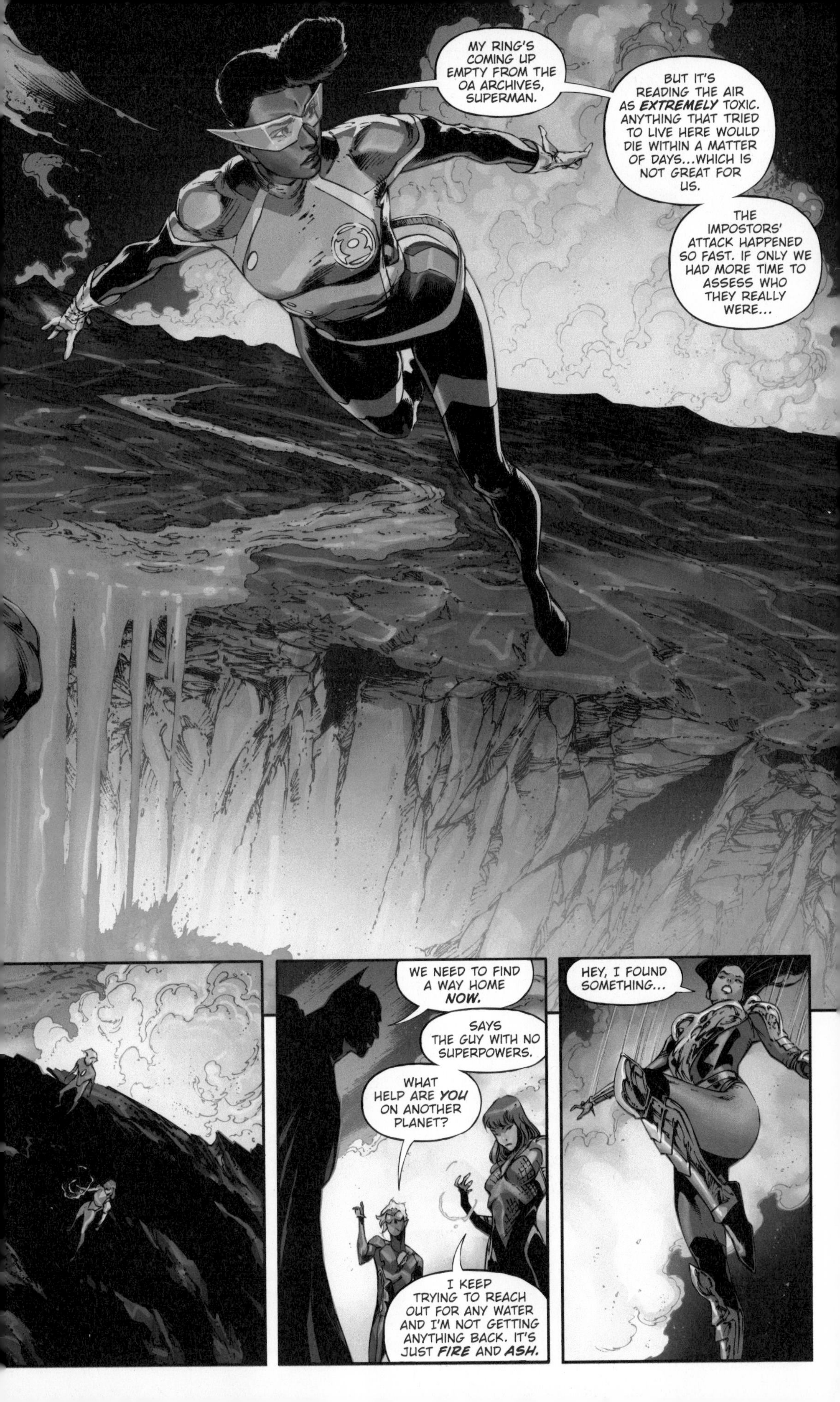
MY RING'S COMING UP EMPTY FROM THE OA ARCHIVES, SUPERMAN.
BUT IT'S READING THE AIR AS EXTREMELY TOXIC. ANYTHING THAT TRIED TO LIVE HERE WOULD DIE WITHIN A MATTER OF DAYS...WHICH IS NOT GREAT FOR US.
THE IMPOSTORS' ATTACK HAPPENED SO FAST. IF ONLY WE HAD MORE TIME TO ASSESS WHO THEY REALLY WERE...
WE NEED TO FIND A WAY HOME NOW.
SAYS THE GUY WITH NO SUPERPOWERS.
WHAT HELP ARE YOU ON ANOTHER PLANET?
I KEEP TRYING TO REACH OUT FOR ANY WATER AND I'M NOT GETTING ANYTHING BACK. IT'S JUST FIRE AND ASH.
HEY, I FOUND SOMETHING...

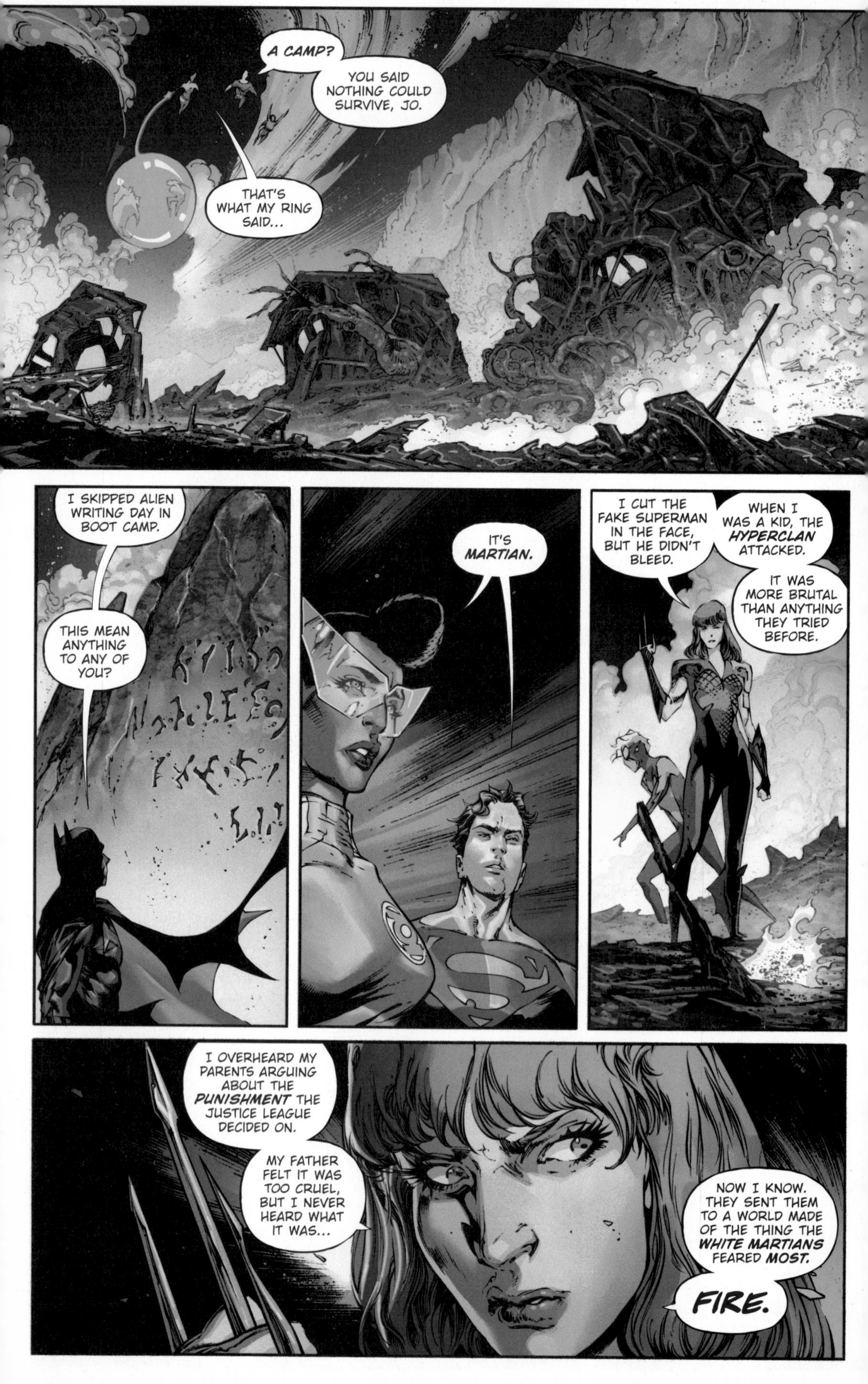
A CAMP?
YOU SAID NOTHING COULD SURVIVE, JO.
THAT'S WHAT MY RING SAID...
I SKIPPED ALIEN WRITING DAY IN BOOT CAMP.
THIS MEAN ANYTHING TO ANY OF YOU?
IT'S *MARTIAN.*
I CUT THE FAKE SUPERMAN IN THE FACE, BUT HE DIDN'T BLEED.
WHEN I WAS A KID, THE *HYPERCLAN* ATTACKED.
IT WAS MORE BRUTAL THAN ANYTHING THEY TRIED BEFORE.
I OVERHEARD MY PARENTS ARGUING ABOUT THE *PUNISHMENT* THE JUSTICE LEAGUE DECIDED ON.
MY FATHER FELT IT WAS TOO CRUEL, BUT I NEVER HEARD WHAT IT WAS...
NOW I KNOW. THEY SENT THEM TO A WORLD MADE OF THE THING THE *WHITE MARTIANS* FEARED *MOST.*
FIRE.

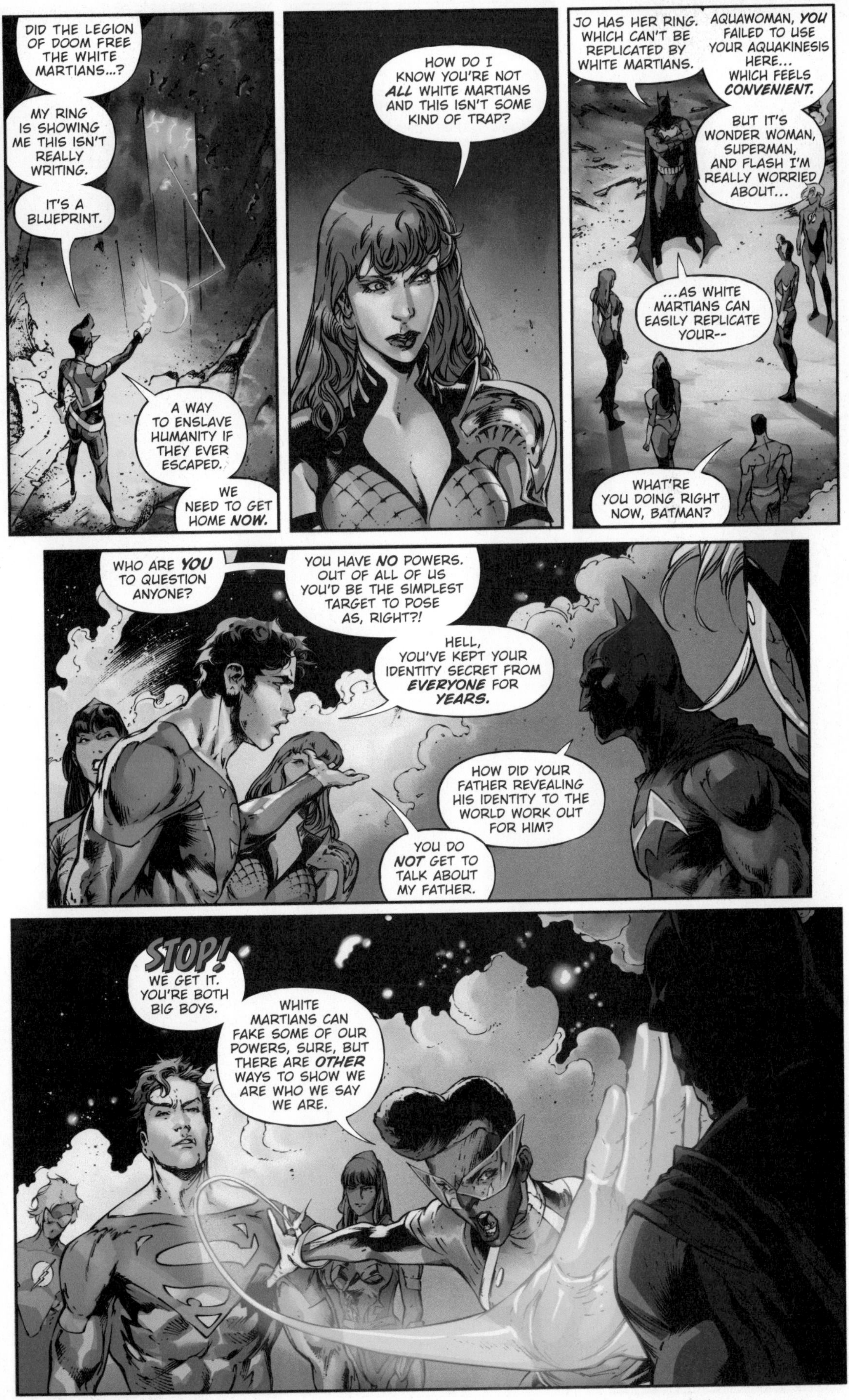

DID THE LEGION OF DOOM FREE THE WHITE MARTIANS...?
MY RING IS SHOWING ME THIS ISN'T REALLY WRITING.
IT'S A BLUEPRINT.
A WAY TO ENSLAVE HUMANITY IF THEY EVER ESCAPED.
WE NEED TO GET HOME NOW.
HOW DO I KNOW YOU'RE NOT ALL WHITE MARTIANS AND THIS ISN'T SOME KIND OF TRAP?
JO HAS HER RING. WHICH CAN'T BE REPLICATED BY WHITE MARTIANS.
AQUAWOMAN, YOU FAILED TO USE YOUR AQUAKINESIS HERE... WHICH FEELS CONVENIENT.
BUT IT'S WONDER WOMAN, SUPERMAN, AND FLASH I'M REALLY WORRIED ABOUT...
...AS WHITE MARTIANS CAN EASILY REPLICATE YOUR--
WHAT'RE YOU DOING RIGHT NOW, BATMAN?
WHO ARE YOU TO QUESTION ANYONE?
YOU HAVE NO POWERS. OUT OF ALL OF US YOU'D BE THE SIMPLEST TARGET TO POSE AS, RIGHT?!
HELL, YOU'VE KEPT YOUR IDENTITY SECRET FROM EVERYONE FOR YEARS.
HOW DID YOUR FATHER REVEALING HIS IDENTITY TO THE WORLD WORK OUT FOR HIM?
YOU DO NOT GET TO TALK ABOUT MY FATHER.
STOP! WE GET IT. YOU'RE BOTH BIG BOYS.
WHITE MARTIANS CAN FAKE SOME OF OUR POWERS, SURE, BUT THERE ARE OTHER WAYS TO SHOW WE ARE WHO WE SAY WE ARE.

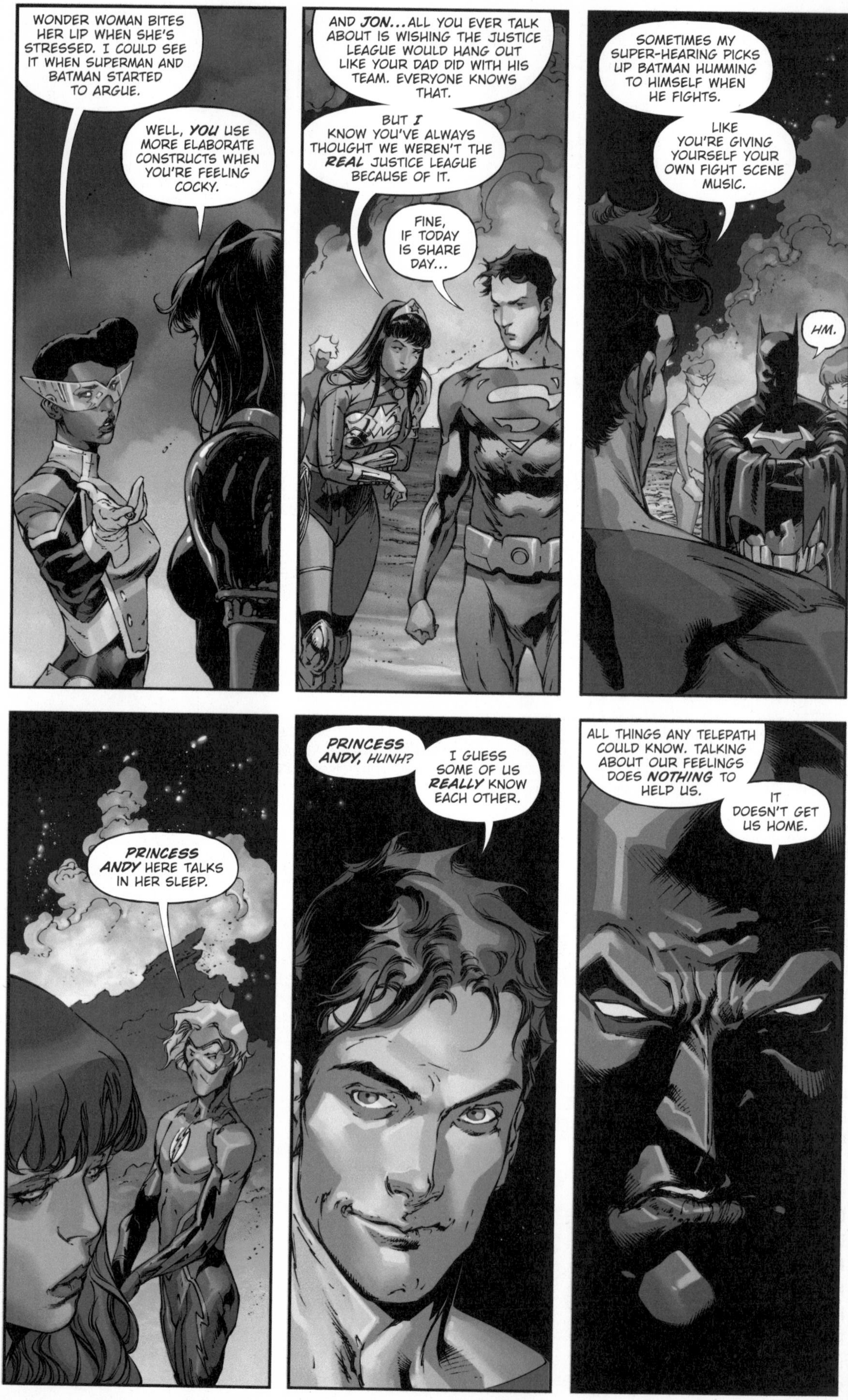
WONDER WOMAN BITES HER LIP WHEN SHE'S STRESSED. I COULD SEE IT WHEN SUPERMAN AND BATMAN STARTED TO ARGUE.
WELL, YOU USE MORE ELABORATE CONSTRUCTS WHEN YOU'RE FEELING COCKY.
AND JON... ALL YOU EVER TALK ABOUT IS WISHING THE JUSTICE LEAGUE WOULD HANG OUT LIKE YOUR DAD DID WITH HIS TEAM. EVERYONE KNOWS THAT.
BUT I KNOW YOU'VE ALWAYS THOUGHT WE WEREN'T THE REAL JUSTICE LEAGUE BECAUSE OF IT.
FINE, IF TODAY IS SHARE DAY...
SOMETIMES MY SUPER-HEARING PICKS UP BATMAN HUMMING TO HIMSELF WHEN HE FIGHTS.
LIKE YOU'RE GIVING YOURSELF YOUR OWN FIGHT SCENE MUSIC.
HM.
PRINCESS ANDY HERE TALKS IN HER SLEEP.
PRINCESS ANDY, HUNH?
I GUESS SOME OF US REALLY KNOW EACH OTHER.
ALL THINGS ANY TELEPATH COULD KNOW. TALKING ABOUT OUR FEELINGS DOES NOTHING TO HELP US.
IT DOESN'T GET US HOME.

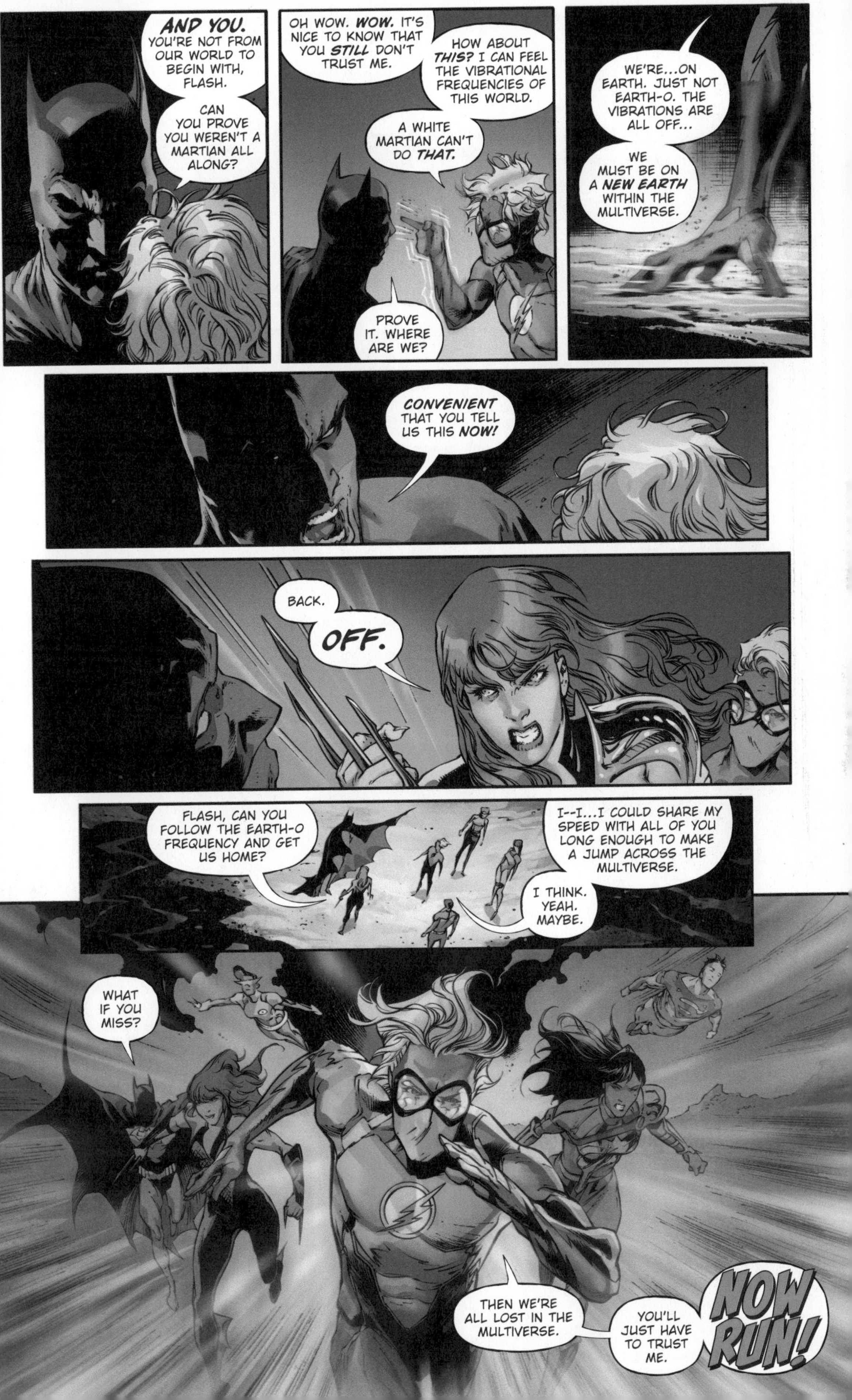
AND YOU. YOU'RE NOT FROM OUR WORLD TO BEGIN WITH, FLASH.
CAN YOU PROVE YOU WEREN'T A MARTIAN ALL ALONG?
OH WOW. WOW. IT'S NICE TO KNOW THAT YOU STILL DON'T TRUST ME.
HOW ABOUT THIS? I CAN FEEL THE VIBRATIONAL FREQUENCIES OF THIS WORLD.
A WHITE MARTIAN CAN'T DO THAT.
PROVE IT. WHERE ARE WE?
WE'RE...ON EARTH. JUST NOT EARTH-O. THE VIBRATIONS ARE ALL OFF...
WE MUST BE ON A NEW EARTH WITHIN THE MULTIVERSE.
CONVENIENT THAT YOU TELL US THIS NOW!
BACK.
OFF.
FLASH, CAN YOU FOLLOW THE EARTH-O FREQUENCY AND GET US HOME?
I--I...I COULD SHARE MY SPEED WITH ALL OF YOU LONG ENOUGH TO MAKE A JUMP ACROSS THE MULTIVERSE.
I THINK. YEAH. MAYBE.
WHAT IF YOU MISS?
THEN WE'RE ALL LOST IN THE MULTIVERSE.
YOU'LL JUST HAVE TO TRUST ME.
NOW RUN!

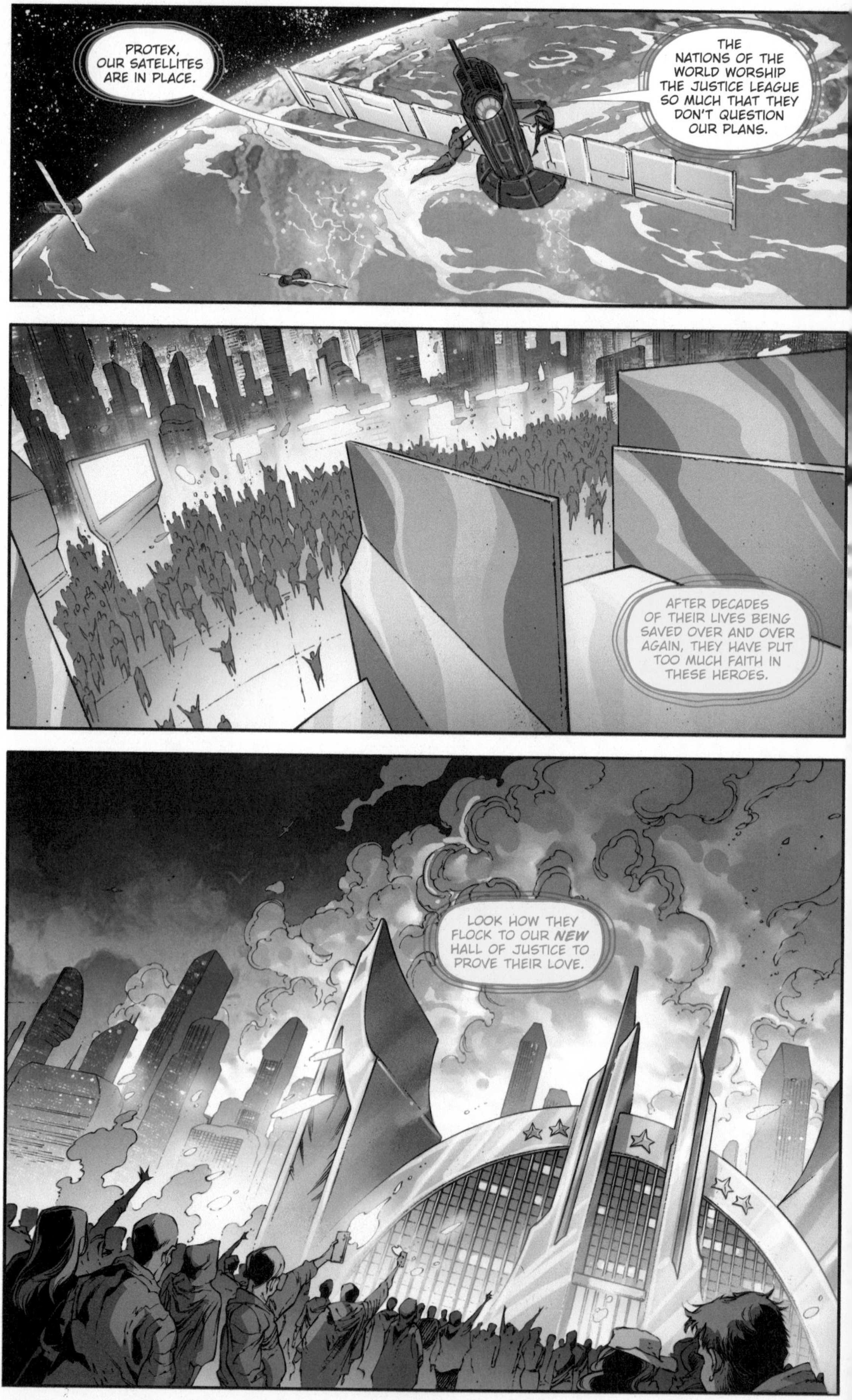
PROTEX, OUR SATELLITES ARE IN PLACE.
THE NATIONS OF THE WORLD WORSHIP THE JUSTICE LEAGUE SO MUCH THAT THEY DON'T QUESTION OUR PLANS.
AFTER DECADES OF THEIR LIVES BEING SAVED OVER AND OVER AGAIN, THEY HAVE PUT TOO MUCH FAITH IN THESE HEROES.
LOOK HOW THEY FLOCK TO OUR *NEW* HALL OF JUSTICE TO PROVE THEIR LOVE.

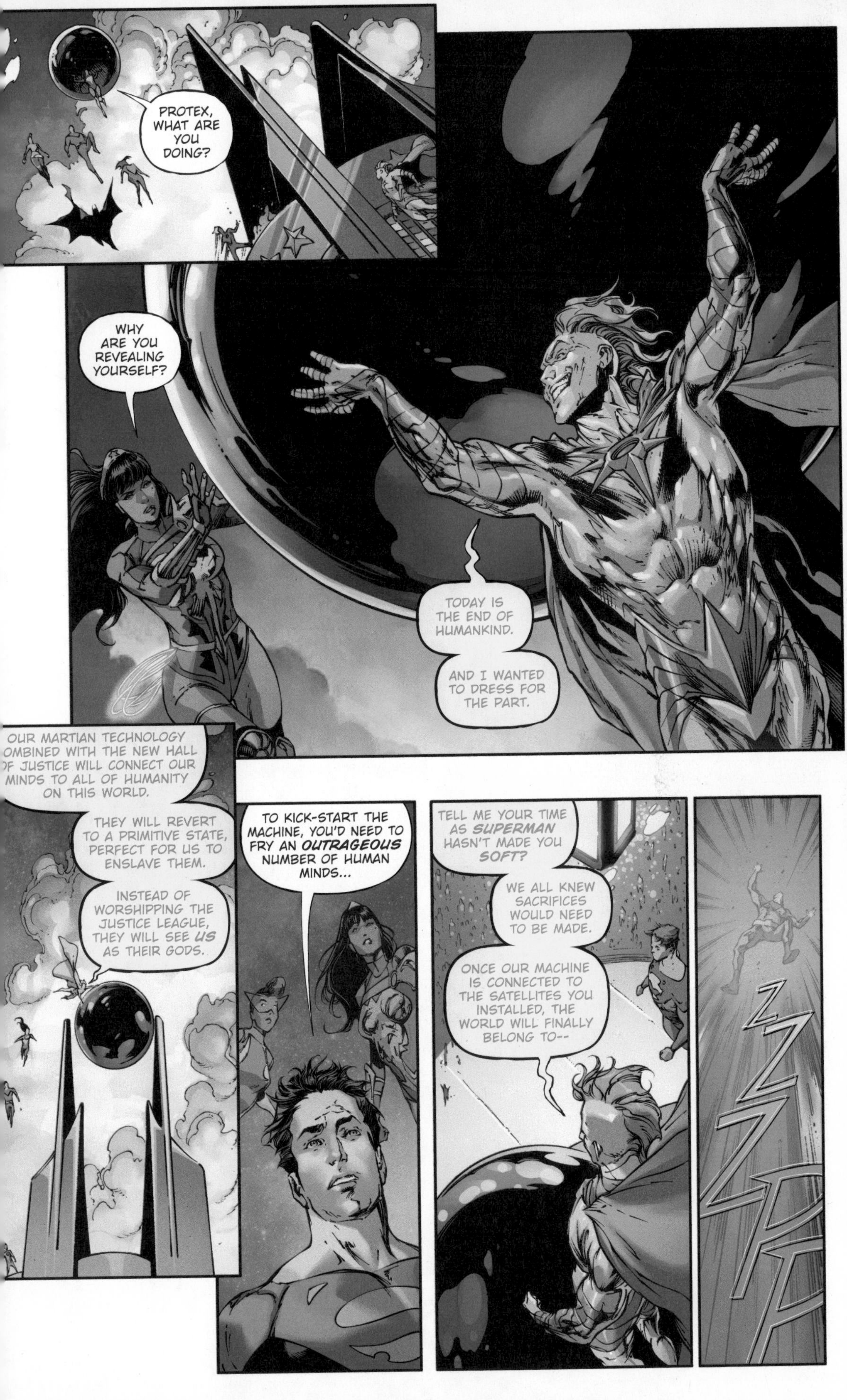
PROTEX, WHAT ARE YOU DOING?
WHY ARE YOU REVEALING YOURSELF?
TODAY IS THE END OF HUMANKIND.
AND I WANTED TO DRESS FOR THE PART.
OUR MARTIAN TECHNOLOGY COMBINED WITH THE NEW HALL OF JUSTICE WILL CONNECT OUR MINDS TO ALL OF HUMANITY ON THIS WORLD.
THEY WILL REVERT TO A PRIMITIVE STATE, PERFECT FOR US TO ENSLAVE THEM.
INSTEAD OF WORSHIPPING THE JUSTICE LEAGUE, THEY WILL SEE US AS THEIR GODS.
TO KICK-START THE MACHINE, YOU'D NEED TO FRY AN OUTRAGEOUS NUMBER OF HUMAN MINDS...
TELL ME YOUR TIME AS SUPERMAN HASN'T MADE YOU SOFT?
WE ALL KNEW SACRIFICES WOULD NEED TO BE MADE.
ONCE OUR MACHINE IS CONNECTED TO THE SATELLITES YOU INSTALLED, THE WORLD WILL FINALLY BELONG TO--
ZZZAP

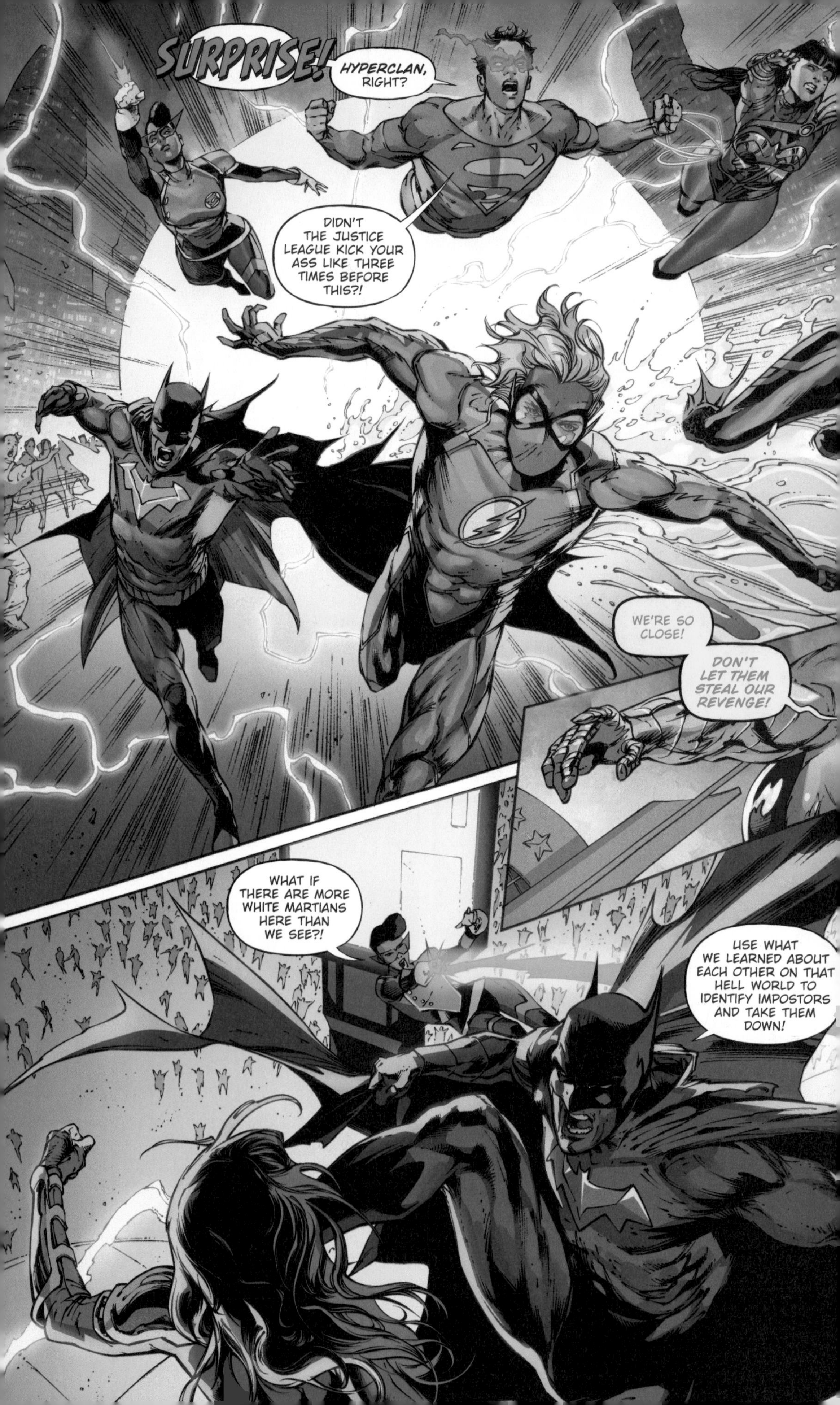

SURPRISE!
HYPERCLAN, RIGHT?
DIDN'T THE JUSTICE LEAGUE KICK YOUR ASS LIKE THREE TIMES BEFORE THIS?!
WE'RE SO CLOSE!
DON'T LET THEM STEAL OUR REVENGE!
WHAT IF THERE ARE MORE WHITE MARTIANS HERE THAN WE SEE?!
USE WHAT WE LEARNED ABOUT EACH OTHER ON THAT HELL WORLD TO IDENTIFY IMPOSTORS AND TAKE THEM DOWN!

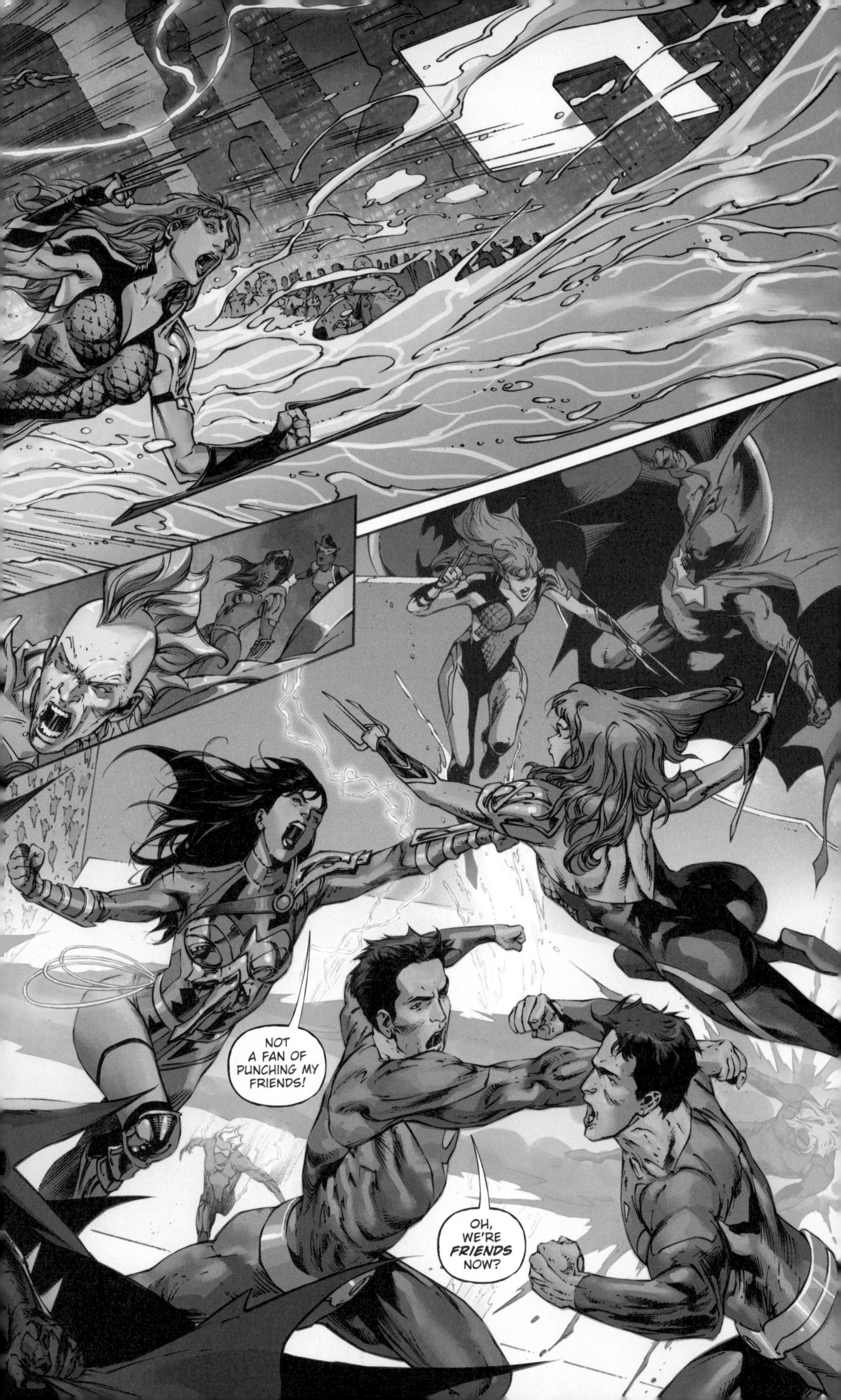
NOT A FAN OF PUNCHING MY FRIENDS!
OH, WE'RE FRIENDS NOW?

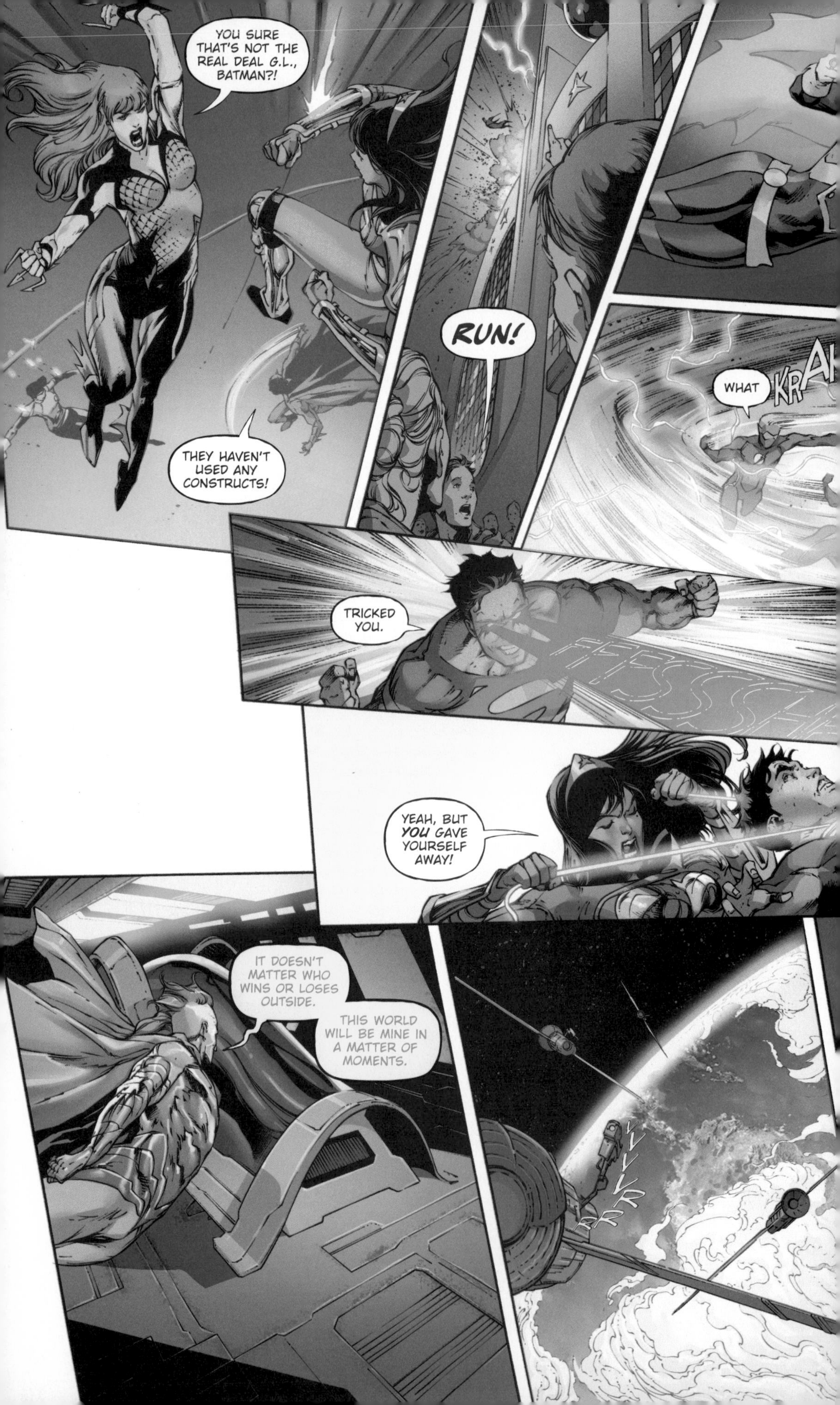
YOU SURE THAT'S NOT THE REAL DEAL G.L., BATMAN?!
THEY HAVEN'T USED ANY CONSTRUCTS!
RUN!
WHAT
KRA
TRICKED YOU.
YEAH, BUT YOU GAVE YOURSELF AWAY!
IT DOESN'T MATTER WHO WINS OR LOSES OUTSIDE.
THIS WORLD WILL BE MINE IN A MATTER OF MOMENTS.
VVVVRRR

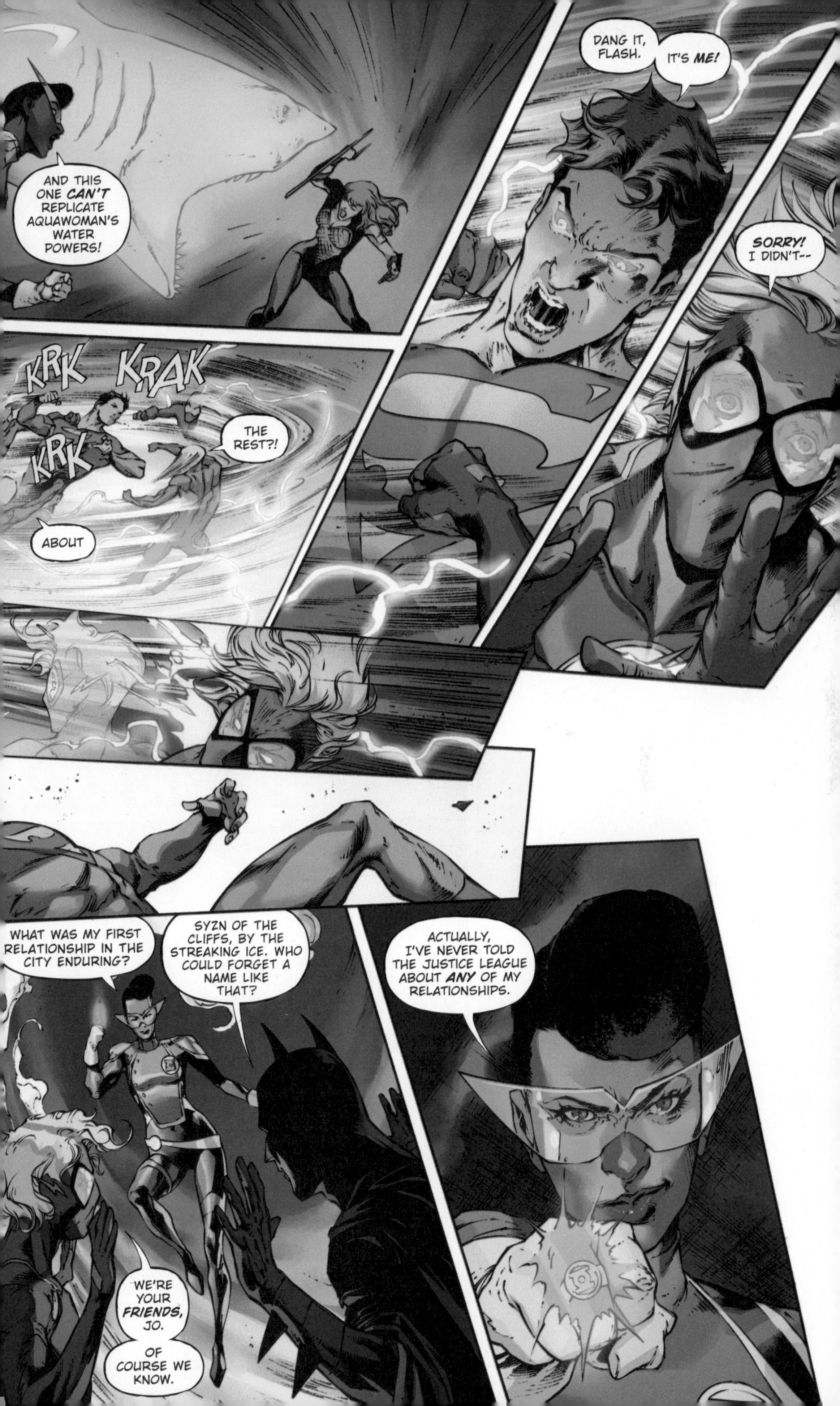
AND THIS ONE CAN'T REPLICATE AQUAWOMAN'S WATER POWERS!
DANG IT, FLASH.
IT'S ME!
SORRY! I DIDN'T--
KRK
KRAK
KRK
THE REST?!
ABOUT
WHAT WAS MY FIRST RELATIONSHIP IN THE CITY ENDURING?
SYZN OF THE CLIFFS, BY THE STREAKING ICE. WHO COULD FORGET A NAME LIKE THAT?
WE'RE YOUR FRIENDS, JO.
OF COURSE WE KNOW.
ACTUALLY, I'VE NEVER TOLD THE JUSTICE LEAGUE ABOUT ANY OF MY RELATIONSHIPS.

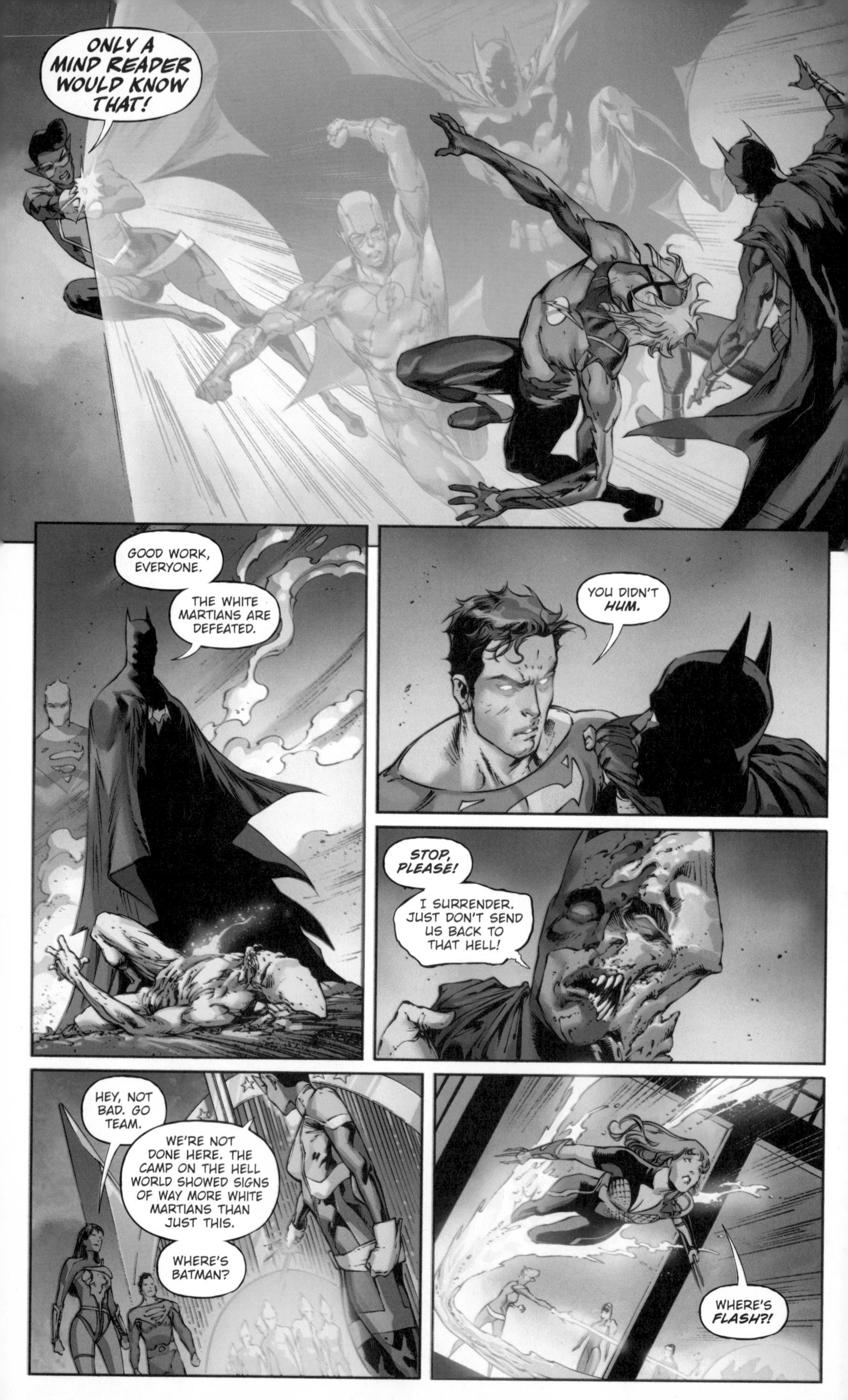
ONLY A MIND READER WOULD KNOW THAT!
GOOD WORK, EVERYONE.
THE WHITE MARTIANS ARE DEFEATED.
YOU DIDN'T *HUM.*
STOP, PLEASE!
I SURRENDER. JUST DON'T SEND US BACK TO THAT HELL!
HEY, NOT BAD. GO TEAM.
WE'RE NOT DONE HERE. THE CAMP ON THE HELL WORLD SHOWED SIGNS OF WAY MORE WHITE MARTIANS THAN JUST THIS.
WHERE'S BATMAN?
WHERE'S *FLASH?!*

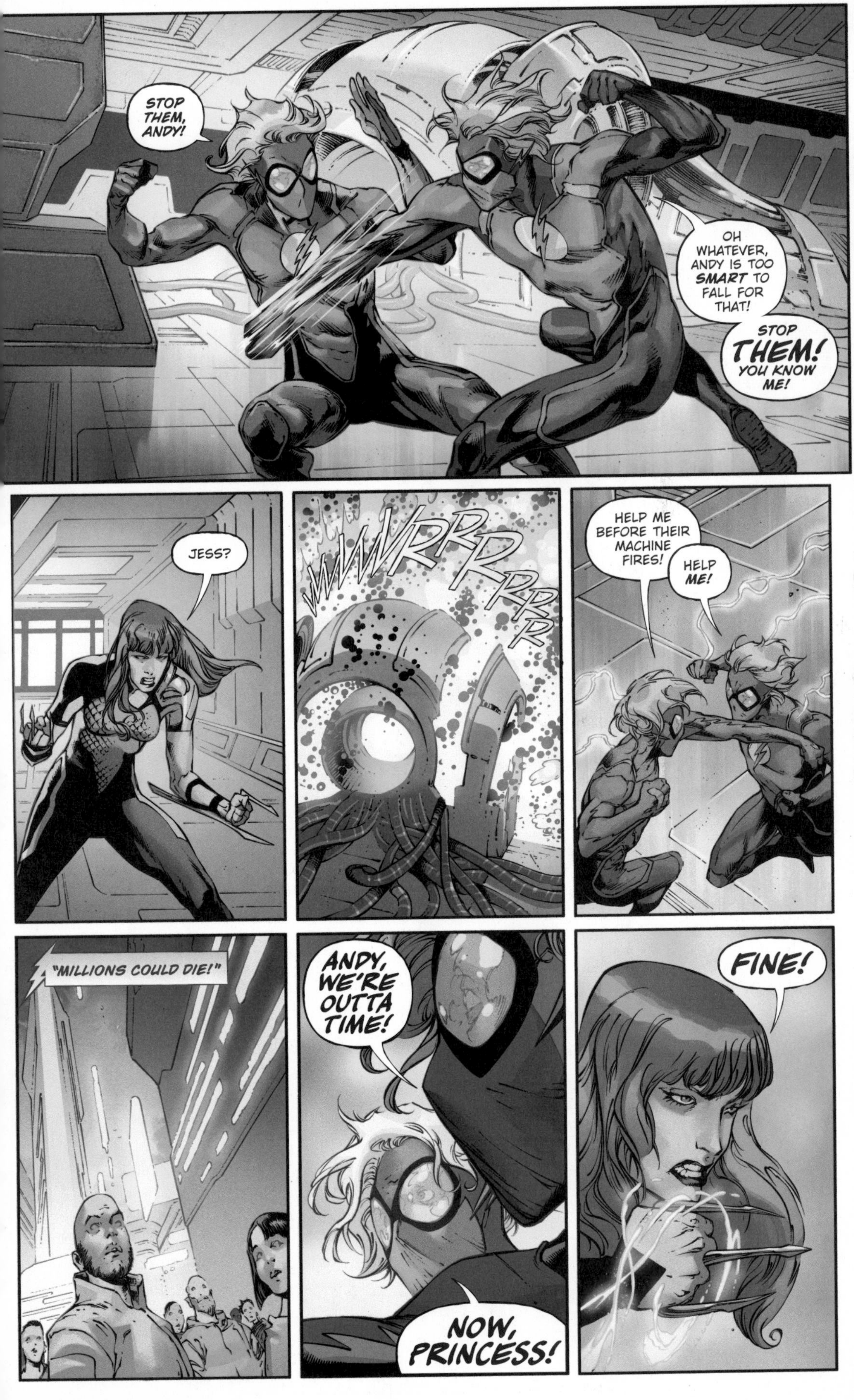
STOP THEM, ANDY!
OH WHATEVER, ANDY IS TOO SMART TO FALL FOR THAT!
STOP THEM! YOU KNOW ME!
JESS?
WWWRRRRRRR
HELP ME BEFORE THEIR MACHINE FIRES!
HELP ME!
"MILLIONS COULD DIE!"
ANDY, WE'RE OUTTA TIME!
NOW, PRINCESS!
FINE!

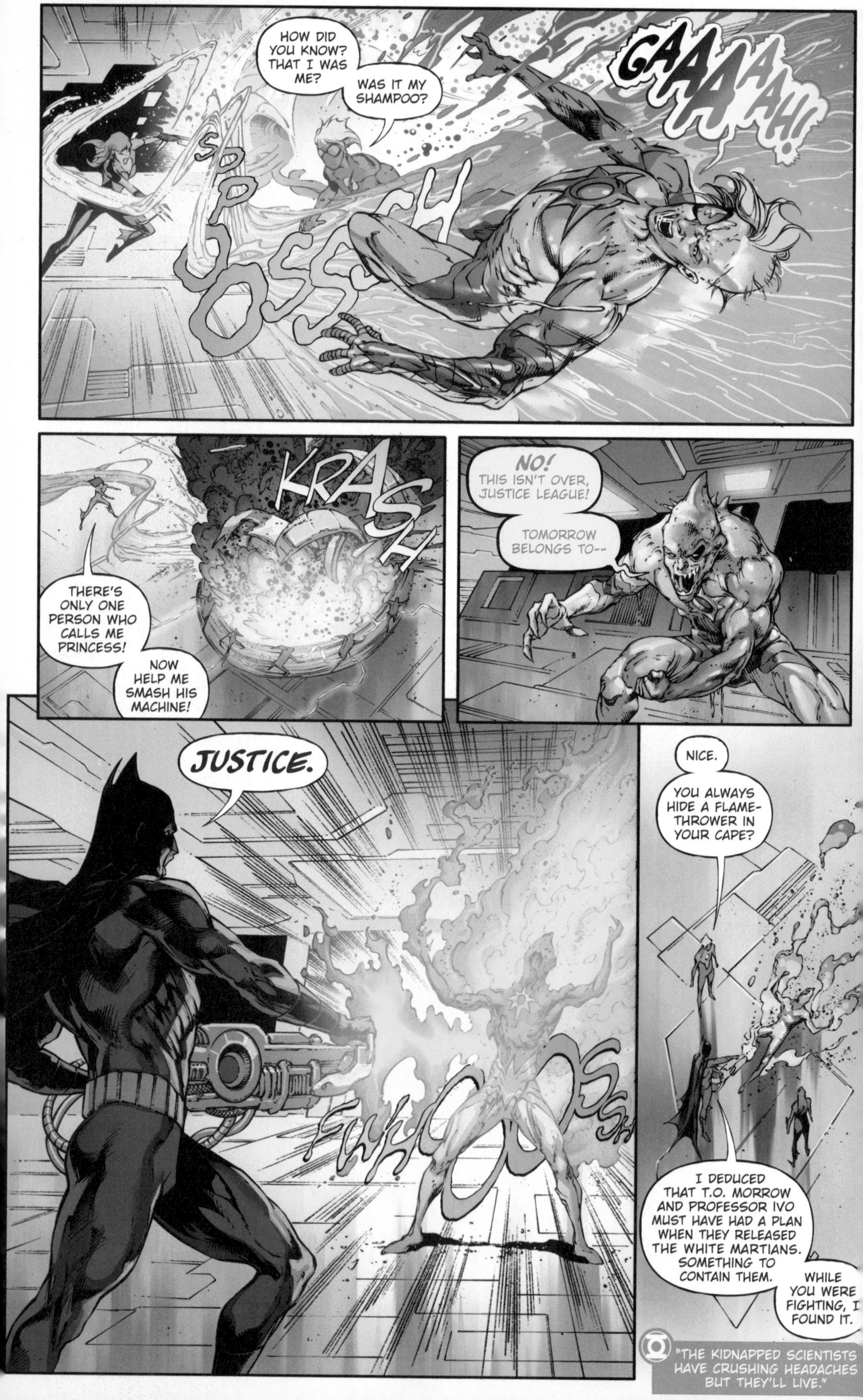
HOW DID YOU KNOW? THAT I WAS ME?
WAS IT MY SHAMPOO?
GAAAAAAH!!
SPOOSSSCH
KRASH
THERE'S ONLY ONE PERSON WHO CALLS ME PRINCESS!
NOW HELP ME SMASH HIS MACHINE!
NO! THIS ISN'T OVER, JUSTICE LEAGUE!
TOMORROW BELONGS TO--
JUSTICE.
FWHOOOSH
NICE.
YOU ALWAYS HIDE A FLAME-THROWER IN YOUR CAPE?
I DEDUCED THAT T.O. MORROW AND PROFESSOR IVO MUST HAVE HAD A PLAN WHEN THEY RELEASED THE WHITE MARTIANS. SOMETHING TO CONTAIN THEM.
WHILE YOU WERE FIGHTING, I FOUND IT.
"THE KIDNAPPED SCIENTISTS HAVE CRUSHING HEADACHES BUT THEY'LL LIVE."

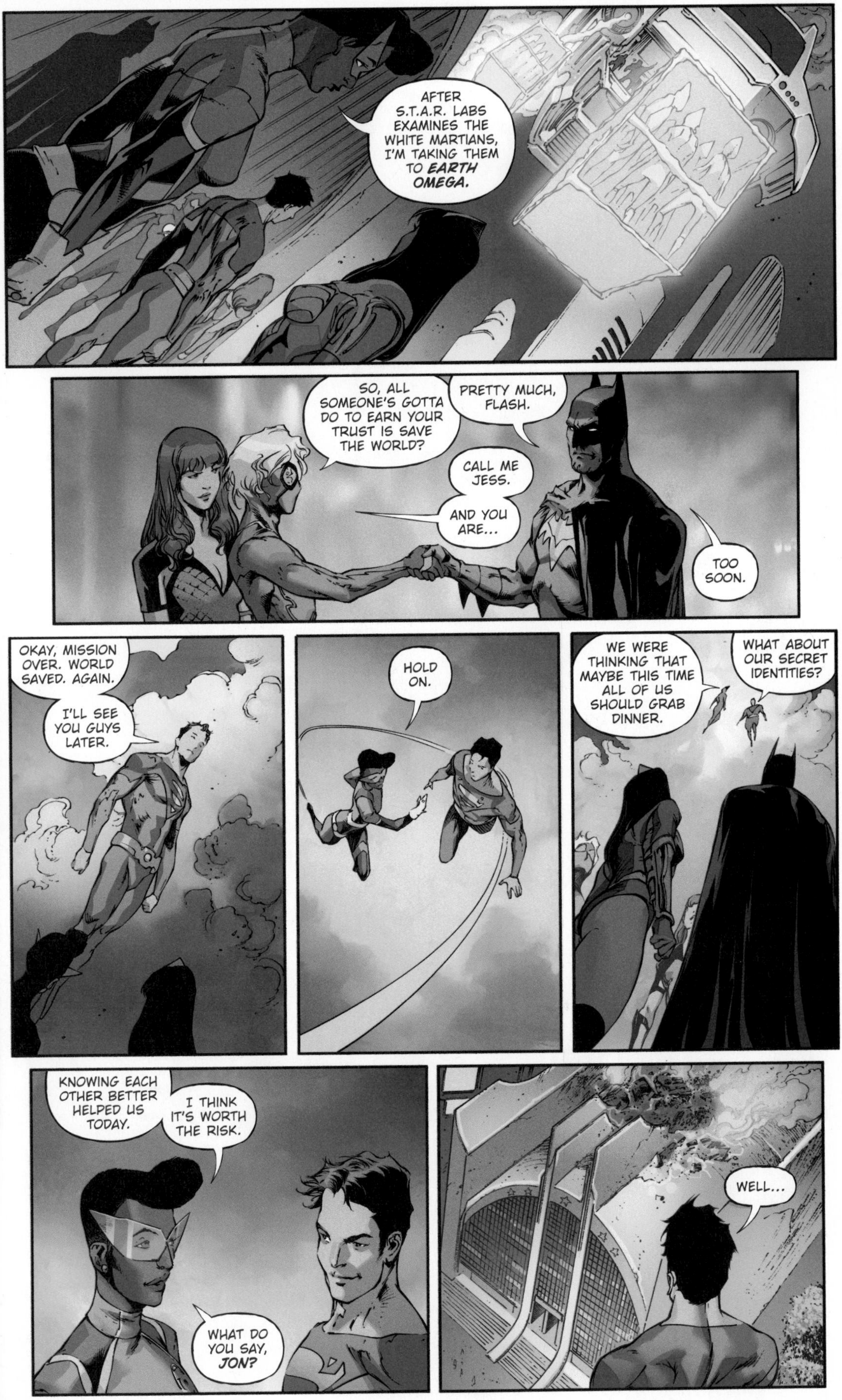
AFTER S.T.A.R. LABS EXAMINES THE WHITE MARTIANS, I'M TAKING THEM TO ***EARTH OMEGA.***
SO, ALL SOMEONE'S GOTTA DO TO EARN YOUR TRUST IS SAVE THE WORLD?
PRETTY MUCH, FLASH.
CALL ME JESS.
AND YOU ARE...
TOO SOON.
OKAY, MISSION OVER. WORLD SAVED. AGAIN.
I'LL SEE YOU GUYS LATER.
HOLD ON.
WE WERE THINKING THAT MAYBE THIS TIME ALL OF US SHOULD GRAB DINNER.
WHAT ABOUT OUR SECRET IDENTITIES?
KNOWING EACH OTHER BETTER HELPED US TODAY.
I THINK IT'S WORTH THE RISK.
WHAT DO YOU SAY, ***JON?***
WELL...

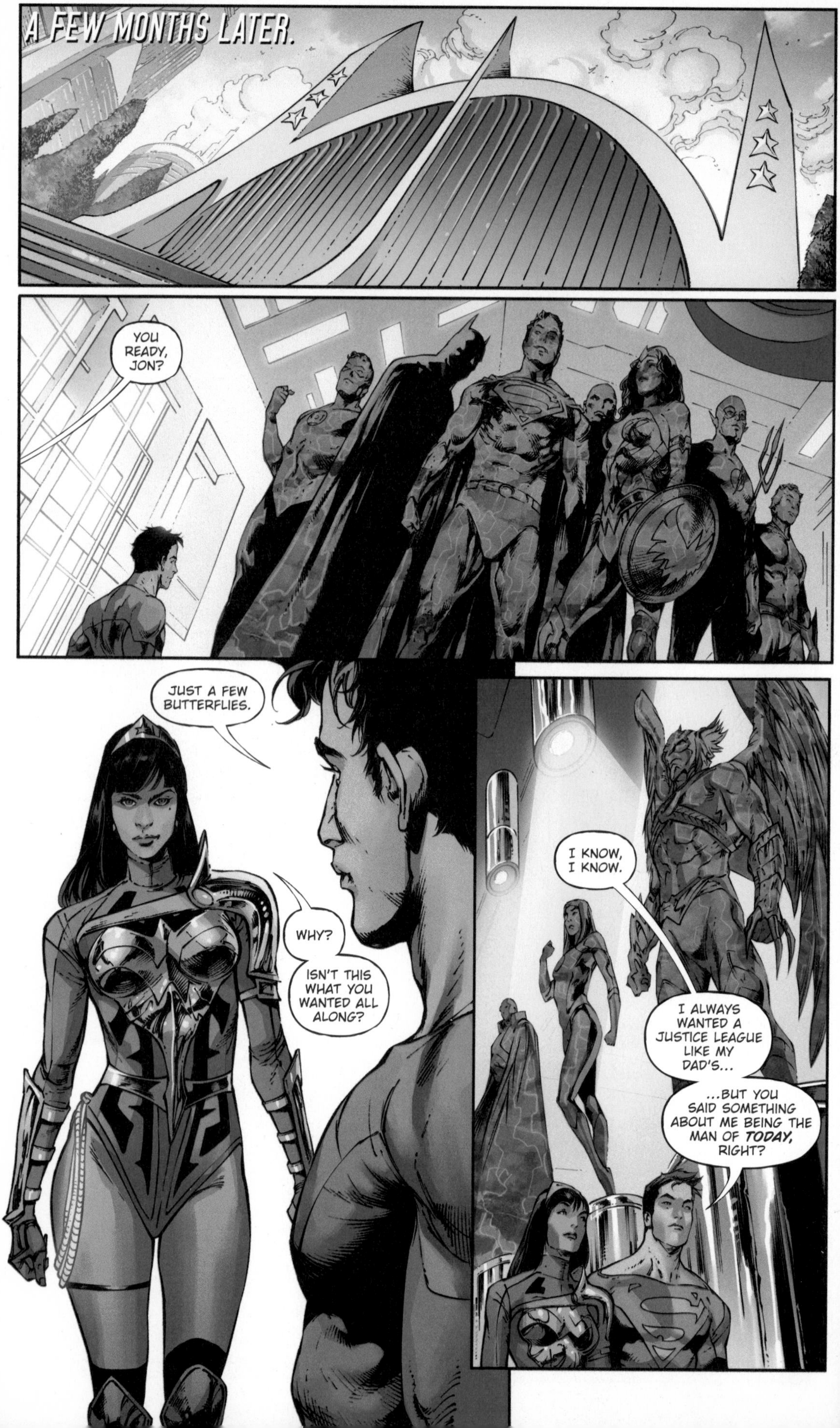
A FEW MONTHS LATER.
YOU READY, JON?
JUST A FEW BUTTERFLIES.
WHY?
ISN'T THIS WHAT YOU WANTED ALL ALONG?
I KNOW, I KNOW.
I ALWAYS WANTED A JUSTICE LEAGUE LIKE MY DAD'S...
...BUT YOU SAID SOMETHING ABOUT ME BEING THE MAN OF *TODAY,* RIGHT?

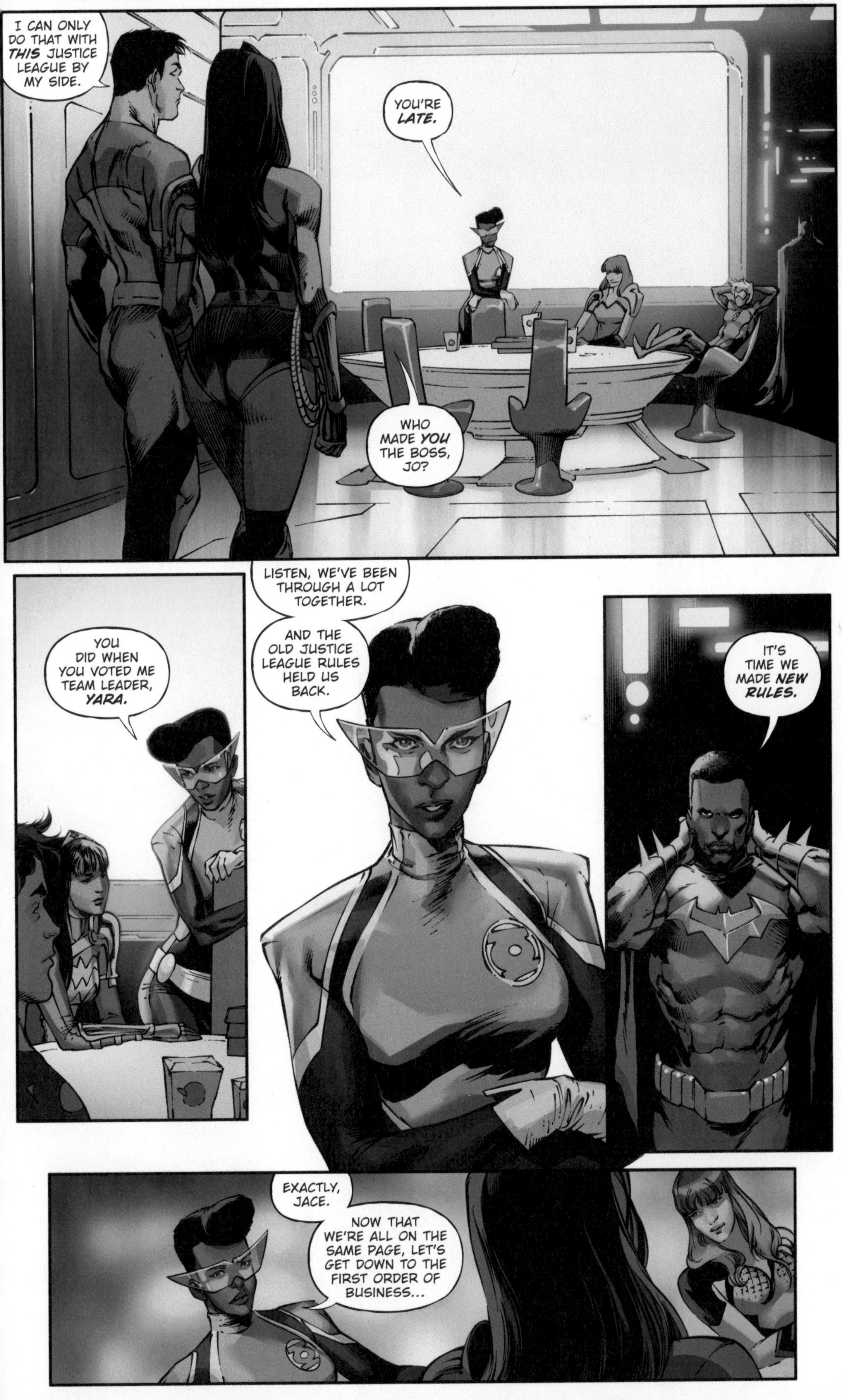
I CAN ONLY DO THAT WITH THIS JUSTICE LEAGUE BY MY SIDE.
YOU'RE LATE.
WHO MADE YOU THE BOSS, JO?
YOU DID WHEN YOU VOTED ME TEAM LEADER, YARA.
LISTEN, WE'VE BEEN THROUGH A LOT TOGETHER.
AND THE OLD JUSTICE LEAGUE RULES HELD US BACK.
IT'S TIME WE MADE NEW RULES.
EXACTLY, JACE.
NOW THAT WE'RE ALL ON THE SAME PAGE, LET'S GET DOWN TO THE FIRST ORDER OF BUSINESS...

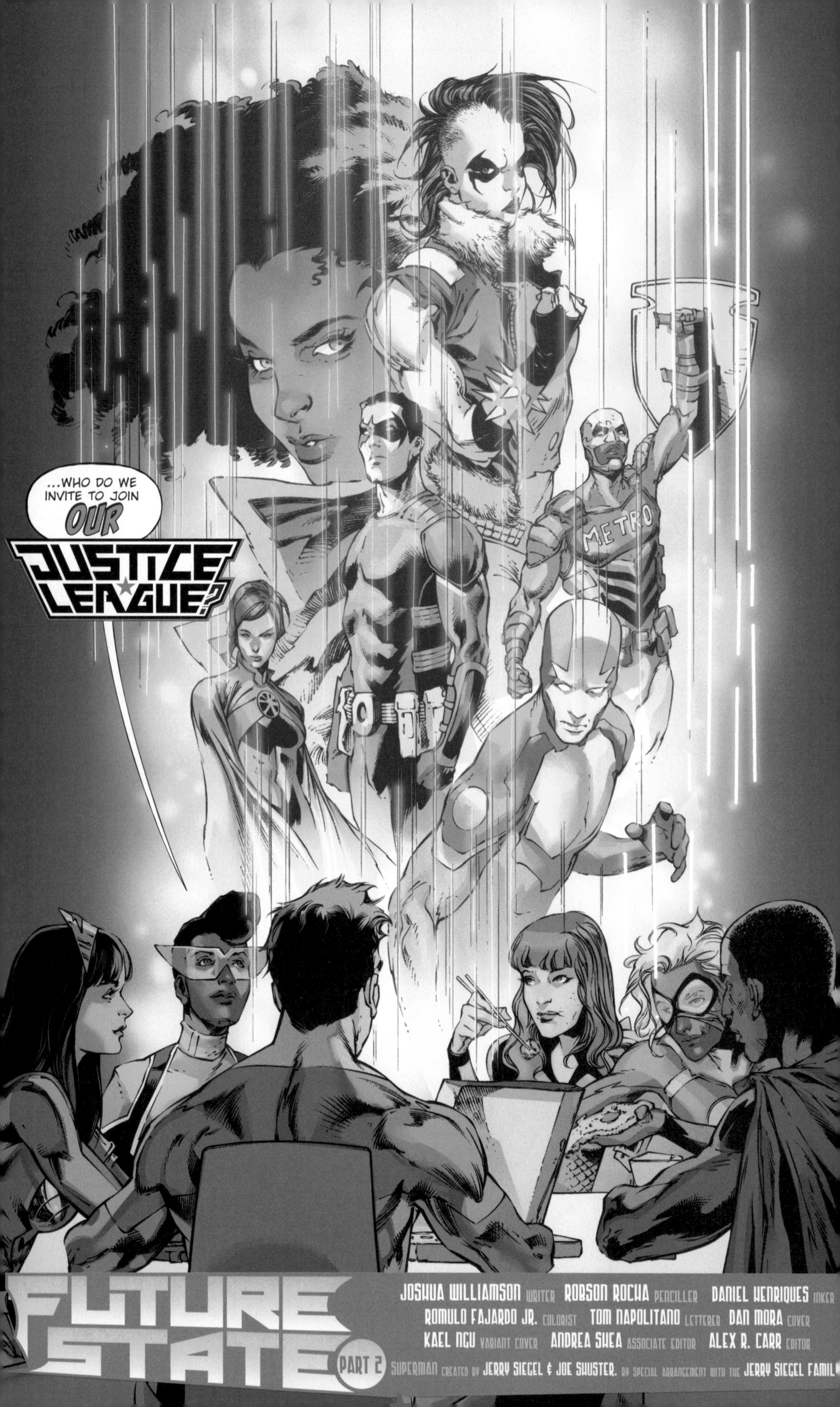

...WHO DO WE INVITE TO JOIN OUR
JUSTICE LEAGUE?
METRO
FUTURE STATE
PART 2
JOSHUA WILLIAMSON WRITER ROBSON ROCHA PENCILLER DANIEL HENRIQUES INKER
ROMULO FAJARDO JR. COLORIST TOM NAPOLITANO LETTERER DAN MORA COVER
KAEL NGU VARIANT COVER ANDREA SHEA ASSOCIATE EDITOR ALEX R. CARR EDITOR
SUPERMAN CREATED BY JERRY SIEGEL & JOE SHUSTER. BY SPECIAL ARRANGEMENT WITH THE JERRY SIEGEL FAMIL

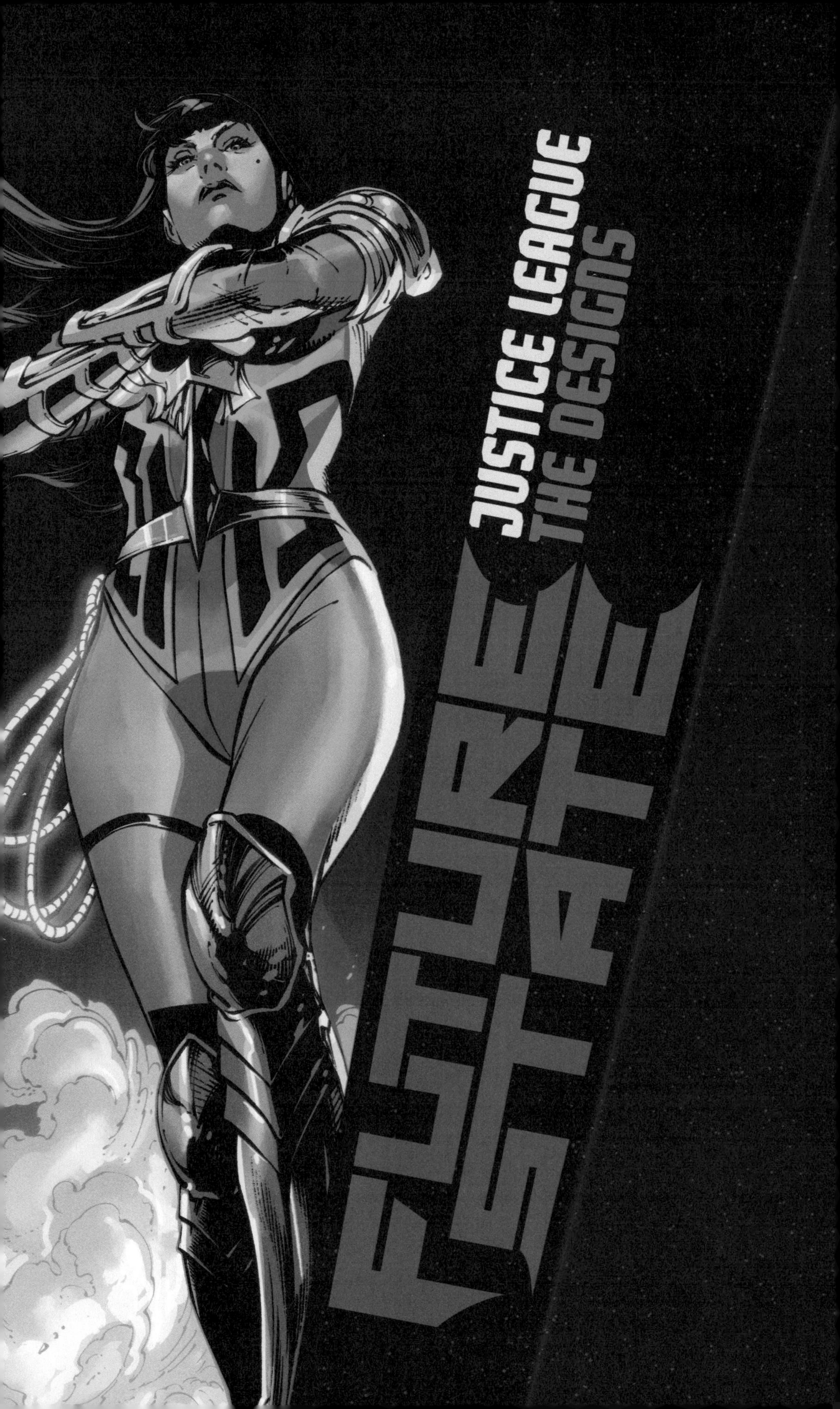
FUTURE STATE
JUSTICE LEAGUE
THE DESIGNS

FUTURE STATE:
AQUAMAN
DESIGNS BY
DANIEL SAMPERE

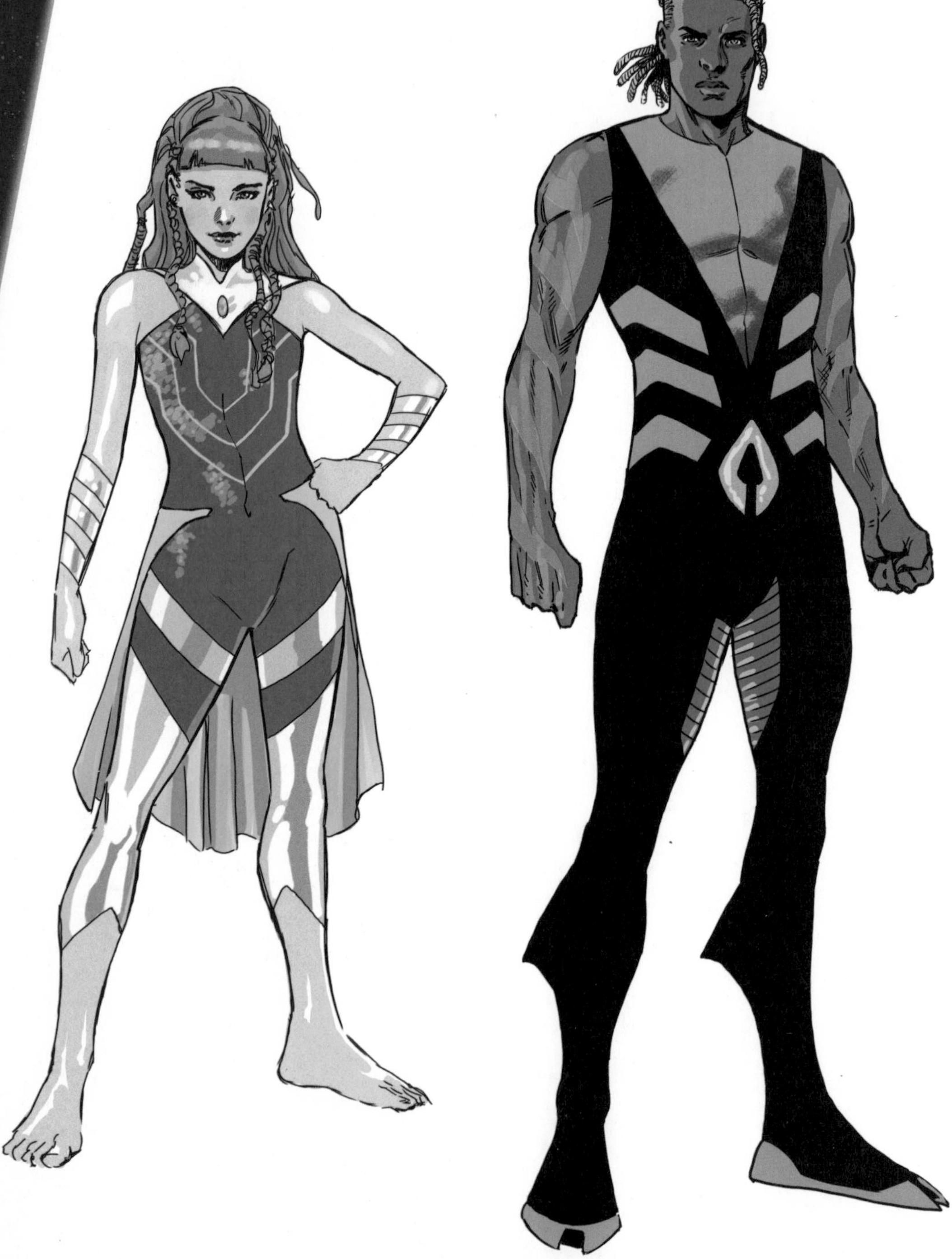